STATE & LOCAL
GOVERNMENT

STATE & LOCAL GOVERNMENT

Ann O'M. Bowman

University of South Carolina

Richard C. Kearney

University of South Carolina

Houghton Mifflin Company ■ **Boston**

Dallas   Geneva, Illinois
Palo Alto   Princeton, New Jersey

Illustration Credits

Illustrations by ANCO-Boston, Inc.
Maps by Sanderson Associates.
Cover photo: © 1987. Bill Gallery/Stock Boston.

Chapter 1: **Page 11,** Eric Tournay/Florida Department of Commerce, Division of Tourism; *Chapter 2:* **Page 30,** Wide World Photos, Inc./Rick Bowmer; *Chapter 3:* **Page 71,** Kitry Krause; *Chapter 4:* **Page 104,** Courtesy *Honolulu Star-Bulletin; Chapter 5:* **Page 124,** Wide World Photos, Inc./W. Alan Greth; *Chapter 6:* **Page 161,** Wide World Photos, Inc./John Swart; *Chapter 7:* **Page 182,** Paul Conklin; *Chapter 8:* **Page 222,** *Time Magazine*/Tony Giles; *Chapter 9:* **Page 273,** Robert Ariail/*The State* (Columbia, S.C.); **275,**Wide World Photos, Inc./Child; *Chapter 10:* **Page 291,** Wide World Photos, Inc./Al Behrman; *Chapter 11:* **Page 316,** Stock Boston/Ellis Herwig; **317,** Stock Boston/Donald Dietz; *Chapter 12:* **Page 342,** Wide World Photos, Inc./Rick McFarland; *Chapter 13:* **Page 383,** Gamma-Liaison/George Bilyk; *Chapter 14:* **Page 418,** Wide World Photos, Inc./Marty Lederhandler; *Chapter 15:* **Page 447,** *Time Magazine*/Steve Liss; *Chapter 16:* **Page 473,** Barry Myers, *Lake City News and Post; Chapter 17:* **Page 486,** Wide World Photos, Inc./Melissa Stevenson; **510,** Robert Ariail/*The State* (Columbia, S.C.); *Chapter 18:* **Page 515,** Robert Ariail/*The State* (Columbia, S.C.); **540,** Wide World Photos, Inc./Morikamenitz.

Printed in the U.S.A.

Library of Congress Catalog Card Number: 89-80919

ISBN: 0-395-46405-6

BCDEFGHIJ-D-99876543210

This book is dedicated to the next generation of students
of state and local government, and especially to
Rachel and Roxanne Bowman
Andrew and Joel Kearney

Contents

Preface   xv

1 New Directions for State and Local Government   1

Places and Images   2
The People: Designers and Consumers of Government   3
The Study of State and Local Government   8
State and Local Government Capacity   10
Is Capacity Enough?   18
Summary   18

2 The Evolution of Federalism   20

Unitary, Confederate, and Federal Systems   21
The Move Toward Federalism   22
The Evolution of American Federalism   24
Models of Federalism   35
The Advantages and Disadvantages of Federalism   40
Local Governments in American Federalism   43
Interstate Cooperation   44
An Enduring Issue of Federalism   46
Summary   47

Politics and Policy 2.1   The Minimum Drinking Age: A Case of Federal Blackmail?   32

Politics and Policy 2.2   Who is Commander in
Chief of the National Guard?   34

3   **Federalism and Public Policy**   **50**

Intergovernmental Financial Relations   51
Reagan's New Federalism   57
Social Welfare Policy and Federalism   61
Higher Education Policy and Federalism   74
Federalism's Evolving Nature   81
Summary   82

Politics and Policy 3.1   A State Takes on a New
Role   73
Politics and Policy 3.2   The New Racism on
Campus   78

4   **State Constitutions**   **84**

The Evolution of State Constitutions   86
Weaknesses of Constitutions   88
Contemporary Constitutional Reform   91
Methods for Constitutional Change   98
State Resurgence and Constitutional Reform   108
Summary   110

Politics and Policy 4.1   The State of New
Columbia?   106
Politics and Policy 4.2   Constitutional Revision in
the Lone Star State   109

5   **Participation and Interest Groups**   **112**

Participation   113
Election-Day Lawmaking   119
Interest Groups   127
Citizen Access to Government   137
Volunteerism   140

The Effects of Citizen Participation   141
Summary   141

Politics and Policy 5.1   Power to the People:
Controlling Growth on Cape Cod   120
Politics and Policy 5.2   The Recall of Arizona's
Governor Mecham   128

6   **Political Parties, Elections, and Campaigns**   **143**

Political Parties   144
Elections   155
Political Campaigns   165
The Democratic Process   171
Summary   171

Profile 6.1   Liberal Does Not Necessarily Mean
Loser   151
Politics and Policy 6.1   The Consequences of
Partisan Fighting   159

7   **Governors**   **173**

The Roles of the Governor   175
Today's Governors   184
Gubernatorial Campaigns   185
Formal Powers   189
Informal Powers   204
Removal from Office   206
Other Executive Branch Officials   207
The Vigor of American Governors   210
Summary   210

Profile 7.1   Governor Madeleine Kunin of Vermont   188
Politics and Policy 7.1   Life After the Governorship   193

8   **The Bureaucracy**   **212**

State and Local Bureaucrats: Who They Are, What
They Do   213

Personnel Policy in State and Local Government:
From Patronage to Merit   215
The Politics of Bureaucracy   229
Budgeting in State and Local Government   234
The Quality and Capacity of Bureaucracies   244
Summary   244

Politics and Policy 8.1   Affirmative Action and the
Alabama Department of Public Safety   220
Politics and Policy 8.2   The Games Spenders Play   239

9   **State Legislatures**   **246**

The Essence of Legislatures   247
Legislative Dynamics   249
How a Bill Becomes Law   258
Legislative Behavior   263
Legislative Reform and Capacity   267
Relationship with the Executive Branch   272
Legislatures and Capacity   277
Summary   277

Profile 9.1   Women's Work: Serving in the State
Legislature   251
Politics and Policy 9.1   The Night of the Long
Knives   261

10   **The Judiciary**   **279**

The Development and Structure of State Court
Systems   281
How Judges Are Selected   285
Judicial Decision Making   298
"New Wave" Courts: Activism in the States   302
New Directions in State Court Reform   305
State Courts Enter the Modern Age   307
Summary   308

Politics and Policy 10.1   Taking Your Case to Small
Claims Court   282
Profile 10.1   Rose Bird and the 1986 Judicial
Retention Elections in California   294

11 The Structure of Local Government   310

Orientations to American Communities   311
Machines, Reform, and Modernization   312
Five Types of Local Governments   315
Interlocal Cooperation   337
The Issue of Governance   338
Summary   339

Politics and Policy 11.1   The Life and Death of a
Nuclear County   318
Profile 11.1   Who's in Charge in Yonkers?   323

12 Local Leadership   340

Community Leadership   341
Local Executives   347
Local Legislatures   353
Political Leadership versus Professional
Leadership   358
Policy Innovation at the Local Level   361
Leadership and Capacity   362
Summary   363

Profile 12.1   Two Mayors: A Contrast in Leadership   349
Profile 12.2   Women as Local Government Leaders   356

13 State and Local Finance   364

The Principles of Finance   365
Revenues   373
The Political Economy of Taxation   384
Borrowing and Debt   389
State and Local Financial Relationships   394
State and Local Finance in the 1990s   397
Summary   398

Politics and Policy 13.1   Florida Lays a Tax Egg   379
Politics and Policy 13.2   Can a State or Local
Government Declare Bankruptcy?   386

14 State-Local Relations   400

The Distribution of Authority   401
State-Local Organizations   408
Metropolitics: A New Challenge for State
Government   410
States and Urban Policy   417
States and Their Rural Communities   420
The Interaction of State and Local
Governments   423
Summary   423

Politics and Policy 14.1   A Battle Royal: State and
Local Land Management Politics   407
Politics and Policy 14.2   States and Their Uneven
Local Economies   422

15 Education Policy   425

The Crisis in Education   426
Intergovernmental Roles in Education   432
Actors in Education Policy   439
Educational Innovation in the States   444
The Continuing Challenge of Public
Education   452
Summary   453

Politics and Policy 15.1   South Carolina: A Model
in Education Reform   444
Politics and Policy 15.2   Voucher Plans:
Privatization for the Schools?   448

16 Economic Development   454

Regional Differences in Economic Prosperity   455
Approaches to Economic Development   457
Issues in Economic Development   458
Tools of Economic Development Policy   461
Competition and Cooperation   463

State Policy Development and
Implementation   465
Current Initiatives   468
Cities and Development   474
The Implications of Economic Development
Policy   481
Summary   482

Profile 16.1   Baltimore: A Tale of Two Cities   462
Politics and Policy 16.1   Major-League Cities   478

17   Criminal Justice   483

How Much Crime Is There?   484
Intergovernmental Roles in Criminal Justice   486
Actors in Criminal Justice Policy   487
Two Policy Areas   490
Correctional Policy   495
Policy Alternatives for States and Localities   504
The Continuing Crisis in Crime and
Corrections   510
Summary   511

Politics and Policy 17.1   The Effects of Federal
Judicial Intervention on Life in a Texas Prison   502
Politics and Policy 17.2   Shock Probation   508

18   Environmental Policy   513

The Political Economy of Environmental
Protection   516
Intergovernmental Relationships in Environmental
Policy   517
Solid Waste Management: Garbage and What to Do
with It   524
Hazardous Waste: The Politics of Confusion   528
Nuclear Waste: The Lingering Horror   534
Environmental Tradeoffs   539
Environmental Challenges for State and Local
Governments   541
Summary   541

Politics and Policy 18.1   The Wake of the Pigeon   519
Politics and Policy 18.2   Nuclear Waste? Let's Bury
It in Southeastern New Mexico   536

References   A-1
Index   A-32

Preface

This is an exciting time to study state and local government. State governments are making front page news with their policy initiatives. Local governments are displaying a new problem-solving vitality. The study of state and local government is enjoying greater prominence, and the visibility comes at a time when state and local governments are experiencing tremendous challenges. "New Federalism" has altered intergovernmental relationships and cut back federal funds. New and troubling public problems have arisen, such as ineffectual schools, prison overcrowding, and environmental degradation. Nonnational governments face rough terrain indeed.

As teachers, we find our classrooms full of students curious about state and local government. These challenging times demand a textbook different in tone and orientation from the standard treatments of the 1970s and 1980s. Existing undergraduate texts fail to capture the immediacy and vitality of state and local government. This book endeavors to do just that, and to foster a continuing student interest and involvement in state and local politics.

The Theme of *State and Local Government*

The book revolves around a central theme: the increased capacity of state and local governments to function effectively in the years ahead. From one end of the country to the other, state and local governments have restructured their institutions, increased their accessibility to citizens, and developed innovative strategies for tackling tough public problems. These are the same levels of government routinely dismissed as outmoded and ineffective a mere two decades ago.

Our confidence in these governments does not blind us, however, to the varying capabilities of the fifty states and the more than 84,000 units of local government. Some are better equipped to function effectively than others. Some state and local governments benefit from talented leadership, enjoy a healthy economy, and are populated by an active citizenry. Others do not fare so well. Comparative analysis of states and localities inevitably leads to an assessment based on first-to-last rankings. The more important point is that, as a group, state and local governments have moved to a higher plane. Even those states and communities perennially clustered at the lower end of various scales have made quantum leaps in their capability.

The Content of *State and Local Government*

This book provides thorough coverage of state and local institutions, processes, and policies. For example, federalism's central importance is recognized in two chapters, one that traces the development of the federal system and another that links contemporary intergovernmental relations with higher education and social welfare policy, giving practical application to theoretical concepts. The text examines the three branches of state government—the executive, legislative, and judicial—with an eye on their performance. Local governments, although creatures of the state in many ways, are not treated as afterthoughts. Two chapters concentrate on localities—one chapter is devoted to the types and structures of local government and the other to leadership. State-local relations are the subject of two other chapters, and localities are also brought in when appropriate throughout the book.

Four policy chapters illustrate the theme of increased state and local government capacity. Two of the policy topics, education and criminal justice, have offered challenges to state and local governments for more than two hundred years. In the 1990s, states and school districts will experiment with a variety of educational innovations such as teacher incentive pay and magnet schools. In criminal justice, the privatization of prisons and new strategies for sentencing and releasing criminals will enliven the policy arena. The other two policy chapters, economic development and environmental policy, present powerful and compelling issues for the next decade. The significance of economic development to nonnational governments is evident as governors embark on international trade missions and local officials offer lucrative incentive packages to entice new industry. And although the national government often dominates environmental policymaking, state and local governments are leaving their indelible marks in this field as well.

Throughout the book, we make an effort to identify contemporary topics and emerging issues. For instance, we examine accidental cities and shadow governments in Chapter 14, the expanding use of the initiative process in Chapter 5, the "congressionalization" of state legislatures in Chapter 9, and the pros and cons of lotteries in Chapter 13.

Features of the Text

Several features make the book accessible to the reader. Each chapter opens with an outline and closes with a summary. A future-oriented conclusion focuses on the theme of government capacity. Within each chapter, two boxes highlight policy issues or provide political profiles. For instance, in Chapter 5, a Politics and Policy box looks at public reaction to fast growth by examining the out-of-control development on Cape Cod. A Profile box in Chapter 12 shows the all-female Missoula County, Montana, commission as an example of the changing composition of local governing bodies. Photographs and cartoons help bring the world of state and local government to life for students.

A glossary of key terms is found in each chapter. In addition, an *Instructor's Manual with Test Items*, written by Professor Harold B. Birch, is available to the instructor. The manual features learning objectives, an overview of each chapter, suggested lecture topics and readings, multiple-choice questions, terms for identification, and essay questions.

Acknowledgments

The book has benefited from the reactions and recommendations of helpful reviewers who, from their vantage points around the country, often reminded us that not all states and localities operate similarly. We thank the following:

Thad Beyle, University of North Carolina, Chapel Hill
James Brooks, New Mexico State University
Jill Clark, University of Texas at Arlington
Sheldon Edner, Portland State University
Robert Friedman, Pennsylvania State University
Barbara Greene, Central Michigan University
David M. Jones, University of Wisconsin Oshkosh
William E. Kelly, Auburn University
Dale Krane, University of Nebraska at Omaha
William A. McClenaghan, Oregon State University
Andrew McNitt, Eastern Illinois University
Mitzi Mahoney, Sam Houston State University
Darryl Paulson, University of South Florida
John Pelissero, Loyola University of Chicago
Richard Scher, University of Florida
Mary Ann E. Steger, Northern Arizona University
Jeff Stonecash, Syracuse University
Janice K. Tulloss, University of Massachusetts–Boston
Nelson Wikstrom, Virginia Commonwealth University

Ann Bowman particularly appreciates the support of the Vanderbilt Institute for Public Policy Studies and the Rice University Department of Political Science during the writing of this book. Richard Kearney gratefully acknowledges the expert assistance of Lori Joye and Sandra Hall in preparing the manuscript, and the steady encouragement and support of Kathy Morgan.

We want to single out Harold B. Birch for his conscientious and knowl-edgeable work on the *Instructor's Manual* and for his comments on the manuscript. The cartoons for this volume were created by the very talented Robert Ariail. The staff at Houghton Mifflin deserves special mention for their assistance in this project. They are top-notch professionals who take a personal interest in their work.

A. O'M. B.
R. C. K.

1

New Directions for State and Local Government

Places and Images

The People: Designers and Consumers of Government
  Ethnic-Racial Composition/Population Growth and Migration/Political Culture

The Study of State and Local Government
  From Sewers to Science: The Functions of State and Local Governments/Our Approach

State and Local Government Capacity
  How State and Local Governments Increased Their Capacity/What Increased Capacity Has Meant/Problems Facing State and Local Governments

Is Capacity Enough?

Imagine a United States in which there are no states, just a broad expanse of land stretching from the Atlantic to the Pacific, bordered by Canada and Mexico. By gathering the knowledge that has been amassed about state governments and local economies and by using sophisticated computer software, we could divide the territory into ideal functional units. In drawing state lines, we could emphasize factors such as population size, income level, and economic activity mix. We might want to make the new states as uniform as possible, to minimize the gap between the "best" and the "worst" states, or we might prefer to capitalize on diversity and create states that complement one another. Whatever our decisions, the result would be states quite unlike those of today.

Of course, we cannot do this. We must accept the states as they are, haphazard as their pattern may seem. Even recent calls for a fundamental restructuring of American government take the existing state pattern as a given. Since the Constitution was drawn up, states have been key components of American **federalism**, a system of government characterized by multiple centers of power (see Chapter 2). Moreover, each of the states contains communities. Communities and therefore some form of local governance have always been with us. Settlements become small towns, small towns grow into cities, and cities develop suburbs. Settled places attract additional people, and the resulting social organization eventually produces a political system. The political systems of the states and communities are the subject of this book.

Places and Images

Each place has its own image. Say *Chicago* and an image immediately springs to mind. *California* inspires a different but distinct mental picture. The image of New Jersey inspired a record album by Bon Jovi that was judged both one of the best and one of the worst in a 1988 readers' poll in *Rolling Stone* magazine. Images are of all kinds. Some states call to mind terrain and climatic images: Minnesota's freshly fallen snow, Oregon's rugged coastline and rain forests, Florida's balmy climate and beaches, Pennsylvania's rolling countryside, Arizona's desert beauty. Others conjure up economic images: West Virginia and coal mining, Nevada and gambling, Michigan and automobile manufacturing, Iowa and agriculture, Montana and ranching, Hawaii and tourism, Massachusetts and high technology.

A community's identity is wrapped up in images and symbols too. Consider the National Basketball Association team nicknames. Of course the Houston team would be the Rockets; Philadelphia, the 76ers; Miami, making its debut in 1988–89, the Heat. But the Los Angeles Lakers or the Utah Jazz? You say that you have been to Los Angeles and you do not remember a lake-dotted city, or that you have visited Utah and you do not recall the sounds of saxophones wafting through the air. Well, the L.A. franchise originated in Minneapolis, which has an abundance of lakes, and the Jazz were in New Orleans before they headed west. These images are strong. In a strange and sad case, violent crime soared in the late 1980s in the nation's capital, home of the NBA's Washington Bullets.

Images are not trivial. They matter because they project and reflect public perceptions, which can be both accurate and inaccurate. They offer a short-hand understanding of a place, a slice of the whole. States and communities have become much more conscious of their images in recent years, and many have launched promotional campaigns to change undesirable perceptions; "Say yes to Michigan" and "Houston Proud" are examples.

One of the most vivid demonstrations of the importance of image occurred in North Dakota in 1989, when legislators gave serious consideration to a resolution that would have dropped the word *North* from the state's name.[1] Supporters of the resolution argued that the change in name would have a significant impact on the state's image to outsiders. The name "North Dakota" was said to summon images of "snowstorms, howling winds, and frigid temperatures."[2] Focus group sessions conducted by the state's director of tourism reported that participants' most common impressions of North Dakota were "cold" and "flat." Even residents of the state were reported to suffer from a kind of mass inferiority complex because of North Dakota's location. The geographical designation "North" was thought to be the problem. Simply going with *Dakota*, a word that means "friend" or "ally" in the Sioux language, would project a warmer image of the state, supporters claimed. (One wag countered that if a warmer image was wanted, the new name ought to be "Palm Dakota.") Ultimately, however, lawmakers were unmoved by the arguments of the proponents. Opponents of the measure cited everything from tradition to identity to cost, and in March 1989 the state Senate defeated the resolution by a 36-to-15 margin. North Dakota remains North Dakota. But this kind of concern with image indicates the importance of identity to state and local governments.

The People: Designers and Consumers of Government

A book on state and local government is not only about places and governments; it is about people—the public and assorted officeholders—and the institutions they create, the processes in which they engage, and the policies they adopt. Thus this volume contains chapters on institutions, such as legislatures; processes, such as elections; and policies, such as education. But in each case, people are the ultimate focus. A legislature is composed of legislators and staff members who deal with constituents; elections involve candidates, campaign workers, and voters (and nonvoters); and education essentially involves students, teachers, administrators, parents, and tax-payers. Thus the word *people* encompasses an array of individuals and roles in the political system.

Figure 1.1 Projected Percentage Change in State Populations, 1990–2000
The general trend during the next decade will be population gain in the Sunbelt and population stability or loss in the Frostbelt. The national rate of growth is expected to be 7.2 percent.

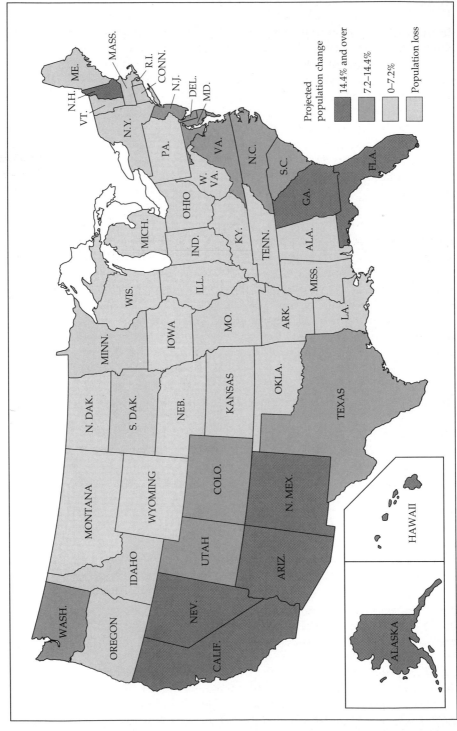

Source: U.S. Bureau of the Census, *Projections of the Population of States, by Age, Sex, and Race: 1988–2010* (Washington, D.C.: U.S. Government Printing Office, 1988), p. 6.

Ethnic-Racial Composition

More than 240 million people live in this country. Some Americans can trace their heritage back to the Mayflower, whereas others look back only as far as a recent naturalization ceremony. Very few can claim indigenous (native) American ancestry. Instead, most Americans owe their nationality to some forebear who came here in search of a better life—or, in the case of a significant minority, the descendants of slaves, to ancestors who made the journey to this country not out of choice but because of physical coercion. The appeal of the United States to economic and political refugees from other countries continues, with Central Americans, Indochinese, and Soviet Jews among the most recent arrivals. One has only to watch the ritual of border crossings, capture, detention, and deportation replayed on nightly newscasts to grasp the strength of the attraction.

The United States is a nation of immigrants. This means ethnic richness and cultural diversity. Large cities, in which immigrants have found economic opportunity, often have distinct ethnic enclaves—Greektown, Little Italy, Chinatown. Some people continue to think of themselves in a hyphenated way, as Polish-Americans or Irish-Americans. In fact, by 1988 some prominent black leaders, the Reverend Jesse Jackson among them, were calling for the use of the term *African-American* as a recognition of the cultural heritage of blacks. Ethnicity and culture still matter, despite the melting pot. This affects state and local government.

Population Growth and Migration

Americans are a mobile lot. From 1980 to 1988, California attracted 2.5 million new residents, Florida became home to 2.3 million newcomers, and 1.1 million people moved to Texas.[3] During the same period, some states in the industrialized Midwest and Northeast experienced out-migration. More than half a million Michigan residents relocated, Illinois and Ohio lost approximately 470,000 each, and 343,000 people packed up and moved from New York. To some extent, the population shifts during the 1980s were a continuation of the Frostbelt-to-Sunbelt migration patterns of the 1970s, when growth in the southern and western regions of the country far outpaced that of the Northeast and Midwest.

Over the next decade, the U.S. Bureau of the Census has projected growth rates of more than 20 percent for Arizona, Nevada, New Mexico, and Florida.[4] (Not all of this increase will result from migration. Natural growth—more births than deaths—is also a factor). Nationally the growth rate is pegged at 7.2 percent. (See Figure 1.1.) At the other end of the scale are Iowa and West Virginia with projected population losses exceeding 7 percent. Other expected nongrowth states during the 1990s include North Dakota (-4.7 percent), Pennsylvania (-2.7 percent), Wyoming (-2.6 percent), and Nebraska (-2.0 percent).

Figure 1.2 Dominant Political Cultures

The political cultures of states reflect population flows and settlement patterns. Recent years have seen an increase in the number of states dominated by an individualistic culture.

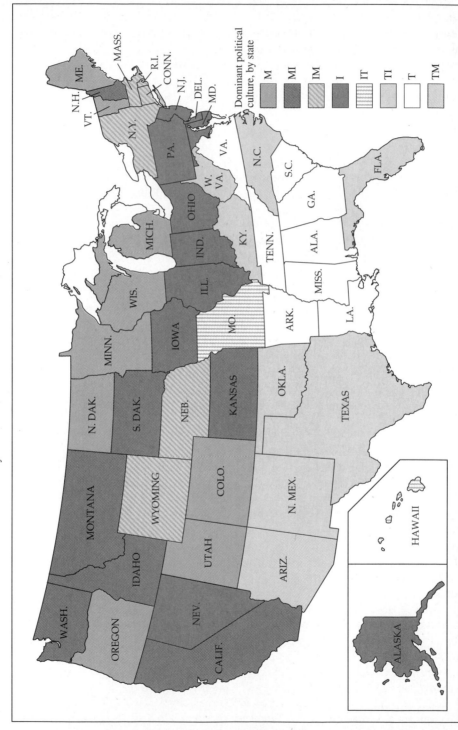

Dominant political
culture, by state

M
MI
IM
I
IT
TI
T
TM

Source: Daniel J. Elazar, *American Federalism: A View from the States,* 3rd ed. (New York: Harper & Row, 1984), p. 135. Copyright © 1984 by Harper & Row Publishers, Inc. Reprinted by permission of the publisher.

Figure 1.1 displays the likely state population changes from 1990 to 2000. Keep in mind that these Census Bureau projections are based on the continuation of existing trends. Unexpected economic conditions or environmental events could upset the anticipated patterns. For example, the Census Bureau had earlier estimated that the population of the District of Columbia would drop from its 1980 level of 638,000 to 376,500 by 2000. But now that the rate of out-migration from the District has slowed, the Census Bureau estimates a 2000 population of 634,000.[5] Population growth and migration carry economic and political consequences for state and local governments.

Political Culture

One of the phrases that a new arrival in town hears from long-time residents is "We don't do things that way here." When it is applied to government, the concept behind this statement is **political culture**—the attitudes, values, and beliefs that people hold toward government.[6] As developed by political scientist Daniel Elazar in the 1960s, the term refers to the way in which people think about their government and the manner in which the political system operates.

According to Elazar, the United States is an amalgam of three major political cultures, each of which has distinctive characteristics. In an *individualistic political culture*, politics is a kind of open marketplace in which people participate because of essentially private motivations. In a *moralistic political culture*, politics is an effort to establish a good and just society. Citizens are expected to be active in public affairs. In a *traditionalistic political culture*, politics functions to maintain the existing order, and political participation is confined to elites. These differing conceptions about the purpose of government and the role of politics lead to different behaviors. Confronted with similar conditions, officials in an individualistic community will resist initiating a program unless public opinion demands it; leaders in moralistic areas would adopt the new program, even without pressure, if they believed it to be in the public interest; and traditionalistic rulers would initiate the program only if they thought it would serve the interests of the elite.

Few states or communities are characterized by pure forms of these cultures. Instead, cultural erosion and synthesis have produced hybrid versions, which the map in Figure 1.2 displays. Because of historical migratory and settlement patterns, seventeen states are predominantly individualistic, seventeen tend toward moralistic cultures, and sixteen have traditionalistic cultures. Generally, traditionalistic cultures have characterized the South, individualistic cultures have developed in the middle and southwestern sections of the country, and moralistic cultures have predominated in the far north, the northwest, and the Pacific Coast. California is an interesting case, because its northern sections attracted central state migrants with an individualistic orientation to politics, while Yankees and their Midwestern descendants took a moralistic political culture to southern California. On the map, a hybridized culture has a two-letter designation. The first letter refers to the dominant culture in the state, the second to the secondary culture. Florida (TI), for example, is dominated by a traditionalistic culture, although pockets of individualistic culture exist.

Political culture is a factor in the differences (and similarities) among communities. One study, for example, found that political culture influenced the accessibility of state government structures and political processes to the public.[7] Other research has linked political culture to policy outcomes; for instance, moralistic states demonstrate the greatest tendency toward innovativeness, whereas traditionalistic states exhibit the least.[8]

Political culture is not the only explanation for why states do what they do, however. Socioeconomic characteristics (income and education levels, for example) and political structural factors (the amount of competition between political parties) also contribute to states' and communities' identities. In fact, sorting out the cause-and-effect relationships among these variables is a daunting job.[9] Suffice it to say that political culture, socioeconomic characteristics, and political structure combine to produce government behavior.

The Study of State and Local Government

The study of state and local governments has typically received short shrift in the survey of American politics.[10] Scholars and journalists tend to focus on glamorous and imperial presidents, a rancorous Congress, and an aging but powerful Supreme Court. National issues capture the lion's share of media attention. Even people who are fierce partisans of nonnational governments frequently feel that the action takes place away from center stage. Yet state and local politics are fascinating theater, precisely because of their involvement in our day-to-day lives. Rather than international battles over the trade imbalance or the debt owed U.S. banks by Third World nations, we have disputes between New York and New Jersey over business exodus and commuter taxes. Instead of record-setting national budget deficits, we have **jurisdictions** that engage in inventive actions to live within their financial means. (A jurisdiction is the territorial limit under a government authority.) Rather than deciding which weapons systems will protect the nation from the attacks of evil empires, local governments are charged with providing for the immediate safety and well-being of citizens—in our homes, on the streets, at the workplace.

The concerns of state and local governments are fundamental, the real concerns of the American public. Perhaps they lack style—admittedly, efficient garbage collection and effective regulation of funeral homes do not make for riveting drama. Yet these are the issues that affect all of us.

From Sewers to Science: The Functions of State and Local Governments

State and local governments are busy. They exist, in large measure, to provide services to the public. This is no easy task. Nonnational governments must offer services efficiently, effectively, and fairly, and do so with limited financial resources. The high costs of inefficient government lead to higher taxes and thus greater citizen displeasure with government, which can lead to tax revolts and taxpayer exodus. A government performs effectively if it accomplishes what it sets out to do. Another expectation is that government function fairly—that its services be delivered in an equitable manner. It is no wonder, then, that state and local governments constantly experiment with new programs and new systems for delivering services, all the while seeking efficiency, effectiveness, and equity. For instance, the massive restructuring of Wyoming's state government begun in 1989 was intended, according to the governor, to produce "a better method of delivering services from the state government to the citizens."[11]

Each year, the Ford Foundation sponsors the "Innovations in State and Local Government" awards to recognize the creativity that abounds in governments throughout the nation. Ten jurisdictions are selected for the prestigious and lucrative ($100,000) prize. The criterion for the awards is that the government's innovation be successful and easily replicated by other jurisdictions. After reviewing the applications of 960 contenders, the 1988 winners and their innovations included

- Illinois's personalized job placement and training program for hard-to-employ individuals in Chicago
- Kentucky's education program for high school dropout parents and their preschool children
- St. Louis's computerized reporting system for the police force
- San Diego's program to make it profitable for developers to preserve and construct low-income residential hotels
- the Tupelo, Mississippi, school district's creative use of private funding to supplement public support
- the use by Fort Collins, Colorado, of "performance zoning," which allows market forces to determine land uses.[12]

Although some of the winning innovations are internal to government operations and carry the promise of increased efficiency, others have a policy goal, such as educational improvement or a stronger economy. The unifying characteristic of the group is the willingness to try something new.

Our Approach

The argument of this book is that state and local governments are resurgent, and that they have a greater capacity to play central roles in the American federal system than ever before. **Capacity** refers to a government's ability to respond effectively to change, make decisions efficiently and responsively, and manage conflict.[13]

In looking at capacity and resurgence, it sometimes makes sense to measure the states against one another. In many instances, however, it is more meaningful to chart a government's performance from one time period to another. Even states that perennially cluster at the bottom of fifty-state rankings have made tremendous strides over the past two decades. Their relative ranking may not have changed substantially, but the improvement in the performance of their governments over time is in many cases noteworthy.

Our stance is tempered by the reality of federalism, by the overlapping spheres of authority of the national and state governments. There are clear instances in which national government intervention in the affairs of a state or local government is defensible. For example, the environmental problems of the 1960s and 1970s exceeded state and local governments' ability to handle them (see Chapter 18), and so corrective action by the national government was generally welcomed. Our approach takes into account intergovernmental relations—the relationships among the three levels of government—particularly the possibilities for cooperation and conflict. Jurisdictions (national, state, or local) possess policymaking authority over an identifiable chunk of territory. Yet they confront innumerable situations in which they must work together to accomplish an objective. The characteristics of cooperation and conflict define the American federal system.

State and Local Government Capacity

Discussions of American government typically proceed from an explicitly national perspective. They examine national actions and assess their impact on lower-level governments. It is important to remember that the discussion can proceed in the opposite direction. That is, we can focus on state and local governments and evaluate their contribution to evolving intergovernmental relations.

This section takes a distinctly nonnational approach. Its underlying premise is that the Reagan administration's "New Federalism," the effort to give many national government powers to the states and cities, was made easier by the existence of increasingly capable state and local governments. Republican presidents as far back as Eisenhower attempted to restore powers to nonnational governments, but had met with little success, primarily because state and local governments were unprepared to handle new responsibilities.[14] With notable exceptions, states and their local governments in the 1950s and 1960s were havens of traditionalism and inactivity.

Those days are as outmoded as a black-and-white television set. Consequently, the Reagan administration encountered state governments able, if

Florida's new capitol, rising up behind the old one, dramatically symbolizes the modernization of state government.

not always willing, to assume additional functions. But federalism in the 1980s meant more than the national government's delegation of unwanted activities. Very important is the fact that states and their local governments have designed and implemented "an explosion of innovations and initiatives."[15] Whether New Federalism will be long lasting or short-lived depends in great measure on the performance of nonnational governments. (New Federalism is discussed in detail in Chapter 3.)

The blossoming of state governments in the 1980s—their transformation from the weak link in the federal chain to viable and progressive political units—resulted from a number of actions and circumstances.[16] In turn, the resurgence of state governments has generated a number of positive outcomes, including increased capacity in local governments. State and local governments will need every bit of their capacity to address the challenges that await.

How State and Local Governments Increased Their Capacity

The national government has shown itself to be increasingly unwilling to confront many of the problems facing our complex society. Admittedly, it has been occupied with concern over the country's global competitiveness. The worsening national debt and the increasing trade imbalance have provided little relief. These problems have come on the heels of two decades of foreign and domestic policy failures, such as the Vietnam War, the War on Poverty, and Watergate. A widespread belief that there is too much power in Washington and that it has been discharged irresponsibly has grown among the public.[17] At the same time, however, states have been demonstrating the capacity to act in a positive manner in policy fields that are of interest and importance to them.

In the 1980s, states also began rethinking their treatment of local governments. Greater realization that local government problems meant state government problems signaled a new era in state-local relations. As states loosened the reins on local governments, allowing them to function more effectively, local capacity increased. As a result, local governments today can better handle the problems they encounter, because they have greater authority to do so. In addition, state governments have increased the financial aid that flows to local governments. Admittedly, a fine line separates state assistance from state interference in local affairs, and state governments continue to struggle to find the optimal balance. (The relationship of states to their local governments is fully examined in Chapters 13 and 14.)

State Reform   While Washington has stumbled, state governments have been quietly and methodically reforming themselves. They have modernized their constitutions and restructured their institutions. During the past twenty years, more than three-quarters of the states have ratified new constitutions or substantially amended existing ones. Formerly thought of as the "drag anchors of state programs" and "protectors of special interests,"[18] these documents have been streamlined and made more workable. Even without wide-scale constitutional reform, tinkering with the documents is almost never-ending through the amendment process. Virtually every state general election finds constitutional issues on the ballot. (State constitutions are discussed in Chapter 4.)

States have also undertaken a variety of internal adjustments intended to improve the operations of state government.[19] Modernized constitutions and statutory changes have strengthened the powers of governors by increasing appointment and removal powers and by allowing longer terms, consecutive succession, larger staffs, enhanced budget authority, and the power to reorganize the executive branch.[20] State bureaucracies are staffed by more professional administrators,[21] and the bureaucracy is increasingly representative demographically of the public.[22] Annual rather than biennial sessions, more efficient rules and procedures, additional staff, and higher salaries have played a part in making state legislatures more professional, capable, and effective.[23] State judicial systems have been the targets of reform as well; the establishment of unified court systems, the hiring of court administrators, and the creation of additional layers of courts are some examples.[24] (State institutions—the governor, state agencies, legislatures, and the courts—are addressed in Chapters 7–10.)

The State and Local Presence in Washington, D.C.   Nonnational governments have energized their lobbying efforts in the nation's capital. The National Governors' Association, the National Conference of State Legislatures, and the Council of State Governments are the three major state-level organizations, and the National League of Cities, the National Association of Counties, the U.S. Conference of Mayors, and the International City Management Association are major players for local governments. Beyond these groups are myriad others representing a variety of state and local officials. For example, there are groups such as the Association of State Highway and Transportation Officials and the National Association of State Development Agencies. In addition, most states and a few of the largest cities have their own liaison offices in Washington.[25]

The intergovernmental lobbies serve an important function in watching out for the interests of their members in the nation's capital. Congress regularly solicits these organizations for information and advice on proposed legislation, and through the State and Local Legal Center, non national governments are increasing their potential impact on the federal judiciary. Beyond lobbying, these groups provide a forum in which jurisdictions can learn from each other.

What Increased Capacity Has Meant

In combination, the forces discussed in the preceding section have enhanced state and local government capacity and led to a resurgence that has generated a variety of positive outcomes. These outcomes work to reinforce the performance of nonnational governments; that is, they are building on their successes. In effect, capacity breeds more capacity.

Improved Revenue Systems   The recession of the early 1980s and the wave of popularly sponsored taxation and expenditure limitations at state and local levels caused states to implement new revenue-raising strategies in order to maintain existing service levels. States also granted local governments more flexibility in their revenue systems. Texas, for example, now allows cities the option of providing property-tax relief to residents while increasing the local sales tax.

State governments over the past decade have first increased user charges, gasoline taxes, and so-called sin taxes on alcohol and tobacco, and only reluctantly raised sales and income taxes. Revenue structures have been redesigned to make them more diversified and more equitable. State "rainy day funds," legalized gambling through state-run lotteries and parimutuels, and aggressive taxation of multinational corporations are examples of diversification strategies. (The last one has fallen into disfavor because of the powerful opposition of the multinationals.) Exemptions of food and medicine from consumer sales taxes and the enactment of property-tax breaks for poor and elderly people characterize efforts at tax equity. (The issue of state and local finances is taken up in Chapter 13.)

Expanding Scope of State Operations   Unlike the national government, which is shedding functions like unwanted pounds, state governments are adding functions. In some instances, states are filling in the gap left by the national government's de-emphasis of an activity. State-sponsored low-income housing programs are a good example of this behavior; increased state regulation of the trucking industry is another.[26] In other cases, states have taken the initiative in ongoing intergovernmental programs by creatively utilizing programmatic authority and resources. In health care, for instance, states are involved in designing and maintaining the mechanisms that channel services to those in need.[27] Many governors now travel overseas to pitch their states' exports and suitability for foreign investment. States are taking on the role of policy innovators and experimenters in the U.S. federal system, and in so doing, they are creating a climate for local government creativity and inventiveness.

Faster Diffusion of Innovations   Among states, there have always been leaders and followers. The same is true for local governments. Now that these governments are doing more policymaking, they are looking more frequently to their neighbors for advice, information, and models. For example, if a state is trying to control the spread of acquired immune deficiency syndrome (AIDS), it is likely to look to New York, California, and Massachusetts, the early leaders in the field. In 1983, New York become the first state to take legislative action, creating a multifunctional AIDS Institute;[28] California and Massachusetts quickly followed suit. These states were the first to address tough problems such as testing for the disease, providing counseling to high-risk groups, and seeking new anti-AIDS drugs. By the end of 1985, more than half of the states had created an AIDS task force of some variety.

Local-level innovations spread quickly too. Attention turned to Rochester, New York, in 1987 when that city overhauled its educational system in hopes of reversing the forces of social disarray in the community.[29] The new plan boosted teacher salaries to the highest in the nation (outside Alaska); in exchange, teachers were asked to take on the additional role of social worker. Miami, San Diego, Pittsburgh, and Toledo have adopted parts of the Rochester plan in their public schools.

State and local governments learn from each other. Communication links are increasingly varied and frequently used. A state might turn to nearby states when searching for policy solutions. Regional consultation and emulation is logical: similar problems beset jurisdictions in the same region; a program used in a neighboring state is more acceptable than one from a distant state; and organizational affiliations bring state and local administrators together with their colleagues from nearby areas.

Interjurisdictional Cooperation   Accompanying the quickening flow of innovations has been an increase in interjurisdictional cooperation. States are choosing to confront and resolve their immediate problems jointly.

Many local governments have forged regional organizations to develop areawide solutions to pressing problems. Such collaboration takes many forms, including informal consultations and agreements, interstate committees, legal contracts, reciprocal legislation, and interstate compacts. An illustration of the latter is the Low Level Radioactive Waste Policy Act of 1980, which enables states to devise regional strategies for the burial of this deadly waste. More informal cooperation was involved when thirteen southern states united to hold a regional presidential primary in 1988. Super Tuesday, as the primary became known, was designed to strengthen the influence of the South in the nomination process. States agreed to participate because they could see some benefit from cooperation.

Increased jurisdictional cooperation fosters a healthy climate for joint problem solving. In addition, when state and local governments solve their own problems, they protect their power and authority within the federal system.

Increased National-State Conflict   An inevitable by-product of more capable state and local governments is intensified conflict with the national government. One source of this trouble has been federal laws and grant requirements that supersede state policy; another is the movement of states onto the national government's turf. National-state conflict is primarily a cyclical phenomenon, but contention has increased in recent years. In fact, it has reached such a pitch that an "intergovernmental regulatory relief act" has been proposed in Congress.[30] If passed, it would require the national government to reimburse the states and local governments for the costs of complying with expensive federal *mandates* (requirements).

Conflict characterizes a variety of policy areas: the removal of the exemption of local governments from federal antitrust laws (laws against business monopolies); disagreement over energy and water resources; the minimum drinking age; the speed limit on interstate highways; air and water quality standards; interstate trucking; severance taxes (fees imposed on the extraction of mineral resources from the earth); registration and taxation of state and municipal bonds; offshore oil drilling; land management and reclamation; and the storage and disposal of hazardous chemical wastes. Even something as basic as agriculture can be a battleground, as the Texas commissioner of agriculture discovered when he unveiled his plan to bypass the U.S. Department of Agriculture and sell beef directly to the European Community.[31]

National-state conflicts are resolved (and sometimes made worse) by the federal judicial system. Cases dealing with alleged violations of the U.S. Constitution by state and local governments are heard in national courts and decided by national judges. Judge Frank Johnson, while a federal district judge in Alabama, ordered the desegregation of a local school district and reform of state prisons and mental health facilities, interventions that did not sit well with a majority of Alabamians.[32]

According to a recent study, the U.S. Supreme Court under Chief Justice

Warren Burger (1969–1986) tended to side with the states in national-state conflicts.[33] Early decisions of the Rehnquist Court (from 1986), however, offer no clear trend for the future. For example, in a 1987 decision, the Supreme Court ruled that states have the power to impose environmental regulations on nationally owned lands.[34] But in 1988 the Court overturned a century-old precedent and ruled that Congress can tax all interest on state and local government bonds.[35] Yet a Court decision in 1989 reaffirmed the states' power to protect consumer interests.[36] Thus, a victory for states in one area is often countered by a defeat in another.

Problems Facing State and Local Governments

Increased capacity does not mean that all state and local problems have been solved. Two tough challenges face nonnational governments today.

Financial Distress   One of the most intractable problems involves money. In the late seventies and early eighties, states got a taste of the havoc that can be wreaked by financial problems. The nationwide recession caused state tax revenues to decline; the national government cut back its financial assistance to state and local governments; and taxpayers, most vividly in California's Proposition 13, indicated their readiness to revolt. By 1983, many states were facing budget deficits for the first time since the Great Depression. States and their local governments were forced to choose between two relatively unappetizing options: reducing service expenditures or raising revenues. Most states responded by combining the least painful varieties of both. Programs were cut, activities that could be deferred were deferred, and hiring freezes were imposed in government agencies. States increased taxes and turned to user fees and lotteries as revenue-raising devices. In the end, national economic recovery eventually lessened the fiscal difficulties of the states. But cyclical peaks and troughs in the national economy and fundamental changes in public finance mean that state and local financial challenges will not disappear.

Ominous clouds have been gathering on the horizon. Illinois was forced to suspend its delivery of income tax refunds to individuals and corporations for several months in 1988 because it ran out of funds.[37] In Louisiana, oil and gas revenues that once financed 40 percent of the state's budget plummeted to 14 percent in 1989.[38] Also in 1989, Louisiana voters resoundingly defeated the governor's plan to restructure the state's revenue system, because they suspected it would mean higher taxes.[39]

The late 1980s were dominated by persistent questions about how long an economic recovery can last and whether a recession is inevitable.[40] States remain susceptible to economic fluctuations. They have proportionately fewer dollars in their rainy day funds than they did a decade ago.[41] Despite their improved revenue systems, states would find it more difficult to ride out economic downturns. Furthermore, as states become the center of innovative programs and take on more responsibilities, spending pressures grow. California and New York had 1985 budgets in excess of $60 billion, and it is not uncommon for medium-sized cities of 100,000 people to have budgets in the $50 million range. Capable state and local governments do operate efficiently, but they still require dollars.

Increased Interjurisdictional Conflict   Conflict is inherent in a federal system, because each of the entities has its own set of interests along with a share of the national interest. When one state's pursuit of its interests negatively affects another state, conflict occurs. Such conflict can become destructive, threatening the continuation of state resurgence. In effect, states end up wasting their energies and resources on counterproductive battles among themselves.

Interjurisdictional conflict develops in two policy areas very dear to state and local governments: natural resources and economic development. States rich in natural resources want to use them in a manner that will yield the greatest return. Oil-producing states, for instance, levy severance taxes that raise the price of oil. States with abundant water supplies resist efforts by arid states to tap into the supply. In both of these examples, the essential question revolves around a state's right to control a resource that occurs naturally and is highly desired by other states. Resource-poor states argue that resources are in fact national and should rightfully be shared among states. The result is a series of seemingly endless battles played out in the federal courts.

In economic development, the conflict is extensive because all jurisdictions want healthy economies. To achieve this, states try to make themselves attractive to business and industry through tax breaks and regulatory relaxation. The conflict arises when they get involved in bidding wars, that is, when an enterprise is so highly valued that actions taken by one state are matched and exceeded by another. Suppose, for example, that an automobile manufacturer is considering shutting down an existing facility and relocating. States hungry for manufacturing activity will assemble a package of incentives such as below-cost land, tax concessions, and subsidized job training in an attempt to attract the manufacturer. The state that wants to keep that manufacturer will try to match these inducements. In the long run, economic activity is simply relocated from one state to another. The big winner is the manufacturer.

This scenario is played out at the local level as well. For instance, when the American Cancer Society decided to leave New York City after three-quarters of a century, Atlanta, Baltimore, Dallas, Denver, Houston, Indianapolis, and Memphis were among the eager suitors. Atlanta's bid—$15 million in tax-free financing from the city, a free parcel of land valued at $2.5 million, and $1 million for moving expenses—secured the prize.[42]

Is Capacity Enough?

Whether state and local governments can become the new heroes of American federalism depends on their ability to solve pressing problems. The interaction of three unique characteristics of our fifty-state system—diversity, competitiveness, and resiliency—suggests that they can.[43] Consider the diversity of the United States. States and their communities have different fiscal capacities (some are rich, some are poor) and different voter preferences for public services and taxes (some are liberal, some are conservative). Along with the national government's reluctance to equalize intergovernmental fiscal disparities, these differences perpetuate diversity. As a result, citizens and businesses are offered real choices in taxation and expenditure policies across different jurisdictions.

Diversity is tempered, however, by the natural competitiveness of a federal system. No state can afford to be too far out of line with the prevailing thinking on appropriate levels of taxes and expenditures. During the 1970s, a high-tax state, Massachusetts, was labeled "Taxachusetts," and poor-service states like Mississippi were castigated for backwardness. Neither state could flourish by being at the extreme end of the scale. States with lower taxes became more attractive than Massachusetts; states with better services became more inviting than Mississippi. Citizens and businesses usually have the option of relocating. Eventually, the workings of government, through an attentive public and enlightened opinion leaders, brought Massachusetts's tax levels and Mississippi's service levels back into line with prevailing thinking. Such competition over taxes and expenditures stabilizes the federal system.[44]

The third characteristic, resiliency, reflects the ability of state governments to recover from adversity.[45] The number of curves thrown at state governments in the form of global economic shifts, national policy redirection, and citizen demands would confound even the most proficient of batters. State governments have shown a remarkable ability to hit the curve ball—perhaps not effortlessly, but certainly consistently. States are survivors. For example, to find the innovative proposals for welfare reform these days, look at the state level, where there has been a veritable burst of activism in policy initiatives.[46] Resiliency is the key.

It is unlikely that the days of unchallenged national dominance will return. The national government is mired in its own problems, such as the unrelenting national debt and mounting trade deficits. Given the increased capacity of state and local governments, it is far more likely that the action will occur beyond the Beltway encircling Washington, D.C.

Summary

State and local governments are moving in new directions. This is facilitated by the coalescing of two developments: a national government intent on limiting its role in domestic programs, and nonnational governments committed to expanding their capacity to function effectively.

Places and people set the context for the operation of state and local governments. The past decade and a half have seen the improvement of state revenue systems, the expansion of the scope of state operations, a faster diffusion of innovations, increased interjurisdictional cooperation, and increased national-state conflict. Two serious challenges await revitalized state and local governments: financial distress and interjurisdictional conflict.

Key Terms

Capacity The ability of government to respond effectively to change, to make decisions efficiently and responsively, and to manage conflict.

Federalism A system of government in which powers are shared between a central (national) government and regional (state) governments.

Jurisdiction The territorial limit under a government authority.

Political culture The attitudes, values, and beliefs that people hold toward government.

2

The Evolution of

Federalism

Unitary, Confederate, and Federal Systems

The Move Toward Federalism
The Articles of Confederation/The Constitutional
Convention

The Evolution of American Federalism
State-centered Federalism/The Growth of
National Power through the Constitution and the
Judiciary/The Growth of National Power through
Congress/Powers Remaining with
the States

Models of Federalism
Dual Federalism (1787-1932)/Cooperative
Federalism (1933-1964)/Contemporary Variations
on Cooperative Federalism (1964 to the present)

The Advantages and Disadvantages of Federalism
The Advantages/The Disadvantages

Local Governments in American Federalism
Dillon's Rule/Home Rule

Interstate Cooperation
Cooperation Under the Constitution/Informal
Cooperation Among the States

An Enduring Issue of Federalism

The men who met in Philadelphia during the hot summer of 1787 to draw up the Constitution were not wild-eyed optimists, nor were they revolutionaries. In fact, they were consummate pragmatists. The Framers held to the belief of English political philosopher Thomas Hobbes that human beings are contentious and selfish, and some of them openly disdained the masses. For example, Gouverneur Morris of New York declared of the American people: "The mob begin to think and reason. Poor reptiles! . . . They bask in the sun, and ere noon they will bite, depend upon it."[1]

Most of the Framers agreed that their goal in Philadelphia was to find a means of controlling lower forms of human behavior while still allowing citizens to have a voice in making the laws they were compelled to obey. The "philosopher of the Constitution," James Madison, formulated the problem in terms of **factions**, groups that pursue their own interests without concern for the interests of society as a whole. Political differences and self-interest, Madison felt, led to the formation of factions, and the Framers' duty was to identify "constitutional devices that would force various interests to check and control one another."[2]

Three practical devices to control factions were placed in the U.S. Constitution. The first was a system of representative government in which citizens would elect individuals who would filter and refine the views of the masses. The second was the division of government into three branches (executive, legislative, judicial). The legislative body was divided into two houses, each with a check on the activities of the other. Equal in power would be a strong chief executive with the authority to veto legislative acts, and an independent judiciary. Finally, the government was structured as a federal system, in which the most dangerous faction of all—a majority— would be controlled by the sovereign states. Insurrection in one state would be put down by the others, acting through the national government.[3] Madison's ultimate hope, according to federalism scholar Richard H. Leach, was that the new Constitution would "check interest with interest, class with class, faction with faction, and one branch of government with another in a harmonious system of mutual frustration."[4]

Sometimes today there appears to be more frustration than harmony, but Madison's dream came true. The American federal system is the longest-lived constitutional government on earth. Its dimensions and activities are vastly different from what the Framers envisioned, but it remains a dynamic, adaptable,and usually effective system for conducting the affairs of government.

Unitary, Confederate, and Federal Systems

Powers and responsibilities can be divided among different levels of government in three ways: a unitary government, a confederacy, or a federal system. In order to understand our federal system, we must know how it differs from the other forms of government.

The great majority of countries (more than 90 percent) have a **unitary government**, in which most if not all legal power is located in the central government. The central government may create or abolish regional or local governments as it sees fit. These subgovernments can exercise only those powers and responsibilities granted to them by the central government. In France, the United Kingdom, Argentina, Egypt, and the many other countries with unitary systems, the central government is very strong and the regional or local jurisdictions are very weak.

A **confederacy** is the opposite of a unitary system. In a confederacy, the central government is very weak and regional governments are powerful. The regional jurisdictions establish a central government to deal with areas of mutual concern, such as national defense and currency production, but they severely restrict the central government's authority in other areas. If they see fit, they may change or even abolish the central government. Although the United States began as a confederacy, and the southern states formed one following secession in 1860, few, if any, national confederate systems exist today. On an international level, however, the United Nations and other cross-national organizations are confederacies.

A federal system falls somewhere between the unitary and confederate forms in the way it divides powers among levels of government. It has a minimum of two governmental levels, each of which derives its power directly from the people and each of which can act directly on the people within its jurisdiction without permission from any other authority. Each level of government is supreme in the powers assigned to it, and each is protected by a constitution from being destroyed by the other.[5] Thus, federalism is a means of dividing the power and functions of government between a central government and a specified number of geographically defined regional jurisdictions. In effect, people hold dual citizenship, in the national government and in their regional government.

In the U.S. federal system, the regional governments are called states. In others, such as that of Canada, they are known as provinces. Altogether there are approximately twenty federal systems in the world, although some are federal in name only, with true political power flowing from a central entity (such as the Communist Party in the Soviet Union).

The drive for independence by the thirteen American colonies was in large measure a reaction to "a history of repeated injuries and usurpations" (according to the Declaration of Independence) under a unitary system of government. The Declaration of Independence proudly proclaimed the colonies' liberation from the "absolute tyranny" exercised over them by the English Crown.

The Move Toward Federalism

The struggle for independence dominated political debate in the colonies, and there was little time to develop a consensus on the form of government best suited to the future needs of American society. Thus, the move toward federalism was gradual. It is interesting that the first independent government established in America was a confederacy; thus, Americans tested two types of government—unitary and confederate—before deciding permanently on the third.

The Articles of Confederation

During the War for Independence, the colonies, now called states, agreed to establish a confederation. A *unicameral* or one-house Congress was created to exercise the authority of the new national government. Its powers were limited to the authority to wage war, make peace, enter into treaties and alliances, appoint and receive ambassadors, regulate Indian affairs, and create a postal system.[6] The states held all powers not expressly granted to the Congress. The governing document, the Articles of Confederation, was effective from 1776 to 1787, and was officially ratified by the new Congress in 1781.

The inherent weaknesses of the confederacy quickly became apparent. The central government was unable to carry out its basic responsibilities, such as paying pensions to war veterans or staffing military garrisons in the western territories, because it did not have the power to force the states to pay their share of the bill. The central government had to rely on the good will of the states for all of its revenues, and therefore often could not honor its financial obligations to private individuals, firms, or foreign governments. Bankruptcy was a chronic concern. Furthermore, the lack of national authority to regulate either domestic or international commerce led to discriminatory trade practices among the states, particularly through the use of protective tariffs. National laws were unenforceable in state courts. These and many other defects caused representatives of the states to come together in Philadelphia in the summer of 1787 to draft a constitution for a new type of government.

The Constitutional Convention

How did the Framers create a long-lasting and successful system of government that seems to have the best features of both unitary and confederate forms? It would be nice to say that they carefully integrated the best theories of various political philosophers into a grand plan for government. Truly the Framers were learned men, well schooled in the theories of politics, and most of them did believe in designing a government that would serve the people and ensure justice. But above all they were pragmatists; they developed a practical compromise on the key issues of the day, including the proper role of the national government and the states. The reconciliation of the interests and powers of the states with the need for a strong national government was an American invention.[7] Today, the United States stands as the prototypical federal system.

The Constitutional Convention turned on the self-interest of large states and small states. The large states supported the Virginia Plan, introduced by Edmund Randolph, which proposed a strong central government spearheaded by a powerful two-house Congress. Because representation in both chambers would be based on population, larger states would be favored. The smaller states countered with the New Jersey Plan, which put forward a one-house legislature composed of an equal number of representatives from each state. There were other differences between the two plans (for example, the Virginia Plan had a single chief executive, whereas the New Jersey Plan had a multimember executive), but the issue of state representation was paramount.

The New Jersey Plan was defeated by a vote of 7 to 3, but the smaller states refused to give in. Finally, Connecticut moved that the lower house (the House of Representatives) be based on the population of each state and the upper house (the Senate) on equal state membership. This Great Compromise was approved, and it ensured that a faction of large states would not dominate the small ones.

The Framers reached another important compromise by specifying the powers of the new central government. Those seventeen powers, to be exercised through Congress, included taxation, regulation of commerce, operation of post offices, establishment of a national court system, declaration of war, conduct of foreign affairs, and administration of military forces.

A third key compromise reached by the Framers concerned the question of who should resolve disputes between the national government and the states: Congress, the state courts, or the Supreme Court? The importance of the decision that the Supreme Court would be the final arbiter was understood only years later, when the Court established the supremacy of the national government over the states through several critical rulings.

The Evolution of American Federalism

Despite the fact that the new Constitution made the national government much stronger than it had been under the Articles of Confederation, the power of the states was still important. As James Madison wrote, "The powers delegated by the proposed Constitution to the federal government are few and defined. Those which are to remain in the State governments are numerous and infinite . . . the powers reserved to the several States will extend to all the objects which, in the ordinary course of affairs, concern the lives, liberties, and properties of the people, and the internal order, improvement, and prosperity of the State."[8]

State-centered Federalism

Indeed, the first decades under the Constitution were an era of **state-centered federalism**. For one thing, the **reserved powers clause** of the **Tenth**

Amendment to the Constitution, ratified in 1791, gave support to the states by openly acknowledging that "the powers not delegated to the United States by the Constitution, nor prohibited by it to the states, are reserved to the states respectively, or to the people." In fact, the Tenth Amendment was an early omen of the eventual triumph of **nation-centered federalism.** As pointed out by constitutional scholar Walter Berns, if the states were intended to be the dominant federal actors, they would not have needed the Tenth Amendment to remind them.[9]

Those who defended the power of the states under the Constitution, or state-centered federalism, expressed their view in terms of three concepts. First, the Constitution was a *compact*, an agreement, among the sovereign states, which maintained their sovereignty, or the right of self-governance. Second, the powers of the national government listed in the Constitution— the **enumerated (delegated) powers**—were to be interpreted narrowly. Third, the national government did not have the exclusive right to determine the scope of its own powers, and the states were obliged to resist any unconstitutional efforts by the national government to extend its authority.[10]

This **compact theory** of federalism became the foundation for states' rights arguments. In particular, it became central to the fight of the southern states against what they considered discrimination by the North. During the 1820s a national tariff that hurt the agricultural economy of the southern states became an issue. The economy of the South had already begun a protracted period of decline while the North prospered. The tariff, which placed high taxes on imported manufactured goods from Europe, hit the South hard, for the South produced few manufactured goods. Rightly or wrongly, the southerners blamed the "tariff of abominations" for many of their economic problems.

In 1828 Vice President John C. Calhoun provided the theoretical foundation for his home state of South Carolina to attack the tariff and other "insults." In Calhoun's view, the United States comprised sovereign states united in a central government through a compact. The powers of the national government had been entrusted to it, not permanently handed over, by the states. Calhoun claimed that the states thus had complete authority to reinterpret the validity of the compact at any time.

Calhoun proposed that if a state found a national law to be in violation of the Constitution, the state had the right to **nullify** or veto the law, making it invalid within that state's borders. This action was known as **interposition**. The federal law in question could then be submitted to the delegates of a national convention for approval or put to a vote in the state legislatures. Most important, Calhoun declared that if a large majority of the states sided with the national government, the nullifying state had the right to *secede* or withdraw from the Union.

Calhoun's full remedy for righting wrongs against the states was complex, and is little more than an interesting historical curiosity today. But in 1832 his theory had considerable impact. That year, after an additional tariff was enacted by the national government, South Carolina nullified it. President Andrew Jackson and the Congress threatened military action to force the state to comply with the law, and Jackson even threatened to hang Calhoun, who by this time had resigned from the vice presidency.[11]

Ultimately, eleven southern states (led by South Carolina) did secede from the Union, and formed the Confederate States of America. The long conflict between state sovereignty and national supremacy was definitively resolved by five years of bloodshed and the eventual readmittance of the renegade states to the Union. The Civil War remains the single most violent event in American history, resulting in more than 620,000 deaths (more than in all our other wars combined) and countless civilian tragedies.

The Growth of National Power through the Constitution and the Judiciary

Although the compact theory of federalism was a factor until the mid-nineteenth century, a *nation-centered* concept of federalism has dominated since then. For the most part, the national government has been the primary force, with the states and localities generally following its lead. Many times the national government has been best positioned to deal with the major problems of governing the nation, and it has been supported by the Supreme Court's interpretations of key sections of the Constitution.

The National Supremacy Clause   The Judiciary Act of 1789, passed by the first Congress, established the U.S. Supreme Court and various lower courts. It also stated that the U.S. Supreme Court would have jurisdiction over state supreme courts when they hold a national law to be unconstitutional, support a state law over the U.S. Constitution, or rule against a right or privilege claimed under national law or the Constitution. The Judiciary Act of 1789 thus established the supremacy of national law and the Constitution, and made the U.S. Supreme Court the final arbiter of any legal disputes between the national government and the states. This act was constitutionally grounded in the **national supremacy clause** (Article VI, Section 2), which provides that the national laws and the Constitution are the supreme laws of the land.

The Necessary and Proper Clause   The fourth chief justice of the United States, John Marshall, was the architect of the federal judiciary during his thirty-four years on the bench. Almost singlehandedly, he made it a coequal branch of government. Several of his rulings laid the groundwork for the expansion of national governmental power. In the case of *McCulloch* v. *Maryland* (1819), two issues were before the bench: the right of the national government to establish a national bank, and the right of the state of Maryland to tax that bank, once it was established.[12] The secretary of the treasury, Alexander Hamilton, had proposed a bill that would allow Congress to charter such a bank for depositing national revenues and facilitating the borrowing of funds. Those who wanted to limit the power of the national government, such as James Madison and Thomas Jefferson, argued that the Constitution did not provide the government with the specific authority to do so.

The crux of the issue was how to interpret the **necessary and proper clause**. The final power delegated to Congress under Article I, Section 8 is the power "to make all laws which shall be *necessary and proper* for carrying into execution the foregoing powers, and all other powers vested by this Constitution in the Government of the United States" (emphasis added). Jefferson argued that "necessary" meant "indispensable," while Hamilton asserted that "necessary" merely meant "convenient." Hamilton argued that in addition to the enumerated powers, Congress also possessed **implied powers**. In the case of the national bank, valid congressional action was implied through the powers of taxation, borrowing, and currency found in Article I, Section 8.

Meanwhile, the state of Maryland levied a tax on the national bank, which had been located within its borders, and the bank had refused to pay. Maryland also claimed that the congressional act creating the national bank was unconstitutional, because it did not accord with Congress's delegated powers, and that the bank was not "indispensable" for the execution of delegated powers.

The bank dispute was eventually heard by Supreme Court Chief Justice Marshall. Marshall was persuaded by the Hamiltonian point of view. He pointed out that the Constitution nowhere stipulates that the only powers that may be carried out are those expressly described in Article I, Section 8. Thus, he ruled that Congress had the implied power to establish the bank, and that Maryland had no right to tax it. Significantly, *McCulloch v. Maryland* meant that the national government had an almost unlimited right to decide how to exercise its delegated powers. Over the years, Congress has enacted a great many laws that are only vaguely, if at all, associated with the enumerated powers, and that stretch the phrase "necessary and proper" beyond its logical limits.

The Commerce Clause   Another important ruling of the Marshall Court extended national power through an expansive interpretation of the **commerce clause** of Article I, Section 8. The commerce clause gives Congress the power "to regulate commerce with foreign nations, and among the several states, and with the Indian tribes." In *Gibbons* v. *Ogden* (1824),[13] two important questions were addressed by Marshall: what *is* commerce, and how broadly should Congress's power to regulate commerce be interpreted?

The United States was just developing a national economy as the industrial revolution expanded. National oversight and regulation of emerging transportation networks and of state activities related to the passage of goods across state lines (interstate commerce) was needed. Marshall defined commerce very broadly, and held that Congress's power to regulate commerce applied not only to traffic across state boundaries but to traffic of goods, merchandise, and people *within* a state.

Gibbons v. *Ogden* was an important ruling because it expanded national power and opened up the prospects for trade by eliminating the constraints of state-created monopolies and other barriers. For example, steamboat navigation and railroads flourished, which tremendously aided the economic development of the United States. The full implications of Marshall's rulings were not realized until many years later, but the Marshall Court was a primary cause of the expansion of national government authority and its eventual supremacy over the states.

There have been two additional constitutional bases for the federal judiciary's furtherance of national government power: the general welfare clause and the Fourteenth Amendment.

The General Welfare Clause The **general welfare clause** of Article I, Section 8 states that "the Congress shall have power to lay and collect taxes, duties, imposts, and excises to pay the debts and provide for the common defense and *general welfare* of the United States" (emphasis added). This clause was interpreted very narrowly before the Great Depression of the 1930s. The early position on the role of the national government in aiding the poor was established by President Franklin Pierce in 1854, in a veto of a bill that would have provided national assistance to insane people who were indigent. Pierce claimed that if Congress provided for these people, it would open the door to those paupers who were not insane. This would eventually find the states turning to the national government for funds to assist the poor.[14] Pierce and most other government officials believed that poor people were responsible for their own plight and that it was up to private charity and nonnational governments to provide limited assistance.

The Great Depression brought massive unemployment and poverty throughout the country, and made necessary a major change in the national government's attitude. Despite their best efforts, the states and localities were staggered by the tremendous loss of tax revenues and by the need to help poor and displaced persons obtain food and shelter. Pierce's worst fears were realized as the states came to Washington, hats in hand. Franklin D. Roosevelt, who won the presidency in 1932, set in motion numerous programs that completely redefined federal responsibility for the general welfare.

Roosevelt's "New Deal" included a massive Federal Emergency Relief Act, establishment of the Tennessee Valley Authority, the National Industrial Recovery Act, the Agricultural Adjustment Act, the National Labor Relations Act, the Wealth Tax Act, the Banking Act of 1935, the Social Security Act, and other statutes that collectively propelled the national government into a position of dominance within the federal system. For instance, the Social Security Act of 1935 allowed the national government to assist the poor and jobless through old-age insurance, unemployment insurance, welfare programs, and health services. It was twice challenged as an unconstitutionally broad interpretation of the general welfare clause, but the Supreme Court on both occasions upheld the use of federal tax revenues to aid the aged, poor, and unemployed. Thus the national role was extended into fields previously within the province of the states, the localities, and the private sector.

The Fourteenth Amendment   Ratified by the states in 1868, the **Fourteenth Amendment** gave former slaves official status as citizens of the United States and of the state in which they lived. It included two other very important principles as well: *due process* and *equal protection* of the laws. "No state shall make or enforce any law which shall abridge the privileges or immunities of the citizens of the United States; nor shall any state deprive any person of life, liberty, or property, without due process of law; nor deny to any person within its jurisdiction the equal protection of the laws." The Fourteenth Amendment has been utilized by the federal courts to increase national power over the states in several critical fields, especially civil rights, criminal law, and election practices.

For example, black residents of the United States were guaranteed citizenship but otherwise profited very little from the Fourteenth Amendment until the 1954 Supreme Court decision in *Brown* v. *Board of Education*. Up to that time the Court had interpreted the amendment very narrowly with respect to civil rights. In *Brown* v. *Board of Education*, however, it held that segregation in the public schools implied unequal treatment of the races and therefore violated the Fourteenth Amendment. Public schools throughout the country were ordered to desegregate "with all deliberate speed."[15] Other public facilities, such as restaurants and bus terminals, were forced to desegregate as well.

The judiciary's application of the Fourteenth Amendment to state and local governments is illustrated by many contemporary cases that have, for example, established the rights of a person accused of a crime (*Miranda* v. *Arizona*), forced states to reapportion their legislature (*Baker* v. *Carr*; *Reynolds* v. *Sims*), declared state laws that prohibit abortion unconstitutional (*Roe* v. *Wade*), and required formal hearings for welfare recipients before benefits are terminated (*Goldberg* v. *Kelly*). (In 1989, the Court adjusted its position on abortion rights in *Webster* v. *Reproductive Health Services*, which reestablished states' rights to restrict access to abortion.) The national judiciary still exerts a major influence on the affairs of state and local governments. During the past few years, more than half of all cases decided by the U.S. Supreme Court have involved state and local governments.

The Growth of National Power through Congress

The U.S. Supreme Court has not been the only force behind nation-centered federalism; Congress has worked hand in hand with the judiciary. The commerce clause represents a good example. Given the simple authority to

Demonstrators in Washington, D.C., show their support for abortion rights as they await the Supreme Court's ruling in *Webster* v. *Reproductive Health Services.* The 1989 decision re-established the states' right to restrict abortion.

control or eliminate state barriers to trade across state lines, Congress now regulates commercial activities within a state's boundaries as well, as long as these activities have substantial national consequences. The states have made literally hundreds of legal challenges to such exercise of the commerce power, but almost all of them have been resolved by the U.S. Supreme Court in favor of the national government.

As the U.S. economy became increasingly complex and the states more and more interdependent, the national government's role in promoting and regulating commerce expanded. Following the Civil War, the national government granted money and land to corporations for the construction of canals and railroads. It also began regulating some of the excesses of business, which nonnational governments were unable to do because they could not pursue a culpable firm across state borders.

Taxing and Spending Power   Other factors have conspired with the nationalization of the U.S. economy to promote the growth of national power, including both world wars and the bitter experiences of the Korean and Vietnam wars. But probably the most controversial source of the rise in national power in recent years is the use of the *taxing and spending power* by Congress to extend its influence over the state and local governments. Under Article I, Section 8, Congress holds the power to tax and spend to provide for the common defense and general welfare. But the **Sixteenth**

Amendment, which grants Congress the power to tax the income of individuals and corporations, moved the center of financial power from the states to Washington, D.C. Through the income tax, the national government raises huge amounts of money, most of which is spent in the states. Like a parent doling out an allowance to a child, Congress has insisted on some sort of accountability in how state and local governments spend these funds.

The Grant-in-Aid   The **grant-in-aid**, which transfers funds for a particular purpose from one level of government to another, is the primary means for distributing national revenues to the states and localities. Attached to federal grants are a variety of conditions to which the recipients must adhere if they are to receive the money. These include requirements for recipient governments to match national contributions (ratios vary up to one state or local dollar for every national dollar), and regulations directly related to the purposes of the individual grant, such as meeting national standards for the quality of drinking water under the Safe Drinking Water Act. (The staggering growth in national grants-in-aid during the 1960s and 1970s and the strings attached to them receive a full discussion in Chapter 3.)

Federal Pre-emption   Besides using the commerce power and the grant-in-aid, the national government has seized power through the process known as **federal pre-emption**. The legal basis for pre-emption is Article VI of the Constitution, the national supremacy clause. Whenever a state law conflicts with a national law, the national law is dominant.

Some federal pre-emption concerns the requirements attached to grants; the minimum drinking age is a case in point (see Politics and Policy 2.1). Congressional passage of a national law that supercedes state legislation is directly pre-emptive. An example is the Air Quality Act, which replaced state standards on permissible levels of air pollutants with national standards. An extreme case of pre-emption is the Voting Rights Act of 1965, which enables the U.S. Justice Department to exercise an advance veto over changes in election procedures and jurisdictions in specified states and localities, and substitute national voting registrars for local ones where abuses in voting rights have occurred. Congress also pre-empts state law when it passes legislation that gives national administrators the power to veto programs, plans, and policies developed by state and local officials.

Gutting of the Tenth Amendment   Actions by the Congress and the federal courts have gradually undermined the Tenth Amendment, which reserves to the states all powers not specifically granted to the national government. In fact, it is very difficult to identify any field of state activity not intruded on by the national government today. Although the Tenth Amendment is a declaration of the original division of powers between nation and states under the Constitution, it bears little relevance to the configuration of American federalism in the 1990s.[16]

POLITICS AND POLICY 2.1
The Minimum Drinking Age: A Case of Federal Blackmail?

In 1984 Congress passed the National Minimum Drinking Age Law, which withheld substantial amounts of federal highway funds from states that did not make twenty-one the legal minimum drinking age by October 1986. In pre-empting state drinking age laws, Congress was responding to arguments (supported by several studies) that raising the drinking age would save lives by reducing fatal alcohol-related traffic accidents among eighteen- to twenty-year-old drivers. Supporters of the drinking age bill, such as Mothers Against Drunk Driving (MADD), further contended that a standard drinking age of twenty-one would eliminate "blood borders" like the boundary between Illinois and Wisconsin, where young people crossed state lines to enter jurisdictions with lower age limits and returned in various stages of inebriation.

Most of the twenty-seven states with lower drinking ages complied fairly quickly, although officials decried the federal "blackmail." Eight states held out. One, South Dakota, filed a suit challenging the constitutionality of the drinking age bill. Governor William Janklow said on NBC's *Today* show that he was in favor of restricting the drinking age to twenty-one and older, "but I'm violently opposed to the federal government thinking it's their responsibility and their duty and their obligation to impose it on the American people." A federal court of appeals dismissed the suit, noting that the states may set any legal drinking age that they want but that the national government has the right to withhold highway funds.

South Dakota and the other laggards eventually complied with the national requirement; Wyoming was the last. Each would have sacrificed millions of dollars if it had refused to raise the drinking age, and the states' highways were in serious need of repair and mainte-nance.[1] Once again the federal courts upheld the power of Congress to attach conditions to federal aid to the states.

[1] Laurie McGinley, "Move to Raise Drinking Age in Wisconsin Reflects Nationwide Pres-sure and Concern," *Wall Street Journal*, May 21, 1986, p. B1.

The one event that temporarily revived the Tenth Amendment in recent years was the decision of the U.S. Supreme Court in *National League of Cities v. Usery* (1976). At issue were the 1974 amendments to the Fair Labor Standards Act (FLSA), which extended federal minimum wage and maximum hour requirements to state and local employees. In a surprising turnaround, the Supreme Court ruled in favor of the states and localities, saying that Congress did not have the constitutional right to impose wage and hour requirements on their basic, or integral, functions, such as law enforcement and firefighting.[17]

Following a spate of litigation in the lower courts aimed at determining just which state and local activities were "integral," and a series of Supreme Court rulings that appeared to contradict the decision in *Usery*, the Supreme Court in 1985 heard the case of *Garcia v. San Antonio Metropolitan Transit Authority*. In *Garcia* the Court reversed its findings in *Usery* and once again applied federal wage and hour laws to nonnational governments. The 5-to-4 Court majority found the *Usery* decision to be "not only unworkable but inconsistent with established principles of federalism."[18]

The *Garcia* case was met with a hail of criticism. The Court had taken itself out of future controversies involving state claims against congressional power exercised under the commerce clause. Now Congress alone would be allowed to determine, through the political process, how extensively it would intrude on what had been state and local prerogatives. One dissenting Supreme Court justice wrote that "all that stands between the remaining essentials of state sovereignty and Congress is the latter's underdeveloped capacity for self-restraint."[19] Congress was thus unshackled from the last chain that restrained it from exercising complete national power in the field of commerce.

Powers Remaining with the States

Has judicial and congressional intervention in the affairs of state and local governments rendered them mere administrative appendages of the national government? Is state sovereignty a relic of the past? Is federalism obsolete in the 1990s? The answer to each of these questions is a resounding no. While the idea of state-centered federalism was effectively squashed by the Civil War, and states' rights are quite limited in the Constitution and in practice, the states do retain considerable power.

The states are explicitly mentioned or directly referred to fifty times in the U.S. Constitution. They are specifically guaranteed territorial integrity, the power to maintain a militia (the National Guard), and various powers related to commerce, taxation, and the administration of justice. States participate in national governance by electing their residents as representatives in Congress. All have two members in the Senate and at least one in the House of Representatives. States also determine the time, place, and manner of holding elections for congressional seats. They participate in

POLITICS AND POLICY 2.2
Who is Commander in Chief of the National Guard?

Each state has a militia called the National Guard. With roots that go back to the first permanent militia in the Massachusetts Bay Colony in 1636, the National Guard assists the states and localities in coping with crime, civil disturbances, and natural disasters. The governor is designated commander in chief of the state Guard by federal and state law. The U.S. Constitution (Article I, Section 8) authorizes Congress "to provide for organizing, arming, and disciplining the militia," but grants the states the right to appoint officers in their respective forces.

The question of who commands the National Guard arises in the context of the Defense Department's "total forces policy," which uses the state militias to fill in for manpower reductions caused by termination of the military draft. In the event of war, National Guard troops would make up close to 50 percent of regular U.S. combat forces. In order to prepare Guard members adequately for such a possibility, state units have been sent to forty-six different countries for six-month training duties. This came under criticism when units were posted to Honduras, El Salvador, and Costa Rica in support of controversial U.S. foreign policy efforts to aid the Contra guerrillas in their fight against the government of Nicaragua. The National Guard was training in and around combat areas, although war had not been declared.[1]

The governors of several

presidential elections through the electoral college, in which each state is allotted presidential votes based on its total number of senators and representatives in Congress. Finally, amendments to the U.S. Constitution must be ratified by three-fourths of the states. Politics and Policy 2.2 shows that even the "guaranteed" powers may not be absolute.

The most direct influence of the states, and their primary importance, stems from the actions they take (or choose not to take) that affect the lives of those who live within their borders. The states provide a broad spectrum of services, from higher education to corrections. They tax us, spend money on us, and employ us. Our state government touches our lives in some way every day.

states, including Maine, Nebraska, Arizona, and Massachusetts, refused to permit their troops to train in Honduras during 1986 and 1987. Mississippi Congressman Sonny Montgomery introduced a measure to halt governors from taking such actions except when their units were needed for local emergencies. The measure passed as an amendment to a defense bill. It was almost immediately challenged in a lawsuit by Minnesota. Hawaii, Maine, Ohio, Vermont, Massachusetts, and seven other states joined the suit, contending the the Montgomery amendment violated the fundamental constitutional right of the states to control their militias.[2]

A federal judge ruled in August 1987 that governors do not have the authority to prevent their militias from training overseas, but the ruling was overturned by the 8th U.S. Circuit Court of Appeals in December 1988. Meanwhile, the national government continues to pressure the states to comply with National Guard training in Central America. When the Governor of Ohio said that he would not allow his militia to be trained in Honduras, the national government responded with a threat to withdraw funding and equipment for the Ohio National Guard. The Pentagon supplies close to 95 percent of the budget of the National Guard.

The final outcome of the confrontation will be determined by the U.S. Supreme Court. The major issue is whether the Framers of the Constitution intended for the states to have full control over their militias as a check on the power of the national government.

[1] Neal R. Peirce, "Debate Grows Over Control of Guard," *P.A. Times* 10 (February 15, 1987): 2.
[2] Ibid.

Models of Federalism

Perceptions of the role of the states in the federal system have shifted from time to time throughout our history. Those who study the federal system have attempted to describe these perceptions through various models, which attempt to present something complex in a form that is readily understandable. These models have been used both to enhance understanding and to pursue ideological and partisan objectives. One complete inventory uncovered 326 models of federalism,[20] but only the best-known ones are reviewed here, to demonstrate that the American federal system and people's perceptions of it change.

Dual Federalism (1787–1932)

The model of **dual federalism** holds that the national and state governments are sovereign and equal within their respective spheres of authority as set forth in the Constitution. The national government exercises those powers specifically designated to it, and the remainder are reserved for the states. The nation and the states are viewed as primarily competitive, not cooperative, in their relationships with one another.

Figure 2.1 shows two ways to conceptualize dual federalism. "Layer cake" federalism[21] is represented in the left half of the figure, and the "coordinate authority" model[22] is on the right. Both demonstrate the separation of national and state authority. In layer cake federalism, the local government is implicitly subsumed by state authority; in the coordinate authority model, this relationship is explicit.

Dual federalism, which has its roots in the compact theory (see pp. 25–26), was dominant for the first 145 years of American federalism, although the Civil War and other events led to substantial modifications of the model during the early 1900s.[23] Until 1860 the functions of the national government remained largely restricted to the delegated powers. Federal financial assistance to the states was very limited. The states had the dominant influence on the everyday lives of their citizens, acting almost unilaterally in such areas as elections, education, economic development, labor relations, and criminal and family law.[24] After the Civil War shattered the doctrines of interposition, nullification, and secession, and dealt the compact theory of state-centered federalism a severe blow, the nation-centered view became paramount. Intergovernmental finance emerged, with the introduction of the federal grant-in-aid. By the end of the era of dual federalism, fifteen grant programs were operational in education, highways, welfare, and other fields. The national government was dominant in banking, economic regulation, and military power.

Figure 2.1   Dual Federalism
In dual federalism, local governments are implicitly (layer cake model) or explicitly (coordinate authority model) located within the realm of state authority.

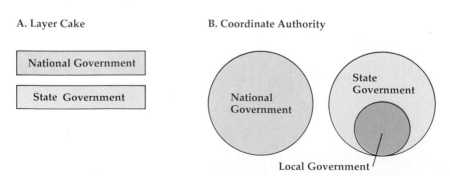

The national government's new activities, however, did not take away the states' traditional functions. They retained responsibility for their historical functions and even enlarged their activities in many fields, such as taxation and regulatory policy. For the most part, national and state governance continued to be carried out separately.

Cooperative Federalism (1933–1964)

The selection of a specific date for the demise of dual federalism is rather subjective, but 1933, when Franklin Roosevelt became president, is as good a date as any. Roosevelt's New Deal buried dual federalism by expanding national authority over commerce, taxation, and the economy.

Cooperative federalism has been called the "marble cake model,"[25] in recognition of the increased sharing of responsibilities and financing by all levels of government. It has also been referred to as the "overlapping authority model" (see Figure 2.2).[26] Beginning with the Great Depression, the national government increasingly cooperated with states and localities to provide jobs and social welfare, to develop the nation's infrastructure, and to promote economic development.

The cooperative aspects of this era were evident in governmental finances. The national government spent huge amounts of money to alleviate

Figure 2.2   Cooperative Federalism
The marble cake and overlapping authority variants of cooperative federalism show that government responsibilities are shared.

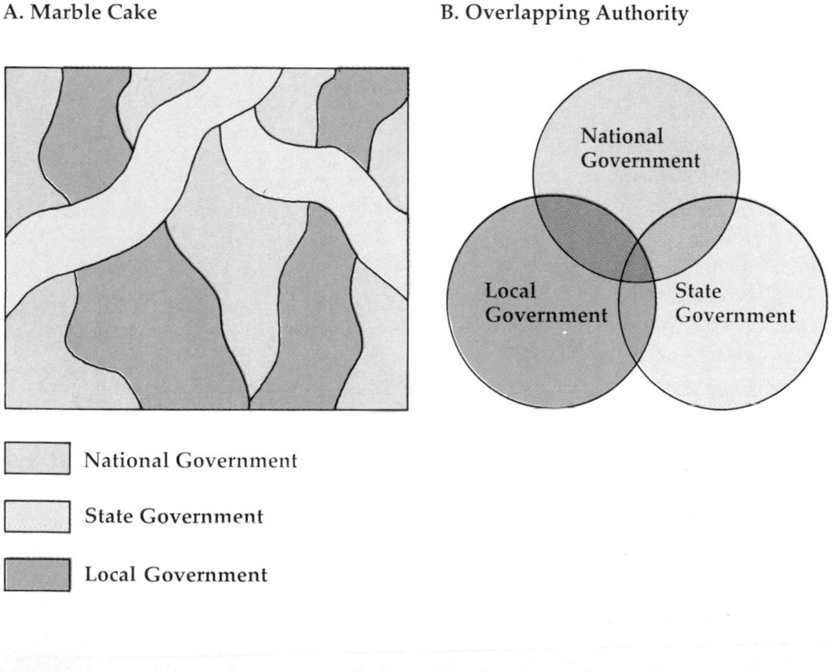

A. Marble Cake

B. Overlapping Authority

National Government

State Government

Local Government

the ravages of the Depression and to get the American economy back into gear. Total federal expenditures rose from 2.5 percent of the gross national product (GNP) in 1929 to 18.7 percent just thirty years later, far surpassing the growth in state and local spending during the same period. The number of federal grants-in-aid rose from twelve in 1932, with a value of $193 million, to twenty-six in 1937, with a value of $2.66 billion. By 1960 there were 132 separate grant programs. A substantial amount of the federal aid was sent directly to local governments, particularly counties and school districts. The variety of grant programs exploded. By 1939 there were grants for maternal and child health, old-age assistance, aid to the blind, fire control, treatment of venereal disease, public housing, road and bridge construction, and wildlife conservation. Before the era of cooperative federalism ended in 1964, programs in airport construction, cancer research, fish restocking, school milk, water pollution, waste treatment, and many other areas were added.

Contemporary Variations on Cooperative Federalism (1964 to the present)

There have been many recent variations on the broad theme of cooperative federalism. All of them stress intergovernmental sharing.[27] Among these variations are creative federalism, picket fence federalism, and New Federalism.

Creative Federalism **Creative federalism** was devised by President Lyndon B. Johnson to promote his dream of a "Great Society." Johnson sought to build the Great Society through a massive national government attack on the most serious problems facing the nation: poverty, crime, poor health care, and inadequate education, among others. The vehicle for the attack was the federal grant-in-aid. More than two hundred new grants were put into place during the five years of Johnson's presidency. The major "creativity" in Johnson's policy of vast government spending involved bypassing the states in distributing funds for some seventy of the new programs. Federal disbursements went directly to cities and counties rather than through the states. Understandably, the states did not appreciate the loss of influence over how localities could spend their national dollars.

Picket Fence Federalism **Picket fence federalism** (see Figure 2.3) is a model offered by former North Carolina governor and present U.S. senator Terry Sanford that illustrates the important role of national, state, and local administrators within functional programs.[28] Officials specializing in a single program area, such as public welfare, have closer attachments to their functional (program) counterparts at all levels of government than to various mayors, governors, and legislators. For example, welfare officials

Figure 2.3   Picket Fence Federalism
The horizontal and vertical "boards" on this fence indicate the common interests of functional program specialists at all three levels of government.

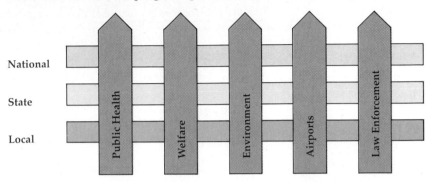

in the federal Department of Health and Human Services share professional training, education, goals, and values with state, county, and municipal social welfare employees. They tend to be more responsive to these associates than to the president, governor, mayor, county executive, or various legislative bodies. As a consequence, coordination and implementation of social welfare policies are likely to be influenced more by functional specialists than by elected officials.

The picket fence model describes many aspects of American federalism from the mid-1960s to the mid-1970s. However, it is overdrawn today, since it fails to account for competing programs and for professionals in the same field who battle over program goals. The model also fails to appreciate the success of government interest groups such as the National Governors' Association and the National League of Cities in challenging program professionals and reasserting executive leadership over bureaucracies.[29]

New Federalism   New Federalism is a model that has been employed with separate but closely related meanings by two different presidents. The New Federalism of Richard Nixon called for a fundamental reordering of national-state-local relations. Partly in reaction to the centralizing excesses of creative federalism, New Federalism was intended to restore power to the states and localities and improve intergovernmental arrangements for delivering services. Among the major policy changes brought about by the Nixon administration were the establishment of ten regional councils to coordinate national program administration across the country, and the simplification and streamlining of federal regulations that apply to state and local government. States and localities were also given greater flexibility in program spending and decision making.

Ronald Reagan's brand of New Federalism is discussed in detail in Chapter 3. Like Nixon's version, it sought to give more power and program authority to states and localities, at least in theory. However, Reagan's main goal—to shrink the size of the national government—soon became obvious.

The Advantages and Disadvantages of Federalism

Federalism, as it has evolved in the United States, is a reasonably effective system of government. That it is not perfect, or well suited to the circumstances of most other nations, is demonstrated by the fact that it exists in only a small number of countries. Federalism offers certain advantages and disadvantages that deserve consideration.

The Advantages

There are five major arguments in favor of a federal system of government.

1. *A federal system facilitates the management of social and political conflict.* First, it broadly disperses political power among governments. The American federal system includes a national government with a *bicameral* (two-chamber) legislative branch. The U.S. Senate represents the geographical diversity of the states, with two senators for each territorial unit, and the House of Representatives is apportioned on the basis of population. This system enables general as well as regional concerns to reach the central government. Local interests are expressed in state capitols through state legislatures and, of course, in city and county councils and other local legislative bodies. Ideally, this allows government to deal with problems before they reach the crisis stage. Many potential centers exist for resolving conflicts. In addition, citizens may express loyalty to more than one government: a person might consider herself an Atlantan, a Georgian, and an American.

Second, a federal system provides numerous bases for political parties to express interests and ideas. This helps maintain a balanced party system. The Democrats may have little influence in the state government of New Hampshire, but they dominate the politics of Massachusetts. A Republican may sit in the White House, but a majority of governors are Democrats. The point is that the federal system helps the political parties remain strong by providing a wellspring for continual rebirth and rebuilding.

Finally, federalism achieves unity through diversity. The United States has a highly diverse population that varies in ethnicity, color, religious preference, and many other factors. These differences are not distributed randomly in the population; people who share certain traits tend to cluster together. Thus, state and local governments represent them. For example, the large and growing Hispanic population of Texas is increasingly gaining representation in the state legislature and in mayoral and city council offices.

2. *Federalism promotes administrative efficiency.* The transfer of responsibility from the national government to states and localities, in order to provide the wide variety of services that citizens demand, helps deliver those services more efficiently. From public elementary education to garbage collection, the government closest to the problem seems to work best in adapting public programs to local needs.

Certainly there are advantages to operating on a large scale in some areas, such as national defense and environmental protection. Functions that do not respect jurisdictional lines are more efficiently carried out by a central government. But a centralized bureaucracy in Washington, D.C., is ill-prepared and probably incapable of designing and implementing services whose scale and dimensions vary from place to place. It is difficult to imagine the local office of the national government in Idaho or Nevada overseeing garbage collection; unit costs would soar. The enormous task of providing mundane public services to the 240 million people living across this vast land calls for a decentralized system. Federalism helps keep the national government from collapsing under its own weight.

3. *Federalism encourages innovation.* A tremendous variety of approaches for solving problems exists in the American federal system. States and localities can customize their policies to the diversity of their residents' demands and needs, and heterogeneity flourishes. New policies are constantly being tested by the more than 84,000 government "laboratories." More and more, state and local governments exchange information on policy approaches, which further encourages experimentation and flexibility across the country. Interestingly, virtually all national government programs have been tested initially at the state or local level. Examples include unemployment compensation, income assistance, and job health and safety programs.

4. *A federal system maximizes political participation in government.* Citizens have opportunities to participate at all three levels of government through elections, public hearings, and other means. The local and state governments serve as political training camps for aspiring leaders, who can test the waters in a school board or county council election and, if successful, move on to bigger electoral prizes in the state or national arena. The great majority of presidents and U.S. senators and representatives got their start in state or local politics. In all, almost one million offices are regularly filled through elections. These opportunities for public participation mean that government is accessible to the people. Citizens can have a meaningful say in decisions that affect their lives. Furthermore, access increases accountability in government, helping to ensure that citizens' demands are taken into consideration during policy formation.

5. *A federal system helps protect individual freedom.* A major reason that the Framers chose a federal system of government was that it provides numerous potential points of opposition to national government policies and political ideology. The fear expressed in eloquent detail by Madison was that a strong central government unchecked by the sovereign states would

encourage a tyranny of the majority. Madison argued that the numerous checks inherent in a federal system would control the effects of faction, making "it less probable that a majority of the whole will have a common motive to invade the rights of other citizens; or if such a common motive exists, . . . more difficult for all who feel it to discover their own strength and to act in unison."[30] From Madison's perspective, the states serve as defenders of democracy by ensuring that no national ideological juggernaut can sweep over the entire nation, menacing the rights of individual citizens.

The Disadvantages

Federalism has performed admirably in the United States, but it is not without flaws. Ironically, its weaknesses are closely related to its strengths.

1. *Federalism may facilitate the management of conflict in some settings, but in others it makes conflict more dangerous.* This has occurred in federal experiments in Nigeria and Canada. In Nigeria, the formal recognition of tribally based regions helped to spawn a devastating civil war in the 1960s. In Canada, recognition by the national government of the ethnically French province of Quebec helped fuel a secessionist movement during the 1970s. The lesson seems to be that a unitary government may be more appropriate for a country marked by strong ethnic, racial, or religious divisions.

2. *Although providing services through governments that are close to the people can promote efficiency, federalism can also hinder progress.* It is extraordinarily difficult, if not impossible, to coordinate the efforts of all state and local governments to combat social and economic problems. Picture trying to get 84,000 squawking and flapping chickens to move in the same direction at once.

3. *Not surprisingly, so many governments lead to duplication and confusion.* Fifty-one separate and independent court systems bring about a great deal of confusion. A complex federal system like our own is a lawyer's sweet dream. A good example is the legal snarl that developed over the will of the multimillionaire Howard Hughes. Born and raised in Texas, Hughes spent much of his life and made the bulk of his fortune in California and Nevada. He died in an airplane, without a will. It took many years, the involvement of the U.S. Supreme Court, and millions of dollars from the estate before Hughes' business affairs and inheritance were settled. Five different state court systems were involved, each with its own unique set of rules and precedents.[31]

4. *Federalism may promote state and local innovation, but it can also hinder national programs and priorities.* The many points of involvement for state and local government can cause obstruction and delay and result in an ineffective national government. An obvious example is the successful opposition of the southern states to voting rights for blacks for more than a hundred years. Federal laws and the U.S. Constitution set forth the right of black Americans to vote, but some states systematically denied them this right until implementation of the national Voting Rights Act of 1965.

5. *Broad opportunity for political participation is highly desirable in a democracy, but it may encourage local biases that damage the national interest.* Chemical and radioactive wastes must be disposed of somewhere, but local officials are quick to scream, "Not in my back yard!" Another example involves smoking and chewing tobacco, which are major causes of illness and high health care costs; representatives from the tobacco-growing states stoutly defend the industry from regulation, taxation, or abolition.

Local Governments in American Federalism

In a formal sense, local governments in the American federal system operate under a unitary system. Municipalities, counties, towns, townships, school districts, and other local governments are created by the states. Their powers depend on what the states decide to let them do. This was a conscious decision on the part of the Framers, who rarely mentioned the role of local governments in their debates on federalism. Local governments are nowhere named in the U.S.Constitution.

Dillon's Rule

Local government powers are derived primarily from the state constitutions. Federal and state courts have consistently upheld the dependency of localities on their state since Iowa Judge John F. Dillon first laid down **Dillon's Rule** in 1868. Dillon's Rule established that local governments may exercise only those powers explicitly granted to them by the state, those clearly implied by these explicit powers, and those absolutely essential to the declared objectives and purposes of the local government. When there is doubt regarding the legality of any specific local government power, the courts will resolve it in favor of the state.[32]

The result of Dillon's Rule is that local governments have relatively little discretionary power. When local officials want to take on a new responsibility or provide a new service, they must first ask the state legislature or the governor for the appropriate authority. This rule applies even to such mundane matters as opening a city skating rink or operating a concession stand at a municipal ballpark.

Home Rule

Thus, in theory and in constitutional law, local governments are cloistered within the walls built by the state. However, most state constitutions have partially opened the doors for at least some types of local governments through home rule. **Home rule** is a legal arrangement by which the state issues local governments a charter that allows discretion and flexibility in carrying out their activities. In effect, it recognizes a form of dual federalism *within* states by formally delegating certain powers to local government.[33] Because the courts have excluded any local powers other than those specifically enumerated, this grant of local authority may be rather limited. Approximately half the states have carried home rule a step further, by granting localities a general range of powers to perform their duties. In these states the localities do not have to make special requests before taking care of traditional city business.

Home rule has resulted in some autonomy for municipalities and counties (it does not usually apply to other forms of local government). Although it has broadened their scope of authority beyond Dillon's Rule, many remain highly dependent on the state. A controversial decision handed down by the U.S. Supreme Court in 1982 reaffirmed the dependency of local governments and restricted broad grants of authority under home rule. In *Community Communications Co.* v. *City of Boulder*, the Court held that local governments do not have immunity from antitrust suits filed under the Sherman Antitrust Act, unless specifically granted by the states.[34] (An antitrust suit seeks to break up a monopoly on some good or service.) Prior to the *Boulder* decision it was widely assumed that local governments, like the states, could not be sued for conduct alleged to have anticompetitive effects on a firm. The *Boulder* case, which involved a city monopoly on cable TV, spawned more than two hundred lawsuits in areas ranging from ambulance service and taxicabs to garbage collection. Because of this, Congress passed a law in 1984 limiting the damages to be paid by localities found to be violating antitrust law. The importance of *Boulder* is that local governments continue to be held to the standards of Dillon's Rule. They have only those powers and immunities specifically granted to them by the states or clearly related to their delegated powers. Immunity from antitrust suits is not within the realm of specified or implied powers under home rule.

Interstate Cooperation

The states often cooperate formally or informally in dealing with common problems. This is known as *horizontal federalism*. Formal methods for cooperation are grounded in the U.S. Constitution. Informal ones have evolved from day-to-day interactions.

Cooperation Under the Constitution

There are four formal provisions for interstate cooperation.

1. *The full faith and credit clause* of the Constitution binds every citizen of every state to the laws and policies of other states. This means, among other things, that a person who has a legitimate debt in North Dakota will be made to pay even if he moves to Montana. Crossing a state boundary does not alter a legal obligation. The courts have interpreted full faith and credit to apply to contracts, wills, divorces, and many other legalities. The clause

does not, however, extend to criminal judgments.

2. *The interstate rendition clause* begins where full faith and credit leaves off, covering those convicted of criminal violations. Governors are required to extradite (return) fugitives to the state in which they were found guilty or are under indictment. Occasionally, however, a governor will refuse to extradite. A typical example is when an escaped felon has become a steadfast, law-abiding citizen in her new state, and has captured public support to continue her free life.

3. *The privileges and immunities clause* states that "the citizens of each state shall be entitled to all privileges and immunities of citizens in the several states." This clause was intended by the Framers to prevent any state from discriminating against the citizens of another state who happen to be traveling or temporarily dwelling outside their own state's borders. Of course, states do discriminate against nonresidents in such matters as out-of-state tuition, hunting and fishing license fees, and residency requirements for voting. The Supreme Court has upheld these and other minor discrepancies, so long as the "fundamental rights" of nonresidents are not violated. Such rights include the right to conduct business, to have access to state courts, and to travel freely across state borders. Floridians cannot keep New Yorkers from settling and working in Tampa any more than Californians could prevent refugees from the Dust Bowl from moving to the Golden State during the Depression.

4. Finally, the *interstate compact clause* authorizes the states to negotiate compacts. Early interstate compacts were used to settle boundary disputes. More than 120 are in effect today in a wide variety of areas, including nuclear power, pest control, and education.

The interstate compact is an effective means of resolving complex problems between states. It has the force of law, is highly flexible, and is adaptable to some of the toughest problems confronting the states. The compact has also become an active vehicle for change. Its usefulness is readily apparent in one of its most recent applications—the management and disposal of low-level radioactive wastes, including laboratory clothing, tools, equipment, concrete, and virtually any other material that has been contaminated with radioactivity. The national government performed poorly in managing these wastes, and the states thought they could do better. Governors and other officials from several states convinced Congress to turn over responsibility for the problem to the states. Generally speaking, interstate compacts in this field have proceeded slowly, but successfully, as the states have assembled themselves into regional groups for the management and disposal of their own nuclear garbage (see Chapter 18).[35]

Informal Cooperation Among the States

A variety of informal methods exist for interstate cooperation. First, there are regional interstate commissions, such as the Appalachian Regional Commission (ARC),[36] which was created by national legislation in 1965 to attack poverty in the states of Appalachia. The ARC coordinates federal aid programs in the region and allocates its own funds for improvements in public health, transportation, and other areas.

States also develop uniform laws to help manage common problems. The National Conference of Commissioners on Uniform State Laws has met regularly since 1892 to develop comparable model statutes on approximately 150 topics, ranging from child support to welfare cheating. States may voluntarily adopt the uniform laws proposed by the conference.

A growing amount of interstate cooperation occurs through information sharing among elected and appointed officials, often through organizations designed to facilitate the exchange of information on assorted problems and proposed remedies. The National Governors' Association, the National Conference of State Legislatures, the Council of State Governments, and many other organizations meet each year to share information. They also publish professional journals, newsletters, and research reports.

The scope and number of cooperative mechanisms have expanded substantially in response to new and more complex problems facing the states. More interstate cooperation is also a product of the resurgence of the states as innovative, effective, and responsive actors within the American federal system. Of course, interstate relations do not always go well—the states get into serious (and not so serious) conflicts and disagreements. Those that the states cannot settle themselves are taken directly to the U.S. Supreme Court for resolution.

An Enduring Issue of Federalism

A single broad issue in American federalism transcends all others: what is the proper balance of power and responsibility between the national government and the states? The debate over this profound question first arose in preconstitutional days, as Jefferson, Madison, Hamilton, and others put forward their views. The Constitution represents a compromise between the most knowledgeable figures of the times, who decided that both levels of government would be sovereign and strong.

In recent times the balance of power and responsibility undeniably has shifted toward the national government. But all the growth in national governmental power and responsibility has not been at the expense of the states and localities. They too have increased their respective scope of activities in the social and economic lives of their citizens. Government has grown at all levels. The states are determined to oppose further federal pre-emptions of their powers and responsibilities. They have fought to protect the health, safety, and physical environment of their citizens, often with standards and commitment that far exceed those of the federal government. They have continued to serve as political laboratories for experiments in service delivery and other fields. As the burdens of governing 240 million Americans have grown, the limitations of the national government have become evident. The states have stepped forward as vigorous and progressive partners in federalism. Dual federalism is a vestige of earlier, simpler times. Effective federalism in the United States today demands a cooperative partnership among nation, states, and localities.

The question of the balance of power and responsibility in American federalism is no less important now than it was two hundred years ago. The focus of the debate has shifted, however, to a pragmatic interest in how the responsibilities of governing should be sorted out among the three levels of government. As pointed out by Samuel H. Beer, an insightful observer of American government, "The American federal system has never been static. It has changed radically over the years, as tides of centralization and decentralization have altered the balance of power and the allocation of functions among the different levels of government."[37] The pendulum marking the balance has swung to and fro over the two centuries of American federalism. Today it swings in the direction of the state and local governments.

Summary

The evolution of American federalism continues in the 1990s. From the early experiment with a confederation of states, to state-centered (compact) federalism, to nation-centered federalism, the trend has generally been in the direction of stronger national government. The states, however, remain very important political actors. The power relationships among the three levels of government are described by various models, including dual federalism, picket fence federalism, and cooperative federalism. Cooperative federalism is the operative model today, under the variant known as New Federalism.

Federalism has certain advantages and disadvantages. Among the advantages are managing conflict and promoting efficiency, innovation, participation, and individual freedom. But federalism can also facilitate conflict, hinder progress, lead to duplication, obstruct national programs, and encourage local bias. Two special concerns in American federalism are the role of local governments and methods for permitting interstate cooperation.

Key Terms

Commerce clause Article I, Section 8 of the U.S. Constitution, which permits Congress to control trade with foreign countries and among the states.

Compact theory *See* state-centered federalism.

Confederacy A league of sovereign states in which a limited central government exercises few independent powers.

Cooperative federalism A model of federalism that stresses the linkages and joint arrangements among the three levels of government.

Creative federalism A model of cooperative federalism in which many new grants-in-aid, including direct national-local financial arrangements, were made.

Dillon's Rule Limits the powers of local government to those expressly granted by the state, or those closely linked to expressed powers.

Dual federalism Theory in which the responsibilities and activities of the national and state governments are separate and distinct.

Enumerated (delegated) powers Those expressly given to the national government in Article I, Section 8 of the Constitution.

Faction Any group of citizens or interests united in a cause or action that threatens the rights or interests of the larger community.

Federal pre-emption The idea that national laws take precedence over state laws.

Fourteenth Amendment Enacted in 1866 to protect the rights of freed slaves, its due process and equal rights provisions now apply to all citizens.

General welfare clause The portion of Article I, Section 8 of the Constitution that provides for the general welfare of the United States.

Grant-in-aid An intergovernmental transfer of funds or other assets.

Home rule The legal ability of a local government to run its own affairs, subject to state oversight.

Implied powers Those that are not expressly granted by the Constitution but that are inferred from the enumerated powers.

Interposition The right of a state to nullify an act of Congress within its own borders.

National supremacy clause Article VI of the Constitution, which makes national laws superior to state laws.

Nation-centered federalism Theory in which the national government is dominant over the states.

Necessary and proper clause Portion of Article I, Section 8 of the Constitution that authorizes Congress to enact all laws "necessary and proper" to carry out its responsibilities.

New Federalism A model that sought to return powers and responsibilities to the states.

Nullification *See* interposition.

Picket fence federalism A model that portrays program specialists in national, state, and local bureaucracies as major policy and administrative actors.

Reserved powers Those powers residing with the states by virtue of the Tenth Amendment.

Sixteenth Amendment Enacted in 1913, this amendment grants the national government the power to levy income taxes.

State-centered federalism Theory in which the national government represents a voluntary compact or agreement between the states, which retain a dominant position.

Tenth Amendment *See* reserved powers.

Unitary government One in which all authority is derived from a central authority.

3

Federalism and Public Policy

Intergovernmental Financial Relations
The Grant-in-Aid/Recent Changes in
National Expenditures

Reagan's New Federalism
A New "New Federalism"/In Retrospect

Social Welfare Policy and Federalism
The Meaning of Poverty/Social Welfare and
Ideology/Current Social Welfare Policy/Types of
Social Welfare Programs/State Innovations in
Social Welfare/Social Welfare Policy
and Federalism

Higher Education Policy and Federalism
Intergovernmental Roles/Actors in Higher
Education Policy/Problems in Higher Education
and What the States Are Doing

Federalism's Evolving Nature

Among the many points made in the preceding chapter, two stand out: the American federal system is constantly evolving, and it is remarkably complex. Federalism is a matter of power, authority, and—very importantly—money. The change and complexity that characterize it have been both legal and financial. Federalism is a question not only of which level of government will do what but of which level will pay for it. Often, the correct answer is "all levels."

This chapter discusses the federalism of the 1980s and what it will mean for federalism in the 1990s. And the chapter focuses on the importance of federalism in *public policy*, which involves actions by governments to solve problems or pursue a particular course to improve society. When Republican Ronald Reagan defeated the incumbent president, Democrat Jimmy Carter, in 1980, a new era in American federalism began. Intergovernmental financial relations have changed, the responsibilities of each level of government have been altered, and states and their local governments have become sources of innovation and creative problem solving. We have entered a period that some have called "fend-for-yourself federalism."[1]

Intergovernmental Financial Relations

"Give me money, that's what I want. . . ." So goes the refrain of an old blues tune that is not about government but might have been. Money has always been important to government, although the word *money* is seldom used. Instead, the talk is of revenues and expenditures. **Revenues** are the funds that governments have at their disposal. They are derived from taxes, fees and charges, and transfers from other levels of government. **Expenditures** are the ways in which the governmental revenues are disbursed. Governments spend money to operate programs, to build public facilities, and to pay off debts. The twentieth century has seen steady increases in both revenues and expenditures at all levels of government.

The Grant-in Aid

By the 1980s, the grant-in-aid (see Chapter 2) had become the primary mechanism for transferring money from the national to state and local governments.[2] The national government makes grants available for a number of reasons: to redistribute wealth, to establish minimum policy standards, and to achieve national goals. But grants are primarily designed to meet the needs of state and local governments, including natural resource and environmental protection, transportation, community and regional development, education, and health care.

Discretion of Recipients   There are two major variations in grants: the amount of discretion (independence) the recipient has in determining how to spend the money, and the conditions under which the grant is awarded. Imagine a spectrum running from maximum discretion to minimum discretion. The grant labels that correspond to these end points are **revenue sharing** and **categorical grants,** respectively. Under revenue sharing, states and communities are allocated funds that they may use for any purpose. A categorical grant, in contrast, can be used by the recipient government only for a narrowly defined purpose, such as removing asbestos from school buildings, acquiring land for outdoor recreation, training managers of bus systems, or constructing waste disposal systems.

Located between revenue sharing and categorical grants on the discretion spectrum are block grants. **Block grants** are *broad-based grants;* that is, they can be used anywhere within a functional area, such as elementary and secondary education, transportation, or training and employment. The difference between categorical and block grants is that the recipient government decides how block grants will be spent. For instance, a local school system can decide whether getting rid of the asbestos in school buildings is more important than buying microscopes for the science laboratory, but the local government cannot spend those block grant dollars outside the functional area of education.

Block grants and revenue sharing give nonnational governments considerable flexibility in responding to pressing needs and preferred goals. These grant mechanisms assume that state and local governments can make rational choices among competing claims.

Conditions for Grants   Grants also vary in the manner in which they are awarded. A **formula grant** makes funding available automatically, based on state and local conditions such as poverty level or unemployment rate. A **project grant** is awarded to selected applicants, based on administrative assessments of the strength of competing proposals. Block grants are distributed on a formula basis; categorical grants can be either formula- or project-based; approximately one-third are formula and two-thirds are project grants.[3] Formula grants offer more discretion to the recipient government than project grants do. (This is not the case for the national government, however. Project grants give the granting agency wide latitude in determining which projects will be funded.)[4]

These two characteristics, the amount of discretion enjoyed by the recipient jurisdiction and the manner in which the grant is awarded, are important for understanding the grant system. Another, less prominent factor also affects intergovernmental financial relations: the existence of *matching requirements.* Some federal grants require the recipient government to use its own resources to pay a certain percentage of program costs. This is designed to stimulate state and local spending and to discourage nonnational governments from participating in a program simply because money is available. For example, if a state government wants funding through the Boating Safety Financial Assistance program administered by the U.S. Department of Transportation, it must contribute 50 percent itself. For a local government to participate in the U.S. Interior Department's Urban Parks program, it must provide from 15 percent to 50 percent of the costs. In each case, the recipient government's commitment to boating safety or urban parks is likely to be higher because of the matching requirements. In 1987, most categorical grants carried a matching requirement.[5] Major exceptions to the trend toward matching grants, however, are in elementary, secondary, and vocational education and in health care programs.

Recent Changes in National Expenditures

During the 1980s, the flow of dollars from the national government to state and local governments slowed down. Although the Reagan administration greatly increased defense expenditures (mostly to pay for new weapons systems), national grants-in-aid to states and localities dropped by $10.4 billion (adjusted for inflation) from 1980 to 1985.[6] Grant expenditures accounted for 3.4 percent of the gross national product when Reagan was elected; eight years later, the figure was 2.4 percent.[7]

Table 3.1 provides both a historical and a projected look at national grant-in-aid expenditures. It is important to remember that the figures in the table have not been adjusted for inflation; the $2.3 billion spent in 1950 was worth vastly more than it would be today. Furthermore, the amounts do not take into account the increase in population since 1950 (in 1950, there were 151 million Americans; in 1988, the figure was estimated at 243 million). The second column of figures in Table 3.1 documents the decreasing proportion of national dollars in the expenditures of state and local governments in the 1980s.

The End of General Revenue Sharing   A principal factor in the decline of national aid to state and local governments during the 1980s was the termination of revenue sharing. Called *General Revenue Sharing* (GRS) when enacted during the Nixon administration, this program was immensely popular with state and local officials. GRS provided funds without strings to state and general-purpose local governments (cities, counties, townships). Given an initial life of five years and $30.1 billion in 1972, it was reauthorized for the same time and amount in 1976. The state portion of GRS (which amounted to one-third of the total) was discontinued in 1980. A similar and much-resisted fate befell the local government portion when the U.S. Congress refused to reauthorize GRS in late 1986.

GRS fell out of favor with Congress mostly because of tax effort. In the eyes of Congress, the availability of GRS funds allowed local governments to keep taxes unnaturally low, since they could use GRS funds to pay bills. If national dollars were going to be used in this way, Congress wanted more control over them. Moreover, the Reagan administration wanted to discontinue GRS because of the national budget deficit. Accordingly, federal funds to localities through GRS fell from $6.8 billion in 1980 to zero in 1988.[8]

Table 3.1   Historical Trends in Federal Grant-in Aid Outlays

	Total grant-in-aid outlays (in billions of dollars)	Federal grants as a percent of state and local expenditures
Five-year intervals:		
1950	$ 2.3	10.4
1955	3.2	10.1
1960	7.0	14.6
1965	10 9	15.2
1970	24.1	19.2
1975	49.8	22.7
Annually:		
1980	91.5	25.8
1981	94.8	24.6
1982	88.2	21.6
1983	92.5	21.3
1984	97.6	20.9
1985	105.9	20.9
1986	112.4	20.5
1987	108.4	18.3
1988	115.3	18.2
1989 (estimate)	123.6	NA
1990 (estimate)	123.6	NA
1991 (estimate)	126.1	NA
1992 (estimate)	129.7	NA
1993 (estimate)	134.0	NA
1994 (estimate)	138.1	NA

Note: Years are fiscal years. Dollar figures are not adjusted for inflation or population growth. NA = Not available

Source: U.S. Office of Management and Budget, *The Budget for Fiscal Year 1990, Special Analysis H* (Washington, D.C.: U.S. Government Printing Office, 1989) p. H-22.

The Continuing Importance of National Funds   The Washington-funded portion of state and local government expenditures peaked in 1978 at 26.5 percent.[9] It dropped to 20 percent in the mid-1980s and has been hovering around 18 percent ever since. Still, it remains an important source of revenue for nonnational governments.

The data in Table 3.2 provide an indication of the magnitude of the fiscal flow in states and regions. Grants to state and local governments averaged approximately $427 per person in 1987. However, the funds were not spread evenly across the country. As the first column of figures in Table 3.2

shows, Alaska and Wyoming, where people are few and far between, received the most per capita. Federal grants poured into these states at the rate of more than $900 per person. At the bottom of the list are Florida and Texas, where federal grant monies averaged slightly under $300 per person. Yet even in the grant-poor states, national funds remain an important source of revenue for state and local governments. (It should be noted that national expenditures in nongrant forms affect state and local economies substantially.[10] In the nongrant category are payments to individuals,

Table 3.2   Federal Grants-in-Aid by State and Region for Fiscal Year 1987

State and region	Per capita grants to state and local governments	Per capita state rank
New England	$499	—
Connecticut	464	17
Maine	580	7
Massachusetts	509	12
New Hampshire	368	42
Rhode Island	558	9
Vermont	573	8
Middle Atlantic	536	—
Delaware	467	15
Maryland	441	23
New Jersey	434	25
New York	669	3
Pennsylvania	442	22
Great Lakes	410	—
Illinois	386	36
Indiana	358	43
Michigan	456	19
Ohio	406	30
Wisconsin	448	21
Plains	418	—
Iowa	385	37
Kansas	342	46
Minnesota	480	14
Missouri	377	40
Nebraska	381	39
North Dakota	624	5
South Dakota	621	6

(cont.)

Table 3.2   Federal Grants-in-Aid by State and Region for Fiscal Year 1987
(*cont.*)

State and region	Per capita grants to state and local governments	Per capita state rank
Southeast	$ 371	—
Alabama	382	38
Arkansas	423	28
Florida	262	50
Georgia	404	31
Kentucky	457	18
Louisiana	430	26
Mississippi	485	13
North Carolina	339	47
South Carolina	374	41
Tennessee	416	29
Virginia	323	48
West Virginia	542	10
Southwest	326	—
Arizona	351	44
New Mexico	519	11
Oklahoma	403	32
Texas	289	49
Rocky Mountain	456	—
Colorado	350	45
Idaho	393	34
Montana	667	4
Utah	467	16
Wyoming	916	2
Far West	437	—
Alaska	1,189	1
California	398	33
Hawaii	425	27
Nevada	391	35
Oregon	456	20
Washington	436	24
U.S. Average	$ 427	

Source: U.S. Advisory Commission on Intergovernmental Relations, *Significant Features of Fiscal Federalism, 1989,* vol. 1 (Washington, D.C.: ACIR, 1989), p. 22.

notably through the social security system; purchases by the national government; and wages and salaries of federal workers.)

The Impact of National Cuts   Cutting grant funds carries a human price. Items excised from the national budget translate into a loss of benefits for the public. The Reagan administration cuts hit poor people particularly hard.[11] For example, public service jobs for the poor were eliminated, funding for low-income students was reduced, unemployed Americans could no longer receive a stipend while enrolled in job training, and rents for public housing increased while the number of new subsidized housing units declined. Governmental actions in Washington, D.C., can translate into real anguish in Gary, Indiana, or Pine Bluff, Arkansas, or in any other community across America.

Complicating intergovernmental financial relations is the 1985 Balanced Budget and Emergency Deficit Control Act (the Gramm-Rudman-Hollings bill), which is aimed at reducing the federal budget deficit. This law mandated that the national budget deficit be reduced to preset levels each year, with the goal of a balanced budget by 1991. Its passage meant that the administration could sequester (fail to spend) authorized funds in order to meet the deficit targets. An additional complication from the perspective of state and local officials was passage of the Tax Reform Act (TRA) in 1986, which immediately affected state tax collections and financing options for economic development.[12] All in all, the mid-1980s brought tremendous insecurity to intergovernmental financial relations.

Reagan's New Federalism

Ronald Reagan made his feelings about federalism quite clear in his 1982 State of the Union message.

> This administration has faith in state and local governments and the constitutional balance envisioned by the founding fathers. Together, after fifty years of taking power away from the hands of the people in their states and local communities, we have started returning power and resources to them.[13]

With this sentiment, the Reagan administration set out on an ambitious quest to devolve power and authority, that is, to turn back a variety of programs to state and local governments. In speaking to the National Conference of State Legislatures, President Reagan used a construction analogy to convey his message. He compared the federal system to a masonry wall composed of bricks (the states) and mortar (the national government). By 1980, the wall, in his view, had become more mortar than bricks.[14] His solution was to chip away at the mortar and let the bricks carry more weight.

A New "New Federalism"

President Reagan's New Federalism represented a departure from President Nixon's federalism of the same name. Nixon was intent on decentralization. For example, his administration wanted to free state and local governments from the conditions attached to federal grants, so it began General Revenue Sharing and consolidated a number of categorical grants into block grants. These actions meant that state and local governments were allowed to make decisions about spending priorities and program implementation.

In contrast, the motivation for Reagan's New Federalism was not only decentralization but, more important, budget cutting. One scholar termed it "a radical departure in intergovernmental fiscal relations characterized by devolution, disengagement, and decremental budgeting."[15] State and local governments were given more freedom to spend an ever-declining amount of federal funds. The strings were cut with a double-edged sword. In other words, state and local governments were forced to assume greater financial responsibility for an array of programs. In effect, the national government said to the states and localities, "If these programs are so important to you, then fund them yourselves." Unfortunately, many state and local governments were not in a position to pay up.

Reagan's Proposals   The first actions under Reagan's New Federalism involved specific proposals to combine existing categorical grants into comprehensive block grants. Reagan was successful in winning congressional approval to merge fifty-seven categorical grants into nine new block grants and to eliminate another sixty categorical grants in 1981.[16] The merger resulted in four health-related block grants: Child and Maternal Health Services, Preventive Health and Health Services, Primary Care, and Alcohol, Drug Abuse and Mental Health. The remaining five block grants were Social Services, Low-Income Home Energy Assistance, Community Services, Community Development for Small Cities, and Elementary and Secondary Education. These nine grants accounted for $7.5 billion of the total $88 billion in national aid to state and local governments during the 1982 fiscal year.[17]

How did this contribute to the goals of New Federalism? The $7.5 billion represented an almost 25 percent decrease from the previous year's allocation for the separate categorical grants.[18] The Reagan administration contended that state and local governments would need less money because the block grants would reduce paperwork. In addition, state governments were to enjoy new freedom in administering the block grants.

Insofar as federalism is concerned, the Reagan administration was never able to recapture the heady days of 1981. For example, in 1982, buoyed by his success the previous year, the President proposed a swap of programs between the national and state governments. This proposal, known as the "turnback," was intended to be the centerpiece of New Federalism. The states were to assume financial and administrative responsibility for two massive programs, Aid to Families with Dependent Children (AFDC) and the food stamp program, and forty smaller ones, such as child nutrition and education for the handicapped in exchange for a national takeover of the Medicaid program. Although national funds would have eased state assumption of the programs initially, the plan called for total state funding of the turned-back programs by 1991. Concern that these arrangements would financially strap all but the wealthiest states effectively stalled the proposal.

Subsequent Reagan concerns for the federal system were more conventional, as the administration abandoned restructuring and focused on funding reductions. For example, its budget proposals for 1986 advocated the termination of GRS for local governments, Urban Development Action Grants (UDAG), Economic Development Administration (EDA) grants and loans for public works and economic development, the Community Development Block Grant (CDBG) program, mass transit operating subsidies, and legal services for the poor. The proposed budget contained spending cuts or freezes in aid programs for the poor and a two-year moratorium on new commitments for low-cost housing or housing assistance.[19] Congress responded by postponing the abolition of GRS for a year, by cutting the CDBG and UDAG programs by 15 percent and 20 percent, respectively, and by making smaller-than-requested cuts in other aid programs.

Executive Order 12612   The final salvo in New Federalism came in the form of an *executive order*—a presidential action that has the effect of law. Executive Order 12612, issued by President Reagan in October 1987, was a product of the recommendations of the Domestic Policy Council. It called for a strict interpretation of the Constitution regarding the distribution of responsibilities between states and the national government. Based on President Reagan's "federalism principles," the Council developed a series of policymaking criteria to guide the national government, including the following ideas:

1. Limiting the size and scope of the national government protects political liberties.
2. The states are well positioned to assume greater responsibilities for governance.
3. Uncertainties about which level, national or state, possesses sovereignty should be resolved in favor of the states.[20]

According to Executive Order 12612, the national government should not take action unless a vital national interest is involved. It included three conditions for determining whether national government action is appropriate:

1. that the activity is within the constitutional authority of the national government;
2. that a problem is of national or significantly large regional scope and thus warrants national action;

3. that the benefits (both economic and noneconomic) derived from national action exceed the action's cost and that national government action is the most efficient solution possible.[21]

The order required federal agencies to test any legislative proposal according to these conditions. In addition, it set new standards for resolving
conflicts between national statutes and state laws, restricting a federal
agency's ability to rule that a federal statute pre-empts state law. The order
also required federal agencies to prepare federalism assessments, which
would gauge the financial, administrative, and legal impact of national
action on the states, to accompany their proposed policies. Since its issu-
ance, Executive Order 12612 has minimized the intrusion of federal agencies
into the state sphere.

In Retrospect

These actions may not have constituted the "Reagan Revolution" that some
people predicted. As two observers noted, "Reagan could not succeed in a
grand-scale dismantling of the whole constellation of grants to local and
state governments."[22] But there has certainly been a redirection of financial
responsibility.

The full force of Reagan's impact was deflected by a number of factors.
One was the organization of certain interests in American society. The
findings of researchers examining programmatic changes during the
Reagan era make this point quite convincingly.[23] Political scientists
Peterson, Rabe, and Wong found that Reagan-sponsored efforts at decentralization were most effectively resisted in programs such as health care,
where well-organized beneficiaries and policy professionals were established. Federal health care programs such as Medicare have become institutionalized, and are thus fairly resistant to threats. In federal housing programs, the administration was able to achieve more of its objectives because
professional and constituent support was limited, and so there is now a
substantially reduced national role in housing. The degree of the administration's success depended on the organization of interests and their relative power.

Another factor limiting Reagan's success was internal to the administration. Administration proposals betrayed a basic ambivalence about intent.
The administration's New Federalism, in all its manifestations, was held
together by the unifying theme of reduced spending, but beyond that
organizing principle, the actions were "inconsistent and incoherent," according to some.[24]

The Reagan years muddied the waters of federalism more than they
clarified them. The remainder of this chapter seeks to make the concept of
federalism more tangible by examining two distinctive policy fields. The
first, social welfare policy, has been dominated and directed by the national

government. It is a highly complex and often confusing area, with shifting goals and strident ideological and partisan debates. In fact, it was conflict over social welfare policies that ultimately sunk Reagan's New Federalism. The second policy, higher education, has been dominated and directed by the states. It is relatively simple to comprehend, and there is fairly broad agreement on goals and objectives.

Although in many respects social welfare and higher education appear at opposite ends of the policy spectrum, they share at least one very important trait. Like almost all public policy fields in American federalism, they involve key contributions by all three levels of government—national, state, and local. Intergovernmental sharing of policymaking and program implementation is central to federalism.

Social Welfare Policy and Federalism

Social welfare policy is intended to assist those people who, for various reasons, need help in coping with the burdens they carry through life. Aid to the poor and disadvantaged is the classic redistributive policy, in which income is transferred from those in the upper economic stratum to those in the lower. It is an accepted principle today that government should provide a safety net for those at the economic margins of society.

The recipients of government assistance are diverse, including such people as an unemployed Hispanic immigrant in a San Antonio barrio whose English is poor and whose prospects for a good job are even poorer, a Vietnamese immigrant living with an extended family in San Francisco while working during the day and studying at night, a fifteen-year old unwed mother in Cleveland who has little formal education and no job skills, a high school graduate in Detroit who was paralyzed because of an automobile accident and will probably never be able to earn a living, an Iowa farm family that has moved to Des Moines to look for work because the bank foreclosed on their mortgage, and an eighty-year-old widow in Phoenix, trying to make ends meet on her monthly social security check. These images are stereotypes, but they reflect some of the many faces of poverty in America. Some poor people do not receive any welfare benefits, but choose to fight their battles by themselves; some need temporary help until they get back on their feet again; and some are likely to be dependent on government assistance for the rest of their lives. Many of the poor work forty-hour jobs at low wages; others have never drawn a paycheck.

The Meaning of Poverty

There are very few cases of absolute deprivation in the United States. The necessities of life—food, clothing, housing—are widely available to all through government programs. The extreme, life-threatening poverty found in Ethiopia or rural Bolivia simply does not occur here. Instead, poverty in America consists of relative deprivation: some people are relatively poor when their wealth and income are compared to those of the middle class.

The national government uses a statistic called the poverty line to define poverty in quantitative terms. It is set at three times the amount of income necessary to purchase essential food. The official poverty line changes each year as the cost of food rises (or, very rarely, falls). In 1989 it was pegged at $12,100 for a nonfarm family of four.[25] The poverty line is important because it helps determine who qualifies for various forms of public assistance.

Poverty in America was once associated largely with old age, but this is no longer true. As the population has grown older and senior citizens have organized as a formidable interest group, higher social security benefits and programs such as Medicare have eased elderly people's financial burdens. Today the most alarming poverty victims are children. One of every four children is born into poverty, and the rate has been rising every year since 1970. Children are 3.7 times more likely then the elderly to be poor.[26]

Childhood poverty is related to a host of factors, the most obvious of which is the "feminization of poverty." This term refers to the startling growth of female-headed households over the past three decades. Single mothers of young children may choose to stay at home and take care of the children, in which case they may have to depend entirely on support from public assistance programs. If they find work, they must somehow contend with the serious shortage and high cost of day-care facilities. Their children often suffer from an unstable environment and deprivation. Poor children are at high risk for criminal behavior and drug abuse.

As we shall see, child poverty is being met with innovative responses by state and local governments. Unfortunately, limited governmental resources are leading inevitably to a generational reckoning in the 1990s, when society will have to decide how to allocate its resources between the old and the young.

Social Welfare and Ideology

Intense debates over political ideology and values have always stormed over the social welfare policy landscape, resulting in confused policy goals, a faulty patchwork of programs, and perpetual crisis. Until recently, conservatives and liberals propounded starkly opposing points of view on the causes of poverty and the appropriate government response.

Conservatives, who generally believe in a restricted role for government, have tended to accept a modern version of the nineteenth-century view that "the giving of relief is a violation of natural law."[27] According to this viewpoint, the poor are victims of their own deficiencies. If they are to rise above poverty, they must hoist themselves up by their own bootstraps. From this perspective, the poor get what they deserve. Charles Murray, in his book *Losing Ground,* lays out the conservatives' classic beliefs on government aid to the poor.[28] He attacks the social welfare system for interfering with the free market, discouraging more productive allocations of public funds, undermining the work ethic, encouraging immoral behavior, and creating a permanent "underclass" of dependent welfare recipients.

For liberals, who generally believe in a broad and active role for government, poverty is a structural problem. People fall into poverty because of factors essentially beyond their control, such as inadequate schooling, poor parents, no job training opportunities, a shortage of job openings, various forms of discrimination, and the up-and-down cycles of a capitalistic economy. According to this view, people cannot help being poor, and so it becomes the responsibility of government to relieve their poverty through public assistance programs.

The Origins of Social Welfare Policy   Our flawed and fragmented social welfare policy today is a reflection of shifting conservative and liberal control over the Congress and the presidency. The basic foundations of the welfare system were laid by the liberal Democratic administration of Franklin D. Roosevelt in response to the Great Depression of the 1930s. Private charity and state and local relief programs were completely inadequate for combatting the unemployment of 25 percent of the population and a collapsed national economy. The national government responded with massive programs designed to provide temporary relief through public assistance payments, job creation, and social security.

Since the 1930s, competing political parties and ideologies have sewn together a patchwork of programs to help the poor and unfortunate. The most generous contributor was President Lyndon B. Johnson's War on Poverty during the 1960s. Johnson greatly expanded the budgets of existing welfare programs and initiated new, expensive efforts to attack poverty, such as the Economic Opportunity Act of 1965, which included Head Start (an educational program for disadvantaged children), the Job Corps, and community action programs. Some of the War on Poverty programs seemed to work, and others clearly did not. Generally, however, the Roosevelt and Johnson policies improved the lot of the poor.[29]

The Republican approach to social welfare policy has consisted mostly of a conservative, hands-off posture. President Richard M. Nixon was an exception. His proposed Family Assistance Plan would have established a federally funded minimum subsistence level for all Americans through direct cash payments to the poor. Most existing welfare programs would have been scrapped in favor of the income maintenance plan, but Nixon's plan was unable to win congressional approval. Democratic President Jimmy Carter sought to resurrect the idea during the late 1970s, but again it failed to capture congressional favor. The conservative President Reagan sought to simplify social welfare policy by turning over control of certain programs to the states and localities, but the major impact of this approach was to halt temporarily some of the escalating welfare costs by cutting back on national funding. Reagan's actions led to an alarming increase in the number of families below the poverty line, even while the national economy registered moderately high growth. When Reagan took office in 1981, approximately 13 percent were in poverty; by 1983 the rate had risen to 15.2 percent. In 1987, following four years of economic growth, 13.5 percent of all Americans were living in poverty. This included 10.5 percent of whites, 33.1 percent of blacks, and 28.2 percent of Hispanics.[30]

A Social Welfare Consensus Interestingly, a social welfare consensus brought together conservatives and liberals into a new coalition for reform in the late 1980s.[31] Conservatives admitted the responsibility of government to help the truly needy and economically vulnerable, and liberals saw the need to attach certain obligations to welfare checks and to address the "behavioral dependency" of the underclass. Behavioral dependency, which means that poor people become dependent on society for their economic well-being through their own choices, is a serious problem for America's underclass, which is disproportionately young, male, and black. Many of these people are school and societal dropouts—borderline illiterates with no job skills. Some become involved in drugs and crime.[32]

The new consensus may reflect a common view of poverty, but there is less agreement on how to solve the problem. There *is* an understanding that different types of poverty should be treated distinctively. For example, children, seniors, working adults, and nonworking adults all have different needs. There is also agreement that government should help those who can climb out of poverty through job training and placement, and that able-bodied welfare recipients have an obligation to seek a job or perform public work.

Beyond these basic elements, the new consensus tends to fall apart. Conservatives seek "better" behavior from the poor, admonishing them to complete high school, get married and stay married, and find employment, even at low wages. Liberals are more willing to utilize social programs to transfer government resources to the poor.[33] Certainly there is no magic solution to the perennial problem of poverty. It will, indeed, always be with us.

Current Social Welfare Policy

After the Great Depression, social welfare policy became the responsibility of the national government, with very limited roles reserved to the states and localities. Today the U.S. government continues to dominate the field by legislating and regulating social welfare programs and by providing the bulk of the money to pay for them. The states, however, have brought the federal programs into action, administered them, and drawn up rules to determine who is eligible for benefits. Cities and counties have been involved in program implementation to a lesser extent.

The trend in the 1990s is for more state and local participation in designing and carrying out social welfare policies. As is the case in most public policy fields, the nonnational governments are the vanguard of innovation and program experimentation. Nevertheless, the money still comes overwhelmingly from Washington, D.C. As Figure 3-1 indicates, the percentage of national funding for social welfare has grown substantially since 1960. (The states also began picking up more local government welfare expenses during the Reagan years.)

There are dramatic variations among the states in levels of social welfare spending. In the largest program, Aid to Families with Dependent Children (AFDC), Alaska spends $550 per recipient each month and California spends $514. At the bottom of the AFDC list are Mississippi and Alabama, which pay only $104 and $113, respectively.[34] States controlled by the Democratic party tend to be more generous than Republican states, and strong party competition drives up benefit levels. Political culture has an impact as well. Moralistic political culture is conducive to high benefit levels, whereas traditionalistic political culture depresses aid to the poor. Individualistic states fall in between the two extremes.

Figure 3.1   Social Welfare Expenditures by Level of Government
The national government is still dominant in social welfare spending.
The uncontrollable growth of such institutionalized programs as
social security and Medicaid has boosted the national government's
percentage of total welfare funding.

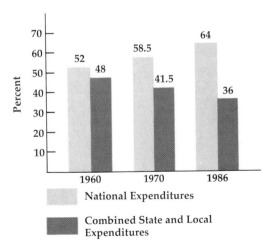

Source: U.S. Bureau of the Census, *Statistical Abstract of the United States, 1989* (Washington, D.C.: U.S. Government Printing Office), p. 347.

Types of Social Welfare Programs

The only way to get even a loose grip on complex intergovernmental social welfare policies is to examine the most significant ones individually. Programs fall into three categories: direct cash transfers, in-kind benefits, and social insurance (see Table 3.3).

Direct Cash Transfers   **Direct cash transfers** are welfare programs that directly convey money, in the form of government checks, to qualifying recipients. Administrative arrangements vary by type of program.

1. *Aid to Families with Dependent Children* (AFDC) was included in the Social Security Act of 1935 to furnish financial aid to poor children whose fathers had died. AFDC payments today go almost entirely (90 percent) to single-parent families in which the living father is divorced

Table 3.3   Major Social Welfare and Social Insurance Programs, 1986

Program category and name	Number of recipients (in millions)	Who funds	Who administers	Total expenditures (in billions)
Direct cash transfer				
AFDC	11.1	National, state	State, local	$ 9.9
SSI	4.6	National	National	12.8
General assistance	1.2	State, local	State, local	35.0
In-kind program				
Food stamps	20.6	National	State, local	12.8
Medicaid	23.3	National, state	State, local	43.9
Social insurance				
Social security	26.2	National	National	272.0
Medicare	32.4	National, state	National, state	75.9
Unemployment compensation	2.4	State, private	State	18.5
Worker's compensation	87.2	State, private	State	24.4

Source: U.S. Bureau of the Census, *Statistical Abstract of the United States, 1989* (Washington, D.C.: U.S. Government Printing Office, 1989), pp. 347, 349, 350, 351, 361.

or separated from or has never married the mother.[35] However, a father who heads a family can also qualify.

AFDC is the most costly and most controversial social welfare program in the United States. Critics claim that it has caused marriages to break up or be consciously avoided and has encouraged young, nonworking, unwed women to get pregnant. No one professes fondness for AFDC, not even the recipients. This helps account for the 13 percent reduction in benefits from 1970 to 1988.[36]

AFDC is jointly funded by national and state governments, and programs are administered at the state and local level. Eligibility standards and payment amounts vary widely.

2. *Supplemental Security Income* (SSI) is entirely financed and operated by the national government. It was created in 1974 by combining three existing programs—Old Age Assistance, Aid to the Blind, and Aid to the Disabled—and its recipients are people who are unable to work because of old age or physical or mental disabilities. The average monthly payment in 1986 was $244.

3. *General assistance* is a state and local program intended to help poor people who do not qualify for AFDC or SSI, such as the nonworking but physically able poor. State benefit levels vary greatly, and twelve states do not offer the program at all.

In-Kind Programs   **In-kind programs** provide benefits "in kind" rather than in cash, in order to address problems of poverty, hunger, and illness.

1. *Food stamps* are coupons that can be used to purchase food. They are paid for by the national government, which also carries half of the administrative expenses. The program was established in 1964, and benefit levels are uniform throughout the United States. Both the working and nonworking poor can qualify.

2. *Medicaid* is a health care assistance program for the poor (AFDC and SSI recipients automatically qualify). It is jointly funded by the national and state governments and is enormously expensive ($43.9 billion in 1986). The Medicaid program provides free health care to uninsured poor people and is the principal source of assistance for long-term institutional care for the physically and mentally disabled. It must be distinguished from Medicare, which grants health-care assistance to the aged (see page 68). Since its inception in 1965, Medicaid has been racked with scandals, and doctors, pharmacists, dentists, and other professionals have been charged with everything from performing unnecessary surgery and inflating fees to filing reimbursements for imaginary patients.

3. *Housing programs* exist in several forms today. The earliest program to provide public housing units was established in 1937, when federal subsidies were given to local governments for the construction of low-rent public housing. Since 1974, the Housing and Community Devel-

opment Act has given rent subsidies directly to the poor, who apply them to private rental units.

4. *Other in-kind programs* include numerous types of public assistance, such as the national school lunch program, Head Start, energy assistance for low-income families, legal services, supplemental food programs, employment assistance, family planning, foster care, and services for the mentally retarded. National, state, and local participation depends on the specific program in question. The diversity of in-kind programs is strong evidence of the complexity of the poverty problem.

Social Insurance   **Social insurance** is distinguished by the fact that recipients contribute financially through the Social Insurance Trust Fund, established by the Social Security Act of 1935. These are not true welfare programs, because participants pay in advance for their future well-being. However, they do help in the broad effort to relieve poverty. Contributions to social insurance come from social security payments by individual workers and by their employers. In 1987 the national government's annual budget devoted 27 percent of all operating expenditures to social insurance programs, up from 5 percent in 1954.[37]

1. *Social security* (officially Old Age, Survivors, Disability, and Health Insurance) is entirely paid for and run by the national government. Monthly payments are mailed to retired people, the disabled, and the spouse and dependent children of a worker who retires, dies, or is disabled. Total cash benefits in 1986 were $260 billion.
2. *Medicare* provides federal health care benefits for people over the age of sixty-five in exchange for a monthly premium. It was created in 1965 through an amendment to the Social Security Act. Medicare costs have escalated rapidly as a result of the growing number of senior citizens and ballooning health care costs. The program was expanded by Congress in 1988 to furnish unlimited coverage for catastrophic illness upon payment of a deductible ($564 in 1988).
3. *Unemployment compensation* was mandated by the Social Security Act of 1935. It requires employers and employees to contribute to a trust fund administered by individual states. Those who lose their jobs through layoffs or dismissals can draw unemployment benefits for as long as thirty-nine weeks.
4. *Worker's compensation* is also a part of the Social Security Act. Financed by employers and administered by the states, it establishes insurance for workers and their dependents to cover job-related accidents or illnesses that result in death or disability.

Social welfare policy clearly exhibits the interdependent nature of the federal system. The national government pays for and operates some programs on its own—social security is one example. State and local governments take care of general assistance. Approximately three of every four social welfare dollars come from Washington, D.C., but the states and localities perform key administrative roles in most public assistance efforts. The private sector also contributes through charities like the United Way and institutions such as private hospitals and clinics.

State Innovations in Social Welfare

The emerging consensus on social welfare policy has two critical goals. One involves the well-being of children and, of necessity, the American family. The other aims to help people replace welfare checks with paychecks. The respective roles of national, state, and local governments in these two policy initiatives are still being sorted out. Undeniably, however, the states and localities were the prime innovators in social welfare policy during the 1980s, and this leadership role is likely to continue during the 1990s.

Saving the Children   By virtue of programs enacted under the Johnson and Nixon administrations, poverty among the elderly has greatly diminished. Medicare, SSI, and other programs halved the poverty rate among seniors from 1964 to 1986.[39] Now the young have replaced the old as our poorest citizens.

There are several important reasons for the sad plight of children. AFDC benefits have declined in terms of noninflationary dollars since 1978. In addition, AFDC does not provide incentives for welfare parents to seek and maintain jobs. Another reason is that more and more children live with a single parent because of high divorce rates, illegitimate births, and irresponsible fathers who refuse to support their offspring. Even if a single mother has the necessary education or skills to secure employment, in the absence of family or friends, her children must be placed in the care of older siblings or left on their own. Few opportunities for subsidized or free day care exist. Finally, too many children are being born not only into poverty but into sickness. Because of inadequate diets, lack of health insurance, and ignorance about prenatal care, many mothers give birth to premature, underweight, and sickly children. Some simply cannot survive.

Children's issues have quietly risen to the top of national and state policy agendas. Historically, the national government has addressed such problems, and it continues to do so today. However, the states and some local governments have their own agendas. Some of the successful program experiments under way today are likely to be adopted into national law in the future.

Even AFDC has been improved. Led by the poorest states, such as Mississippi and Georgia, state contributions have been increased. In 1988 the national government passed the Family Support Act, which requires most AFDC recipients to participate in state-run jobs, training, or education programs, among other things. Congress also boosted the income of low-income working parents by eliminating their federal income tax obligations under the Tax Reform Act of 1986.

To deal with the growing problem of absentee fathers, the Family Support Act of 1988 requires the states to withhold court-ordered child support payments from the wages of absent parents, even if the parent has not fallen behind in payments. States are also required to establish paternity for children born out of wedlock, through blood tests and other laboratory techniques. The result is that more fathers are being held financially responsible for their offspring. The states now have additional authority to speed judicial and administrative procedures for obtaining paternal support, to establish guidelines for judges to determine the appropriate size of child support awards, and to monitor support payments.

The national Family Support Act of 1988 borrowed heavily from state experience and innovations. Wisconsin blazed the trail with its Child Support Assurance System, under which any parent not living with his or her minor children is legally obligated to share a portion of his income. One child claims 17 percent of the noncustodial parent's annual gross income; the rate rises with the number of children. Payments may be withheld from the parent's paycheck or from income tax refunds. In addition to assuring that absentee parents meet their legal obligations, the Wisconsin plan is expected to relieve AFDC caseloads by 20 percent.[39]

The issue of day care for children of working parents has also received a great deal of attention from the state and local governments, while the national government has struggled in vain to produce child-care legislation. State and local governments are subsidizing day care programs through tax breaks and are experimenting with various child-care arrangements. In Virginia, a state agency has been created to provide day care for young children from poor and single-parent families. States are also taking the lead in improved prenatal care, in an effort to reduce the nation's shameful infant mortality rate of ten deaths for every thousand live births (which exceeds the rate of sixteen industrialized nations).[40] South Carolina reduced its infant mortality rate from 18.5 in 1978 to 13.2 in 1986 through health care programs for young and economically deprived mothers and mothers-to-be.

Workfare: Turning Welfare Checks into Paychecks   The AFDC program helps support 3.7 million families with 7 million children. In the past, money has been handed over to recipients by the national and state governments, and little has been required in return. The idea behind workfare is to help these parents find jobs. Jobs should produce more household income than AFDC, improved self-images for recipients, and financial savings for taxpayers and the national government.

Workfare is not a new idea. The Nixon administration's 1967 Work Incentive (WIN) program required employable AFDC recipients to register for work, or for education and training courses aimed at making them more employable. But WIN was a failure. Few recipients actually participated through doing public work (such as cleaning parks or painting government buildings). Some did get jobs, but they tended to be the most easily employable recipients anyway, and most jobs were low-wage, with few opportunities for advancement.[41] In 1981, Congress converted WIN into something resembling a block grant by permitting the states to restructure the program and implement their own workfare variations.

Workfare was the centerpiece of the 1988 Family Support Act. Under this legislation, the first major overhaul of welfare policy in over fifty years, states must implement a Job Opportunities and Basic Skills (JOBS) program by 1990. JOBS seeks to combine job-related education, training, and services with a requirement that welfare parents obtain employment. Able-bodied AFDC parents of children over three must participate. States will help them with child-care and transportation costs. In two-parent welfare families, one adult must contribute sixteen hours of work per week to the state if the search for a job fails. States are permitted to fashion their own approach to JOBS, and must match national government funds by at least 50 percent. States not complying with JOBS provisions risk losing national AFDC funds.

At first blush, the Family Support Act might appear to represent continued national government dominance of welfare policy. But in fact, the major elements of the act were born and raised in the states and adopted at

Welfare recipients in Baltimore renovate their own low-income housing complex, learning useful skills. Baltimore's program gets people off welfare and saves the city and national government a lot of money.

the national level at the insistence of the governors.[42] The states had conducted a number of workfare experiments on their own during the 1980s. California's GAIN (Greater Avenues for Independence) has been one of the most widely praised programs. It contains several phases and options for recipients. If an initial job search leads to nothing, the AFDC recipient is formally assessed and brought into a contractual arrangement that stipulates the obligations of the recipients and of the county administering the program. Education, training, and additional job search typically follow. If a job is still not to be had, the recipient must work for one year in a public or nonprofit position designated by the county to earn the AFDC check. Some of the workfare jobs lead to regular jobs; others are mindless busy-work.[43]

So far the state workfare experiments have been small-scale programs intended to extract knowledge. There is basic consensus that workfare is well intentioned. As the old saying goes, "Give a man a fish and you have fed him for a day. Teach him to fish and he can feed himself for life." But there is some disagreement on how workfare has performed so far. The U.S. General Accounting Office (GAO) conducted a study of sixty-one programs operating in 1985 in thirty-eight states.[44] It criticized the programs for serving only a minority of AFDC recipients and for overconcentration on low-wage and part-time jobs that paid too little to get people off welfare. The GAO found that the states and localities were overly reliant on federal funds, placing comparatively little of their own financial resources into the effort. Some states prohibited work programs for women with preschool children, even though this group of recipients is the most likely to benefit from work experience.

An evaluation of six state workfare programs by the Manpower Demonstration Research Corporation (MDRC) was more positive.[45] Observing that the states had made substantial improvements over the old WIN program, the MDRC authors praised them for increasing rates of recipient participation and for offering low-cost employment services in spite of limited resources. Significantly, projected AFDC savings were expected to exceed program costs within two to five years. The MDRC concluded that state workfare experiments were a "moderate success."

Social Welfare Policy and Federalism

Enormous social welfare challenges confront national, state, and local governments. The pivotal issue in terms of federalism is which level of government should have primary responsibility for the poor and unfortunate. Historically, the national government has done so. But it is testimony to the dynamism of the federal system that the answer is no longer so certain. Politics and Policy 3.1 describes how one state is trying to ensure health care for all its citizens.

POLITICS AND POLICY 3.1
A State Takes on a New Role

Massachusetts ventured into uncharted policy territory when it enacted a universal health insurance plan for its citizens. The 1988 law provides health insurance for more than 600,000 Massachusetts residents who are without coverage, including disabled children and adults, college students, unemployed people, and the employed but uninsured.[1]

The new law is quite complex. The largest single group of uninsured people is those who work for small businesses, and an interest group of small business owners mounted the fiercest opposition to the plan. To satisfy some of their concerns (primarily cost-related), Massachusetts organized a new group insurance purchasing pool for firms with six or fewer employees. In addition, the state is offering two-year tax credits to firms with fifty or fewer workers as an incentive to offer insurance. By 1992, workers will be able to choose between insurance coverage from the workplace or from the state pool. Companies that do not offer coverage have to pay a penalty into the state fund. Insurance coverage for the unemployed will be subsidized by a new state trust fund.

Once passage of the universal health insurance plan was secured, proponents faced an equally tough problem: figuring out a way to pay for it. An initial source of funding, a five-cent increase in the cigarette tax, will have to be supplemented with other revenues. And, because Massachusetts developed a $250 million gap between budgeted expenditures and actual revenues in 1989–90, the prospect of additional dollars for universal health insurance dimmed.[2] The likelihood that the state might be forced to scale down its ambitious program loomed. The Massachusetts law was the first of its kind, and other states are closely watching its implementation.

[1] Richard A. Knox, "Amid Fanfare, Health Care Becomes Law," *Boston Globe*, April 22, 1988, pp. 1, 43–44.
[2] "9 States Biting Financial Bullet to Tune of $6 Billion Debt," *Houston Post*, May 16, 1989, p. A-14.

State and local officials are caught in a dilemma. On the one hand they are physically and emotionally close to the problems of the poor, and subject to the demands of their constituents. On the other hand, they do not have the financial resources necessary to alleviate poverty within their boundaries. It would help if poverty and related problems were clearly definable and solvable, but they are not. It would also help if the national government were in better financial shape, but it is constrained by enormous debts and trade imbalances.

Poverty is a very complex economic, social, and behavioral phenomenon that demands multiple, intergovernmental responses. Because state and local governments cannot manage social welfare policy by themselves, they must tap revenue-raising capacity of the national government for what is, after all, a national problem. Indeed, this is one policy area in which some degree of standardization and centralization is called for. Poor people in New Mexico should not be treated worse than their counterparts in New Jersey. Standardization of some benefits and centralization of policymaking by the national government tend to diminish inequities in state and local funding of social welfare programs.[46] The states and localities are best at policy experimentation, innovation, and administration within their own jurisdictions. They contribute meaningfully to social welfare policy, but they cannot solve the problems of the poor and disadvantaged on a national level.

Higher Education Policy and Federalism

The goals of higher education policy have changed in response to the needs of American society, but they remain clear in contrast to social welfare policy goals. Controversy arises, to be sure, but never has it taken on the intensity and partisan rancor of social welfare policy arguments. This is mostly because higher education goals are clear and understandable, and the means to achieve them are widely agreed upon. Higher education policy strives to embrace learning, to promote social and economic mobility, to instill cultural and moral values, and, most recently, to assist the states in economic development. The last goal springs from the need to upgrade and retool the work force, and from the growing recognition that universities, through research and development, foster economic innovation and growth.[47]

Unlike social welfare policy, which was developed and funded initially at the national level, higher education was first the responsibility of the private sector, states, and localities. Colleges and universities developed initially as private institutions available to the socioeconomic elite. A major landmark in the popularization of higher education was the Morrill Act of 1862, in which the national government established the public land-grant college system in order to teach agriculture and "mechanical arts." These colleges were largely vocational in nature, and were aimed at increasing the levels of knowledge and efficiency on the farms and in the factories. Private colleges such as Yale, Harvard, and Columbia remained the premier institutions for education in the classics for some time, but gradually the land-grant institutions began to expand the scope of their curricula, and eventually to achieve a level of education equal to and in some cases better than that of the best private colleges. Any list of America's most prestigious universities today will have at the top such land-grant institutions as Penn State, Cornell, and the universities of Wisconsin, Minnesota, and California.

Today there are approximately 3,330 institutions of higher education in the United States, not counting the numerous two-year (junior college) and vocational (technical) schools. Enrollment exceeds 12.2 million students. State-supported colleges and universities predominate. Over 78 percent of students are enrolled at public institutions today, compared to only 49 percent in 1947.[48]

Intergovernmental Roles

Public higher education is predominantly a state government responsibility. Its increased significance to state economic well-being means that more state involvement is apt to come in the years ahead. Some state government activities, such as increased commitment of resources, will be welcomed. Others, such as bureaucratic, political, and ideological intrusions, are uninvited and unwanted by professional educators.

The national government's presence in higher education policymaking is probably more pronounced than most people realize. The Morrill Act donated national lands for state schools. Various G.I. bills have entitled returning war veterans to a college education at government expense and helped fuel tremendous expansion in higher education facilities for a burgeoning student population. Financial aid to veterans was severely curtailed after President Nixon terminated the military draft, but other programs provide students with grants and loans (the most important being the National Defense Education Act, the Basic Educational Opportunity Grant, and guaranteed student loans). Although the Reagan administration substantially cut back funding of these programs, they still sustain thousands of college students. The national government also supports higher education with research grants that help develop new programs, support faculty and graduate students, pay indirect costs, and purchase research materials and laboratory equipment. Finally, although the national government does not operate a national university like most governments around the world, the Defense Department provides huge sums of money for professional training, military officer training, correspondence courses, and the military service academies.

In 1986 the national government spent $12.2 billion on its assorted programs in higher education. However, this made up only 12.6 percent of all expenditures, a decline from 16.6 percent in 1970 (see Figure 3.2). The state

Figure 3.2   National, State, and Local Expenditures for Higher Education
The national government's share of support for higher education has been declining over the past twenty years, forcing universities to look more to state and local governments, and particularly to private sources.

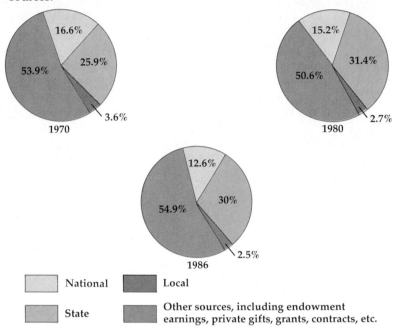

1970

1980

1986

National

State

Local

Other sources, including endowment earnings, private gifts, grants, contracts, etc.

Source: U.S. Bureau of the Census, *Statistical Abstract of the United States, 1989* (Washington, D.C.: U.S. Government Printing Office), p. 125.

share was 30 percent. Other sources of money for higher education are tuition, endowments, private gifts, and grants and contracts.

Given the national government's limited financial support, it is little wonder that its policy impacts are mostly indirect. Research grants can affect the disposition of institutional resources through matching requirements and other conditions, but otherwise national influence on decision making within colleges and universities is quite limited. Public higher education remains primarily a state government undertaking dominated by state and university officials.

Actors in Higher Education Policy

The president is the chief spokesperson and fund raiser for a university, and is often the most influential lobbyist for university causes both in the legislature and in the business world. But he must share influence over the university with many other people. The president is usually appointed by, and responsible to, a university governing board called the *regents* or *trustees*. Some states select the members of these boards through popular elections, but most provide for appointment by the governor and/or legislature. Seats on the governing board are typically filled with prominent university supporters from government and business. Private institutions, although recipients of state charters and various amounts of state financial aid, operate with a greater amount of autonomy.

A few states still administer higher education policy through individual governing boards for each public college and university, but most have opted for an umbrella agency to develop broad policy directions and to coordinate curricular and other relations among the various higher education institutions.[49] Usually referred to as the *state commission on higher education,* the statewide governing board is appointed by the governor in almost all states. Its members must simultaneously advocate higher education policy and spending and represent the governor's own higher education preferences. Twenty-two states have eliminated the governing boards for individual institutions by consolidating their functions into a statewide board.

Legislatures have elevated their policy role in higher education, primarily through expenditure decisions. Universities are certain to find faithful friends and strong supporters among the legislators who represent the district in which the campus is situated. But college officials are seldom given a blank check, as legislative committees are taking more seriously their responsibility to ensure that higher education, like other activities of state government, strives for greater efficiency and effectiveness.

The governors have become the most important policy actors in higher education. As we have mentioned, they appoint governing board members in most states, and in some cases they sit on these boards as *ex officio* members (appointed by virtue of their office). The chief executive also exercises direct influence over university affairs through the budgetary process. Gubernatorial support for increased appropriations or a new building on campus usually counts heavily in the legislature.

The increased scope of gubernatorial interest in higher education issues has been widely noted. A Carnegie Foundation study found that "the Governor, in many states, is now the one dominant figure in higher education."[50] In some instances gubernatorial involvement has gone beyond the bounds of propriety. In well-known cases, governors have brazenly attempted to dismiss members of governing boards and university presidents. Others have fired football or basketball coaches or the athletic director. Usually, however, the governor's involvement is positive, and clearly in the best interest of higher education. To many chief executives, the union between campus and state economic development is a marriage made in heaven.[51] Politics and Policy 3.2 looks at an issue that officials at all levels will have to pay attention to in the next few years.

POLITICS AND POLICY 3.2
The New Racism on Campus

Some twenty-five years after the civil rights movement opened up the doors to a college education for large numbers of black students across the nation, there are signs of a new racism on campus. Its form is less open than the ugly, violent clashes between white and black students, particularly in the South, during the early years of campus integration, but it is no less disturbing to university faculty and administrators.

Indications of the new racism are found in campus flyers and graffiti, and in the occasional verbal and physical conflict between blacks and whites. A pattern of racism appears to be developing, rather than just a few isolated incidents, and it is found in institutions of all types and sizes, even the most prestigious such as Penn State and the universities of Michigan and Massachusetts.

The growing hostility between black and white students is evident in their common complaints. Blacks charge white students and faculty with making racial slurs and with other forms of discrimination. They note the problems of adjusting to a predominantly white student body, and complain that the colleges are not doing enough to help them. White students gripe about the special treatment that some blacks receive, including relaxed admission standards and extra financial aid. Whites assert that black students tend to blame racism for any and all problems they confront.

Freeing campuses of racial problems will be an important challenge for officials at the state and university level. Some universities are coping with racism by emphasizing the study of nonwestern cultures in their required curriculum. Administrators are taking strong stands against racial harassment in any form, and instituting special programs to hire more black faculty as role models. The biggest problem, according to many observers, is overcoming white indifference to the plight of black students.

Source: Denise K. Magner, "Blacks and Whites on the Campuses: Behind Ugly Racist Incidents, Student Isolation and Insensitivity," *The Chronicle of Higher Education* 35 (April 26, 1989): A1, A28-A33. Copyright 1989, The Chronicle of Higher Education. Reprinted with permission.

Problems in Higher Education and
What the States Are Doing

Public attention is gradually shifting from primary and secondary school reform, which is well under way, to America's institutions of higher learning. Pressures for change are building, and an agenda is developing for future policy actions at all levels of government. Five major policy problems can be identified.

Quantity   The quantity issue has to do with how states should coordinate and administer their complex systems of higher education. In some states, individual institutions are the norm. In others, particularly the territorially large ones, a main "flagship" campus has numerous sister campuses spread about the state. In some states the "little sisters" have far outgrown the original campus in size and quality.

Academic, administrative, political, and "turf" conflicts, among others, plague higher education. Two-year schools want to become four-year colleges, which themselves aspire to become full-fledged graduate universities. Regional institutions fight for their share of the higher education budget. Duplication of graduate degree programs unnecessarily strains budgets, as do superfluous and debt-ridden small regional campuses. States must decide how to coordinate and manage such issues and what organizational arrangements to employ. Diverse responses have ensued. Most states have created statewide governing boards for centralized planning and budgeting, program evaluation, and policy recommendations. There is a long and highly valued history of institutional autonomy in higher education, but obvious benefits can be derived from some administrative centralization and control. In states where individual governing boards continue to exist, they are becoming more active in policy matters and less the pawns of the university president. Special coordinating mechanisms are being utilized in some states. For example, at least nine have created new boards to organize university-based activities in high technology.

Quality   A second and increasingly important policy problem is quality—how to make and keep higher education relevant to society and a significant contributor to the state's quality of life and economic development. Higher education will always be elitist in the sense that those who derive direct benefits from it are largely students from middle- and upper-income families. Even students from lower socioeconomic backgrounds who attend college are elite, since they must have the intellect and ambition necessary to secure scholarships and other forms of financial aid. However, higher education offers benefits to the society at large beyond the immediate confines of the campus. An important question is how colleges and universities should be linked to society, and which objectives should be paramount.

During the 1960s and early 1970s, higher education institutions were criticized for selling their souls to the defense industry and to business interests. Such allegations are much rarer today, when universities are widely accepted as resources for attracting new investments and promoting economic development. As one education expert explains, "Having a first-class university is essential. A state that lacks one is putting itself out of business as far as economic development goes. . . . In a world of growing economic competition and social complexity, it is the university to which the state turns for assistance."[52]

The dilemma is how to graduate well-educated students with a sense of public ethics while working with government and business to promote economic development. Universities need businesses for grant and contract revenues and for opportunities to test research and theory in applied settings. Businesses need universities for fresh ideas and talented human resources. Cooperation strongly benefits both parties and furthers state economic development. The models for this kind of relationship are California's Silicon Valley and North Carolina's Research Triangle, but almost every state has formed some formal means to promote partnerships in technology and business innovation. Nonetheless, institutions of higher education must not seek capitalistic relevance at the price of failing to transmit historical, social, and cultural knowledge.

Faculty   A third higher education policy problem is how to recruit and keep outstanding faculty, especially in math and science, given the tradition of low salaries in academia. The lack of qualified math and science instructors in colleges is related to curriculum choices of students. Between 1975 and 1984, the proportion of freshman choosing to pursue a science or math major fell from 13 percent to 8 percent.[53]

The problem of recruiting and retaining qualified faculty can be solved by offering higher salaries to professors and financial incentives to graduate students. More research and teaching fellowships and higher graduate student stipends offer a useful start. This is an area where some federal financial assistance would have tangible results. Of course, it is primarily up to the states to see that professors and promising graduate students receive the necessary financial inducements.

Politicization   A fourth policy problem is the politicization of higher education. As in primary and secondary education (see Chapter 15), conflict has moved beyond the confines of the professional community (faculty, administrators, and governing boards) and into the legislative and gubernatorial arenas. The trend toward greater politicization in college and university funding and policy decisions is largely a function of economic considerations, ranging from how to keep institutions operating during hard times to how to foster economic development. Universities are perceived by political leaders as state resources that should be utilized efficiently to promote growth and prosperity. The "ivory tower" has become more like a corporate boardroom, with legislators and the governor constituting the board of directors.

State intrusion into the previously sacred affairs of colleges and universities can be harmful. Bureaucratic interference in the form of unnecessary or unworkable rules and regulations can obstruct effective university operations. Politicians may attempt to influence hiring decisions or facility locations, and community groups or individual politicians may try to influence internal institutional matters such as what subject matter is or is not taught or which guest speakers should or should not be invited to campus. Such intrusions cause academicians to hoist the banner of academic freedom to defend themselves.[54]

The politicization of higher education is apt to persist as long as the game has such high stakes for political and business leaders. The worst kind of counterproductive intervention can be eliminated if university presidents and governing boards educate potential intervenors about their proper role in higher education and the need to maintain academic freedom.

Student Costs   Finally, higher education confronts the problem of spiraling student costs. College costs have risen much faster than inflation since 1980. In 1987, the average expenses for room, board, and tuition totaled $32,000 for four years. That is expected to rise to $100,000 by the year 2000 if present rates of increase continue. The leap in college costs has been particularly evident in private universities, which are now well out of the financial reach of most prospective students. Combined with the national government's cutbacks on grants and low-interest loans to children of low-income families, rising education costs mean that a college education is becoming unfeasible for more and more young people.

An interesting approach that would help parents save for their children's college education has been taken by Michigan, which in 1986 became the first state to enact a prepaid tuition program. Parents lay out a lump sum of several thousand dollars for an infant, and when the child reaches eighteen, the entire tuition bill for four years will be paid up at any state higher education institution. (Wyoming enacted a similar plan in 1987.)

Just as Socrates urged students of all ages to examine their own lives in order to be truly knowledgeable, so must our colleges and universities undergo a perpetual process of self-examination to deal with ever-present political and economic pressures.

Federalism's Evolving Nature

Social welfare and higher education are very different in terms of historical development, goals and objectives, and level of government control. The national government, however uncomfortably, dominates social welfare policy. Suggested swaps and turnbacks to the state and local governments reflect this discomfort. The vitality of the nonnational governments can be seen in their growing willingness to accept greater responsibility for the social welfare of their citizens. Reductions in federal funding and greater state autonomy have made social welfare a fast-evolving policy field. It will take time to determine whether decentralization of poverty policy ultimately shortchanges the poor. Time will also tell whether the states and localities can meet what might be their most difficult challenge in federalism.

Higher education policy is also evolving, but much more slowly and with little tension between levels of government. The national, state, and local governments are basically comfortable with their respective roles. Certainly more federal money would be welcomed, but not at the expense of policy autonomy. Control over higher education policy is crucial to the states, because universities are keys to state economic development.

Together, the two policy fields examined in this chapter illustrate the necessity for intergovernmental sharing of the burdens of governance in a highly diverse and complex society. Federalism permits numerous possibilities for conflict and cooperation in the exercise of power.[55] But in the end, all 84,000 American governments are in the same situation. As President John F. Kennedy observed many years ago, state, local, and national governments are "allies under the Constitution [and] must work closely together . . . for the benefit of our country, which all of us seek to serve."[56]

Summary

A recent analysis of intergovernmental relations concluded that "federalism is under siege."[57] The Reagan years left an indelible mark on American federalism, because of the administration's emphasis on shifting responsibility out of Washington and into state capitals. The fundamental ideas of New Federalism will mature under the Bush administration.[58] For the states, the next decade offers both challenges and opportunities as their relationship with the national government continues to evolve. As the Massachusetts universal health insurance plan aptly demonstrates, the states do not lack good ideas. But what they frequently need is more money. If the trend toward reduced national expenditures continues, state capacity could be sorely tested.

Social welfare and higher education policy are two important illustrations of federalism in practice. Although these two policy fields differ in many respects, both involve key contributions from all three levels of government. This intergovernmental sharing of responsibilities is central to federalism.

Key Terms

Block grant A form of financial aid from one level of government to another for use in a functional area.

Categorical grant A form of financial aid from one level of government to another to be used for a narrowly defined purpose.

Direct cash transfer The transfer of cash, such as in the form of a social security check, from one level of government to an individual, citizen beneficiary.

Expenditures Allocations of government monies.

Formula grant A funding mechanism that automatically allocates monies based on conditions in the recipient government.

In-kind program The payment of a noncash social welfare benefit, such as food stamps or clothing, to an individual recipient.

Project grant A funding mechanism that awards monies based on the strength of an applicant government's proposal.

Revenues Monies raised by governments from taxes, fees, enterprises, and payments from other levels of government.

Revenue sharing A "no-strings" form of financial aid from one level of government to another.

Social insurance A benefit program made available by a government to citizens in need, as a right of those citizens.

4

STATE

CONSTITUTIONS

The Evolution of State Constitutions
The First State Constitutions/Legislative
Supremacy/The Growth of Executive Power

Weaknesses of Constitutions
The Trouble with Long Constitutions/
Substantive Problems

Contemporary Constitutional Reform
The Essential State Constitution/
Constitutions Today

Methods for Constitutional Change
Informal Constitutional Change/Formal
Constitutional Change

State Resurgence and Constitutional Reform

Does a citizen have the right to freedom of expression in a private shopping mall? Specifically, does a citizen have the constitutionally protected right to collect shoppers' signatures on a petition opposing a United Nations resolution against Zionism, even if the shopping center owners object? The U.S. Supreme Court has said no on two occasions.[1] But in 1979 the Supreme Court of California ruled that citizens do have the right to petition in private shopping centers as part of their protected right to free speech.[2] The owners of the Prune Yard Shopping Center appealed to the U.S. Supreme Court, hoping for a reversal of the California decision, but the decision was upheld.The Court based its ruling on the principle that state constitutions can create broader rights of free speech than those guaranteed in the federal constitution.

The *Prune Yard* case illustrates the new *judicial federalism*, in which state supreme courts are increasingly grounding their rulings on the language of their state, rather than the national, constitution. It also reflects the fact that state constitutions are once again becoming the guardians of civil liberties, as they were throughout the early history of the United States.

All state constitutions serve as instruments of political power. They set forth the basic framework and operating rules for government, distribute power to the three branches, limit the scope of governmental authority, and protect individual rights. Constitutions represent the *fundamental law* of a state, superior to statutory law. They provide a set of rules for the game of state government, and those who master the regulations and procedures have a strong advantage over novices. Everything that a state government does and represents is rooted in its constitution. Only the federal constitution and federal statutes take priority over it. This is why the constitution is called the fundamental law.

In the American system of *dual constitutionalism*, in which there are both national and state constitutions, the national government is supreme within the spheres of authority specifically delegated to it in the U.S. Constitution. Powers granted to the national government are denied to the states. In theory, state governments possess the inherent power to act in all other areas, as long as such actions are not contrary to any provisions of the U.S. Constitution or to acts of Congress. Thus, state constitutions are supreme for all matters not expressly within the jurisdiction of the national government or forbidden by federal constitutional or statutory law. In practice, however, congressional and federal court interpretations have expanded the powers of the national government and, in some fields, eroded the powers of the states.

The earliest state constitutions were simple documents reflecting an agrarian economy, single-owner businesses, and horse-and-buggy transportation. As American society and the economy changed, it became necessary to alter the rules of state government. Constitutional reform has been a regular theme throughout the American experiment in federalism. It has occurred in several waves, the first beginning around 1800. Some reforms have reflected changing political fortunes; newly powerful groups have pressed to revise the constitution to reflect their interests, or one or another political party has gained control of state government and sought to solidify its power. Constitutional reforms have promoted different views of politics and the public interest, as when Progressive reformers rallied for honest and efficient government in the late nineteeth and early twentieth centuries.[3] Since the 1960s, constitutional revisions have concentrated power in the governor's office, unified court systems, and generally sought to make state government more efficient, effective, responsive, and capable of adapting to changing social and economic forces.

The Evolution of State Constitutions

When the states won their independence from Great Britain more than two hundred years ago, there was no precedent for writing constitutions. The thirteen colonial charters provided the foundation for the new state constitutions. The thirteen original colonial charters were brief documents (around five pages each) that the Crown granted to trading companies and individuals for governance of settlements in the new territories. As the settlements became full colonies, these charters were expanded to incorporate the "rights of Englishmen"—political and civil rights first enumerated by the Magna Carta in 1215. They also laid down some basic principles of colonial government.[4]

The First State Constitutions

Following the War of Independence, the former colonies drafted their first constitutions in special revolutionary conventions or in legislative assemblies first brought together during the war. With the exception of Massachusetts, the new states put their constitutions into effect immediately, without popular ratification.

In content, most of these documents simply extended the colonial charters, removing references to the king and inserting a bill of rights. The constitutions of Connecticut and Rhode Island for example, differed only slightly from those states' colonial charters. All the documents incorporated the principles of limited government: a weak executive branch, the separation of powers, checks and balances, a bill of rights to protect the people and their property from arbitrary government actions, and (except for Pennsylvania) a bicameral legislature.[5] The earliest constitutions were not progressive. Essentially, they called for government by an aristocracy. Officeholding and voting, for instance, were restricted to white males of wealth and property.[6]

Only one of the thirteen original state constitutions, that of Massachusetts, survives (although it has been amended 116 times). It is the oldest active constitution in the world. Its longevity can be attributed in large part to the foresight of its drafter, John Adams, who grounded the document in extensive research of governments that took him all the way back to the Magna Carta. Even after many amendments, the Massachusetts constitution reflects a composite of the wisdom of the foremost political philosophers of the eighteenth century: John Locke, Jean-Jacques Rousseau, and the Baron de Montesquieu.[7]

Legislative Supremacy

The first state constitutions reflected the framers' fear and distrust of the executive, a result of their experiences with the colonial governors. The governors were not all tyrants, but because they represented the British Crown and Parliament, they became a symbol of oppression to the colonists. As a result, the guiding principle of the new constitutional governments was **legislative supremacy**, and the legislatures were given overwhelming power at the expense of governors. Most governors were to be elected by the legislature, not the people, and were restricted to a single term of office. (In Pennsylvania, executive power was exercised through a multimember board.) State judiciaries also were limited in authorized powers, and like governors, judges were to be elected by the legislature. The pre-eminence of legislative power was so great that an English observer, Lord James Bryce, was moved to remark: "The legislature . . . is so much the strongest force in the several states that we may almost call it the government and ignore all other authorities."[8]

The Growth of Executive Power

Disillusionment with the legislatures soon developed, and spread rapidly through the states during the early 1800s. There were many reasons for disenchantment, including the legislatures' failure to meet the new demands caused by rapid population growth and the Industrial Revolution; the growing amount of legislation that favored private interests; and a mounting load of state indebtedness, which led nine states to default on their bonds in a single two-year period.

Gradually the executive branch began to accumulate more power and stature through constitutional amendments that provided for popular election of governors, who were given longer terms and the authority to veto legislative bills. The constitutions of states admitted to the Union during the early 1800s established stronger executive powers at the outset. This trend toward centralization of power in the executive branch continued during the 1830s and 1840s, the so-called Jacksonian era; however, the Jacksonian principle of popular elections to fill most government offices resulted in a fragmented state executive branch. The governor now had to share authority with a lieutenant governor, an attorney general, a treasurer, and other popularly elected officials, and with numerous agency heads appointed by the legislature. Although the growth of the governor's powers continues today, the divided nature of the executive branch still makes it difficult for an individual to exercise those powers.

As executive power grew, levels of public confidence in state legislatures continued to erode, and this was reflected in constitutional revision. Also affecting constitutional change were broader social and economic forces in the United States, such as the extension of suffrage and popular participation in government, the rise of a corporate economy, the Civil War and Reconstruction, the growth of industry and commerce, the process of urbanization, and a growing movement for government reform. States rapidly replaced and amended their constitutions from the early 1800s to 1920 in response to these and other forces. The decade immediately after the Civil War saw the highest level of constitutional activity in American history, much of it in the southern states; between 1860 and 1870, twenty-seven constitutions were supplanted or thoroughly revised as Confederate states ratified new documents after secession, then redrew the documents after Union victory to incorporate certain conditions of readmission to the United States.

Constitutional change after Reconstruction was driven by the Populist and Progressive reform movements. During the late 1800s the Populists championed the causes of the "little man," including farmers and laborers. They sought to open up the political process to the people through such constitutional devices as the initiative, the referendum, and recall (see Chapter 5). The Progressives, who made their mark during the 1890–1920 period, were kindred spirits whose favorite targets were concentrated wealth, machine politics, and boss rule in the cities. They focused on corruption at the state level as well, particularly in New York, Wisconsin, and California. In these and other states, reformers successfully promoted constitutional revisions such as regulation of campaign spending, party activities, and conflicts of interest; replacement of party conventions with direct primary elections; and selection of judges through nonpartisan elections.

Weaknesses of Constitutions

In spite of the numerous constitutional amendments and replacements enacted during the nineteenth and twentieth centuries, by 1950 the states were buffeted by a rising chorus of criticism of their fundamental laws. Ironically, many states were victims of past constitutional change, which left them with documents that were excessively long, frustratingly inflexible, and distressingly detailed. In general, state constitutions still provided for a feeble executive branch, because they granted limited administrative authority to the governor, permitted the popular election of numerous other executive branch officials, and organized the executive into a hodgepodge of semiautonomous agencies, boards, and commissions. State judiciaries remained uncoordinated and overly complex, while legislatures suffered from archaic structures and procedures. Statutory detail, out-of-date language, local amendments (those that apply only to designated local governments), and other problems contaminated the documents.

The Trouble with Long Constitutions

From the first constitutions, which averaged 5,000 words, state documents expanded into enormous tracts of verbiage averaging 27,000 words by 1967. (The U.S. Constitution has 8,700 words.) Some of this growth resulted from increasing social and economic complexity, and from a perceived need to be very specific about what the legislatures could and could not do. The states did have to delineate their residual powers (those not delegated to the national government), identify the scope of their responsibility, and define the powers of local governments. But some constitutions went too far. Louisiana's exceeded 253,000 words. Georgia's contained around 583,500 words, if local provisions were counted, surpassing Tolstoy's *War and Peace* in length. Even today the constitution of South Carolina limits local government indebtedness but lists seventeen pages of exceptions. Maryland's constitution devotes an article to off-street parking in Baltimore. Oklahoma's sets the flash point for kerosene at 115 degrees for purposes of illumination,[9] and California's deals with a compelling issue of our time—the length of wrestling matches.

Not surprisingly, lengthy state constitutions tend to be plagued by contradictions and meaningless clauses. Article II, Section 13 of Pennsylvania's constitution states that "the sessions of each House and of committees of the whole shall be open, unless when the business is such as ought to be kept secret." Other constitutions suffer from superfluous formality, legal jargon, redundancy, and poor grammar. Some constitutions address problems that are no longer with us, like the regulation of steamboats[10] or the need to teach stock feeding in Oklahoma public schools.

Verbose constitutions fail to distinguish between the fundamental law and issues that properly should be decided by the state legislature.[11] Excessive detail leads to litigation, as the courts must rule on conflicting provisions and challenges to constitutionality; this unnecessarily burdens the courts with decisions that should be made by the legislature. Once incorporated in a constitution, a decision becomes as close to permanent as anything can be in politics. Unlike a statute, which can be changed by a simple legislative majority, constitutional change requires an extraordinary majority, usually two thirds or three-fourths of the legislature. This hampers the legislature's ability to confront problems quickly and makes policy change more difficult. Too many amendments may also deprive local governments of needed flexibility to cope with their own problems. Too much detail generates confusion, not only for legislatures and courts but also for the general public. It encourages political subterfuge to get around archaic or irrelevant provisions, and breeds disrespect or even contempt for government.

Many detailed provisions are intended to favor or protect special interests, such as public utilities, farmers, timber companies, religious groups, and many others. A 1966 study by Lewis Froman found that the longest constitutions are in those states with the strongest interest groups.[12] A more recent study, however, by David Nice, discovered no statistical relationship between interest group strength and long, detailed constitutions.[13] Rather, Nice found long constitutions in states with little competition between political parties. He suggests that one-party states are characterized by intraparty dissension and unstable political coalitions that produce unpredictable legislative outcomes. These conditions mean that interest groups try to insulate their pet agencies and programs from uncertainty by placing protective provisions for them in the constitution. This is less likely to occur where a strong opposition party exists "to serve as watchdog, critic, and disciplinary force."[14] According to Nice's study, urbanization is also a factor in the length of state constitutions; because urban states are economically and socially more complex than rural states, their governments may attempt to cope with details by modifying their constitutions.[15]

Substantive Problems

In addition to contradictions, anachronisms, wordiness, and grants of special privilege, the substance of state constitutions has drawn criticism. Specific concerns voiced by reformers include the following:

- *The long ballot*. Elected executive branch officials are not beholden to the governor for their jobs, and so the governor has little or no formal influence on their decisions and activities. Reformers who seek to strengthen the governor's powers wish to restrict the executive branch to a maximum of two elected leaders, the governor and the lieutenant governor.
- *A glut of boards and commissions*. This reform of the Jacksonian period was intended to expand opportunities for public participation in state government and to limit the powers of the governor. In the late twentieth century, it leads to fragmentation and a lack of policy coordination in the executive branch.
- *A swamp of local governments*. There are more than 84,000 municipalities, counties, and special-purpose districts in the states. Sometimes they work at cross purposes, and nearly always they suffer from overlapping responsibilities and absence of coordination.
- *Restrictions on local government authority*. Localities in some states have to obtain explicit permission from the state legislature before providing

a new service, tapping a new source of revenue, or exercising any other authority not specifically granted them by the state.

- *Unequal treatment of racial minorities and women.* Constitutional language sometimes discriminates against blacks, Hispanics, and women by denying them certain rights guaranteed to white males.
- *Long delays in the administration of justice.* Court systems are in a condition of anarchy in some states, where no one seems to have control over case management, judicial interactions, or administration. The result is lengthy delays in the disposition of cases.

Contemporary Constitutional Reform

Shortly after World War II, these problems began to generate increasing commentary on the sorry condition of state constitutions. One of the most influential voices came in 1955 from the Commission on Intergovernmental Relations, popularly known as the Kestnbaum Commission. In its final report to the President, the commission stated that

> it is significant that the Constitution prepared by the Founding Fathers, with its broad grants of authority and avoidance of legislative detail, has withstood the test of time far better than the constitutions later adopted by the States. . . . The Commission believes that most states would benefit from a fundamental review of their constitution to make sure that they provide for vigorous and responsible government, not forbid it.[16]

Another important voice for constitutional reform was the National Municipal League, which developed a **Model State Constitution** in 1921 that is now in its sixth version.[17] Among other prestigious organizations pressing for reform in the 1950s and 1960s were the American Assembly, the National Governors' Conference (now the National Governors' Association), the Public Administration Service in Chicago, the Committee on Economic Development, and the League of Women Voters.

Thomas Jefferson said that each generation has the right to choose for itself its own form of government. He suggested that a new constitution every nineteen or twenty years would be appropriate. Based on the large number of constitutional changes since 1960, it would appear that the states have taken his remarks to heart. Every state has altered its fundamental law in some respect during this period, and new or substantially revised constitutions have been put into operation in more than half the states. During the 1970s alone ten states held conventions to consider changing or replacing their constitution. One of these was Louisiana, which set a record by adopting its eleventh constitution; Georgia is in second place with nine. Table 4.1 provides a summary of state constitutions today.

Extensive constitutional revision, which is likely to continue into the 1990s, has brought many documents closer to conformity with the National Municipal League's Model State Constitution, which serves as an ideal to

Table 4.1 State Constitutions

State	Number of constitutions*	Effective date of present constitution	Estimated length (number of words)	Number of amendments Submitted to voters	Number of amendments Adopted
Alabama	6	Nov. 28, 1901	174,000	679	471
Alaska	1	Jan. 3, 1959	13,000	30	21
Arizona	1	Feb. 14, 1912	28,876	191	105
Arkansas	5	Oct. 30, 1874	40,720	160	73
California	2	July 4, 1879	33,350	768	460
Colorado	1	Aug. 1, 1876	45,679	231	109
Connecticut	4	Dec. 30, 1965	9,564	26	25
Delaware	4	June 10, 1897	19,000	—	117
Florida	6	Jan. 7, 1969	25,100	68	44
Georgia	10	July 1, 1983	25,000	20	18
Hawaii	1	Aug. 21, 1959	17,453	86	78
Idaho	1	July 3, 1890	21,500	186	106
Illinois	4	July 1, 1971	13,200	9	4
Indiana	2	Nov. 1, 1851	9,377	67	36
Iowa	2	Sept. 3, 1857	12,500	49	46
Kansas	1	Jan. 29, 1861	11,865	114	86
Kentucky	4	Sept. 28, 1891	23,500	56	27
Louisiana	11	Jan. 1, 1975	51,448	36	22
Maine	1	March 15, 1820	13,500	184	156
Maryland	4	Oct. 5, 1867	41,349	231	199
Massachusetts	1	Oct. 25, 1780	36,690	143	116
Michigan	4	Jan. 1, 1964	20,000	44	15
Minnesota	1	May 11, 1858	9,500	203	109

State		Date			
Mississippi	4	Nov. 1, 1890	24,000	141	70
Missouri	4	March 30, 1945	42,000	107	68
Montana	2	July 1, 1973	11,866	21	13
Nebraska	2	Oct. 12, 1875	20,048	278	184
Nevada	1	Oct. 31, 1864	20,770	168	103
New Hampshire	2	June 2, 1784	9,200	272	141
New Jersey	3	Jan. 1, 1948	17,086	49	36
New Mexico	1	Jan. 6, 1912	27,200	224	114
New York	4	Jan. 1, 1895	80,000	272	205
North Carolina	3	July 1, 1971	11,000	34	27
North Dakota	1	Nov. 2, 1889	20,564	215	124
Ohio	2	Sept. 1, 1851	36,900	244	144
Oklahoma	1	Nov. 16, 1907	68,800	264	124
Oregon	1	Feb. 14, 1859	26,090	361	183
Pennsylvania	5	1968	21,675	24	19
Rhode Island	2	May 2, 1843	19,026	98	52
South Carolina	7	Jan. 1, 1896	22,500	639	455
South Dakota	1	Nov. 2, 1889	23,300	181	94
Tennessee	3	Feb. 23, 1870	15,300	55	32
Texas	5	Feb. 15, 1876	62,000	459	304
Utah.	1	Jan. 4, 1896	11,000	124	75
Vermont	3	July 9, 1793	6,600	208	50
Virginia	6	July 1, 1971	18,500	23	20
Washington	1	Nov. 11, 1889	29,400	147	80
West Virginia	2	April 9, 1872	25,600	102	62
Wisconsin	1	May 29, 1848	13,500	167	124
Wyoming	1	July 10, 1890	31,800	96	56

*All information is through December 31, 1987. The constitutions referred to in this table include those Civil War documents customarily listed by the individual states.

Source: The Book of the States, 1988–89 (Lexington, KY.: Council of State Governments, 1983), pp. 14–15. Reprinted with permission.

strive for. The authors of the Model State Constitution recognized that in fact no document can be suitable for all the states, because they differ too much in society, economics, and political culture. But there are certain basic principles that reformers believe should be found in a sound constitution. These may change over time, as indicated by the several revisions of the model constitution itself. A good constitution strikes a balance between the need for stability and the requirement for enough flexibility to deal with emerging problems. It is brief, readable, and simple enough for the average citizen to understand. It is logical, and devoid of the unnecessary obscurity and jargon associated with the law profession. Where possible, familiar language is used in place of technical and legal terms.[18]

The Essential State Constitution

The Model State Constitution has twelve basic articles, which are embodied to a greater or lesser extent in the various state constitutions today. The following list provides a brief description of each article and how its contents are changing.

Bill of Rights   These individual rights and liberties closely resemble, and in some cases are identical to, those delineated in the first eight amendments to the U.S. Constitution. For example, all state constitutions protect citizens from deprivation of life, liberty, and property without "due process of law." Originally, the national Bill of Rights protected citizens only from actions by the U.S. government. State constitutions and courts were the principal guardians of civil liberties until 1868, when the adoption of the Fourteenth Amendment extended the protective umbrella of the national courts over the states.[19] By implication, some states had failed to uphold their trust.

In the 1980s, however, there was a renewed assertion of guarantees of individual rights by some activist states. At a minimum state constitutions must protect and guarantee those rights found in the U.S. Bill of Rights. But state constitutional provisions may guarantee additional or more extensive rights to citizens. Seventeen states now have equal rights amendments that guarantee sexual equality and prohibit sex-based discrimination. The U.S. Constitution does not guarantee a right of privacy, but ten states do. Utah and North Dakota have recently protected the right to keep and bear arms. Californians enjoy the right to fish, and residents of New Hampshire hold the right to revolution.

The major reason for the rebirth of state activism in protecting civil liberties and rights has been the conservatism (relative to the Warren Court) of the U.S. Supreme Court since 1969, when Warren Burger became chief justice. One commentator accused the Supreme Court of having abdicated its role as "keeper of the nation's conscience."[20] As we have noted, the states' power to write and interpret their constitutions more aggressively than the U.S. Constitution in protecting civil rights and liberties has been upheld by the Supreme Court, as long as the state provisions have "adequate and independent" grounds.[21]

Two cases from California illustrate how states can interpret their constitutional protections differently from principles that have issued from the U.S. Supreme Court. In *People* v. *Anderson* (1972), the California Supreme Court declared the state's death penalty to be unconstitutional, even though the death penalty is permissible under certain conditions according to the U.S. Supreme Court. At issue in this case was constitutional language. The U.S. Bill of Rights prohibits "cruel *and* unusual punishment," whereas California's bans "cruel *or* unusual punishment."[22] Thus California's provision is more restrictive. (It should be noted that the Golden State's electorate reacted to this ruling by amending the state constitution to permit the death penalty.[23]) The second case involved identical national and state constitutional language concerning search and seizure of evidence. In 1973, California's high court held that the U.S. Supreme Court had inaccurately interpreted the Fourth Amendment. The identical state provision was interpreted to afford greater protection from illegal search and seizure than the U.S. Supreme Court had granted (*U.S.* v. *Robinson*).[24]

Power of the State   This very brief article simply says that the powers enumerated in the constitution are not the only ones held by the state—that the state indeed has all powers not denied to it by the state or national constitution.

Suffrage and Elections   This article provides for the legal registration of voters and for election procedures. Recent extensions of voting rights and alterations in election procedures have been made in response to U.S. Supreme Court decisions and to national constitutional and statutory changes. Generally, states have improved election administration, liberalized registration, voting, and office-holding requirements,and shortened residency requirements. The voting age is eighteen years in all states; the age for holding legislative office is typically twenty-one, but varies depending on the office. Some states have amended this article to require the disclosure of campaign expenditures. Others have imposed campaign contribution and spending limitations, and a few have provided for partial public financing of election campaigns.

The Legislative Branch   This section sets forth the powers, procedures, and organizing principles of the legislature. In a pair of decisions in the 1960's, the U.S. Supreme Court ordered that state legislatures be apportioned on the basis of one person, one vote. That is, legislators must represent approximately the same number of constituents—House members the same as other House members and senators the same as other senators. District lines must be redrawn every ten years, after the national census has revealed population changes.

States have taken numerous actions in this section to approach greater conformity with the Model State Constitution, including increasing the length and frequency of legislative sessions, streamlining rules and procedures, and authorizing special sessions. Instead of stipulating specific dollar amounts for legislators' pay and fringe benefits (which are soon rendered inappropriate by inflation), most state constitutions now establish a procedure to determine and occasionally adjust the compensation of legislators. Specific pay levels are implemented through statute.

Interestingly, the model constitution for many years recommended a unicameral legislature as a means to overcome complexity, delay, and confusion. In the most recent revision of its book, the National Municipal League tacitly recognized the refusal of the states to follow this suggestion (only Nebraska has a single house general assembly) by providing recommendations appropriate for a bicameral body.

The Executive Branch   The powers and organization of the executive branch, which are outlined in this section, have seen many notable modifications. Essentially, executive power continues to be centralized in the office of the governor. Governors have won longer terms and the right to run for re-election. Line item vetos, shorter ballots, the authority to make appointments within the executive branch, and the ability to reorganize the state bureaucracy have also increased gubernatorial powers (see Chapter 7). Several states have opted for team election of the governor and lieutenant governor. Some have lowered the minimum age for the top two officers from thirty to twenty-five years.

The Judicial Branch   All states have revised court organization and procedures and election of judges substantially. A large majority have unified their court systems under a single authority, usually the state supreme court. Court procedures have been modernized under the office of the court administrator. Many states now select judges through a merit plan rather than by gubernatorial appointment, legislative election, or popular election (see Chapter 10). The states have also established commissions to investigate charges against judges and to recommend discipline or removal from the bench when necessary.

Finance   This article consists of provisions relating to taxation, debt, and expenditures for state and local government. A wave of tax and expenditure limitations swept across the states during the late 1970s and early 1980s, and tax relief has been granted to the aged and the handicapped in many states.

Local Government   Here, the authority of municipalities, counties, and other local governments is granted. Most states have increased local authority through home rule provisions, which give localities more discretion in providing services. Local taxing authority has also been extended. Mechanisms for improved intergovernmental cooperation, such as consolidated city and county governments and regional districts to provide services, have been created.

Public Education   In this article the states provide for the establishment and maintenance of free public schools for all children. Higher education institutions, including technical schools, colleges, and universities, are commonly established in this section. Some states have constitutional provisions for other functions, such as highways and transportation, health care, housing, and law enforcement.

Civil Service   The Model State Constitution sets forth a *merit system* of personnel administration for state government, under which civil servants are hired, promoted, paid, evaluated, and retained on the basis of competence, fitness, and performance instead of political party affiliation or other such criteria. All states must include certain public workers in merit systems, as mandated by federal law, but there is a great deal of variability in how states deal with other employees (see Chapter 8).

Intergovernmental Relations   Some states stipulate, as recommended by the Model State Constitution, specific devices for cooperation among various state entities, among local jurisdictions, or between the state and its localities. They may detail methods for sharing in the provision of certain services, or they may list cost-sharing mechanisms such as local option sales taxes. As the need for intergovernmental cooperation has grown, some states have substantially expanded the length of this article.

Constitutional Revision   In this section the methods for revising, amending, and replacing the constitution are described. Generally, the trend has been to make it easier for the voters, the legislature, or both to change the constitution. For example, several states have enabled voters to implement revisions through citizen initiative petitions (see Chapter 5). All states except Delaware ensure citizen participation in the constitutional amendment process through initiatives or by requiring voter ratification of all changes.

Constitutions Today

In general, state constitutions in the 1990s conform more closely to the Model State Constitution than those of the past did. They are shorter, more concise, simpler, and contain fewer errors, anachronisms, and contradictions. They give the state legislatures more responsibility for determining public policy through statute, rather than through constitutional amendment. The two newest states, Alaska and Hawaii, have documents that follow the model constitution quite closely.

However, much work remains to be done. Some state constitutions are still riddled with unnecessary detail because new amendments have continually been added to the old documents, and obsolete provisions and other relics can still be found. But there are more important deficiencies, which demand the attention of legislators and citizens in states whose constitutions inhibit the operations of state government and obstruct the ability to adapt to change. The governor's formal powers remain weak in some jurisdictions; a plethora of boards and commissions makes any thought of executive management and coordination a pipe dream; local governments chafe under the tight leash of state authority; and many other problems persist. Constitutional revision must be an ongoing process if the states are to be able to cope with the changing contours of American society.

The case of Mississippi is instructive. For several years a growing coalition of reformers has sought to rewrite the Magnolia State's archaic fundamental law. The document was written in 1890 and has been amended seventy times. Some discriminatory provisions are still included, even though they were nullified by the national government in the 1950s and 1960s (for example, a poll tax and a ban against interracial marriages). Mississippi's constitution is widely accused of hobbling gubernatorial authority, sustaining an unwieldy state bureaucracy, and restricting local governments. In 1985, Governor Bill Allain established a constitutional study commission, which recommended sweeping changes that were supported by the next governor, Ray Mabus. However, entrenched senior leaders in the House and Senate have stifled Mabus's efforts to let the voters decide on proposed amendments through a referendum. Critics contend that without far-reaching government reform, Mississippi will remain at the bottom of the list of states in terms of capability, accomplishments, and quality of life.[25]

Methods for Constitutional Change

There are only two methods for altering the U.S. Constitution. The first is the *constitutional convention*, at which delegates representing the states assemble to consider modifying or replacing the Constitution. Despite periodic calls for a national constitutional convention, only one has taken place—in Philadelphia more than two-hundred years ago. However, the states fell just two votes short of calling a convention during the mid-1980s over a proposal to require the national government to balance its budget. Two-thirds of the states must agree to call a convention; three-fourths are required to ratify any changes in the constitution.

The second means of amending the U.S. Constitution is through the *initiative process*, wherein Congress, by a two-thirds vote of both houses, agrees to send one or more proposed changes to the states. Again, three-fourths of the states must ratify the proposals. Since 1787 more than one thousand amendments have been submitted to the states by Congress. Only twenty-six have been approved. Note that neither method for amending the U.S. Constitution provides for popular participation by voters.

Informal Constitutional Change

One informal and four formal methods for amending state constitutions exist. The informal route is *interpretation* of constitutional meaning by the state legislature, executive branch, or courts, or through usage and custom. The force of habit can be a powerful influence, specific constitutional provisions notwithstanding.

State supreme courts play the most direct role in changing constitutions through interpretation. In large measure, a constitution is what the judges say it is in their decisions from the bench. The power of the state supreme courts to review executive actions, legislative actions, and decisions of lower courts is known as **judicial review**. This power evolved in the states much as it did on the national level—through the courts' own insistence that they hold this authority. During recent years, as the U.S. Supreme Court has become more conservative and less activist in its interpretations of the law, some state courts have moved in the opposite direction.

We have already noted that state supreme courts have the authority to interpret and apply state guarantees of civil rights and liberties more broadly than the U.S. Supreme Court's interpretation of the Bill of Rights in the U.S. Constitution. The U.S. Supreme Court does not review state court decisions that rest on "adequate and independent" state grounds, that is, decisions clearly and properly based on state constitutional provisions.[26] In practice, state supreme courts are often guided by constitutional rulings of the U.S. Supreme Court and high courts in other states. Because courts apply similar constitutional language to many common issues, it is natural for them to share their experiences in legal problem solving.[27] Interaction and the sharing of legal precedents between state and national courts have existed since the earliest days of our federal system. Of course, the national courts are supreme under the U.S. Constitution and will strike down any serious constitutional contradictions between the nation and the states, but since the advent of the Burger Court, the U.S. Supreme Court has shown "a studied deference to the work of the state judiciaries."[28]

Several states, including California, New York, and Washington, have recently earned reputations as judicial activists. However, it is safe to say that the majority of state supreme courts continue to base their rulings on national precedents and decisions. Some state justices are simply too set in their ways to embark on a new legal voyage. Others fear national court reversal of rulings based on independent state grounds, or perhaps feel that judicial activism would sit poorly with the voters, who could turn them out of office.[29]

Formal Constitutional Change

The four formal procedures for constitutional change are legislative proposal, initiative, constitutional convention, and constitutional commission.

All of them involve two basic steps, *initiation* and **ratification**. The state legislature, or in some cases the voters, propose (initiate) a constitutional change. Then, in all states but one, the proposed amendment is submitted to the voters for approval (ratification). The exception is Delaware, where the legislature can implement a constitutional revision without a vote of the people.

Legislative Proposal   This is the most common road taken to revision; over 90 percent of all changes in state constitutions have come through **legislative proposal**, which is permitted in all fifty states (see Table 4.2). Since 1970, around 70 percent of legislatively proposed constitutional changes have been ratified by the voters.

The specifics of legislative proposal techniques vary, but most states require either two-thirds or three-fifths of the members of each house to

Table 4.2   State Constitutional Changes and Methods of Initiation, Selected Years

Method	1970-71	1974-75	1978-79	1982-83	1984-85
Total Proposals					
All methods	403	352	395	345	238
Legislative proposal	392	332	319	330	211
Initiative	5	13	17	15	17
Constitutional convention	6	7	51	0	10
Constitutional commission	0	0	8	0	0
Total Adopted					
All methods	224	256	277	258	158
Legislative proposal	222	244	223	255	144
Initiative	1	8	6	3	8
Constitutional convention	1	4	48	0	6
Constitutional commission	0	0	0	0	0
Percent Adopted					
All methods	56	73	70	75	66
Legislative proposal	57	74	70	77	68
Initiative	20	62	35	20	47
Constitutional convention	17	57	94	—	60
Constitutional commission	—	—	0	—	—

Source: Data for each year from same year's edition of *The Book of the States* (Lexington, Ky: Council of State Governments). Reprinted with permission. Copyright by The Council of State Governments.

approve a proposal before it is sent to the voters for ratification. Twelve states require two consecutive legislative sessions to consider and pass a proposed amendment. The procedure can become quite complicated. Connecticut's constitution, for example, states that modification can come only after a three-fourths vote in each house during one session, *or* a majority vote in each house for two consecutive sessions, between which an election was held. South Carolina's legislative proposal must be passed by two-thirds of the members of each house; then it is sent to the people during the next general election. If a majority of voters show approval, the proposal returns to the next legislative session, in which a majority of legislators have to concur.

Almost all states accept a simple majority for voter ratification of a proposed revision. In New Hampshire, however, two-thirds of the voters must approve of the proposal. Hawaii, Illinois, Louisiana, Nebraska, New Mexico, and Tennessee also apply some restrictions to simple majority rule. Tennessee, for instance, requires approval by a majority of the citizens casting a vote for governor, and New Mexico mandates a three-fourths vote for amendments concerning suffrage and education matters.

Legislative proposal is probably best suited to revisions that are relatively narrow in scope. Some legislatures, however, such as South Carolina's, have presented a series of proposals to the voters over a period of years, and thereby significantly revised the document. The disadvantage to such a strategy is that it tends to result in a patchwork of amendments that can conflict or overlap with other constitutional provisions. This spawns additional revisions, which lead to increased litigation in the state supreme court. Thus, if the legislative proposal is used too frequently, it complicates and lengthens the constitution.

Initiative   Seventeen states permit their citizens to initiate and ratify changes in the constitution on their own, bypassing the legislature (see Table 4.3). Oregon was the first to use this method, in 1902. Only four of these states are east of the Mississippi River, which reflects the fact that the **initiative** was a product of the Progressive reform movement of the early 1900s. Most of the territories admitted as states during this period chose to permit the initiative (known as constitutional initiative in some states). Twenty-three states also authorize the initiative for enacting the statutory change (see Chapter 5).

The initiative is used much less frequently than legislative proposal in amending constitutions (see Table 4.2). It is also less successful in terms of the percentage that are adopted by the voters. On average, from 1970 to 1985, only about one-third of the initiatives were written into state constitutions. Perhaps the most famous initiative in recent years was California's Proposition 13, enacted in 1978, which unleashed a wave of tax and expenditure limitations across the states.

The initiative requires that a proposed constitutional amendment receive a certain percentage or number of signatures by registered voters before it

Table 4.3   States Authorizing Constitutional Amendment by Citizen Initiative

State	Number of signatures required on initiative petition
Arizona	15% of total votes cast for all candidates for governor in last election
Arkansas	10% of voters for governor in last election
California	8% of total voters for all candidates for governor in last election
Colorado	5% of total legal votes for all candidates for secretary of state in last general election
Florida	8% of total votes cast in the state in the last election for presidential electors
Illinois*	8% of total votes cast for candidates for governor in last election
Massachusetts	3% of total votes cast for governor in preceding biennial state election (not fewer than 25,000 qualified voters)
Michigan	10% of total voters for all candidates in last gubernatorial election
Missouri	8% of legal voters for all candidates for governor in last election
Montana	10% of qualified electors, the number of qualified electors to be determined by number of votes cast for governor in preceding general election
Nebraska	10% of total votes for governor in last election
Nevada	10% of voters who voted in entire state in last general election
North Dakota	4% of population of the state
Ohio	10% of total number of electors who voted for governor in last election
Oklahoma	15% of legal voters for state office receiving highest number of voters in last general state election
Oregon	8% of total votes for all candidates for governor in last election at which governor was elected for four-year term
South Dakota	10% of total votes for governor in last election

* Only Article 6, "The Legislature," may be amended by initiative petition.

Source: Adapted from *The Book of the States, 1988-89* (Lexington, KY.: Council of State Governments, 1988). Reprinted with permission. Copyright by The Council of State Governments.

can be placed on a statewide ballot for a ratification vote. Oklahoma requires 15 percent of the votes cast in the race for the statewide office that received the highest number of votes in the last general election. Eight states specify that the petition signatures must be collected widely throughout the state, as a means of ensuring that an initiative that favors one region does not become embodied in the constitution. In Montana, 10 percent of the petition signatures must come from two-fifths of the state's legislative districts.

In general, a petition for constitutional amendment is sent to the office of the secretary of state for verification that the required number of registered voters have signed their names. Then the question is placed on a statewide ballot in the next general election. Ratification requires a majority vote of the people in most states, although four have further requirements for approval. For instance, Nevada mandates a majority popular vote on an amendment in two consecutive general elections.

If the formal legislative process is circumvented altogether and propositions are placed directly on the general election ballot, it is called a **direct initiative**. If a legislature participates by voting on the citizen proposal, as it does in Massachusetts, or if it otherwise contributes substantively to the amendment process, the procedure is known as an **indirect initiative**. Eight states allow indirect initiatives.

The initiative is useful in making limited changes to the state constitution, and in recent years has addressed some controversial issues that state legislatures have been loath to confront. Colorado voters, for example, adopted an initiative to prohibit the use of public funds for abortions. Other controversial proposals in the 1980s included legalized gambling, a unilateral nuclear arms freeze, gun control, and prayer in the public schools.

A major advantage of the initiative is that it permits the people's will to counter a despotic or inertia-ridden legislature. For instance, Illinois voters in 1978 reduced the size of the House of Representatives from 177 to 118 after the legislature voted itself a huge pay raise during a period of economic hardship. Another advantage is that this method appears to enhance citizen interest and participation in government. However, the initiative can be abused by special interests with selfish motives who seek to gain privileges, and under crisis conditions it can result in ill-conceived, radical changes to the constitution. The initiative can also result in just the kind of excessive detail and poorly drafted verbiage that is so widely condemned by constitutional scholars and reformers.[30]

Constitutional Convention   Legislative proposals and initiatives are quite specific about the type of constitutional change that is sought. Only those questions that actually appear on the ballot are considered. In contrast, a **constitutional convention** assembles delegates who suggest revisions or even an entirely new document, then submit the proposed changes to the voters for ratification. The convention is especially well suited to consider far-reaching constitutional changes or a new fundamental law. Convention proposals are less likely to be ratified by the people than legislative proposals are, but they have higher success rates than initiatives.

The states have held more than 230 constitutional conventions during their history. The convention is the oldest method for constitutional change in the states, and is available in all fifty of them. The process begins when the electorate or the legislature decides to call for a constitutional convention. No state permits a convention to be called through the petition process; the legislature must either call a convention unilaterally or place the issue before the people on the general election ballot. A third possibility exists in a growing number of states, where the question of calling a convention must be regularly voted on by the electorate, as Thomas Jefferson once proposed. Alaskans and Iowans consider a constitutional convention every ten years; in New York and Maryland, the convention issue is submitted to the voters every twenty years. Fourteen states have such a systematic review provision in their constitutions. In all states, the legislature can decide on its own to submit to the voters the question of whether to hold a constitutional convention, and in some, including Virginia and Maine, the legislature may call a convention without asking for voter concurrence. Except in Delaware, proposals emerging from the convention must be ratified by the voters before they become part of the constitution.

Delegates to a convention are usually elected by the voters from state house or senate districts. The total number of delegates has varied from 40 in Virginia to 481 in New Hampshire, but it averages 170. Recently, most delegates have been elected on a nonpartisan basis, although some states provide for partisan ballots. Generally, partisan election selects delegates

The 1978 Hawaii constitutional convention lasted two and a half months. Several proposed amendments were submitted to the electorate.

with more years of experience in politics, whereas nonpartisan selection is associated with fewer professional politicians.[31]

Conventions are usually dominated by middle-aged and elderly white males with high levels of formal education.[32] Many are professionals; the percentage of lawyers alone typically ranges from 25 to 50 percent. There is normally a substantial number of educators and businesspeople and a smattering of homemakers.[33] This delegate composition is not surprising, since convention calls are strongly supported by higher socioeconomic groups in urban areas.[34] Recent conventions have been more representative of state population characteristics, however. Hawaii's 1978 convention, for instance, comprised more ethnic, female, and occupationally diverse members than the delegate pool in 1968. The 1980 constitutional convention that met in the District of Columbia to design a charter in anticipation of future statehood was certainly the most diverse in delegate characteristics of any such convention to gather on these shores; almost every minority imaginable was represented. The document they produced was "as much a manifesto for social reform" as a charter for governance.[35] It included clauses that guaranteed, among other things, the rights to employment and to abortion on demand. Politics and Policy 4.1 looks at the possibility of granting statehood to the District of Columbia.

The characteristics of a delegate pool are important for several reasons. First, the delegates need knowledge of and experience in state government and politics if they are to contribute meaningfully to the debate and drafting of proposed amendments. It is usually not too difficult to attract qualified people for service; the experience is important, unique, and a privilege, and it is not as time-consuming as running for and serving in the legislature. Second, the delegates should represent a cross section of the state's population insofar as possible. If the delegate pool does not reflect gender, racial, regional, ethnic, and other salient characteristics of the population, the fruit of its labor may lack legitimacy in the eyes of substantial numbers of voters. Finally, partisanship should be avoided where possible. Partisan differences can wreck consensus on major issues and destroy the prospects for voter ratification of suggested amendments that emerge from the convention, as experiences in Michigan, Illinois, and New York aptly show.[36] Of course, delegates elected on a partisan ticket are more likely to divide along party lines than those selected through nonpartisan election.

It would be the very rare convention that did not experience some divisions, partisan or not. The basic conflict is frequently between those who favor comprehensive constitutional change—reformers—and supporters and protectors of the status quo. Splits can also develop between urban and rural interests, regional interests, and blacks and whites. One study of constitutional conventions in six states found that a large majority of delegates began the convention with an idealized view that the debates and decisions would be above party politics and generally statesmanlike.[37] Most delegates kept that perspective throughout their respective conven-

POLITICS AND POLICY 4.1
The State of New Columbia?

More than two hundred years after the American Revolution, "No taxation without representation" is still a rallying cry. The 750,000 residents of the District of Columbia pay almost $2 billion annually in federal taxes yet have no voting members in Congress. The District's nonvoting House member, Walter E. Fauntroy, contends that, "It is wholly inconsistent to espouse the virtues of democracy around the world while denying democracy to three-quarters of a million taxpaying Americans in the nation's capital."[1]

Article I, Section 8 of the U.S. Constitution designates the District of Columbia as the seat of the national government. The Framers believed that a separate district would keep the state hosting the national capital from exercising special pressure on Congress, and would prevent the national government from being dependent on any one state for services and security. Under the Constitution, Congress holds exclusive authority over the District. Since 1974, the District has operated under a home rule charter under which Congress retains veto power over its legislative and budgetary affairs.

During the 1980s, two major attempts to achieve statehood for the district failed: a constitutional amendment was approved by only sixteen of the necessary thirty-eight states, and a House of Representatives committee bill did not pass in the full chamber. The constitutional and political arguments against statehood are formidable. The constitutional issues involve the Twenty-third Amendment, which gives the District three electoral votes in a

tions, with the exception of those attending the highly politicized Illinois and New York assemblies, who tended to emerge with more cynical views.

Voter approval of convention proposals is problematic. If partisan, racial, regional, or other disagreements dominate media reports on the convention, voter approval is difficult to obtain. People naturally tend to regard suggestions for sweeping changes in the basic structures and procedures of government with skepticism. If they have not been regularly involved with and informed of the progress of the convention, they may be reluctant to give their approval to the recommendations.

Delegates usually understand these dynamics and are sensitive to how their proposed changes may affect the general public. They must, for example, carefully consider how to present the proposed amendments for ratifi-

presidential election. It would probably have to be repealed, requiring approval by a difficult three-fourths of the states. Also, New Columbia would be situated on sixty-seven acres of land originally ceded to the national government by Maryland, which might have to consent formally to the use of the land for a new state.

The political objections to statehood are powerful and probably will be the determining factor. The District has no meaningful agriculture or industry (except government) and therefore would require a special subsidy from the national government to pay for its operations. New Columbia would have the highest per capita income of any state except Alaska, yet would rank first in the percentage of people on welfare. Its population would be overwhelmingly black (70 percent), liberal, and Democratic, characteristics that do not appeal to Republicans and conservatives. Other features that bother opponents are the murder rate, which is one of the highest among American cities and twice that of the most homicidal state (Texas), and the fact that the District crawls with lawyers—one out of every twenty-five residents. An additional source of political opposition has been the corruption scandals that have rocked the city government since 1987, tarnishing the reputation of the District's mayor, Marion Barry, and many of his associates. Even if supporters of statehood overcome these political obstacles, any congressional action in favor of it is certain to be challenged on constitutional grounds.

[1] Eric Pianin, "Tiny and Crowded, New Columbia Would Be a Unique State," *Washington Post*, June 23, 1987, pp. B1, B5.

cation. There are two choices: the all-or-nothing strategy of consolidating all changes in a single vote, and the piecemeal strategy, which presents each proposal as a separate ballot decision. In recent years, voters have tended to reject inclusive packages. Each suggested change is certain to offend some minority, and when all the offended minorities coalesce, they may well comprise a majority of voters.[38] In 1968, for example, Maryland voters soundly rejected a new constitution, but separate amendments later submitted to the people were approved.

However, separate proposals do not ensure victory. Texas's eight constitutional amendments each met defeat in 1975 for several reasons, including conflicts among the delegates, popular discontent with the legislature (which had formulated the proposals), and a general perception that since the state had a large budget surplus and low taxes, there was no pressing need for change (see Politics and Policy 4.2). Florida's voters rejected a series of eight proposed amendments in 1978, largely because the proposals were so complex that people could not understand them.[39]

Constitutional Commission   Often called a *study commission*, the **constitutional commission** is usually established to study the existing document and to recommend changes to the legislature. It may be created by statute, legislative resolution, or executive order of the governor in all states, but not by initiative. Little or no citizen participation is associated with this method of constitutional change. Depending on the mandate, the study commission may examine the entire constitution with a view toward replacement or change, it may focus on one or more specific articles or provisions, or it may be given the freedom to decide its own scope of activity. Commission recommendations are only advisory to the legislature and/or governor, which helps account for this method's popularity with elected officials. Some or all of the recommendations may be submitted to the voters; others may be completely ignored. Only in Florida can a commission send its proposals directly to the voters.[40]

Some constitutional commissions, called *preparatory commissions*, are created to do the groundwork for a forthcoming constitutional convention. Typically, they arrange for convention staff, lay out a schedule, and in some cases submit suggestions for constitutional change to the convention.

Commission size averages twenty members, who are private citizens or public officials and who are usually appointed by the governor or by the governor and the legislature. Selection may reflect such factors as geography, political party, and occupation. Meetings are normally held over a period of about one and one-half years, usually in the state capital.

Only twenty-three commissions have operated since 1970. Service on a constitutional commission can be a thankless task, as legislators sometimes ignore the commission's recommendations or employ them as a symbolic device for relieving political pressure. But when used properly, commissions can furnish high-quality research inexpensively and relatively quickly.

State Resurgence and Constitutional Reform

Few tasks in government are more difficult than modernizing a constitution. It requires "sustained, dedicated, organized effort; vigorous, aggressive and imaginative leadership; bipartisan political support; education of the electorate on the issues; judicious selection of the means; and seemingly endless patience."[41] In the words of constitutional scholar W. Brooke Graves, "The advocate of constitutional reform in an American state should be endowed with the patience of Job and the sense of time of a geologist."[42]

POLITICS AND POLICY 4.2
Constitutional Revision in the Lone Star State

Texas tried an interesting experiment in 1974: its first constitutional convention in almost one hundred years. The state legislature organized *itself* as a convention—the first (and probably last) time this had been done in the United States. The House and Senate convened as a unicameral body, with the Speaker of the House as convention president.

The legislator-delegates did a good job. They proposed a new constitution of only 17,500 words, to replace a badly written, scrambled 63,000-word document with more than 200 amendments. The new document won the backing of most newspapers, civic and professional organizations, "good government" groups, and the deans of all eight law schools at Texas universities. Strangely, however, the proposed constitution failed to gain enough votes to emerge from the convention and be placed on the ballot for popular ratification.

After spending some $4 million and many months in debate, the Texas convention became the first in history to reject its own product. There were two major reasons for the fiasco. First, the convention hobbled itself with a rule that required a two-thirds vote for approval of each proposal to be submitted to the voters. This was too high a margin. Second, the fact that delegates were legislators made for divisive convention politics. They began with hard feelings over the election of the Speaker as president of the body, and compromise proved impossible. At the final vote, the "cockroaches"—those opposed to revising the constitution—outnumbered reform supporters by three.

The Texas saga continued the following year, when, under virulent public criticism and pressure, the legislature reorganized the rejected document into eight constitutional amendments and submitted them to the voters in the general election. All eight were rejected by large margins (more than 2.5 to 1), which led Lieutenant Governor William P. Hobby to remark, "There's not enough of the [constitutional] body left to have an autopsy."

Source: Janice C. May, "Texas Constitutional Revision: Lessons and Laments," NATIONAL CIVIC REVIEW 66 (February 1977): 64-69. Reprinted with permission.

Constitutions reflect the political culture, the way of life, the values, principles, and ideals of the state community. They define the political institutions and how important decisions will be made by them. They establish the basis for citizenship and the authority of state government.[43] They set forth the fundamental law of the state, subordinate only to the U.S. Constitution and national legislation. The solemn duty of framing the original state constitutions, which was so effectively discharged by our predecessors, must be matched by the continuous oversight of present and future generations. Changes are necessary to adjust state governments to the vagaries of life in the 1990s and beyond.

According to the U.S. Advisory Commission on Intergovernmental Relations, the constitutional changes enacted in the states during the three decades since the Kestnbaum Commission report have generally resulted in documents that "are shorter, more clearly written, modernized, less encumbered with restrictions, more basic in content and have more reasonable amending processes. They also establish improved governmental structures and contain substantive provisions assuring greater openness, accountability and equity."[44] The states have made a great deal of progress in modernizing their governments. As state constitutional scholar Richard Leach has put it, "There are not many constitutional horrors left."[45] In fact, there is growing evidence that the states are again becoming important guardians of individual rights and liberties.

Terry Sanford, former governor of North Carolina and presently U.S. senator, has referred to old-style constitutions as "the drag anchors of state programs, and permanent cloaks for the protection of special interests and points of view."[46] These constitutions held back progress and delayed the states' resurgence as lead players in the drama of American federalism. Recent constitutional amendments have reflected, and indeed caused, profound changes in state government and politics. Since the genesis of modern reform in the mid-1960s, some forty states have adopted new constitutions or substantially amended existing ones. Problems persist, and future constitutional tinkering and replacements will be necessary. But in most states, the constitutional landscape is much cleaner and more functional than it was twenty-five years ago.

Summary

As instruments of political power, constitutions establish the basic structure and operating rules for state government. Most states have modernized their constitutions during the past twenty-five years, bringing them closer to the Model State Constitution, by among other things strengthening executive power and making the documents clearer and more concise. Many constitutions, however, remain outdated and in need of reform. Constitutions can be revised through legislative proposal, initiative, or constitutional convention. All methods require voter approval.

Key Terms

Constitutional commission A meeting of delegates appointed by the governor or legislature to study constitutional problems and propose solutions.

Constitutional convention An assembly of delegates chosen by popular election or appointed by the legislature or the governor to revise an existing constitution or to create a new one.

Direct initiative A procedure by which the voters of a jurisdiction propose the passage of constitutional amendments, state laws, or local ordinances, bypassing the legislative body.

Indirect initiative Similar to the direct initiative, except that the voter-initiated proposal must be submitted to the legislature before going on the ballot for voter approval.

Initiative Proposed law or constitutional amendment that is placed on the ballot by citizen petition.

Interpretation An informal means of revising constitutions in which members of the executive, legislative, or judicial branch apply constitutional principles and law to the everyday affairs of governing.

Judicial review The power of the U.S. Supreme Court or state supreme courts to declare unconstitutional actions of the executive and legislative branches and decisions of lower courts.

Legislative proposal The most common means of amending a state constitution, wherein the legislature proposes a revision, usually by a two-thirds majority.

Legislative supremacy The legislature's dominance of the other two branches of government.

Model State Constitution The experts' ideal of the structure and contents of a state constitution.

Ratification The formal approval of a constitution or constitutional amendment by a majority of the voters of a state.

5

Participation and Interest Groups

Participation
Why and How People Participate/
Nonparticipation/The Struggle for the Right
to Vote/Voting Patterns/Should Nonvoting
Be a Concern?

Election-Day Lawmaking
The Initiative/The Recall

Interest Groups
Types of Interest Groups/Interest Groups in
the States/Techniques Used by Interest Groups/
Local-Level Interest Groups

Citizen Access to Government
Types of Official Access/The Impact of
Citizen Access

Volunteerism

The Effects of Citizen Participation

The mountain town of New Vineyard, Maine, almost became defunct in 1989, a victim not of economic calamity but of a bad case of apathy. Not enough of the town's 607 residents would participate in local government.[1] The annual town meeting, the symbol of direct democracy, where residents gather to set policy for the community, drew only a handful of residents. With no citizens willing to serve on the town's governing body, the board of selectmen, there could be no New Vineyard, and it looked like state government would have to step in and provide basic services to residents of the 187-year-old town.

Participation

Democracy assumes citizen **participation**—taking action to influence government. Although the New Vineyard case is an extreme example, there is persistent evidence that citizens are not much interested in participation. We have grown accustomed to reports of low voter turnout and public hearings that no public attends. On the surface, government works just fine with limited participation: the interests of the active become translated into public policy, and those who are inactive can be safely ignored, because they do not vote. If, however, some traditional nonvoters, such as low-income, less-educated citizens, went to the polls, then vote-seeking candidates might be forced to pay more attention to their interests, and public policy might be nudged in a different direction. In this light, it is important to understand both why many people do participate and why others do not.

Why and How People Participate

In a representative democracy, voting is the most common form of participation. For many citizens, voting is a matter of civic responsibility. It is a fundamental facet of citizenship—after all, it is called "the right to vote." Citizens go to the polls to elect the officials who will govern them. But there are other methods of participation. Consider a citizen who is unhappy because the property taxes on her home have increased substantially from one year to the next. What options are available to her besides voting against incumbent officeholders at the next election? As shown in Figure 5.1, she can be either active or passive, and her actions either constructive or destructive. Basically, she has four potential responses: loyalty, voice, exit, and neglect.[2]

According to this formulation, voting is an example of *loyalty*, a passive but constructive response to government action. It shows the irate taxpayer's underlying support for her community despite her displeasure with specific tax policies. An active constructive response is *voice:* the aggrieved property owner could contact officials, work in the campaign of a candidate who promises to lower tax assessments, or (assuming that others in the community share her sentiments) participate in antitax groups and organize demonstrations.

Destructive responses (those that undermine the citizen-government relationship) are similarly passive or active. If the citizen simply shrugs and concludes that "you can't fight city hall," she is exhibiting a passive response termed *neglect*. She has virtually given up on the community and does not participate. A more active version of giving up is to *exit*; that is, to leave the community altogether (this is often referred to as "voting with your feet"). The unhappy citizen will relocate in a community that is more in line with her tax preferences.

Every citizen confronts these participatory options. It is much healthier for the political system if citizens engage in the constructive responses, but some individuals are likely to conclude that constructive participation is of little value to them and opt for neglect or, in more extreme cases, exit.

Figure 5.1   Possible Responses to Dissatisfaction in the Community
Each of these participatory options affects public policy decisions in a community. Citizens who choose the *voice* option frequently find themselves in the thick of things.

Active

VOICE	EXIT
• Contacting officials • Discussing political issues • Campaign work • Campaign contributions • Participation in neighborhood groups • Participation in demonstrations	• Leaving or contemplating leaving the jurisdiction • Opting for privatized alternatives to government services

Constructive   *Destructive*

• Voting • Speaking well of the community • Showing support for the community by attending public functions	• Nonvoting • Feeling that fighting city hall has no impact • Distrust of city officials
LOYALTY	**NEGLECT**

Passive

Source: William E. Lyons and David Lowery, "The Organization of Political Space and Citizen Responses to Dissatisfaction in Urban Communities: An Integrative Model," *The Journal of Politics* 49 (May 1986): 331. Reprinted by permission.

Nonparticipation

What explains the citizens who choose neglect as their best option? One explanation for nonparticipation in politics is socioeconomic status. Individuals with lower levels of income and education tend to participate less than wealthier, more educated individuals do.[3] Tied closely to income and education levels is occupational status. Unskilled workers and hourly wage earners do not participate in politics to the same degree that white-collar workers and professionals do. Individuals of lower socioeconomic status may have neither the interest nor the resources to become actively involved in politics.

Other explanations for nonparticipation have included age (younger people have participated less than middle-aged individuals), race (blacks have participated less than whites), and gender (women have participated less than men). However, of these factors, only age continued to affect political activity in the 1980s. Black political participation actually surpasses that of whites when socioeconomic status is taken in consideration,[4] and the gender gap in the types and levels of political participation has virtually disappeared.[5]

The explanation for nonparticipation does not rest solely with the individual. Institutional features—that is, the way the political system is designed—may suppress participation. For example, local governments that have instituted nonpartisan elections, in which candidates run without party affiliation, have removed an important mobilizing factor for voters. Voter turnout tends to be lower in these elections than in partisan contests. Some state governments still have not modernized their voter registration procedures to make the process quick and easy, which discourages potential registrants. City council meetings scheduled at 10:00 A.M. put a tremendous strain on workers who must take time off from their jobs if they want to attend; consequently, attendance is low. Local governments in which it is difficult for citizens to contact the appropriate official with a service request or complaint are not doing much to facilitate participation. Features like these play an often unrecognized role in dampening participation.

The Struggle for the Right to Vote

State constitutions in the eighteenth and early nineteenth centuries entrusted only propertied white males with the vote. They did not allow public involvement in government, and the eventual softening of restrictions on suffrage did not occur without a struggle. Even after requirements for property ownership and wealth were dropped, women and blacks were still denied the right to vote.

In an effort to attract women to its rugged territory, Wyoming enfranchised women in 1869. Suffragists—people who were actively fighting for female suffrage—scored a victory when Colorado extended the vote to women in 1893. Gradually, other states began enfranchising women and in 1920 the Twentieth Amendment to the U.S. Constitution, forbidding states to deny the right to vote "on account of sex," was ratified.

Although the Fifteenth Amendment (1870) extended the vote to blacks, some southern states clung defiantly to traditional ways that denied blacks and poor people their rights. Poll taxes and literacy tests kept the poor and uneducated, regardless of race, from voting. Furthermore, southern Democrats designed the "white primary" to limit black political influence. In the one-party South, the Democratic primary elections, where candidates for the general elections were chosen, were the scene of the important contests. Thus, blacks were still barred from effective participation, because they could not vote in the primaries. The general election amounted to little more than ratification of the party's choices, because so few elections were contested by the Republicans. In *Smith* v. *Allwright* (1944), the U.S. Supreme Court ruled that since primaries were part of the machinery that chose officials, they were subject to the same nondiscriminatory standards as general elections, and the days of the white primary came to an end.

Segregationists in the South continued their battle against the pressures of modernization and fairness.[6] Although the number of black voters increased steadily during the mid-twentieth century, substantial discrimination remained. The outlawing of the white primary forced racists to resort to more informal methods—physical intimidation was one—of keeping blacks from the polls. Blacks gained access to the polls primarily through national enactments such as the Civil Rights Act of 1964 and the Twenty-fourth Amendment (1964), which made poll taxes unconstitutional.

The **Voting Rights Act of 1965** finally broke the back of the segregationists' efforts. Under its provisions, federal poll watchers and registrars were dispatched to particular counties to investigate voter discrimination. To this day, counties covered under the Voting Rights Act (all of nine southern states and parts of seven other states) must submit to the U.S. Department of Justice any changes in election laws, such as new precinct lines or new polling places.

Over time, judicial interpretations, congressional actions, and Justice Department rules have modified the Voting Rights Act. One of the most important modifications has been to substitute an "effects" test for the original "intent" test. In other words, if a governmental action has the *effect* of discouraging minority voting, whether intentionally or not, the action must be rejected. Civil rights activists welcomed this change, because proving the intent of an action is much more difficult than simply demonstrating its effect.

Voting Patterns

Figure 5.2 demonstrates the fact that voter turnout has been steadily declining for a number of years. Note, however, that the data show voter turnout

Figure 5.2   Voter Turnout as a Proportion of Voting-Age Population, 1958–1988
Voter turnout typically drops by 15 to 20 percentage points from a presidential year to an off-year election.

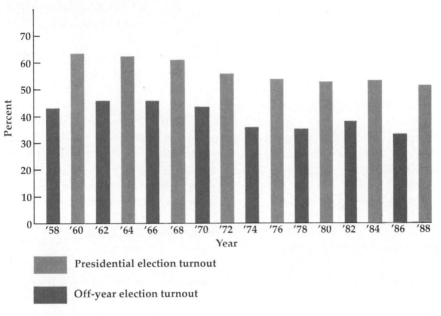

Presidential election turnout

Off-year election turnout

Source: U.S. Bureau of the Census, *Statistical Abstract of the United States* (Washington, D.C.: U.S. Government Printing Office, 1964, 1976, 1988).

as a percentage of the voting-age population. Not all people who have reached the age of eighteen are in fact eligible to vote (for example, convicted felons who have not had their civil rights restored are ineligible) and the percentages in Figure 5.2 tend to understate the percentage of eligible voters who show up at the polls. But even with that distinction, it is true that twenty and thirty years ago, over 60 percent of the voting-age population customarily turned out for a presidential election. Since 1972, when eighteen-year-olds were given the right to vote, the proportion has dropped to under 55 percent. In off-year elections, when there is no presidential race, voter turnout has declined from the mid-40 percent range to the low 30s.

Voter turnout is affected by several factors. First, it varies according to the type of election. A presidential race usually attracts a higher proportion of eligible voters than a local election does. Turnout for elections is higher when a presidential contest is on the ballot than in off-years, when many state races appear. Second, attractive candidates running a close race seem to increase voter interest. When each candidate has a chance to win, voters sense that their vote will matter more than in a race with a sure winner.

There are noteworthy differences among states in proportions of both voting-age population registered and voter turnout. Nationally, 66.3 percent of the voting-age population was registered to vote in 1986. But when we look at the figures for individual states, wide variation appears. Compare two states with very similar voting-age populations: Oklahoma, with 2.4 million, and South Carolina, with 2.5 million. In 1986, 82.6 percent of the voting-age population in Oklahoma was registered; in South Carolina, the figure was 52.6 percent.[7]

States can also be differentiated according to voter turnout rates. States with moralistic political cultures typically experience higher voter turnout than states with traditionalistic political cultures do. For example, Utah voters have historically turned out for state elections at about twice the rate of Georgia voters. States with competitive political parties tend to turn out a higher proportion of voters; each party needs to mobilize individuals who identify with it in order to win. Finally, the states can affect turnout by the way in which they administer the elections. People who are registered tend to vote. Making registration easy, as it is in Wisconsin, where voters can register at the polls on election day, is one way to bolster turnout.

The Issue of Nonvoting

Many people are staying home on election day, feeling annoyed that *Wheel of Fortune* will be pre-empted by election returns on television that evening. When asked why they did not vote, these citizens are likely to offer responses ranging from "It was too much trouble" to "I didn't like either of the candidates" to "My vote won't change the system." To them, voting simply was not in their interest. In the U.S. political system, this is a choice that individuals can make.

Many other citizens are concerned about the extent of nonvoting, as shown by the drive to increase voter turnout, which takes two principal forms: (1) public relations efforts, such as public service advertisements in which celebrities tell us why they vote, and (2) procedures that make registration and absentee voting easier. Almost half (twenty-four) of the states have adopted a system whereby voters can register by mail.[8] Some have moved the closing date for registration nearer to the actual date of the election, giving potential voters more time to register. This is important, because campaigns tend to heighten the public's interest in the election. A potential voter is not encouraged to participate when he or she is told at the registration office that "the books have closed" for next week's election. Most states now close their registration books fewer than thirty days before an election, and four states allow registration on election day.[9] North Dakota is the only state in the nation that does not require voter registration.

Absentee balloting has also been made easier than it was in the past. Most states still require a voter applying for an absentee ballot to supply an acceptable reason, such as being away on business or in school, but some have lifted these restrictions and allow any voter to vote in absentia. These states include Alaska, California, Iowa, Kansas, Oregon, and Washington.[10]

Ironically, the effects of nonvoting are not always clear. First of all, higher turnout might not affect election results. An analysis of the 1988 presidential election indicated that if nonvoters had voted, the outcome would not have changed.[11] Second, as Figure 5.1 showed, the potential participant has other options. Although voting is declining, people are engaging in other forms of participation.

Election-Day Lawmaking

What happens when the government does not respond to the messages that the people are sending? More and more, the answer is to transform the message into a ballot proposition and let the citizens make their own laws. As explained in Chapter 4, *initiatives* are proposed laws or constitutional amendments that are placed on the ballot by citizen petition, to be approved or rejected by popular vote. An initiative lets citizens enact their own laws, bypassing the state legislature. For example, citizens used an initiative to control growth in Massachusetts, as noted in Politics and Policy 5.1. This mechanism for legislation by popular vote was one of several reforms of the Progressive era, roughly 1890 to 1920. Other Progressive reforms included the popular referendum and the recall. The **popular referendum** allows citizens to petition to vote on actions taken by legislative bodies.[12] It provides a means by which the public can overturn a legislative enactment. (A popular referendum is different from a general **referendum**—a proposition that requires voter approval before it can take effect. Constitutional amendments and bond issues are examples of general referenda.) The **recall** election requires elected officials to stand for a vote on their removal, before their term has expired. Recall provides the public with an opportunity to force an official out of office.

The key characteristic shared by initiative, popular referendum, and recall is that they are actions begun by citizens. The Progressives advocated these mechanisms to expand the role of citizens and to restrict the power of intermediary institutions such as legislatures, political parties, and elected officials.[13] Their efforts were particularly successful in the western part of the United States (see Figure 5.3), probably because of the difficulty of amending existing state constitutions in the East and an elitist fear of the working class (the industrialized immigrants in the Northeast and the rural sharecroppers in the South). The newer western states, in contrast, were quite open, both procedurally and socially. In 1898, South Dakota became the first state to adopt the initiative process. The first time the initiative was actually used was in Oregon in 1902, when citizens successfully petitioned

POLITICS AND POLICY 5.1
Power to the People: Controlling Growth on Cape Cod

Cape Cod is a popular New England vacation spot—maybe too popular. In the summertime, the Cape is the destination of thousands upon thousands of vacationers and tourists. The crush of people has, quite naturally, led to extensive development of this Massachusetts coastal area. Sacrificed to development are saltmarshes, woods and ponds, quiet harbors, and modest bungalows. In their place are shopping malls, condos, and horrific traffic. To the political leaders of the Cape and to the development-related interests (developers, builders, realtors, lawyers), these conditions have been acceptable, even desirable. To the average Cape Codder, they are not.

A report on environmental conditions indicated that the aquifer supplying water to the Cape was in danger of becoming polluted. The report offered, as an initial measure, a temporary moratorium on growth to buy time to reassess the problem. Political leaders and the development community ridiculed the idea, and it appeared that development would continue at its breathtaking pace.

But the thinking of local big shots was out of synch with that of most Cape Codders. Opinion polls taken by newspapers indicated that a substantial majority of residents supported a moratorium on development. Rather than waiting for their leaders to catch on, a citizens' group, the Association for the Preservation of Cape Cod, pushed to get a nonbinding initiative for a one-year moratorium on the local November 1988 ballot. Former U.S. senator Paul Tsongas, who had chaired the committee that produced the environmental report and who had become caught in the resulting conflict, stated: "I challenge you to find another example in the history of the Republic when an issue evokes such deep passion in people, is supported by two-thirds to three-quarters in polls and never was supported by any elected official at any level."

The growth moratorium question passed overwhelmingly and Cape Cod officials learned their lesson. Sometimes it does not pay for public officials to get out of step with the public.

for ballot questions on mandatory political party primaries and local option liquor sales. Both of the initiatives were approved.

Today, twenty-three states allow the initiative. A few use the indirect initiative, which gives the legislature an opportunity to consider the proposed measure. If the legislature fails to act, or if it rejects the measure, the proposal is put before the voters at the next election. But most states use the direct initiative. Popular referendum is provided for in twenty-five states, and recall of state officials in fifteen. These figures understate the use of these mechanisms throughout the country, however, because many states without statewide initiative, popular referendum, and recall allow their use at the local government level.[14]

The Initiative

The first step in the initiative process is the *petition*. A draft of the proposed law (or constitutional amendment) is circulated along with a petition, which citizens must sign. As noted in Chapter 4, the petition signature requirement varies by state, but usually falls between 5 and 10 percent of the number of votes cast in the preceding statewide election. In California, more than 600,000 registered voters' signatures are needed for a measure to make a statewide ballot.

California, which has been referred to as "the world's largest direct democracy," has transformed the signature-gathering process into a science.[15] Its first innovation was to replace standard door-to-door canvassing with an operation based in shopping malls, where proponents buttonhole shoppers to explain the initiative and ask them to sign the petitions. California's most recent contribution to the signature-gathering process has been to use direct mail: petition forms are simply mailed to a preselected, computer-generated list of likely signers. This is a costly but simple method of collecting signatures. The Golden State's methods are making their way to other states.

The Return of Initiatives   The 1950s and 1960s saw little use of the initiative process, but grassroots fervor of three kinds of groups reactivated the process in the 1970s: environmental activists, consumer advocates, and tax limitation organizations. In 1976, for example, measures to restrict nuclear power were on the ballot in seven states. The propositions were defeated in every instance. Yet the environmental groups' pioneering efforts eventually bore fruit: antinuclear measures have been much more successful in recent years, as demonstrated in the 1989 vote to shut down a nuclear power plant outside Sacramento, California. Second, consumer activists promoted initiatives aimed at tightening regulations on business and corporate interests. And as mentioned, the most influential modern initiative was California's Proposition 13 (1978), which rolled back property taxes in the state and

Figure 5.3   State Use of the Initiative

In the past fifty years, only Wyoming (1968) and Florida (1978) have joined the ranks of initiative states.

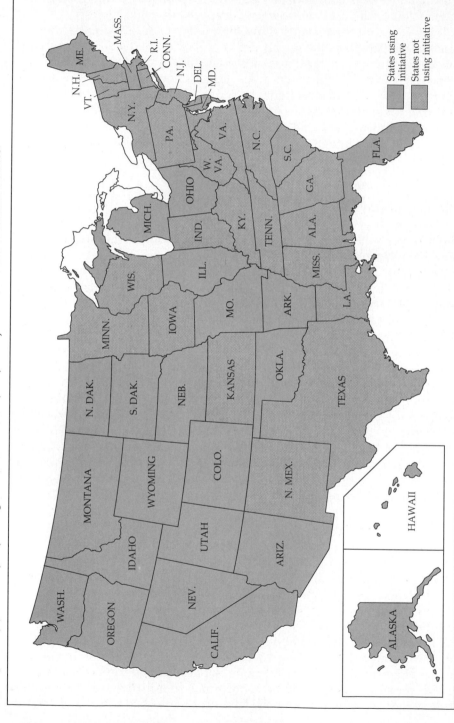

States using
initiative

States not
using initiative

Source: Ann OM. Bowman and Richard C. Kearney, *The Resurgence of the States* (Englewood Cliffs, N.J.: Prentice-Hall, 1986), p. 115. © 1986. Reprinted by permission of Prentice-Hall, Inc., Englewood Cliffs, N.J.

spawned an immediate wave of tax reduction propositions across the land. In states with the initiative, tax limitation advocates began to dust off old petition forms and crank up the signature-collection machinery.

Other factors have contributed to the increased popularity of initiatives. Some observers believe that wavering public confidence in government, shaken by political chicanery, among other things, has led citizens to take matters into their own hands. Historically, the initiative process has been used more during times of economic strain, such as the late 1970s and early 1980s. In addition, new methods of signature collection have brought the initiative process within the reach of any well-financed group with a grievance or concern. These factors combine to make the current climate ripe for election-day lawmaking.

Recent Initiatives   The initiatives of the past few years have dealt with both new and old subjects. The year 1986 saw the birth of the initiative for English as a state's official language, which was approved by California voters 73 percent to 27 percent. An even bigger issue in 1986 was gambling.[16] Voters in five states were asked to approve a state lottery (the measure passed in Florida, Idaho, Montana, and South Dakota; it was defeated in North Dakota). In addition, there were ballot questions on pari-mutuel betting at race tracks and casino gambling. Other topics that appeared that year were tax limitation measures, anti-abortion propositions, and caps on liability awards.

Similar issues dominated the 1988 round of ballot questions. The success of the English-language initiative in California spurred similar campaigns in Arizona, Colorado, and Florida, and as in California, the measures were approved by the voters. The public was not in as much of a tax-cutting mood in 1988 as it had been: Colorado voters rejected a proposal dubbed a "taxpayer bill of rights," which would have cut income taxes 10 percent, limited property taxes, and required referenda on future tax increases except in emergencies; in South Dakota and Utah, initiatives to lower taxes were rejected. Nevada voters bucked the trend, however, and approved a constitutional ban on personal income taxes.[17] Other issues also appeared on 1988 ballots. Anti-abortion forces rejoiced over their success in Arkansas, Colorado, and Michigan, where voters enacted or upheld measures that barred state financing for abortions.[18] Florida voters rejected a plan that would have imposed a $100,000 cap on "pain and suffering" awards in personal injury lawsuits.[19]

Two topics that created a firestorm of attention in California were AIDS and automobile insurance. The AIDS initiative would have required doctors to report to the state anyone testing positive for the AIDS virus, so that the state could trace and inform the sexual partners of the infected person. The measure would also have ended California's prohibition against AIDS tests for employment and insurance purposes. It was opposed by most medical organizations as potentially undermining AIDS research and by gay activists as a violation of civil rights.[20] Although voters rejected this initiative, they did approve a narrower proposition that would allow AIDS testing of suspects in certain sex crimes without their consent.

The AIDS initiatives generated heated debate, but the more acrimonious case was automobile insurance initiatives. Voters were confronted with five different insurance questions.[21] Proposition 103, advocated by consumer interests, proposed a 20 percent rollback in car insurance rates for one year and required the elected state insurance commissioner to approve future rate hikes. Four alternative measures, including one backed by trial lawyers and two favored by the insurance industry, quickly surfaced. "Let the money dance" might have been the motto of the groups promoting the different propositions. Initial reports showed that about $75 million was spent on behalf of the five insurance intiatives.[22] Supporters of Proposition 103 were reportedly outspent twenty-three to one by opponents.[23] Voters sorted their way through the maze of conflicting information and exaggerations from all sides in the initiative campaigns and ultimately approved Proposition 103. As one analysis concluded, "Democracy never looked so ugly."[24]

Harvey Rosenfield, leader of the movement to pass California's Proposition 103 in November 1988, celebrates the success of a "voter revolt." The initiative to cut car insurance rates unleashed a flurry of insurance reform movements around the country.

Possible Overuse of Initiatives   In the 1988 elections, there were 238 ballot questions (including initiatives and referenda) in forty-one states. California led the way, with twenty-nine statewide issues on the ballot, along with a bewildering array of local questions. Has democracy run amok? Is the placement of twenty-nine statewide issues on the ballot outrageous? The California situation raises troubling questions about the use of initiatives in particular and the wisdom of direct democracy more generally. By resorting to initiatives, citizens can bypass (or, in the case of indirect initiatives, prod) an obstructive legislature. Initiatives can be positive or negative; that is, they can be used in the absence of legislative action or they can be used to repudiate actions taken by the legislature. (In extreme cases, an initiative may be directed at the lawmaking institution itself. A 1984 initiative in California restructured the legislature's rules, restricted the power of each house's leadership, and trimmed the legislative budget by 30 percent. The courts eventually ruled the proposition unconstitutional.[25]) But is the initiative process appropriate for resolving tough public problems? Seldom are issues so simple that a yes-or-no ballot question can adequately reflect appropriate options and alternatives. A legislative setting, in contrast, fosters the negotiation and compromise that produce workable solutions. Legislatures are deliberative bodies, not instant problem solvers.

Related to this concern is the question of whether the public is too ill-informed to make intelligent choices or whether it falls prey to emotional appeals. Well-financed business and religious groups have used the initiative process to their advantage. The executive director of the publication *Initiative Quarterly* argues that the initiative is no longer "the people's tool but a special interest process—pure and simple."[26] For example, Scientific Games Inc., a major lottery-ticket maker, spent $1.5 million in California and Oregon to promote the petitions for lotteries in those states.[27] The firm virtually bankrolled the signature collection process.

Taken to its extreme, the initiative process can become electronic democracy. Honolulu has conducted experimental "electronic town meetings" in which the pros and cons of particular issues are presented on television. Voters then either mail in ballots or record their opinion with a telephone call.[28] The advantages offered by specially targeted direct mail appeals and instantaneous voting are not lost on legislators. The Alaska Legislature has pioneered the use of a teleconferencing system that allows its committees to receive audio and computer messages as testimony from citizens around the state.[29]

Legislators are of two minds when it comes to direct citizen involvement in policymaking. On the one hand, having the public decide a controversial issue such as abortion or school prayer helps legislators out of tight spots. On the other hand, increased citizen lawmaking intrudes on the central function of the legislature. The National Conference of State Legislatures, lawmakers' primary interest group, is seeking ways "to prevent usurpation of lawmakers' prerogatives" in the states that allow initiatives.[30] Given the popularity of initiatives, legislators must proceed cautiously with actions that would make them more difficult to use. So far, efforts to increase the signature requirements or to limit the kinds of topics an initiative may address have been unsuccessful. A citizenry accustomed to the initiative process does not look kindly on its dismantling.

The Recall

Recalls, too, were once a little-used mechanism in state and local governments. Only fifteen states provide for recall of state officials; in six of these, judicial officers are exempt. City and county government charters, even in states without recall provisions, typically include mechanisms for recall of local elected officials. In fact, the first known recall was aimed at a Los Angeles city council member in 1904.[31] Recalls have a much higher petition signature requirement than initiatives do; it is not uncommon to require a signature minimum of 25 percent of the votes cast in the last election for the office of the official sought to be recalled. (Kansas, for example, requires a 40 percent minimum.)

Recall efforts usually begin with a public perception of official misconduct. When a judge in Madison, Wisconsin, said from the bench during a hearing in a juvenile sexual assault case in 1977, "Given the way women dress, rape is a normal reaction," outraged citizens organized a group to promote his recall.[32] The group, the Committee to Recall Judge Archie Simonson, was composed of individuals who were already members of groups such as the National Organization for Women and the Women's International League for Peace and Freedom. Their coalition launched a hard-fought campaign that resulted in the recall of the judge.

Once enough signatures have been collected and verified, a recall election is held. In some states, the ballot contains wording such as "Should Official X be recalled on the following charges?" (A brief statement of the charges would follow.) A majority vote is required to remove an official, and the vacancy created by a successful recall is filled by a subsequent special election or by appointment. In other states, the recall ballot is more like an election ballot. There is no simple yes-or-no vote on the official; instead, his or her name appears on a ballot along with those of challengers. To continue in office, the subject of the recall must receive the most votes. The ballot used to recall the mayor of Omaha, Nebraska, in 1987 appears in Figure 5.4.

The number of recalls grew in the 1980s, the most notable being the ouster of Arizona governor Evan Mecham in 1987. Mecham's case was particularly interesting because it involved a number of possibilities: Mecham simultaneously faced recall, impeachment (formal charges by the House of Representatives), and a criminal indictment for violating campaign finance laws.[33] Politics and Policy 5.2 examines the case, which shows that even the threat of recall can be an effective weapon.

The rationale for the recall process is straightforward: public officials should be subject to continuous voter control.[34] As the organizer of the

Figure 5.4   Sample Recall Ballot
Omaha voters recalled their mayor, Michael Boyle, in 1987 with this ballot.
Former mayor Boyle resurfaced in 1989 in a race for mayor but was
defeated.

OFFICIAL BALLOT

A X CITY OF OMAHA	B X SPECIAL ELECTION	C X JANUARY 13, 1987
OFFICIAL BALLOT **SPECIAL CITY ELECTION** **HELD JANUARY 13, 1987** **Shall Michael Boyle be removed from the Office of Mayor by recall?** ☐ **FOR** THE RECALL OF MICHAEL BOYLE ☐ **AGAINST** THE RECALL OF MICHAEL BOYLE		

Source: Office of the Election Commissioner, Omaha, Nebraska.

successful campaign to recall the mayor of Omaha stated, "We've shown you can fight city hall."[35] Whether it is used or not, the power to recall public officials is valued by the public. A recent national survey indicated that two-thirds of those polled favored amending the U.S. Constitution to permit the recall of members of Congress.[36] Perhaps the public, rather than being uninterested in politics, is in fact quite interested and would like mechanisms that make it easier to participate.

Initiatives and recalls have helped open up state and local government to the public. Ironically, increased citizen participation can jam up the machinery of government, thus making its operation more cumbersome. Advocates of greater citizen activism, however, would gladly trade a little efficiency to achieve their goal. In the long run, citizen participation makes for government vitality.

Interest Groups

Interest groups offer another participatory venue for Americans. Joining a group is a way for individuals to communicate their preferences—their interests—to government. Interest groups attempt to influence govern-

POLITICS AND POLICY 5.2
The Recall of Arizona's Governor Mecham

Start with a plurality victory in a three-way race for governor, add a barrage of misjudgments and misdeeds, and in a state with a tradition for populist politics, you have the ingredients for a recall.[1] Evan Mecham, who had been defeated several times in previous statewide elections, surprised political observers by winning the Arizona Republican gubernatorial primary in 1986. The subsequent general election featured Mecham, a Democrat, and a Democrat running as an independent. Mecham won with 40 percent of the vote.

The storm clouds gathered at Mecham's inauguration. His first major action as governor was to cancel a holiday in honor of Dr. Martin Luther King, Jr., which had been authorized by the previous governor, and that was just the beginning. His insults of working mothers, blacks, and gays earned him national notoriety. The Republican-dominated legislature was up in arms over his selection of "individuals of questionable character" for high-level appointments and his submission of a state budget designed to obliterate a variety of programs.[2] The business community, suffering from the boycott of Arizona by conventions (as a result of the King holiday

mental decisions and actions by pressuring decision-making bodies to put more guidance counselors in public elementary schools, to clamp restrictions on coastal development, to keep a proposed new prison out of a neighborhood, or to strengthen state regulations on the licensing of family therapists. Success is getting the group's preferences enacted. As we shall see, some groups are more successful than others. In some states, interest groups dominate the policymaking process.

In considering the role of groups in the political system, we must remember that people join groups for reasons other than politics. For instance, a teacher may be a member of a politically active state education association because the group offers a tangible benefit such as low-cost life insurance, but he may disagree with some of the political positions taken by the organization. In general, motivations for group membership are individually determined.[37] This point was confirmed in recent research on Farm Bureau membership in five midwestern states.[38] Farm bureaus provide services and material benefits to members, and they represent agricultural interests in the state capital. No single all-encompassing explanation for fluctuations in membership levels could be determined.

cancelation), moved away from Mecham. The relationship of Mecham's administration to the press was later described as "almost warlike."[3]

The Mecham Watchdog Committee began gathering signatures on petitions to recall the governor in July 1987. (Arizona law prohibits the circulation of recall petitions until the official has served six months in office.) It was a grassroots operation, hindered by lack of resources and by the need to collect 216,000 signatures in four months, but it was wildly successful, and a recall election was scheduled for May 1988. The success of the recall effort owed much to the unrelenting stream of negative events surrounding the governor, including rumors of corruption. The legislature began to collect evidence for impeachment proceedings, and a state grand jury returned criminal indictments against Mecham for violating campaign finance laws.

In the end, Mecham avoided a recall election when he was removed from office in April 1988 following his conviction by the Arizona Senate in an impeachment trial. But supporters of the recall were not perturbed. The recall effort had paved the way for the impeachment.

[1] Richard R. Johnson, "Recall in Action: The Mecham Recall in Arizona," paper presented at the annual meeting of the American Political Science Association, Washington, D.C., 1988.
[2] Paula D. McClain, "Arizona 'High Noon': The Recall and Impeachment of Evan Mecham," *PS: Political Science and Politics* 21 (Summer 1988): 631.
[3] Johnson, "Recall in Action," p. 13.

Types of Interest Groups

Interest groups come in all types and sizes. If you were to visit the lobby of the state capitol when the legislature was in session, you might find the director of the state school boards association conversing with the chairperson of the education committee, or the lobbyist hired by the state hotel-motel association exchanging notes with the representative of the state's restaurateurs. If a legislator were to venture into the lobby, she would probably receive at least a friendly greeting from the lobbyists and at most a serious heart-to-heart talk about the merits of a bill. You would be witnessing efforts to influence public policy. Interest groups want state government to enact policies that are in their interest, or, conversely, not to enact policies at odds with their interest. And although the primary target of the groups' pressure is the legislature, state agencies, because of their rulemaking function, also receive their share of attention. For example, interest groups use the rule review process (in which a legislative committee reviews agency rules) as a point of possible influence.[39]

The interests represented in the capitol lobby are as varied as the state itself. One that is well represented and powerful is business. Whether a lobbyist represents a single large corporation or a consortium of businesses, when he or she talks, state legislators listen. From the perspective of business groups (and other economically oriented groups), legislative actions can cost or save their members money. Therefore, the Chamber of Commerce, industry groups, trade associations, financial institutions, and regulated utilities maintain a visible presence in the state capitol during the legislative session. Of course, business interests are not monolithic and on occasion find themselves on opposite sides of a bill.

Other interests converge on the capitol. Representatives of labor, both of established AFL-CIO unions and professional associations such as the state optometrists' group or sheriffs' association, frequent the hallways and committee meeting rooms. They too are there to see that the legislature makes the "right" decision on the bills before it. For example, if a legislature were considering a bill to change the licensing procedures for optometrists, you could expect to find the optometrists' interest group immersed in the debate.

Many other interest groups are active in state government, and a large number of them are ideological in nature. In other words, their political activity is oriented toward some higher good, such as clean air or fairer tax systems or consumer protection. Members of these groups do not have a direct economic or professional interest in the outcome of a legislative decision. Instead, their lobbyists argue that the public as a whole benefits from their involvement in the legislative process.

Interest Groups in the States

The actual interest group environment is different from one state to another. Not only does the composition of the involved groups change, but also the degree of influence they exert. Table 5.1 classifies states according to the strength of interest groups in their politics. In only ten states are interest groups considered weak.

An important study by political scientists more than two decades ago identified five different patterns of interest group influence in the states.[40] Some states had a very simple pattern in which a *single dominant interest* prevailed; an example was the Anaconda Company's power in Montana politics. Related to that pattern was the *alliance of dominant groups,* in which two or three major economic interests controlled state politics. Maine with its "big three"—electric power, timber, and textile and shoe manufacturers—was a case in point.

Michigan offered a different type of system. There, *conflict between two dominant groups* characterized state politics. The groups were the automobile manufacturers and the automobile workers—a classic management-labor conflict. States in which political parties were weak and no single

Table 5.1   Interest Group Strength

States in which interest groups are *strong*

Alabama	Nebraska
Alaska	New Hampshire
Arkansas	New Mexico
Florida	North Carolina
Georgia	Oklahoma
Hawaii	Oregon
Iowa	South Carolina
Kentucky	Tennessee
Louisiana	Texas
Mississippi	Washington
Montana	West Virginia

States in which interest groups are *moderately strong*

Arizona	Missouri
California	Nevada
Delaware	Ohio
Idaho	Pennsylvania
Illinois	South Dakota
Indiana	Utah
Kansas	Vermont
Maine	Virginia
Maryland	Wyoming

States in which interest groups are *weak*

Colorado	New Jersey
Connecticut	New York
Massachusetts	North Dakota
Michigan	Rhode Island
Minnesota	Wisconsin

Source: Adaptation of tables on pages 106–12 from *State Politics, Parties and Policy* by Sarah McCally Morehouse. Copyright © 1981 by Holt, Rinehart & Winston, Inc. Reprinted by permission of the publisher.

group of economic interests prevailed produced what the political scientists called a *triumph of many interests*; California was a prime example. The final pattern included states in which interest groups paled by comparison to political party power. Connecticut was a state where *party dominance* existed.

For the most part, interest group politics is defined by its state context.[41] First of all, an inverse relationship exists between interest groups and political parties. In states where political parties are strong, interest groups tend to be weak; in states characterized by weak political parties, interest groups tend to be strong.[42] Strong parties provide leadership in the policymaking process, and interest groups function through them. In the absence of party leadership and organization, interest groups fill the void, becoming important recruiters of candidates and financiers of campaigns, and consequently they exert tremendous influence in policymaking. Although the inverse relationship between parties and groups generally holds true, politics in states like New York and Michigan offer an interesting variation. In these states, groups are active and can be influential, but they work with the established party system in a kind of symbiotic relationship.[43]

A second, related truth adds a developmental angle to interest group politics. As states diversify economically, politics are less likely to be dominated by a single interest. Because the interest group environment is becoming more cluttered, *hyperpluralism,* or a multiplicity of groups, is resulting.

Kansas, which is undergoing economic diversification and urbanization, is also experiencing a change in the representation of interests.[45] Thirty years ago, the influential economic interests in Kansas policymaking were primarily banks, utilities, pipeline companies, railroads, and farm groups. The interest group universe has expanded significantly since then. Now, visitors to the state capitol in Topeka are likely to encounter lobbyists for the health-care industry, education, local governments, insurance, telecommunications, and social services as well as the traditional interests. In addition, there are an increasing number of "single-interest" groups, such as Kansans for Pari-Mutuel (a group promoting dog racing), Kansans for Life (anti-abortion activists), and Traffic Safety Now. The increase in the number of groups and the types of interests represented in Topeka does not necessarily signal a decline in the influence enjoyed by the dominant interests, however. Surveys of both legislators and lobbyists identify the constellation of interests surrounding banking, agriculture, education, business, utilities, the legal profession, and medical and health interests as the "consistently influential" forces in Kansas politics.[46] But now there are more groups clamoring for a piece of the action.

Kansas is not unique. Interest group politics in many states is becoming more pluralistic. As states increasingly become the arena in which important social and economic policy decisions are made, more and more groups will go to statehouses, hoping to find a receptive audience.

Techniques Used by Interest Groups

Interest groups want to have a good public image. It helps a group when its preferences can be equated with what is "good for the state" (or the community). Organizations use slogans like "What's good for the timber industry is good for Oregon" or "Schoolteachers have the interest of New York City at heart." Some groups have taken on the label "public interest groups" to designate that their main interest is that of the public at large. Groups, then, invest resources in creating a good image.

Being successful in the state capitol or at city hall involves more than a good public image, however. For example, interest groups have become effective at organizing grassroots networks that exert pressure on legislators. To maximize their strength, groups with common interests often establish coalitions. They also hire representatives who can effectively promote their cause. To ensure that legislators will be receptive to their pressures, groups will try to influence the outcome of elections by supporting candidates who reflect their interests.

Lobbying Lobbying is the attempt to influence government decision makers. States have developed official definitions to determine who is a lobbyist and who is not. A common definition is "anyone receiving compensation to influence legislative action."[47] A few states, like Nevada, North Dakota, and Washington, require everyone who attempts to influence legislation, even if he or she is not being paid, to register as a lobbyist, but most exclude public officials, members of the media, and people who speak only before committees or boards from their definition.

In most states, lobbyists are required to file reports indicating how and on whom they spent money. Concern that lobbyists would exert undue influence on the legislative process spurred states to enact new reporting requirements and impose tougher penalties for their violation. By 1988, the only states that did not require lobbyists to file reports on expenditures were Arkansas, Georgia, Louisiana, Utah, and Wyoming.[48] At the other end of the spectrum, Idaho and Nebraska required lobbyists to report their sources of income, total and categorized expenditures, the names of the individual officials who received their monies or gifts, and the legislation they supported or opposed.

To influence legislators in their decision making, lobbyists need access, so they cultivate good relationships with lawmakers. A study of interest group activity in North Dakota identified two primary functions of lobbyists: to provide testimony and to help legislators understand issues.[49] In Michigan, legislators and lobbyists alike agreed that providing information was "a strong source of power to lobbyists."[50] Legislators want to know how a proposed bill might affect the different interests in the state and their legislative districts, and what it is expected to achieve. Social lobbying—wining and dining legislators—still goes on, but it is being supplemented by the provision of information. A study of western states revealed a new breed of lobbyists trained as attorneys and public relations specialists, skilled in media presentation and information packaging.[51]

The influence of lobbyists specifically and interest groups generally is a subject of much debate. The popular image is one of a mythical lobbyist whose very presence in a committee hearing room can spell the fate of a bill. His will is done, however, because the interests he represents are widely considered vital to the state, because he has assiduously laid the groundwork, and because legislators respect the forces he can mobilize if necessary. Few lobbyists cast this long a shadow, and their interaction with legislators is seldom this mechanical. Much contemporary interest group research suggests that patterns of influence are somewhat unpredictable and highly dependent on the state context.[52]

Political Action Committees Political action committees (PACs) made extensive inroads into state politics in the 1980s. Narrowly focused subsets of interest groups, PACs are political organizations that collect funds and distribute them to candidates. (Their electoral influence is covered in Chapter 6.) PACs serve as the campaign financing arms of corporations, labor unions, trade associations, and even political parties. They grew out of long-standing laws that made it illegal for corporations and labor unions to contribute directly to a candidate. Barred from direct contributions, these organizations set up "political action" subsidiaries to allow them legal entry into campaign finance.

Recent research on interest groups in Iowa offers insights into PACs.[53] The categories of PACs and their relative share of the total number are business (45 percent), employee (26 percent), noneconomic (14 percent), professional (12 percent), and agriculture (3 percent). About one half of the business PACs were established by finance or insurance interests and utilities or telecommunications groups. Health-care specialists dominate the professional PACs. The noneconomic committees are composed largely of single-issue organizations, such as an anti-abortion or an antigambling PAC. The most noteworthy aspect is how important a source of campaign funds PACs have become. In 1984, PACs (excluding those affiliated with political parties) contributed 51 percent of the $1.6 million raised by candidates for the Iowa legislature.[54] The fourteen PACs listed in Table 5.2 accounted for more than half of the PAC money that was pumped in legislative campaigns.

The impact of PACs on state politics is just beginning to become clear. Some Michigan legislators, for example, consider PACs a potentially dangerous influence in state politics, because their money "buys a lot of access that others can't get."[55] One very likely possibility is that an independent interstate network of groups with money to spend could emerge as a real threat to political parties as recruiters of candidates and financiers of campaigns. This concern has led to calls for stricter state regulation of PACs in the years to come.

Local-Level Interest Groups

Interest groups function at the local level as well. Because so much of local government involves the delivery of services, local interest groups devote a great deal of their attention to administrative agencies and departments. Groups are involved in local elections and in community issues, to be sure, but their major focus is on the actions of government: policy implementation and service delivery.[56]

Table 5.2   Leading PAC Contributors to State Legislative
Candidates in Iowa, 1984

PAC name	Total amount contributed
Taxpayers United	$50,900
Iowa Realty PAC	41,750
Iowa Bankers PAC	40,600
Construction Survival Club	39,850
Iowa Medical PAC	30,650
Hawkeye/Bank PAC	29,451
Northwestern Bell–Iowa PAC	28,296
Professional Optometric League	28,200
Iowa State Education Association	25,250
Iowa State United Auto Workers PAC	23,000
Savings and Loan PAC	21,745
Iowa Committee of Automotive Retailers	20,550
Iowa Life Underwriters PAC	20,000
Iowa Industry PAC	18,300

Source: Charles W. Wiggins and Keith E. Hamm, "Iowa: Interest Group Politics in an Undistinguished Place," paper presented at the annual meeting of the Midwest Political Science Association, Chicago, 1987. Reprinted by permission of the authors.

National surveys of local officials have indicated that although interest groups are influential in local decision making, they do not dominate the process.[57] The kinds of groups that appear on the local scene and their relative influence, according to local officials, are listed in Table 5.3. As at the state level, business groups are considered to be the most influential. Business-related interests, such as the local Chamber of Commerce or a downtown merchants' association, appear to wield power in the community. A very different yet increasingly influential group at the local level is the neighborhood-based organization. Groups that might not have been on the list twenty years ago include women's organizations, ideological groups (such as the Moral Majority), and homosexual rights groups. Thus far, these groups have not achieved the degree of influence accorded business and neighborhood groups.

Neighborhood organizations deserve a closer look. Some have arisen out of issues that directly affect neighborhood residents—a local school that is scheduled to close, a wave of violent crime, a proposed freeway route that will destroy homes and businesses. Others have been formed by govern-

Table 5.3   Local Interest Groups Ranked by Degree of Influence, According to Local Officials

1. Business-oriented groups (e.g., Chamber of Commerce, businesspersons' associations)
2. Neighborhood groups
3. Political parties
4. Civic groups (e.g., League of Women Voters, service clubs)
5. Professional organizations (e.g., bar association)
6. City service groups (e.g., transit, health, housing, education)
7. Labor unions
8. Civil rights groups (e.g., NAACP, Urban League)
9. Ethnic groups (nonblack, Hispanic)
10. Environmental groups
11. Women's political groups
12. Ideological nonparty groups (e.g., Moral Majority, ACLU)
13. Gay/lesbian political groups

Source: Howard A. Faye, Allan Cigler, and Paul Schumaker, "The Municipal Group Universe: Changes in Agency Penetration by Political Groups, 1975–1986," paper presented at the annual meeting of the American Political Science Association, Washington, D.C., 1986. Reprinted by permission of the authors.

ment itself as a way of channeling citizen participation. For example, in 1974, the city council in Birmingham, Alabama, divided the city into ninety-three neighborhood associations. These groups provide a formal mechanism whereby residents can voice their concerns about the quality and quantity of municipal services.[58] One result has been to give voice to neighborhoods that had been underrepresented.

Neighborhood groups, as well as others lacking a bankroll but possessing enthusiasm and dedication, may resort to tactics such as **direct action,** which includes protest marches at the county courthouse or standing in front of bulldozers in an effort to block their progress. Direct action is usually designed to attract attention to a cause, and it tends to be a last resort, a tactic employed when other efforts at influencing government policy have failed. The nation witnessed a stunning example of extreme direct action when riots broke out in poor, predominantly black sections of Miami and Tampa in the 1980s. In each instance allegations of police brutality triggered violent upheaval, and in each case the eventual uneasy calm that settled over the neighborhood brought with it promises of increased government assistance.

Citizen Access to Government

Citizens have opportunities to participate in government in ways that do not involve voting or joining organizations. State and local governments have undertaken extensive measures to open themselves to public scrutiny and to stimulate public input. In other words, citizen access to government has been increased. Many of these mechanisms are directly connected with the policymaking process. At the very least, they enable government and the citizenry to exchange information, and thus they contribute to the growing capacity of state and local governments. At most, they may alter political power patterns and resource allocations.[59]

Types of Official Access

Many of the accessibility measures adopted by state and local governments are the direct result of public demands that government be more accountable. These measures reflect citizens' rejection of "policymaking behind closed doors" and "government by announcement," where the public is removed from the process and hears about it only after a decision has been made. Other accessibility measures have resulted from an official effort to involve the public in the ongoing work of government.

Open Meeting Laws   Florida's 1967 "sunshine law" is credited with sparking a surge of interest in openness in government, and today **open meeting laws** are on the books in all fifty states. These laws do just what the name implies—they open meetings of government bodies to the public. These laws apply to both the state and local level and affect the executive branch as well as the legislative branch. They are taken rather seriously, especially by the press. In fact, some city council members have complained that they cannot have lunch with their colleagues because it would violate their state's open meeting law. They overreact a bit: their luncheon meeting would violate state law only if they discussed city business.

Basic open meeting laws have been supplemented by additional requirements in many states. More than forty states require advance public notice of the meeting, thirty-seven insist that minutes be taken, thirty-five levy penalties against officials who violate the law, and thirty-one void actions taken in meetings held contrary to sunshine provisions.[60] These "brighter sunshine" laws make a difference. Whether a meeting is open or closed is irrelevant if citizens are unaware that it is occurring. If no penalties are assessed for violation, then there is less incentive for officials to comply.

Open Records Laws   In the same spirit as open meetings are provisions for open records. After the enactment of an open records law in Wisconsin in the nineteenth century, states gradually began to facilitate public access to government documents. All states now have some form of an open records law.

Open records laws are frequently called freedom-of-information acts. They are designed to make it easier for the public to obtain public records, although documents that are damaging to the public interest can be withheld. The trick is to determine just what is damaging and what is not. The courts are often called upon to make that determination when the press has requested information and a government agency has refused to provide it, as in the case of lists of contributors to state university foundations. Other exemptions to the open records requirement are documents dealing with individual matters such as juveniles, adoptions, paroles, and medical and mental health.

Administrative Procedure Acts   Government bureaucracies are increasingly the scene of important decisions. After state legislation is passed or a city ordinance is adopted, an administrative agency typically is responsible for implementation. This process involves the establishment of rules and regulations and as such is a powerful responsibility. In practice, agencies often have wide latitude in translating legislative intent into action. For example, if a new state law creates annual automobile safety inspections, it is the responsibility of the state's Department of Motor Vehicles to make it work. Bureaucrats might determine the items to be covered in the safety inspection, the number and location of inspection stations, and the fee to be charged. These items are just as important as the original enactment.

To ensure public access to this critical rule-making process, states have adopted **administrative procedure acts,** which usually require public notice of the proposed rule and an opportunity for citizen comment. Virtually all states provide for this "notification and comment" process, as it is known. In addition, some states give citizens the right to petition an administrative agency for an adjustment in the rules.

Advisory Committees   Another form of citizen participation that is popular in state and especially local governments is the **advisory committee,** in the form of citizen task forces, commissions, and panels. Regardless of name, these organizations are designed to study a problem and to offer advice, usually in the form of recommendations. People chosen to serve on an advisory committee tend to have expertise and interest in the issue, and in most cases political connections. Take the hypothetical case of a mayor's Citizens Advisory Committee on the Environment. It is likely to be composed of local environmentalists, scientists, representatives of industry, and supporters of the mayor, and will probably focus on "hot" environmental issues in the community, such as clean-up of a nearby river, waste disposal, or smog. Whatever the focus, the mayor will expect some sort of policy statement and recommendations.

Citizen advisory committees are useful because they provide a formal arena for citizen input. For example, New York City is divided into fifty-nine community boards that offer advice on planning.[61] Rather than leaving the growth and development of their community to chance or market forces or the desires of monied interests, citizens have an opportunity to offer their views on the preferable future. If officials heed public preferences, citizen advice can become the basis for public policy. Furthermore, a statewide committee might hold public forums in different locations around the state so that interested people can offer their opinions and ideas. These organizations also provide the governor, the legislature, or local officials with a "safe" course of action. In other words, in a politically explosive situation, a governor can say, "I've appointed a citizen's task force to study the issue and report back to me with recommendations for action." This buys time, with the hope that the issue will gradually cool down. Another benefit of these organizations is that they ease citizen acceptance of subsequent policy decisions, since the governor can note that an action "was recommended by an impartial panel of citizens." This is not to suggest that citizen advisory committees are merely tools for manipulation by politicians, but they do have uses beyond citizen participation.

Citizen Surveys   One effective way of determining what is on the public's mind is to ask people, and this can be done in a systematic manner through citizen surveys. By sampling the population, government officials can obtain a reading of the public's policy preferences and its evaluation of governmental performance. In the 1970s, for example, Washington used mail, telephone, and newspaper surveys to establish citizen preferences for the state's future. For local governments, citizen surveys have provided information on the effectiveness and quality of public services.[62] This is far more systematic than simply relying on complaints as a means of identifying problems.

An important feature of citizen surveys is that they can counteract some of the bias that clouds most avenues of participation. As noted in the beginning of this chapter, political participation is generally an activity undertaken by those of middle to upper socioeconomic status. Nonparticipants seldom transmit their opinions to government. In a carefully designed citizen survey, those whose opinions are often muted have a better opportunity to be heard.

The Impact of Citizen Access

But the impact of citizen access is not always as much as hoped for. The national General Revenue Sharing act of 1972 required jurisdictions to create citizen advisory committees to help elected officials decide how the funds should be allocated in the community. Citizen input was to help determine whether the jurisdiction used its revenue-sharing money to purchase police cars, to rehabilitate low-income housing, or whatever. But most studies have found that these committees had a minor impact, at best, on allocation decisions.[63] They were less than full partners in the process.

This is a troublesome aspect of citizen participation. The system has been opened up, making government more accessible than ever before. Citizens have increased opportunities for participation, but their influence may be difficult to discern. A critical factor in the fate of citizen access programs is the commitment of government officials to the concept. Sincerely encouraging and promoting citizen access is likely to produce a different outcome from some sort of cosmetic treatment designed to satisfy the conditions of a grant.

Volunteerism

Voluntary action is participatory activity unrelated to the ballot box, groups, and access. People and organizations donate their time and talents to supplement or even replace government activity. **Volunteerism** is a means of bringing fresh ideas and energy, whether physical or financial, into government while relieving some of the service burden.

Washington created the first statewide volunteerism office in 1969, and by the mid-1980s forty other states had followed suit. One of the most ambitious efforts is Volunteer for Minnesota, which assists local communities in the design of a program, including the actual recruitment, training, and placement of volunteers.[64]

Local governments use volunteers in a variety of ways. Generally, volunteerism is most successful when citizens can develop the required job skills quickly or participate in activities they enjoy, such as library work, recreation programs, or fire protection.[65] In addition to helping provide services to others, volunteers can be utilized for "self-help," that is, engage in activities in which they are the primary beneficiaries. For example, some New York City neighborhoods take responsibility for the security and maintenance of nearby parks. Residential crime-watch programs are another variety of self-help. In both these instances, the volunteers and their neighborhoods benefit. Overall, studies show, volunteerism is especially successful in rural areas and small towns.[66]

Nongovernmental volunteerism can be an important supplement to government programs. For instance, an energetic new volunteerism campaign is under way in the Denver area. Unaffiliated with government, Metropolitan Denver GIVES is attempting to increase the amount of charitable giving and personal volunteering in the region.[67] Its effort is expected to be the prototype for similar campaigns in other metropolitan areas, such as Cleveland, Baltimore, and San Francisco.

The Effects of Citizen Participation

Return to the four quadrants of Figure 5.1. Constructive participatory behaviors, whether active or passive, invigorate government. The capacity of state and local governments depends on a number of factors, one of which is citizen participation. Underlying this argument is the implicit but strongly held belief shared by most observers of democracies that an accessible, responsive government is a legitimate government.

An example makes the point. In 1986, the Florida legislature enacted Visions 2000 to encourage community goal setting. Funding was available so that citizens could engage in debate and consider a number of scenarios for the proper direction for their communities.[68] Researchers studying eight Florida communities discovered that without widespread citizen involvement, the goal-setting process can easily become a vehicle for special interests. When that occurs, the public is not likely to feel any loyalty to the resulting plan. And they are not likely to accord much legitimacy to the government that endorsed the process. This could lead to the destructive behaviors displayed in Figure 5.1: neglect or exit.

A mobilized public can generate system-wide change. From the perspective of government officials and institutions, citizen participation can be a nuisance because it can disrupt established routines. The challenge is to incorporate citizen participation into ongoing operations. In a democracy, citizen involvement is the ultimate test of the legitimacy of that government. State and local governments, more often than not, pass that test.

Summary

Citizen participation affects the vitality of American state and local governments. Whether through voting or signing initiative petitions or marching in a demonstration, the power of the people is a force to be reckoned with. One of the ironies of the political system is that increased citizen activism may not make government run more smoothly. In fact, citizen participation may make government messy, increasing delays and conflict. The dramatic upsurge in election-day lawmaking, for example, has led some observers to question the wisdom of direct democracy in contemporary America.

As this chapter demonstrates, an array of participatory options are available to the citizen. Constructive actions include voting, signing petitions, joining groups, and attending meetings. One point to keep in mind is that many but not all citizens participate in the political system. Paying some attention to the reasons for nonparticipation and designing corrective measures may in the long run sustain government capacity.

Key Terms

Administrative procedure acts Acts that standardize administrative agency operation as a means of safeguarding clients and the general public.

Advisory committee An organization created by government to involve members of the public in studying and recommending solutions to public problems.

Direct action A form of participation designed to draw attention to a cause.

Interest group An organized body of individuals with shared goals and a desire to influence government.

Lobbying The process by which groups and individuals attempt to influence policymakers.

Open meeting laws Statutes that open the meetings of government bodies to the public.

Open records laws Statutes that facilitate public access to government documents.

Participation Actions through which ordinary members of a political system attempt to influence outcomes.

Political action committee (PAC) An organization that raises and distributes campaign funds to candidates for elective office.

Popular referendum A special type of referenda whereby citizens can petition to vote on actions taken by legislative bodies.

Recall A procedure that allows citizens to vote elected officials out of office before their term has expired.

Referendum A procedure whereby a governing body submits proposed laws, constitutional amendments, or bond issues to the voters for ratification.

Volunteerism A form of participation in which individuals or groups donate time or money to a public purpose.

Voting Rights Act of 1965 The law that effectively enfranchised racial minorities by giving the national government the power to decide whether individuals are qualified to vote and to intercede in state and local electoral operations when necessary.

6

Political Parties, Elections, and Campaigns

Political Parties
  Political Parties in Theory and in Reality/Party
  Organization/The Two-Party System/Interparty
  Competition/Is the Party Over?

Elections
  Primaries/Runoff Elections/General
  Elections/Nonpartisan Elections/The 1988 State
  Elections/The 1990 State Elections

Political Campaigns
  A New Era of Campaigns/Campaign Finance

The Democratic Process

The Republican National Committee collectively cringed when David Duke, former grand wizard of the Ku Klux Klan, campaigned as a Republican for a seat in the Louisiana legislature in 1989.[1] In a rarity in races for the state legislature, party VIPs, including former President Reagan and President Bush, entered the fray on behalf of the other Republican candidate. Duke, a skilled media campaigner who had been defeated in two previous tries for the legislature and in 1988 had run for president as a member of the Populist party, charmed many of the district's voters using carefully couched racial and antitax sentiment. He won the election, with 51 percent of the vote.[2] Afterwards, voters voiced their resentment that national politicians had interfered in a state legislative race.

Political parties, elections, and campaigns are the stuff of representative democracy. On election day, the Democratic and Republican parties offer us slates of candidates to lead us. Candidates campaign hard for the glamorous jobs of governor, state legislator, mayor, and a variety of other state and local positions. In some states, even candidates for judicial positions compete in partisan races. But party involvement in our system of government does not end on election day—the institutions of government themselves have a partisan tone. Legislatures are organized along party lines; governors offer Republican or Democratic agendas for their states; county commissioners of different ideological stripes fight over the best way to provide services to local residents. Through the actions of their elected officials, political parties play a major role in the operation of government.

Political Parties

Lately the condition of contemporary American political parties has been described with words such as *decline, decay,* and *demise.* A more precise description uses the word *transformation,* which reflects the change that parties are experiencing but stops short of an epitaph. Even the experts are unsure of what lies ahead for political parties. One 1987 book on the subject, *The Party's Just Begun,* lays out a blueprint for party *renewal.*[3] And although we will stop short of similar words—*rejuvenation, revitalization*—we acknowledge that political parties are still evolving.

Political Parties in Theory and in Reality

One ideal against which political party systems can be measured is called the **responsible party model.** This has several basic principles:

1. Parties should present clear and coherent programs to voters.
2. Voters should choose candidates according to the party programs.
3. The winning party should carry out its program once in office.

144

4. Voters should hold the governing party responsible at the next election for executing its program.[4]

According to the model, political parties carve out identifiable issue positions, base their campaign appeals on them, and endeavor to enact them upon taking office. Voters select candidates who represent their preferences and hold officeholders accountable for their performance.

Even a casual observer of the American scene would recognize that U.S. political parties fall somewhat short of the responsible party mark. For example, American political parties stand for different things in different places, so a single, coherent program is unworkable. Although Democratic politicians tend to be more liberal than their Republican counterparts, it would be difficult to find an abundance of liberals in a Democrat-controlled southern state legislature. Furthermore, voters display a remarkable penchant for **ticket-splitting,** that is, for voting for a Democrat for one office and a Republican for another in the same election. Many voters are fond of saying that they "vote for the person, not the party."

Parties in the United States function as umbrella organizations that shelter loose coalitions of relatively like-minded individuals. A general image for each party is discernible: the Republicans are considered the party of big business, the Democrats the party of workers. But even though many people identify with the party of their parents, they hold that identification increasingly lightly. In what used to be called "the solid South," a label that indicated the region's historically overwhelming support for the Democratic party, one finds fewer and fewer "yellow dog Democrats"—people who would vote for the Democratic nominee "even if he was a yellow dog." Republicans, once regarded as oddities in the region, have become respectable. One classic South Carolina tale recalls an election in 1924 in which the Republican candidate received 1,100 of the 50,000 votes cast for president. A leading Democratic politician reportedly commented that he was "astonished to know that they were cast and shocked to know that they were counted."[5] Now the Republican party considers the South a good source of partisan support.

Party Organization

Political parties are decentralized organizations. There are fifty state Republican parties and fifty state Democratic parties. Each state also has local party organizations, most typically at the county level. Although they interact, each of these units is autonomous, a situation that is good for independence but not so good for party discipline. Specialized partisan groups, including College Democrats, Young Republicans, Democratic Women's Clubs, Black Republican Councils, and so on, have been given official recognition.[6] Party organizations are further decentralized into precinct-level clusters, which bear the ultimate responsibility for turning out the party's voters on election day. Figure 6.1 shows a typical state party organization.

Figure 6.1   Typical State Political Party Organization
Most state political party organizations look something like this. Party
workers at the bottom of the chart are direct links to voters.

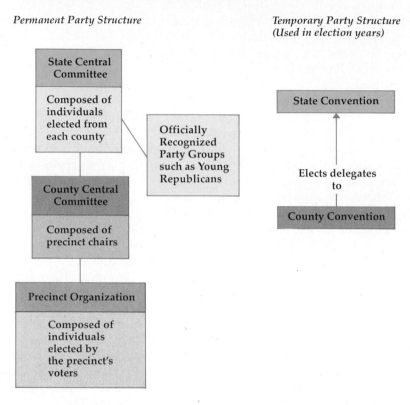

State Parties Each state party has a charter or by-laws to govern its operation. The decision-making body is the state committee, sometimes called a
central committee, which is headed by a chairperson and composed of
members elected in party primaries or at state party conventions. State
parties, officially at least, head their party's push to capture statewide
elected offices, but despite attempts to formulate platforms and develop a
party-centered fund-raising appeal, they do not play a leading role in campaigns. Instead, their efforts are aimed at promoting good feelings about the
party and protecting it from partisan attacks by the other party.
    State party organizations vary widely in their organizational vitality and
resources. Approximately one-quarter of them employ salaried chairpersons, and most have staffs numbering between three and ten people, and
annual budgets in the $250,000-to-$500,000 range.[7] Republican organiza-

tions generally outstrip Democratic ones in these measures of organizational strength.

Local Parties   County party organizations are composed of committee members chosen at the precinct level. These workers are volunteers whose primary reward is the satisfaction of being involved in politics. The work is rarely glamorous. Party workers are the people who conduct voter registration drives, drop off lawn signs for residents' front yards, organize candidate forums, and stand at the polls and remind voters to "Vote Democratic" or "Vote Republican."

Local parties are less professionally organized than state parties. Although half of the local organizations maintain campaign headquarters during an election period, less than one-quarter operate year-round offices.[8] County chairpersons report devoting a lot of time to the party during election periods, but otherwise the post does not take much of their time. Most lead organizations without any full-time staff, and vacancies in precinct offices are common.

The extremes in local party organization are exemplified in Los Angeles and Chicago. One analysis describes Los Angeles County in this manner: "In neither party is the Los Angeles county committee a powerful entity. Its powers are ambiguous; its meetings bog down with trivia; its funds are limited and its patronage resources more so. In each party, rival factions time after time frustrate even the appearance of solidarity in supporting a full slate of party nominees."[9] The Chicago Democratic party historically has been at the opposite end of the organizational spectrum: "The Chicago machine is both rare and impressive in the range of services offered, the cohesiveness and permanence of its structure, the professionalism and experience of its members at all levels, and, of course, its electoral successes. The difficulties the opposition party faces make its position virtually hopeless."[10]

Most local parties are more akin to the Los Angeles County model than to the Chicago Democrats (who are much less cohesive than they used to be). Table 6.1 ranks the states in terms of the strength of their local political party organizations, which are held together by committed, public-oriented volunteers.

The Makeup of Parties   Although conservatism has experienced renewed popularity throughout the nation, the ideology of the leaders of the two parties remains distinct. A survey of Houston party leaders confirms this fact.[11] More than twice as many Republicans (56 percent) as Democrats (25 percent) labeled themselves conservatives. Liberal ideology, a grand tradition in American politics but a victim of almost hysterical denunciation in the late 1980s, clearly belongs more to Democrats (24 percent) than to Republicans (5 percent). Many of the party leaders identified themselves as "moderates," a designation that is a hybrid. Fully 51 percent of Houston's Democratic leaders and 40 percent of the Republicans classified themselves like this. Figure 6.2 shows the ideological distribution.

Table 6.1   States Ranked According to the Strength of Their Local Parties

Democrats		Republicans	
Rank	State	Rank	State
1	New Jersey	1	New Jersey
2	Pennsylvania	2	New York
3	New York	3	Indiana
4	Delaware	4	Pennsylvania
5	Indiana	5.	Maryland
6	Rhode Island	6	Arizona
7	Ohio	7	Ohio
8	New Hampshire	8	California
9	Connecticut	9	New Mexico
10	Illinois	10	Connecticut
11	Maryland	11	Delaware
12	Michigan	12	Illinois
13	Hawaii	13	Washington
14	Idaho	14	Michigan
15	Washington	15	Hawaii
16	Maine	16	Rhode Island
17	Florida	17	Iowa
18	North Dakota	18	Minnesota
19	Alaska	19	North Dakota
20	Utah	20	Wisconsin
21	Minnesota	21	Wyoming
22	New Mexico	22	Nevada
23	Tennessee	23	North Carolina
24	California	24	West Virginia
25	North Carolina	25	Maine

Source: J. L. Gibson, "Whither the Local Parties," *American Journal of Political Science* 29, no. 1 (February 1985): 154–55. Reprinted by permission of the University of Texas Press, and the author.

Figure 6.2 also depicts seeds of Democratic discontent: ideological factions, or subgroups within the larger organization. Whereas the Republican ideological distribution resembles a ladder of increasing conservatism, the Democratic distribution shows that moderate party leaders buffer two equally distributed camps holding divergent ideologies. It is difficult to reconcile liberal and conservative preferences into a coherent set of policy recommendations. While the Republicans find themselves in agreement on issues, Democrats are much more divided. This difficulty is reflected in the Houston leaders' responses to these policy alternatives: (a) spend less and reduce social services, or (b) continue to provide such services. Alternative *a* was favored by 83 percent of the Republican activists; alternative *b* was preferred by 16 percent. Of the Democrats, 43 percent selected alternative

Table 6.1 States Ranked According to the Strength of Their Local Parties *(cont.)*

Democrats		Republicans	
Rank	State	Rank	State
26	Wisconsin	26	Idaho
27	Iowa	27	Virginia
28	Oregon	28	Colorado
29	Vermont	29	Oregon
30	Arizona	30	Tennessee
31	Colorado	31	New Hampshire
32	Virginia	32	South Carolina
33	West Virginia	33	South Dakota
34	South Dakota	34	Alaska
35	Wyoming	35	Montana
36	South Carolina	36	Kansas
37	Missouri	37	Oklahoma
38	Massachusetts	38	Massachusetts
39	Montana	39	Mississippi
40	Oklahoma	40	Arkansas
41	Kentucky	41	Texas
42	Nevada	42	Missouri
43	Alabama	43	Utah
44	Arkansas	44	Nebraska
45	Kansas	45	Vermont
46	Georgia	46	Louisiana
47	Mississippi	47	Alabama
48	Texas	48	Kentucky
49	Nebraska	49	Florida
50	Louisiana	50	Georgia

a and 43 percent chose alternative *b*. Houston Republicans are united by an ideological bond; Houston Democrats are not. This illustrates one of the problems that a local party faces in becoming a meaningful, policy-oriented organization.

A factional challenge to local Republican parties has come from evangelical Christian activists who want to move the party to even greater conservatism. In Douglas County (Omaha), Nebraska, for example, conservative Christians had gained sufficient power by 1988 to oust the moderate head of the party.[12] The moderates responded by forming their own political action committee to promote the Republican electoral cause. This experience is representative of what is occurring in many other locales, in states such as North Carolina, Minnesota, Georgia, and Michigan.

Political parties continually face the problem of factions. The challenge for party leadership is to unite the factions into a winning force. Profile 6.1

Figure 6.2   Ideological Distribution of
Houston's Party Leaders
There are a few lonely liberals in the
Republican party. Even among Democrats, in
Houston anyway, liberals make up only
one-quarter of the leadership.

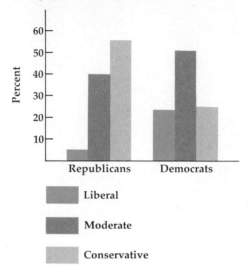

Liberal

Moderate

Conservative

Source: Richard W. Murray and Kent L. Tedin, "Emerging Competition in the Sunbelt," in William Crotty, ed.,
Political Parties in Local Areas (Knoxville: University of
Tennessee Press, 1986), p. 54. Reprinted with permission of the University of Tennessee Press.

highlights a faction that is on the verge of becoming a significant force in the
Northeast.

The Two-Party System

General elections in the United States are typically contests between candidates representing the two major political parties. It has been this way for
the past century and a half. The Democratic party has been in existence
since the 1830s, when it emerged from the Jacksonian wing of the Jeffer-
sonian party.[13] The Republican party, despite its label as the "Grand Old
Party," is newer; it developed out of the sectional conflict over slavery in the
1850s.

There are numerous reasons for the institutionalization of two-party
politics. Explanations that emphasize sectional dualism, such as East versus
West or North versus South, have given way to those that focus on the
structure of the electoral system. Parties compete in elections in which there
can be only one winner. Most legislative races, for example, take place in

PROFILE 6.1
Liberal Does Not Necessarily Mean Loser

A group of Connecticut political activists is challenging the late 1980s wisdom that to be branded a liberal is the kiss of death in a political campaign. The thinking that "liberal equals loser" grew out of the 1988 presidential campaign, when the Republican nominee, George Bush, effectively used the word *liberal* as a club to attack the Democratic nominee, Michael Dukakis. Suddenly schoolchildren were teasing each other with the taunt "you liberal."

In Connecticut, liberal Democrats have formed a populist coalition that is demonstrating remarkable success in legislative elections. The coalition, known as LEAP, draws its members from progressive unions, consumer activist groups, and environmental and women's groups. From its modest beginnings in 1980, it has emerged as a force to be reckoned with. In 1986 LEAP supported forty candidates for the state legislature, and thirty-four of them won.

How has LEAP been so successful in bucking the rising tide of antiliberalism? One answer is organization.

Industrious LEAP workers give new meaning to the phrase "canvassing the neighborhood." They target voters who are favorably disposed to their message, and they make certain, through extensive grassroots campaigning, that those voters hear it.

Bolstered by their growing numbers in the legislature, LEAP-affiliated lawmakers have successfully pushed bills that make voter registration easier, require doctors to accept Medicare reimbursement rates, and guarantee female state employees pay parity. Other causes that have been part of the LEAP agenda are gay rights and lower utility bills.

LEAP will probably have a long-lasting impact on Connecticut politics, and its influence is spreading. LEAP coalitions have arisen in four other New England states, and organizers have convened the first Northeast Progressive Elected Officials convention. The rest of the nation is likely to hear more from LEAP.

Source: Michael Winerip, " 'Liberal' Is Not a Dirty Word to All," *New York Times*, October 18, 1988, p. 14. Copyright © 1988 by The New York Times Company. Reprinted by permission.

single-member districts, in which only the candidate with the most votes wins; there is no reward for finishing second or third. This discourages the development of additional parties. Another very plausible explanation has to do with tradition: Americans are accustomed to a political system composed of two parties, and that is how we understand politics.

The assessment of former Alabama governor George Wallace that "there ain't a dime's worth of difference between Democrats and Republicans" raises questions about the need for alternative parties. Third parties (also called nonmajor or minor parties), are an unsuccessful but persistent phenomenon in American politics. There may not be substantial differences between the two major parties, but for the most part their positions reflect the public mood. When third party options are presented to voters in national elections, voters stick to the two major parties. Third parties also suffer because the two established parties have vast reserves of money and resources at their disposal; new parties can rarely amass the finances or assemble the organization necessary to make significant inroads into the system.

Third parties have occasionally achieved isolated success in certain states. For example, the Socialist party elected a few state representatives in New York in the early 1900s, and the Progressive party of Robert La Follette in Wisconsin and the Farmer Labor party in Minnesota strongly influenced the politics of those states before World War II. More recently, third parties have been formed by dissatisfied factions that have split off from a major party. This was the case with the Conservatives, who broke with the New York Republican party because it was not conservative enough for them, and with the Freedom Democratic party of Mississippi, which developed in the 1960s as an alternative to the racist official Democratic party.[15] Today, the Libertarian party and its antigovernment candidates are the most active third party.

Small vote totals tell the story of third-party electoral performance. In the eight years from 1976 to 1984, third-party candidates and independents captured less than 1 percent of the vote in state legislative races.[16] This is hardly a showing that will set the major parties on edge. In only five states (led by New York, with 9.2 percent) did nonmajor party candidates receive more than 2 percent of the vote. One factor that appears linked to third-party voting is the educational level of the state. States with more highly educated citizens are more receptive to partisan alternatives.[17]

Interparty Competition

Most states exhibit substantial two-party competition. In other words, when you look at a general election ballot, you will find that both the Democrats and the Republicans are offering credible candidates. Gone are the days when one party virtually ran state government without any opposition. The extension of interparty competition to states that have lacked it is a healthy development in American politics. Citizens who are dissatisfied with the performance of the party in power have another choice.

Patterns of Competition   In measuring party competition, an important consideration is which party controls the major policymaking institutions in the state: the governor's office and the state legislature. The information in Figure 6.3 indicates party control of these institutions by state for the period 1965–88. The assignment of states to different categories takes into consideration the closeness of the gubernatorial election and the size of the partisan majorities in the legislature.[18]

Five possible categories of competition exist: Democratic dominant, Democratic majority, competitive two-party, Republican majority, and Republican dominant. We can eliminate the last category, however, because the Republican party did not dominate the politics of any state during the twenty-four-year period. In fact, the Republican party controlled only New Hampshire and South Dakota for a majority of those years, and even these stars of Republicanism had Democratic governors for one-third of the period.

The Democrats are a different story. Georgia and Mississippi stand out among the five Democratic-dominant states, because Republicans operate at a tremendous disadvantage in state politics. When Georgia Republicans won seven seats in the House in 1988, bringing their total to thirty-six (out of 180), it was an electoral coup. An editorial in the *Atlanta Journal and Constitution* was headlined "Something Is Gaining on State's Democrats."[19] Ten states are considered Democratic-majority states; Democrats usually win, but Republicans put up a spirited fight and have some victories to build on.

The majority of the states (thirty-two) have competitive two-party politics but the institutional patterns vary. In some states, such as Oregon, one party has controlled the governor's office while the other has prevailed in the legislature. In others, such as California, Massachusetts, and Tennessee, Democratic control of the legislature has been offset by partisan balance in the governor's office. Exemplifying a pattern of almost perfect competition are states like Illinois, Ohio, and Pennsylvania, where institutional control has oscillated between the two parties.

Consequences of Competition   Two-party competition is spreading at a time when states are becoming the battleground for the resolution of difficult policy issues. Undoubtedly, as governors set their agendas and legislatures outline their preferences, cries of "partisan politics" will be heard. But in a positive sense, such cries symbolize the maturation of state institutions. Partisan politics will probably encourage a wider search for policy alternatives and result in innovative solutions. Consider this comment on the waning days of single-party politics in Georgia, where Republicans are making inroads into traditionally Democratic territory:

> [Georgia Democrats are] being stalked by a critter not native to these parts, an animal with hot breath, heavy footsteps and contempt for the state's

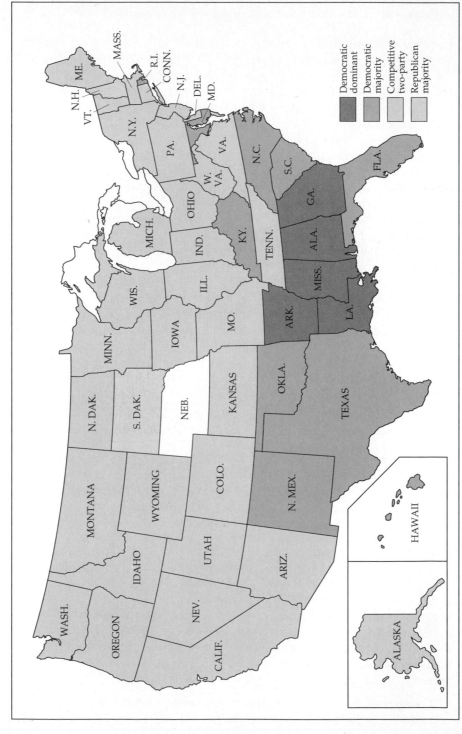

Figure 6.3   Party Competition in the States, 1965–1988

Interparty competition is on the increase. As recently as a decade ago, many of the competitive two-party states would have been in a one-party majority category. (Nebraska, with its nonpartisan legislative elections, is not included.)

Democratic dominant
Democratic majority
Competitive two-party
Republican majority

Source: Adapted from Malcolm E. Jewell and David M. Olson, *Political Parties and Elections in American States,* 3rd ed. (Pacific Grove, Calif.: Brooks/Cole Publishing Co., 1988), pp. 26–27. Used by permission of Brooks/Cole Publishing Co.

154

ancient, ossified buddy system. . . . Sooner or later, the state's
unresponsive Democrats will learn the meaning of competition. The faster
complacency dies at the Capitol, the better off Georgians will be.[20]

Heated partisan competition turns a dull campaign into a lively contest.
Public interest picks up and voter turnout increases. In the view of many,
two parties are better than one.

Is the Party Over?

This impertinent question is intended to spark debate. Have political parties, as we know them, outlived their usefulness? Should they be cast aside
as new forms of political organization and communication emerge?

As some have argued, a more educated populace that can readily acquire
political information is likely to be less reliant on party cues.[21] Today's
generation is less loyal to political parties than its grandparents were and is
not so likely to vote along party lines. A *dealignment*, or weakening of
individual partisan attachments, has occurred. Parties also no longer rule
the roost when it comes to campaign finance. Challenges come from PACs
that pour huge amounts of money into campaigns and candidates, and from
political operatives who use new technology creatively to build individual
election teams.

Political parties are not sitting idly by as their function in the political
system is challenged. Research has shown that party organizations are
making their operations more professional and have more money to spend
and more staff to spend it.[22] The past several years have seen the development of party-centered advertising campaigns and a renewed commitment
to get-out-the-vote drives.[23] In a few states that have publicly funded campaigns, parties as well as candidates have been designated recipients of
funds. States formerly dominated by one party now find themselves with a
resilient second party on their hands. All in all, it appears that parties are
still viable parts of the political system.

Elections

Elections are central to a representative democracy. State and local governments have traditionally relied on them for choosing top leaders. In most
states, voters choose the governor, lieutenant governor, legislators, the
attorney general, the secretary of state, and the state treasurer; in some,
they also choose the heads of the agriculture and education departments
and public utility commissioners. At the local level, the list of elected
officials includes mayors and council members, county commissioners,
county judges, sheriffs, tax assessors, and school board members. For state
and local governments to function effectively, elections must provide talented, capable leaders.

Primaries

For a party to choose a nominee and put her name on the general election ballot, a winnowing of potential candidates must occur. In the pre-Jacksonian era, party nominees were chosen by a legislative caucus, a conference of the party's legislators. Caucuses gave way to the mechanism of state party conventions, which were similar to national presidential nomination conventions, without most of the spectacle; popularly elected delegates from across a state convened to select the party's nominees. Then the Progressive movement made an effort to open up the nomination process and make it more democratic. Political parties adopted the **primary system,** whereby voters directly choose among several candidates to select the party's nominees for the general election.

Twelve states still allow for party conventions in particular instances, such as nominations for lieutenant governor (Michigan) and selection of nominees by third parties (Kansas).[24] Connecticut, the last state to adopt primaries, operates a unique "challenge" system, whereby nominees for various state offices are selected at a convention, but if a contest develops at the convention and a second candidate receives as much as 20 percent of the votes, the convention's nominee and the challenger square off in a primary.[25]

Primaries can be divided into two types, closed and open. The only voters who can participate in a **closed primary** for a particular party are those who are registered in that party. An **open primary** does not require party membership; any voter who is qualified to vote in the general election can participate. However, even this basic distinction lends itself to some variation. For example, the ease with which voters can change party affiliation and participate in the closed primary of the other party varies. In seventeen states, a voter is an enrolled member of one party (or is an independent and may or may not be eligible to vote in either party's primary) and can change that affiliation only well in advance of the primary election.[26] Ten other closed-primary states allow more flexibility, to accommodate shifts in voters' loyalties.

Open primaries account for (and perhaps contribute to) fleeting partisan loyalties among the public. The key difference among states with open primaries is whether a voter is required to identify which party's primary he is participating in. Eleven states require voters to request a specific party's ballot at the polling place. Nine other open primary states make no such demand; voters secretly select the ballot of the party in which they wish to participate.

A few states fall outside the strict closed or open classification. Two western states, Alaska and Washington, use what is referred to as a **blanket primary.** Under this system, voters can vote in the primaries of both parties in a single election. In other words, voters may cross over from one party's primary ballot to the other's. A voter could select from among Democratic candidates for governor and Republican candidates for the legislature, in effect participating in both primaries. In a sense, this is the ultimate open primary.

The other variation on the primary pattern is found in Louisiana, which uses a single nonpartisan primary for its statewide and congressional races. Voters can choose from among any of the candidates, regardless of party affiliation. If no one candidate receives a majority of the votes in a race, the top two vote-getters face each other in a runoff election. The nonpartisan

Table 6.2 State Primary Types

States with Closed Primaries (17)	Arizona California Connecticut Delaware Florida Kentucky Maryland Nebraska Nevada	New Mexico New York North Carolina Oklahoma Oregon Pennsylvania South Dakota West Virginia
States with Flexible Closed Primaries (10)	Colorado Iowa Kansas Maine Massachusetts	New Hampshire New Jersey Ohio Rhode Island Wyoming
States with Open Primaries Requiring Party Selection (11)	Alabama Arkansas Georgia Illinois Indiana Mississippi	Missouri South Carolina Tennessee Texas Virginia
States with Open Primaries (9)	Hawaii Idaho Michigan Minnesota Montana	North Dakota Utah Vermont Wisconsin
States with Blanket Primaries (2)	Alaska	Washington
States with Nonpartisan Primaries (1)	Louisiana	

Source: Malcolm E. Jewell and David M. Olson, *Political Parties and Elections in American States,* 3rd ed. (Pacific Grove, Calif.: Brooks/Cole Publishing Co., 1988), p. 90. Based in part on Craig L. Carr and Gary L. Scott, *American Politics Quarterly* 12 (October 1984): 465–76, copyright 1984 by Sage Publications, Inc. Reprinted with permission of Brooks/Cole Publishing Co. and Sage Publications, Inc.

primary is particularly disruptive to political party power. Table 6.2 groups the states according to their primary type.

The distinction between closed and open primaries obviously affects party influence in elections, but does it have any impact on the outcome? In other words, if we had completely open primaries, would different candidates win? There are no definitive answers to this question, but preliminary research on presidential primaries offers some compelling evidence. Primary structure does not seem to affect electoral outcomes very dramatically.[27] One possible but not very likely upset would occur if voters of one party overwhelmingly voted in the other party's primary election. This actually happened in the 1986 Democratic gubernatorial primary in Alabama, which is explained in Politics and Policy 6.1.

Runoff Elections

A **runoff election** is a second election that is held if no one candidate for an office receives a majority of votes in the primary. Runoffs became a controversial topic during the late 1980s because of the contention that different people win than would win in a system without runoffs.

Primary election runoffs have a distinct regional flavor to them. They are used by parties in nine states: Alabama, Arkansas, Florida, Georgia, Mississippi, North Carolina, Oklahoma, South Carolina, and Texas. (As we have noted, Louisiana switched from a partisan to a nonpartisan runoff election in 1975.) These have traditionally been one-party—Democratic—states, so the greatest amount of competition for an office has occurred in the Democratic party's primaries, where as many as ten candidates might enter the race. In these states, a candidate must receive more than 50 percent of the votes in the primary to become the party's nominee. When many candidates compete, it is quite probable that no one will be able to amass a majority of the votes, so the top two vote-getters face each other in a runoff election. This process ensures that the party's nominee is preferred by a majority of the primary voters. In the past, Democratic nominees in runoff states typically faced only nominal, if any, Republican opposition in the general election, so winning the Democratic nomination was tantamount to being elected to office. The general election was a virtual formality.

Myths about Runoffs   Three myths have grown up around the runoff primary.[28] One is the idea that "the leader loses"—that the candidate who finishes first in primary voting is likely to lose in the runoff to the second-place finisher. Another is the "incumbent loses" myth, which suggests that an incumbent who cannot win the necessary majority in the primary is destined to lose in a runoff. Finally, some people believe in the "minority disadvantage" myth (a variation on the "leader loses" idea), which declares that a minority candidate who leads in the primary tends to lose in the runoff. Concern that these theories (especially the last one) might actually have some basis in fact has led to calls for abolishing runoff elections.

POLITICS AND POLICY 6.1
The Consequences of Partisan Fighting

In the words of an Alabama state senator, "It's the craziest thing I've ever seen. It could only happen in Alabama politics." He was referring to the tumultuous Democratic party runoff primary in 1986, in which the gubernatorial candidate with fewer votes was actually declared the winner.

How could this happen? The two candidates in the runoff, Lieutenant Governor Bill Baxley and Attorney General Charlie Graddick, engaged in what was by all accounts a nasty, mud-slinging race for the Democratic nomination. In the runoff, Graddick amassed 8,756 more votes than Baxley. But his electoral glory was short-lived: a five-member Democratic party panel charged Graddick, a former Republican, with violating the 1965 Voting Rights Act by encouraging 16,000 Republicans to cross over and vote illegally in the Democratic runoff.

The problem then facing party leaders was how to determine Graddick's replacement. Two options existed: to schedule another runoff election or to select Baxley as the nominee. The party leaders opted for the latter, despite the fact that Alabamians favored a runoff, and voters were unhappy with the decision and with the Democrats in general. A parade of judicial rulings followed.

In the final analysis, the only real winner in this situation was the Republican candidate, Guy Hunt. Hunt benefited from the ill feelings associated with the Democrats and their electoral games. He won the general election to become the first Republican governor in Alabama since 1874.

Source: Bill Peterson, "Confusion Reigns in Alabama Over Gubernatorial Nominee," *Washington Post,* September 20, 1986, p. A1. Copyright © 1986 *The Washington Post.* Reprinted by permission.

Analysis of election results does not lend much credence to the myths. Research on 215 runoffs in Georgia from 1965 to 1982 found that with the exception of some celebrated cases, primary leaders went on to win the runoff.[29] Also, although incumbents are more vulnerable in runoffs than nonincumbent primary leaders are, they still win more often than they lose. The Georgia findings included few cases in which a minority candidate competed in a runoff, but initial results showed no discernible disadvantage for these candidates.

Are Runoffs Divisive?   Theoretically, the rationale for the runoff primary is majority rule. Political circumstances have changed since several southern states adopted the runoff primary system in the 1920s, and the Democratic party is no longer unchallenged in the region. The growth of Republicanism produced an increasing number of meaningfully contested general elections during the 1970s and 1980s. Has the runoff primary outlived its usefulness? Worse yet, does it systematically disadvantage the political party using it? In other words, do runoffs generate such divisiveness within the party that its nominee is weakened in the general election?

A recent study of this issue supports the speculation that candidates who emerge from a bloody intraparty runoff are systematically disadvantaged in the general election.[30] Being involved in a runoff costs Democratic gubernatorial candidates in the South approximately 4.56 votes per hundred cast, on average, in the subsequent general election. (Incumbency tends to restore some of the deficit, however.) The reasons for this are complex, but they seem to reflect the factionalized majority party's inability to overcome the rancor that the two-primary structure produces.

The increasing competitiveness of the Republican party in the South has produced more crowded primaries and thus has led to greater use of runoffs in the GOP as well. Thus, the Republicans may eventually be susceptible to the kind of divisiveness that afflicts the Democrats.

General Elections

Primaries and runoffs culminate in the general election, through which candidates become officeholders. Virtually all states hold general elections in November of even-numbered years. A few states—Kentucky, Mississippi, New Jersey, and Virginia among them—schedule their gubernatorial elections in odd-numbered years.

General elections typically pit candidates of the two parties against one another. The winner is the candidate who receives a majority of the votes cast. In a race in which more than two candidates compete (which occurs when an independent or a third-party candidate enters a race), the leading vote-getter is less likely to receive a majority (more than half) of the votes cast. Instead, the candidate with the most votes—a **plurality**—wins.

Political parties have traditionally been active in general elections, mobilizing voters in support of their candidates. Over time, however, their role has diminished, as general election campaigns have become more candidate-centered and geared to the candidate's own organization.[31] One new twist in the past decade has been the emergence of legislative party caucuses as major factors in general elections. In California, for example, the Democratic and Republican leaders in both houses raised over $7.5 million to distribute to their partys' nominees for the legislature in 1986.[32] That year in Illinois, the four party caucuses (two parties, two houses) spent nearly $3 million. Ohio's House Republican Campaign Committee conducts seminars on issues and on campaign management for the party's House nominees. In some states, the formal state party organization has given way to the legislative party caucus.

Nonpartisan Elections

A **nonpartisan election** removes the political party identification from the candidate in an effort to "depoliticize" the electoral campaign. Elections that have been made nonpartisan include those for many judicial offices and for many local-level elections. The special task of judges—adjudicating guilt or innocence, determining right and wrong—does not lend itself to partisan interpretation. The job of local governments—delivering public services— has also traditionally been considered nonideological. Nonpartisan local elections are likely to be found in municipalities and in school districts and special districts.

Under a nonpartisan election system, a first election (like a primary) selects leading candidates, and a second election (like a general election) selects officeholders. The occurrence of nonpartisan local elections is largely a function of region. Although 73 percent of cities use nonpartisan elections, according to a recent survey, the regional percentages range from 94 in the West to 21 in the Northeast.[33] Large cities are no more likely to conduct partisan elections than smaller ones are; those that do, however, such as New York City and Chicago, attract attention.

The three leading Democratic candidates for mayor of Chicago in 1989—Acting Mayor Eugene Sawyer, Richard M. Daley, and Lawrence Bloom—debate the issues. Daley won the primary and went on to win the general election. Voting in both elections was largely divided along racial lines.

The Impact of Nonpartisan Elections   Most studies have concluded that nonpartisanship depresses turnout in municipal elections that are held independently of state and national elections. The figures are not dramatic, but in what are already low-turnout elections, the difference can run as high as 15 to 20 percent of municipal voters.[34] Nonpartisan elections seem to produce a more socioeconomically elite city council and more Republican members. One fascinating finding is that although a nonpartisan election structure seems to result in a different type of city council, the policy outcomes appear unaffected.[35] In terms of policies, nonpartisanly elected city councils are not noticeably different from partisan ones.

What It Takes to Get Elected   In the absence of political parties, candidates are forced to create their own organizations in order to run for office. They raise and spend money (much of it their own), and they seek the endorsements of newspapers and business and citizen groups. Money matters; this fact of political life cannot be understated. But endorsements are also important in local campaigns. Recent research on the impact of newspaper endorsements in six cities (Dallas, Fort Worth, San Antonio, Memphis, Peoria, and Charlotte) during a thirty-year period ending in 1980 confirmed their influence.[36] The researchers reported "considerable success for candidates receiving a newspaper endorsement."[37]

An incumbent backed by a newspaper is an almost unbeatable combination. Consider the *Tampa Tribune*'s evaluation of the three candidates competing for the mayor's post in 1987.[38] The paper claimed that one of the contenders had "served without particular distinction on the city council a few years ago." Another challenger was said to have an "absolute genius for driving people crazy." The incumbent, however, won the newspaper's resounding endorsement, because she had "demonstrated high intelligence, a talent for creative problem-solving, a strong individualistic bent, a quiet but fierce determination, and a deep and honest regard for the welfare of all [Tampa residents]." The endorsed incumbent defeated her opponents handily.

In running for a nonpartisan local office, candidates do not enjoy the good will, especially the money and grassroots support, that automatically accompanies a candidate affiliated with a major political party. In some communities, local groups function as unofficial parties in that they identify candidates whom they prefer and undertake efforts on behalf of those candidates. Citizens' groups can also be an important factor in local elections. In Austin, Texas, for example, two ideologically based citizens' groups play important roles in influencing election outcomes.[39] Liberals come together in an umbrella organization, the River City Coordinating Council, and the conservative perspective is represented by the Austin Area Research Organization. These groups provide informal support to preferred candidates. A study of Austin municipal elections from 1975 to 1985 indicates that the endorsement of these groups is "worth more than 10 percentage points of the vote."[40]

The 1988 State Elections

Although the presidential election garnered the lion's share of media attention and public interest in 1988, there were a number of significant state elections throughout the country. The outcomes of these elections, and those in 1990, will influence the vitality of state government during the next decade.

Gubernatorial Races   Twelve of the fifty governors' seats were up for election in 1988. Most states schedule their statewide elections in non-presidential election years, so that the presidential race does not divert attention from state races and so they can minimize the possible **coattail effect,** by which a popular presidential candidate can sweep state candidates of the same party into office. (A coattail effect did not occur in 1988.) Two-thirds of the contested gubernatorial seats were occupied by Republicans, one-third by Democrats. When the elections were over, the Democrats showed a net gain of one seat, bringing the total number of Democratic governors to twenty-eight. Changes in party control occurred in the governorships in Indiana and West Virginia (from Republican to Democratic) and Montana (from Democratic to Republican). This gain by the Democrats interrupted a recent pattern of Republican success in gubernatorial contests. For example, in the 1986 general election, Republicans picked up eight seats.

One of the more interesting races took place in Utah, where three candidates—a Republican, a Democrat, and an independent—battled for the governor's office. On election day, the Republican incumbent was returned to office with only 40 percent of the vote. Sixty percent of the Utah voters preferred someone other than the incumbent, but because two opposition candidates shared the vote, the candidate with the plurality won the election. The entry of an independent into a standard two-party contest confounded the process. Early polls showed the Democratic challenger with a lead of as much as twenty percentage points over the Republican incumbent, so the independent apparently siphoned off support expected to go to the Democratic candidate.[41]

Legislative Races   The 1988 elections did not yield dramatic shifts in partisan control of state legislatures. Almost 6,000 legislative seats were in contention. In a typical election year, as many as 300 partisan shifts might occur. In 1984, for instance, Republicans took 330 seats from the Democrats,[42] and thus gained control of seven additional legislative chambers. Nowhere was the impact as dramatic as in Connecticut, where the 1984 elections shifted the Senate from a two-thirds Democratic majority to a two-thirds Republican majority. The Connecticut House of Representatives experienced a similar reversal in partisan control that year too. However, in the 1986 elections the Republicans lost ground in the Connecticut legislature, and the Democrats recaptured control.

Before the 1988 elections, Democrats controlled the senates of thirty-one states and the houses of thirty-seven states. Overall, there were twenty-eight Democrat-controlled state legislatures. Republicans counted sixteen senates and twelve houses under their leadership. (Two state senates were evenly split between the parties.) In only eight states did Republicans control both houses.

The 1988 results did not substantially disrupt this pattern of partisan control. Only two houses actually shifted from one party to the other: in Montana, where Republicans held a narrow margin in the House, Democrats gained three seats to become the majority party; in Vermont, the Republicans gained enough seats to regain majority status. Indiana voters produced an electoral puzzle of sorts. The 100-member House went from a 52–48 Republican margin to an even 50–50 split. Since there was no majority party around which to organize the legislative session, leaders agreed to share power by alternating Speakers in a sort of "Speaker du jour" plan.[43] Each legislative committee was to have two chairs, a Republican and a Democrat. In practice, though, this system proved to be rather unworkable and led to calls for increasing the size of the House by one member so that a tie could never happen again.[44]

The 1990 State Elections

The 1990 state elections carry a special significance because of *reapportionment*. Reapportionment of state legislatures and the U.S. Congress will take place in 1991 (on the basis of the 1990 census), so the party that controls each statehouse will be in a position to influence the drawing of district lines. Chapter 9 includes a detailed discussion of the highly politicized science of redistricting. Since state legislatures approve (and in many states actually draw) district maps, the party in power is ideally situated to improve its electoral fortunes. Both the Republican and the Democratic parties have promised intense competition for high-stakes state legislative races in 1990.

One of the issues certain to ignite the 1990 campaigns is abortion. After the U.S. Supreme Court's 1989 decision that turned a good deal of control over abortion back to the states, both pro-choice and anti-abortion forces mobilized their troops for statehouse sieges. Gubernatorial and legislative candidates face intense pressure from both sides. The abortion issue is especially tricky for candidates because within the parties, divisions run deep. Taking an unequivocal stand on the abortion question will alienate some voters and attract others. It is precisely the kind of ideological issue that state politicians would prefer to avoid, but avoidance appears impossible.

Political Campaigns

Like so many things these days, political campaigns aren't what they used to be. State and local campaigns are no longer unsophisticated operations run from someone's dining room table. The 1980s ushered in a new era of campaign technology and financing in which information is accessible to almost everyone through television and the mailbox. As a consequence, some argue, campaigns have taken on a different and decidedly negative tone.

A New Era of Campaigns

Campaigns of the past conjure up images of fiery oratory and county fairs. In South Carolina, for instance, candidates for statewide office used to be required by law to speak at every county seat, a practice that became widely known as the "traveling political circus." But today, campaigns orchestrated by rural courthouse gangs and urban ward-bosses have given way to stylized video campaigning, which depends on the mass media and political consultants.

Mass Media Mass media, especially television, are intrinsic aspects of modern statewide campaigns. Even candidates for local offices are increasingly using mass media to transmit their messages. Campaigners can either buy air time and newspaper space for advertising or get it free by arranging events that reporters are likely to cover. These range from serious (a candidate's major policy statement) to gimmicky (a candidate climbing into the ring with a professional wrestler to demonstrate his "toughness"); either way, they are cleverly planned to capture media attention.

Using the media is an increasingly sophisticated venture. Florida state senator Bob Graham, running in a crowded field for the Democratic gubernatorial nomination in 1978, developed what is now considered a classic approach: he held a series of "work days," spending a day each week pumping gas, clerking at a convenience store, loading trucks, digging ditches, handling baggage. The media followed him everywhere, and a disproportionate share of media attention helped him to win the nomination and ultimately the governorship. During his eight-year stint as governor, and now as a U.S. senator, Graham continues to devote one day a month to such work days.

A candidate seeking free media attention needs to create visual events, be quotable, and relentlessly attack opponents or targeted problems. But as the magazine *Campaigns and Elections* advises, he or she must integrate gimmicks with a message that appeals to the electorate. In one of its 1988 issues, this magazine contained articles aimed at candidates on "making a name for yourself," "nailing the opposition," and "effective targeting."[45]

Free media time is seldom sufficient. Candidates, particularly those running for higher-level state offices and for positions in large cities, rely on paid advertisements to reach the public. One estimate indicated that the average 1986 gubernatorial candidate produced and aired twenty to thirty different political commercials.[46] These are not inexpensive to produce or to air, although there is some variation in advertising rates around the country. A thirty-second spot on the most popular television program of 1986, *The Cosby Show,* was reported to cost $800 for all of South Dakota but $30,000 for New York City alone.[47]

Paid media advertisements in the 1980s seemed to be of two distinct varieties, generic and negative. Generic advertisements include

1. *the sainthood spot,* which glorifies the candidate and her accomplishments;
2. *the testimonial,* in which other people (celebrities, average citizens) attest to the candidate's abilities;
3. *the bumper-sticker policy spot,* which emphasizes the campaign's popular and noncontroversial themes (good schools, lower taxes, more jobs); and
4. *the feel-good spot,* which identifies and capitalizes on the spirit of a place and its people (e.g., "Vermont's a special place," "Nobody can do it better than Pennsylvania").[48]

Negative advertising, which has been renamed by its practitioners in a bit of linguistic chicanery as "comparative" advertising, is easily recognizable. The public has been inundated with the *flip-flop ad* and the *not-on-the-job ad,* in which an opponent's voting record and attendance rate, respectively, are presented. Comedy spots ridiculing the opponent, another type of negative ad, are difficult to produce and can backfire, but when they work, they linger in voters' minds. Another negative ad is the *hit-and-run,* in which the opponent is linked to unpopular people, causes, or events.

Media advertising is important because it is frequently the only contact a potential voter has with a candidate. A candidate's personal characteristics and style—important considerations to an evaluating public—are easily transmitted via the airwaves. The image of the candidate (in the 1980s, it was almost invariably of hardworking family men and women who will get the job done) is what we carry into the voting booth.[49]

Political Consultants   Along with increased media usage, a new occupational specialty sprang up during the 1970s and 1980s: political consulting. Individuals with expertise in polling, direct mail, fund-raising, advertising, and campaign management hire themselves out to campaigns, in which use of new campaign technology makes their expertise invaluable. The occupation is undoubtedly here to stay, and several colleges and universities now offer degree programs in practical campaigning.

The final responsibility of a political consultant is to get his candidate(s) elected. In today's campaigning, this means creating the right "packaging" and ensuring that adequate funds are available. Packaging involves issues as central as identifying the campaign theme (contemporary favorites include "leadership," "integrity," and, especially for gubernatorial and mayoral candidates, "business acumen") and as trivial as choosing the candidate's neckwear.

Consultants form the core of the professional campaign management team assembled by candidates for state offices. They identify and target likely voters, both those who are already in the candidate's camp and need to be reminded to vote and those who can be persuaded. They carefully craft messages to appeal to specific voters, such as the elderly, homeowners, and environmentalists. Any number of factors influence the result of an election, such as the presence of an incumbent in a race and the amount of funds a challenger has accumulated, but one significant factor is the ability to frame or define the issues during the campaign. Even in a quietly contested state legislative race, district residents are likely to receive mailings that state the candidates' issue positions, solicit funds, and perhaps comment unfavorably on the opposition. The candidate who has an effective political consultant to help set the campaign agenda and thereby put her opponent on the defensive is closer to victory.

Campaign Finance

To campaign for public office is to spend money—a lot of money. Lewis Lehrman spent over $13 million dollars, much of it his own, and lost his 1982 bid for the governorship of New York to Mario Cuomo. The pricetag for Cuomo's campaign was not small either: $5 million.[50]

The average cost of winning the governor's job in the thirty-six states that held gubernatorial elections in 1986 was estimated to be $7 million.[51] Of course, the total amounts in New York and California are substantially higher than they are in Georgia and Rhode Island; it costs more to run for office in the most populous states. For example, the 1986 gubernatorial election in Texas, in which a former incumbent successfully unseated the current incumbent, cost $35 million.[52] But when campaign costs are broken down to a cost per vote, it is the less populous states in which expenses mount up. The cost per vote of the 1982 gubernatorial elections in New York and California was slightly over $2. In Georgia, it was $4; in Rhode Island, in 1984, it was $8.50. Those costs pale by comparison to those in Alaska, where candidates for top state offices frequently have spent at a rate of more than $20 per vote.

Spending in legislative races has also increased. For example, candidates for the Florida House of Representatives in 1980 were spending 50 percent more (after accounting for inflation) than their counterparts in 1972.[53] In 1983, New Jersey Assembly candidates averaged $20,000 in expenditures; two years later, the figure had climbed to $37,000.[54] California, as might be expected, was the site of the first million-dollar campaign for a legislative seat, and it is not uncommon for a competitive legislative campaign there to consume half a million dollars. At the other end of the scale are legislative races in New Hampshire, where an average candidate's expenditures in 1986 were less than $3,000. (Keep in mind, however, that the job pays $100 a year.)[55]

Just how important is money? One knowledgeable observer concluded: "In the direct primaries, where self-propelled candidates battle for recognition, money is crucial. Electronic advertising is the only way to gain visibility. Hence the outcome usually rewards the one with the largest war chest."[56] This does not bode well for an idealistic but underfunded potential candidate. Winning takes money, either the candidate's or someone else's. If it is someone else's, it may come with a string or two attached.

State Efforts at Campaign Reform   Concern over escalating costs and the influence of wealthy special interests in campaigns has led reform groups such as Common Cause to call for improved state laws to provide comprehensive and timely disclosure of campaign finances, impose limitations on contributions by individuals and groups, create a combined public/private financing mechanism for primaries and general elections, and establish an independent commission to enforce tough sanctions on violators of campaign finance laws.[57]

States have performed impressively on the first of these recommendations: all states have some sort of campaign financing reporting procedure. In response to the fourth recommendation, twenty-six states have established independent commissions to oversee the conduct of campaigns, although they have found it somewhat difficult to enforce the law and punish violators. One study of state election commissions identified only four—in California, Connecticut, Florida, and New Jersey—as displaying "consistency and vigor" in their enforcement behavior.[58]

The other recommendations have proved more troublesome. States have grappled with the issue of costly campaigns but have made only modest progress in controlling costs. A 1976 decision by the U.S. Supreme Court in *Buckley* v. *Valeo* made these efforts more difficult; the Court ruled that governments cannot limit a person's right to spend to spread his views on particular issues and candidates. In essence, this means that a candidate has unlimited power to spend his own money on his own behalf and that other individuals may spend to their heart's content to promote their own opinions on election-related issues. The Court did let stand state limits on an individual's contributions to candidates and parties, however, and if a candidate accepts public funds, he is then bound by whatever limitations the state may impose.

Some states have established actual limits on the amount of money that organizations and individuals can contribute to a political race. For example, in New York, corporations are limited to a contribution maximum of $5,000 per calendar year, and individuals (other than an official candidate) are restricted to $150,000. Florida limits corporations, labor unions, and

PACs to $1,000 to $3,000 (depending on the type of race) per candidate. The same limits apply to individuals, excluding the candidate's own contributions. Some states, such as Arizona, Connecticut, North Dakota, Pennsylvania, and Texas, have gone even further by prohibiting contributions from corporations and labor unions.[59] A totally different philosophy pervades the politics of a large number of states that continue to operate their election systems without any limitations on contributions. In California, Colorado, Illinois, Louisiana, and Utah, to name a few, organizations and individuals can contribute as much as they wish.

States have also considered the other side of the campaign financing equation: expenditures. Virtually all states require candidates and political committees to file reports documenting the expenditure of campaign funds. Nine states impose limits on a candidate's total expenditures. (Hawaii uses voluntary spending limits.) In Delaware, for example, statewide candidates are allowed to spend up to twenty-five cents times the number of qualified voters in the primary, and twice that figure in the general election. Michigan takes a different approach. There, publicly funded candidates (governor and lieutenant governor) are restricted to $1 million per election, with another $200,000 allowable for specific purposes. In the vast majority of states, however, candidates campaign without any spending limits.

The Need for High Financing   Does any of this really matter? Should the general public be concerned about the spiraling costs of competing for elected posts?

Recent research has confirmed several longstanding truths about the costs of campaigning.[60] Close elections cost more than elections in which one candidate is sure to win, since uncertainty regarding the outcome is a spur to spending. A candidate quickly learns that it is easier to get money from potential contributors when the polls show that she has a chance of winning. Also, elections that produce change—that is, in which an incumbent is unseated or the out-party gains the office—typically cost more. Taking on an existing officeholder is a risky strategy, and it drives up election costs. An open race in which there is no incumbent represents an opportunity for the party out of office to capture the seat, so the party and its candidate are likely to invest heavily in the race, which triggers similar spending by the in-party in an effort to protect the seat. It is no wonder that costs continue to rise.

Major candidates, especially incumbents, do not have to look too hard to find campaign money. PACs loom larger and larger as heavy financiers of state election campaigns. For instance, the average winning candidate for the Iowa Senate in 1976 reported approximately $6,300 in contributions, about one-quarter of which came from PACs.[61] By the 1984 elections, Senate winners averaged $13,000 in contributions, and the PAC portion had grown to two-thirds of the total. Iowa is not unusual in this regard; studies of legislative campaign financing in Arizona, Kansas, and Missouri confirm the trend.[62]

Public Funding as a Solution   Almost half the states have begun experimenting with public funding of campaigns. Individuals voluntarily contribute to a central fund, which is divided among candidates or political parties. The system is fairly easy to administer and is relatively easy for voters. In most of the public-funding states, citizens can use their state income tax form to earmark a portion (a dollar or two) of their tax liability for the fund. A check-off system like this does not directly increase taxpayers' tax burden. In a few states, the public fund is amassed through a voluntary surcharge, or additional tax (usually $1, although California allows surcharges of $5, $10, and $25). Indiana has opted for a different approach: revenues from the sale of personalized motor vehicle license plates support the fund.

In addition to check-offs and surcharges, some of the public-funding states, including Idaho and Minnesota, offer taxpayers a tax credit (usually 50 percent of the contribution, up to a specified maximum) when they contribute to political campaigns. A more popular supplement to public funding is a state tax deduction for campaign contributions, as used in California, Hawaii, Montana, Oklahoma, and North Carolina. A final and not widely explored approach is a direct state appropriation of funds. Maryland, for instance, does not use check-offs or surcharges but relies on a direct state appropriation to candidates for state, county, and Baltimore city offices.[63]

Public campaign financing is supposed to rid the election process of some of its evils. Proponents argue that it will democratize the contribution process by freeing candidates from excessive reliance on special interest money. Other potential advantages include expanding the pool of potential candidates, allowing candidates to compete on a more equal basis, and reducing the cost of campaigning.[64] A study of legislative races in Wisconsin indicated that as a proportion of total contributions, public dollars increased and PAC money declined.[65] By contributing to the fund, average citizens may feel that they have a greater stake in state elections.

Despite the claims offered in support of public funding, it is not universally embraced. One study of legislators in eight states found that an almost equal proportion favored public funding of gubernatorial campaigns (46.2 percent) as opposed it (46.4 percent).[66] The reaction to public funding of legislative races was more one-sided: 55 percent were against, 36 percent supported it. Opponents claim that public funding will introduce new biases into state elections while stifling competition and protecting incumbents.[67] Evidence from states with public-funding systems indicates that the mechanism itself—a check-off or a surcharge—largely determines the success of the program. When a check-off is used, the percentage of contributing taxpayers reaches the 20 to 25 percent level. With a surcharge, the participation rate falls below 5 percent. New Jersey offers a successful example. Forty percent of tax filers contribute to a general fund that is allocated to gubernatorial candidates for specific campaign activities.[68] Taxpayer participation of the magnitude found in New Jersey suggests that public funding can be a useful alternative to private fund-raising.

The Democratic Process

Elections are the key to the resurgence of state and local governments. It is through elections that we select the individuals who will serve as governors and mayors, legislators and council members, and in many places, as judges. If the elections process is flawed, the modernized institutions of government that you will read about in the next several chapters cannot function effectively. It is the people that we put into office who will make a difference in the quality of state and local government.

Elections usually involve political parties and they almost always involve campaigning. Both of these elements have changed substantially in the past several years. Many of these changes have been positive, such as the increase in interparty competition; some have been negative such as the skyrocketing costs of campaigning. Are these processes producing the kinds of leaders needed to take state and local governments into the twenty-first century? No one has a definitive answer, but it is certainly a subject for debate. Perhaps the true test of the capacity of state and local governments will be their ability to resolve some of the difficult questions surrounding the electoral process.

Summary

Political parties, elections, and campaigns are part of the process of democratic government. This machinery is what keeps government on track and working in the public's interest. It is exciting to observe and even more exciting to participate in. Elections are the stable part of the machinery; political parties are undergoing a transformation, and campaigns have taken on an entirely new look. Interparty competition is on the rise at the same time that PACs are increasing their financial influence in campaigns in many states. In other states, the legislative party caucus is emerging as a real force in campaigns and elections. This tremendous fluidity makes it difficult to assess the impact of these changes on state and local government. It is important that they have a positive effect so that nonnational governments can maintain their vitality.

Key Terms

Blanket primary A primary in which a voter is allowed to vote for candidates of both parties in a single election.

Closed primary A primary in which only voters registered in the party are allowed to participate.

Coattail effect The tendency of a winning presidential candidate to carry state candidates of the same party into office.

Nonpartisan election An election without party labels.

Open primary A primary in which voters may vote for either party's candidates.

Plurality The number of votes (though not a majority) cast for the winning candidate in an election with more than two candidates.

Primary system The electoral mechanism for selecting party nominees to compete in the general election.

Responsible party model A theoretical ideal in which political parties are issue-oriented, candidates toe the party line, and voters respond accordingly.

Runoff election A second election conducted if no candidate receives a majority of votes in the first election.

Ticket-splitting Voting for candidates of different political parties in a general election.

7

Governors

The Roles of the Governor
Policymaker/Chief Legislator/Chief
Administrator/Ceremonial/Leader
Intergovernmental Coordinator/Economic
Development Promoter/Party Leader

Today's Governors

Gubernatorial Campaigns

Formal Powers
Tenure/Appointment Power/Veto
Power/Budgetary Power/Reorganization
Power/Staffing Power/The Relevance of the
Formal Powers

Informal Powers
Tools of Persuasion/Characteristics of a
Successful Governor

Removal from Office

Other Executive Branch Officials
Attorney General/Lieutenant
Governor/Treasurer/Secretary of State

The Vigor of American Governors

Louisiana is known for its bayous, Cajun cooking, and remarkable governors. Perhaps the best known was fire-breathing Huey P. Long, who taxed the oil companies to finance a massive program for building bridges, roads, hospitals, and schools. His promises of "a chicken in every pot" and "every man a king" captured the attention of the nation's poor during the Great Depression and made him a legitimate contender for the presidency of the United States until his assassination in 1935.

High-rolling Edwin Edwards served as governor of Louisiana for eight years during the 1970s and was elected to a third term in 1983. Shortly thereafter he was indicted by a federal grand jury for allegedly raking in $2 million from a hospital-permit scheme. Well known for gambling, he offered 8-to-5 odds that he would not be indicted, and 2-to-1 odds that if he was indicted, he would be acquitted. Edwards was also well known for making outrageous statements. At one time, he proclaimed himself "more popular than Jesus Christ," but he was defeated in the Democratic primary for governor in 1987 by Charles "Buddy" Roemer.

Roemer was cut from a different cloth from most of his predecessors, but proved to be no less remarkable. He entered the governor's office with a dramatic reform agenda that included reorganizing the state's inefficient executive branch, rectifying far-reaching waste, fraud, and abuse, and reversing Louisiana's economy, which had been devastated by a decline in oil and natural gas prices. Although it is too soon to evaluate "the Roemer revolution," the election of this Harvard-educated reformer represents a drastic change in the tone of government in the Bayou State.

It has been said that the American governorship was "conceived in mistrust and born in a straitjacket." The excesses of some colonial governors appointed by the English Crown resulted in strong dislike and distrust of executive power by the early American settlers, so the first state constitutions placed political power in the legislative branch. Early governors were typically elected by the legislature rather than the voters, were restricted to a single one-year term of office, and had little authority.[1] Two states, Pennsylvania and Georgia, even established a plural (multi-member) executive. Slowly the governorships became stronger through longer terms, popular election, and the power to veto legislation, but power did not come easily. The movement for popular democracy during the Jacksonian era led to the election of other executive branch officials, and then reaction to the excesses of Jacksonian democracy resulted in numerous independent boards and commissions in the executive branch. Although governors did gain some power, they were not able to exercise independent authority over these executive boards and commissions.

In the early 1900s, along with their efforts to democratize national politics and clean up the corrupt city political machines, Progressive reformers launched a campaign to reform state government. Their principal target was the weak executive branch. Efforts to improve the state executive branch have continued throughout the twentieth century. Today we are in the latter stages of a long, highly comprehensive wave of reform that began

174

around 1965 and has affected all the states. Its essential goal has been to increase the governors' powers to make them more commensurate with the office's increased duties and responsibilities. As a result, constitutional and statutory changes have fortified the office of the chief executive, reorganized the executive branch, and streamlined the structure and processes of the bureaucracy. The capacity of governors and the executive branch to apply state resources to solve the problems of the 1990s has thus been greatly enhanced.[2]

The Roles of the Governor

In performing his or her duties, the governor wears the hats of policymaker, chief legislator, chief administrator, ceremonial leader, intergovernmental coordinator, economic development promoter, and political party leader. Sometimes several of these hats must be balanced atop the governor's head at once. All things considered, these roles make the governorship one of the most difficult and challenging yet potentially rewarding jobs in the world.

Policymaker

A governor is the leading formulator and initiator of public policy in his state from his first pronouncements as a gubernatorial candidate until the final days in office. The governor's role as chief policymaker involves many other players, including actors in the legislature, bureaucracy, courts, and voting public, but few major policies that the governor does not initiate are enacted, and success or failure depends largely on how competently the governor designs and develops policy. The governor must also follow through to see that adopted policies are put into effect as originally intended.

Some issues are transitory in nature, appearing on the agenda of state government and disappearing after appropriate actions are taken.[3] These issues are often created by external events, such as federal court decisions that mandate a certain state action, a new national law requiring a state response, or an act of nature such as a tornado, flood, or earthquake. A recent example is the minimum drinking age; congressional legislation forced the states to comply with the twenty-one-year drinking age if they were to continue receiving federal grants for highways.

Most policy issues, however, do not emerge suddenly because of happenstance. Perennial concerns face the governor each year: education, corrections, social welfare, transportation. Cyclical issues also appear, increase in intensity, and slowly fade away.[4] Examples of this type are consumer protection, energy conservation, and ethics in government.

Several recent factors contribute to strong policy leadership from the chief executives, including larger and more able staffs that are knowledgeable in important policy fields; strengthened formal powers of the office, such as longer terms and the veto power; and the assistance of the National Governors' Association (NGA), which offers ideas for policy and program development. Of no small importance is the high caliber of individuals who have won the office in recent years.[5] With increasing frequency governors have even assumed the mantle of national policy leadership, most recently in public education and welfare reform.

Chief Legislator

This gubernatorial role is closely related to that of policymaker, because legislative action is required for most of the chief executive's policies to be put into effect. In fact, the governor cannot directly introduce bills; party leaders and policy supporters in the House and Senate must actually put the bills in the hopper. Dealing with legislators is a demanding role for a governor, consuming more time than any other role and representing for many the single most difficult aspect of the job.[6]

Executive-Legislative Tensions   Developing a positive relationship with the legislature requires great expenditures of a governor's time, energy, and resources. Several factors hinder smooth relations between the chief executive and the legislature, including partisanship and personality clashes. Even the different natures of the two branches can cause conflict. Governors are elected by a statewide constituency and therefore tend to take a broad view of issues, whereas legislators represent relatively small geographical areas and are attentive to a much smaller group of voters.

Often the governor must deal with a one- or two-house majority from the opposing political party. According to one study, the amount of strife between the two branches is influenced by three factors: the size of the majority and the minority parties, the personalities of the governor and legislative leaders, and the nearness of an election year.[7] When the opposition party is strong, the governor must seek bipartisan support in order to get favored legislation passed. Frequently a governor facing a large legislative majority from the opposing party has only the veto and the possibility of mobilizing public support as weapons against the legislature. Personality clashes can make partisan conflict worse. For example, when Republican Ronald Reagan served as governor of California, he worked closely with the Democrat-controlled legislature. When roadblocks appeared, Reagan initiated discussions over disputed issues, and compromise often resulted. Yet a later Republican, George Deukmejian, who had a reputation for being an aloof and unbending conservative, often was not able to break stalemates with the Democratic legislature. The approach of statewide elections can bring gubernatorial-legislative deadlock, as incumbents may be extremely cautious or overtly partisan in trying to please (or at least not to offend) the voters. These three conflict-producing factors are intensified during debates on the budget, when the principal policy and financial decisions are made.

Even in states where the governor's own party enjoys a large majority in both houses of the legislature, factions are certain to develop along ideological, rural-urban, geographical, or other divisions.[8] Ironically, a very large legislative majority can create the greatest problems with factionalism, largely because there is no substantial opposition to unite the majority party. Apparently a legislative majority of 60 to 70 percent helps a governor; beyond that, the majority party tends to degenerate into intraparty rivalries beyond the governor's control.[9] As Governor Michael Dukakis of Massachusetts lamented in the face of a 4-to-1 majority of his own party in the legislature, "You've got Democrats, you've got moderate Democrats, you've got suburban Democrats, you've got urban Democrats, you've got rural Democrats, and you don't have any Republicans."[10] Figure 6.3 (page 154) displays the variation in party competition among the states. Figure 7.1 shows the parties of the current governors.

Executive Influence on the Legislative Agenda   Despite the difficulties in dealing with the legislature, most governors do dominate the policy agenda. The governor's influence begins with the state-of-the-state address, which kicks off each new legislative session. During the session, she might threaten to veto a proposed bill or appeal directly to a particular legislator's constituency.

Most of the drama, however, takes place behind the scenes. The governor might promise high-level executive branch jobs or judgeships (either for certain legislators or for their friends) to influence legislative votes. Or she might offer some sort of **pork barrel** reward, such as making sure a certain road in a legislator's district is paved or approving state funds for the local Corn Queen Festival. Private meetings, breakfasts, or lunches in the governor's mansion flatter and solicit support from small groups or individual legislators. Successful governors are usually able to relate to representatives and senators on a personal level. Many are former members of the state legislature, so they know which strings to pull to win over key supporters.

In addition, all governors have one or more legislative liaisons, who are assigned to lobby for the administration's program. Members of the governor's staff testify at legislative hearings, consult with committees and individuals on proposed bills, and even write floor speeches for friends in the legislature.[11] Most governors, however, are careful not to be perceived as unduly interfering in the internal affairs of the legislature. For example, chief executives generally do not become involved in legislative elections for majority and minority leadership positions, or they act only in a quiet and very selective way.[12] Too much meddling can bring a political backlash that undermines a governor's policy program. The role of chief legislator, then, requires a balancing act that ultimately determines the success or failure of the governor's agenda.

Figure 7.1 The Governors by Party, 1990
Democrats hold an advantage of twenty-nine to twenty-one in governorships, but have lost the Old South states of Alabama and the Carolinas.

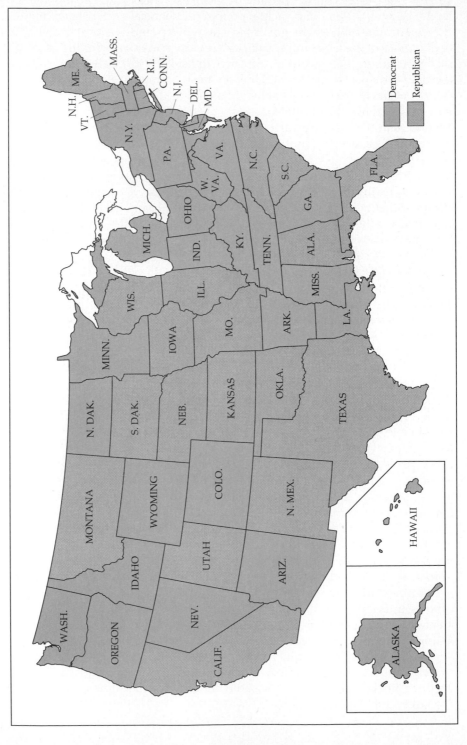

Democrat   Republican

Chief Administrator

As chief executive of the state, the governor is (in name, at least) in charge of the operations of numerous agencies, boards, and commissions. In the view of many voters, the governor is directly responsible not only for pivotal matters such as the condition of the state's economy, but also for such mundane things as the number and depth of potholes on state highways. The governor's role as chief administrator has become more important over the past twenty-five years. Governors are increasingly sensitive to their administrative role, and most spend more time and energy on administrative concerns than on any other role except policymaker and chief legislator.

The new attention given to the management of state government is a product of many factors, including the growth in the size and economic dimensions of state government and the rise of the federal grant-in-aid as the principal method for transferring national dollars to states and localities. Constitutional and statutory reforms since 1965, including the concentration of executive power in the office of the governor and the consolidation of numerous state agencies, have considerably strengthened the governor's capacity to manage the state. (See Chapter 8 for further discussion of the bureaucracy.) The recruitment of executive support staff to help manage personnel, planning, and budgeting has also been helpful.

Governors perform a wide variety of duties in carrying out their role of chief administrator. One observer has summarized them as follows:

1. Initiating or changing policy
2. Setting a proper administrative tone and keeping morale high among the bureaucracy and the governor's staff
3. Mediating policy disputes between and within state agencies
4. Promoting policies and policy issues to state employees, to the voters, and to the legislature
5. Recruiting top state executive branch employees
6. Allocating resources within the state through the budgetary process, establishing programs, and controlling and regulating state agencies.[13]

In many ways the governor's job is comparable to that of the chief executive officer of a large corporation. He must manage thousands of workers, staggering sums of money, and complex organizational systems. There are, however, important differences. For one thing, the governor is not nearly so well paid; the typical company president makes hundreds of thousands of dollars per year, whereas the average gubernatorial salary in 1988 was $74,629. More important, governors confront several critical factors that constrain their ability to manage.

Restraints on Management   The reforms of the executive branch during the past twenty-five years have allowed far more active and influential management, but significant restraints still exist. For example, the separation-of-powers principle dictates that the governor share his authority with the legislature and the courts. Changes in state agency programs, priorities, or organization typically require legislative approval, and the legality of such changes may be tested in the courts. The governor's ability to hire, fire, motivate, and punish is severely restricted by merit system rules and regulations, independent boards and commissions with their own personnel systems, and other elected executive branch officials, who pursue their own administrative and political agendas. Thus, the great majority of employees in the executive branch are outside the governor's formal sphere of authority. Career bureaucrats who have established their own policy direction and momentum over many years see governors come and go, but usually march to their own tune. Another restraint is that governors sometimes simply have little time to oversee the executive branch agencies. Policymaking, legislative relations, and public relations all can be enormously time-consuming, and are more immediately gratifying.

One of the most critical functions of the governor's role as chief administrator is crisis management. Immense problems may come crashing down on the chief executive as a result of natural or manmade disasters. Some governors are unfortunate enough to have a series of crises, none of their own making, befall the state during their administration. For instance, during Milton Shapp's eight years in office, Pennsylvania suffered two terrible floods, two hurricanes, extraordinarily severe winters, major ice storms, serious forest fires, drought, and forest devastation caused by an invasion of the gypsy moth.[14] Shapp could be forgiven for feeling like a biblical victim of God's Holy Wrath.

Governors as Managers   Because of the considerable political liabilities associated with the role of chief administrator, some of today's governors seek to avoid this responsibility. These are the **custodial (caretaker) governors**, who choose passive, perfunctory administrative roles. They generally concern themselves with ensuring that administrative agencies conduct their affairs ethically and with a reasonable degree of competence and are prepared to respond to a crisis.[15] Yet an increasing number of governors have assumed active management roles.

The growing ranks of **managerial governors** actively seek to provide policy leadership in state government, and to convince the bureaucracy to follow them. Strong managerial governors during the past twenty years have included Nelson Rockefeller and Mario Cuomo of New York and Lamar Alexander of Tennessee. All were highly goal-directed chief administrators who managed to make a strong impact on their state bureaucracies.[16] Carrying out the administrative role energetically and competently while paying enough attention to the competing gubernatorial roles to be re-elected appears to be the key.[17]

Former Pennsylvania governor Milton Shapp employed a unique approach to managing state government effectively while keeping his finger on the public pulse. He set up a citizens' hotline, a toll-free number that residents could call to discuss their problems and concerns with state government. This enabled Shapp and his staff to determine which services were being provided as intended and which were not.[18]

The constraints on the governor's managerial activities are not likely to lessen in the 1990s, nor are the potential political liabilities. The governors who courageously wade into the bureaucratic fray must invest a great deal of time and scarce political resources, yet they risk an embarrassing defeat that can drag their administration into debilitation and disrepute. Meanwhile, social and economic changes make the management of state government increasingly complex, and the need for active managerial governors more critical than ever before.

Ceremonial Leader

Some governors thrive on ceremony and others detest it, but all spend a large portion of their time on it. Former governors remember ceremonial duties as the second most demanding of the gubernatorial roles, just behind working with the legislature.[19] Cutting the ribbon for a new highway, laying the cornerstone of a high-rise office building, welcoming foreign businesspeople, receiving the queen of the Frog Jump Festival, announcing "Be a Good Neighbor Week," opening the state fair, and handing out high school or college diplomas are the kind of ceremonial duties that take a governor all over the state and often consume a larger portion of the workweek than any other role. Some former governors report spending more than half their time in duties relating to ceremony and public relations.[20]

To many management-oriented governors, the ceremonial role comprises a series of tedious events that divert them from more important responsibilities. They prefer to ask the lieutenant governor or another state official to perform these tasks for them. But a chief executive otherwise embroiled in struggles with the legislature and the bureaucracy may welcome a chance to shake hands and visit with the people. Moreover, the ceremonial role brings favorable publicity and cultivates voter support for the next election by keeping the governor in the spotlight and in touch with constituents.

Intergovernmental Coordinator

During the 1960s and 1970s many governors began to question whether their delegations in Congress were adequately representing state interests. The main factor that caught the governors' attention was the enormous growth in intergovernmental financial relations, as the number and size of federal grants-in-aid to states and localities mushroomed.

The governor serves as the major point of contact between his or her state and the president, Congress, and national agencies. For example, Governor Steve Cowper of Alaska coordinated cleanup efforts with the U.S. Coast Guard, the Environmental Protection Agency, and Exxon Corporation following the disastrous Alaskan oil spill in April 1989. State-to-state relations in order to manage conflicts or settle disputes over water pollution and other environmental concerns are carried out through the governor's office. At the local level, governors are involved in allocating grants-in-aid, promoting cooperation and coordination in economic development activities, and a variety of other matters.

The governor's role of intergovernmental coordinator is most visible at the national level, where she is aided by the National Governors' Association and the state's Washington office. In the 1960s the NGA was transformed from a social club into a lobbying and research organization with considerable clout. It now meets several times a year in full session and in regional groupings. The NGA's Center for Policy Research analyzes important issues and distributes its analyses to the states, and the State Services Branch offers practical and technical assistance to governors. In addition, more than thirty-two states have established Washington offices to fight for their interests in Congress, the White House, and, perhaps most important, the many federal agencies that interact with states on a daily basis.[21] A

Governors discuss critical issues of public policy during a recent meeting of the National Governors' Association. The NGA facilitates cooperation and mutual problem solving among state chief executives.

governor's official inquiry can help speed up the progress of federal grant-in-aid funds or gain special consideration for a new federal defense facility.

The governor's role as intergovernmental coordinator is becoming more important with each passing year. It reflects the elevated position of the states in the scheme of American federalism and increasing state importance in national and international affairs. Acting together, the governors have exercised national policy leadership on critical issues such as radioactive waste management (see Chapter 18), public education (see Chapter 15), welfare reform (see Chapter 3), and economic development (see Chapter 16).

Economic Development Promoter

As promoter of economic development, a governor works to recruit industry from out of state and promote economic growth from sources within the state. Governors attend industrial fairs, visit headquarters of firms interested in locating in the state, telephone promising business contacts, and welcome business leaders. The role may take the governor and the state economic development team to Japan, Korea, Europe, and other places, but it mostly entails making the state "good for business" through improvements in infrastructure and other strategies designed to entice out-of-state firms and encourage in-state businesses to expand. Often the governor's office of economic development directs a public relations campaign organized around themes such as "Arkansas Means Business" or "Maryland— The Incentives Have Never Been Better."

When a state enjoys success in economic development, the governor usually receives (or at least claims) a major portion of the credit. For example, Michael Dukakis campaigned for the Democratic nomination for president in 1988 by emphasizing Massachusetts's surge in high-technology industry, which turned a $300 million budget deficit into a surplus of $217 million (before economic growth leveled off and a budget shortfall reappeared in early 1989). Tennessee's governor, Lamar Alexander, convinced Nissan to build small trucks and General Motors to construct its state-of-the-art Saturn plant in his state rather than in any of numerous competing states. Sometimes the personal touch of a governor can mean the difference between an industrial plum and economic stagnation; or, in the case of Illinois, it can determine the nature of a summer's sports entertainment. Vigorous lobbying by Governor James R. Thompson in 1988 helped keep the White Sox in Chicago.

Party Leader

By claiming the top elected post in the state, the governor becomes the highest-ranking member of his or her political party. This role is not as powerful as it was several decades ago, when the governor had strong influence over party nominations for seats in the state legislature and executive branch. The widespread adoption of primaries, which have replaced party conventions, has put nominations largely in the hands of the voters. Still, the party remains useful to the governor for three principal reasons.[22] First, legislators from the governor's own party are more likely to help push executive programs successfully. Second, communication lines to the president and national cabinet members are more likely to be open when the president and the governor are members of the same party. Finally, the party remains the only effective means by which to win nomination to the governor's office.

A growing number of states have been removed from the ranks of one-party Democratic or Republican systems and placed on the two-party competitive list. The Republican party has become a major force in Texas politics after many years of Democratic dominance, while Indiana's legislature has gone from almost completely Republican to a 50–50 mix. This means that governors must work with the opposition if their legislative programs are to pass. In state legislatures still heavily dominated by one party, the governor must try to build a majority coalition of factions in support of his legislative agenda.

Today's Governors

As the foregoing discussion demonstrates, being governor is a high-pressure, physically demanding, emotionally draining job. As scholar Larry Sabato states, "Governors must possess many skills to be successful. They are expected to be adroit administrators, dexterous executives, expert judges of people, combative yet sensitive and inspiring politicians, decorous chiefs of state, shrewd party tacticians, and polished public relations managers."[23] The job is difficult from a professional perspective, but it is also hard on the governor's private life. It consumes an enormous amount of waking hours, at the expense of family activities and hobbies.

Fortunately, governorships are attracting better-qualified chief executives than ever before. These "New Breed" governors, first described by Larry Sabato in *Goodbye to Goodtime Charlie: The American Governorship Transformed*,[24] are a far cry from the figureheads of the eighteenth and nineteenth centuries and the back-slapping, cigar-smoking wheeler-dealers of the first half of the present century. Sabato's study of 357 governors holding office from 1950 to 1981 revealed "a thoroughly trained, well regarded, and capable new breed of state chief executive."[25] The trend continues into the 1990s, personified by "New South" governors Ray Mabus of Mississippi, Bill Clinton of Arkansas, and Buddy Roemer of Louisiana. Table 7.1 provides a list of the 1989 governors.

The governor of today is younger, better educated, and better prepared for the job than his or her predecessors. The average age was forty-six to forty-eight during the 1970s, compared with fifty-one during the 1940s. (The minimum age ranges from eighteen in California and Washington to thirty in most states.) Formal education has averaged around eighteen years since 1950 (the general population averages 11.1 years),[26] and approximately two-thirds of the governors since 1960 have held law degrees. About one-half of today's governors paid their political dues in state legislatures, gaining an understanding of important issues confronting the state, a working familiarity with influential figures in government and the private sector, and a practical knowledge of the legislative process and other inner secrets of state government. Thirty percent have served previously as an elected state official, and some 26 percent have a background in law enforcement (serving as solicitor, sheriff, or attorney general). Around 15 percent have held a local elective office. The attractiveness of the governor's office is evident in the fact that four recently elected chief executives, including James Florio of New Jersey, left a congressional seat to take office. Only 8 percent of the governors serving from 1970 to 1987 did not hold a previous position in government.[27]

Although still predominantly white Anglo-Saxon males, today's governors are more representative of population characteristics than former chief executives were. In 1989, Virginia elected the first black governor since Reconstruction, L. Douglas Wilder. Several Hispanics have served as governors in recent years, including Tony Anaya of New Mexico and Bob Martinez of Florida. In earlier years, several women succeeded their husbands as governor, but since 1974 five women have won governorships on their own: the late Ella Grasso (Connecticut, 1974, 1978), Dixy Lee Ray (Washington, 1976), Martha Layne Collins (Kentucky, 1983), Madeleine Kunin (Vermont, 1984, 1986, 1988), and Kay Orr (Nebraska, 1986). (In addition, Rose Mofford became governor of Arizona in 1988 when Evan Mecham was forced out of office.) Profile 7.1 looks at Kunin's career.

Gubernatorial Campaigns

The lure of the governorship must be weighed against the financial costs. It has become immensely expensive to campaign for the office. Because candidates can no longer rely on their political party to support them, they must solicit huge sums of money from donors to pay for the new technology of campaigning—political consultants, opinion polls, advertisements in the print and broadcast media, telephone banks, and direct mailings. Moreover, the growing attractiveness of the office has led to more competitive (and expensive) primary and general election races. During the spring 1986 party primaries, 107 candidates actively sought the governor's office in only fifteen states, and fifteen individuals filed for their state's top office in Nebraska alone. To date, the most costly governor's race was the 1986 election in Texas, in which Bill Clements, Jr., defeated incumbent governor Mark White; $34.6 million was spent. This official figure does not include

Table 7.1   1990 Occupants of the Nation's Statehouses

State	Governor	Party	Year of next election
Alabama	Guy Hunt	Republican	1990
Alaska	Steve Cowper	Democratic	1990
Arizona	Rose Mofford	Democratic	1990
Arkansas	Bill Clinton	Democratic	1990
California	George Deukmejian	Republican	1990
Colorado	Roy R. Romer	Democratic	1990
Connecticut	William A. O'Neill	Democratic	1990
Delaware	Michael N. Castle	Republican	1992
Florida	Bob Martinez	Republican	1990
Georgia	Joe Frank Harris	Democratic	1990
Hawaii	John Waihee	Democratic	1990
Idaho	Cecil D. Andrus	Democratic	1990
Illinois	James R. Thompson	Republican	1990
Indiana	Evan Bayh	Democratic	1992
Iowa	Terry E. Branstad	Republican	1990
Kansas	Mike Hayden	Republican	1990
Kentucky	Wallace G. Wilkinson	Democratic	1991
Louisiana	Charles "Buddy" Roemer	Democratic	1991
Maine	John R. McKernan, Jr.	Republican	1990
Maryland	William Donald Schaefer	Democratic	1990
Massachusetts	Michael S. Dukakis	Democratic	1990
Michigan	James J. Blanchard	Democratic	1990
Minnesota	Rudy Perpich	Democratic	1990
Mississippi	Ray Mabus	Democratic	1991
Missouri	John Ashcroft	Republican	1992

hidden donations, such as free transportation, telephones, and other in-kind contributions.

Several expenditure patterns have been identified in gubernatorial races. Elections tend to cost more when the contest

- is close.
- involves unseating an incumbent.
- involves a partisan shift (a Democrat succeeds a Republican, or vice versa).

Table 7.1   1990 Occupants of the Nation's Statehouses *(cont.)*

State	Governor	Party	Year of next election
Montana	Stan Stephens	Republican	1992
Nebraska	Kay A. Orr	Republican	1990
Nevada	Richard H. Bryan	Democratic	1990
New Hampshire	Judd Gregg	Republican	1990
New Jersey	James J. Florio	Democratic	1993
New Mexico	Garrey E. Carruthers	Republican	1990
New York	Mario M. Cuomo	Democratic	1990
North Carolina	James G. Martin	Republican	1992
North Dakota	George Sinner	Democratic	1992
Ohio	Richard F. Celeste	Democratic	1990
Oklahoma	Henry Bellmon	Republican	1990
Oregon	Neil Goldschmidt	Democratic	1990
Pennsylvania	Robert P. Casey	Democratic	1990
Rhode Island	Edward DiPrete	Republican	1990
South Carolina	Carroll A. Campbell, Jr.	Republican	1990
South Dakota	George S. Mickelson	Republican	1990
Tennessee	Ned Ray McWherter	Democratic	1990
Texas	William P. Clements, Jr.	Republican	1990
Utah	Norman H. Bangerter	Republican	1992
Vermont	Madeleine M. Kunin	Democratic	1990
Virginia	L. Douglas Wilder	Democratic	1993
Washington	Booth Gardner	Democratic	1992
West Virginia	Gaston Caperton	Democratic	1992
Wisconsin	Tommy G. Thompson	Republican	1990
Wyoming	Mike Sullivan	Democratic	1990

■ is held in a highly populated state, particularly if it is also large in territory (e.g., Texas, California, New York).[28]

On a cost-per-vote basis, races in states with a widely scattered population or hard-to-reach media markets, such as Alaska or Nevada, tend to be most expensive. Cost per vote in the 1986 gubernatorial elections ranged from $26.24 in Alaska to only 74 cents in South Dakota.[29]

Money means a lot in politics, but it doesn't mean everything. One contemporary veteran of political campaigns reflects that "everyone knows

PROFILE 7.1
Governor Madeleine Kunin of Vermont

The first woman governor of Vermont, and the seventh in the nation, was born in Zurich, Switzerland, in 1933 to a German-Jewish father and a Swiss mother. As the Nazis advanced through Europe during the summer of 1940, Madeleine (May) Kunin escaped to the United States with her brother and widowed mother.

Beginning her career as a journalist, Kunin became interested in politics after spending the year 1970 in Switzerland, at the time when Swiss women were struggling to win the right to vote in national elections. Determined to get involved in American politics, she began her climb up the political ladder, later observing that "You have to build your credentials as a candidate, not just as a woman."[1] Kunin, a Democrat, won a seat in the Vermont House of Representatives in 1972 and was twice re-elected. Her first success in statewide politics was winning the lieutenant governorship in 1978 and 1980, serving under Republican governor Richard Snelling.

When Snelling announced that he would not run for another term, Kunin threw her hat into the ring. Even after Snelling reversed himself and re-entered the race, Kunin stayed in the contest against the popular incumbent, losing the vote 56 percent to 44 percent but attracting many supporters. "There's an important message there for women candidates who may face tough races the first time around," she said. "There are degrees of losing, and if you lose respectably in a tough race, you can emerge

that half the money spent in a political campaign is wasted. The trouble is that nobody knows which half."[30] Lewis Lehrman spent $13.9 million in the 1982 race in New York, which he lost, and Tom Bradley sacrificed $8.7 million to lose in California that same year. Perhaps participants are finally beginning to discover which half is wasted. According to expenditure reports for 1982–87, the rate of increase for costs of governors' races is slowing. A principal reason may be that the new campaign technologies are now in place throughout the states. The tremendous leap in campaign expenditures during the 1970s and 1980s may have been a one-time phenomenon.[31]

An incumbent governor running for re-election stands an excellent chance of victory; approximately 80 percent have retained their seats since 1970. Incumbents enjoy a number of important advantages, including the opportunity to cultivate both popularity with the voters and campaign

again."[2] She did again emerge, winning the governor's seat in 1984 against a different Republican candidate with only 50.2 percent of the vote. Kunin then easily won re-election in 1986 and 1988.

Kunin has been an effective governor, winning a number of impressive legislative battles. In her first term alone, she achieved a 25 percent increase in education funding, a rural enterprise zone law, a state venture capital fund, and won an environmental fight with the state's powerful ski industry. Although Kunin has often concentrated on gender-neutral issues, in 1989 she came to the forefront of the abortion rights debate, becoming one of the nation's highest ranking public officials to speak out strongly for abortion rights.[3]

Governor Kunin has developed her own political style. Voters see Kunin as a down-to-earth person and simply call her Madeleine.

Executive branch employees find her management style open and frank. Some critics say she is too open to various points of view, calling her "straddlin' Madeleine." Kunin counters, "What is different for women is that . . . as we exercise power we are judged not only on our own terms, but we continue to be measured against traditional male standards." Is a female governor different? "The most obvious difference, of course, is that being a woman is an issue at all," Kunin responds.[4]

[1] Marge Runnion, "Once a Refugee from Nazi Europe, Madeleine Kunin Takes Charge as Vermont's First Woman Governor," *People Weekly*, April 1, 1985, pp. 102–3.
[2] Nancy Day, "Madeleine Kunin," *Working Woman*, July 1986, p. 74.
[3] John Milne, "Kunin Gains as Abortion Debate Deepens," *Boston Globe*, July 16, 1989, pp. 31, 33.
[4] Day, p. 74.

donations from interest groups. However, re-election is no sure thing. Economic and budget woes led Texas voters to toss Mark White out of office in 1986, and "Tony the Taxer" Earl lost the Wisconsin governorship in 1986 because of political fallout from a tax increase.

Formal Powers

A variety of powers are attached to the governor's office. Governors' **formal powers**—those provided for in the state's constitution—include the tenure of the office, the power of appointment, the power to veto legislation, the responsibility for preparing the budget, the authority to reorganize the executive branch, and the right to use professional staff in the governor's office. These powers give governors the *potential* to carry out the duties of office as they see fit. However, the formal powers vary considerably from state to state. Some governors' offices are considered strong and others weak. Also, the fact that these powers are available does not mean that they are used fully or even partly. Equally important are the **informal powers** that governors have at their disposal. These are potentially empowering features of the job or the person that are not expressly provided for in law. Many of the informal powers are associated with personal traits on which the chief executive relies to carry out the duties and responsibilities of the office.

Both sets of powers have increased over the past several decades, and governors are more influential than ever before because of their enhanced formal powers and the personal qualities they bring to the state capital. The most successful governors are those who employ their informal powers to maximize the formal powers. The term for this concept is *synergism,* which means a condition in which the total effect of two distinct sets of attributes working together is greater than the sum of their effects when acting independently. An influential governor is one who can skillfully combine formal and informal powers to maximum effectiveness.

Tenure Power

There are two aspects of the governor's tenure power: the duration (number of years) of a term of office, and the number of consecutive terms that an individual governor may serve. Both have been slowly but steadily expanding over the past two hundred years. From the onerous restriction to a single one-year term of office placed on ten of the first thirteen governors, the duration has moved to the standard today of two or more four-year terms (see Table 7.2). In addition, gubernatorial elections have become distinct from national elections, as most states now hold them in non-presidential election years. This ensures that the voters focus their attention on issues important to the state rather than allow national politics to contaminate state election outcomes.

The importance of longer consecutive terms of office is readily apparent. A two-year governorship condemns the incumbent to a perpetual re-election campaign. As soon as the winner takes office, he or she must begin planning for the next election. For a new governor, the initial year in office is typically spent getting used to the job. In addition, the first-term, first-year chief executive must live with the budget priorities adopted by his or her predecessor. A two-year governorship therefore does not encourage success in the roles of chief legislator or policy leader. Nor does it enable the governor to have much effect on the bureaucracy, whose old hands are likely to treat the governor as a mere bird of passage, making him virtually a lame duck when his term begins. As Governor Alfred E. Smith of New York observed after serving four two-year terms during the 1920s, "One hardly has time to locate the knob on the Statehouse door."[32]

Table 7.2   Tenure Provisions for Governors

Four-year term, no restrictions on re-election	Arizona California Colorado Connecticut Idaho Illinois Iowa Massachusetts Michigan	Minnesota Montana New York North Dakota Texas Utah Washington Wisconsin Wyoming
Four-year term, restricted to two terms	Alabama Alaska Arkansas Delaware Florida Georgia Hawaii Indiana Kansas Louisiana Maine Maryland Missouri	Nebraska Nevada New Jersey North Carolina Ohio Oklahoma Oregon Pennsylvania South Carolina South Dakota Tennessee West Virginia
Four-year term, consecutive re-election prohibited	Kentucky Mississippi	New Mexico Virginia
Two-year term, no restrictions on re-election	New Hampshire Rhode Island	Vermont

Source: The Book of the States, 1986–87 (Lexington, Ky.: Council of State Governments, 1986). Reprinted with permission. Copyright by The Council of State Governments.

In contrast, the governor who is restricted to a single four-year term is a bit less confined in carrying out his responsibilities. Still, he has only two years to put his programs and priorities in place, sandwiched on one side by the initial "learning year" and on the other by the lame-duck period. The incumbent needs another four-year term to design new programs properly, acquire the necessary legislative support to put them into place, and get a handle on the bureaucracy by appointing competent political supporters to top posts. Eight years in office also enhances the governor's inter-governmental role, particularly by giving him or her sufficient time to win leadership positions in organizations such as the National Governors' Association. The record of an eight-year chief executive stands on its own, uncontaminated by the successes or failures of the office's previous inhabitant.

The average time actually served by governors has grown steadily since 1955 as a result of fewer restrictions on tenure. The longest gubernatorial incumbencies of recent years are those of Richard D. Lamm of Colorado, who retired after twelve years, and Illinois governor Jim Thompson, who started his fourth four-year term in 1986. When he finishes his present term, Thompson will set a twentieth-century record. (He has decided not to run again.) Long periods in office strengthen the governor's position as policy leader, chief legislator, chief administrator, and intergovernmental coordinator, as shown by the policy legacies left on their respective states by Lamm and Thompson.

There is still some resistance to unlimited tenure. More than one re-election creates fears of political machines and possible abuses of office. More pragmatically, a long period of a "safe governorship" can result in stagnation and a loss of vigor in the office. Even in states that do not restrict governors to two consecutive terms, an informal custom of not seeking a third term exists. As demonstrated in Politics and Policy 7.1, life does go on after the governorship.

Appointment Power

Surveys of past governors indicate that they consider appointment power to be the most important weapon in their arsenal when it comes to managing the state bureaucracy. The ability to appoint one's own people to top positions in the executive branch also enhances the policy management role. When individuals who share the governor's basic philosophy and feel loyal to the chief executive's programs direct the operations of state government, the governor's policies are more likely to be successful. Strong appointment authority can even help the governor's legislative role. The actual or implicit promise of important administrative and especially judicial positions can generate a surprising amount of support from ambitious lawmakers.

Unfortunately for today's governors, Jacksonian democracy lives on in the plural executive. Most states continue to provide for popular election of numerous officials in the executive branch, including insurance commissioners, public utility commissioners, and secretaries of agriculture. Proponents of popular election claim that these officials make political decisions and therefore should be directly responsible to the electorate. Opponents contend that governors and legislators can make these decisions more properly, based on the recommendations of appointed executive branch professionals who are not beholden to special interests.

Life After the Governorship

For those unable or unwilling to seek re-election, life after the governor's mansion often means a lucrative law practice or a return to a business career. All told, approximately 60 percent of governors retire from political life upon leaving the office. Former governor Lamar Alexander of Tennessee, for example, moved his family to Australia for six months to be "as far away from Nashville and still be on earth."

Alas, the transition from chief executive to ordinary citizen is not always easy. Former Utah governor Calvin L. Rampton, asked what he missed most, replied, "I miss my airplane and my highway patrol driver. I never realized how much of a man's life he spends on looking for a parking place."[1] After fourteen years as governor of Michigan, William Milliken rented a car to brush up on his rusty driving skills. Driving in New York City, he abruptly cut in front of a cab driver. The cabbie rolled down his window and made an obscene gesture at the governor. Milliken later remarked, "I realized then that my transition out was complete."[2]

Other former governors stay active in politics. In the past the governorship served as a natural stepping-stone to the U.S. Senate. In 1988, fourteen senators were former governors. But today's governors are less likely to seek a seat in the Senate. After the heady experience of the power, prestige, and perquisites of the top political post in the state, becoming merely one among a hundred senators (and starting on the bottom rung of the seniority ladder) is not an altogether pleasing prospect.

Former governors have also acquitted themselves well as state and federal judges, national cabinet heads, vice presidents, and foreign ambassadors. Between 1976 and 1988, former governors Jimmy Carter and Ronald Reagan occupied the White House. Another, Michael Dukakis, ran unsuccessfully for the presidency in 1988 as a sitting governor. Governors appear to be well suited for the presidency in many respects, given their experience in balancing budgets and dealing with the other demanding responsibilities of a chief executive. Their only recognized shortcoming is in the field of foreign affairs. Yet even here governors develop expertise by interacting with foreign officials while promoting state economic development. All things considered, life after being governor can be interesting and rewarding.

[1] National Governor's Association, Center for Policy Research, *Reflections on Being Governor* (Washington, D.C.: NGA, 1981), p. 185.
[2] George Weeks, "Gubernatorial Transition: Leaving There," *State Government* 57 (March 1984): 73–78.

Perhaps the "correct" answer depends on the office under consideration. Those offices that tend to cater to special interests, such as agriculture, insurance, and education, probably should be appointive. Less substantive offices (secretary of state, treasurer) probably should be appointive as well. However, it makes sense to elect an auditor and an attorney general, because they require some independence in carrying out their responsibilities. (The auditor oversees the management and spending of state monies; the attorney general is concerned with the legality of executive and legislative branch activities.)

Many governors are further weakened by their inability to appoint the heads of state agencies, boards, and commissions. These high-ranking officials make policy decisions in the executive branch, but they may owe their jobs in whole or in part to the legislature, which appoints them with (or, in some cases, without) the consent of the governor. Even though nominally in charge of these agencies, the governor may have limited authority.

The fragmented nature of power in the executive branch diminishes accountability and frustrates governors. Former Oregon governor Tom McCall once lamented that "we have run our state like a pick-up orchestra, where the members meet at a dance, shake hands with each other, and start to play."[33] When the assorted individuals are not appointed by the chief executive, their performance may lack harmony, to say the least.

Most reformers interested in "good government" agree on the need to consolidate power in the governor's office by reducing the number of statewide elected officials and increasing the power of appointment to policy-related posts in the executive branch. But the number of elected executive branch officials has remained virtually the same since 1965.[34] Table 7.3 shows the range and number of separately elected officials. The largest number is in North Dakota, where twelve statewide offices are filled through elections: governor, lieutenant governor, secretary of state, attorney general, agricultural commissioner, chief state school officer, treasurer, labor commissioner, tax commissioner, two insurance commissioners, and utility commissioner. At the bottom of the list are the reformer's ideal states, Alaska, Maine, and New Jersey, all of which elect only the governor. The average number of elected officials is about eight.[35]

Why has it been so difficult to abolish multiple statewide offices? Primarily because incumbent tax commissioners, agricultural commissioners, and others have strong supporters in the electorate. Special interest groups, such as the insurance industry, benefit from having an elected official—the insurance commissioner—representing their concerns at the highest level of state government. They can be counted on for solid resistance to proposals to make the office appointive. Additional resistance may be credited to the legacy of Jacksonian democracy; many citizens simply like having an opportunity to vote on a large number of executive branch officials.

Appointment powers are weakened by separately elected or appointed officials, but governors do select nearly 50 percent of the top executive

Table 7.3 Separately Elected State Officials

Office	Number of states electing
Governor	50
Attorney general	43
Lieutenant governor	42
Treasurer	38
Secretary of state	36
Education (superintendent or board)	29
Auditor	25
Secretary of agriculture	12
Public utilities commissioner	11
Controller	10
Insurance commissioner	8
Land commissioner	5
Labor commissioner	4
Mines commissioner	1
Adjutant general (National Guard)	1

Source: Adapted from *The Book of the States, 1984–85* (Lexington, Ky.: Council of State Governments, 1984), pp. 72–73.

branch personnel. Governors have been particularly adept at winning appointment power for top posts in new state agencies for human services, the environment, natural resources, highways, and agriculture, although approval of one or both houses of the legislature usually must be obtained[36] (see Table 7.4).

Professional Jobs in State Government The vast majority of jobs in the states are filled through objective civil service (merit system) rules and processes. Governors usually are quite content to avoid meddling with civil service positions (see Chapter 8), and a few have actually sought to transfer many **patronage** appointments—those based on personal or party loyalty —to an independent, merit-based civil service.[37] Gubernatorial sacrifice of patronage power is comprehensible in view of the time and headaches associated with naming political supporters to jobs in the bureaucracy. There is always the possibility of embarrassment or scandal if the governor accidentally appoints a person with a criminal record, a clear conflict of interest, or other problems, and those who are denied coveted appointments are likely to be angry. One governor is quoted as stating: "I got into a lot of hot water because I refused to appoint some of the more prominent

Table 7.4   Appointment Powers of the Governors

Very strong	Connecticut	New York
	Delaware	North Carolina
	Hawaii	Pennsylvania
	Kentucky	Vermont
	Massachusetts	Virginia
	Minnesota	West Virginia
	New Jersey	
Strong	Arkansas	Iowa
	California	Maryland
	Colorado	Ohio
	Illinois	South Dakota
	Indiana	Tennessee
Moderate	Arizona	Montana
	Georgia	Nebraska
	Kansas	New Hampshire
	Louisiana	Rhode Island
	Maine	Utah
Weak	Alabama	New Mexico
	Alaska	North Dakota
	Idaho	Oklahoma
	Michigan	Oregon
	Mississippi	Washington
	Missouri	Wisconsin
	Nevada	Wyoming
Very weak	Florida	
	South Carolina	
	Texas	

Source: The Book of the States, 1980–81 (Lexington, Ky.: Council of State Governments, 1980), pp. 195–97, and updated by the authors. Reprinted with permission. Copyright by The Council of State Governments.

Democrats around the state." According to another, who was about to name a new member of a state commission, "I now have twenty-three good friends who want on the Racing Commission. [Soon] I'll have twenty-two enemies and one ingrate."[38] A governor benefits from a stable, competent civil service that hires, pays, and promotes on the basis of knowledge of the job rather than party affiliation or friendship with a legislator or other politician.[39]

The Power to Fire The power of the governor to hire is not accompanied by the power to fire. Except in cases of extreme misbehavior or corruption, it is very difficult to remove a subordinate from office. For instance, if a governor attempts to dismiss the secretary of agriculture, he or she can anticipate an orchestrated roar of outrage from legislators, bureaucrats, and farm groups. The upshot is that "the political costs of firing can be greater than those of living with the problems."[40] In settings where the governor indirectly appoints top officials, it may be nearly impossible to dismiss an undesirable employee. For example, in Missouri the governor appoints eight members of the State Board of Education, who then choose a commissioner of education. The governor cannot sanction or remove the commissioner except through the State Board.[41] In the case of merit-selected civil servants, formal dismissal procedures bypass the chief executive.

Good appointments to top agency posts are the best way for a governor to influence the bureaucracy. By carefully choosing a competent and loyal agency head, the governor can more readily bring about significant changes in the programs and operations of that agency. Where appointment powers are circumscribed, the chief executive must muster his or her informal powers to influence activities of the state bureaucracy, or rely on the reasoned judgment of professional civil servants.

Veto Power

The power to veto bills passed by the legislature is an important method for exercising the role of chief legislator. It is also a means for influencing the bureaucracy; the governor can strike out an appropriation for a particular agency's programs if that agency has antagonized the governor. Often the mere threat of a veto is enough to persuade a recalcitrant legislature to see the governor's point of view and compromise on the language of a bill. Vetos are not easy to override. Most states require a majority of three-fifths or two-thirds of the legislature, depending on the type of veto the governor has employed.

Types of Vetos There are several variations of the veto. The **package veto** is the governor's rejection of a bill in its entirety. All governors except North Carolina's hold package veto authority. (Almost every year the incumbent governor asks the North Carolina legislature for this power, and the request is just as regularly rejected.) The package veto is the oldest form available to governors, having been adopted first in the original constitutions of New York and Massachusetts.

A **line item veto** allows the governor to strike out one or more sections of a bill, permitting the remaining provisions to become law. It is not available at the national level, much to the frustration of recent presidents. The item veto was first adopted by Georgia and Texas in 1868, and quickly spread to other states.[42] Only Indiana, Maine, Nevada, New Hampshire, Rhode Island, Vermont, and, of course, North Carolina forbid this gubernatorial power. Eleven states permit a hybrid form of item veto in which the governor may choose to reduce the dollar amount of a proposed item in order to hold down state expenditures or cut back support for a particular program.

A **pocket veto,** which is available in fifteen states, allows the governor to reject a bill by refusing to sign it after the legislature has adjourned. In three states (Hawaii, Utah, Virginia) the legislature can reconvene to vote on a pocket veto. Otherwise, the bill dies. A governor might use the pocket veto to avoid giving the legislature a chance to override a formal veto, or to abstain from going on record against a proposed piece of legislation.

A fourth type of veto is the **executive amendment,** formally provided for in fifteen states and informally used in several others. With this power a governor may veto a bill, recommend changes that would make the bill acceptable, and then send it back to the legislature for reconsideration. If the legislature concurs with his or her suggestions, the governor signs the bill into law.[43]

Use of the Veto   The actual use of the veto varies by time and state. Some states, such as California and New York, often record high numbers of vetos, while others, like Virginia, report few. On average, governors veto around 5 percent of the bills reaching their desks.[44] The variation reflects tensions and conflicts between the governor and the legislature. The largest number of vetos typically occurs in states with divided party control of the executive and legislative branches. During the mid-1980s, Governors Bruce Babbitt of Arizona and John Carlin of Kansas liberally employed the veto in dealing with legislatures dominated by the opposition party.

Although the overall rate of veto utilization has remained steady, the percentage of successful legislative overrides has increased in the past two decades from 2 percent to 8 percent or more, depending on the year.[45] This is an indication of the growing strength and assertiveness of state legislatures, an increase in conflict between the executive and legislative branches, and the prevalence of split-party government. Different party affiliations of the governor and the legislative majority probably provoke more vetos than any other situation, as party ideology and platforms openly clash.

Where mutual respect and cooperation prevail between the two branches, the governor rarely needs to threaten or actually use the veto. Most governors interact with the legislature throughout the bill adoption process. Before rejecting a bill, the governor will request comments from key legislators, affected state agencies, and concerned interest groups. He may ask the attorney general for a legal opinion. And before actually vetoing proposed legislation, the governor usually provides advance notification to legislative leaders.[46]

Budgetary Power

The governor's budget effectively sets the legislative agenda at the beginning of each session. By framing the important policy issues and attaching price tags to them, the governor can determine the scope and direction of budgetary debates in the legislature and ensure that they reflect his or her overall philosophy on taxing and spending. All but three governors now have the authority to appoint (and remove) the budget director and to formulate and submit the executive budget to the legislature. In Mississippi, South Carolina, and Texas budget authority is shared with the legislature or with other elected executive branch officials. In Mississippi and Texas, two budgets are prepared each year, one by the governor and one by a legislative budget board.

Since full budgetary authority is normally housed in the office of the chief executive, the governor not only drives the budgetary process in the legislature but also enjoys a source of important leverage in the bureaucracy. The executive budget may be used to influence programs, spending, and other activities of state agencies.[47] For example, uncooperative administrators may discover that their agency's slice of the budget pie is smaller than expected, while those who are attentive to the concerns of the governor may receive strong financial support. Rational, objective criteria usually determine departmental budget allocations, but a subtle threat from the governor's office does wonders for agency cooperation.[48]

Reorganization Power

Reorganization power is primarily relevant in the governor's role of chief administrator. It refers to the governor's ability to create and abolish state agencies, departments, and other offices and to reallocate administrative responsibilities among them. Reorganizations are usually aimed at the upper levels of the bureaucracy, in order to streamline the executive branch and thereby make it work more efficiently and effectively. The basic premise is that the governor, as chief manager of the bureaucracy, needs the authority to alter administrative structures and processes to meet changing political, economic, and citizen demands. For instance, serious and recurring problems in delivering social services may call for a new social services department with expanded powers. A governor with strong reorganization power can do this without approval of the legislature.

Traditionally, legislatures have been responsible for organization of state government, and in the absence of a constitutional amendment to the contrary or a statutory grant of reorganization power to the governor, they still are. A survey of thirty-nine governors during the mid-1960s asked what powers they lacked that could help them be more effective. Forty-six percent named reorganization,[49] second only to appointment power (67 percent). Apparently many of the legislatures paid attention and recognized the need to grant their chief executives more discretion in organizing the bureaucracy.

Today, twenty-four states specifically authorize their chief executive to reorganize the bureaucracy through **executive order.** This means that the governor can make needed administrative changes when she deems it necessary. All governors are permitted through constitution (eight states), statute (thirty-six), or custom (six) to issue directives to the executive branch in times of emergency, such as natural disasters or civil unrest.[50]

Administrative reorganization takes place under the assumption that properly designed government improves the effectiveness of performance by cutting down on duplication, waste, and inefficiency.[51] A reorganization in Iowa in the mid-1980s is a case in point. Governor Terry Branstad's restructuring program eliminated fifty departments and forty-two boards and commissions, along with almost a thousand state government positions. Total savings have been estimated at $40 million.[52]

Types of Reorganization   Virtually all states have some form of cabinet structure to advise the governor and to coordinate policies and programs. There are three possible formats within a cabinet structure. The first, the **cabinet system,** is composed of state agency heads representing the most important departments, such as administration and finance, corrections, health, social services, transportation, public works, agriculture, natural resources, and labor. The department heads may meet regularly as a cabinet, or at the call of the governer. Such meetings can improve coordination, communications, and interpersonal relations among executive branch officials. Some governors, including James Hunt of North Carolina and Pierre du Pont of Delaware, have held regular cabinet retreats away from the immediate pressures of the capital.[53]

A second format is the **subcabinet system,** which is currently in use in approximately half the states. Here, agency heads are assigned to functional groups to provide the governor with administrative and policy advice in specific fields such as economic development, human services, and the environment. Subcabinets are helpful for concentrating attention on the most pressing items on the state policy agenda and exploring methods for coordinating attacks on especially difficult problems that cut across agency lines, such as hazardous waste spills or drug-related violence.

A third organizational format is the **task force,** an ad hoc assemblage of agency heads, other high-level officials, and sometimes private individuals brought together on a temporary basis to confront a special problem or issue. For instance, Governor William Milliken created a task force on high technology to offer advice on improving Michigan's technological base for industrial development. Several states have used this form of organization to manage block grants or to plan for the possibility of a natural disaster.[54]

A growing number of states are making use of all three organizational formats to cope with increasingly complicated economic and technological policy issues. New experiments with executive branch reorganization are also appearing. For example, New Jersey governor Thomas Kean focused on internal (intradepartmental) restructuring of state agencies in 1982. A team of managers from the public and private sectors found that too many midlevel managers were clustered in the agencies, making the organization chart resemble "a nuclear reactor rather than a pyramid."[55] An evaluation of changes implemented during the subsequent reorganization, which included streamlining management levels, grouping similar functions together, and reallocating resources, found most public managers agreeing that improved performance resulted. An advantage of the New Jersey approach is that legislative approval is not normally required for intradepartmental reorganization.

The Politics of Reorganization Reorganization is a politically charged process. Mere talk of it sounds alarms in the halls of the legislature, in the honeycombs of state office buildings, and in the offices of interest groups. Reorganization attempts usually spawn bitter controversy and conflict inside and outside state government as assorted vested interests fight for favorite programs and organizational turf. As a consequence, reorganization proposals are frequently defeated or amended in the legislature, or even abandoned by a discouraged chief executive. James L. Garnett's study of state reorganizations attempted between 1900 and 1975 discovered that almost 70 percent resulted in rejection of the plan in part or in its entirety.[56] Even when enacted, reorganizations may generate extreme opposition from entrenched interests in the bureaucracy, and in the final analysis be judged a failure. In the memorable words of former Kansas governor Robert F. Bennett: "In the abstract, [reorganization] is, without a doubt, one of the finest and one of the most palatable theories ever espoused by a modern day politician. But in practice . . . it becomes the loss of a job for your brother or your sister, your uncle or your aunt. It becomes the closing of an office on which you have learned to depend. . . . So there in many instances may be more agony than anything else in this reorganization process."[57] Most governors who have fought the battle for reorganization would concur. Perhaps this helps explain the rarity of far-reaching executive branch restructurings in the 1980s.

Staffing Power

The governor relies on staff for policy analysis and advice, liaison with the legislature, and assistance in managing the bureaucracy. Professional staff members are a significant component of the governor's team, composing a corps of political loyalists who help the governor cope with the multiple roles of the office. From the handful of political cronies and secretaries of several decades ago, the staff of the governor's office has grown in number and in quality. The average size of professional and clerical staff rose from eleven in 1956 to thirty-four in 1979.[58] It is approaching fifty today. In the larger, more highly populated states, such as New York and California, staff may number well over one hundred.[59] The principal staff positions of the governor's office may include the chief of staff, legislative liaison, budget director, planning director, scheduler, legal counsel, press secretary, and intergovernmental coordinator. Some governors have also established strong offices of policy management along the lines of the national Office of Management and Budget.

A question of serious concern, especially in the states whose governors have large staffs, is whether too much power and influence is being placed in the hands of nonelected officials. Clearly, professional staff members have been highly influential in developing and promoting policies for the governor in some states, particularly in cases where the governor lets the staff have free rein. In other states the chief executive is very much in control, relying on staff primarily for drafting bills and providing technical information.[60] By their physical and intellectual proximity to the governor, staff members are in a highly advantageous position to influence their boss. By serving as the major funnel for policy information and advice, they can affect the governor's decisions by controlling the flow of information.

Nonetheless, the dramatic growth in the scope and number of activities engaged in by contemporary governors demands a certain amount of staff. The institutionalized governorship appears to be a practical necessity of governance in the larger, highly populated states, and a probable future development in the smaller ones as well.

The Relevance of the Formal Powers

Table 7.5 categorizes the states on the strength of the governor's formal powers of office. As we have noted, governors have won stronger powers during the past twenty-five years. But how helpful are the formal powers? In spite of the major transformation of the governor's office, governors remain relatively weak because of the setting of state government. They must function within a highly complex and politically charged environment with formal authority that is quite circumscribed. Because of the nature of our federal system, the national government effectively strips them of control over many policy and administrative concerns. Moreover, the business of state government is carried out in a fishbowl, open to regular scrutiny by the media, interest groups, and other interested parties.[61] Notwithstanding the continued constraints on the exercise of their authority, however, today's governors as a group are more effective than their predecessors in carrying out their varied responsibilities. The formal powers of the office have been substantially strengthened, and highly qualified people are serving as chief executives.

Table 7.5   Formal Powers of the Governors

Very strong	Hawaii	New Jersey
	Maryland	New York
	Massachusetts	Pennsylvania
	Minnesota	Utah
Strong	Alaska	Iowa
	Arizona	Maine
	California	Michigan
	Colorado	Montana
	Connecticut	South Dakota
	Delaware	Tennessee
	Idaho	Wyoming
	Illinois	
Moderate	Alabama	North Dakota
	Arkansas	Ohio
	Florida	Oklahoma
	Georgia	Oregon
	Indiana	Rhode Island
	Kansas	Vermont
	Kentucky	Virginia
	Louisiana	Washington
	Missouri	West Virginia
	Nebraska	Wisconsin
	New Mexico	
Weak	Mississippi	North Carolina
	Nevada	South Carolina
	New Hampshire	Texas

In theory, governors with strong formal powers, such as those in New Jersey, Maryland, and Minnesota, should be more effective than their counterparts in Texas, New Hampshire, and Nevada. In practice that tends to be true—but not always. The potential for power and influence must not be confused with action. A governor with strong formal powers enjoys the capacity to serve effectively, but she may choose not to do so, or for various reasons be unable to utilize the formal powers properly. Alternatively, a governor with weak formal powers can nonetheless be an effective, strong chief executive if she actively and skillfully applies the levers of power given to the governor in the constitution.

Informal Powers

No doubt a governor with strong formal powers has an advantage over one without them. But at least equally important for a successful governorship is the exploitation of the informal powers of the office. These are the authoritative and influence-wielding aspects that are not directly attached to any office through statute or constitution, but are associated with the human being who happens to occupy the governor's mansion.

The informal powers help transform the capacity for action into effective action. They react in synergy with the formal powers to create a successful governorship. An incumbent chief executive in the "strong governor" state of New York will be hopelessly weak unless he also uses his personal assets in performing the multiple roles of the office. Alternatively, a chief executive in a "weak governor" state such as South Carolina can be remarkably successful if he fully employs his informal powers[62] to become a "change master"—one who excels in persuading his state to adopt new ideas.[63]

The informal powers are not as easy to specify as the formal powers are. However, they generally include such tools of persuasion as popular support, public relations and media skills, negotiating and bargaining skills, prestige of the office, special sessions, pork barrel and patronage, and such personal characteristics as youth, ambition, experience, energy, and leadership.

Tools of Persuasion

Popular support refers to public identification with and support for the governor and his or her program. It may be measured in terms of the margin of victory in the primary and general election or the results of public opinion polls. A governor can parlay popular support into legislative acceptance of the policy mandate and otherwise channel the pressures of public opinion to his or her advantage. For example, a reluctant legislature can be convinced to support a certain program by a direct appeal to the voters, who may in turn apply pressure to their elected representatives.

Popular support can be generated and maintained through a second informal power, *public relations and media skills.* As the leading political figure in the state, the governor commands the regular attention of the press, radio, and television. Any governor can call a press conference at a moment's notice and get a substantial turnout of the state's major media representatives. Some chief executives appear regularly on television or radio to explain their policy positions and initiatives to the people. Others write a weekly or monthly newspaper column for the same purpose. Frequent public appearances, telephone calls, and correspondence can also help the governor develop and maintain popular support; the media can be a strong ally in carrying out the governor's programs and responsibilities. But media relations are a two-way street. The media expect the governor to be honest, forthright, and available. If he instills respect and cooperation, observes political scientist Coleman B. Ransome, Jr., the governor's media relations can be "of incalculable value in his contest for the public eye and ear."[64]

Negotiating and bargaining skills help the governor to convince legislators, administrators, interest groups, and national and local officials to accept his point of view on whatever issue is at hand. These skills are of tremendous assistance in building voting blocks in the legislature. They also help persuade industrialists to locate in the state, and effectively represent a state's interests before the national government.

Prestige of the office helps the governor open doors all over the world that would be closed to an ordinary citizen. National officials, big-city mayors, corporate executives, foreign officials, and even the president of the United States recognize that the governor sits at the pinnacle of political power in the state, and they treat her accordingly. Within the state the governor typically makes use of the prestige of the office by inviting important individuals for an official audience, or perhaps to a special breakfast, luncheon, or dinner at the mansion.

The governor's informal power to call the legislature into *special session* can be employed to focus public and media attention on a particular part of the legislative program or on a pressing issue. In this way the governor can delineate the topics that will be considered, thereby forcing the legislature's hand on divisive or controversial matters, such as insurance reform or a tax increase. In conjunction with popular support and media and public relations skills, this can work effectively to bend legislative will.

Pork barrel and *patronage* are aspects of the seamier side of state politics. Although they are utilized much less frequently than they were before the civil service reforms of the first half of this century, governors are still known to promise jobs, contracts, new roads, special policy consideration, electoral assistance, and other favors to legislators and other politicians for their support. All governors have some discretionary funds to help out a special friend who has constituents in need. And although patronage appointments are severely limited in most states, a supportive telephone call from the governor's mansion can open the door to an employment opportunity.

Characteristics of a Successful Governor

The *personal characteristics* that make for an effective governor are discussed frequently but seldom specified, because it is nearly impossible to measure them. Research by political scientists indicates that age is the only statistically significant predictor of gubernatorial performance: younger governors have been more successful than older ones.[65] However, there is general agreement that leadership is a very important quality of effective governors. Leadership traits are difficult to define, but former Utah governor Scott

Matheson identified the best governors as "men and women who have the right combination of values for quality public service—the courage to stick to their convictions, even when in the minority, integrity by instinct, compassion by nature, leadership by perception, and the character to admit wrong and when necessary, to accept defeat."[66]

A successful governor blends these qualities with the formal and informal powers of office in order to do a job well. For example, following the political campaign to win the election, the governor must conduct an internal campaign to win the loyalty and support of state employees if he is to be effective.[67] This campaign requires the governor to convey his key values to the bureaucracy, the legislature, and the people. For example, Dick Riley of South Carolina emphasized the theme of education improvement, promoting education reform through a one-cent sales tax increase by using the convincing slogan "A Penny for Their Thoughts." In Florida, Governor Bob Graham fought a "Save the Everglades" campaign to protect an important vanishing natural resource.[68]

Successful governors, particularly in "weak governor" states, know how to limit their policy agenda. Realizing that all things are not possible, they focus on several critical issues and marshal their formal and informal resources behind them. Eventually, the determined governor can wear down opponents. A successful governor exercises leadership by convincing the public that their interests are his interests, and that he is the person to pursue their vision. He prevails in the legislature by building winning blocks of votes, and he leads the bureaucracy through personal example. Above all else, a successful governor must be persuasive.

In sum, the formal powers of the office are important to any governor, but even strong formal powers do not guarantee success. They must be combined with the informal powers to be effective. For example, as chief legislator a governor may seek passage of a favorite bill by employing her budgetary and staffing powers. She may even threaten to veto any related bills. But in order to win over the necessary majority of legislators' support, the governor's negotiations and bargaining skills and personal leadership qualities may be critical.

Removal from Office

All states but one provide in their constitutions for the impeachment of the governor and other elected officials (in Oregon, they are tried as regular criminal offenders). Usually impeachment proceedings are initiated in the House of Representatives and the impeachment trial is held in the Senate. A two-thirds vote is necessary for conviction and removal of the governor in most states.[69] Of the more than 2,100 governors who have held office, only sixteen have been impeached, and only eight actually convicted.

As discussed in Politics and Policy 5.2, the most recent impeachment and conviction occurred in 1988 in Arizona, in the case of Governor Evan

Mecham. The Arizona House voted to hold an impeachment trial, and Mecham was convicted by the Senate on charges of misusing state money and trying to stop an investigation of a murder threat against one of his aides. Mecham was removed from office and replaced by Secretary of State Rose Mofford. He was later tried on six felony counts of perjury, but was found innocent.

Other modern governors have left office under a cloud of criminal allegations, including Illinois governor Otto Kerner, Maryland chief executives Spiro T. Agnew and Marvin Mandel, David Hall of Oklahoma, and Edwin Edwards of Louisiana. One of the most sordid governorships in recent years was Ray Blanton's in Tennessee. Blanton was convicted of conspiracy, extortion, and mail fraud and charged with numerous additional offenses, including selling liquor licenses and selling pardons to state prison inmates. These are the gubernatorial black sheep—the oddities of contemporary state government, who make interesting reading in the scandal sheets as political throwbacks to the Goodtime Charlies of yesteryear. They deflect proper attention from the vast majority of hard-working, honest chief executives who typify the American state governorship today.

Other Executive Branch Officials

The states elect more than 450 officials to their executive branches, not counting the fifty governors. This includes forty-three attorneys general, forty-two lieutenant governors, thirty-eight treasurers, thirty-six secretaries of state, and an assortment of other officers ranging from the Texas railroad commissioner to the commissioner of public law in New Mexico. The four most important statewide offices are described here.

Attorney General

The attorney general is the state's chief legal counsel. He or she renders formal written opinions on legal issues (such as the constitutionality of a statute, administrative rule, or regulation) when requested to do so by the governor, agency heads, legislators, local prosecutors, or other public officials. In most states, the attorney general's opinions have the force of law unless they are successfully challenged in the courtroom.

The attorney general represents the state in cases where the state government is a legal party, and conducts litigation on behalf of the state in federal and state courts. He or she can initiate civil and criminal proceedings in most states. Increasingly, attorneys general have been actively involved in legal actions related to the national government's statutes and administrative activities in controversial fields such as hazardous and nuclear wastes, the legal minimum drinking age, and the maximum speed limit for state highways. Another relatively new responsibility is the administration of consumer protection programs. As federal regulatory activities faded away during the Reagan years, the states, acting through their attorneys general, became the "new cops on the beat," policing everything from deceptive advertising to antitrust violations.[70] Increasingly, these officials constitute an aggressive group of highly competent attorneys, often working together through the auspices of the National Association of Attorneys General, to assert and protect the role of the states in American federalism.

Lieutenant Governor

This office was originally created by the states for two major reasons: to provide for orderly succession to a governor who is unable to fill out a term owing to death or other reasons, and to provide for an official to assume the responsibilities of the governor when the incumbent is temporarily incapacitated or out of the state. Seven states do not see the need for the office: Arizona, Maine, New Hampshire, New Jersey, Oregon, West Virginia, and Wyoming. (In addition, Tennessee does not have an elected lieutenant governor; the Speaker of the Senate is given the title.) Others attach little importance to it, as indicated by a very low salary ($6,800 per year in South Dakota) or the absence of official responsibilities. The historical reputation of the lieutenant governor was that of a do-nothing, and one former occupant of the office in Nevada characterized his major responsibility as "checking the obituaries to see if I should be in Carson City."[71]

However, over the past fifteen years the lieutenant governorship in the majority of states has become a more visible, demanding, and responsible office. This trend is likely to continue as state governance grows increasingly complex and as additional states adopt the team election of governor and lieutenant governor. Many lieutenant governors hold important powers in the state senate, including serving as presiding officer and making committee appointments. They are official members of the cabinet or the governor's top advisory body in twenty-one states.[72] Virtually all lieutenant governors accept special assignments from the chief executive, some of them quite visible and important. For example, Michigan's lieutenant governor acts as the state's affirmative action officer and chairs the Equal Employment and Business Opportunity Council. In Illinois, the lieutenant governor is responsible for the affairs of senior citizens and chairs the Small Business Council and the Job Development Team.[73] In general, lieutenant governors' salaries, budget allocations, and staff have grown markedly during the past two decades.

A lingering problem is that twenty-one states continue to elect the governor and lieutenant governor independently. This can result in conflict and controversy when the chief executive is out of state and the two officeholders are members of opposing political parties or hold different governing philosophies. On several recent occasions a lieutenant governor, assuming command, has proceeded to make judicial appointments, veto legislation, convene special sessions of the legislature, and take other actions at odds with the governor's wishes. When California governor Jerry Brown left the state to campaign for the presidency in the mid-1970s, for instance, Lieutenant Governor Mike Curb did all of these things.

In order to avoid partisan bickering and politicking in the top two executive branch offices, twenty-two states now require team election. New York was the first to adopt this innovation, in 1953; twenty-one others have followed the lead of the Empire State, most recently Iowa in 1988. In addition to avoiding embarrassing factionalism, team election has the advantages of promoting party accountability in the executive branch, making continuity of policy more likely in the event of gubernatorial death or disability, and ensuring a measure of compatibility and trust among the two state leaders. (With team election, the lieutenant governor must relinquish duties involving the legislature.)

Does the lieutenant governorship help or hinder a politician who wishes to achieve the state's top political office? Like everything else in state politics, it depends. A lieutenant governor running for the higher office does enjoy the advantage of name recognition and, potentially, a positive association with a popular governor's program. Alternatively, he or she can be linked negatively with an unpopular former governor, and may even lose the race for this reason. Over the past thirty-five years, more than seventy lieutenant governors have won their state's top elective office. On balance, the lieutenant governorship seems to offer a boost to an aspiring chief executive.

Treasurer

The treasurer is the official custodian of state funds. He or she collects revenues and makes disbursements of state monies. The treasurer's signature is on the paycheck of all state employees and on citizens' state tax refunds. Another important duty is the investment of state funds, including state employee pension monies.

The failure to make profitable investments can cost the treasurer his job. In March 1989, West Virginia treasurer A. James Manchin was impeached by the House of Delegates for losing $279 million in state funds through bad investments.

Secretary of State

In a majority of states the duties of this office are rather perfunctory. They mostly entail record-keeping and election responsibilities. Secretaries of state typically register corporations, securities, and trademarks, and commission people to be notary publics. In their election-related responsibilities, they determine the ballot eligibility of political parties and candidates, receive and verify initiative and referendum petitions, supply election ballots to local officials, file the expense papers and other campaign reports of candidates, and conduct voter registration programs. The typical secretary of state also maintains state archives, registers driver's licenses, files agency rules and regulations, publishes statutes and copies of the state constitution, and registers lobbyists.

The Vigor of American Governors

For the past two and a half decades the states have been deeply involved in reforming their executive branches. The overriding goal has been to enhance the capability of the governor as chief executive and to make the office more efficient, effective, accountable, and responsive. The reforms discussed in this chapter have indeed extended the formal powers of the office and have improved the contemporary governor's performance in the demanding roles of policymaker, chief legislator, chief administrator, intergovernmental coordinator, and so on. The capacity of the executive branch has been expanded to meet the challenges of the 1990s and beyond.

In addition, today's governors are better educated, more experienced in state government, and more competent than their predecessors. They are better able to employ the informal powers of their office in meeting multiple and complex responsibilities. In a word, there is greater *vigor* in the American governorships than ever before. The governors are actively engaged in national and international politics while they serve as the focal point of political activities in their states. They will be capable champions of the states in the 1990s.

Summary

The American governorship has been transformed as the states enter the decade of the 1990s. Today's governors tend to be very active in their various roles, including those of policymaker, chief legislator, and chief administrator. The governor's office, historically weak in formal powers, has been significantly strengthened during the past twenty-five years. Terms of office have been extended, appointment and veto powers increased, and budgetary authority enhanced, among other things. Governors also apply various informal powers in executing their duties. These include tools of persuasion such as bargaining and negotiating skills, and personal characteristics such as leadership skills.

Key Terms

Cabinet system The organization whereby the heads of the major executive branch agencies or departments meet formally with the governor on matters of public policy and administration.

Custodial (caretaker) governor A chief executive who maintains the basic operations of state government and deals with emergencies as they arise.

Executive amendment A type of veto used by the governor to reject a bill, and also to recommend changes that would cause the governor to reconsider the bill's approval.

Executive order A rule, regulation, or policy issued unilaterally by the governor to affect executive branch operations or activities.

Formal powers Powers of the governor derived from the state constitution.

Informal powers Powers of the governor derived from nonconstitutional sources.

Line item veto The governor's formal power to veto separate items in a bill instead of the entire piece of proposed legislation.

Managerial governor A chief executive who actively leads and manages state government policy and administration.

Package veto The governor's formal power to veto a bill in its entirety.

Patronage The informal power of a governor (or other officeholder) to make appointments on the basis of party membership, and to dispense contracts and other favors to political supporters.

Pocket veto The governor's power to withhold approval or disapproval of a bill after the legislature has adjourned for the session, thus vetoing the measure.

Pork barrel Favoritism, by a governor or other elected official, in distributing government monies or other resources to a particular program or jurisdiction.

Subcabinet system The organization whereby the heads of specified state executive branch agencies or departments meet formally with the governor on matters that concern a particular problem, government function, or policy field.

Task force A temporary group of state executive branch agency or department heads who meet with the governor to address short-term policy or administrative problems.

8

The Bureaucracy

State and Local Bureaucrats: Who They Are, What They Do

Personnel Policy in State and Local Government: From Patronage to Merit
The Merit System/State and Local Advances/
Representative Bureaucracy/
Comparable Worth/Sexual Harassment/
Unions and Collective Bargaining

The Politics of Bureaucracy
Joining Administration and Politics/The Public
Interest/Bureaucratic Responsiveness/
Professionals in State and Local Government

Budgeting in State and Local Government
The Budget Cycle/The Actors in Budgeting/
Pervasive Incrementalism/Types of Budgets

The Quality and Capacity of Bureaucracies

This chapter is about state and local **bureaucracy,** or public administration, and the millions of men and women who work as public employees. Bureaucracy—the much maligned "fourth branch" of government—is the most poorly understood of all political institutions. It encompasses the many departments, agencies, and offices of state and local government. Mindless and ill-informed criticism is regularly leveled at bureaucracy from all quarters. Presidents Jimmy Carter and Ronald Reagan made "bureaucrat bashing" a popular national game, and blamed all sorts of social, economic, and political ailments on the national bureaucracy.

State and local bureaucracies have come in for their own share of vitriol from governors, legislators, the media, and the general public. Who has not blamed the bureaucracy for an annoying problem such as long lines at the automobile license renewal department, a computer foul-up on college fees or class schedules, or a street repaved, then torn up a week later to lay sewer lines?

Those who study, write about, and practice public administration are concerned with the nagging problems of delivering services in a timely, efficient, and effective manner. Some are also troubled by the rather abstract but in the long run more difficult problems of **accountability** and **responsiveness.** How, in an increasingly complex world, can we make state and local bureaucracy accountable to other political institutions and to the public? How can we ensure that bureaucracy is responsive to the needs of society, groups, and individuals, without undue favoritism? There are no easy answers to these questions, nor will there ever be.

A theme of this chapter is that state and local bureaucracy should not be treated as a scapegoat for all the social, economic, and political maladies that befall us. The quality and capacity of public administration have improved markedly in America's states, municipalities, and counties during the past twenty-five years in terms of the characteristics of employees and the efficiency, effectiveness, and professionalism with which they perform their duties. States and localities are providing a wider range of services, in greater quantity, to more people than ever before. They are much more accountable and responsive to political actors and to the public than they are popularly perceived to be. In truth, dedicated public employees who work for the people should be saluted, not castigated, for jobs well done under difficult conditions.

State and Local Bureaucrats: Who They Are, What They Do

There are nearly 14 million employees in states and localities. Their numbers have grown steadily since accurate counts were first compiled in 1929, in contrast to the number of federal bureaucrats, which has remained fairly

Figure 8.1   Distribution of Public Employment, 1929–1986
Since the end of World War II, the percentage of state and local
employees, as a proportion of the total government work force, has
increased.

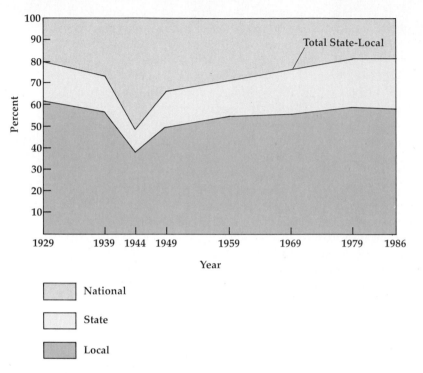

National

State

Local

Source: U.S. Bureau of the Census, *Public Employment,* selected years, Series GE 84
(Washington, D.C.: U.S. Government Printing Office).

stable at just under 3 million* since 1969.[1] The distribution of government
employees is also of interest. The national percentage of civilian government employment has declined from its World War II high of 51.5 percent
in 1944 to less than 18 percent today. Correspondingly, the state and local
proportions have inched upward to around 23 percent and 59 percent,
respectively (see Figure 8.1). Government work tends to be highly labor-
intensive, with the exception of national defense programs, which rely
heavily on expensive technology. As a result of this and of inflation, personnel expenditures for states and localities have risen even faster than the
number of workers. Total payroll costs for state and local governments
exceeded $256 billion in 1986.[2]

    Of course, the number of employees varies greatly among jurisdictions.
Generally speaking, states and localities with high populations and high
levels of per capita income provide more services and thus employ larger

*The figures on federal employees are somewhat misleading, because the enormous number of
contract employees who perform work for the national government is not included.

numbers of workers than smaller, less affluent jurisdictions. Employment figures are further influenced by the number and scope of programs undertaken by governments and by the distribution of activities and service responsibilities between states and their local jurisdictions.

Such figures do not adequately account for the real individuals who work for states, cities, counties, and school districts. These include the police officer on patrol, the welfare worker finding a foster home for an abandoned child, the eleventh-grade English teacher, the highway patrol officer, and your professor of state and local government (in public institutions). Their tasks are as diverse as their titles: sanitation engineer, zookeeper, heavy equipment operator, planner, physician, and so on. The diversity of state and local government work rivals that of the private sector. From the sewer maintenance worker to the commissioner of social services, all are public servants—bureaucrats. Approximately one of every five working Americans is employed by government at some level.

Personnel Policy in State and Local Government: From Patronage to Merit

National actions have had a pronounced influence on state and local personnel practices. National laws and court decisions have determined the parameters within which personnel policies can be set. Today, however, personnel policy innovations are more likely to come from the state and local jurisdictions, although national influence remains important.

In the nation's first decades, public employees came mainly from the educated and wealthy upper class and were generally hired on the basis of fitness for office. During the presidency of Andrew Jackson (1829–37), who wanted to open up national government jobs to all segments of society, the *patronage* system was used to fill many positions. Hiring could depend on partisan alliances rather than qualifications. Jackson himself continued to give jobs to competent people, but the door was open for favoritism in federal hiring practices.

Moreover, patronage was entrenched in many states and cities where jobs were awarded almost entirely on grounds of partisan politics, personal friendships, or family ties. This made appointees accountable to the governor, mayor, or whoever appointed them, but it did nothing to ensure honesty and competence. By the beginning of the Civil War, "spoils" embraced American governments at all levels. The quality of public employees plummeted.

The Merit System

The concept of the **merit system** originated with the campaign for passage of the Pendleton Act of 1883. Scandals rocking the administration of an alcoholic president, Ulysses S. Grant, spawned a public backlash that peaked with the assassination of President Garfield by a man seeking a political appointment. The Pendleton Act set up an independent, bipartisan *civil service* commission to make objective, merit-based selections for national job openings. The merit system was originally limited to 10.5 percent of all civilian executive branch positions, but future presidents gradually extended its coverage to approximately 90 percent. The system, which is far from perfect, was thoroughly overhauled by the Civil Service Reform Act of 1978. Nonetheless, the negative effects of patronage and spoils politics in national selection practices were mostly eliminated. **Neutral competence** became the primary criterion for obtaining a national government job, as public servants were expected to perform their work competently and in a politically neutral manner.

New York was the first state to enact a merit system, in 1883, the year of the Pendleton Act, and Massachusetts followed in 1884. The first municipal merit system was established in Albany, New York, in 1884; Cook County, Illinois, became the first county with a merit system, in 1895. Ironically, both Albany and Cook County (Chicago) later were consumed by machine politics and spoils-ridden urban governance.

By 1949, twenty-three states and numerous local governments had enacted merit-based civil service systems. Congressional passage of the 1939 amendments to the Social Security Act of 1935 had given additional impetus to such systems. This legislation obligated the states to set up merit systems for employees in social service and employment security agencies and departments that were at least partly funded by national grants-in-aid under the Social Security Act. Therefore, all states are required to establish a merit system for a sizable segment of their work force (around 20 percent); most of them (thirty-five) have in fact developed comprehensive systems that encompass virtually all state employees (see Table 8.1). Common elements of these modern personnel systems include recruitment and selection in accordance with knowledge, skills, and ability; regular performance appraisals; equal employment opportunity; and position classification.

Some merit systems work better than others. In a handful of states and localities, merit systems are mere formalities, lifeless skeletons around which a shadowy world of patronage, spoils, favoritism, and incompetence flourishes.[3] Rigid personnel rules, a lack of training programs, and inadequate salaries and retirement plans continue to plague some jurisdictions. Political control over merit system employees is limited everywhere, because most cannot be fired without considerable difficulty.

State and Local Advances

On balance, however, state and local personnel systems have been greatly improved over the past twenty-five years, and the process continues.[4] Nonnational governments are experimenting with merit pay plans and other incentive systems, collective bargaining innovations, new perform-

Table 8.1   Comprehensive State Merit Systems

Alabama	Kansas	New York
Alaska	Kentucky	Ohio
Arizona	Louisiana	Oklahoma
California	Maine	Oregon
Colorado	Maryland	Rhode Island
Connecticut	Massachusetts	South Dakota
Delaware	Michigan	Tennessee
Georgia	Minnesota	Utah
Hawaii	Nevada	Vermont
Idaho	New Hampshire	Washington
Illinois	New Jersey	Wisconsin
Iowa	New Mexico	

Source: 1979 Annual Statistical Report on State and Local Personnel Systems (Washington, D.C.: U.S. Office of Personnel Management, June 1980), p. 43, updated by the authors.

ance appraisal methods, senior executive systems, comprehensive training programs, the decentralization of personnel functions, and many other concepts. In the 1980s, virtually every state had some sort of civil service reform effort under way.

These reforms are designed to make the executive branch more responsive to the chief executive, to improve service capacity, to elevate efficiency and effectiveness in providing services, and to enhance flexibility for chief executives, agency heads, city managers, and other officials. Reformers remain dedicated to the principle of protecting the civil service from unnecessary and gratuitous interference by politicians with patronage considerations in mind. But they also want to increase the capacity of government executives to manage programs and people in their bureaucracies.

As we shall see, state and local governments have taken the lead in addressing such controversial questions as affirmative action, comparable worth, and sexual harassment. State and local work forces tend to be more representative of the general population than the national work force with respect to race, gender, and other traits. Also, the level of professionalism, indicated by graduate degrees, government work experience, and membership in professional organizations, has risen dramatically among nonnational government employees.

Representative Bureaucracy

The concept that the structure of government employment should reflect major sexual, racial, socioeconomic, religious, geographic, and related components in society is called **representative bureaucracy.** The assumptions behind this idea are (1) that a work force representative of the values, points of view, and interests of the people it governs will be responsive to their special problems and concerns, and (2) that a representative bureaucracy provides strong symbolic evidence of a government "of the people, by the people, and for the people." These assumptions have been widely debated. Empirical research indicates that which agency a person works for and which profession he or she belongs to are better predictors of public policy preferences than racial, sexual, and other personal characteristics.[5] However, the symbolic aspects of representative bureaucracy are important. A government that demonstrates the possibility of social and occupational mobility for all sorts of people gains legitimacy in the eyes of its citizens and expands the diversity of views taken into account in bureaucratic decisions.

One of the most controversial questions in public personnel policy is how to achieve a representative work force, particularly at the upper hierarchy of government organizations. *Equal employment opportunity* (EEO)—the policy of prohibiting employment practices that discriminate for reasons of race, sex, religion, age, physical handicap, or other factors not related to the job—is embodied in the Fourteenth Amendment to the U.S. Constitution, the Civil Rights Acts of 1866, 1871, and 1964, the Equal Employment Opportunity Act of 1972, the Age Discrimination and Rehabilitation Acts of 1973, and several U.S. Supreme Court decisions interpreting these acts. This policy has been the law for well over a hundred years, yet progress was very slow until the past twenty years or so.

Affirmative Action   In order to enhance the effects of EEO, governments take special steps to hire and retain those categories of workers that have been discriminated against in the past. These measures, known as **affirmative action,** are required under certain conditions by the U.S. Equal Employment Opportunity Commission (EEOC), the regulatory body created to enforce EEO.[6] They include goals, timetables, and other preferential selection and promotion devices to make the work forces of public and private organizations more representative of racial, sexual, and other characteristics of the available labor pool.

Under affirmative action, the absence of overt discrimination in employment is not sufficient; organizations must implement preferential hiring schemes to redress existing imbalances. The legitimacy of affirmative action policies imposed on employers by the EEOC has been upheld in several important U.S. Supreme Court decisions, including *Regents of the University of California* v. *Bakke* (1978) and *United Steelworkers of America* v. *Weber* (1979). *Bakke* involved a white male who was denied admission to medical school even though his test scores were higher than those of some nonwhites who were admitted under a quota system.[7] *Weber* upheld an arrangement between a firm and a union to reserve half of all slots in a training program for blacks.[8] Politics and Policy 8.1 looks at another instance of the courts upholding affirmative action.

Affirmative action remains highly controversial. Establishing specific numerical goals and timetables for hiring and promoting minorities does not necessarily correspond with selection or promotion of "the best person for the job." In other words, affirmative action appears to conflict with the merit principle. Furthermore, it has alienated a large proportion of the white male population, who feel that they have become victims of "reverse discrimination."

The Lack of Consensus   Although the U.S. Supreme Court and federal appeals courts have ruled on numerous affirmative action cases, no coherent interpretation of the policy's legal standing has been forthcoming. For example, the language of the 1972 amendment to the Civil Rights Act of 1964 prohibits state and local governments from depriving any individual of equal protection of the laws. That same act forbids employees to grant preferential treatment to any individual or group on the basis of race, color, religion, sex, or national origin. Yet a hiring quota clearly denies equal protection of the laws to white males by granting preferential treatment to certain other categories of people. In upholding affirmative action plans, the U.S. Supreme Court examined the history of the Civil Rights Act of 1964, as amended, and determined that Congress *intended* to authorize affirmative action as a means of achieving equal employment opportunity.

A 1984 court case shows the complexity of issues surrounding this policy. In 1980 Memphis, Tennessee, signed a federal court consent decree (an agreement among parties to a lawsuit) to increase the percentage of black firefighters to approximately the same as the proportion of blacks in the Shelby County labor pool. Facing a fiscal crisis a year later, the city announced that the fire department and other agencies would lay off a substantial number of employees, using the time-honored principle of "last hired, first fired." This meant, of course, that the new black firefighters would be the first to go.

In this case, *Memphis* v. *Stotts* (1984), a federal district court, upheld by the appeals court, prohibited the city from implementing the layoff plan if it would reduce the percentage of black firefighters.[9] The city complied, laying off white workers or reducing them in rank. On final appeal, the U.S. Supreme Court held that the district and appeals courts' actions were improper, since the original affirmative action consent decree did not mention layoffs. Moreover, the Court interpreted Title VII of the Civil Rights Act of 1964 as applying only to individuals who could prove that they themselves had been victims of illegal discrimination. There was no evidence that the Memphis blacks protected from layoff had ever suffered discrimination by the city.

The *Stotts* case had important implications for affirmative action plans containing hiring and promotion goals. The Reagan administration, consistently in opposition to affirmative action in any form, immediately called on state and local governments to terminate policies that did not favor individual, identifiable victims of proven discrimination. Almost all refused to

POLITICS AND POLICY 8.1
Affirmative Action and the Alabama Department of Public Safety

Continued resistance to affirmative action as a government policy is illustrated in the case of *United States* v. *Paradise* (1972). The National Association for the Advancement of Colored People (NAACP) filed a class action suit against the Alabama Department of Public Safety (ADPS), alleging that it had systematically and blatantly refused to hire blacks as state troopers, thus violating the equal protection clause of the Fourteenth Amendment. The U.S. District Court agreed with the charges and imposed a hiring quota of one black trooper for every white trooper until blacks made up 25 percent of the state trooper force. The court also prohibited ADPS from practicing any race- or color-based discrimination against any employees or job applicants.

By 1979 a number of black troopers had been hired, but white troopers were receiving preferential treatment in job testing and training, and black troopers were being disciplined more harshly. The black dropout rate was high, which held the proportion of black troopers well below one-quarter. Moreover, no blacks had been promoted to upper ranks. The court ordered the promotion of black troopers on a one-for-one basis with white troopers until an appropriate number filled upper-level positions. Two years later, no blacks had been

comply. State and local officials evidently feel that EEO, implemented through a policy of affirmative action, is of sufficient benefit to be retained. Ironically, the states and localities have become staunch supporters of a policy originally imposed by the national government over their strong resistance.

Further evidence of the Supreme Court's new conservatism on affirmative action is the 1989 case of *Martin* v. *Wilks*, in which the Court ruled that past affirmative action settlements (consent decrees) may be challenged by white employees.[10] In this case, an eight-year-old agreement by Birmingham, Alabama, to increase the number of black firefighters hired and promoted was reopened to consider allegations of reverse discrimination. Similar affirmative action agreements established over the past twenty years are likely to be challenged across the country.

Progress toward representative bureaucracy continues, but at a slow pace. Stabilization and, in some jurisdictions, shrinkage of government work forces in the first half of the 1980s restricted job opportunities for women and minorities. Nonetheless, the commitment to building a repre-

promoted. ADPS agreed to review its promotion exam at the level of corporal for discriminatory effects against blacks, and reported that of sixty blacks taking the test, only five made grades in the fiftieth percentile. The court decided to disallow the exam as racially discriminatory. ADPS proposed to promote four blacks and eleven whites to corporal, but the court ordered one-for-one promotion of blacks (a decade after the original *Paradise* decision, only four of the sixty-six corporals were black, and no blacks had entered the higher ranks). Finally, ADPS promoted eight blacks and eight whites to corporal.

Alabama's resistance to affirmative action was finally easing when the Reagan administration entered the picture. The Justice Department appealed to the U.S. Supreme Court, claiming that although the district court's hiring quotas were legal, its quotas on promotion violated the Fourteenth Amendment by denying white troopers equal protection of the laws. In a 5–4 decision, the Supreme Court affirmed the legality of the promotion quotas in this case, citing ADPS's "pervasive, systematic, and obstinate discriminatory exclusion of blacks" from the upper ranks. Thus, affirmative action quotas for both hiring and promotions are legal to remedy the effects of past discrimination.

Source: U.S. v. *Paradise* 94 L. Ed. 2d 203 (1987); *U.S. Law Week* 55 (February 24, 1987): 4211–55. Used by permission.

sentative work force appears to be firmly in place in the great majority of state and local governments. This commitment is indicated both by observation (for instance, the number of female city managers rose from seven in 1971 to more than one hundred in 1986) and by scholarly research on improvements in and attitudes toward minority employment.[11] In 1964 only 2 percent of the top administrative posts were held by women and 2 percent by nonwhites. Fourteen years later the proportions were 12 percent and 9 percent, respectively. These percentages, although low, far exceed those for female and black senior executives in the private sector.[12]

Comparable Worth

A conspicuous public personnel policy issue that garnered a great deal of media attention during the latter half of the 1980s is **comparable worth.** Just about everyone would agree with the principle of equal pay for equal

The affirmative action plan of the Birmingham, Alabama, fire department was ruled illegal by the Supreme Court in 1989. Affirmative action will likely be under legal pressure for many years to come.

work: two individuals with equivalent experience and seniority, performing the same job, should receive equal compensation. Comparable worth takes this principle a big step further by stipulating that individuals performing different jobs of equal *value* should be compensated equally. For example, a vehicle maintenance worker should receive the same salary as a clerical employee if the work both people are doing is of equal worth to their employer.

The Debate over Comparable Worth   Comparable worth has become a prominent personnel issue because pay inequities are related to gender. Women tend to be concentrated in low-paying jobs: secretary, nurse, waitress, and so on. Nationwide, full-time working women earn an average of around 64 cents for every dollar made by men.

Advocates of comparable worth hold that women are segregated into a small number of low-paying occupations because of sex-based discrimination. From birth to adulthood, females are socialized into the "proper" occupational choice. Because their options are limited, they are paid wages that do not reflect their true value to the employer. Proponents of comparable worth argue that jobs should be comparatively evaluated for their relative worth, based on education, training, skills, effort, responsibility, and other factors associated with performance of the job. Wages should be adjusted to bring female-dominated positions in line with male-dominated jobs.

Opponents of comparable worth dispute the assertion that society segregates women into low-paying occupations. They claim that women accept these jobs freely because of personal preferences. Many women, the critics point out, leave the work force periodically to marry, have children, and provide child care. They do not accrue experience and years of service at a rate that merits the same compensation as men. Opponents also state that comparable worth is not feasible in a practical sense, as it would interfere with the forces of supply and demand that set wages in the labor market. If wages were set by some other means, tremendous disparities would occur, wreaking havoc on the nation's employers. Spokespersons for local chambers of commerce become apoplectic over the mere thought of the billions of dollars that a national comparable worth plan could cost American business.

Finally, those in opposition argue that the real answer to job segregation is for women to seek out occupations that historically have been dominated by men. Little girls should be encouraged to become doctors, engineers, and police officers, not nurses and secretaries. Otherwise, the concentration of women in a narrow range of jobs will continue, whether or not they are better paid.

Comparable Worth in Court   A pair of court cases brought the issue to national attention in the early 1980s. In 1981, the U.S. Supreme Court seemingly upheld sex discrimination claims based on the theory of comparable worth. In the case of *Gunther* v. *County of Washington*, the Court's 5–4 majority ruled that Title VII of the 1964 Civil Rights Act, which prohibits sex discrimination, applies to jobs that are similar. The suit involved a female guard in the Washington County, Oregon, jail. She based her suit on a job evaluation study that judged female jailers' work to be 95 percent as difficult as male jailers' work, but the women were paid 30 percent less.

The second case was *AFSCME* v. *State of Washington* (1983). AFSCME, the largest public employee labor union, filed suit against Washington after a comparable worth study conducted by the state found substantial sex-based pay inequities, which the state did little about, primarily because of budget problems. A district court judge ruled in favor of AFSCME and instructed Washington to award several years' back pay and higher salaries to some 15,500 female employees. The judge found that Title VII did in fact call for equal pay for jobs of equal value. On appeal, however, a federal court overturned the lower court's ruling. A union appeal to the U.S. Supreme Court was dropped in December 1985, when the plaintiffs and the state of Washington reached an out-of-court settlement. Under the terms of the agreement, 34,000 workers in female-dominated state jobs are to receive an estimated $482 million in pay adjustments over a six-year period.[13]

Washington's willingness to implement a comparable worth policy was emulated by other states. Minnesota's comparable worth plan, adopted in 1983, called for an appropriation of $21.8 million for wage adjustments for more than 8,000 employees. New Mexico joined the group later that year by allocating $3.2 million to elevate the pay ranges of twenty-three female-dominated occupations. Iowa became the fourth state in 1984, with an appropriation of $10 million.[14]

By the late 1980s, at least ten states had a written comparable worth policy in place, and twenty had conducted pay equity studies. This was in stark contrast to the national government, which was moving at a snail's pace on the issue. In the private sector, large firms had begun quietly making pay adjustments in female-dominated jobs, while continuing to fight in the political arena against a national comparable worth policy.

Sexual Harassment

Sexual harassment has long been a problem in public and private employment, but it has only recently gained widespread recognition. Sexual harassment can consist of any of a variety of incidents: obscene or sexually oriented jokes that a listener finds personally insulting, unwanted touching or other physical contact of a sexual nature, implicit or overt sexual propositions, or (in one of its worst forms) extortion of a subordinate by a supervisor who demands sexual favors in return for a promotion or other employment-related considerations. Sexual harassment can occur once or over time through continuing behavior.

Although sexual harassment is difficult to define comprehensively, there is no doubt that it is common in the workplace. Typically, surveys of women discover that at least half of the respondents report being a victim.[15] Unfortunately for the recipient of unwanted sexual attention, there are seldom any witnesses. It becomes one person's word against another's. When one of the parties is the supervisor of the second party, a formal complaint is often decided in favor of the boss.

Sexual harassment is illegal according to the federal courts; it constitutes sex discrimination under Title VII of the 1964 Civil Rights Act. It is considered a form of punishable employee misconduct under national civil service rules, and it is increasingly being prosecuted in the private sector.

Much of the official activity aimed at stopping sexual harassment has been precipitated by the states. Michigan was the first to adopt a sexual harassment policy, in 1979; in a very short time, thirty-three additional states adopted statewide sexual harassment policies through legislation or executive orders. Another six states have policies in place in individual agencies and departments. Twenty-nine offer employee training programs that help workers and supervisors identify acts of sexual harassment, establish procedures for effectively addressing it, and enforce prompt, appropriate disciplinary action against offenders.[16]

The costs of sexual harassment go well beyond the personal discomfort or injury suffered by victims. The problem also results in significant financial costs to organizations, whose employees lose productive work time. Such misconduct is widely considered unacceptable today in a national work force that is almost 50 percent female. Most states have responded promptly once the problem has gained recognition. Local governments are following suit, in some instances because state legislation forces them to, but more frequently because local officials also recognize the seriousness of the problem.

Unions and Collective Bargaining

The growth and development of unions in the United States was until recently a private-sector phenomenon, boosted by national legislation in the early 1930s that protected the rights of workers in industry to organize and engage in **collective bargaining** with their employers over wages, fringe benefits, and working conditions. Workers then organized in record numbers. By the late 1950s, however, private-sector union growth halted. A slow but steady decline in the percentage of organized employees continued into the late 1980s for a number of reasons, including the shift in the U.S. economy from manufacturing to the services (banking and finance, retail sales, fast food, and so on).

Unions in Government   Unions in the public sector did not receive any formal recognition through national action until 1962, when President John F. Kennedy issued an executive order that recognized the rights of federal employees to join unions and to be recognized by federal agencies. Today the labor rights of national workers are covered under several executive orders and the Civil Service Reform Act of 1978. These employees enjoy most of the rights and privileges of their counterparts in industry, with two important exceptions: most federal workers do not have the right to negotiate over wages and fringe benefits, and none have the right to strike.

Unionization in state and local government developed and flourished in the 1960s and 1970s, some thirty years after the heyday of private-sector unionism. During the 1960s, the number of public employee union members more than tripled. Why the sudden growth? In retrospect, several reasons are apparent.

First, the rise of unionism in government was spurred by the realization by state and local employees that they were underpaid and otherwise maltreated in comparison to their counterparts in the private sector, who had progressed so well with unionization and collective bargaining. Second, the bureaucratic and impersonal nature of work in large government organizations encouraged unionization to preserve the dignity of the workers. A third reason for the rise of state and local unionism was the employees' lack of confidence in many civil service systems. Not only were pay and benefits inadequate, but grievance processes were controlled by management, employees had little or no say in setting personnel policies, and "merit" selection, promotion, and pay often were influenced by management favoritism. Fourth, public employees got caught up in the revolutionary fervor of the sixties. They saw other groups in American society making noise and winning concessions from government authorities, and decided to join in.

Perhaps most important, the growth of unions in government was promoted by a significant change in the legal environment of labor relations. The rights of state and local employees to join unions and bargain collectively with management were guaranteed by several U.S. Supreme Court rulings, state legislation, local ordinances, and various informal arrangements that became operative during the 1960s. Wisconsin was the first state to permit collective bargaining for state workers, in 1959. By 1975, forty-one states specifically allowed at least one category of state or local government employees to engage in collective bargaining.

The Extent of Unionization The extent of unionization and collective bargaining is greatest in the states of the industrial Midwest and Northeast —the same areas so fertile for the growth of private-sector unions. A handful of traditionalistic states, including Arizona, Mississippi, Utah, Virginia, and the Carolinas, continue to resist the incursion of state and local unions (see Table 8.2). Public employees in these jurisdictions have the legal and constitutional right to join a union, but their government authorities do not have a corresponding duty to bargain with them over wages, benefits, or conditions of work.

As of the late 1980s, approximately 40 percent of all state government workers belonged to unions; 50 percent of local government employees were organized. The highest proportions of union workers were found in education, highways, public welfare, hospitals, police protection, fire protection, and sanitation.[17]

The surge in the fortunes of state and local unions was partially arrested in 1973, when a severe recession slowed the growth of government employment. A decline in revenues also halted the rapid gains in salary levels that had accompanied the growth of unions and collective bargaining. Further resistance to unions came from the taxpayer revolt of the late 1970s and a second recession in the early 1980s. Fiscal and taxpayer resistance helped stiffen the backbones of public officials, who had been criticized in some jurisdictions for giving the unions too much. In addition, a union-led campaign to convince the Congress to enact mandatory collective bargaining legislation for all state and local governments was derailed by a 1976 U.S. Supreme Court decision, *National League of Cities* v. *Usery*, which appeared to declare the pending bill unconstitutional.[18] From that decision to 1989, only three additional states passed statutes that enabled major categories of state and local workers to engage in collective bargaining.

Table 8.2   Collective Bargaining Rights in the States

Comprehensive	Partial	No bargaining
Alaska	Alabama	Arizona
California	Georgia	Arkansas
Connecticut	Idaho	Colorado
Delaware	Indiana	Louisiana
Florida	Kentucky	Mississippi
Hawaii	Maryland	North Carolina
Illinois	Missouri	South Carolina
Iowa	Nevada	Utah
Kansas	New Mexico	Virginia
Maine	Oklahoma	
Massachusetts	Tennessee	
Michigan	Texas	
Minnesota	Wyoming	
Montana		
Nebraska		
New Hampshire		
New Jersey		
New York		
North Dakota		
Ohio		
Oregon		
Pennsylvania		
Rhode Island		
South Dakota		
Vermont		
Washington		
West Virginia		
Wisconsin		

Comprehensive = full bargaining rights for all state and local employees
Partial = bargaining rights for one or more employee groups

As a result of these factors, unionism in state and local government has leveled off. Substantial gains in membership and bargaining rights are not likely during the next several years. Nonetheless, unions remain an important and highly visible component of many state and local government personnel systems.

The Impact of Collective Bargaining in State and Local Government   The outcomes of bargaining between a union and a firm in the private sector are largely determined by market forces, such as the supply and demand for labor. In government, political factors are much more important. The technical process of negotiating over wages and other issues is very similar to that in business and government. But the setting makes government labor relations much more complex, mostly because the negotiating process culminates in the political allocation of *public* resources.

Jay F. Atwood has identified four factors that make government labor relations highly political.[19] First, public officials are under greater pressure than private employers to settle labor disputes. Public services are highly visible and often monopolistic in nature; for example, there are no other convenient suppliers of police and fire protection. Elected officials who confront a controversial labor dispute in an "essential service" may fear it will derail their opportunity for re-election.

Second, public employee unions have considerable political clout. Their members can influence election outcomes, particularly at the local level. A recalcitrant mayor or city council member who opposes a hefty wage increase may suffer defeat at the polls in the next election if the municipal union members vote as a bloc. Unions may actively engage in politics through raising money, writing letters to the editor about candidates, knocking on doors to get out the vote, formally endorsing candidates, or using any of the other electoral techniques employed by interest groups. Some of the larger unions have professional lobbyists to represent them in the state capitol or in city hall.

A third politicizing factor in government labor relations is the symbiotic relationship that can develop between unions and elected officials. In exchange for special consideration at the bargaining table and perhaps elsewhere, the unions can offer public officials two valued commodities: labor peace and electoral support.

Finally, a hard-pressed union can apply the strike or a related job action (such as a slowdown or picketing) as a political weapon. In the private sector, a strike is not likely to have widespread public repercussions unless it involves goods or services that the nation relies on for its economic well-being (such as air transportation or coal mining). In government, a strike can directly involve the health and safety of all the citizens of a jurisdiction. For instance, a general strike involving police officers, firefighters, and sanitation workers has the potential to turn a city into filthy, life-threatening anarchy.

Strikes and other job actions by public employees are illegal in most jurisdictions, although nine states permit work stoppages by "nonessential" workers under strictly regulated conditions. However, teachers, health-care workers, and others regularly walk off the job anyway. The annual number of state and local work stoppages during the past ten years has averaged four hundred. The nightmare of a defenseless populace terrorized by acts of violence during a police strike, or the stench of garbage piling up on city streets for weeks during the hot months of July and

August, has convinced many an elected official to seek a prompt settlement to a labor-management impasse.

Because of these politicizing factors, one might expect that unions in government are extravagantly successful at the bargaining table. In fact this is not the case at all. Public employee unions have raised wages and salaries an average of 4 to 8 percent, depending on the service under consideration (that is, teachers earn around 5 percent more if represented by a union, firefighters around 8 percent). This is much lower than the union-associated wage impacts that have been identified in the private sector.[20] Greater success has come in winning better fringe benefits, particularly generous pensions.[21]

Certain personnel impacts have also been associated with collective bargaining in government. Clearly, unions have gained a stronger voice in management decision making. All personnel-related issues are potentially negotiable, from employee selection and promotion procedures to retention in the event of a reduction in force. Civil service rules, regulations, and procedures have been altered by many employers as a result of collective bargaining—often for the better. Certainly the rights of public employees have been strengthened.

Generally speaking, civil service systems and collective bargaining have reached an accommodation. The principle of merit in making personnel decisions is still in place, and usually is supported strongly by the unions. In an increasing number of jurisdictions, unions are cooperating with management to increase productivity in government services, through a process known as productivity bargaining. Perhaps the best way to characterize the impacts of unions in government is through a "diversity thesis": the effects vary over time and place, depending on numerous variables that range from how management is structured to the personalities found on either side of the bargaining table.[22]

The Politics of Bureaucracy

In an ideal world, political officials popularly elected by the people make all decisions regarding public policy. Then it becomes the duty of public administrators in the executive branch—the bureaucrats—to carry out these decisions through the agencies of state and local government. In the real world of bureaucratic politics, the line dividing politics and administration is transparent. Politicians have a hand in administrative matters, and administrators play politics at the state capitol and in city hall.

Joining Administration and Politics

Bureaucrats are intimately involved in making public policy, from the design of legislation to its implementation. The bureaucracy is often the seed bed for policy ideas that grow to become law, in large part because they are more familiar with agency and departmental problems and prospects than anyone else in government. It is not unusual, for instance, for law enforcement policy to originate with police administrators, or higher education policy with university officials.

Once a bill does become law, state and local employees must interpret the language of the legislation in order to put it into effect. Because most legislation is written in very general terms, civil servants must apply a great deal of **bureaucratic discretion** in planning and delivering services and otherwise managing the affairs of government. In a very real sense, the ultimate success or failure of a public policy depends on the administrators who are responsible for its implementation. Experienced legislators and chief executives understand this, and bring relevant administrators into the legislative process at a very early stage. Their knowledge and expertise is invaluable in developing a policy approach to a specific problem, and their cooperation is essential if a policy enacted into law is to be implemented as the lawmakers intend.

Thus, bureaucratic power derives from knowledge, expertise, and discretionary authority. It also comes from external sources of support for agency activities, such as the chief executive, legislators, and interest groups. Those who receive the benefits of government programs—the clientele—are also frequently organized into pressure groups. All government programs benefit some interest—agricultural policy for the farm community; social welfare policy for the poor; education policy for parents, students, teachers, and administrators—and these **clientele groups** often are capable of exerting considerable influence in support of policies that benefit them. Their support is critical for securing the resources necessary to develop and operate a successful government program. They serve as significant political assets to state agencies and municipal and county departments that are seeking new programs or additional funding from legislative and executive bodies, and they can become fearsome political infighters when their program interests are threatened.

The problem of politics and administration, then, has two dimensions. First, political intrusion in administrative affairs should be minimized, so that administrative decisions and actions can be based on neutral, professional competence, not the politics of favoritism. Second, elected officials have the very important responsibility of ensuring that administrative decision makers are accountable and responsive to the public interest. Generally speaking, political officials manage to avoid this responsibility. Other political activities absorb so much of their time and energy that they have little left for probing the affairs of the bureaucracy. Even when elected officials want to approach the bureaucracy, they are partially constrained by merit systems, which protect public employees from dismissals, demotions, or other adverse personnel decisions. In addition, most government agencies perform their duties competently and require little oversight.

An example of the merger of politics and administration is the lobbying of public administrators by legislative officials. This occurs when legislators and council members perform casework for members of their constituency. Although on occasion the legislator-lobbyist seeks favorable treatment that borders on illegality, the bulk of legislative casework is a response to a citizen's inquiry or complaint, or a request for clarification of administrative regulations.[23] Such legislative casework is useful in that it promotes both feedback on the delivery of services and helpful exchanges of information with elected officials.

In sum, state and local politics are intricately joined with administration. Public policy is made and implemented through the interaction of elected officials, interest groups, and public administrators. Nonetheless, the vast majority of administrative decisions are based on the neutral competence and professionalism of public employees. An important question remains: are administrators responsive to the public interest in their decision making?

The Public Interest

Everyone agrees that government programs should be conducted in accordance with the "public interest." The dilemma for state and local administrators lies in defining this concept. In fact there are numerous, competing public interests with no clear set of priorities among them. Public administrators may be expected to respond to the "general" interest of the people, but who is authoritative (or presumptuous) enough to identify it? Administrators also must listen to their immediate superiors, elected and appointed officials at all levels, clientele groups, and public interest groups, and they must be aware of national and state constitutional, statutory, and administrative law.

Often various publics make demands at once. Take the case of the county animal control officer. Her job is to keep unowned and unattended animals off the streets and to destroy those that are not claimed within a reasonable period of time. Citizens call to complain about stray cats and barking dogs. Owners criticize her for making them pay to retrieve their animals. In order to have adequate space and to keep within the budget for feeding and maintenance expenses, she has to destroy unclaimed animals, which prompts regular outcries from the local animal rights groups. Yet failure to destroy the animals means a budget fight with the county administrator or county council, or a rabies epidemic that could involve state health department officials.

The point is that public administrators are required to identify and balance a variety of interests in carrying out their responsibilities. For practical purposes, there is no single, clearly identifiable public interest, nor should there be. In a sense, the bureaucracy plays an important role in integrating political demands made from a variety of interests within American government.[24] This is largely accomplished by applying professional values and expertise in formulating standard operating procedures and work routines.

Bureaucratic Responsiveness

The concept of **bureaucratic responsiveness** is just as murky as that of the public interest, in part because the two are so closely linked. In essence, state and local bureaucrats are expected to be answerable, or accountable, to the public interest (however defined) for their actions. The bureaucracy must be responsible and accountable for what it does and does not do. Three basic types of administrative responsibility can be identified: objective, subjective, and professional.

Objective Responsibility   Objective responsibility means that an administrator is legally or officially responsible for some thing or action. In other words, by virtue of the constitution, a law, an administrative regulation, or some other formal requirement, x is accountable to y for z. Objective responsibility is achieved through the formal organizational structure (hierarchy), and various political controls placed on the bureaucracy by executive, legislative, and judicial structures and processes. For example, *sunset laws* require the termination of government agencies, boards, or commissions that are unable to justify their existence on a periodic basis, and administrative procedures laws require government agencies to give written notice and solicit public comment before changing or eliminating administrative regulations. (See Chapter 9 for more on sunset laws.) Reorganization of the state executive branch, as described in Chapter 7, is intended to enhance objective responsibility by reducing the number of state agencies, centralizing authority in the governor's office, and other actions aimed at making high-level bureaucratic actors more directly accountable to the governor.

Similar structural reorganization efforts took place in local governments across the United States during the municipal reform movement, especially in middle-sized jurisdictions like Dayton, Ohio, and Little Rock, Arkansas (see Chapter 12). These included nonpartisan elections to eliminate the influence of political parties in urban government, at-large elections to discourage political machines and pork barrel politics, the establishment of the city manager form of government, and the development of modern personnel and budgeting systems. Although results are difficult to evaluate, a recent national survey of municipal department heads found that respondents from reorganized ("reformed") cities were more likely to stress efficiency, effectiveness, and equity in the delivery of services than were their colleagues in old-style cities. The respondents from reorganized localities were also judged to be more responsive to the needs of individual citizens and minorities.[25]

Subjective Responsibility   The second category of administrative responsibility, subjective responsibility, concerns a personal feeling of moral obligation: a bureaucrat should *feel* responsible for behaving legally and properly. This is associated with a public employee's sense of loyalty or conscience. Almost all states and many of the larger local governments have enacted laws that set forth standards on what conduct is and is not considered ethical. Unfortunately, such ethics laws have been of limited use. They tend to issue grand exhortations and to impose moral judgments that cannot be enforced.

Professional Responsibility   A more pragmatic means of seeking bureaucratic responsiveness is through professional responsibility.[26] This concept is constructed on, first, the professional public servant's dedication to and confidence in the expert knowledge and skills that he has developed and, second, the use of his knowledge and skills in conformity with standards and norms established by the profession in pursuit of the public interest.

Professionals in State and Local Government

The growth and development of professionalism in government is a controversial phenomenon that has generated much discussion among scholars.[27] Virtually every profession in the United States is represented in state and local government. Some, such as law, medicine, and teaching, have been recognized for many years. Newer professions include certified public accounting, social work, librarianship, and city planning. And there is the emerging profession of public administration itself.

The Rise of Professionalism   The proportion of professionals in state and local government employment has risen steadily, and an increasing number of government workers hold graduate degrees or professional licenses. The professions and government are highly interdependent. Indeed, only government can provide employment for some professionals, such as military specialists and city managers. It is not uncommon for a particular profession's values and goals to dominate a public organization; examples include doctors in a state department of public health and engineers in a state highway department. In local government, the city management profession has exerted substantial influence over policies, programs, and techniques.

Critics bemoan professionalism in government. It is said that each profession has its own view of the world, grounded in its education process and specialized knowledge. Some fear that a professionalized bureaucracy pursues its own limited notion of what is in the public interest (and in the interest of the profession) rather than balancing the interests of the citizenry, clientele groups, and elected officials. Others have associated the dangers of professionalism with those of bureaucracy generally, by saying that professionalized agencies are not accountable to the public interest and that the original goals of public agencies and programs are displaced by professional goals.[28]

Professionalism and Bureaucratic Responsiveness   Actually, a strong case can be made that professionalism encourages bureaucratic responsiveness.[29] Professional responsibility, as embodied in the public-serving norms and standards of the professions, can lead the administrator to respond neutrally, objectively, and competently to competing interests in government. Professional norms, standards, and codes of ethics provide the public administration professional with a means for deciphering and responding to a multifaceted public interest by promoting accountability for work behavior and encouraging a sense of personal duty.[30]

An excellent example of the value of professionalism can be found in case studies of urban service delivery, in Houston, Chicago, San Antonio, Oakland, Detroit, and other cities. The studies find that bureaucratic rules, usually developed in accordance with professional standards, serve as the basis for allocating services in police and fire protection, recreation, street repair, and other areas. This finding is important, because it indicates that urban services are generally provided without discrimination on the basis of wealth or race.[31] When the municipal department of roads and streets, for example, must decide which transportation routes to repave, the decisions are seldom made on the basis of political favoritism. Instead, a formula that takes into account such factors as date of the last repaving, intensity of public usage, and the condition of the road is applied.

Professional organizational goals and the public interest do not necessarily conflict. Indeed, they have evolved and interacted over time. Public administrators tend to be committed to their profession but more strongly committed to their immediate employer and to the broader institutions and processes of American government.[32] Other factors also should alleviate apprehension. First, there is healthy debate in most professions regarding the interpretation of ethics, values, and goals. Second, representative bureaucracy helps restrain professional dominance by ensuring that professionals in public organizations have diverse backgrounds. This enhances the legitimacy of agency decision making and expands the diversity of views taken into account. Finally, there are the numerous formal and informal constraints on professional and bureaucratic discretion noted earlier, including interest groups and the checks and balances of the three branches of government.[33]

The public seems to agree that state and local professionals are doing a good job in delivering services. Charles T. Goodsell presents evidence that some three-fourths of Americans are satisfied with their treatment in receiving government services.[34] Satisfaction varies by level of government, with opinion of the national government declining since 1972, and that of states and localities generally increasing (see Figure 8.2).

Budgeting in State and Local Government

The budget is the source of life itself for state and local organizations. Without a budgetary appropriation, they would cease to exist. The monies are allocated, usually on an annual basis, by legislative bodies, but the

Figure 8.2   From Which Level of Government Do You Feel You Get
the Most for Your Money?
The percentage of the American public that feels the national
government is doing the best job has dropped since the early 1970s,
because of scandals such as Watergate and a general dissatisfaction
with national government activities.

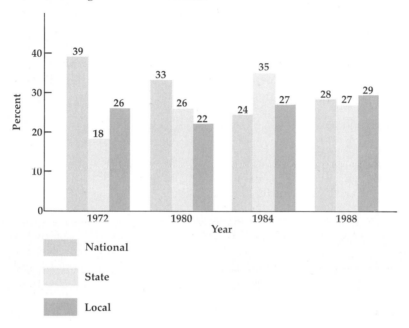

Source: U.S. Advisory Commission on Intergovernmental Relations, *Changing
Public Attitudes on Governments and Taxes,* selected years (Washington, D.C.:
ACIR).

politics of the budgetary process involve all the familiar political and bureaucratic players: chief executives, interest and clientele groups, other
government employees, the general public, and, of course, the recipients of
legislative appropriations—the state highway department, the municipal
police department, the county sanitation office, and so on. In a phrase,
budget making is a highly charged political poker game with enormous
stakes.

An often-quoted definition of politics is Harold Lasswell's famous line,
"Politics is who gets what, when, where, and how."[35] The budget document provides hard dollars-and-cents data for this statement. It is a political
manifesto—the most important one you will find in state and local government. It is a policy statement of what government intends to do (and not to
do) for the next year, and the amount of the taxpayers' resources that it will
dedicate to each program and activity. The outcomes of the budgetary
process represent the results of a zero-sum game—for every winner there is
a loser—because public resources are limited. An extra million dollars for

higher education can mean that much less for corrections; an expensive new fleet of sanitation trucks requires higher taxes from the homeowner.

The Budget Cycle

The process of governmental budgeting is best understood as a cycle with overlapping stages, five of which can be identified: preparation, formulation, adoption, execution, and audit (see Figure 8.3). Several stages are going on at any single time. For example, during the implementation stage of the 1990 budget, the 1989 budget is being audited and the 1991 budget is being prepared or formulated.

Figure 8.3   The Budget Process
The budget process is a cycle consisting of five stages. It has built-in "checks and balances," since all spending is approved or audited by more than one agency or branch.

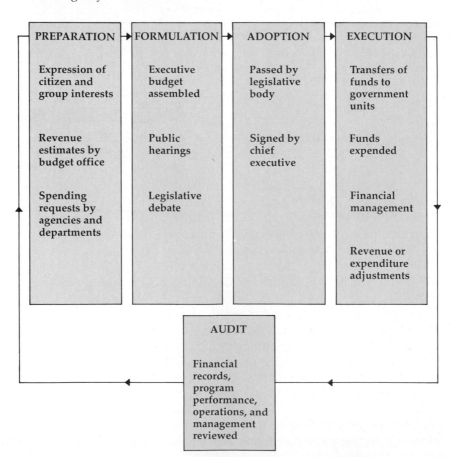

PREPARATION	FORMULATION	ADOPTION	EXECUTION
Expression of citizen and group interests	Executive budget assembled	Passed by legislative body	Transfers of funds to government units
Revenue estimates by budget office	Public hearings	Signed by chief executive	Funds expended
Spending requests by agencies and departments	Legislative debate		Financial management
			Revenue or expenditure adjustments

AUDIT

Financial records, program performance, operations, and management reviewed

Budgets are normally based on a *fiscal* (financial) *year* rather than on a calendar year. Fiscal years for all but four states run from July 1 through June 30 (the exceptions are Alabama, Michigan, New York, and Texas). Eight states, including Oregon, Montana, and Kentucky, have biennial budget cycles. Most local governments' fiscal years also extend from July 1 to June 30, but a substantial minority budget on the calendar year. (The national government's budget cycle begins on October 1 and ends on September 30).

The initial phase of the budget cycle involves demands for slices of the budget pie and estimates of available revenues for the next fiscal year. State and local agency heads join the chorus of interest groups seeking additional funding. Large state agencies are typically represented by their own lobbyists, or "public information specialists." State and local administrators are also involved in estimating revenues based on past tax receipts and expected economic conditions. Preliminary revenue expectations are communicated to state agencies or municipal departments, which then develop their individual spending requests for the fiscal year. Revenue projections are revised as new data become available.

Formulation, or development, of the budget document is the responsibility of the chief executive in most states and localities. Exceptions include states in which the balance of power rests with the legislature, such as Arkansas, Mississippi, and South Carolina, and local governments in which budgeting is dominated by a council or commission. The executive budget of the governor or mayor is prepared by budget office staff and submitted to the chief executive for the final touches. The executive budget is then presented to the appropriate legislative body for debate and review.

The lengthy review process that follows allows agencies, departments, interest groups, and citizens to express their points of view. Finally, the budget is enacted by the legislative body. The state legislature or city council must ensure that the final document balances revenues with expenditures. Balanced-budget requirements are contained in the constitutions or statutes of most states, and operate through precedent in the others. These requirements usually apply to local governments as well. Balanced-budget requirements force state and local governments to balance expenditures with revenues, but they may be circumvented to some extent.[36] One increasingly popular device is the "off-budget budget," in which costs and revenues for public enterprises such as government corporations and development banks are exempt from central review and are not included in budget documents and figures.[37] Before the budget bill becomes law, the chief executive must sign it. Last minute executive-legislative interactions may be needed to stave off executive vetoes or to override them. Once the chief executive's signature is on the document, the budget goes into effect as law, and the execution phase begins.

During budget execution, monies from the state or local "general fund" are periodically transferred to agencies and departments to meet payrolls, purchase goods and materials, fulfill service contracts, write checks for welfare recipients and pensioners, and try to achieve program goals. Accounting procedures and reporting systems continually track revenues and outlays within the agencies. If revenues have been overestimated, the chief executive must make adjustments to keep the budget in the black. He or she may draw on a "rainy day fund" to meet a shortfall, or, if the deficit is a large one, order service reductions or layoffs. In a crisis the governor may call the legislature into special session, or the mayor may request a tax increase from the city council.

The final portion of the budget cycle involves several types of audits, or financial reviews, each with a different objective. Fiscal audits seek to verify that expenditure records are accurate and that financial transactions have been made in accordance with the law. Performance audits examine agency or department activities in relation to goals and objectives. Operational and management audits review how specific programs are carried out and assess administrators' performance. The auditors may be employed by the executive or the legislative branch. Some jurisdictions retain professional auditors from the private sector in order to ensure objectivity.

The Actors in Budgeting

There are three main actors in the budget process: agencies, the chief executive, and the legislative body. The role of the agency or department is to defend the base—the amount of the last fiscal year's appropriation—and to advocate spending for new or expanded programs. Agency and department heads are professionals who believe in the value of their organization and its programs, but they often find themselves playing some Byzantine games to get the appropriations they want, as set forth in Politics and Policy 8.2.

Aaron Wildavsky describes the basic quandary of agency and departmental representatives as follows:

> Life would be simple if they could just estimate the costs of their ever-expanding needs and submit the total as their request. But if they ask for amounts much larger than the appropriating bodies believe is reasonable, their credibility will suffer a drastic decline. . . . So the first decision rule for agencies is: do not come in too high. Yet the agencies must also not come in too low, for the assumption is that if the agency advocates do not ask for funds they do not need them.[38]

What they usually do, according to Wildavsky, is carefully evaluate the fiscal-political environment. They take into consideration what happened last year, the composition of the legislature, policy statements by the chief executive, the strengths of clientele groups, and other factors. Then they put forward a figure somewhat larger than they expect to get.[39]

The chief executive has a very different role in the budget process. In addition to tailoring the budget to his program priorities as closely as possible, he acts as an economizer. Individual departmental requests must

POLITICS AND POLICY 8.2
The Games Spenders Play

The following are suggestions for state and local officials to maximize their share of the budget during negotiations and hearings with the legislative body.

Massage your constituency. Locate, cultivate, and utilize your clientele groups to further the organization's objectives. Encourage them to offer committee testimony and contact legislative members on your behalf.

Always ask for more. If your agency or department doesn't claim its share of new revenues, someone else will. The more you seek, the more you will receive.

Spend all appropriated funds before the fiscal year expires. An end-of-year surplus indicates that the elected officials were too generous with you this year; they will cut your appropriation next time.

Conceal new programs behind existing ones. Incrementalism means that existing program commitments are likely to receive cursory review, even if an expansion in the margin is substantial. An announced new program will undergo comprehensive examination. Related to this game is . . .

Camel's nose under the tent, in which low program start-up costs are followed by ballooning expenses down the road. (The U.S. defense industry has mastered this one.)

Here's a knife; cut out my heart while you're at it. When told that you must cut your budget, place the most popular programs at the front of the line for the chopping block. Rely on your constituency to organize vocal opposition.

A rose by any other name. Conceal unpopular or controversial programs within other program activities. Give them appealing names (call a sex education class "Teaching the Values of Family").

Let's study it first (or maybe you won't be re-elected). When told to cut or eliminate a program, argue that the consequences would be devastating and should be carefully studied before action is taken.

Smoke and mirrors. Support your requests for budget increases with voluminous data and testimony. The data need not be especially persuasive or even factual, just overwhelming.

be reconciled, which means that they must be cut, since the sum total of requests usually greatly exceeds estimated revenues. Of course, an experienced governor or mayor recognizes the games played by administrators; he knows that budget requests are likely to be inflated in anticipation of cuts. In fact, various studies on state and local budgeting indicate that the single most influential participant is the chief executive.[40] Not surprisingly, astute administrators devote both time and resources to cultivating the chief executive's support for their agency's or department's activities.

The role of the legislative body in the initial stage of the budget cycle is essentially to respond to the initiatives of the chief executive. The governor, mayor, or city manager proposes, and the legislature or council reacts. Later in the budget cycle, the legislative body performs an important function through its review of agency and department spending and its response to constituents' complaints.

Pervasive Incrementalism

In a perfect world, budgeting would be a purely rational enterprise. Objectives would be identified, stated clearly, and prioritized; alternative means for accomplishing them would be considered; revenue and expenditure decisions would be coordinated within the context of a balanced budget.

That is how budgeting *should* be done. But state and local officials have to allocate huge sums of money each year in a budgetary environment in which objectives are not clear and are often conflicting and controversial. It is nearly impossible to prioritize the hundreds or thousands of policy items on the agenda. Financial resources, time, and the capacity of the human brain are severely constrained.

In order to cope with complexity and minimize political conflict over scarce resources, decision makers muddle through.[41] They simplify budget decision making by adopting decision rules. For example, instead of searching for the optimal means for addressing a public problem, they search only until they find a feasible solution. As a result, they sacrifice comprehensive analysis and rationality for **incrementalism,** in which small adjustments (usually an increase) are made to the funding base of existing programs. Thus the policy commitments and spending levels of ongoing programs are accepted as a given—they become the base for next year's funding. Decisions are made on a very small proportion of the total budget: the increments from one fiscal year to the next. If the budget has to be cut, it is done decrementally; small percentage adjustments are subtracted from the base. Political conflict over values and objectives are held to a minimum.

The hallmarks of incremental budgeting are consistency and continuity: the future becomes an extension of the present, which is itself a continuation of the past. Long-range commitments are made, then honored indefinitely. This does not mean that state and local budget making is a simple affair. On the contrary: it is as tangled and intricate as the webs of a thousand spiders.

Types of Budgets

A budget document can be laid out in various ways, depending on the purposes one has in mind: control, management, or planning.[42] Historically, *control,* or fiscal accountability, has been the primary purpose of budgeting, incrementalism the dominant process, and the line item budget the standard document.

Control Through Line Item Budgets   The **line item budget** facilitates control by specifying the amount of funds each agency or department receives and monitoring how those funds are spent. Each dollar can be accounted for with the line item budget, which lists every object of expenditure, from earth-moving vehicles to toilet paper, on a single line in the budget document. A police department's line items would typically include firearms, ammunition, gasoline for squad cars, uniforms, telephone costs, and so forth.

Line item budgets are useful for finding out where the money goes and tracking the annual incremental changes, but they do not tell us how effectively the money is spent. They do not inform us on important matters such as the impact of police spending on crime rates or clearance (arrest) rates, nor do they provide a clue as to the performance of a new program intended to reduce violent crimes or parking violations. Line item budgets facilitate incrementalism by emphasizing changes in the same expenditure categories year after year.

Budgeting for Management and Planning   Budget formats that stress *management* and *planning* are intended to help budget makers move beyond the narrow constraints of line items and incrementalism toward more rational and flexible decision-making techniques that focus on program results. Chief executives and agency officials seek to ensure that priorities set forth in the budget are properly carried out by organizational units—the management aspect of budgeting. The planning part involves orienting the budget process toward the future by anticipating needs and contingencies. A budget format that emphasizes planning is one that specifies objectives and lays out a financial plan for attaining them.

Several techniques permit budgeting for management and planning. The most important are performance budgets; planning, programming, and budgeting systems (PPBS), which require identification of program objectives and output measures; and zero-based budgeting (ZBB), which reviews the expenditure base each year. All of these systems are designed to address a single fiscal year's operating revenues and expenditures. Most state and local governments also use **capital budgets,** which allocate funds over a period of years to pay for expensive one-time projects. These budget systems are much more demanding than the simple line item budget, but if properly implemented, they can significantly improve agency management and planning.

In **performance budgeting,** the major emphasis is on activities, or programs. The idea is to focus attention on how efficiently and effectively work is being done rather than on what things are acquired. Whereas line item budgets are input-oriented, performance budgets are output-oriented. For example, the performance of a state highway department can be evaluated by examining the unit costs of resurfaced highways or rebuilt bridges. By focusing on program objectives and work performance, performance budgets can assist managers, elected officials, and citizens in assessing the efficiency of government operations. This form of budget has been criticized, however, because suitable measures of program performance are difficult to find. For example, a new garbage truck might double the amount of trash collected in a given time period, but it might also leave a trail of garbage in its wake. Is this improved performance? State and local governments usually try to employ several indicators to gauge the efficiency and effectiveness of their programs, and they have made a great deal of progress in performance measurement. Still, it remains very difficult to judge the quality of service delivery in those government activities, such as social services and criminal justice, that deal with changes in human behavior and attitudes.

Planning, Programming, and Budgeting Systems   Introduced by Secretary of Defense Robert McNamara in the early 1960s, planning, programming, and budgeting systems (PPBS) attempt to move public budgeting one step closer to the rational allocation of dollars among competing agencies, departments, and programs. The process of PPBS involves identifying (planning) goals and objectives, designing programs to put them into effect, and budgeting to finance each program adequately. President Lyndon B. Johnson ordered all national agencies to adopt PPBS in 1965. Many states and several large cities experimented with the technique as well, although it is rarely in use today in its original format.

Rational planning and decision making form the backbone of PPBS. Because it is intended to enhance management flexibility and planning by extending the scope of budget decision making beyond the present fiscal year, PPBS has been very useful in making military hardware decisions and other choices with clearly defined parameters. However, the process is very time-consuming, complex, and expensive.[43] It has been quietly set aside as a budgeting technique by the national government, and in the several states and localities that continue to use it, PPBS has been substantially modified.[44]

Zero-Based Budgeting   Zero-based budgeting, or ZBB, was first applied to a government setting in Georgia in the early 1970s by then-governor Jimmy Carter. When Carter won the presidency in 1976, he ordered its usage throughout the national government. By 1985 more than twenty states had adopted the technique in whole or in part.

ZBB directly attacks incrementalism by formally and regularly re-examining the primary objectives and baseline funding of programs. Thus, all programs compete each fiscal year, on an equal footing, for scarce government dollars. The base expenditures for existing programs are evaluated and may be cut or even eliminated.

Unfortunately, ZBB is a very time-consuming activity for managers. Reassessing all programs in a single jurisdiction is impossible in most settings, and most expenditures are uncontrollable in the short term anyway, because they have been allocated for ongoing programs. In general, the widely trumpeted promise of ZBB has gone unrealized. The technique has been useful, however, when applied on a limited basis in state and local government. For example, if legislators and administrators can examine 20 percent of existing programs each year, they will reduce demands on their time and energy.[45]

No new budgeting technique that promises to wipe out incrementalism is on the horizon, but the innovations discussed above have nudged the budget process in the direction of rationalism and comprehensiveness.[46] States and localities have moved beyond the limited control function of budgeting in a quest for improvements in management and planning. Incrementalism remains the norm, but program performance is now taken into consideration along with dollar outlays for personnel and material goods. Efficiency and effectiveness measures are increasingly used to evaluate how well governments use the taxpayers' dollars, and budgeting has been linked to planning beyond the immediate constraints of the next fiscal year. Perhaps of equal importance, state and local governments are developing tailor-made budget systems by incorporating the elements of performance budgeting, PPBS, and ZBB that best suit their needs.[47]

Capital Budgets   The budget formats described above are utilized for operating allocations that are depleted within a year. Capital outlays are made over a longer period of time and are composed of "big ticket" purchases such as hospitals, university buildings, libraries, new highways, and major computer systems. They represent one-time, nonrecurring expenditures that call for special funding procedures, or a capital budget. Because such items cannot be paid for within a single fiscal year, governments borrow the required funds, just as most individuals borrow when buying a house or an expensive automobile. The debt is paid back in accordance with a predetermined schedule.

Capital projects are funded by selling general obligation or revenue bonds. *Bonds* are certificates of debt sold by a government to a purchaser, who eventually recovers the initial price of the bond plus interest. *General obligation bonds* are paid off with a jurisdiction's regular revenues (from taxes and other sources). The "full faith and credit" of the government is pledged as security. *Revenue bonds* are usually paid off with user fees collected from use of the new facility (for example, a parking garage, auditorium, or toll road). Payments for both types of bonds are scheduled over time, which usually ranges from five to twenty years. The costs of operating a new facility, such as a school or recreation area, are met through the regular operating budget and/or user fees.

Capital budgeting lends itself to a more rational approach than operating budgets. Payments must be scheduled years in advance, and most state and local governments have constitutional or statutory limitations on how much they can borrow. This means that capital purchases must be anticipated and prioritized well into the future by agency heads, program administrators, and elected officials.

The Quality and Capacity of Bureaucracies

In spite of the amount of criticism hurled at government bureaucracies by the popular media, elected officials, and others, the quality of public administration in state and local government has improved markedly. Of course, there is considerable variance among jurisdictions; the quality of administration is higher in those that are affluent, industrialized, and urban. Patronage systems have been replaced by merit-based personnel systems. Bureaucracies are more representative of race, gender, and other characteristics of the American people. Pay disparities based on gender are gradually being rectified through comparable worth, and some forty states now have comprehensive labor relations policies in place.

Administrative quality is a critical factor in support of the resurgence of the states and the revitalization of localities. State and local governments have the capacity to do more things on a grander scale than ever before, and this trend is continuing in the 1990s. The basics of providing services, from picking up dead animals to delivering healthy human babies, depend on government employees for high standards of performance and professionalism. Increasingly, those who work in state and local bureaucracies represent the values of professionalism and neutral competence.

Summary

Much of the popular criticism of state and local bureaucracy is misplaced. Innovation and capacity-building are two important characteristics of bureaucracy in state and local government. Advances include merit systems, representative bureaucracy, fair pay policies, labor-management relations policies, and increased professionalism and responsiveness in public administration. Budgeting in the nonnational governments is more oriented toward management and planning, although exercising financial controls is still important.

Key Terms

Accountability The extent to which public employees answer to the higher authority of elected officials and the people.

Affirmative action Special efforts to recruit, hire, and promote members of disadvantaged groups in order to eliminate the effects of past discrimination.

Bureaucracy The administrative branch of government, consisting of all government offices and public workers.

Bureaucratic discretion The ability of public employees to make decisions interpreting law and administrative regulations.

Bureaucratic responsiveness The willingness of bureaucratic employees to react to demands from elected officials, interest groups, the general public, and other policy actors.

Capital budget A budget that plans large expenditures for long-term investments, such as buildings and highways.

Clientele group A group that benefits from a specific government program, such as the poor in welfare programs.

Collective bargaining A formal arrangement in which representatives of labor and management negotiate wages, benefits, and working conditions.

Comparable worth The principle of equal compensation for jobs of equal value to an organization.

Incrementalism A decision-making approach in the budgetary process in which last year's expenditures are used as a base for this year's budget figures.

Line item budget A budget that lists detailed expenditure items such as typewriters and automobiles, with no attention to goals or objectives of spending.

Merit system An organization of government personnel providing for hiring and promotion on the basis of knowledge, skills, and abilities rather than patronage or other influences.

Neutral competence The concept that public employees should perform their duties competently and without regard for political considerations.

Performance budgeting Budgeting that is organized to account for the outcomes of government programs.

Representative bureaucracy The concept that all major groups in society have the right to participate in government work.

9

State Legislatures

The Essence of Legislatures
Legislative Functions/A History of Legislative
Malfunction

Legislative Dynamics
The Senate and the House/Legislative
Districts/Legislative Pay/Legislative
Leadership/Legislative Committees

How a Bill Becomes Law
The Birth of a Bill: Idea and
Introduction/Committee Action/Floor Action/
The Other Chamber/The Governor

Legislative Behavior
Legislative Norms/Legislative Cue-taking

Legislative Reform and Capacity
The Ideal Legislature/The Effects of Reform

Relationship with the Executive Branch
Dealing with the Governor/Overseeing the
Bureaucracy

Legislatures and Capacity

Twenty years ago, who would have thought that long-haired student activists would become power brokers in a state legislature? Well, in Wisconsin that is precisely what happened. The Wisconsin legislature is controlled by Democrats who have made a career out of politics.[1] The legislators' hair may be shorter today, but their enthusiasm and commitment to a progressive agenda are undiminished. Since their ascent to power, the legislature has revamped the state university system, made the state tax code more progressive, and passed tough environmental and consumer protection laws. Focusing on social issues in the 1980s, it has enacted gay rights and sexual privacy laws, comparable-worth provisions for state employees, and marital property rights statutes. Far from feeling the antigovernment sentiment of recent times, these legislators thrive on government.

The Essence of Legislatures

"They're ba-a-ck." The announcement by the little girl in the movie *Poltergeist II* about her other-world friends could easily be applied to state legislators converging on the state capitol year after year. Every January (or February or April in a few states; every other January in a few others) state legislatures reconvene in session to do the public's business. More than seven thousand legislators hammer out solutions to intricate and often intransigent public problems.

Legislative Functions

Legislatures engage in three principal functions: *policymaking, representation,* and *oversight.* The first, policymaking, includes enacting laws and allocating funds. During the late 1980s, legislators debated such issues as surrogate motherhood, automobile insurance reform, and prison overcrowding. These deliberations resulted in the revision of old laws, the passage of new laws, and changes in spending. This is what policymaking is all about. Legislatures do not have sole control of the state policymaking function—governors, courts, and agencies also determine policy, through executive orders, judicial decisions, and administrative regulations, respectively—but they are the dominant policymaking institution in state government.

In their second function, legislators are expected to represent their constituents—the people who live in their district—in two ways. At least in theory, they are expected to speak for their constituents in the state capital—to do "the will of the public" in designing policy solutions. This is not an easy task. On "quiet" issues, a legislator seldom has much of a clue as to what the public's will is. On "noisy" issues, constituents' will is rarely unanimous. Individuals and organized groups with different perspectives may write to or visit their legislator to urge her to vote a certain way on a pending bill. In the other method of representation, legislators act as their constituents' facilitators in state government. For example, they may help a citizen deal with an unresponsive state agency. This kind of constituency service, or casework, as it is often called, can pay dividends at re-election time, since voters tend to look favorably on a legislator who has helped them out.

The oversight function is one that legislatures have taken on recently. Concerned that the laws they passed and the funds they allocated frequently did not produce the intended effect, legislators began to pay more attention to the performance of the state bureaucracy. Legislatures have adopted a number of methods for checking up on agency implementation and spending. The oversight role takes legislatures into the administrative realm, and, not surprisingly, is little welcomed by agencies, although legislatures see it as a logical extension of their policymaking role.

A History of Legislative Malfunction

The dawning of the twentieth century found state legislatures in poor shape, and they continued to languish well into the 1960s. One widely cited criticism was that state legislatures used horse-and-buggy methods to solve jet-age problems.[2]

Malfunctioning legislatures were the result of three conditions: not enough pay, not enough time, and not enough help.[3] Until the mid-1960s, pay was so low that legislative service attracted only the independently wealthy, the idle, and young careerists on the rise. (For example, lawyers who were just beginning their practice often campaigned for the legislature as a way of getting their name known, in hopes that it might bring some business their way.) Annual legislative salaries ranged from $100 in New Hampshire to $10,000 in New York. Serving in the legislature was a part-time vocation, and most members had to supplement their salaries with other jobs. Others collected unemployment compensation, and some sought income from legal fees, retainers from corporations, public utilities, or interest groups, or outright payoffs from lobbyists for votes or other assistance in the legislative process.

The length and frequency of legislative sessions was also a problem. Some were restricted to as few as thirty-six days in session (Alabama, for example), and most met on a biennial basis. For instance, the Texas constitution required the legislature to meet once every two years for 140 days. (Critics have suggested that the constitution really meant for the legislature to meet once every 140 years for two days.) As the policy problems confronting state government became more numerous and complex, legislators found themselves overburdened with work and without the time to give much more than cursory examination to most of the proposed legislation that passed across their desks.

As for help, legislatures in the early 1960s were woefully understaffed and poorly equipped to process information, to study problems, or to respond to the needs of citizens. Many states did not make transcripts of committee hearings or floor debates, and thus had no formal legislative history. Some states turned to organizations like the state bar association for assistance in drafting bills. Without enough staff, legislatures lacked an independent research capability. It was virtually impossible for them to accumulate information and systematically analyze possible solutions to contemporary problems. Instead, they tended to rely on the governor and the executive branch and on lobbyists for special interests, who set the policy agenda and controlled the flow of information.

State legislatures could not function as effective policymaking institutions under these conditions. Although there was a pervasive sense that matters had to improve, it took two factors to shake legislatures out of their lethargy. One was federal court decisions in *Baker* v. *Carr* (1962) and *Reynolds* v. *Sims* (1964), which mandated reapportionment of both the lower and upper houses of state legislatures. Compliance with these rulings eventually changed the composition of legislatures. The other was the activities of private reform groups such as the Committee for Economic Development and the Citizens' Conference on State Legislatures, which promoted the modernization of state legislatures to make them more capable institutions. The success of the reformers has produced legislative assemblies that are far more professional than they were in the past.

Legislative Dynamics

State legislative bodies are typically referred to as "the legislature," but their formal titles vary. In Colorado, it is the General Assembly that meets every year; in Massachusetts, it is the General Court, and in Oregon, it is the Legislative Assembly. The legislatures of forty-three states meet annually; in seven (Arkansas, Kentucky, Montana, Nevada, North Dakota, Oregon, and Texas), they meet every two years. The length of the legislative session varies widely. For example, the Massachusetts General Court convened on January 1, 1986, and did not adjourn until January 6 in the following year; that is 371 calendar days in session. In New Mexico, the legislature gathered in Santa Fe on January 21, 1986, and was out of town by February 20, 1986, for a total of 30 calendar days in session.[4]

The Senate and the House

State legislatures have two houses or chambers, similar to those of the U.S. Congress. Forty-nine states are bicameral; the exception is Nebraska, which in 1934 established a unicameral legislature. Bicameralism owes its existence to the postcolonial era, in which an "upper house," or Senate, represented the interests of the propertied class, and a "lower house" represented everyone else. Even after this distinction was eliminated, states stuck with a bicameral structure, ostensibly because of its contribution to the concept of checks and balances. It is much tougher to pass "bad old bills" when they have to survive the scrutiny of two legislative houses. Having a bicameral structure, then, reinforces the status quo. Unicameralism might improve the efficiency of the legislature, but efficiency has never been a primary goal of a consensus-building deliberative process.

In the forty-nine bicameral states, the upper house is called the Senate; the lower house is usually the House of Representatives. The average size of a state Senate is forty members; Houses typically average about one hundred members. As with most aspects of state legislatures, chamber size varies substantially, from the Alaska Senate with twenty members to the New Hampshire House with four hundred representatives. For senators, the term of office is usually four years, and approximately one-quarter of the states use a two-year Senate term. In many states, the election of senators is staggered. House members serve two-year terms, except in Alabama, Louisiana, Maryland, and Mississippi, where four-year terms prevail.

There are 7,461 state legislators in this country: 1,995 senators and 5,466 representatives. Democrats outnumber Republicans 60 percent to 40 percent; men outnumber women 83 percent to 17 percent; and whites outnumber nonwhites 95 percent to 5 percent. Even this small proportion of women and nonwhites represents a substantial increase, however, from their virtual absence from most pre-1970s legislatures. (Profile 9.1 examines the issue of women in the legislature.) In terms of occupations, lawyers and business owners predominate, followed by employees of someone else and farmers.[5] Figure 9.1 shows the breakdown in professions.

Legislative Districts

Legislators are elected from districts. Each state is divided, or apportioned, into legislative districts, and the delineation of these districts is an intensely political process. Legislative decisions about districting effectively structure the balance of power in a state. In the 1960s, for example, the less populated panhandle area of Florida was overrepresented in the legislature at the expense of the heavily populated southern area of the state. The balance of power lay with the northern rural region.

Malapportionment   Political decisions on districting have often resulted in this sort of **malapportionment,** or unequal representation. For example, before reform, some states had simplified the senatorial districting system by allocating an equal number of senators to each county. (This resembles the U.S. Senate, which has two senators per state.) Because counties vary in population size, some senators were representing ten or twenty times as many constituents as their colleagues were. New Jersey offered one of the most extreme cases. In 1962 one county contained 49,000 residents and another had 924,000, yet each county was allocated one senator and each

PROFILE 9.1
Women's Work: Serving in the State Legislature

Select seven state legislators at random and one of them is likely to be a woman. By 1989, 17 percent of America's state legislators were women. This proportion has slowly but steadily risen during the past twenty years. In the 1960s, female legislators tended to be Republicans and entered politics because of a moral commitment and encouragement by friends and relatives. They were more likely to be found in New England and western states. There were very few women legislators in highly populous, urbanized states, which were characterized by a high degree of competition for comparatively lucrative legislative seats.

Much of this has changed. Although far from achieving gender parity in the legislature, women are a more visible and forceful presence. Every state has female legislators. The representation of women is greatest in New Hampshire (32 percent), Maine (31 percent), Vermont (31 percent), Arizona (30 percent), and Colorado (29 percent). Women occupy 14 percent of the legislative leadership posts and 11 percent of the committee chair positions.

Surveys show that women state legislators think of their female constituents as a special responsibility. And although their legislative interests run the gamut, they often identify issues such as equal pay, comparable worth, child abuse, day care, child support, and infant mortality as legislative priorities. Admittedly, women legislators do not function as a single entity. A number of issues divide them: abortion, the Equal Rights Amendment, party affiliation, and questions of government funding and fiscal responsibility.

Women are no longer oddities in the legislature, but just how rapidly they will increase their numbers is uncertain. After all, incumbency is the fast track to elective office, and there are still comparatively few female incumbents. Open seats are the most winnable legislative slots, and they are typically hotly contested, so the road to legislative parity is not easy for women.

Sources: Center for the American Woman and Politics, "Women in Elective Office 1989," Eagleton Institute of Politics, Rutgers University, May 1989; Carol Nechemias, "Changes in the Election of Women to U.S. State Legislative Seats," *Legislative Studies Quarterly* 12 (February 1987): 125–42; Katherine E. Kleeman, "Women in State Government: Looking Back, Looking Ahead," *State Government* 60 (September/October 1987): 199–203; Carol Mueller, "Consensus Without Unity," *State Government* 60 (September/October 1987): 230–34.

Figure 9.1   The Statehouse as a Second Job,
1986
A 1986 survey determined that 11 percent of
legislators do not have an outside occupation,
and the proportion of full-time legislators is on
the rise.

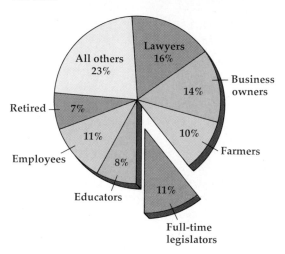

Source: Elizabeth Kolbert, "As Workload Grows,
Number of Part-time Legislators Falls," *New York
Times,* June 4, 1989, p. 13. Copyright © 1989 by The
New York Times Company. Reprinted by permission.

senator had one vote in the Senate.[6] This kind of imbalance meant that a small group of people had the same institutional power as a group that was nineteen times larger. This disproportionate power is inherently at odds with representative democracy, in which each person's vote carries the same weight.

Until the 1960s, the federal courts ignored the legislative malapportionment issue. It was not until 1962, in a Tennessee case in which the malapportionment was especially egregious (House district populations ranged from 2,340 to 42,298), that the courts stepped in. In that case, *Baker* v. *Carr,* the U.S. Supreme Court ruled that the Fourteenth Amendment guarantee of equal protection applies to state legislative apportionment.[7] With that ruling as a wedge, the Court held that state legislatures should be apportioned on the basis of population. In *Reynolds* v. *Sims* (1964), Chief Justice Earl Warren summed up the apportionment ideal by saying, "Legislators represent people, not trees or acres."[8] Consequently, districts should reflect population equality: one person, one vote. This decision, which overturned the apportionment practices of six states, caused a **reapportionment** fever to sweep the country, and district lines were redrawn in every state.

State legislatures are reapportioned after the United States census, which is taken every ten years. This allows population fluctuations—growth in some areas, decline in others—to be reflected in redrawn district lines. Most legislatures do the job themselves, although about one-fifth of the states use an impartial commission to develop a reapportionment plan.

Reapportionment has become a sophisticated operation in which statisticians and geographers use computer mapping to assist the legislature in designing an optimal districting scheme. Allowable deviation from the population equality standard varies, but 7 percent appears to be the maximum. Although "one person, one vote" is the official standard, some unofficial guidelines are also taken into consideration. Ideally, districts should be geographically compact and unbroken. Those who draw the lines pay close attention to traditional political boundaries like counties and to the fortunes of political parties and incumbents. As long as districts adhere fairly closely to the population-equality standard, federal courts tolerate the achievement of unofficial objectives.

Gerrymandering   In apportioning a legislature, the tradition has always been to draw district lines so as to maximize the strength of the party in power. The art of drawing district lines creatively was popularized in Massachusetts in 1812, when a political cartoonist for the *Boston Gazette* dubbed one of Governor Elbridge Gerry's district creations a **gerrymander** because the district, carefully configured to reflect partisan objectives, was shaped like a salamander.

The U.S. Supreme Court returned to the reapportionment issue in 1986 in an Indiana case. *Davis* v. *Bandemer* affirmed the state's apportionment plan, which was designed, according to the Republican Speaker of the House, "to save as many Republicans as possible."[9] The significance of this case, however, lies less in the actual ruling than in the judicial portent. By accepting the case, the Court declared that gerrymandering, previously considered a political matter beyond the Court's jurisdiction, is a judicial issue. Thus, reapportionment plans following the 1990 census will probably encounter court challenges on the grounds of gerrymandering.

Legislatures also have to pay some attention to how their reapportionment schemes affect minority voting strength. It is not unusual for legislatures to design some districts to facilitate the election of blacks or Hispanics. A less felicitous (and illegal) legislative intent might be to design districts so as to dilute minority strength. In some southern states, reapportionment plans intended to aid the election of blacks have had the unintended consequence of helping Republicans.[10] A study of South Carolina Senate reapportionment, for instance, demonstrated that "packing" blacks into districts diluted the Democratic vote of nearby districts, thus allowing Republicans to win.[11] Both blacks and Republicans have benefited from such reapportionment. Figure 9.2 shows how the drawing of district lines can affect the fortunes of three groups: white Democrats, black Democrats, and white Republicans.

Figure 9.2   Electoral Geography
The circle in the center shows a hypothetical distribution of black
Democrats (BD), white Democrats (WD), and white Republicans
(WR) in an area. The dotted lines in the other circles demonstrate
how the drawing of district lines affects electoral outcome.

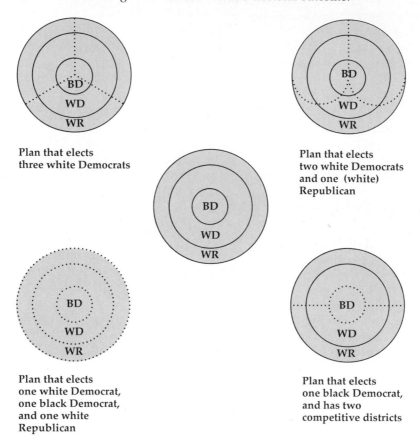

Plan that elects
three white Democrats

Plan that elects
two white Democrats
and one (white)
Republican

Plan that elects
one white Democrat,
one black Democrat,
and one white
Republican

Plan that elects
one black Democrat,
and has two
competitive districts

Source: Kimball Brace, Bernard Grofman, and Lisa Handley, "Does Redistricting
Aimed to Help Blacks Necessarily Help Republicans?" *The Journal of Politics* 49
(February 1987): 175. Reprinted by permission.

Reapportionment provided an immediate benefit to previously underrepresented urban areas, and increased urban representation led to a growing responsiveness in state legislatures to the problems and interests of
cities and suburbs. Where reapportionment had a partisan effect, it generally benefited Republicans in the South and Democrats in the North. Other
impacts of reapportionment have included the election of younger, better-
educated legislators and, especially in southern states, better representation
of blacks.[12] In addition, state legislatures, in the opinion of those who

served during the reapportionment period of 1967–77, took a discernibly liberal turn.[13] All in all, reapportionment is widely credited with improving the representativeness of American state legislatures.

Legislative Pay

Legislative compensation has increased handsomely in the past two decades, again with some notable exceptions. Before the modernization of legislatures, salary and per diem (money for daily expenses) levels were set in the state constitution, and thus impossible to adjust without a constitutional amendment. By the late 1980s, only nine states continued to have constitutional restrictions on legislative compensation.[14] Lifting these limits placed legislatures, as the policymaking branch of state government, in the curious position of setting their own compensation levels. Recognizing that this power is a double-edged sword—the legislators can vote themselves pay raises and the public can turn around and vote them out of office—almost half of the states have established compensation commissions or advisory groups to make recommendations on legislative remuneration.

As of 1989, annual salaries of legislators (excluding per diem) ranged from a low of $100 in New Hampshire to a high of $57,500 in New York.[15] Eight states paid their legislators over $30,000 annually. Compare these figures with the more modest pay levels of legislators in Arizona ($15,000), Georgia ($10,125), and Maine ($9,000). States with more generous compensation typically demand more of a legislator's time than do low-paying states, however. Table 9.1 charts the change in legislative compensation in selected states.

Table 9.1   Changes in Legislative Pay in Selected States

State	Biennial salary				Annual salary	
	1943–44*	1952–53	1962–63	1972–73†	1982–83	1988–89
Arkansas	$1,000	$1,200	$2,400	$2,400 (bi)	$ 7,500	$ 7,500
Colorado	1,000	2,400	4,800	7,600 (an)	14,000	17,500
Iowa	1,000	2,000	n.a.	5,500 (an)	13,700	14,600
Minnesota	1,000	3,000	4,800	9,600 (bi)	18,500	24,174

* In 1943–44, all four states had biennial legislative sessions. By 1982–83, only Arkansas continued this tradition.
† The 1972–73 figures reflect biennial salaries in Arkansas and Minnesota and annual salaries in Colorado and Iowa.
Source: Data for each year from same year's edition of *The Book of the States* (Chicago and Lexington, Ky.: Council of State Governments).

Legislative Leadership

Legislatures need leaders, both formal and informal. Each chamber usually has four formal leadership positions. In the Senate, a president and a president pro tempore (who presides in the absence of the president) are in charge of the chamber; in the House, the comparable leaders are the Speaker and the Speaker pro tempore. These legislative officials are chosen by the members. Both houses have two political party leadership positions: a majority leader and a minority leader.

The leaders are responsible for making the legislature run smoothly and seeing that it accomplishes its tasks. In a typical chamber, the presiding officer appoints committee members, names committee chairs, controls the activity on the floor, allocates office space and committee budgets, and, in

Table 9.2   Standing Committees of the Legislature

Both houses of state legislatures typically have standing committees dealing with these substantive issues:

> Agriculture
> Banking/Financial Institutions
> Business and Commerce
> Communications
> Education
> Elections
> Energy
> Environment and Natural Resources
> Ethics
> Government Operations
> Health
> Insurance
> Judiciary and Criminal Justice
> Local Affairs
> Public Employees
> Rules
> Social/Human Services
> Transportation

In addition, both houses have standing committees that address the raising and allocating of state funds. These committees may have different names in different chambers:

> Appropriations
> Finance and Taxation
> Ways and Means

some states, selects the majority leader and the holders of other majority-party posts.[16] The actual influence of the leadership varies from one chamber to another. One factor that affects leaders' power is whether the positions are rotated or retained. Leaders who have the option of retaining their position can build power bases; rotation replaces one set of leaders with another on a regular basis, and so the leaders are lame ducks when they assume the posts.

Leadership in legislatures is linked to political parties. In states with competitive political parties, legislative behavior and decisions have a partisan cast. There are Democratic and Republican sides of the chamber and Democratic and Republican positions on bills. The parties meet in caucuses to design their legislative strategies and generate camaraderie. In states dominated by one political party, partisanship is less important. In one-party settings, the dominant party typically develops splits or factions at the expense of party unity. However, when the vastly outnumbered minority party begins to gain strength, the majority party usually becomes more cohesive. In the Texas House, traditionally a bastion of Democratic party strength, Republicans now hold about one third of the seats. This has caused the Democrats to coalesce and organize a truly partisan Democratic caucus.[17] As a result, legislative voting patterns among Democrats show less fractionalization.

One reward for party loyalty comes when pork barrel projects are dispersed. The way this process works in the Democratic-controlled North Carolina legislature is instructive.[18] Requests for local appropriations (to construct a civic center in district x, a sewer system in district y) are consolidated into an omnibus "pork" bill. The leaders determine what is in and what is out. Which projects are included depends largely on partisanship (Democrats get more than Republicans) and loyalty (party members who occasionally vote with Republicans get less than "true" Democrats).

Legislative Committees

The workhorse of the legislature is the committee. Under normal circumstances, a committee's primary function is to consider bills—that is, to hear testimony, perhaps amend the bills, and ultimately approve or reject them. A committee's action on a bill precedes debate in the House or Senate.

All legislative chambers are divided into committees, and most committees have created subcommittees. Committees can be of several types. A *standing committee* regularly considers legislation during the session. A *joint committee* is made up of members of both houses. Some joint committees are standing; others are temporary and are convened for a specific purpose, such as investigating a troubled agency or a particularly challenging public policy problem. Most states use *interim committees* during the period when the legislature is not in session to get a head start on an upcoming session. The number of committees varies, but most Senates and Houses have standing committees on the topics listed in Table 9.2.

A substantive standing committee tends to be made up of legislators who are interested in that committee's subject matter.[19] Thus you find farmers on the Agriculture Committee, teachers on the Education Committee, bankers on the Commerce Committee, lawyers on the Judiciary Committee, and so on. These legislators bring knowledge and enthusiasm to the committee; they also bring a certain bias since they tend to function as advocates for their career interests.

The central concern of a standing committee is its floor success—getting the full chamber to accede to its recommendations on a bill. There are a number of plausible explanations for a committee's floor success.[20] For one thing, a committee with an ideological composition like that of the chamber is likely to be more successful than one whose members are at odds with the chamber. Also, committees full of legislatively experienced members ought to have more floor success than committees composed of legislative novices. And committees that have a reputation for being tough have more floor success with their bills than committees that are easy and pass everything that comes before them.

How a Bill Becomes Law

A legislative bill starts as an idea and travels a long, complex path before it emerges as law. It is no wonder that of the 431 bills introduced in the Ohio legislature in 1986, only 43 had become law by the end of the session.[21]

We seldom think of meat processing and bill processing as similar, but legislative veterans frequently comment that there are two items that people should not see being made: sausage and laws. This comparison is probably unfair to the meat processing industry. Figure 9.3 diagrams the law-making process.

The Birth of a Bill: Idea and Introduction

Bills do not emerge out of thin air; they come from the recommendations of interest groups and their lobbyists, state agencies, constituents, and citizen groups. Governors are initiating legislation at an ever-increasing rate.

Suppose that an organization you have joined, Students Opposed to Toxins (SOT), has come up with a plausible solution to the toxic waste problem plaguing your state. The first step is to find a legislator who would be willing to introduce your solution in the form of legislation. In other words, you have to find someone to sponsor the bill. Introduction ("putting the bill in the hopper") gives the proposal legislative life.

The new bill will be assigned a number (for example, House Bill 1520) and given *first reading*. In this stage, it is announced to the House (this usually involves reading its title) and referred by the Speaker to a committee. Committee referral matters. The Speaker can assign H.B. 1520 to the Com-

Figure 9.3   How a Bill Becomes Law
At each of the stages in the process, supporters and opponents of a
bill clash. Most bills stall at some point and fail to make it to the end.

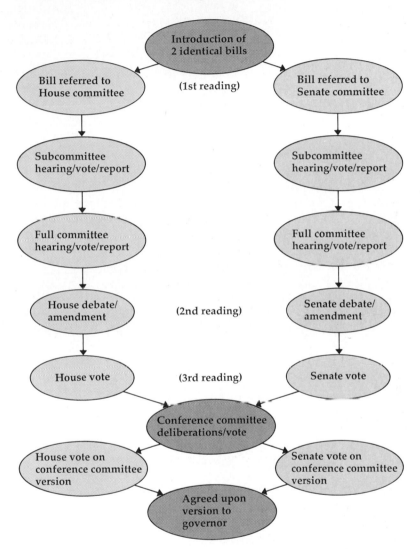

mittee on Environment, which is likely to be receptive to its contents, or to
the Committee on Commerce, which may be less than enthusiastic about it.
If the bill goes to Environment, it will be scheduled for a hearing. If it goes to
Commerce, it stands a good chance of being assigned to a subcommittee
that will never meet. If no action is taken in committee, the bill has been
pigeonholed or *bottled up,* and it will in all likelihood die there. (This potential
for committees to become bill graveyards has caused many legislatures to

adopt procedures to force a committee to hear a bill.) If H.B. 1520 will cost the state money, it will be referred to the Committee on Appropriations in addition to a substantive committee.

Committee Action

For the sake of argument, let's assume that good fortune visits SOT, and that the Speaker is an environmentalist (or fears the wrath of the Environment Committee chairperson if the bill is assigned to Commerce), and refers H.B. 1520 to the Committee on Environment. The bill will be assigned by the committee chairperson to a subcommittee for study and recommendation. The committee staff, knowledgeable about environmental issues, will evaluate it. At the subcommittee hearing, you and SOT will have a chance to present arguments in favor of it, and the bill's sponsor will also attend, probably rushing into the hearing room from another committee meeting. Opponents will also be heard. As a consequence of the discussion, members of the subcommittee may offer amendments to the bill. This is another critical point, as some amendments may not be supportive of the bill's content. For example, if a subcommittee member raises his hand and suggests that the subcommittee strike everything after the enacting clause (the introduction), he has proposed an *unfriendly amendment,* effectively killing the bill by deleting all of its substance. For the sake of this example, let's assume that only friendly, clarifying amendments are attached to H.B. 1520 and that the subcommittee recommends it favorably to the full committee.

The Committee on Environment will schedule the bill, with the subcommittee's amendments, for a full committee hearing. You can be sure that the bill's opponents, unhappy at failing to get the bill pigeonholed or reported unfavorably by the subcommittee, will have contacted the members of the full committee to make their case. Anticipating this, SOT should engage in its own lobbying of committee members in support of the bill. (You cannot expect the merits of the bill to carry the day. You have to convince committee members that voting for H.B. 1520 is in their interest.) Both the bill's sponsor and the groups that testified before the subcommittee typically reappear at the full committee hearing.

Given the number of bills introduced and the proportion that ultimately become law, SOT should be pleased that its idea has gotten this far. Since so many legislatures operate with absolute limits on session length, they often run out of time before they can consider all of the bills that have been introduced.[22] Time is an interesting concept in a legislature, and skillful legislators use time to their advantage. Common explanations for legislative action (or inaction) are "because of a lack of time" or "owing to time pressures." Politics and Policy 9.1 takes a look at legislative time and committee behavior.

POLITICS AND POLICY 9.1
The Night of the Long Knives

Time and tradition form a curious bond in a legislative organization. Time is critical in the sense of deadlines, and tradition matters in terms of informal norms. The Virginia House of Delegates' "Night of the Long Knives" illustrates both.

State legislatures typically impose deadlines for action on bills that have been introduced and referred to committees. The Virginia House of Delegates, controlled largely by conservative Democrats, has such a time limit, and proposals pending before the Courts of Justice Committee find themselves subjected to curious treatment because of it. Each session, the committee engages in an "annual bill-killing marathon" that reportedly leaves "the dreams of many liberals and Republicans shredded like so much confetti" —hence the name "the night of the long knives." On the evening of the deadline, committee members convene to deal with pending legislation. In five hours one February night in 1987, they disposed of two hundred bills, at an average rate of one and a half minutes of deliberation per bill. Fifty bills met their death, one hundred were passed by (thus leaving them for dead), and fifty were approved.

It is the spirit of the affair that attracts attention. Members of the committee (in the 1987 session, all male and all lawyers) are renowned for their wit and their merciless skewering of hapless bills. Few bills (or their sponsoring legislators) emerge unscathed. But the process plays an important role in filtering out bad or premature legislative proposals.

Most legislatures have a committee that performs a similar function. In some states it is the Appropriations Committee that serves as the "killer" committee, and that, by simply setting the funding level at zero dollars, in effect kills a bill. In other legislatures it is the Calendar Committee, which schedules only the bills it deems worthy for floor action. In each instance, these committees have taken on an informal role beyond their formal one.

Source: From R. H. Melton, "Night of Long Knives Guts Va. Proposals," *Washington Post,* February 8, 1987, p. D3. Copyright © 1987 *The Washington Post.* Reprinted by permission.

Let's assume that H.B. 1520 is supported by the committee, although it is subjected to a variety of amendments. Someone on the committee might move that the committee offer a substitute for H.B. 1520. It will probably be wise for the sponsor to accept the motion, because reporting a committee substitute adds the weight of the committee to what was originally an individually sponsored bill. The next critical juncture is getting the bill through the scheduling committee, often called the Committee on Rules and Calendar. While the Committee on Environment was considering H.B. 1520, twenty other committees were also considering bills. The Rules and Calendar Committee is a point at which bills can pile up. Some may languish on the back burner while the committee schedules the bills it prefers or considers most pressing for floor debate. SOT has to make certain that H.B. 1520's sponsors (the Environment Committee and the original sponsor) actively urge the Rules and Calendar Committee to schedule the bill for prompt floor action.

Floor Action

Some time usually passes between standing committee passage and floor action, so SOT and other supporters of the bill should use the time to contact legislators to acquaint them with the positive features of H.B. 1520. Again, you can be certain that the bill's opponents have not conceded defeat. Opposing interests will be lobbying hard against H.B. 1520.

When the bill is scheduled for floor action, it is given *second reading*, which means that it is put formally before the House for its consideration. Arguments for and against ensue, and amendments are offered and accepted or rejected. If H.B. 1520 survives this part of the process, its supporters can breathe a sigh of relief. True, it still faces *third reading*, which is a vote on final passage, but in most states second reading spells a bill's fate. Third reading becomes a formality, and you may find that some of H.B. 1520's opponents vote for the bill at this point, in grudging recognition that they have lost the battle. (This maneuver often confuses voters when they try to evaluate a legislator's voting record. A legislator may be actively opposed to a particular bill right up until third reading, at which time he votes in favor of it.) Virtually all states require a *roll-call vote* on third reading, which means that an individual legislator's vote is recorded. Watching the electronic toteboard flash a green (yes) or a red (no) light next to a legislator's name is the key moment for the bill and for SOT members.

The Other Chamber

H.B. 1520 now goes to the Senate, where it will experience a similar routine of referral, committee hearings, and floor action. Because this can be a lengthy process, SOT would have been well served to have had a senator introduce a companion bill to H.B. 1520 at the beginning of the session, so the bills could move through the two houses simultaneously. Whichever bill passes first can be substituted for the companion in the other chamber, if the other chamber agrees. This saves time, an important commodity in legislatures with short sessions.

If the Senate further amends H.B. 1520, the two versions of the bill will have to be reconciled. If the House refuses to accept the Senate's amendments, the presiding officers of the two chambers appoint a *conference committee* to devise some kind of compromise. This can be a challenging process, depending on the extent of disagreement and the intensity of the conferees' views. Their compromise is called a conference committee report and is voted on by both houses. If both chambers approve the conference committee report, the bill is *enrolled*—certified and signed by the presiding officers—and sent to the governor for her signature.

The Governor

The law-making process is not over until the governor acts (or fails to act). Bills passed by the legislature can be signed by the governor, vetoed by the governor, or not acted on by the governor. If the governor signs H.B. 1520, it becomes law. If the governor vetoes it, it still has a chance to become law, if the legislature can *override* the veto. An override typically requires an extraordinary majority (a two-thirds vote) in both houses. If the legislature feels strongly about H.B. 1520, it might be able to muster the necessary votes. But if the governor's veto comes after the legislature has adjourned, a special session must be called to consider the veto. (This is why some legislatures do not officially adjourn until the governor has acted on all bills.) If the session has ended and the governor has not acted on H.B. 1520, in most states the bill becomes law without the governor's signature (the unsigned bill is a symbolic gesture of the governor's lack of support). In other states, the governor's inaction is a *pocket veto* of the bill (see Chapter 7), and the bill is dead.

After reading about the law-making process, you might be amazed that any good idea survives to become law. In one sense, that is a valid assessment, because without pushes and nudges along the way—without active and skillful lobbying, without the support of key legislators, and without fortuitous timing—few bills would become law. A consensus has to be built around the issue, and the bill has to be widely perceived as the appropriate solution, before proposed legislation becomes statutory.

Legislative Behavior

Legislatures have their own dynamics, their own way of doing things. Senate and House rulebooks spell out what can and cannot be done in the same way that an organization's by-laws do. Legislatures, for the most part, function as self-regulating institutions; it is especially important, therefore, that participants know what is expected of them. To make certain that the chamber's rules are understood, most legislatures conduct orientation sessions for new members.

Legislative Norms

An understanding of the legislature involves not only knowledge of formal structures and written rules but also an awareness of informal norms and unwritten policies. For example, nowhere in a state's legislative rules does it say that a freshman legislator is prohibited from playing a leadership role, but the unwritten rules of most legislatures place a premium on seniority. A primary rule of legislative bodies is that "you gotta go along to get along," a phrase that emphasizes teamwork and "paying your dues." Legislators who are on opposite sides of a bill to regulate horse racing might find themselves on the same side of a bill outlawing the sale of the handguns known as Saturday night specials. Yesterday's opponent is today's partner. Because of this, no one can afford to make bitter enemies in the legislature and expect to flourish. For example, legislators learn early that concealing the real purpose of a bill in order to secure its passage will get them in trouble.[23] During the 1988 session, a freshman legislator from Tennessee wrote in his diary that he planned to watch one of his colleagues more closely, because "he slipped in an amendment increasing legislative pensions without disclosing what he was doing."[24]

Those who aspire to rise from rank-and-file legislator to committee chairperson and perhaps to party leader or presiding officer find consensus-building skills quite useful. These skills come in handy because many norms are intended to reduce the potential for conflict in what is inherently a setting full of conflict. For instance, a freshman legislator is expected to defer to a senior colleague. Although an energetic new legislator might chafe under such a restriction, one day he will have gained seniority and will take comfort in the rule. Legislators are expected to honor commitments made to each other, which encourages reciprocity: "If you support me on my favorite bill, I will be with you on yours." A legislator cannot be too unyielding. Compromises, sometimes principled but more often political, are the backbone of the legislative process. Very few bills are passed by both houses and sent to the governor in exactly the same form they had when they were introduced.

It is worth noting that the internal organization of legislatures varies, as a study of three legislatures—New York, Connecticut, and California—emphasizes.[25] New York has a stable organizational system in which seniority is the major criterion for advancement. Empire State legislators tend to be careerists who expect a long tenure in office. In Connecticut, where an unstable system prevails and few career incentives exist, members stay in the legislature a short time and then return to private life. California has an unstable system that is not seniority-oriented, and talented legislators can advance quickly; therefore, California legislators tend to be politically ambitious, and the system allows them to act as entrepreneurs. The informal rules in these three legislatures are quite different, and the institutions tend to attract different types of legislators. Table 9.3 classifies the New York legislature as career-oriented, Connecticut as a dead end, and California as a springboard.[26] The groupings are based on the compensation and advancement potentials of twenty-five legislatures.

Informal rules are designed to make the legislative process flow more smoothly. Legislators who cannot abide by the rules, those who refuse to "go along," find it difficult to get along. They are subjected to not-so-subtle behavior modification efforts, such as powerful social sanctions (ostracism and ridicule) and legislative punishment (bottling up their bill in committee or assigning them to an unpopular committee), to promote adherence to norms.

Legislative Cue-Taking

Much has been written about how legislators make public policy decisions, and a number of explanations are plausible. Legislators may adopt the policy positions espoused by their political party. They may follow the dictates of their conscience—that is, they do what they think is right. They may yield to the pressures of organized interest groups. Legislators may be persuaded by the arguments of other legislators, such as a committee chairperson who is knowledgeable about the policy area or a trusted colleague who is considered to be savvy, or they may succumb to the entreaties of the governor, who has made a particular piece of legislation the focus of her administration. Of course, legislators may attempt to respond to the wishes of their constituents. On a significant issue—one that has received substantial media attention—they are likely to be subjected to tremendous cross-pressures.

One remarkably candid assessment of how legislators make public policy decisions was offered by a freshman in the Tennessee House of Representatives. He identified two often unspoken but always present considerations: "Will it cost me votes back home?" and "Can an opponent use it against me [in the] next election?"[27] These pragmatic concerns intrude on the more idealistic notions of decision making. They also suggest a fairly cautious approach to bold policy initiatives.

Assuming that legislators are concerned about how a vote will be received back home, it seems logical that they would be particularly solicitous of public opinion. Some research on the subject, however, has shown that state legislators frequently hold opinions at odds with those of their constituents.[28] Moreover, they misperceive what the public is thinking, so it is difficult for them to act as mere **delegates** and simply fulfill the public's will. To improve the communications link, some legislators use questionnaires to

Table 9.3   The Proportion of Full-time Legislators in Three
Types of Legislatures

Type of legislature	Percentage of members identifying themselves as "legislator"
Career	
Maryland	0
Michigan	69
Minnesota	1
Missouri	20
New York	55
Ohio	31
Pennsylvania	64
Wisconsin	62
Dead end	
Connecticut	7
Georgia	2
Iowa	0
North Carolina	0
Oklahoma	3
Oregon	5
Rhode Island	0
South Dakota	0
Texas	3
Vermont	0
Virginia	0
West Virginia	0
Springboard	
Alaska	0
California	36
New Jersey	0
South Carolina	0
Washington	0

Source: Adapted from Peverill Squire, "Career Opportunities and Membership Stability in Legislatures," *Legislative Studies Quarterly* 13 (February 1988): 75. Reprinted by permission of the Comparative Legislative Research Center, and the author.

poll constituents about their views, and some hold town meetings at various spots in the district to assess the public's mood.

It is quite probable that freshmen legislators feel more vulnerable to the whims of the public than legislative veterans do. The new legislator therefore devotes more time to determining what the people want, while the experienced legislator "knows" what they want (or perhaps knows what they need), and thus functions as a **trustee**—someone who follows his or her own best judgment. Since the vast majority of legislators are returned to office election after election, it appears that there is some validity to this argument. Recent research on Oklahoma and Kansas legislators, for example, found that the members' personal values were consistently important in their decision choices.[29]

In the final analysis, the issue under consideration appears to be the determining factor in how legislators make decisions. "When legislators are deeply involved with an issue, they appear to be more concerned with policy consequences" than with constituency preferences.[30] In this situation, legislators are not simply bent on re-election. But if legislators are not particularly concerned about an issue that is important to their constituents, they will follow their constituents' preference. In that sense, they act as **politicos,** adjusting as the issues and cues change.

Legislative Reform and Capacity

It was not easy to get state legislatures where they are today. During the 1970s, fundamental reforms occurred throughout the country, as legislatures sought to increase their capacity and to become more professional. The modernization process never really ends, however.

The Ideal Legislature

In the late 1960s, the Citizens' Conference on State Legislatures (CCSL) studied legislative performance and identified five characteristics critical to legislative improvement.[31] Ideally, a legislature should be functional, accountable, informed, independent, and representative; the acronym is FAIIR.

The *functional* legislature has virtually unrestricted time to conduct its business. It is assisted by adequate staff and facilities, and has effective rules and procedures that facilitate the flow of legislation. The *accountable* legislature's operations are open and comprehensible to the public. The *informed* legislature manages its workload through an effective committee structure, legislative activities in between sessions, and a professional staff, and it conducts regular budgetary review of executive branch activities. The *independent* legislature runs its own affairs independently from the executive

Table 9.4   FAIIR Rankings of State Legislatures

Overall	State	Functional	Accountable	Informed	Independent	Represen-tative
1	Calif.	1	3	2	3	2
2	N.Y.	4	13	1	8	1
3	Ill.	17	4	6	2	13
4	Fla.	5	8	4	1	30
5	Wis.	7	21	3	4	10
6	Iowa	6	6	5	11	25
7	Hawaii	2	11	20	7	16
8	Mich.	15	22	9	12	3
9	Nebr.	35	1	16	30	18
10	Minn.	27	7	13	23	12
11	N.Mex.	3	16	28	39	4
12	Alaska	8	29	12	6	40
13	Nev.	13	10	19	14	32
14	Okla.	9	27	24	22	8
15	Utah	38	5	8	29	24
16	Ohio	18	24	7	40	9
17	S.Dak.	23	12	15	16	37
18	Idaho	20	9	29	27	21
19	Wash.	12	17	25	19	39
20	Md.	16	31	10	15	45
21	Pa.	37	23	23	5	36
22	N.Dak.	22	18	17	37	31
23	Kans.	31	15	14	32	34
24	Conn.	39	26	26	25	6
25	W.Va.	10	32	37	24	15

Source: Citizens' Conference on State Legislatures, *The Sometime Governments: A Critical Study of the 50 American Legislatures,* 2nd ed. (Kansas City, Mo.: CCSL, 1973).

branch. It exercises oversight of agencies, regulates lobbyists, manages conflicts of interest, and provides adequate compensation for its members. Finally, the *representative* legislature has a diverse membership that effectively represents the social, economic, ethnic, and other characteristics of the constituencies.

CCSL evaluated the fifty state legislatures and scored them according to the FAIIR criteria. The rankings, which appear in Table 9.4, offered a relatively scientific means of comparing one state legislature with another. Overall, the "best" state legislatures were found in California, New York, Illinois, Florida, and Wisconsin. The "worst," in the assessment of CCSL, were Alabama, Wyoming, Delaware, North Carolina, and Arkansas.

The CCSL report triggered extensive self-evaluation by legislatures around the country. The results are readily apparent. In terms of the CCSL

Table 9.4   FAIIR Rankings of State Legislatures *(cont.)*

Overall	State	Functional	Accountable	Informed	Independent	Represen-tative
26	Tenn.	30	44	11	9	26
27	Ore.	28	14	35	35	19
28	Colo.	21	25	21	28	27
29	Mass.	32	35	22	21	23
30	Maine	29	34	32	18	22
31	Ky.	49	2	48	44	7
32	N.J.	14	42	18	31	35
33	La.	47	39	33	13	14
34	Va.	25	19	27	26	48
35	Mo.	36	30	40	49	5
36	R.I.	33	46	30	41	11
37	Vt.	19	20	34	42	47
38	Tex.	45	36	43	45	17
39	N.H.	34	33	42	36	43
40	Ind.	44	38	41	43	20
41	Mont.	26	28	31	46	49
42	Miss.	46	43	45	20	28
43	Ariz.	11	47	38	17	50
44	S.C.	50	45	39	10	46
45	Ga.	40	49	36	33	38
46	Ark.	41	40	46	34	33
47	N.C.	24	37	44	47	44
48	Del.	43	48	47	38	29
49	Wyo.	42	41	50	48	42
50	Ala.	48	50	49	50	41

criteria, states have made tremendous strides in legislative institution-building. A re-examination of the criteria reveals these facts:

1. *Staffing.* Individual legislators have vastly more staff resources at their disposal than they did twenty years ago. Many states provide year-round staff for legislators (especially senators) at the state capital, and some states make personnel available in a legislator's district office. (A few states limit staff to the session only.) Professionals serve on at least some legislative committees in all states, and the legislative leaders' staff has increased. This has helped make legislatures more independent and informed.

2. *Compensation.* Serving in the legislature is more lucrative than it was twenty years ago. In about one-quarter of the states, legislators can afford to be full-time, or professional, legislators. Legislative leaders typically enjoy a higher level of remuneration than members. For example, when the Tennessee legislature increased annual legislative

salaries by 32 percent (from $12,500 to $16,500), it tripled the salaries of House and Senate speakers (from $18,500 to $47,500).[32]

3. *Time.* Annual sessions are the rule, not the exception. However, thirty-eight state legislatures continue to operate with constitutional or statutory limits on session length. In order to remain ready to respond to a crisis, some legislatures that have the authority to do so will recess temporarily rather than adjourn. In this way the presiding officers can call legislators back into session without the formality of a special session.[33]

4. *Committee structure.* In response to CCSL recommendations, most states have tinkered with legislative committee structure. Over time, however, they have not pared their committees back as drastically as CCSL advocated. Legislators are stretched thin when they are assigned to four committees. However, legislatures do use their committees more effectively, especially by scheduling committee meetings during the period when the legislature is not officially in session.

5. *Facilities.* Legislative surroundings have improved, in some states quite dramatically. New legislative buildings have been constructed, and some states, like Florida, have erected new capitols. Legislators have private offices, ample meeting space, and computerized bill-tracking and vote-tallying systems.

6. *Leadership.* Legislatures have experienced substantial democratization in the years since the CCSL study. Legislative leaders' control over "information, favors, and finances" has diminished,[34] and there is an increasing tendency to rotate leadership assignments.

7. *Rules and procedures.* Legislatures have begun to realize that their rules and procedures are not cast in stone. Periodic review of rules and procedures is not uncommon. For example, legislatures have imposed limitations on the number of bills that can be introduced, instituted more equitable committee hearing procedures, and established deadlines for committee action.

8. *Size.* CCSL reformers argued that a legislature composed of between 100 and 150 senators and representatives would be about right. Almost 40 percent of today's legislatures exceed that size, and, not unexpectedly, large legislatures balk at reducing the number of legislators. One noteworthy reduction came when Illinois voters cut their House by one-third, to 118 representatives. But size is a tricky issue. A large legislature reduces the citizen-to-legislator ratio and thus increases the potential for representation, although it probably functions less efficiently than a small one. Which value should be maximized?

9. *Ethics.* Legislatures have made substantial efforts to improve ethical behavior in the institution. They have adopted financial disclosure and conflict-of-interest laws for members, and a few have begun to impose restrictions on a former legislator's ability to hire himself out as a legislative lobbyist.

The Effects of Reform

The jury is still out on whether increased professionalism in state legislatures represents an unqualified victory. Initial research suggested that legislative professionalism had an independent, positive effect on social welfare policy.[35] In other words, policymaking in professional legislatures seemed to be more responsive to the needs of lower-income citizens. However, some subsequent research arrived at a different conclusion: professionalized legislatures did not seem to affect the direction of state public policy.[36] More recent studies have sought to clarify the relationship between the characteristics of a legislature and its public policy outputs. They have led to the recognition that legislative characteristics *and* a variety of other factors, such as a state's socioeconomic conditions and executive branch strength, affect policy decisions.[37]

In the late 1980s, legislative capacity gained attention. Recent analysis has confirmed the significance of the variables that CCSL used. Legislatures that are closer to the FAIIR standards appear to have greater capacity than the remaining "less FAIIR" institutions do.[38]

Political scientist Alan Rosenthal, who has closely observed legislative reform, has warned that "the legislature's recent success in enhancing its capacity and improving its performance may place it in greater jeopardy than before."[39] That certainly was not an intended effect of the reform efforts. Rosenthal's argument is that a constellation of demands pulls legislators away from the legislative core. That is, the new breed of legislators gets caught up in the demands of re-election, constituent service, interest groups, and political careerism and thus neglects institutional matters such as structure, procedure, staff, image, and community. The legislature as an institution suffers, because it is not receiving the necessary care and attention from its members.

Consider the idea of a citizen-legislator, one for whom service in the legislature is a part-time endeavor. Since the onset of reform, the proportion of legislators who are lawyers, business owners, or insurance or real estate executives has dropped from almost one-half to slightly over one-third.[40] This has been accompanied by a rise in the number of full-time legislators. Take another look at Table 9.3. Roughly two-thirds of the legislators in Michigan, Pennsylvania, and Wisconsin identify themselves as "legislators," with no other occupation.

The critical issue is whether the decline of the citizen-legislator is a desirable aspect of modernization. Should a state legislature represent a broad spectrum of vocations, or should it be composed of career politicians? One perspective is this: "If I'm sick, I want professional help. I feel the same way about public affairs. I want legislators who are knowledgeable and professional."[41] Another view is represented by a Michigan legislator who believes that his careerist colleagues have lost touch with their constituents: "When you spend all your time in Lansing, you're more influenced by the lobbyists than by your constituents."[42]

In effect, state legislatures are becoming more like the U.S. Congress. Legislators are staying in the legislature in record numbers. Modernization has made the institution more attractive to its members, and thus turnover rates are declining. Do we really want fifty mini-Congresses scattered across the land? Today's legislatures are more "FAIIR" than in the past, but reform has also brought greater professionalization of the legislative career, increased polarization of the legislative process, and more fragmentation of the legislative institution.[43]

Relationship with the Executive Branch

In Chapter 7, you read about strong governors leading American states boldly into the twenty-first century. In this chapter, you have read about strong legislatures charting a course for that same century. Do these institutions ever collide in their policymaking? Is there conflict between the legislature and the governor in a state? Of course there is. As one observer noted, "Conflict is the chief manifestation of a new calculus of political and institutional power in state government today."[44]

Interinstitutional tension is inevitable, but it is not necessarily destructive. It is inevitable because both governors and legislators think that they know what is best for the state. It is not necessarily destructive because during the posturing, bargaining, and negotiating that produces a consensus, they may actually arrive at the "best" solution.

Dealing with the Governor

The increased institutional strength of the legislature and its accompanying assertiveness have made for strained relations with a governor accustomed to being the political star. When a legislature is dominated by one party and the governor is of the other party, a condition referred to as **split party control** of state government, the ingredients for conflict are assembled. This is a fairly new phenomenon in the Democrat-dominated southern states, which elected their first Republican governors since Reconstruction during the 1970s (the Carolinas and Texas) and 1980s (Alabama and Louisiana). In some states in the Rocky Mountain area, the reverse was the case. During the 1980s, popular Democratic governors and Republican-dominated legislatures governed Arizona, Colorado, Utah, and Wyoming. The result of split party control can be finger-pointing and blame-shifting.

But having a governor and a legislature controlled by the same party does not necessarily make for easy relations. In fact, it may actually increase the strain between the two branches. Especially in states where the two parties are competitive, legislators are expected to support the policy initiatives of their party's governor. Yet the governor's proposals may not mesh with individual legislators' attitudes and ambitions.

Executives have a media advantage over deliberative bodies like a legislature. We saw media-use developed to a veritable art form at the national level during the Reagan years, when the media conveyed images of the president as leader, and the Congress as a collection of self-interested politicians. A similar situation exists at the state level. The governor is the visible symbol of state government, and as a single individual fits into a media world of thirty-second sound bites. The Colorado Senate president explains it from a distinctly legislative perspective: "We never win in Colorado in the public's eye. We, the legislature, are always the bad guys, and the governor is the white hat, and he has been very successful in making that appeal to the public through the news media."[45] In contrast, media images of the legislature often portray deal-making, pork barrel politics, and general silliness.

Another weapon of the governor is the veto. In 1987 the Wisconsin legislature found out just how powerful this can be, when the Republican governor used 290 partial vetoes (the deletion of specific items) to virtually

This cartoon captures the popular image of the legislature. It has been difficult for legislators to dispel this impression.

rewrite the budget produced by the Democratic legislature.[46] The governor's explanation was that the legislature was testing him by passing a budget bill that was "porked up."[47] In the 1988 session, the legislature changed its strategy; according to the Speaker of the House, "We put more controversial items in bills where he couldn't use his partial veto, where he had to veto the whole bill or sign it."[48]

Sometimes governors who have previously served as legislators seem to have an easier time dealing with the law-making institution. For example, Governor Madeleine Kunin of Vermont assumed the office after three terms in the legislature and one term as lieutenant governor, "knowing the needs of legislators, the workings of the legislative process, the sensitivities of that process."[49] Usually about two-thirds of the governors have had legislative experience. In 1988, for example, thirty-one of the fifty governors had put in time in the legislative ranks.

The legislature is not without its weapons. In recent years a popular battleground has been the state budget. Legislatures have enacted a number of measures designed to enhance their control and to reduce the governor's flexibility in budgetary matters.[50] For example, some states now require the governor to get legislative approval of budget cutbacks in the event of a revenue shortfall. Others have limited the governor's power to initiate transfers of funds among executive branch agencies. These actions reflect the continuing evolution of legislative-executive relations.

Overseeing the Bureaucracy

Legislative involvement with the executive branch does not end with the governor. State legislatures are increasingly venturing into the world of state agencies and bureaucrats, with the attitude that "we've authorized the program, we've allocated funds for it, so let's see what's happening." Legislative oversight involves four activities: policy and program evaluation, legislative review of administrative rules and regulations, sunset legislation, and review and control of federal funds received by the state.[51]

Policy and Program Evaluation   Legislatures select auditors to keep an eye on state agencies and departments (in a few states, auditors are independently elected officials). Auditors are more than superaccountants; their job is to evaluate the performance of state programs as to their efficiency and effectiveness (sometimes known as the postaudit function). They conduct periodic performance audits to measure goal achievement and other indicators of progress in satisfying legislative intent, a process that has been credited with both saving money and improving program performance.[52] The key to a useful auditing function is strong legislative support (even in the face of audits that turn up controversial findings) and at the same time a guarantee of a certain degree of independence from legislative interference.[53]

Legislative Review of Administrative Rules   All state legislatures are involved in reviewing administrative rules and regulations, but they vary in the way they do it. They may assign the review function to a special committee (such as a Rule Review Committee) or to a specific legislative agency, or they may incorporate the review function in the budgetary process.

Legislative review is a mechanism through which administrative abuses of discretion can be corrected. Legislative bills frequently contain language to the effect that "the Department of Youth Services shall develop the necessary rules and regulations to implement the provisions of this act." This gives the agency wide latitude in establishing procedures and policies. The legislature wants to be certain that in doing so, the agency does not overstep its bounds or violate legislative intent. If it is found to have done so, then the legislature can overturn the offensive rules and regulations through modification, suspension, or veto, depending on the state.

This is a true gray area of legislative-executive relations, and court rulings at both the national and state level have found the most powerful of these actions, the **legislative veto,** to be an unconstitutional violation of the separation of powers. If legislative vetoes and similar actions are determined to be unconstitutional, more states will return to the traditional

Legislative service is not all fun and games, as these weary Connecticut legislators, many of them buried in paper, will agree.

means of reviewing agency behavior—through the budgetary process. Increasingly, legislatures are requiring state agencies to furnish extensive data to justify their budget requests, and they can use their financial power to indicate their displeasure with agency rules and regulations.

Sunset Legislation   Half the states have established **sunset laws** that set automatic expiration dates for specified agencies and other organizational structures in the executive branch. An agency can be saved from termination only by an overt renewal action by the legislature. Review occurs anywhere from every two years to every twelve years, depending on individual state statute, and is conducted by the standing committee that authorized the agency or by a committee established for sunset review purposes (such as a Government Operations Committee).

During the 1970s, sunset legislation was widely hailed as an effective tool for asserting legislative dominion over the executive branch, but fifteen years' experience with the technique has produced mixed results, and some states have repealed their sunset laws. Agency reviews tend to be time-consuming and costly. Nevertheless, they do acquaint the legislature with the intricacies of agency operations. Termination, however, is more a threat than an objective reality.

State Legislative Review   Since the early 1980s, legislatures have played a more active role in directing the flow of federal funds once they have reached the state. Before this time, the sheer magnitude of federal funds and their potential to upset legislatively established priorities caused great consternation among legislators. The executive branch virtually controlled the disposition of these grant funds by designating the recipient agency and program. In some cases, federal money was used to fund programs that the state legislature did not support. Federal dollars were simply absorbed into the budget without debate and discussion, and legislators were cut out of the loop. By making federal fund disbursement part of the formal appropriations process, however, legislators have redesigned the loop.

If legislatures are to do a decent job in forecasting state priorities, some control of federal funds is necessary. With reduced federal aid to states, it is critical for legislators to understand the role that federal dollars have played in program operation. When funding for a specific program dries up, it is the legislature's responsibility to decide whether to replace it with state money.

How effectively are legislatures overseeing state bureaucracies? As with so many questions, the answer depends on who is asked. From the perspective of legislators, their controls increase administrative accountability. A survey of legislators in eight states found legislative oversight committees, the postaudit function, and sunset laws to be among the most effective bureaucratic controls available.[54] Another effective device, and one that legislatures use in special circumstances, is legislative investigation of an agency, an administrator, or a program. But from the perspective of the governor, many forms of legislative oversight are simply meddling, and as such they undermine the separation of powers.[55]

Legislatures and Capacity

State legislatures are fascinating institutions. Although they share numerous traits, each maintains some uniqueness. Despite their newfound seriousness of purpose, legislatures still address items that most observers would deem trivial. The highly reformed Florida legislature, for example, devoted some of its precious 1988 session time to the question of whether Myakka fine sand should be designated the official state soil.[56] That same legislature, however, gave considerable time and energy to much more compelling problems, such as medical malpractice insurance, education finance, and prison overcrowding.

The demands placed on state legislatures are unrelenting. Challenges abound. The ability of the legislatures to function effectively in these times depends on institutional capacity. The extensive modernization that virtually all legislatures underwent in the 1970s is evidence of institutional renewal. Structural reforms and a new breed of legislator have altered state legislatures and are sending them in the direction of increased capacity.

Summary

Overcoming a history of legislative malfunction, state legislatures have embarked on an aggressive effort at reform and modernization. These changes have affected their three major functions: policymaking, representation, and oversight. Today's legislatures have become more functional, accountable, informed, independent, and representative, or FAIIR.

Legislatures are deliberative bodies with their own informal rules and behavioral norms. Today's legislator is more likely than ever before to consider herself or himself a full-time legislator, and that has led to some debate over whether the institutions are becoming "congressionalized." Legislatures' relationship with governors and the executive branch continues to move in the direction of greater interaction.

Key Terms

Delegate A legislator who functions as a conduit for constituency opinion.

Gerrymander The process of creatively designing a legislative district to enhance the electoral fortunes of the party in power.

Legislative veto An action whereby the legislature overturns a state agency's rules or regulations.

Malapportionment Skewed legislative districts that violate the "one person, one vote" ideal.

Politico A legislator who functions as a delegate or a trustee as circumstances dictate.

Reapportionment The redrawing of legislative district lines to conform as closely as possible to the "one person, one vote" ideal.

Split party control The situation in which the governorship is controlled by one party and the legislature by the other party.

Sunset laws Statutes that set automatic expiration dates for specified agencies and other organizations.

Trustee A legislator who votes according to his or her conscience and best judgment.

The Judiciary

The Development and Structure of State Court Systems
The Three Tiers/Structural Reforms

How Judges Are Selected
Legislative Election/Partisan Popular Election/Nonpartisan Popular Election/Merit Plans/Gubernatorial Appointment/Which Selection Plan Is Best?/Removal of Judges

Judicial Decision Making
In and Out of the Trial Court/Inside the Appellate Court/Influence of the Legal System on Judicial Decision Making/Personal Values and Attitudes of Judges

"New Wave" Courts: Activism in the States
Judicial Activism/Current Trends in State Courts

New Directions in State Court Reform
Financial Improvements/Dealing with Growing Caseloads/Focus on the Judges

State Courts Enter the Modern Age

In June 1989, Kentucky joined the ranks of a growing number of states that have altered their means of financing public schools. Kentucky's supreme court declared unconstitutional the existing property-based school finance system, because it created and maintained a substantial gap in school spending between wealthy and poor districts. The ruling was based on a provision in Kentucky's constitution that obliges the legislature to establish an equitable system of public education. Because funding disparities meant that schools were not equal either in per-pupil expenditures or in quality of facilities, the court ordered the legislature to make local property tax rates uniform and to devise a way of guaranteeing equal educational opportunities for all children in the state.

Skiing can be a dangerous sport, as anyone who has braved the slopes can attest. In an increasingly litigious society like ours, lawsuits by injured skiers are commonplace. Montana's legislature, responsive to the state's powerful ski resort interests, enacted a "skier responsibility" law that prevented skiers from recovering damages from ski operators if their injury resulted from "any risk inherent in the sport of skiing." Since that clause covered just about all contingencies, skiers were effectively left without legal recourse. But in 1988 the Montana supreme court threw out the law, finding that it protected ski operators from legal damages even when they were at fault. In cases in which ski operators are found negligent because of malfunctioning equipment, unusual hazards on the slopes, or other dangers, they are now held liable for damages.[1]

All sorts of conflicts and problems find their way to state and local courts, from the profound (public education) to the mundane (skiing). Sometimes, as in Kentucky and Montana, state supreme courts act as policy makers. As the third branch of government, the judiciary is the final authority on the meaning of laws and constitutions and the ultimate arbiter of disputes between the executive and legislative branches. It also makes public policy through rulings on questions of political, social, and economic significance. As noted in Chapter 4, state courts have become more active policymakers in recent years and have increasingly based important decisions on state consitutions rather than on the national Constitution. And like the other branches of state government, their structures and processes have been greatly reformed and modernized in recent years.

The work of the fifty state court systems is divided into three major areas: civil, criminal, and administrative. In **civil cases,** one individual or corporation sues another over an alleged wrong. Typical civil actions are property disputes and suits for damages arising from automobile or other accidents. **Criminal cases** involve the breaking of a law by an individual or a corporation. The state is usually the plaintiff; the accused is the defendant. Murder, assault, embezzlement, and speeding are common examples. **Administrative cases** concern court actions such as probating wills or determining custody of a child of divorced parents.

The Development and Structure of State Court Systems

State courts have evolved in response to changes in their environment. In colonial days, they developed separately, influenced by local customs and beliefs in their colonies. A shortage of trained lawyers and an abiding distrust of English law meant that the first judges were laymen who served on a part-time basis. It did not take long for the courts to become overwhelmed with cases: case overloads were reported as long ago as 1685.[2] More than three hundred years later, backlogs still plague our state judiciaries.

As the population and the economy grew, so did the amount of litigation. Courts expanded in number and in degree of specialization. Their names reflected the problems they were designed to address: small claims court, juvenile court, traffic court. However, their development was not carefully planned. Rather, new courts were added to existing structures. The results were predictably complex and confusing, with overlapping, independent jurisdictions and responsibilities. For instance, Chicago offered an astounding array of jurisdictions, estimated at one time to number 556.[3] State court systems were beset not only by numerous overlapping and independent jurisdictions but by a host of other serious problems, including administrative inefficiency, congestion, and excessive delays. In short, the American system of justice left much to be desired.

The organization of the state courts is important because it affects the quality and quantity of judicial decisions and the access of individuals and groups to the legal system. It also influences how legal decisions are made. An efficiently organized system, properly staffed and administered, can do a better job of deciding a larger number of cases than a poorly organized system can. Court structure is of great interest to those who make their living in the halls of justice, namely lawyers and judges. It can also be an issue of concern to others who find themselves in court.

The Three Tiers

States today have a three-tiered court structure: limited jurisdiction courts, trial courts, and appellate courts. Each tier, or level, has a different *jurisdiction*, or range of authority. Courts in the lowest tier—*limited jurisdiction courts*—have **original jurisdiction** over specialized cases, such as those involving juveniles, traffic offenses, and small claims (see Politics and Policy 10.1). This means that these courts have the power to hear certain types of cases first, in contrast to **appellate jurisdiction,** which means the courts review cases on appeal after they have been tried elsewhere. Most states have three to five courts of limited jurisdiction, with names that reflect the type of specialized case: traffic court, police court, probate court, municipal

POLITICS AND POLICY 10.1
Taking Your Case to Small Claims Court

Almost all states offer a relatively simple and inexpensive way to settle minor civil disputes without either party having to incur the financial and temporal burdens of lawyers and legal procedures. Small claims courts are usually divisions of county, city, or district trial courts. The plaintiff (the person bringing the suit) asks for monetary recompense from the defendant (the individual or firm being sued) for some harm or damage. Claims are limited to varying amounts, depending on the state. The average maximum is around $900. Some states allow claims as high as $3000. The cost of taking a case to small claims court is usually $25 or less.

The proceedings are informal. Each party presents the relevant facts and arguments to support their case to a judge. The party with the preponderance of evidence on his or her side wins. Most disputes involve tenant-landlord conflicts, property damage, or the purchase of merchandise (e.g., shoddy merchandise or the failure of a customer to pay a bill).

According to a 1978 study by the National Center for State Courts, the plaintiff usually wins. About half the time defendants do not show up to plead their case and thereby lose by default. In contested cases, plaintiffs win around 80 percent of the time. Of course,

court, and so on. Criminal cases usually are restricted by law to violations of municipal or county ordinances and are punishable by a small fine, a short jail term, or both.

The middle tier of the state judiciary is composed of *major trial courts,* which exercise general authority over civil and criminal cases. Most cases are filed initially under a major trial court's original jurisdiction. However, trial courts also hear cases on appeal from courts of limited jurisdiction. Major trial courts are often organized along county or district lines. Their names vary widely: circuit courts, superior courts, district courts, courts of common pleas.

The upper tier consists of **supreme courts** (sometimes called courts of last resort) and, in most states, **intermediate appellate courts.** Oklahoma and Texas have two supreme courts, one for criminal cases and the other for civil disputes. Thirty-five states have intermediate appellate courts (Alabama, Oklahoma, Oregon, Texas, Pennsylvania, and Tennessee have two, typically one each for criminal and civil cases). Most are known as superior

collecting the award is quite a different matter, and sometimes requires the services of the local sheriff.

The Consumer's Union, the publisher of *Consumer Reports* magazine, offers an instruction booklet on small claims court. It recommends the following steps in handling your case:

1. *Properly identify your opponent.* The legal name of a business may not be the same as the advertised name. Look at the business license, which must be posted. Individuals can often be identified through automobile registration files.
2. *Send a warning letter* stating your claim, the facts of the case, and that you will file a suit in small claims court if you do not receive a satisfactory reply within a specified period of time.
3. *Find the court.* Try the telephone book under small claims, municipal, or county courts.

Another option is to call the state or local office of consumer affairs.

4. *File a claim and pay the filing fee.* Follow the exact procedures specified.
5. *Notify the defendant.* The court will usually do this for you, but if its initial effort does not meet with success, it becomes your responsibility. The local sheriff may deliver the notification for a fee.
6. *Assemble the evidence.* This includes all relevant documents, photographs, witnesses, and objects.
7. *Consider an out-of-court settlement* if offered by the defendant.
8. *Present your case to the judge.* A dress rehearsal in front of a friend or family member is advised.

Source: "Role of the Small-Claims Court," *Consumer Reports,* November 1979, pp. 666–70. Copyright 1979 by Consumers Union of United States, Inc., Mount Vernon, NY 10553. Reprinted by permission from CONSUMER REPORTS.

courts or courts of appeals. Their work generally involves cases on appeal from lower courts. Thus, these courts exercise appellate jurisdiction. State supreme courts also have original jurisdiction in certain types of cases, such as those dealing with constitutional issues.

Appellate court decisions are rendered by a panel of judges, in contrast to a single judge or a jury, which decides lower court cases. Majority rule determines case outcomes. Usually, the judges write majority and minority opinions. The typical supreme court consists of a chief justice and six associate justices, although several states have a total of nine justices and some have only five. The number of intermediate appellate court justices varies widely from state to state.

Intermediate appellate courts constitute the most notable change in the structure of the state court system during the past twenty-five years. They are intended to increase the capability of supreme courts by reducing their caseload burden, speeding up the appellate process, and improving the quality of judicial decision making. The bulk of the evidence points to moderate success in achieving each of these objectives.[4] Case backlogs and delays have been reduced, and supreme court justices arc better able to spend an appropriate amount of time on significant cases.

If a state supreme court so chooses, it can have the final word on any state or local case except one involving a national constitutional question, such as First Amendment rights. Some cases can be filed in either federal or state court. For example, a person who assaults and abducts a victim and then transports him across a state line can be charged in state court with assault and in federal court with kidnapping. Some acts violate nearly identical federal and state laws; possession or sale of certain illegal drugs is a common example. Other cases fall entirely under federal court jurisdiction, such as those involving mail theft, treason, or violation of currency laws. Thus, there is a *dual system* of courts in the United States. Generally, state courts adjudicate, or decide, matters of state law, while federal courts deal with national law. The systems are separate and distinct. Although state courts cannot decide against federal law, they can base certain rulings on the national constitution. For example, it is very unusual for a case decided by a state supreme court to be heard by the U.S. Supreme Court or any other federal court. This occurs only when the case involves a federal question, that is, an alleged violation of federal constitutional or statutory law.

Structural Reforms

The court reform movement that swept across the states in the 1960s and 1970s sought, among other things, to reorganize the state courts into more rational, efficient, and simplified structures. One important legacy of that movement is the *unified court system.*[5]

Although the three tiers of state courts appear to represent a hierarchy, in fact they do not. Courts in most states operate with a great deal of autonomy. They have their own budgets, hire their own staff, and use their own procedures. Moreover, the decisions of major and specialized trial courts usually stand unchallenged. Only around 5 percent of lower court cases are appealed, mostly because great expense and years of waiting are certain to be involved.

Unified court systems consolidate the various trial courts with overlapping jurisdictions into a single administrative unit and clearly specify each court's purpose and jurisdiction. This makes the work of the courts more efficient, saving time and money and avoiding confusion. Instead of having each judge running his or her own fiefdom, rule making, record keeping, budgeting, and personnel management are standardized and centralized, usually under the authority of the state supreme court.

Such centralization relieves judges from the mundane tasks of day-to-day court management so that they can concentrate on adjudication. Additional efficiencies are gained from *offices of court administration,* which exist in all states. Some of these offices do little more than collect and disseminate statistics, but administration in an increasing number of states involves actively managing, monitoring, and planning the courts' resources and operations.

In spite of consolidation and centralization, a great variety of court structures and processes continues to characterize the states, as shown in Figure 10.1. Generally, the most modern systems are found in the western states, including Alaska and Hawaii. Further improvements could usefully be made in most states, but the staggering number of changes made in state court structures and procedures in recent years has produced a system that "would hardly have been recognizable twenty-five years ago."[6]

How Judges Are Selected

In large part, the quality of a state court system depends on the selection of competent, well-trained judges. According to the American Bar Association (ABA), the leading professional organization for lawyers, judges should be

Figure 10.1   Simplicity and Complexity in State Court Systems
State court systems can vary from the simple to the very complex, as illustrated by these two models.

Simple System	Complex System

Appellate Courts

Supreme Court	Supreme Court District Courts of Appeals Intermediate Appellate Courts

Trial Courts of General Jurisdiction

Circuit Courts	Circuit Courts Court of Record

Trial Courts of Special Jurisdiction

District Courts Land Court Tax Appeal Court	Civil Courts of Record Criminal Courts of Record Civil and Criminal Courts of Record Courts of Record County Judges' Courts Juvenile and Domestic Relations Courts Small Claims Courts Justice Courts Municipal Courts Metropolitan Courts

chosen on the basis of solid professional and personal qualifications, regardless of their political views and party identification.[7] Judges should have "superior self-discipline, moral courage, and sound judgment."[8] They should be good listeners, broadly educated, and professionally qualified as lawyers. An appellate or general trial court judge should also have relevant experience in a lower court or as a courtroom attorney. Even the three states* that do not require judges to be members of the state bar rarely permit anyone who is not a lawyer to receive an appointment to the bench.[9]

For a great many years, however, controversy has swirled over the selection of state judges. Should they be elected by popular vote? Should they be appointed by the governor? By the legislature? Many critics insist that judicial selection be free from partisan politics and interest group influence. Others claim that judges should be accountable to the people or to elected officials for their decisions.

The conflict between judicial independence and accountability is manifest in the five types of selection systems used in the states: legislative election, partisan popular election, nonpartisan popular election, merit plans, and gubernatorial appointment. Thirty-nine states use a single selection system for all appellate and major trial court judges. The other states take separate approaches to selecting judges, depending on the tier. Table 10.1 shows these selection techniques. Some states have rather elaborate systems. Oklahoma, for example, utilizes a merit plan for the supreme court and court of criminal appeals, partisan elections for its other appellate courts and district courts, and city council appointment of municipal judges.

Legislative Election

This method is found in only four states, all of them original colonies. In Rhode Island, South Carolina, and Virginia, the legislature elects judges from among announced candidates by majority vote. Connecticut's judicial candidates are nominated by the governor, then appointed by legislative vote. Not surprisingly, the vast majority of judges selected under this plan are former legislators (in South Carolina, the proportion is close to 100 percent).[10] In these four states, a judgeship is viewed as a highly valued reward for public service and a prestigious cap to a legislative career.

Few people other than legislators approve of legislative election. Indeed, the method seems open to criticism. The public has no role in choosing judges or re-electing them, so accountability is minimal. The judges may be independent, but since the major criterion for selection is service as a legislator, they often lack other qualifications. Legislative service has little connection to the demands of a judgeship.

---

*The three states are Massachusetts, New Hampshire, and Rhode Island, which also have no U.S. citizenship, residence, or minimum age requirements.

Partisan Popular Election

Judges for courts in one or more tiers run for popular election on a party ballot in fifteen states. More than half of the partisan election states are located in the South; Mississippi was the first to adopt this system, in 1832. All except one (New Mexico) are in the eastern half of the United States. This plan enjoyed popularity during the Jacksonian era as a means of ensuring a judiciary answerable to the voters.

In theory, partisan election maximizes the value of judicial accountability. Judges, identified by party label, must run for office, on the same ticket as candidates for other state offices. Like other candidates, they must raise and spend money for their election campaigns and publicly deal with political issues. The ABA Code of Judicial Conduct forbids judicial campaigning on legal issues, but this prohibition is sometimes overlooked in close contests and where crime-related concerns claim voters' attention. A more serious problem occurs when judges elected on a partisan ballot are accused of pandering to special interests during election campaigns and favoring them in court decisions. In Texas, for instance, supreme court justices deciding a $10.3 billion judgment against Texaco in favor of Penn zoil were criticized for accepting huge campaign contributions from both parties. Nonpartisan elected judges are open to similar charges.

Nonpartisan Popular Election

In eleven states, appellate judges are elected from a ballot on which party identification is not listed; thirteen states use this method for trial court judges. This selection technique won favor during the first half of the twentieth century, when reformers sought to remove partisanship from the election of judges and certain other officials in state and local government. Political parties are prohibited from openly taking sides in nonpartisan judicial elections. In fact, however, they sometimes play a covert role in such contests. Approximately 95 percent of all judges have a political party preference;[11] most list it in the official biographies that are available to interested voters during campaigns.

Nonpartisan elections tend to reduce voter participation, since party identification is an important voting cue for many citizens. However, voter turnout is very low in most judicial elections, whether partisan or nonpartisan. This is a major criticism of both methods of electing judges: the winners are not truly accountable to the people, which is the principal advantage commonly associated with elections. Low rates of voter interest and participation combine with low-key, unexciting, and issueless campaigns to keep many incumbent judges on the bench as long as they run for re-election. In addition, popular elections have recently been criticized for the growing amount of money necessary to win a state judgeship. In some

Table 10.1   Appellate and Major Trial Court Selection Plans

State	Appellate Courts					Major Trial Courts				
	Leg. elec.	Gub. appt.	Part. elec.	Non-part. elec.	Merit plan	Leg. elec.	Gub. appt.	Part. elec.	Non-part. elec.	Merit plan
Ala.			X					X		
Alaska					X					X
Ariz.					X			X		X
Ark.			X					X		
Calif.					X			X		
Colo.					X					X
Conn.	X					X				
Del.		X					X			
Fla.					X				X	
Ga.			X				X	X		
Hawaii					X					X
Idaho					X					X
Ill.			X					X		
Ind.					X		X			
Iowa					X					X
Kans.					X			X		
Ky.				X					X	
La.			X					X		
Maine		X					X			
Md.					X					X
Mass.					X					X
Mich.				X					X	
Minn.				X					X	
Miss.			X					X		
Mo.					X			X		X

Source: Adapted from *The Book of the States, 1985–86* (Lexington, Ky.: Council of State Governments, 1985), pp. 161–163, updated by the authors.

cases, the implication is that judges have sacrificed their independence and professionalism for crass electoral politics.

It is useful to look at Texas's partisan election system to see the problems with both partisan and nonpartisan elections. As we have noted, judicial candidates in the Texas system appear to be some of the biggest offenders. During the lengthy court battle between Pennzoil and Texaco during the 1980s, Pennzoil and its attorneys legally contributed over $315,000 to the

Table 10.1 Appellate and Major Trial Court Selection Plans *(cont.)*

	Appellate Courts					Major Trial Courts				
State	Leg. elec.	Gub. appt.	Part. elec.	Non-part. elec.	Merit plan	Leg. elec.	Gub. appt.	Part. elec.	Non-part. elec.	Merit plan
Mont.				X					X	
Nebr.					X					X
Nev.				X					X	
N.H.		X					X			
N.J.		X					X			
N.Mex.					X					X
N.Y.		X	X						X	
N.C.			X						X	
N.Dak.				X					X	
Ohio				X					X	
Okla.				X	X				X	
Ore.				X					X	
Pa.			X						X	
R.I.	X									X
S.C.	X					X				
S.D.					X				X	
Tenn.			X		X				X	
Tex.			X						X	
Utah					X					X
Vt.					X					X
Va.	X					X				
Wash.				X					X	
W.Va.			X						X	
Wis.				X					X	
Wyo.					X					X

campaigns of Texas supreme court justices. Texaco, which lost the lawsuit, doled out $190,000. In the eyes of some observers, Texas "justice" was for sale. In early 1988, Chief Justice John Hill resigned from the bench in protest and headed a drive to replace the election process with a merit plan (see below). Hill himself had spent more than $1 million to win election to the Texas Supreme Court in 1984.[12]

Following the trend set in executive and legislative contests, judicial campaign spending has also skyrocketed in other states that elect judges.

Hamilton County, Ohio, District Court Judge Norbert A.
Nadel hears testimony seeking to block Pete Rose's
scheduled hearing with baseball commissioner A. Bartlett
Giamatti on Rose's alleged betting on baseball games.
After ruling in Rose's favor in June 1989, Nadel was
accused of pandering to the voters, since he faced
re-election in 1990.

The 1987 Ohio race for supreme court chief justice cost $2.7 million, $1.7 million of which was spent by the loser. (In 1980 the two chief justice candidates
spent only $99,192). The largest campaign contributors are usually lawyers
and other groups with a stake in judges' decisions. In Ohio, labor unions,
business interests, and the medical profession were the biggest givers.[13]

It looks as though judges running for election are forfeiting their independence in certain legal disputes while offering accountability only to the

highest bidders instead of to the general public. Neither independence nor accountability is achieved, if this indeed is the case. According to the president of the Ohio State Bar Association, "The people with money to spend who are affected by court decisions have reached the conclusion that it's a lot cheaper to buy a judge than a governor or an entire legislature, and he can probably do a lot more for you."[14]

If it is, as some people argue, unethical for a judge to rule on a case in which she or he has accepted money from one or more of the interested parties, then it would be difficult to bring together enough judges to hear cases in Texas and Ohio. As a direct consequence of the burgeoning costs of judicial elections, other states are joining Texas in actively considering alternative selection plans, or at least in imposing spending and contribution ceilings for judicial contests.

Merit Plans

Dissatisfaction with the other methods for selecting judges has led to the popularity of so-called *merit plans*. Incorporating elements of gubernatorial appointment and elective systems, merit plans attempt to provide a mechanism for appointing qualified candidates to the bench while permitting the public to evaluate a judge's performance through the ballot box.

Recommended by the ABA in 1937 and strongly supported today by virtually the entire legal community, merit plans have been adopted by all but two of the states that have changed their selection systems since 1940. Missouri became the initial adopter in 1940; Kansas followed eighteen years later. Since then another twenty states have adopted merit plans, and others are considering merit selection.

The Missouri Plan Commonly referred to as the Missouri Plan, the basic merit plan involves three steps:

1. A judicial nominating commission meets and recommends three or more names of prospective judges to the governor. Members of this bipartisan commission usually include a sitting judge (often the chief justice), representatives chosen by the state bar association, and laypersons appointed by the governor. In a few states nominations are made by a group of judges.

   The nominating commission solicits names of candidates, investigates them, chooses those it believes to be the three or more best-qualified individuals, and then forwards their names and files to the governor.
2. The governor appoints the preferred candidate to the vacant judgeship.
3. A retention election is held, usually after one or two years, in which the newly appointed judge's name is placed before the voters on a nonpartisan ticket. The voters decide whether the judge should be

retained in office. If he or she is rejected by a majority vote, the judicial nominating commission begins its work anew. Subsequent retention elections may be held every eight or twelve years, depending on the merit plan's provision.

Various hybrids of the basic plan are used in several states. For example, the California Plan for choosing appellate judges begins when the governor identifies a candidate for a vacancy on the bench and sends that person's name to the Commission on Judicial Appointments. The commission, composed of two judges and the attorney general, hears testimony regarding the nominee and votes to confirm or reject. The new judge is then accepted or rejected in a retention election in the next regularly scheduled gubernatorial contest.[15] Thus, although the governor appoints, the new judge is subject to confirmation by both the Commission on Judicial Appointments and the voters.

The object of merit plans is to permit the governor some appointive discretion while removing politics from the selection of judges. If they work as intended, popular and legislative elections or direct gubernatorial appointment (which are highly politicized procedures) are replaced by a careful appraisal of candidates' professional qualifications by an objective commission. The process is intended to ensure the basic independence of judges and accountability to the people.

The Politics of Merit Selection   The merit plan looks great on paper, but in practice it has not fulfilled its promise. First of all, it certainly has not dislodged politics from its pre-eminent position in judicial selection. A judgeship is too important a political office in any state ever to be immune from politics. It is a prized job, and an important point of judicial access to numerous individuals, firms, and interest groups, especially the powerful state bar association.

Studies of judicial nominating commissions show that politics is rampant in the review and nomination of candidates.[16] For better or worse, the legal profession often dominates the process. Counting the judge who presides over the nominating commission, lawyers make up a majority in at least nine of the states with merit plans. Bar association lobbying is often the prime reason merit plans are adopted in the first place. However, the legal profession is not monolithic in its politics, and it often divides into two camps, plaintiff's attorneys and defendant's attorneys.

Furthermore, the governor's influence can be exceptionally strong. The laypersons he or she appoints to the nominating commission may hold the judge in awe, but they are there to represent the governor's point of view and sometimes to promote specific candidates.[17] In six states, the majority of commission members are laypeople. The judge may also respect the governor's preferences, particularly if he owes his appointment to that chief executive.

A second criticism of merit plans in action is that the procedure intended to ensure judicial accountability to the people—the retention election—rarely generates any voter interest and almost never results in an incumbent judge being turned out of office.[18] Turnout in retention elections is normally very low, sometimes even lower than the abysmal participation levels in local bond referenda. Fewer than 3 percent of incumbent judges have been voted out in retention elections—only thirty-three judges in forty-five years. In effect, merit selection has been a lifetime appointment in most states, and some have argued that this was its intended purpose.[19]

Recently, however, voter backlashes have occurred against judges whose decisions are distinctly out of step with public opinion. In November 1986, California Chief Justice Rose Bird and two associate justices were swept from the state supreme court by large margins in retention elections, as explained in Profile 10.1. The defeat of judges in retention elections is more likely in other states as well; twenty-seven of the thirty-three losses have come since 1972.

The final charge leveled against merit plans is that in spite of reformers' claims to the contrary, they do not result in the appointment of better-qualified judges or of more women and minorities. When background, education, experience, and decision making are taken into account, judges selected by the merit plan are very comparable to those selected with other plans.[20] Virtually all are white males. Most leave private practice for the bench in their forties and stay there until retirement, often moving up the three tiers of courts. Approximately 20 percent come from a family in which the father or grandfather held political office (often a judgeship).[21] Almost all state judges are qualified attorneys. A substantial majority were born, raised, and educated in the state in which they serve. A majority are members of the Democratic party, but the percentage of Republican judges increased during the 1980s.

Gubernatorial Appointment

This is the method of choice in six states for appellate or major trial courts, or both. Usually the Senate is required to confirm gubernatorial appointees. All six states using this method are former colonies, reflecting the early popularity of the plan. As a method, gubernatorial appointment rates fairly high on independence, since the judge is appointed without popular or legislative participation, but it is weak on accountability, because the judge is beholden to only one person for his or her job.

Although only six states formally recognize it, gubernatorial appointment is in fact the most common method for selecting a majority of appellate and major trial court judges in the United States. Judges in states with popular elections or merit plans often resign or retire from office just before the end of their term.[22] Under most state legal systems, the governor has the power to make interim appointments to vacant seats until the next scheduled election or the commencement of merit plan selection processes.

PROFILE 10.1
Rose Bird and the 1986 Judicial Retention Elections in California

Long considered one of the nation's most liberal and activist courts, the California Supreme Court was skewered by a conservative attack in the November 1986 judicial retention elections. Three of the six judges on the ballot were decidedly defeated by the voters.

The battle against Chief Justice Rose Bird and Associate Justices Joseph Grodin and Cruz Reynoso was led by conservative Republican governor George Deukmejian and supported by the state's Republican political establishment. Bird, Grodin, and Reynoso were appointees under the administration of former Democratic governor Jerry Brown (1974–82). Their defeat turned the ideological bent of the Supreme Court 180 degrees. Deukmejian now had appointed five of the seven justices, all conservatives.[1]

Bird in particular had been the object of criticism and controversy; she held on to the chief justiceship in her initial retention election in 1978 by only 1.7 percent of the vote. Five unsuccessful efforts were made to recall her between 1978 and 1985.[2] The criticism began as soon as she was appointed by Governor Brown. With no prior judicial experience, she was the first woman on the California Supreme Court. Bird soon made

The governor's temporary appointee then enjoys the tremendous advantage of running as an incumbent for the next full term. Gubernatorial appointment is also used to replace a judge who dies before the expiration of his or her term.

A study of state trial courts in California by Philip L. Dubois found that 84.3 percent of the judges selected for the superior court from 1959 to 1978 were initially appointed by the governor to fill vacancies, in spite of the formal requirement for nonpartisan election.[23] The importance of such initial selection is evident in the astounding success of these California judges when running for election to a full term: 99.4 percent won.[24]

What criteria does a governor apply in making appointments to the bench? Political considerations usually come first. The governor can use the appointment to reward a faithful legislator, to shore up support in certain regions of the state, or to satisfy the demands of party leaders and the state legal establishment.[25] Of course, a poor choice can sometimes backfire

a number of substantive and symbolic changes in the state court system, including hiring many women and minorities with scant administrative or judicial experience. The changes were very unpopular with court employees and the legal establishment. Bird was widely accused of poor leadership and administration.[3]

But it was their work on the bench that ultimately brought down Bird and the others. A series of rulings by the liberal court majority significantly extended the rights of the accused and of convicted felons. Bird voted to overturn or declare invalid all sixty-one capital punishment cases brought to the court during a period when polls showed 80 percent support for the death penalty in California. Grodin voted to overturn thirty-five of the forty cases in which he ruled, and Reynoso ruled

against the death penalty in forty-four out of forty-five cases. (No executions have taken place since 1967 in California.)[4]

Exit polls after the retention election indicated that the capital punishment issue was the major cause of the three judges' defeat.[5] This may have indicated the effectiveness of Deukmejian's campaign for governor; he ran ads urging citizens to vote yes on the death penalty by voting against retaining Bird and her two colleagues. In this case, at least, a merit selection plan clearly held judges accountable to public opinion.

[1] John Culver, "California Supreme Court Elections: 'Rose Bird and the Supremes,'" *Comparative State Politics Newsletter*, February 1987, p. 13.
[2] Ibid.
[3] Edwin Chen, "Rose Bird Runs for Her Life," *The Nation*, January 18, 1986, pp. 10–13.
[4] Culver, p. 13.
[5] Ibid.

politically, so governors must pay close attention to the judge's background, education, experience, and legal philosophy.[26]

Dubois's California study sheds some light on how governors choose judges. Although California formally uses a merit plan for appellate courts, its governor has so much input in the judge selection process that it is useful to look at the way certain governors made their choices. Dubois examined the governorships of three distinct individuals: Edmund G. "Pat" Brown (1958–66), Ronald Reagan (1966–74), and Edmund G. "Jerry" Brown, Jr. (1974–82). He found that all three governors used a similar process to identify, evaluate, and select judges. Each one's staff received nominations from legislators, lawyers, interest groups, and other interested individuals (including the candidates themselves), then checked out each nominee's background. Consultations were held with judges, lawyers, and legislators from the local district where the vacancy existed. Names of the most promising candidates were sent to the California State Bar for confidential assessment and rating.[27] Each governor selected more than 80 percent of his appointees from candidates within his own political party who shared his general political ideology.[28] Differences in educational background and legal experience were minimal. All three governors picked a majority of appointees from private law practice, although Governor Jerry Brown did select a greater percentage of women and minorities than did his father or Governor Reagan.

Which Selection Plan Is Best?

The ongoing debate over which of the five selection systems is best is unlikely to be decided convincingly. Legislative election and gubernatorial appointment are probably the least desirable, because judges selected under these systems tend to come from a rather specific political occupation (the legislature), and the general public has little opportunity to hold these judges accountable. None of the three remaining systems produces "better" judges or decisions. Elections emphasize accountability, while merit plans favor judicial independence. Figure 10.2 compares the five methods in terms of accountability and independence. Politics, of course, is what raises all judges into office, regardless of the selection method. Ultimately, the voters and their elected representatives must determine the selection system that is most acceptable.

Removal of Judges

Like anyone else, judges can break the law, go mad, suffer senility, or become physically incapable of carrying out their responsibilities. If a judge displays serious deficiencies, he or she must be removed from the bench. Forty-five states provide for the rather clumsy process of impeachment, wherein charges are filed in the state House of Representatives and a trial is conducted in the Senate. Other traditional means for removing justices include the legislative address (nineteen states) and popular recall (five states).[29] In the legislative address, both houses of the legislature by two-thirds vote must ask the governor to dismiss a judge. Popular recall requires a specified number of registered voters to petition for a special election to recall the judge before the term has expired. These traditional mechanisms are slow, cumbersome, uncertain, and as a consequence seldom used.

In recent years, states have begun utilizing more practical methods for removing judges. Problems related to senility and old age are dealt with in at least thirty-seven states by a mandatory retirement age (generally seventy years) or by the forfeiture of pensions for judges serving beyond the retirement age. Most states have established special entities to address behavioral problems. *Courts of the judiciary*, whose members are all judges, and *judicial discipline and removal commissions*, composed of judges, lawyers, and layper-

Figure 10.2 Accountability and Independence in Judicial Selection Systems

The five methods of selecting judges allow for widely varying degrees of judicial accountability and independence. In most cases, a high degree of one characteristic means a low degree of the other. In the figure, a high level of color in a particular box shows a high level of accountability or independence for that method.

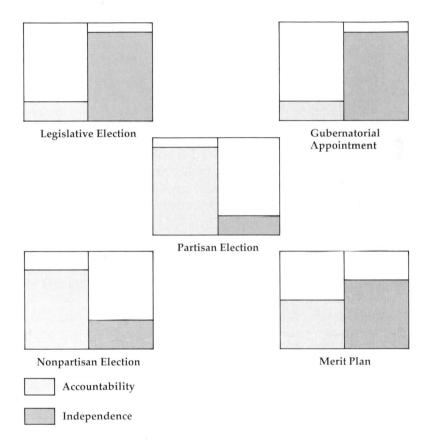

sons, are authorized to investigate complaints about judges' qualifications, conduct, or fitness. These entities may reject allegations if they are unfounded, privately warn a judge if the charges are not serious, or hold formal hearings. Hearings may result in dismissal of the charges, recommendation for early retirement, or, in some states, outright suspension or removal.[30]

The discipline, suspension, or removal of state court judges is uncommon, but it becomes necessary in all states at one time or another. Judges have been found guilty of drunkenness and drug abuse, sexual misconduct with witnesses and defendants, soliciting and accepting bribes, and just about every other kind of misconduct. Sometimes judicial ethics seem to be seriously in short supply. In 1988, fifteen Philadelphia municipal judges resigned or were removed from office in connection with taking bribes and other scandals. Eleven Cook County, Illinois, judges were convicted in the late 1980s as a result of Operation Greylord, which investigated various charges of judicial corruption, including the buying and selling of verdicts.

Judicial Decision Making

What factors influence the rulings of state court judges? Why are some judges widely recognized as "liberal" and others as "tough on crime"? Why does a prosecutor prefer to file her case before one judge rather than another? Isn't justice supposed to be blind, like its symbol of the woman holding the scales?

Judges, alas, are mortal beings just like the rest of us. The legal formalities and mumbo jumbo of the courtroom tend to mask the fact that judges' decisions are no less discretionary and subjective than the decisions of a governor, legislator, or agency head. Before we examine the factors that affect judicial decision making, however, we must distinguish between the legal settings of appellate courts and trial courts.

In and Out of the Trial Court

It has been estimated that 90 percent of all civil and criminal cases are actually resolved outside of the courtroom. In many civil cases, the defendant never appears in court to defend himself, and so he implicitly admits his guilt and loses the case by default. Other civil cases are settled in a pretrial conference between the defendant and the plaintiff (for instance, payments on an overdue debt might be rescheduled).

The process of settling criminal cases out of court at the discretion of the prosecutor and the judge is called **plea bargaining.** Although some defendants plead guilty as originally charged, acknowledging guilt for a lesser charge is more typical in criminal proceedings. With the possible exception of the victim and the general citizenry, everyone potentially benefits from plea bargaining, a fact that accounts for its extensive use. The accused gets off with lighter punishment than she would face if the case went to trial and she lost. The defense attorney frees up time to take on additional legal work. The prosecuting attorney increases his conviction rate, which looks good if he has political ambitions. The judge helps cut back the number of cases awaiting trial. Even police officers benefit by not having to spend time testifying (and waiting to testify) and by raising the department's clearance rate (the number of cases solved and disposed of).

Out-of-court settlements through plea bargaining are negotiated in a very informal atmosphere in the judge's chamber, or between attorneys in the halls of the court building, or over drinks in a neighboring tavern. This is a disturbingly casual way to dispense justice. The process is secretive and far removed from any notion of due process. The prosecuting (district) attorney enjoys enormous discretion in making deals. Often her propensity to settle depends on the length of her court docket or her relationship with the accused's attorney, not on the merits of the case. All too often an innocent person pleads guilty to a lesser offense for fear of being wrongly convicted of a more serious offense, or because he cannot post bail and doesn't want to spend any unnecessary time behind bars. Equally unsettling is the fact that plea bargaining can soon put a guilty person back on the streets looking for another victim.

Nonetheless, plea bargaining is widely practiced. It is almost inevitable when the prosecutor's case hinges on weak evidence, police errors, a questionable witness, or the possibility of catching a bigger fish. Negotiation of a guilty plea for a lesser offense can occur at any stage of the criminal justice process. Sometimes it is abetted by a judge, who promises a light sentence for a guilty plea.

If the accused is unable to reach a compromise with the prosecuting attorney, she faces **bench trial** by a single judge or a **trial by jury.** Both involve a courtroom hearing with all the legal formalities. In some jurisdictions and for certain types of cases, the defendant has a choice. In other situations state legal procedures specify which trial format will be utilized. For murder cases, a jury is always mandatory.

In a bench trial, the judge alone hears all arguments and makes rulings on questions of law. Jury trials depend on a panel of citizens who share decision-making power. Although at least one study has found that juries and judges come to identical decisions in more than 75 percent of criminal cases,[31] the uncertainty introduced by twelve laypersons is usually great enough to convince a defendant to choose a bench trial. Fewer than 1 percent of all cases are resolved by jury trial.

Attorneys seek to limit the unpredictable nature of juries by extensively questioning individuals in the jury pool. Each side in the dispute has the right to strike the names of a certain number of potential jurors without giving a specific reason. Others are eliminated for cause, such as personal knowledge of the case or its principals. In high-stakes cases, the jury selection process involves public opinion surveys, individual background investigations, and other costly techniques.

Inside the Appellate Court

Appellate courts are substantially different from trial courts. No plaintiffs, defendants, or witnesses are present. The appeal consists of a review of court records and arguments, directed by the attorneys, who frequently are not the same lawyers who originally represented the parties. There is no bargaining and no opportunity for predecision settlement. Appellate court rulings are issued by a panel of at least three judges. Unlike decisions in most trial courts, appellate court decisions are written and published. The majority vote prevails. Judges voting in the minority have the right to make a formal, written dissent that justifies their opinion.

There is marked variation in the dissent rates characterizing state appellate courts. Some courts maintain a public aura of consensus on even the most controversial matters by almost always publishing unanimous opinions. Other courts are racked by public battles over legal questions. Personal, professional, partisan, political, and other disagreements can spill over into casework.[32] Supreme courts in states such as California, New York, and Michigan have a history of contentiousness, while others, like those in Rhode Island and Maryland, are paragons of harmony. Dissent rates appear to be related to state social and political factors, such as urbanization and partisan competition. More dissent occurs in courts with a large number of justices[33] and in states with intermediate appellate courts.

On the average, state appellate court dissent rates are much lower than those in federal courts. This reflects the tradition of unanimity in some states, the similar backgrounds of state justices, and the way in which cases are managed. For example, unanimous decisions are partly a result of the common practice of coping with heavy caseloads by making one judge responsible for writing the opinion on each case. The other judges tend to concur without detailed review.

Influence of the Legal System on Judicial Decision Making

Judicial decision making is influenced by factors associated with the legal system, including how state courts are organized, accepted legal procedures, caseload pressures, and the ease with which interested parties gain access to the legal process.

1. *Organization of the court system.* Where court organization includes an intermediate appellate court, supreme court judges benefit from more time to consider important cases. The level, or tier, of court is another structural characteristic that influences decision making. Trial court judges enforce legal norms and routinely *apply* the law as it has been written and interpreted over the years. The trial court permits interpersonal contact among the judge, the jury, and the parties (usually individuals and small businesses). Divorce cases, personal injury cases, and minor criminal cases predominate in trial courts.

Appellate courts are more apt to *interpret* the law and create public policy. Cases typically involve governments and large corporations. State constitutional issues, state-local conflicts, and challenges to government regulation of business are the kinds of issues likely to be found in appellate courts. From time to time a particular case in a high court has an enormous impact on public policy, as judges depart from established precedent or offer new interpretations of the law. Rulings on capital punishment, affirmative action, and the financing of public education offer good examples.

Precedent means that the principles and procedures of law applied in one situation should be applied in any similar situation. Lower courts are supposed to follow the precedents established by higher courts. Although an individual decision may seem unimportant in itself, when taken in the context of other, similar cases, it helps judicial policy evolve. Through this practice the doctrine of equal treatment before the law is pursued. When lower court judges refuse to follow precedent or are ignorant of it, their decisions are likely to be overturned on appeal.

Where do judges look to find existing precedent? Within a state, supreme court decisions set the norms. Supreme courts themselves, however, must scan the legal landscape beyond state boundaries. In the past, decisions of the U.S. Supreme Court heavily influenced them. Increasingly, however, state supreme courts look to one another for precedent. According to a study by Gregory A. Caldeira, state appellate judges have taken a cue from legislators in borrowing from the experiences of other states.[34] They especially tend to rely on the more professional, prestigious supreme courts, such as those of California, Massachusetts, and New York, whose decisions are generally applicable in other states and times. State courts also tend to rely on courts in the same region of the country, where cultural and other environmental factors are similar. The closer two supreme courts are geographically, the more likely they are to communicate.[35] This sort of judicial cross-fertilization puts legal distance between the state and federal supreme courts.

2. *Legal procedures.* In addition to precedent, other legal procedures affect judicial decision making. These include the formal and informal rules of interaction between appellate judges on a panel and between trial court judges and the lawyers and litigants who appear before them. Another important procedural factor is the degree of administrative oversight exercised over a lower court by a higher one.

3. *Caseload pressures.* Caseload affects the decisions of judges. The number of cases varies in accordance with crime rates, socioeconomic characteristics of the jurisdictions, state laws, the number of judges, and many other variables. It stands to reason that the quality of judicial decision making is inversely related to caseload. Judges burdened by too much litigation are hard-pressed to devote an appropriate amount of time and attention to each case before them.

4. *Access to the system.* The final characteristic that affects judicial decisions is the access of individuals, organizations, and groups to the court system. Wealthy people and businesses have more ability to pay for resources (attorneys, legal research, etc.) and therefore enter the legal system with an advantage over poorer litigants. Special interest groups also enjoy certain advantages in affecting judicial decisions, by virtue of their specialized knowledge in areas of litigation, such as environmental or business regulation. Lobbying by interest groups is much less prominent in the judicial branch than in the legislative and executive branches, but groups can affect outcomes by providing financial aid to litigants in important cases and by

filing *amicus curiae* (friend of the court) briefs supporting one side or the other in a dispute.

Most of the legal-system factors influencing judicial decision making are subject to manipulation by elected officials, who can add judges, pass laws, alter procedures, and ease caseloads through various reforms. However, the second set of factors related to decision making in the courts, judges' values and attitudes, are rather immutable.

Personal Values and Attitudes of Judges

Simply put, judges do not think and act alike. Each is a product of his or her individual background and experiences, which in turn influence decisions made in the courtroom. Studies of state supreme court justices have found that decisions are related to the judges' party identification, political ideology, religion, ethnicity, age, and sex. In other words, personal characteristics predispose a judge to decide cases in certain ways.

For example, Stuart Nagel found that Democratic judges tend to favor the claimant in civil rights cases, the government in tax disputes, the employee in worker's compensation cases, the government in business regulation cases, the defendant in criminal contests, the union in a disagreement with management, and the tenant in landlord-tenant cases. Republicans tend to support the opposite side on all these issues.[36] Female judges are more supportive of women in feminist issues and in general are more liberal than their male colleagues.[37] Obviously, these distinctions do not hold in all situations, but the point is that "justice" is a complex concept subject to individual interpretation. No wonder attorneys try to shop around for the most sympathetic judge before filing a legal action.

"New Wave" Courts: Activism in the States

During the 1950s and 1960s, the U.S. Supreme Court was far and away the leading judicial actor in the land. Under the chief justiceship of Earl Warren (1953–69) and his liberal majority, the Court handed down a long series of rulings that overturned legally imposed racial segregation, mandated legislative reapportionment, extended voting rights, and expanded the rights of accused criminals. Significant reversals of state court decisions were commonplace.

Beginning with Chief Justice Warren Burger (1969–86) and a growing faction of conservative judges, however, the Supreme Court changed direction in the 1970s and 1980s. By 1988, a conservative majority was firmly in control. This was reflected in the Court's new hesitance to intrude in many areas and in some backtracking on Warren Court "minimum standards." The Supreme Court's caution created a vacuum of sorts, which some activist state high courts rushed to fill.

Judicial Activism

Judicial activism is a term that has value-laden and ideological dimensions.[38] It is usually associated with political liberalism, and is therefore decried by conservatives. Historically, however, conservative judges have also been accused of activism. For example, New Deal liberals loyal to President Franklin D. Roosevelt argued for judicial restraint by the Court's Republicans who sought to dismember FDR's social and economic programs. Recently, liberals accused the U.S. Supreme Court under Chief Justices Warren Burger and William Rehnquist of reversing rulings made by the Warren Court.

An objective definition of judicial activism, then, points to court-generated change in public policy that is perceived as illegitimate by opponents who favor the status quo.[39] Judicial activism is in the eye of the beholder; it holds a pejorative association for some people and a positive one for others, depending on the issue at hand.

Regardless of one's feelings on the matter, state supreme courts have clearly become *more* activist by expanding into new policy areas. They are more likely to be involved in the policymaking process by making decisions that affect policy in the executive branch, and they even appear to pre-empt the lawmaking responsibility of the legislature. Ironically, some of the most spectacular examples of state court activism are based on prior rulings by the U.S. Supreme Court. In fact, it has been estimated that state supreme courts since 1970 have issued more than three hundred opinions that have taken certain minimum standards established by the federal Supreme Court and expanded them within the jurisdiction of the states. Examples include the following:

- California, Connecticut, and Massachusetts courts have expanded women's right to abortion on demand and the right to financial aid from the state for abortions.
- At least twelve state courts have directly challenged the 1973 Burger Court decision in *San Antonio Independent School District* v. *Rodriquez*, which held that inequalities in the financing of public education due to disparities between wealthy and poor school districts are not in violation of the constitutional guarantee of equal protection of the law. Courts in New Jersey, Idaho, Wyoming, Georgia, Arkansas, and other states have found that property-tax-based finance systems discriminate against children in poor districts and deny them their right under the state constitution to equal educational opportunity.
- Courts in New York, Wisconsin, Mississippi, and elsewhere have rejected a Burger Court ruling that permits prosecutors to introduce evidence obtained through a defective search warrant.
- The California Supreme Court has upheld the right of people to collect petition signatures in a private shopping center, after the U.S. Supreme Court ruled that owners of shopping malls could prohibit such activities.

■ The supreme court of Oregon has rejected a U.S. Supreme Court decision that provided guidelines for declaring certain printed and visual materials to be obscene. The Oregon court noted that its state constitution had been authored "by rugged and robust individuals dedicated to founding a free society unfettered by the governmental imposition of some peoples' views of morality on the free expression of others." "In this state," declared the Oregon Supreme Court, "any person can write, print, read, say, show or sell anything to a consenting adult even though that expression may be generally or universally considered 'obscene.' "[40]

How can the state courts override the decisions of the highest court in the land? The answer is that they are grounding their rulings in their own constitutions instead of in the national constitution. The Bill of Rights protections of many states are more precise and broader in scope than the rights set forth in the first ten amendments to the U.S. Constitution. In several decisions, the Burger Court specifically upheld the right of the states to expand on the minimum rights and liberties guaranteed under the national document. It is generally believed that Chief Justice William Rehnquist, who replaced Warren Burger in 1986, is sympathetic to this position.[41] Of course, when there is an irreconcilable conflict between state and federal law, the latter prevails.

Current Trends in State Courts

The new wave of state court activism is not carrying all the ships of state with it; a majority of state supreme courts remain caught in the doldrums. Some of them are so quiet, as one wag suggested, "that you can hear their arteries harden." But even traditionally inactive courts, in states such as Wisconsin and Mississippi, have been stirred into independent actions recently, and the trend is likely to continue in the 1990s.[42] The U.S. Supreme Court will probably have a conservative majority for many years to come, which will permit the state courts to explore the legal landscape further. State court activism seems to be contagious, as courts utilize their own information and case networks instead of those of the Supreme Court.

Of course, judges cannot seize issues as governors and legislators can; they must wait for litigants to bring them to the courthouse. And although judges can issue rulings, they must depend on the executive and legislative branches to comply with and enforce those rulings. Nonetheless, state supreme courts are becoming more active in the policymaking process. A case in point is the supreme court of New Jersey, which has clearly departed from several U.S. Supreme Court rulings on issues including free speech, mandatory drug testing, and public financing of abortion rights for poor women. The reluctance of the federal court to address important and controversial issues comprehensively has resulted in more cases for state supreme courts to decide.

If there is a danger in the new wave of court activism, it is that some courts may try to go too far in policymaking, intruding into the domain of executive and legislative actors. Judges have little expertise in the substance of public policy or in the policymaking process. They have no specialized staff to perform in-depth research on particular policy issues, and they cannot realistically depend on lawyers to do policy research for them. Attorneys are trained and practiced in legal reasoning, not social science or political science.[43] If justices overstep their authority, in the opinion of the voters, they can be held accountable through the appropriate judicial selection or retention procedures, as the fate of Chief Justice Rose Bird and two of her colleagues in California shows.

New Directions in State Court Reform

We have already discussed several important judicial reforms: intermediate appellate courts, court unification and consolidation, administrative improvements, merit selection plans for judges, and more practical means for disciplining and removing judges. Administrative and organizational issues remain important, as shown by the growing number of states that are centralizing court budgeting and finance.

Financial Improvements

More than half of the states have assumed full financial responsibility for the operation of state and local courts. In 1969 the states paid only about 25 percent of all costs; counties and municipalities took care of the remainder. The alternative to full state funding—state and local sharing of costs—tends to be associated with spending disparities among courts and among judicial districts, and with a lack of mechanisms for evaluating and controlling court operations.

First recommended by the American Bar Association in 1972, centralized budgeting has been adopted by approximately twenty states. Also referred to as *unified court budgeting*, this reform entails a consolidated budget for all state and local courts, prepared by the chief administrative officer of the state court system, that details all personnel, supplies, equipment, and other expenditures.[44] It is intended to enhance financial management and help maintain judicial independence from the executive and legislative branches, which lose their authority to alter the judiciary's budget. A unified court system, centralized financing, and unified budgeting are all similar in that the objective is to bring a state's entire court system under a single authoritative administrative structure.

Dealing with Growing Caseloads

Recently, court reformers have been attending to the need to deal more effectively with excessive caseloads. State courts can confront more than fifty thousand cases each year. Some judges must participate in more than three hundred opinions per year. Delays of two years or more have not been uncommon for appellate court hearings.

Backlogs are caused by numerous factors, including the greater propensity of losing parties to appeal lower court decisions, the tremendous growth in litigation, and poor caseload management procedures. The paramount concern is that long delays thwart the progress of justice. The quality of evidence deteriorates as witnesses disappear or forget what they saw, and victims suffer from delays that prevent them from collecting damages for injuries incurred in a crime or an accident. Even accused (and perhaps innocent) perpetrators can be harmed by being held in prison for long periods while awaiting trial.

Reducing excessive caseloads is not a simple matter. Common sense dictates establishing intermediate appellate courts and adding new judgeships, but apparently intermediate appellate courts tend to attract more appeals by their very existence.[45] New judges speed up the trial process in lower courts, but this can actually add to appellate backlogs. Expanding the number of judges in an appellate court is also problematic; hearings may actually take longer because of more input or factional divisions among judges.[46]

The stubborn persistence of case backlogs has led to some interesting and highly promising new approaches.

1. *Alternatives to formal litigation.* Pennsylvania and at least twelve other states use trained arbiters to help settle civil cases pending before appellate courts. Other techniques include third-party mediation by retired judges or attorneys and voluntary binding arbitration. For example, in South Carolina most civil cases under appeal are eligible for binding settlement by a three-member panel of retired judges or lawyers. A two-year appellate court backlog in civil cases was reduced to four to five months after this system was first implemented.[47]
2. *Punitive court rules.* These provide for monetary fines to be levied by judges against lawyers and litigants guilty of delaying tactics.[48]
3. *Case management systems.* This is probably the most promising innovation. Although individual systems vary widely, a typical approach is *multitracking,* which distinguishes between simple and complex, and frivolous and potentially significant cases, and treats them differently. Complex and significant cases are waved on down the traditional appellate track. Simple and frivolous cases take a shorter track, usually under the direction of staff attorneys. Experiments with multitracking have been successful in reducing case delays in Arizona, Maine, New Hampshire, and several other states.

Other innovations are improving the quality and quantity of court operations as well. Electronic databases are being used to store case information and legal research and to transmit information from law offices to courts. Videotaping of witnesses' testimony is becoming commonplace. Arraignment procedures, during which suspects are formally charged, are also videotaped to save time or to prevent potential problems from a disruptive defendant.[49] Kentucky has instituted "video courtrooms" in which trials are filmed by TV cameras. This creates a more accurate trial record and costs much less than a written transcript by a court stenographer.[50]

Focus on the Judges

Finally, judges are receiving some long overdue attention. Judicial salaries declined markedly during the 1960s and 1970s compared to inflation and to the earnings of attorneys. One study found that whereas the salaries of lawyers increased by 9 percent in noninflationary terms from 1974 to 1984, the salaries of state supreme court justices dropped 15 percent.[51] Workloads burgeoned while compensation declined.

At first glance, judicial salaries seem high enough. In 1988 appellate judges earned from just over $50,000 in Montana to $115,000 in New York. The average was approximately $74,000. Trial court judges were paid 10 to 20 percent less. However, these amounts are substantially below what an experienced, respected attorney can expect to make. For a successful lawyer to give up private practice for the bench, she or he must be willing to take a considerable cut in income. Unlike legislators, state judges are permitted very little outside income. Therefore, it is reasonable to ask whether the best legal minds will be attracted to judgeships, when judicial compensation is relatively low.[52] This is a dilemma at all levels and in all branches of public service, from the municipal finance officer to the highway patrol officer, since most state and local government compensation lags behind pay for comparable jobs in the private sector. If we expect our judges, law enforcement officers, and other public employees to be honest and productive, they must be compensated adequately. Recent salary increases for state judges seem to recognize this principle.

State Courts Enter the Modern Age

As in the case of the other two branches of government, state judicial systems have been touched significantly by reform. Court systems have been modernized and simplified, intermediate appellate courts have been added, processes have been streamlined, judicial selection has been moved toward the merit ideal, and case delays have been reduced. Disciplinary and removal commissions make it easier to deal with problem judges. As a result, courts are entering the 1990s with more independence from political pressures and favoritism and more accountability for their actions. Justice at times may still appear to be an ephemeral ideal, but it is more likely to be approximated in state judicial decisions today than ever before.

The changes in state court systems during the past quarter-century have not gone far enough in some cases, but it is still remarkable that so much has happened in such a short period of time to such a conservative, slow-moving institution of government. The courts, like the rest of society, are no longer immune to the technological age and its prime tool, the computer.

Court modernization and reform have been accompanied by increased judicial activism. The "new wave" state courts have far surpassed the federal courts in public policy activism. They sometimes blatantly disagree with federal precedents and insist on decisions grounded in state constitutional law rather than in the national constitution. In sum, the resurgence of the states has not left the state courts behind.

Summary

The state courts are political institutions with public policy implications. They sort out hundreds of thousands of conflicts each year on an astonishing variety of topics. Like the executive and legislative branches, the judiciary has come in for its share of criticism. Byzantine court organization, judicial selection systems, and excessive delays are just three examples of problems confronting state courts during the past two decades.

The trends in court organization are toward greater centralization, control, and efficiency. Merit plans are replacing other judicial selection methods. Various court reforms have cut down case backlogs. "New wave" activist courts have developed in the states, and reform continues to improve the operation of state judiciaries.

Key Terms

Administrative case A legal dispute not involving a civil suit or a criminal matter.

Appellate court A court that considers appeals of a lower court's decision.

Appellate jurisdiction The power of a court to review cases previously decided by a lower court.

Bench trial Trial by a single judge, without a jury.

Civil case A case that concerns a grievance involving individuals or organizations, not the breaking of a law.

Criminal case A case that involves the breaking of a law.

Intermediate appellate court A state appellate court that relieves the case burden on the supreme court by hearing certain types of appeals.

Judicial activism Judges' making of public policy through decisions that overturn existing law or effectively make new laws.

Original jurisdiction The power of a court to hear a case first.

Plea bargaining Negotiation between a prosecutor and a criminal defendant's counsel that results in the defendant's pleading guilty to a lesser charge or pleading guilty in exchange for a reduced sentence.

Precedent The legal principle that previous court decisions influence future decisions.

Supreme court The highest court, beyond which there is no appeal except in cases involving federal law.

Trial by jury A trial in which a jury decides the facts and makes a finding of guilty or not guilty.

11

The Structure of Local

Government

Orientations to American Communities

Machines, Reform, and Modernization
Urbanization and Industrialization/Political
Machines/The Advent of Reform

Five Types of Local Governments
Counties/Municipalities/Towns and Townships/
Special Districts/School Districts

Interlocal Cooperation

The Issue of Governance

The Board of Estimate, a central feature of New York City's government for almost a century, was ruled unconstitutional by the U.S. Supreme Court in 1989. More powerful than the city council, the board made land-use decisions, awarded municipal contracts and franchises, and helped shape the city's budget.[1] At issue before the Court was the representation of New York City's five boroughs on the board. Each borough had one representative, despite their vastly different population sizes. The Court ruled that this structure violated the principle of "one person, one vote," and thus unleashed a long, involved process to restructure New York City's government.

American local governments were not planned according to some grand design. Rather, they grew in response to a combination of citizen demand, interest group pressure, and state government acquiescence. As a consequence, no scientific system of local governments exists. What does exist is a collection of autonomous, frequently overlapping jurisdictional units. Consider the Pittsburgh metropolitan area. Packed into its 3,000 square miles are 4 counties, 195 cities (55 of which have fewer than 1,000 residents), 117 townships, 331 special districts, and 92 school districts.[2] That is a lot of local government.

What do citizens want from local governments? The answer is, to be governed well. As this chapter demonstrates, "governed well" is hard to define.

Orientations to American Communities

In the early days of the United States, communities were idealized as *civic republics*.[3] In a civic republic, community government is based on the principle of mutual consent. Citizens share fundamental beliefs and participate in public affairs. Their motivation for civic involvement is less materialistic self-interest than altruistic concern for community welfare.

Although this conception continued to have theoretical appeal, its reality was threatened by the growing and diverse nineteenth-century populace, which preferred to maximize individual liberty and accumulation of wealth. An economically inspired conception of the community, that of the *corporate enterprise,* gradually emerged. Economic growth and the ensuing competition for wealth sparked extensive conflict.[4] Local governments created rules and mediated between the clashing interests.

These two theoretical orientations, the community as a civic republic and the community as a corporate enterprise, remain viable. A new orientation is emerging, however—one that portrays the community as a *consumer market*,[5] in which citizens are consumers of public services and governments are providers. This idea places increased emphasis on quality of life and cost-effectiveness. Whether this orientation will demonstrate the staying power of the other two is uncertain, but the consumer-market model is attracting substantial scholarly attention.

A quarter-century ago, a study conducted in Michigan pointed out four types of communities, as identified by officials and candidates for local public offices.[6] The four types were:

1. *the boosteristic city:* the city as a promoter of economic growth.
2. *the amenities city:* the city as a provider and preserver of life's comforts.
3. *the caretaker city:* the city as a maintainer of traditional services.
4. *the brokerage city:* the city as an arbiter of conflicting interests.

Even today these types can be loosely associated with certain kinds of places. For example, many medium-sized communities stretching from the South Atlantic seaboard through the Southwest to the Pacific Coast display characteristics of boosterism—an avid devotion to growth and expansion. Upper-middle-income suburbs of large central cities prefer to focus on conserving community amenities such as residential landscaping. Small towns in all regions that are content to remain small are caretaker communities. Large cities experiencing population loss and economic stresses are where a brokerage style of government is likely to emerge. Of course, all communities have governments; in fact, they have a variety of governments. To understand how local governments affect citizens, we must first look at the ways in which they have developed.

Machines, Reform, and Modernization

As the American republic was developing on a grand scale, pushing west with a vision of manifest destiny, new communities emerged along the way and the original settlements of colonial America matured. The five largest cities in the country in 1800 were New York, Philadelphia, Baltimore, Boston, and Charleston, South Carolina, ranging in population from 61,000 (New York City) to 19,000 (Charleston).[7] The United States was primarily rural well into the nineteenth century. It was not until 1850 that any city other than New York contained more than 100,000 residents.

The modest waterfront communities of the eighteenth century became some of the leading metropolises of the twentieth century. Their development signaled significant transformations in their governments, transformations that reflected a recurring theme in local government: what are the best arrangements for governance?

Urbanization and Industrialization

As communities grew in both population and land area, the *town meeting*, in which all citizens of the town were able to take part in government, became increasingly cumbersome. Granted, local government in the early days was essentially an informal operation. There were few government-provided services; instead, governance was largely in the hands of civic elites. Whenever a community need arose, prominent citizens would form committees to address it. In this way docks and streets were built, town watchmen were organized, and charity was distributed to the poor.[8]

The minimal array of services and the often inferior quality of services that were available contributed to a relatively poor quality of life in nineteenth-century urban areas. The urbanization that accompanied industrialization exacerbated these problems. A burgeoning population required cities to provide sanitation facilities, an adequate water supply, a competent police force, and usable streets. As demand grew, community leaders responded by expanding services, thereby extending the scope of local government. But this was done in a piecemeal manner and produced an unsystematic cluster of boards and departments. Local leaders were hindered in their efforts to create effectively functioning governments by state legislative restrictions; legislatures, dominated by rural interests in most states, exerted a powerful influence and consciously kept urban governments ineffectual.

The crush of immigrants from Germany and Ireland during the 1840s and 1850s, and later from Italy, Poland, and Russia, challenged governance by urban civic elites. The inability of existing local governments to respond to the pressures of urbanization and industrialization produced chaos, which contributed to the development of political machines.

Political Machines

Political machines flourished in northeastern and midwestern cities that were heavily populated by immigrants. Enterprising politicians were able to use the bloc voting of immigrant groups in partisan elections to gain control of political parties and eventually of local governments. These politicians formed alliances and coalitions to create powerful political organizations dubbed machines.

Machine government delivered the vote of ethnic groups, dispensed material benefits such as jobs to loyal party workers, and lacked any underlying ideology. It was in effect the triumph of *quid pro quo* ("something for something") government. Businesses friendly to the machine were awarded padded city contracts and franchises and in return kicked back a portion of what they were paid by the city to the machine. "Bosses," such as Tweed in New York, Curley in Boston, Crump in Memphis, and Pendergast in Kansas City, were cunning politicians who created seemingly invincible machines that ruled local government unchecked.

Political machines were not without societal value, however. To new arrivals in America, they offered friendship, social welfare, and an opportunity for political influence that immigrants would not otherwise have had.

The Advent of Reform

Political machines did not operate without opposition. Gradually, the opposition developed into a full-fledged reform movement, part of the Progressive Era. From the perspective of the reformers, machine government was two things: corrupt and inefficient. They sought to clean up and modernize local government.

Rescuing a "Poisoned System"   In many ways, the reform-machine conflict represented a clash of cultures. Reformism was supported by middle- and upper-class Anglo-Saxon Protestants, many of whose families had lived in America for generations. They resurrected earlier conceptions of the city, espousing a belief in a "public interest" and in "the city as a whole." Reformers argued that local government had become too political and that what was needed was a government designed along the lines of a business corporation. In the words of one reformer, party government had led to the "injection of political virus" into municipal government, which had "poisoned the system."[9]

Many analyses of the reform movement question the reformers' motivations, since their sense of "public interest" directly benefited themselves.[10] Quite simply, they intended to replace a government structure responsive to the working class and ethnic groups with one responsive to themselves.[11] In a sense, machine politicians and reformers were locked in a battle for the hearts and minds of America's city dwellers.

Clean, Efficient Government: Reform Style   To achieve their goals, reformers advocated fundamental structural changes in local government. These changes were intended to destroy the political machines, and included:

- the abolition of partisan local elections (the popular catchphrase of the day was, "There's no Republican or Democratic way to pave a street") in favor of nonpartisan elections.
- the installation of a professionally trained chief administrator or "city manager" to replace party hacks to run local government.
- the use of an at-large (citywide) election mechanism for choosing the governing body, rather than election by district or ward.
- the institution of a merit or civil service system for local government employment, to replace patronage appointments.
- a reduction in the number of local elective positions.

The Impact of the Reform Movement   The reform movement gradually gathered steam and eventually generated a new kind of city government. (Actually, vestiges of reformism can be found in virtually all types of local government, from counties to school districts.) Boston was the first major eastern city to adopt nonpartisan elections (1909), and Dayton, Ohio, was the first large city to install the city manager system (1913). The reform movement was aided by extensive educational outreach efforts through research organizations like the New York Bureau of Municipal Research. Machines began to disappear, and by 1980 even the most resilient, the Daley machine in Chicago, had lost its magic.

Reformed city government—with nonpartisan, at-large elections of the governing body, a manager firmly handling the technical side of government, and employees hired on the basis of merit—is in its fullest flower in the newer, more homogenous suburban Sunbelt communities.[12] The older central cities of the Northeast and Midwest have adopted elements of a reformed system but have resisted total conversion and remain proudly more "political" than their reformed counterparts.

Research on the effects of a reformed city government structure has not produced completely consistent findings, but the preponderance of evidence suggests that citizen participation is lower in reformed governments than in nonreformed ones, minority groups are less represented in reformed governments than in nonreformed ones, and the influence of city bureaucracy increases in reformed governments, while that of the elected governing body decreases. Reform changed the structure of American local governments and, some would argue, increased government capacity. Yet it carried a price, as these findings suggest. Consequently, local governments continue to experiment with structural modifications.

Five Types of Local Governments

Local government is the level of government that fights crime, extinguishes fires, paves streets, collects trash, maintains parks, provides water, and educates children. Some local governments are engaged in all of these activities; others provide only some of these services. A useful way of thinking about them is to distinguish between general-purpose and single-purpose local governments. **General-purpose local governments** are those that perform a wide range of governmental functions. These include counties, municipalities, and towns and townships. **Single-purpose local governments,** as the label implies, have a specific purpose and perform one function. School districts and special districts are single-purpose governments.

Regardless of the purpose of a local government, it is important to remember that it has a lifeline to state government. That is, state government gives local government its legal life. This is not quite the equivalent of a hospital patient hooked up to a life-support system, but it is a basic condition of subnational government organization. Local citizens may instill a local government with its flavor and its character, but state government makes local government official.

Being so close to the people offers special challenges to local governments. Citizens are well aware when trash has not been collected or when

Local governments are designed to fit the setting. In rural communities, such as in Iowa farm areas (above), local governments perform a set of basic activities like public safety, education, and road maintenance. In an urban environment like Des Moines (above right), local governments take on a much wider array of functions.

libraries do not carry current best sellers. They can contact local officials and attend public hearings. Local government can be very interactive.

Counties

Counties are general-purpose units of local government. With a few exceptions, most Americans are in a county right now. The exceptions occur in Connecticut and Rhode Island, where there are no official county governments; Washington, D.C., which is a special case in itself; municipalities in Virginia that are independent jurisdictions and are not part of the counties that surround them; and cities like Baltimore and St. Louis, which, as the result of past political decisions, are not part of a county. Even in places where you do not ever hear about county government—New York City, Philadelphia, Boston, and San Francisco—you are actually in one; long-time consolidated city-county government structures exist in these major cities. State governments have carved up their territory into 3,041 discrete subunits called counties (except in Louisiana, where counties are called parishes, and Alaska, where they are called boroughs).

Not All Counties Are Alike   Seldom does anyone confuse Los Angeles County, California, with Gilmer County, West Virginia. Obviously, counties can be differentiated according to their urban/rural nature.[13] There are

three types of *metropolitan* counties, some of which contain large cities (the core counties) and others of which abut the core county (the fringe counties). The core county is likely to serve as the work destination of the residents of the fringe counties. Fewer than 10 percent of the counties in America are core or fringe, but these are the counties that we hear about most—places like Dade County (Miami), Cook County (Chicago), and Fulton and DeKalb counties (Atlanta). The third kind of metropolitan county is the single-county metropolitan area. It differs from the core and fringe counties because its largest cities do not attract commuters from nearby areas. (Approximately 15 percent of American counties fall into this category.)

Even though most Americans live in metropolitan areas, most counties are *nonmetropolitan,* and there are three types of these too. Those that contain one or more growing small cities (the urbanized counties) act as service centers for surrounding rural areas. These are the nonmetropolitan equivalents of the metropolitan core counties. Counties categorized as "less urbanized" are those with populations in the 2,500-to-20,000 range, containing only one small city. The most rural of all the counties are the "thinly populated centers," and they have no incorporated places with more than 2,500 residents. In northern Wyoming or almost anywhere in Nevada, "less urbanized" and "thinly populated" are very real concepts. Politics and Policy 11.1 tells the story of the life and death of a nonmetropolitan county in Nevada.

Why We Have County Governments   Counties were created by states to function as their administrative appendages. In other words, counties were expected to manage activities of statewide concern at the local level. Their basic set of functions traditionally included property tax assessment and

The Life and Death of a Nuclear County

One of the shortest-lived counties in America was also one of the most unusual. Bullfrog County was created by the state of Nevada to serve as the designated site for high-level nuclear waste disposal. Its creation represented an effort by Nevada to capitalize on an unwanted activity. The county had no residents and no buildings. Bullfrog County was created on June 30, 1987, and died a nonnuclear death less than a year later.

Bullfrog's genesis is interesting. As Nevada leaders began to realize that their state would probably be designated by the national government for the unwanted disposal site, they cast about for ways to reap benefits from the designation. Because the national government compensates jurisdictions for the tax revenues they lose from the existence of certain federal facilities, Nevada legislators decided to carve a new twelve-square-mile county out of existing Nye County.

Bullfrog was to be no ordinary county. Under the provisions of the legislative enactment, the governor was to appoint the county commissioners (after all, there were no residents of the county), and Carson City (the state capital, located 270 miles away) was to be the county seat. The real rationale for Bullfrog County was its exceptionally high property-tax rate. When it came time for the national government to reimburse Bullfrog (in reality, the state of Nevada) for lost revenue, the amount would be significant.

As might be expected, officials of Nye County, which would have received the federal compensation if no Bullfrog County existed, were none too pleased. The nuclear waste disposal facility would still be located in their midst, but they would receive no federal payments. Nye County promptly sued the state, claiming that the creation of Bullfrog County violated thirty-seven provisions of the Nevada and U.S. constitutions.

As public debate ensued, state officials gradually began to rethink their support of Bullfrog. Nevada's image, already characterized by gambling and prostitution, took on a nuclear glow. Another factor was a change in the national government's provisions for the distribution of compensation, which rendered Bullfrog County expendable. The governor withdrew his support, and when a state judge ruled that the creation of the county was unconstitutional, few supporters remained to appeal the decision.

Source: Dana Titus, "Bullfrog County: A Nevada Response to Federal Nuclear-Waste Disposal Policy," *Publius: The Journal of Federalism* 20 (Winter 1990). Reprinted with permission.

collection, law enforcement, elections, land transaction record keeping, and road maintenance.[14] The county courthouse was the center of government.

The twin pressures of modernization and population growth placed additional demands on county governments. As a result, their service offerings have expanded. Counties these days handle health care and hospitals, pollution control, mass transit, industrial development, social services, and consumer protection.[15] They are increasingly regarded less as simple functionaries of state government and more as important policymaking units of local government. Organizational change and reform have occurred at the county level: state governments have awarded greater decision-making authority and flexibility to counties through *home rule* (see Chapter 2). By 1980, thirty states had adopted home rule provisions for at least some of their counties.[16]

Even with their gradual empowerment, counties, like other local governments, continue to chafe at the traditionally tight reins of state government control. In a recent survey, county officials blamed "state requirements without state funding" for many of the problems plaguing their government.[17] Also ranking high on their list of complaints were "state limits on authority." The issue of empowerment is unlikely to fade away during the 1990s.

How County Governments Are Organized   The typical structure of county government is based on an elected governing body, usually called a board of commissioners or supervisors, which is the central policymaking apparatus in the county. The board enacts county ordinances, approves the county budget, and appoints other officials (such as the directors of the county public works department and the county parks department). One of the board members acts as presiding officer. This form of government is the most popular; about three-quarters of America's counties use it. A typical county commission has three or five members and meets in regular session twice a month.

The board is not omnipotent, however, because a number of other county officials are elected as well. In most places, these include the sheriff, the county prosecutor (or district attorney), the county clerk (or clerk of the court), the county treasurer (or auditor), the county tax assessor, and the coroner. These officials can become powerful political figures in their own right by controlling their own bureaucratic units. Figure 11.1 sketches the typical organizational pattern.

There are two primary criticisms of this type of organization. First, there is no elected central executive official, like the mayor of a city or the governor of a state. County government is run by a board. Second, there is no single professional administrator to manage county government, the way a city manager does in a municipality. Elected officials are responsible for administering major county functions.

These criticisms have led to two alternative county structures. In one, called the *county council–elected executive plan,* the voters elect an executive

Figure 11.1 Traditional Organization of County Government
The most common form of county government lacks a central
executive.

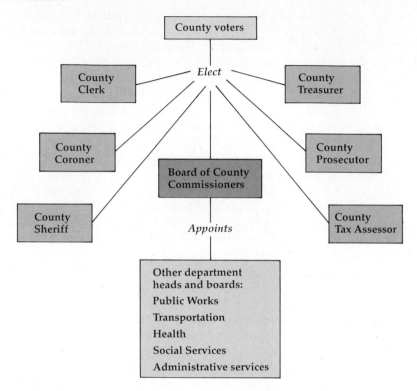

officer in addition to the governing board. This creates a clearer separation
between legislative and executive powers and is, in effect, a two-branch
system of government. The board still has the power to set policy, adopt the
budget, and audit the financial performance of the county. The executive's
role is to prepare the budget, administer county operations (in other words,
implement the policies of the board), and appoint department heads. In the
other alternative structure, the *council-administrator plan*, the county board
hires a professional administrator to run the government. The advantage of
this form of government is that it brings to the county a highly skilled
manager with a professional commitment to efficient, effective government.

Determining the most effective structural arrangements for county government is an ongoing issue. Defections from the long-standing commission form of county government and experimentation with alternatives
continue.

Hot Topics in County Government Myriad problems confront county
governments. Table 11.1 lists the most pressing of these, according to

Table 11.1 The Most Pressing Problems for County Government

Problem	Percentage of counties in which the problem is "very important"
Promotion of business and industrial development	70.8
Financial management	63.2
Roads	61.2
Toxic waste management	51.0
Public transportation	45.7
Jail expansion	40.4
Law enforcement planning	36.5
Land-use planning and zoning	35.0

Source: Barbara P. Greene, "Counties and the Fiscal Challenges of the 1980s," *Intergovernmental Perspective* 13 (Winter 1987): 16.

county officials. In almost every county, the promotion of business and industrial development is the most critical concern. County governments are increasingly devoting time and resources to promoting their area as a place to do business. Other concerns include financial management (primarily achieving a balance between revenues and expenditures), roads (a long-time county concern), and toxic waste management (a new problem). Public transportation, jail expansion, law enforcement planning, and land-use planning and zoning are very important issues in at least one-third of America's counties.

County Performance The last word on counties has not been written. Since the 1970s they have been said to be improving, modernizing, or exhibiting some other positive behavior. Granted, counties are now more prominent than they were in the old days, when they were considered the shadowy backwaters of local governments. As urban populations spill beyond the suburbs into the unincorporated territory of counties, the pressure on government grows.[18]

One reform that has long been touted as a means of achieving more efficient local government in an area is the consolidation of city and county governments into one unified structure. (The consolidation issue is explored fully in Chapter 14.)

Travis County, Texas (where Austin is located), has joined with its cities in an effort to improve governmental performance. These jurisdictions intend to reduce the layers of government, minimize the reliance on single-purpose governmental units, provide regionwide planning and coordination of service delivery, improve the fiscal health of the region, and increase governmental accountability to the public.[19] To accomplish these objectives, they will begin with partial consolidation of certain government functions through contracts between communities. Gradually, other services will be added, culminating in the consolidation of Travis County with its cities and with neighboring counties.

This process began in the late 1980s, and it remains to be seen how well the march toward consolidation will fare. One obstacle to local structural innovation is that changes in Texas state laws will be needed to accommodate these local-level improvements. Being "creatures of the state" is a fact of life for local governments.

Municipalities

Municipalities are cities; the words are interchangeable, and they refer to a specific, populated chunk of territory operating under a charter from state government. Cities differ from counties in how they were created and in what they do. Historically, they have been the primary units of local government in most societies—the grand enclaves of human civilization. Augustine wrote of a city of God and Cotton Mather of a heavenly city, but more recent formulations speak of ungovernable[20] and unheavenly[21] cities. Whatever the appropriate image, they are fascinating places.

Creating Cities   A city is a legal recognition of settlement patterns in an area. In the most common procedure, residents petition the state for a charter of incorporation. The area slated for incorporation must meet certain criteria, such as population or density minimums. In most cases, a referendum is required, so citizens are able to vote on whether they wish to become an incorporated municipality. Frequently, citizens are also asked to vote on the name of the municipality and its form of government. If the incorporation measure is successful, then a charter is granted by the state, and the newly created city has the legal authority to elect officials and to provide services to its residents.

New cities are created every year. In 1986, twenty-five places incorporated (and five cities disincorporated, or ceased to exist).[22] One of the largest new cities was Encinitas, California, with a population at birth of almost 40,000.

Like counties, cities are general-purpose units of local government. Unlike counties, they typically have greater decision-making authority and discretion. Most states have enacted home rule provisions for cities, although in some states, only cities that have attained a certain population size can exercise this option. The issue of city government authority is examined in Profile 11.1.

In addition, cities generally offer a wider array of services to their citizenry than most counties do. Public safety, public works, parks, and

PROFILE 11.1
Who's in Charge in Yonkers?

Yonkers, New York, the site of a decade-long dispute over the location of low-income housing, offers compelling insights into the impact of other levels of government on community decision making. Yonkers, a city that numbers 21,100 blacks among its 194,000 residents, was found guilty in federal court in 1985 of having practiced intentional and unlawful discrimination in housing and education for forty years.[1] The federal judge imposed school and housing desegregation remedies for Yonkers. It was the implementation of the housing order that sparked controversy.

The Yonkers city council was not pleased with the court ruling and was not particularly enthusiastic about having to carry it out. After two years of delay, it selected seven sites in predominately white neighborhoods for the first two hundred units of low-income housing. After fierce objections from property owners in the selected neighborhoods, the city council voted, by a margin of 4–3, to reverse its earlier decision, thereby defying the court order.

The national government's response was swift. The judge found the four council members who opposed the order in contempt of court and levied heavy fines on them and on the city of Yonkers. Council members defended their action, arguing that it was they who governed Yonkers, not a federal judge. State government quickly got into the fray: the state of New York, concerned over the mounting fines, dispatched its Emergency Financial Control Board to take control of the city's spending. Governor Mario Cuomo announced his readiness to take the extraordinary action of removing the rebellious council members from office, if necessary.[2]

The governor never had to make good on his threat, because once the board began preparing to lay off 447 city employees and shut down the public library, the city council ended its defiance and approved the housing plan.[3] Intervention by other levels of government provokes the question, Who's in charge in Yonkers? Is it the city council elected by Yonkers citizens, or is it a federal judge appointed by the president?

[1] James Feron, "Yonkers Desegregation Panel Likely," *New York Times*, July 13, 1988, p. 8.
[2] Elizabeth Kolbert, "Cuomo Says Councilmen in Yonkers May Be Removed for Defying Court," *New York Times*, August 30, 1988, p. 24.
[3] Janet M. Levine, "Defying Interference: Yonkers and Public Housing," paper presented at the annual meeting of the Southern Political Science Association, Memphis, November 1989.

recreation are standard features, supplemented in some cities by publicly maintained cemeteries, city-owned and operated housing, city-run docks, and city-constructed convention centers. It is city government that picks up garbage and trash, sweeps streets, inspects restaurants, maintains traffic signals, and plants trees.

City Governmental Structure   City governments operate with one of three structures: a mayor-council form, a city commission form, or a council-manager form. In each structure, an elected governing body, typically called a city council, has policymaking authority. What differentiates the three structures is the manner in which the executive branch is organized.

1. *Mayor-council form.* In the mayor-council form of government, executive functions such as the appointment of department heads are performed by elected officials. This form of government can be subdivided into two types, depending on the formal powers held by the mayor. In a strong-mayor–council structure, the mayor is the source of executive leadership. Strong mayors run city hall like governors run the statehouse. They are responsible for daily administrative activities, the hiring and firing of top-level city officials, and budget preparation. They have a potential veto over council actions. In a weak-mayor–council structure, the mayor's role is as an executive figurehead. The council (of which the mayor may be a member) is the source of executive power. The council appoints city officials and develops the budget, and the mayor has no veto power. He performs ceremonial tasks such as speaking for the city, chairing council meetings, and attending ribbon-cutting festivities. A structurally weak mayor can emerge as a powerful political figure in the city, but only if she possesses informal sources of power. Figure 11.2 highlights the structural differences between the strong- and weak-mayor–council forms of city government.

Mayor-council systems are popular in large cities (where populations are greater than 250,000) and in small cities (with populations under 10,000). Approximately half of the cities in the United States use a mayor-council structure. Some large cities, in which the administrative burdens of the mayor's job are especially heavy, have established a position of general manager or chief administrative officer.

2. *City commission form.* Under the city commission form of government, illustrated in Figure 11.3, legislative and executive functions are merged. Commissioners not only make policy as members of the city's governing body, but they also head the major departments of city government. They are both policymakers and policy executors. One of the commissioners is designated as mayor simply to preside over commission meetings.

The commission form of government was created as a reaction to the mayor-council structure. Its origins lie in the inability of a mayor-council government in Galveston, Texas, in 1900, to respond to the chaos caused by a hurricane that demolished the city and killed 6,000 people. The Texas legislature authorized the creation of a totally new form of city government —the commission form—and by 1904, the new city government had entirely rebuilt Galveston.[23] The success of the commission led to its adoption

Figure 11.2   Mayor-Council Form of Government
The primary difference between these two structures is in the power
and authority possessed by the mayor. Strong mayors are more
ideally situated to exert influence and control.

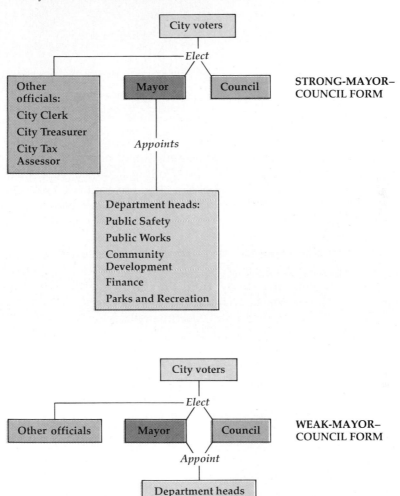

first by other Texas cities (Houston, Dallas, Fort Worth) and, within a
decade, by 160 other municipalities (such as Des Moines, Pittsburgh, Buffalo, Nashville, and Charlotte). Its appeal was its ostensible reduction of
politics in city government.

But almost as fast as the commission form of government appeared on
the scene, disillusionment with it set in. One problem stemmed from the
predictable tendency of commissioners to act as advocates for their own
departments. Each commissioner wanted a larger share of the city's budget
allocated to his department. Another problem had to do with politicians
acting as administrators; elected officials may not turn out to be good

Figure 11.3   City Commission Form of Government
Executive leadership is fragmented under a commission form of
government. Individually each commissioner heads a department; together
they run city hall.

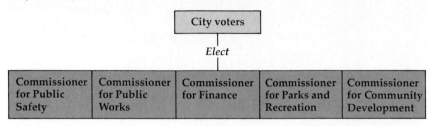

managers. As quickly as it had appeared, the commission form declined.
One study showed that of the almost two hundred cities reporting a commission structure in 1970, over 42 percent had replaced it with another form
by 1980.[24] By the late 1980s, few cities operated with a commission structure. Notable among them were Mobile, Topeka, Tulsa, Portland (Oregon),
and Chattanooga.

3. *Council-manager form.* The third city government structure, the council-
manager form, emphasizes the separation of politics (the policymaking
activities of the governing body) from administration (the execution of the
policies enacted by the governing body). Theoretically, the city council
makes policy, and administrators execute policy. Under this structure, the
council hires a professional administrator to manage city government. Figure 11.4 sketches this structure.

The administrator (usually called a city manager) appoints and removes
department heads, oversees service delivery, develops personnel policies,
and prepares budget proposals for the council. These responsibilities alone
make the manager an important figure in city government. But add to them
the power to make policy recommendations to the city council, and the
position becomes very powerful. When offering policy recommendations to
the council, the manager is walking a thin line between politics and administration. Managers who, with the acquiescence of their council, carve out
an activist role for themselves may be able to dominate policymaking in city
government.[25] In council-manager cities, the two contending parties typically have a working understanding about just how far the manager can
venture into the policymaking realm of city government.[26]

The council-manager form of city government predominates in cities of
10,000 to 25,000 people, especially in homogeneous suburban communities
and in the newer cities of the Sunbelt region.

Which Form of City Government Is Best?   Experts disagree about many
things, and one of them is which city government structure is best. Most
would probably agree that structures lacking a strong executive officer are
generally less preferable than others. By that token, the weak-mayor–
council and the commission forms are less favorable. The strong-mayor–

Figure 11.4   Council-Manager Form of Government
The council-manager form places administrative responsibility in the hands of a skilled professional. The intent is to make the operation of city government less political.

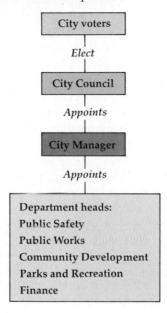

council form of government is extolled for fixing accountability firmly in the mayor's office, and the council-manager system is credited with professionalizing city government by bringing in skilled administrators to run things. It is up to the people to decide which form of government they want, and they have been doing just that.

In 1974, voters in Albuquerque replaced their council-manager form of government with a strong-mayor–council structure. In 1984, Rochester, New York, voters rejected their long-standing council-manager form in favor of an empowered mayor. Not all proposed switches meet with success, of course. In Toledo in 1986, for example, voters defeated a proposal to abandon the council-manager plan in favor of a strong mayor. Voters in Kansas City in 1989 rejected a plan to change from a weak-mayor to a strong-mayor structure. The best advice may be for a city to use whichever form of government works while remaining receptive to structural improvements.

Pressing Issues in City Government   The pressing issues in city governments these days revolve around expansion, contraction, and representation. The first two issues apply not only to territory but also to finances. Cities generally want to maintain, and most prefer to expand, their sphere of influence, which they can achieve by annexing territory lying outside city limits. They are also casting about for revenues, especially since the flow of federal funds has slowed to a drip. Thus, annexation of revenue-rich territory solves two problems. Finally, cities are trying to determine just what fair representation is. How should representatives to city government be chosen? The three issues are discussed below.

1. *Annexation.* Land is important to city governments, for it is crucial to their economic and political well-being.[27] Annexation has historically been a popular means of adding territory and population. In the past thirty years, many cities have found themselves squeezed by the rapid growth and incorporation of territory just outside city limits, and therefore beyond their control. What is worse (from a central city's perspective), some of these suburban cities have begun to threaten the central city's traditional dominance of the metropolitan area. People and jobs are fleeing the central city. To counteract this trend and to assure themselves of adequate space for future expansion, some cities have engaged in annexation efforts.

Not all cities can annex, however. They run up against two realities: the existence of incorporated suburbs (which makes that territory nonannexable) and the strictures of state laws. State governments determine the legal procedures for the annexation process, and they can make it easy or hard. Texas is a state that makes it easy for cities to annex, and not surprisingly, big Texas cities (in terms of population) have vast territories: Houston covers 556 square miles, Dallas 333 square miles, and San Antonio 263 square miles.

In Texas, cities use their power of **extraterritorial jurisdiction** (ETJ) to supplement annexation. Under ETJ, they can control subdivision practices in unincorporated bordering territory. (The amount of territory varies from a half mile for small cities to five miles for cities with over 25,000 people.)[28] Additionally, a Texas city can annex up to 10 percent of its territory annually without a referendum. The city simply has to provide adequate notice to the about-to-be-annexed residents. Houston has elevated this practice to an art form: it has annexed along major transportation arteries extending out of the city, thereby astronomically increasing its extraterritorial jurisdiction and reserving for itself vast territories for future annexation.[29]

South Carolina is an example of a state where it is difficult for cities to annex. Cities typically have to wait for land owners in an adjacent area to petition to be annexed. Even if a majority of the land owners request annexation, if the proportion is less than 75 percent, referendum elections must be held. State law requires that the annexation be approved by referendum by both the existing city and the area to be annexed.[30] This is known as a "dual majority," and it effectively makes annexation difficult.

Some of America's most prominent cities have rather confined city limits. For example, of the fifty most populated cities in the country, twenty-two control less than one hundred square miles of territory. The most extreme cases are Newark (covering 24.1 square miles), Miami (34.3), Buffalo (41.8), San Francisco (46.4), and Boston (47.2).[31] In the older, established metropolitan areas there is little room for a central city to expand, because it is hemmed in by incorporated suburbs.

2. *Finances.* City governments, just like other local governments, have to

balance their fiscal resources against their fiscal needs. Unlike the national government, these governments have to operate within the constraints of a balanced budget. The option of ending the fiscal year in debt or printing new money does not exist for them. As a result, they have become fairly creative at finding new sources of revenue in hard times.

A 1989 National League of Cities (NLC) survey of 360 city finance directors indicated just how serious the revenue issue is in city governments.[32] One-quarter of the cities reported that their general fund revenues had declined from 1988 to 1989. Minor declines can be covered (for example, most cities begin the fiscal year with some money in the bank), but more substantial declines can upset the balance between revenues and expenditures.

Table 11.2 reports the percentage of cities in which the imbalance between revenues and expected expenditures was worse than minus 5 percent. It is evident from the table that the proportion of cities experiencing imbalances nearly doubled between 1988 and 1989. The regional breakdowns indicate that the problem was somewhat more acute for cities in areas other than the Northeast, but for the most part, the percentages were fairly constant across regions. The population breakdowns present quite a different picture. Small- to medium-sized cities, those in the 10,000-to-99,999 categories, have been hardest hit by the revenue-expenditure imbalance, and this is a growing problem. In a slightly more advantageous situation are large cities —those with populations of 300,000 or more. Only 8 percent of them showed a serious imbalance in 1989, although the percentage was rising.

Table 11.2   The Proportion of Cities Expecting Revenue-Expenditure Imbalances Worse than −5 Percent

	Percentage of Cities		
	1987	1988	1989
All cities	11	8	15
Broken down by region			
Northeast	5	3	9
Midwest	14	5	16
South	10	15	15
West	14	5	17
Broken down by population size			
300,000 and over	3	0	8
100,000–299,999	10	12	10
50,000–99,999	14	9	16
10,000–49,999	12	7	19

Source: Douglas D. Peterson, *City Fiscal Conditions in 1989* (Washington, D.C.: National League of Cities, 1989), pp. 16–17. Reprinted by permission of the National League of Cities.

Given these figures, what can cities do to adapt? The survey asked just that question. The responses from city officials appear in Table 11.3. The most relied-upon corrective action was to increase fees and charges. Almost 70 percent of the cities did so during the previous fiscal year. A city might increase the cost of a building permit or charge more for health inspections at restaurants. The cost of parking in a metered space or in a city-owned parking garage can be hiked. (Commuting students at urban colleges with inadequate parking have probably marveled at how adept city officials are at the "make students pay" strategy.) Cities can boost revenues in a variety of seemingly small ways. More than one-third of the cities indicated that they were imposing new fees and charges. A city service that used to be free, such as a city park, may now have an admission fee.

An alternative to raising more money is to cut costs. Cities in the NLC survey indicate that this too is a popular option. Over 40 percent of the cities reduced the growth rate of their operational spending (expenditures for city services), and almost the same proportion cut their capital spending (items such as construction projects). Cities are setting spending priorities, and many people are concerned that in doing so, they will assign social services, such as programs for the poor, a low priority.

The list in Table 11.3 suggests that cities are responding inventively to declining revenues. City officials bite the political bullet and increase fees and taxes; they try to achieve savings in service delivery in a number of ways. This is a city government issue that will not go away.

3. *Representation.* Representation in city government is another fundamental concern. How can citizens' preferences be effectively represented in city hall? In the colonial days of town meetings and civic republics, it was simple: a citizen showed up at the meeting hall, voiced his opinion, and the majority ruled. When this proved to be unwieldy, a system of representative democracy seemed just the ticket.

In city governments, city council members are elected in one of two ways: either at large or by districts (also called wards). In **at-large elections,** a city voter can vote in each council race. In **district elections,** a city voter can vote only in the council race in her district. From the perspective of candidates, the at-large system means that a citywide campaign must be mounted. With districts, the candidate's campaign is limited to a specific area of the city. As discussed earlier in the chapter, the structural reform movement advocated at-large elections as a means of weakening the geographic base of political machines.[33] Candidates running in citywide races must appeal to a broad cross-section of the population to be successful.

There are significant consequences for the use of at-large electoral systems. An in-depth study of almost one thousand city council members across the country revealed that at-large members tend to be wealthier and more highly educated than council members elected from districts.[34] At-large council members also differ from district members in their relationships with constituents. Council members elected at large devote less time to answering individual complaints and direct their attention to a citywide and business constituency.

Table 11.3   Budget Adjustments Reported by Cities

		Factors influencing reported action*						
Budget adjustments reported by cities	Percent reporting action last year	Loss of general revenue sharing	Federal tax reform	Loss of other federal funds	Change in state funds	Federal mandates	State mandates	Other factors
Increased fees and charges	69	27	3	10	14	14	19	80
Reduced growth rate of operating spending	43	46	9	19	26	9	16	68
Increased property tax rates	41	48	12	17	27	17	35	64
Implemented new fees and charges	36	30	3	12	16	13	16	75
Reduced capital spending	36	57	10	19	22	6	10	54
Contracted out services	32	11	2	4	4	5	7	85
Reduced number of city employees	24	39	8	19	23	6	11	70
Froze municipal hiring	19	41	6	22	21	7	12	77
Imposed/raised impact or development fees	18	27	3	9	13	5	19	78
Increased rates of other taxes (other than property, income, or sales)	13	46	9	16	23	11	18	82
New tax or taxes	10	39	3	6	15	9	21	79
Reduced service levels (e.g., hours of operation)	7	44	13	9	17	4	17	87
Shifted service responsibilities to another government	6	10	0	0	0	0	5	76
Increased sales tax rates	5	28	6	11	17	6	17	67
Increased income tax rates	3	50	17	8	8	25	0	50

*Totals sum to more than 100 percent because many cities reported multiple factors for a single decision.
Source: Douglas D. Peterson, *City Fiscal Conditions in 1989* (Washington, D.C.: National League of Cities, 1989), p. 20. Reprinted by permission of the National League of Cities.

Most U.S. cities (approximately 60 percent) use an at-large method for electing their council members. The popularity of the method decreases as city population size increases, however. For example, only 15 percent of cities with populations above the half-million mark use at-large elections. This approach to city council representation is increasingly under attack for diminishing the likelihood that a member of a minority group can be elected. Research on 313 cities indicated that when cities shifted from an at-large system to a district or mixed format (a combination of at-large and district seats), more blacks were elected to the council.[35] Other research has amplified those findings, especially in cities where the black population is more than 20 percent.[36]

Some studies have shown that changing the electoral system from at-large to districts produces an overall increase in citizen participation, in terms of greater attendance at council meetings, higher voter turnout, and a larger number of candidates.[37] It is not altogether clear that changing to districts will translate into policy benefits for the previously underrepresented sectors of the city, however.[38] Research has shown that in terms of policy attitudes, there is really no significant difference between council members elected at large and those elected from districts.[39]

Towns and Townships

The word *town* evokes an image of a small community where everyone knows everyone else, where government is informal, and where local leaders gather at the coffee shop to make important decisions. This is both accurate and inaccurate. Towns generally are smaller, in terms of population, than cities or counties. The extent of their governmental powers depends on state government, but even where they are relatively weak, town government is increasingly becoming more formalized.

How Do We Know a Town When We See One?   Towns and townships are general-purpose units of local government, distinct from county and city governments. Only twenty states, primarily in the Northeast and Midwest, have official towns or townships. In some states these small jurisdictions have relatively broad powers, and in others they have a more circumscribed role. Many of the New England towns offer the kinds of services commonly associated with cities in other states.

New England towns, along with those in New Jersey, Pennsylvania, and to some degree Michigan, New York, and Wisconsin, enjoy fairly broad powers. In large measure, they act like other general-purpose units of government. In the remainder of the township states (Illinois, Indiana, Kansas, Minnesota, Missouri, Nebraska, North Dakota, Ohio, and South Dakota), the nature of township government is more rural. Rural townships tend to stretch across thirty-six square miles of land (conforming to the surveys done by the national government before the areas were settled), and their service offerings are often limited to roads and law enforcement. The closer these rural townships are to large urban areas, the more likely they are to offer an expanded set of services to residents.

Townships and the Future   The demise of the township form of government has long been expected. As rural areas become more populated, they will eventually meet the population minimums necessary to become municipalities. However, if they experience substantial population loss and with it their reason for existence, they may die a natural death, and county governments will assume service provision. The issue is whether townships are superfluous. Despite predictions, though, townships have proved to be remarkably resilient. According to the Census Bureau, there were 16,700 of them in 1987, down only 100 from the 1977 figure.

Townships have not sat idly by as commentators speculated on their dim future. They formed an interest group, the National Association of Towns and Townships, to lobby on their behalf in Washington, D.C. As general-purpose units of local government, townships qualified for General Revenue Sharing (GRS) funds from the national government when those funds were still available, and were thus helped through times of financial stress. The U.S. Advisory Commission on Intergovernmental Relations (ACIR) went so far as to opine that townships were being "propped up by GRS largesse."[40]

Now that GRS has run its course, the long-anticipated demise of some townships may come to pass. In fact, one observer has called for a triage strategy for allocating funds to small towns.[41] This approach would concentrate funds on towns with the prospect of survival, not on those that are dying or those that are flourishing.

Special Districts

Special districts are supposed to do what other local governments cannot or will not do. They are created to meet service needs in a particular area. If, for example, residents of an unincorporated area want fire protection but the closest city refuses to extend its coverage and the county is unable to provide adequate service, the residents may establish a special fire district. The process usually requires the residents to petition the state to hold a referendum on the question. If the vote is favorable, a fire service district will be established, employees will be hired, and fire protection will be provided. Residents will pay a special tax or fee for the operation of the district. There are approximately 29,000 special districts around the country, and that number is increasing.

Not all special districts are organized alike. Ninety percent of them provide a single function, such as irrigation or mosquito control. Governing bodies can be independently elected or, in the case of weaker special districts, appointed by another government, such as the county. The budget and staff size of special districts ranges from miniscule to mammoth. Some of the more prominent include the Port Authority of New York and New Jersey, the Chicago Transit Authority, the Washington Public Power Supply System, and the Los Angeles County Sanitation District.

Yes, But Do We Really Need Them? Special districts overlay existing general-purpose local governments, and some question their necessity. The ACIR puts the question bluntly: "If general-purpose local governments are set up to perform a broad spectrum of functions and if they collectively cover practically every square foot of territory in a state, why [are] special districts needed at all?"[42] The answer has traditionally focused on the deficiencies of general-purpose local governments.[43] Three general categories of "deficiencies" are worth examining.

First are the technical conditions of a general-purpose local government. In some states, cities cannot extend their service districts beyond their boundaries. Moreover, the problem to be addressed may not fit neatly within a single jurisdiction. A river that runs through several counties may periodically overflow its banks in heavy spring rains. The problem affects small portions of many jurisdictions. A flood control district covering only the affected areas may be a logical solution. Furthermore, there are problems of scale. A general-purpose local government simply may not be able to provide electric service to its residents as efficiently as a special utility district that covers a multitude of counties. Finally, there may be prohibitions against jurisdictional coventuring. For example, some states do not allow their counties to offer services jointly with other counties. To manage a two-county library, a special two-county library district has to be established.

A second set of deficiencies has to do with financial constraints. Local general-purpose governments commonly operate under debt and tax limitations. Demands for additional services that exceed a jurisdiction's revenue-raising ceiling or lead to the assumption of excessive debt cannot be accommodated. By using special districts, existing jurisdictions can circumvent the debt and tax ceilings. Special districts, more than general-purpose governments, are well suited for service charge or user fee financing, in which the cost of the service can be directly apportioned to the consumer, as with water or sewer charges.

Technical and financial deficiencies of general-purpose local governments help to explain the creation of special districts, but political explanations shed even more light. Restrictive annexation laws and county governments with limited authority are political facts of life that encourage the use of special districts. For residents of an urban fringe area, a public service district (which may provide more than one service) may be the only option. Some special districts owe their existence to a federal mandate. For example, national government policy has spurred the creation of soil conservation and flood control districts throughout the country.

Once created, a special district may become a political power in its own right. In places where general-purpose governmental units are fully equipped legally, financially, and technically to provide a service, they may encounter resistance from special-district interests fighting to preserve the district.

Uneasiness about Special Districts   The arguments in favor of special districts revolve around their potential for efficient service provision and the likelihood that they will be responsive to constituents whose demands are not otherwise being met.[44] But for the most part, scholarly observers look at special districts with a jaundiced eye. The most frequently heard complaint is that special districts lack accountability. The public is often unaware of their existence, and so they function free of much scrutiny. It has been said that special districts "operate in dim lights at the outermost fringes of public consciousness."[45]

The proliferation of special districts complicates the development of comprehensive solutions to public problems. For example, by 1979, the most populous county in Texas, Harris County, was the home of 327 water districts. Flooding is a serious problem in the county, and the plethora of water districts has not helped to solve it.[46] The presence of an array of districts makes it difficult for general-purpose governments to set priorities.[47] It is not uncommon for cities and counties to be locked in governmental combat with the special districts in their area. There is a natural tendency for these governmental units to be turf-protecting, service-providing rivals.

Cognizant of these concerns, state governments are looking more closely at special districts and the role they play in service delivery. Colorado, Arizona, and Florida have taken actions that give their general-purpose local governments more input into the state's decision to create special districts.[48]

School Districts

School districts are a type of single-purpose local government. They are a special kind of special district, and as such are considered one of the five types of local government. The trend in school districts follows the theory that fewer is better. Before the Second World War, over 100,000 school districts covered the countryside. Many of these were rural, one-school operations. In many small towns, community identity was linked to the local schoolhouse. Despite serving as a source of pride, small districts were so expensive to maintain that mergers occurred throughout the nation, and by 1987 there were only 15,000 districts.

School Politics   The school board is the formal source of power and authority in the district. The board is typically composed of five to seven members, usually elected in nonpartisan, at-large elections. Their job is to make policy for the school district. One of the most important policy decisions involves the district budget—how the money will be spent.

School districts are governed by boards and managed by trained, full-time educational administrators. Like city governments, school districts invested heavily in the reform model of governance, and the average district has become more professional in operation in the past thirty years. An appointed chief administrator (a superintendent) heads the school district staff, the size of which is dependent on the size of the district.

During the 1970s, the criticism of school districts was that professional experts had seized control of the educational system, thus reducing the governing function of school boards to mere rubber-stamping of administrators' recommendations.[49] This appears to be less true as time passes. The 1980s were a time of rediscovery of public education, and this has led to a repoliticization of school districts. The issue of who is in charge, however, has another claimant: the parents of schoolchildren.

Parental influence in school district policy is most clearly emerging in the matter of school choice. School districts around the country are beginning to adopt measures that allow parents to decide whether their child will attend the school in the neighborhood or one elsewhere in the district. In effect, schools are competing for students. They are anxious to attract students, because district and state funds are allocated on a per-pupil basis. To attract students, some schools specialize in a particular academic area, such as arts or sciences; others emphasize certain teaching styles. As one administrator put it, "Public schools of choice is an on-rushing train."[50] The tradition of neighborhood schools, disrupted by busing and redrawing of school boundary lines in efforts to achieve racial balance, is being further eroded.

Advocates of parental choice claim that the approach offers poor families some of the options that wealthy families have always had with private schools. They argue that competition among schools will generate creativity and responsiveness among teachers and principals. Opponents of parental choice voice concerns about equity. They fear that students left in the less preferred schools (perhaps because their parents cannot afford to take them to a distant school and the school district does not provide transportation) will receive lower-quality education.

School District Concerns   There are always controversies in education. The burning issues in school districts range from corporal punishment to the drop-out rate, but one recurring central issue is finances. Although the relationship is a bit more complex than "you get what you pay for," there is widespread agreement that children in well-funded school districts are better off than those in poorly funded ones.

A history of serious disparities in school funding, caused by great differences in the available property taxes that provide most of the revenue, has led to the increasing financial involvement of state government in local school districts. State governments use an **equalization formula** to distribute funds to school districts in an effort to reduce financial disparities.

Under the formula, poorer school districts receive a proportionately larger share of state funds than wealthier districts do. Although these programs have increased the amount of funding for education, they have not eliminated the interdistrict variation. Wealthier districts simply use the state guarantee as a foundation on which to heap their own resources. Poorer school districts continue to operate with less revenue. Chapter 15 looks in depth at school administration, innovations in education, and school finances.

Interlocal Cooperation

Local governments of all stripes are re-examining the "go it alone" approach to problem solving. Central cities and suburban town governments are banding together, and cities and counties are joining in efforts to forge areawide solutions to contemporary problems. Governments of all types are expanding their involvement with the private sector. This is not to say that concerns over turf or interjurisdictional jealousies are things of the past, but there is a new appreciation of common problems.

A large portion of interlocal cooperation is fairly modest in application. Adjoining cities may operate a sanitary landfill together; a city and a county may agree to use the same jail facility; three school districts may share student transportation vehicles. Despite their seeming inconsequential nature, even these small steps represent service delivery alternatives that were seldom examined in the past.

The explanation for such cooperative behavior is in large part financial. Simply put, the cost of independently providing a service may exceed the preference for it. Another part of the explanation is uneasiness about existing arrangements, and perhaps a dawning awareness that cooperative approaches may be more effective than individual jurisdictional solutions. Whatever the explanation, the phenomenon appears to be growing.

In the past, areawide solutions were attempted through the organizational mechanism of a regional planning council. These councils, as noted in Chapter 14, owed their genesis to national-level decisions about how local governments should act. As is often the case with externally imposed solutions, the regional planning council concept met with indifference at best, opposition at worst, in local governments around the country. As a result, these "glamour organizations of the 1960s [have] become major disappointments all over the country."[51] Local governments are much more likely to succeed in jurisdictional cooperation when they themselves initiate it.

The kind of interlocal cooperation that is catching on now has been given the label "intercommunity partnerships."[52] The key to these partnerships is that they involve private-sector organizations, the academic community, and citizen leagues. An example is the Intergovernmental Cooperation Program (ICP) in the Pittsburgh area. The central purpose of the ICP is "to identify emerging issues that offer timely opportunities for inter-governmental cooperation, to assemble resources for designing cooperative projects, and to monitor the implementation of cooperative projects."[53] The ICP has created a weighty agenda for itself.

Less formal than the ICP are coalitions that pursue common objectives. In the Seattle metropolitan area, in an effort to secure passage of referenda on low-income housing and a downtown art museum, supporters of each project established an informal alliance for joint fund-raising, political organizing, and marketing.[54] The motto for this unlikely coalition is "art, like low-income housing, serves the public interest."[55] Another coalition composed of naturalists, business interests, and civic activists emerged in support for a bond issue to upgrade the local zoo. These efforts in Seattle have generated a strategic consensus on behalf of interlocal cooperation that is likely to spread. Local governments are inveterate borrowers of good ideas from other local governments.

The Issue of Governance

Intercommunity partnerships return us to the governance issue raised early in this chapter and alluded to throughout it. How do we know when a community is well governed? We have seen communities restructure their governments with the intent of improving governance. Voters defeat incumbents and elect new council members in a similar effort. Conflict over local government spending priorities ensues. There is no set of universally accepted criteria for evaluating the quality of governance. The National Municipal League, a group that got its start during the reform movement, annually bestows its "All-American City" designation on a few select communities that display "civic energy."[56] Perhaps the key to governance is energy.

One attempt to isolate characteristics that are plausibly related to governance settled on seven elements.[57] According to this study, well-governed communities exhibit

1. tranquility among public officials—an absence of squabbles and bloodletting;
2. continuity in office of top-level managerial officials—a stable corps of administrative personnel;
3. use of analytical budgeting and planning processes—reliance on comprehensive, multiyear methods;
4. participative management—less commitment to hierarchical models and more employee-oriented management;
5. innovativeness—receptivity to new ideas;
6. active public-private partnerships—a minimization of the traditional barrier between government and the private sector;
7. citizen input into government decisions—the use of formal mechanisms to increase public involvement in government.

The governance question goes back to Plato and Aristotle, and we are unlikely to resolve it here. These seven elements offer some guidance for continued rumination about government structure and function.

Summary

Communities can be considered civic republics, corporate enterprises, or consumer markets. The prevailing orientation affects the structure of government, and the structure in turn affects the way government functions.

The American landscape is awash in local governments, all delivering services to the public. General-purpose governments (counties, cities, townships) cover the country. Superimposed on them are thousands of single-purpose governments (special districts, school districts). These governments continue to tinker with their structures in an effort to find the right balance between the twin goals of efficiency and responsiveness. Local government structure is constantly evolving, as New York City has recently learned.

Key Terms

At-large elections Citywide (or countywide) contests to determine the members of a city council (or county commission).

District (ward) elections Elections in which the voters in one district or ward of a jurisdiction (city, county, school district) vote for a candidate to represent that district.

Equalization formula A means of distributing funds (primarily to school districts) to reduce financial disparities among districts.

Extraterritorial jurisdiction The ability of a city government to control certain practices in an adjacent unincorporated area.

General-purpose local governments Local governments that provide a wide range of functions.

Political machine An informal organization that controls the machinery of government through favoritism, service to constituents, and intimidation.

Single-purpose local governments Local governments that perform a specific function, such as a school district.

12

Local Leadership

Community Leadership
The Meaning of Leadership/Community Power

Local Executives
Mayors/City Managers

Local Legislatures
City Council Members: Old and New/Councils in
Action: Increasing Conflict/Reshaping a Council:
The Case of Houston

Political Leadership versus
Professional Leadership
Council-Manager Interactions/Perceptions of
Governmental Systems

Policy Innovation at the Local Level

Leadership and Capacity

A battle for prominence is brewing in the Bay Area. San Francisco, the historical leader of the region, is being challenged by San Jose, which, although long considered a "second city" in the area, has blossomed into what its mayor hopes will be the urban center of Silicon Valley.[1] Located fifty miles from San Francisco, with a population expected to surpass San Francisco's by 1990 and with an upswing in cultural and commercial activity, San Jose is emerging as a leading city.

Reggie Jackson once said about his role on the New York Yankees: "I'm the straw that stirs the drink." He was talking about leadership. Leadership is just as critical to local governments as it is to baseball teams. It can make the difference between a championship season and one that is a struggle.

The terms that conjure up images of leadership in local government circles these days include initiative and inventiveness, risk-taking, high energy level, persistence, entrepreneurship and innovation, vision. These words share a common element: they denote activity and engagement. Leaders are people who "make a difference."[2]

Community Leadership

A federal system gives state and local governments the option of leadership. Suffolk County, New York, can ban nonbiodegradable packaging, and Madison, Wisconsin, can declare itself a nuclear-free zone. Actions like these typically spread to like-minded communities, and if substantial support exists, state governments and eventually the national government may follow.

Communities can be leaders in the federal system if two conditions exist. First, the local citizenry must be receptive to leading most other communities on a specific issue. Second, skilled local officials must be able to translate that willingness into action. Burlington, Vermont, offers an interesting example: after an eight-year stint as mayor, Bernard Sanders said in 1989, "We're leading the state in terms of tax reform, affordable housing, child care, environmental protection, women's rights, children's programs, cultural activities, speaking out on national and international issues."[3] Many attribute the city's leadership in the state to Mayor Sanders's actions.

Of course, community leadership often is not easy. In an effort to reverse the recent trend of being cast adrift by the national government, big-city mayors set out on an ambitious quest to woo the 1988 presidential candidates and get urban issues back on the national agenda. This task was more difficult than it was thirty years ago, because as a whole, mayors have lost their clout as big players in the political system.[4] Mayor-centered political organizations cannot deliver the vote as they did in the past (Mayor Richard J. Daley's delivery of the Chicago vote on behalf of John F. Kennedy in 1960 is a prime example), and what influence they have accounts for a smaller proportion of the total vote. However, even though it is more difficult for mayors to exert influence on the national scene, they persevere.

The Meaning of Leadership

Whether or not a community chooses a leadership role in the federal system, every community needs leaders. Good leadership is good leadership, whether in the public or the private sector. *In Search of Excellence,* a study of sixty-two private-sector organizations, identified several interrelated factors that made for excellent companies, and by inference for excellent governments.[5] These included

1. an organizational tendency toward action;
2. closeness to the customer;
3. autonomy and entrepreneurship;
4. productivity through employees;
5. a hands-on, value-driven approach; and
6. a simple organization with a lean staff.

The authors did not spell it out, but essentially, each of these characteristics is about leadership. In fact, in a sequel to *In Search of Excellence,* the authors acknowledge that leadership is the "one element that connects all the others."[6]

In the same vein, another study focused on leaders and their behavior, and found that effective leadership in organizations involves four strategies:[7]

The job of mayor is demanding but fulfilling. Kathryn J. Whitmire, Houston's mayor in the 1980s, enjoys the challenges.

1. *Attention through vision:* creating a focus for what needs to get done.
2. *Meaning through vision:* communicating the vision, gaining its acceptance, and giving its meaning to the organization's employees.
3. *Trust through positioning:* developing a set of actions necessary to implement the leader's vision.
4. *Deployment of self through positive self-regard:* recognizing personal strengths and compensating for weaknesses, nurturing one's own skills, and matching individual skills with organizational needs.

The findings from these studies offer some important lessons for local government officials. As the models recommend, good leaders tend to be people who aim for results. They think in terms of desired outcomes.[8] Leaders are also people-oriented: they interact positively with others and are able to mobilize them in support of their objectives.

The final word on leadership belongs to scholars at the Center for Excellence in Local Government. In trying to identify the essential kernel that is leadership, they relayed a comment about former Baltimore mayor (now Maryland governor) William Donald Schaefer: "Schaefer just doesn't run Baltimore, he *is* Baltimore. The same goes for other excellent leaders. They *are* what they lead."[9]

Community Power

Real questions about who is running the show in local government do arise. At the risk of being accused of naiveté, we might suggest that "the people" run government, local and otherwise. Unfortunately, there is much evidence to persuade us otherwise. But we should not become too cynical, either. Citizen preferences do have an impact on public policy decisions. Can we assume, therefore, that those who occupy important positions in government, such as the mayor and the city council, are in fact in charge? Are they the leaders of the community? This is a question that has interested scholars for over sixty years.

In sorting through the issue of "who's running the show," two theories predominate. One, the **elite theory,** argues that a small group of leaders called an elite possesses power and rules society. In the **pluralist theory,** power is dispersed among competing groups, whose clash produces societal rule.

The Elite Theory   One of the earliest expositions of the elite theory argued that in any society, from underdeveloped to advanced, there are two classes of people: a small set who rule and a large clump who are ruled.[10] The rulers allocate values for society and determine the rules of the game; the ruled tend to be passive and ill-informed, and they are unable to exercise any direct influence over the rulers. This division is reflected elsewhere in society. In organizations, for example, power is inevitably concentrated in the hands of a few people.[11] Given the pervasiveness of elite systems, should we expect decision making in communities to be any different?

A famous study of community power in Middletown (actually Muncie, Indiana) in the 1920s and 1930s discovered an identifiable set of rulers.[12] The researchers, sociologists named Lynd, determined that "Family X" (the Ball family) was at the core of this ruling elite. Through their economic power, Family X and a small group of business leaders called the shots in Middletown. Government officials simply did the bidding of Family X and its cohorts.

Another widely read study of community power confirmed the basic tenets of elitism. Floyd Hunter's study of Regional City (Atlanta) in the 1950s and 1970s isolated the top leadership—a forty-person economic elite—that dominated the local political system.[13] Hunter argued that an individual's power in this city was determined by his role in the marketplace. Local elected officials simply carried out the policy decisions of the elite. To illustrate the point, Hunter compared the relatively limited power enjoyed by the mayor of Atlanta to the extensive power possessed by the president of one of Atlanta's major corporations, Coca-Cola.[14]

Assuming for a moment that the elitist interpretations of community power are accurate, where do they take us? Do not be confused about the intent of an economic elite—they are not running the community out of a sense of benevolence. The following statement captures the larger meaning of elitism: "virtually all U.S. cities are dominated by a small, parochial elite whose members have business or professional interests that are linked to local development and growth. These elites use public authority and private power as a means to stimulate economic development and thus enhance their own local business interests."[15] To many, this is a fairly disturbing conclusion.

The Pluralist Theory   The findings of these sociologists did not square with the prevailing orthodoxy of American political science: pluralism. Not everyone saw community power through the elitist lens, and many questioned whether the findings from Middletown and Regional City applied to other communities.

Pluralist theory views the decision-making process as one of bargaining, accommodation, and compromise. No monolithic entity is in control; instead, authority is fragmented. There are many leadership groups, any one of which, given the importance of the issue at hand, can become involved in decision making. Granted, the size, cohesion, and wealth of these groups vary. But no group has a monopoly on resources. Pluralism sets forth a much more accessible system of community decision making than the grimly deterministic tenets of elitism do.

A study conducted in New Haven, Connecticut, by Robert Dahl was considered to be a refutation of the sociologists' findings, particularly those of Hunter.[16] According to Dahl, decisions in New Haven were the product of the interactions of a system of groups with more than one center of power.

Except for the mayor, no one leader was influential across a series of issue areas, and influential actors were not drawn from a single segment of the community.

Further explication of the pluralist model acknowledged that although community decision making is limited to relatively few actors, the legitimacy of such a system hinges on the easily revoked consent of a much larger segment of the local population.[17] In other words, the "masses" may acquiesce to the leaders, but they can also rise up when they are displeased. Success in a pluralistic environment is determined by a group's ability to form coalitions with other groups. Pluralism, then, offers a more hopeful interpretation of community power.

A Return to New Haven: Is It All in the Approach?   New Haven, the setting for Dahl's affirmation of pluralist theory, has been examined and re-examined by skeptical researchers. Some of the debate between elitists and pluralists is a function of methodology, that is, the approach that is used in studying community power. Sociologists have tended to rely on what is called a **reputational approach.** They go into a community and ask informants to name and rank the local leaders. Those whose names repeatedly appear are considered to be the movers and shakers. This approach is criticized on the grounds that it does not measure leadership per se, but the reputation for leadership. Political scientists approach the power question differently, through a **decisional method.** They focus on specific community issues and try to determine, using a variety of sources, who is influential in the decision-making process. It is easy to see that the two different approaches can produce divergent findings.

Users of the decisional method claim that it allows them to identify overt power rather than just power potential.[18] Additionally, it offers a realistic picture of power relationships as dynamic rather than fixed. Defenders of the reputational method argue that when researchers select key issues to examine, they are being arbitrary. Also, it may be that a study of decision making ignores the most powerful actors in a community—those who are able to keep issues *off* the agenda, who are influential enough to keep certain issues submerged.[19]

New Haven was found by Dahl to be a pluralist's delight. Convinced that the finding was affected by Dahl's methods, another researcher, G. William Domhoff, examined New Haven and emerged with a contrary view of the power structure.[20] He claimed that Dahl missed the big picture by focusing on issues that were of minor concern to the New Haven elite, so that Dahl's finding of an accessible decision-making process where many groups were involved was not an adequate test of the presence of an elite. Domhoff investigated the urban redevelopment issue and discovered that the long-time mayor, whom Dahl had seen as leading an executive-centered coalition, was being actively manipulated by a cadre of local business leaders. New Haven, Domhoff contended, is not quite the pluralistic paradise it was made out to be.

The Dynamics of Power   The work of Hunter and Dahl remains significant, but neither elitism nor pluralism adequately explains who's running the show. In fact, some observers claim that "no single descriptive statement applies to community leadership in general in the United States today."[21] Not all communities are organized alike, and even within a single community, power arrangements shift as time passes and conditions change. One group of political scientists, Agger, Goldrich, and Swanson, argued that an understanding of community power requires an assessment of two variables: how power is distributed to the citizens and the extent to which there is ideological unity among the political leaders.[22]

The effort of a Chicago growth coalition to promote the 1992 World's Fair offers an instructive example of how the power structure sometimes loses.[23] The 1992 Fair Corporation, a well-connected nonprofit group of economically powerful and socially prominent people, wanted to bring the next world's fair to Chicago. World's fairs have value to a community, secondarily from the show and spectacle, but primarily because of the long-term development consequences. To land the fair, the group had to convince the city's political leadership of the event's importance. They were in the process of doing so when the political dynamics suddenly changed. A supportive mayor, Jane Byrne, was defeated in 1983, and the new mayor, Harold Washington, was indifferent to the project. That was just the wedge that opponents of the fair needed. In the words of one commentator, "Chicago's new reform-minded black mayor and more open city council gave legitimacy to Fair critics."[24] Grassroots and political opposition intensified. Eventually enough questions were raised that the state legislature refused to allocate the funds necessary to continue planning for the fair, and the 1992 Fair Corporation was forced to admit defeat. In this instance, power had shifted to a temporary coalition of forces.

If the elite can be beaten in Chicago, is there likely to be a triumph of pluralism in communities across the land? Probably not. The penetration of the government's domain by private economic interests in American communities is deep.[25] Clarence Stone uses the concepts of "systemic power" and "strategic advantage" to explain why community decisions so frequently favor upper-strata interests.[26] The starting point of his argument is that public officials operate in a highly stratified socioeconomic system in which there is a small upper class, a large, varied middle class, and a relatively small lower class. According to Stone, "Public officeholders are predisposed to interact with and to favor those who can reciprocate benefits."[27] Two considerations define the environment in which public officials operate: electoral accountability (keeping the majority of the public satisfied) and systemic power (the unequal distribution of economic, organizational, and social resources). Decision makers are likely to side with majority preferences on highly visible issues, but on less visible ones, the upper strata will win most of the time. In other words, they enjoy a strategic advantage.

The final word on community power structures has not been written.

That some interests, especially those of the economically powerful, seem to prevail more often than others is certain. Yet different communities have developed different arrangements for governance.[28] The question of who's in charge remains an interesting one.

Local Executives

The mantle of leadership in city government falls most often on chief executives: mayors and managers. Although it is possible for chief executives to eschew a leadership role, it is unlikely.

Mayors

Mayors tend to be the most prominent figures in city government, primarily because their position automatically makes them the center of attention. Occasionally a city council member emerges as a leader on a specific issue or stirs up some interest with verbal attacks on the mayor (which many observers will interpret as jockeying for position to run against the mayor at the next election). This occurred in Chicago in the mid-1980s, when city alderman Edward Vrdolyak locked horns with incumbent mayor Harold Washington in his bid to win the office. But for the most part, attention is drawn to the mayor.

Differences Between Strong and Weak Mayors   Because of the structure of local government, some mayors have a greater opportunity for leadership than others. They are referred to as **strong mayors,** while those who lack the leadership-inducing structure are referred to as **weak mayors.** It is important to note that these labels refer to the structure of the position, not to the person who occupies it. A structure simply creates opportunities for leadership, not the certainty of it. True leaders are those who can take what is structurally a weak-mayor position and transform it into a strong mayorship.

As explained in Chapter 11, a strong-mayor structure establishes the mayor as the sole chief executive who exercises substantive policy responsibilities. In this kind of structure, there is no city manager who could expand on an administrative role and become a policy rival to the mayor. A strong mayor is directly elected by the voters, not selected by the council; serves a four-year, not two-year, term of office; and has no limitations on re-election. She also has a central role in budget formulation, extensive appointment and removal powers, and veto power over council-enacted ordinances.[29] The more of these powers a mayor has, the stronger her position is and the easier it is for the mayor to become a leader.

A weak-mayor structure does not provide these elements. It is designed so that the mayor shares policy responsibilities with a manager and serves a limited amount of time in office. (In an especially weak-mayor system, the job is passed around among the council members, each of whom takes a turn at being mayor.) A weak-mayor structure often implies strong council involvement in budgetary and personnel matters. The city of Milwaukee uses a strong-mayor structure, while in Kansas City a weak-mayor structure is in use; the leaders of these two cities are examined in Profile 12.1.

The mayoral structures of most American cities reveal a suspicion about powerful elected executives and a preference for weak mayors. Granted, in some cities, the mayor is structurally strong and has the powers that the average governor has at the state level. However, in most cities, if the mayor is to become a leader, he has to exceed the job description.

An example of a mayor who was able to do just that is Pete Wilson, who was mayor of San Diego from 1971 to 1982. In terms of structure, the San Diego mayor is weak, since he has to share power with a manager. Mayor Wilson quickly learned that "his ability to lead the city depended on his power of persuasion, not the formal power of the charter."[30] Wilson was able to capitalize on a time of flux in community core values—the citizens were rethinking issues such as growth rates and development patterns— and use his talents to restructure the role of the mayor informally. During this period, San Diegans voted down charter amendments that would have formally established a strong-mayor structure. Instead, Wilson made internal organizational changes, such as creating a city council subcommittee system and expanding the staff of the mayor's office, that effectively diminished the manager's power. Within three years of taking office, Wilson was the acknowledged leader of San Diego—in a city that ten years before had no city officeholders among its thirty-person power structure.

Requirements for Leadership What transforms a mayor into a leader? Three factors stand out. One is the individual's ability to use the resources of the office effectively. This is a special challenge for structurally weak mayors. Another factor is the personal and political skills of the individual. The ability to use the media skillfully, to exploit connections with state and national officials, and to maintain popularity with the electorate is what a leader needs. And not enough can be said about timing, the third leadership factor and the one most beyond the control of the mayor. The times (which really means the conditions) have to warrant the leadership transformation. In the final analysis, Pete Wilson's personal and political skills notwithstanding, he "was the right person at the right time in San Diego."[31]

Problems can arise when a strong person occupies a structurally weak mayoral post. If politically powerful citizens in the city want a star, they design a government structure to accommodate stardom. But if they have installed a structure intended to minimize individual leadership, a would-be leader finds his efforts at establishing a statewide reputation disrupted by squabbles back home.

PROFILE 12.1
Two Mayors: A Contrast in Leadership

You do not spend twenty-eight years as mayor of a major city without making some enemies. And, you do not get re-elected six times, averaging 69 percent of the vote, without having some friends. Just ask Henry Maier, who served as mayor of Milwaukee from 1960 to 1988.[1] Maier says it took him years "to lick the council" on some of his agenda items,[2] but even when the local press was blasting the mayor as "power mad," the people of Milwaukee revered him. Maier was widely regarded as an effective chief executive who managed Milwaukee through often demanding social and economic times. The revitalization of the downtown area is impressive evidence of his leadership.

Exhibiting quite a different style and operating in a very different structural setting is Richard Berkley, who has been mayor of Kansas City, Missouri, since 1979. The mayor is described by observers as "warm and fuzzy."[3] The council-manager form of government does not invest him with much power; unlike Mayor Maier, Berkley has no administrative responsibilities (they belong to the city manager). He is a member of the city council, and the only real powers he has are appointing council committees, naming individuals to advisory boards, and voting last in council discussions. Leadership is not thrust on this mayor; any leadership role he plays is primarily self-determined.

Berkley has opted for an active role, and, like Maier, finds himself guiding the city through turbulent times. By all accounts, he has been quite successful. He has built the coalitions that are necessary for a weak mayor's survival, and has used the structure so masterfully that during his bid for a third term, critics coined the phrase "Teflon mayor," because nothing seemed to stick to him.[4]

[1] Dirk Johnson, "Milwaukee Mayor Outlives Problems and Politicians in His 28-Year Reign," New York Times, March 29, 1988, p. 8.
[2] Jane Mobley, "Politician or Professional? The Debate over Who Should Run Our Cities Continues," Governing 1 (February 1988): 42–48.
[3] Jane Mobley, "The Warm and Fuzzy Mayor of Kansas City Takes on the Urban Agenda," Governing 1 (October 1987): 38–46.
[4] Ibid., p. 43.

Mayoral Types Of course, not everybody wants to be a leader. Some mayors are comfortable just being mayor; they may find the position appealing because of the social benefits that accompany the office. And a mayoral style that is acceptable in one community might not fit in other places. One typology identified four styles of mayoral behavior:[32]

- *the crusader mayor,* who wants to solve urban problems and produce signficant policy innovations but is hindered by weak political and financial resources;
- *the entrepreneurial mayor,* who, like the crusader, is predisposed to activism in urban policymaking but, unlike the crusader, is blessed with strong political and financial resources;
- *the boss mayor,* who, unlike the crusaders or entrepreneurs, is not particularly interested in solving urban problems but has strong political and financial resources at his disposal; and
- *the broker mayor,* who lacks both resources and will and therefore devotes time to balancing and adjusting demands and conflicts.

Given these variations in resources and predispositions, we can expect different responses to common problems. The crusading mayor will devote his energies to symbolic politics and crisis management. Given a deficient resource base, he has to build a supportive constituency in order to pursue his objectives. This type of mayor often does not seek re-election, because he is frustrated that the policy return does not justify the energy expended. The entrepreneurial mayor, in contrast, has the luxury of resources to go with her activist style. This kind of mayor is most likely to be considered a leader. The entrepreneur can control the policy agenda and build the necessary political alliances to centralize power in her office.[33] Mayors with ample resources but without the inclination to engage in innovative policymaking tend to focus on enhancing their own political base. Policymaking is pragmatic, not ideological, for these boss mayors. And finally, broker mayors, who lack resources and policymaking verve, really function as mediators and referees in the city government system. This is not the stuff of which local government leadership is made.

Black Mayors Black mayors were interesting in the past simply because there were so few of them, but today their uniqueness has worn off. By the late 1980s, there were black mayors in almost three hundred cities across the country. (About fifty were women.) Black mayors are interesting now because of the different nature of the challenge they confront and the subtle shift in their orientation to it. Called a "new generation," these mayors consider themselves problem solvers, not crusaders; political pragmatists, not ideologues.[34]

A roll call of the black mayors who were "firsts"—that is, the first blacks to be elected to the mayor's office in a major city—includes some powerful names from the past: Carl Stokes in Cleveland; Richard Hatcher in Gary, Indiana; Kenneth Gibson in Newark; Ernest Morial in New Orleans; Harold

Washington in Chicago. Some powerful names of the present are also on the list: Coleman Young of Detroit, Maynard Jackson of Atlanta, and Tom Bradley of Los Angeles. For many of these pioneering mayors, a prominent item on the agenda has been civil rights.

For second-generation black mayors, the focus tends to be citywide development issues rather than civil rights and empowerment of minorities.[35] According to Richard Arrington, the mayor of Birmingham, "what black voters want now is a chunk of the city's commercial and economic development boom."[36] In addition, second-generation black mayors have found that winning the election means building coalitions among white voters. Table 12.1 lists big-city black mayors and the black population percentage.

The defeat in 1987 of Harvey Gantt, the first black mayor of Charlotte, North Carolina, demonstrates the fragility of biracial coalitions in city politics. Charlotte's population is 30 percent black. Gantt, with overwhelming support in the black community, had won in 1983 with 36 percent of the white vote and in 1985 with 46 percent. His white challenger unseated him when Gantt's proportion of the white vote dropped to 34 percent and turnout among black voters declined. In Chicago, results from the 1989 mayoral race raised disturbing questions about racial polarization in the voting there: more than 90 percent of the black voters voted for black candidates; more than 90 percent of the white electorate voted for white candidates.[37]

Table 12.1   Big-City Black Mayors

City	Percent black	Mayor
New York City	25	David Dinkins
Los Angeles	17	Tom Bradley
Philadelphia	38	Wilson Goode
Detroit	63	Coleman Young
Baltimore	55	Kurt Schmoke
Washington, D.C.	70	Marion Barry
Cleveland	44	Michael White
New Orleans	55	Sidney Barthelemy
Seattle	9	Norman Rice
Atlanta	67	Maynard Jackson
Oakland	47	Lionel Wilson
Newark	58	Sharpe James
Birmingham	56	Richard Arrington

*As of 1989. Listed in descending order according to city size.

Source: Data for percentages of blacks from U.S. Department of Commerce, *County and City Data Book, 1983* (Washington, D.C.: U.S. Government Printing Office, 1983).

City Managers

City managers exemplify the movement to reformed city government. They are the embodiment of the professional, neutral expert whose job it is to run the day-to-day affairs of the city.

In the original conception, managers were to implement but not formulate policy. Administration and politics were to be kept separate. The managers' responsibility would be to administer the policies enacted by the elected officials—the city councils—by whom they were hired (and fired). But it is impossible to keep administration and politics completely separate. City managers are influenced not only by their training and by the councils that employ them but by their own political ideology.[38] When it comes to making choices, they balance professional norms, the politics of the issue, and their own predispositions. This means that city managers typically end up being far more influential on the local government scene than their neutral persona might suggest.

Managers as Policy Leaders   As time has passed and more governments have adopted the council-manager form, the issue of whether the city manager should be a policy leader or a functionary of the city council has become paramount. Should a city's policy initiation and formulation process involve a well-trained, highly competent administrator?

The International City Management Association, the city managers' professional association (and lobbyist), says yes: the role of the manager is to help the governing body function more effectively.[39] The manager-in-training is taught that "the manager now is also expected to be a full partner in the political side of the policymaking process."[40] Ways in which the manager can assume a larger role in policymaking include proposing community goals and service levels; structuring the budget preparation, review, and adoption process so that it is linked to goals and service levels; and orienting new council members to organizational processes and norms.

One indisputable role is as an information source for the busy, part-time city council. For instance, suppose that some enterprising college students are requesting a change in a city ordinance that prohibits street vendors. The council asks the manager to study the pros and cons of street vending. At a subsequent meeting, he reports on other cities' experiences: Has it created a litter problem? Does it draw clientele away from established businesses? How much revenue can be expected from vendor licensing fees? The manager offers alternative courses of action (allow street vending only at lunchtime; restrict pushcarts to Main Street) and evaluates their probable consequences. In some councils, the manager is asked to make a formal recommendation, but in others his recommendation is more along the lines of "Well, what do you think?" At some point, a vote will be called and the council will make a formal decision.

Managerial Types   Let us reconsider San Diego in the 1970s. From the perspective of mayoral leadership it was a success story, but from the view of city management it was a disaster. During Mayor Pete Wilson's eleven-year tenure, San Diego went through five city managers.[41] Few of the new breed of managers trained to be policymakers wanted to return to the weakened managerial position that Wilson had instituted.

Like mayors, city managers are not cut from one mold. The trick is to match the managerial "type" with the right community. Four general local managerial types have been identified:[42]

- *the community leader,* who sees himself or herself as an agent for community change, as an innovator, full of energy and idealism;
- *the chief executive,* the experienced community leader whose innovativeness and idealism have been tempered by pragmatism;
- *the administrative innovator,* an inward-focused manager who is interested in change within the organization by promoting technical and procedural improvements; and
- *the administrative caretaker,* who values order and routine and concentrates on the housekeeping functions of local government.

For any of these administrators to be successful, he or she must fit with the community. We can match the managerial types with the four community types introduced in Chapter 11. The brokerage community, for example, would benefit from the enthusiasm and commitment of a community leader, who could put his skills to work resolving conflicts. The boosteristic community would be a good place for the savvy chief executive who has been around; in such a setting, the manager's job would entail promoting the community and managing growth, two functions that often do not complement one another. The amenities community would be an ideal spot for an administrative innovator, an environment in which his skills would be valued; preserving the quality of life and providing services efficiently would probably be the major responsibilities of the post. Finally, the caretaker community and the administrative caretaker are made for each other—a community prefers minimal government, and the manager wants little challenge.

When managerial type and community type correspond, local government should function well. The perfect fit is difficult to achieve, however. City councils get replaced, local tax bases suffer disruptions, and managers shift their orientation to the job. Communities search for the perfect manager; managers seek out the perfect community.

Local Legislatures

Local legislatures include city councils, county commissions, town boards of aldermen or selectmen, special district boards, and school boards. They are representative, deliberative bodies. In this section we focus on city councils, because that is where most of the research has taken place, but many of the points made are applicable to the other local legislative bodies.

City Council Members: Old and New

A former member of the Concord, California, city council defines "the good old days" on local governing boards with this comment: "When I first came on the city council, it was like a good-old-boys' club."[43] The standard description was that the city council was a part-time, low-paying haven for public-spirited white men who did not consider themselves politicians. Most councils used at-large electoral mechanisms, so that individual council members had no specific territorially based constituency. Council members considered themselves volunteers.[44] Research on city councils in the San Francisco Bay area cities in the 1960s found that these volunteer members were fairly unresponsive to public pressures and tended to vote their own preferences.

These days, circumstances have changed. As pointed out in Chapter 11, city councils are less white, less male, and less passive than they were in the past. Some of this is due to modifications in the electoral mechanism. Many cities, such as San Antonio, have abandoned citywide elections and switched to district (or ward) elections. Only the mayor of San Antonio, a council-manager city, is currently elected at large. Other cities have chosen to retain some at-large seats while dividing the city into electoral districts. Houston, a strong-mayor city, is an example: of the fourteen members of the Houston city council, five are elected at large, and nine are elected from districts. (Table 12.2 shows the wide variation in council size and in the number of members elected at large and from districts.) In both San Antonio and Houston, and in cities across the nation, changes in the election mechanism signaled a change in council composition. There are more blacks, Hispanics, and women on city councils than ever before, and they are taking their governance roles quite seriously. Profile 12.2 looks at a Montana county governed by women.

Councils in Action: Increasing Conflict

When members of the council came from the same socioeconomic stratum (in some communities, members of the at-large council all came from the same neighborhood) and when they shared a common political philosophy, governing was a lot easier. The council could meet before the meeting (usually at breakfast) and discuss the items on the agenda. That way they could arrive at an informal resolution of any particularly troubling items and thus transform the actual council meeting into a rubber-stamp exercise. No wonder that the majority of council votes were unanimous; members were merely ratifying what they had already settled on.

Table 12.2   City Councils of Selected Large Cities

	1984 population	Council size	Number at large	Number districts
Los Angeles	3,096,721	15	0	15
Chicago	2,992,472	50	0	50
Houston	1,705,697	14	5	9
Philadelphia	1,646,713	16	0	16
Detroit	1,088,973	9	9	0
Dallas	974,234	6	6	0
San Diego	960,452	7	0	7
Phoenix	853,266	9	1	8
San Antonio	842,779	11	1	10
Baltimore	763,570	19	1	18
San Francisco	712,753	11	11	0
Indianapolis	710,280	7	2	5
Memphis	648,399	13	6	7
Milwaukee	620,811	16	0	16
Jacksonville	577,971	19	5	14
Boston	570,719	13	4	9

Source: Adapted from International City Management Association, *The Municipal Year Book 1987* (Washington, D.C.: ICMA, 1987); and National League of Cities, *Directory of City Policy Officials* (Washington, D.C.: NLC, 1986).

Council members elected by districts report more factionalism and less unanimity than their counterparts elected at large do. Data from surveys of council members in 218 cities in 42 states shed more light on this question.[45] Conflict on councils revolves around three types of rivalries: development interests versus others, business versus neighborhoods, and tax-cutters versus opponents. The level and focus of such conflict are detailed in Table 12.3. The growing tendency of cities to move away from complete reliance on at-large electoral mechanisms suggests that council conflict will be on the rise.

Reshaping a Council: The Case of Houston

Houston, the nation's fourth largest city, has weathered several changes in the structure of its government. It adopted the plural-executive commission structure during the reform movement but abandoned it for a fling

PROFILE 12.2
Women as Local Government Leaders

City councils these days average slightly under 20 percent women members.[1] The number of women on county commissions has not quite reached that proportion, but you would not know it if you examined the Missoula County, Montana, commission. There, the three-member county governing board is all female.

As far as anyone can determine, Missoula County in 1985 became the first county in the nation to be run by women. It has not been easy for the Missoula County commissioners to succeed, not because of any managerial deficiencies or political liabilities but because of skepticism about their ability to govern effectively. The commissioners' ideologies range from conservative Republican to liberal Democrat, but the basis for skepticism was the fact that the commissioners were women. As one commissioner stated, women "have to be twice as good and twice as smart" to be considered successful in the political arena.

Has their sex affected governance in Missoula County? The commissioners themselves say yes. They believe that they have brought to the job characteristics such as a nurturing style and trustworthiness, which have helped them forge a solidarity that has contributed to effective performance. But they and other observers readily admit that their biggest problem has been poor relations with other elected county officials, especially men. Clashes with other elected officials is nothing new for county commissioners, male or female. What is new is its basis in conflict between the sexes. The commissioners have been accused of looking for sexism; they claim that they have not had to look for it, because it is a fact of daily life.

When the accomplishments of this group are tallied, there is little dispute that they have been an effective county commission. That portends well for increasing the number of women on local governing boards.

[1] Susan Welch and Timothy Bledsoe, *Urban Reform and Its Consequences* (Chicago: University of Chicago Press, 1988), p. 131n.

Source: Richard D. Manning, "How Three Women Took Over Missoula County and the 'Gender Factor' Became an Edge," *Governing* 1 (May 1988): 44–50. Reprinted by permission.

with the council-manager form from 1942 to 1946. During the late 1940s, it adopted a strong-mayor structure. In 1979, the eight-member, elected at-large council system was junked in favor of the fourteen-member system described above. This change represented a definite revision in terms of council composition. In 1981, a new mayor, Kathryn J. Whitmire, was elected with the explicit intent of executive-branch reform.[46] Thus, a newly aggressive council encountered a mayor with a mission. The consequences were predictable: the mayor thought the council was intent on encroaching on her authority, and the council was convinced that the mayor was engaging in empire-building.

In the ensuing years, the mayor and the council have hammered out a working relationship that entails greater council involvement in the affairs of city government. The old "council as [a] rubber stamp of the mayor and the city's business interests" is gone.[47] This is not to say that an expanded role for the council has been created without bitter antagonism between the executive and the legislative branch—far from it. But the council's larger role reflects a recognition of its representational function and an appreciation of the need for institutional partnerships.

Table 12.3 Council Members' Perceptions of Council Conflict

Rivalry	Very important	Somewhat important	Not very important	
Development interests vs. others	44	41	15	
Business vs. neighborhoods	32	42	27	
Tax cutters vs. opponents	27	45	28	
One area vs. another	20	39	42	
Liberals vs. conservatives	19	40	40	
Business vs. labor	12	33	56	
Whites/anglos vs. others	12	27	62	
Democrats vs. Republicans	12	26	63	
Political machine vs. reformers	12	25	64	
	None	Some	Sharp	
Factions on the council	19	36	45	
Unanimous votes	75	50–74	25–49	<25
(% of time)	42*	31	14	12

*Forty-two percent of the cities have unanimous votes 75 percent or more of the time, 31 percent have them 50–74 percent of the time, and so forth.

Source: Susan Welch and Timothy Bledsoe, *Urban Reform and Its Consequences* (Chicago: University of Chicago Press, 1988), p. 96. Reprinted by permission of The University of Chicago Press.

Political Leadership versus Professional Leadership

The issue of politics versus administration is not confined to the local level of government. Congress battles with federal agencies and state legislatures fight with state agencies. There is a natural struggle between officials who make policy and those who implement it, and between those who allocate funds and those who spend them. What distinguishes the local level is the relentlessness of the conflict. The elected representatives of the public—the city council—are pitted against the best professional management that money can buy—the city administrator and his staff. In strong-mayor cities, the dynamic is slightly different, since an elected official heads the bureaucracy. In that setting, the chief executive balances a political role with an administrative one. In both instances, the functioning of local government depends on the creation of a workable relationship.

Council-Manager Interactions

The interactions between the council and the manager cover more than the traditional division of politics and administration. Interviews with elected and administrative officials in five North Carolina cities convinced one researcher that this dichotomy did not describe reality.[48] Every city revealed instances when administrators engaged in policymaking (for example, when they initiated proposals and drafted the budget) and when council members intruded on the administrative sphere (say, with legislative oversight of program implementation). A more realistic model of council-manager interaction posits four functions of the government process: mission, policy, administration, and management. Figure 12.1 depicts these dimensions.

The *mission* function involves setting goals and establishing the purpose and direction of city government. The *policy* function covers middle-range actions such as passing ordinances, making spending decisions, and creating programs. The *administration* function includes policy implementation, service delivery, and promulgation of regulations. The *management* function involves the day-to-day operations of city government—organizational procedures and actions.

The mission function is primarily the province of elected officials, just as the management function belongs to administrative personnel (although the council is an "interested observer" in hiring and firing decisions and contract awards). Predictably, the policy and administration functions are more difficult to sort out. Elected officials and managers share these functions to a considerable extent. Managers make policy recommendations; elected officials field citizen complaints and participate in some implementation decisions.[49] The key to effective government is a mutual understanding of the mixed responsibilities in policy and administration.

Figure 12.1 Four Dimensions of the Governmental Process
Local government officials, both elected and appointed, want to protect their turf—their designated dimension.

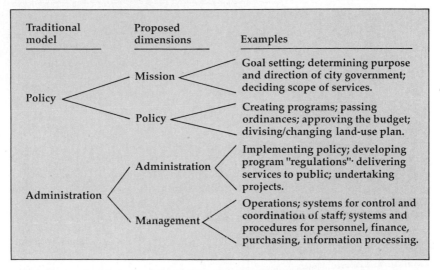

Traditional model	Proposed dimensions	Examples
Policy	Mission	Goal setting; determining purpose and direction of city government; deciding scope of services.
	Policy	Creating programs; passing ordinances; approving the budget; divising/changing land-use plan.
Administration	Administration	Implementing policy; developing program "regulations"· delivering services to public; undertaking projects.
	Management	Operations; systems for control and coordination of staff; systems and procedures for personnel, finance, purchasing, information processing.

Source: James H. Svara, "The Complementary Roles of Officials in Council-Manager Government," in International City Management Association, *The Municipal Year Book 1988* (Washington, D.C.: ICMA, 1988), p. 24. Reprinted by permission.

Perceptions of Governmental Systems

This chapter and the preceding one emphasize government structure. The basic point is that structure reflects orientations to and expectations of government. A strong-mayor system reflects a polity in which accountability is valued and politics is not a dirty word. A council-manager form is characteristic of a polity that emphasizes professional management and efficiency. This distinction certainly does not mean that a strong-mayor system is inevitably less efficient or that a council-manager form is not accountable to the public. It simply suggests that the orientations and expectations are different.

This is borne out in the internal workings of local governments. Table 12.4 shows the degree to which council members and department heads agree with four statements about the way their governments work.[50] Responses from officials in council-manager cities tend to be at odds with responses from those in strong-mayor systems.

To the basic question of whether the council and the chief executive officer (a manager in the council-manager cities, a mayor in the strong-mayor cities) have a good working relationship, there is striking variation in answers of officials in the two structures. Virtually all of the council members and three-quarters of the department heads in council-manager sys-

Table 12.4   Perceptions of Council–Chief Executive Relations

| | Form of government* | | | |
| | Council-manager[†] | | Strong-mayor–council[‡] | |
Description	Council members agree (%)	Department heads agree (%)	Council members agree (%)	Department heads agree (%)
The council and manager (or mayor) have a good working relationship	100.0	75.7	56.5	52.1
The manager [or] mayor provides council with sufficient alternatives for policy decisions	76.9	90.9	29.1	56.2
The council effectively draws on the expertise of professional staff	76.9	76.1	54.2	47.9
Intervention by a council member is necessary to get adequate response to citizen complaints	34.6	7.5	66.7	14.6

*The forms of government in this table included six council-manager and five strong-mayor–council cities.
[†]In the council-manager cities, twenty-six council members and sixty-seven department heads responded.
[‡]In the strong-mayor–council cities, twenty-four council members and forty-eight department heads responded.
Source: James H. Svara, "The Complementary Roles of Officials in Council-Manager Government," in International City Management Association, The Municipal Year Book 1988 (Washington, D.C.: ICMA, 1988), p. 25. Reprinted by permission.

tems report good working relationships. In strong-mayor systems, only about half of the council members and the department heads report this. Council members in council-manager systems are much more satisfied with the process of arriving at policy alternatives than are council members in strong-mayor structures. In compelling affirmation of the different nature of service delivery and constituency relations in the two forms, nearly twice as many council members in strong-mayor structures report that council intervention is necessary to get the bureaucracy to respond to citizen complaints.

These findings suggest that structural differences can have consequences. It is important to remember, however, that individuals who work within structures are the essential factor. As we saw with San Diego, leaders can make structures work for them (sometimes by performing minor surgery on the structure to ensure that it does). As the mayor of Rochester, New York, a city that switched from a council-manager system to a strong-mayor form, commented, "The bottom line is good people committed to good governance."[51]

Policy Innovation at the Local Level

Earlier in this book, it was argued that state and local governments function as sources of innovation. Reflect on the words of President Reagan in his January 1988 state-of-the-union message; he mentioned "a thousand sparks of genius" and suggested that some of these sparks would catch fire and "become guiding lights."[52]

To be innovative means simply to try something new. But to do something new implies taking risks. Innovators often behave in an entrepreneurial manner. True leaders—individuals who are unequivocally perceived as leaders by relevant observers— tend to be innovative and entrepreneurial.[53] They do things that others cannot or will not do.

Innovative communities are those that do things first, that are receptive to creative solutions to problems. The first scholarly explorations of this phenomenon involved the fluoridation of public water systems. Before 1951, fluoridation was used on an experimental basis by a small number of cities. As word spread (that is, as community leaders and health professionals in these cities transmitted information to their counterparts in other cities), fluoridation became fashionable, and eventually fluoridated water systems became the norm. The critical variable determining which cities took the lead in this instance seemed to be the position taken by the executive leaders.[54] If the mayor or city manager strongly advocated fluoridation, the community was more likely to support it.

Studies of structural innovations in government suggest that if important communities adopt a new structure, other communities are more receptive to it.[55] And research on innovations in "quality of life" demonstrates that the compatibility of an innovation with the existing policy climate in the city contributes to its adoption rate.[56] Some communities specialize; that is, they develop reputations for innovativeness in certain areas, such as environmental protection or government structure.

One example of a recent local government innovation is the restriction or banning of billboards. With the aim of reducing visual pollution, cities across the nation, especially those in the growing Sunbelt areas, have enacted antibillboard ordinances. In 1987, voters in Jacksonville, Florida, approved a measure that will remove all billboards from city streets by 1992.[57] Other cities are following suit, although not to the point of total removal. Denver, for example, has frozen the allowable number of billboards at the 1988 level and has mandated the removal of those along historic boulevards. Houston and Phoenix have taken similar actions.

Another example of innovation is found in environmental issues. In 1988 Suffolk County, New York, became the first jurisdiction in the country to outlaw the use of nonbiodegradable containers. The ban includes "clam-shell" packaging for fast foods, plastic-foam meat trays, and certain plastic grocery sacks.[58] This was not aberrant behavior for Suffolk County; in 1981, it was the first to prohibit the nonreturnable bottle. The Long Island county's innovativeness is partly the result of a waste problem. As in other jurisdictions, the local waste dumps are at capacity and scheduled for closure, and plastic packaging of the kind that has been banned cannot be safely incinerated. Innovation is the product of need: the county had to do something to reduce the volume of waste.

Some innovations have symbolic value. Madison, Wisconsin, the home of the University of Wisconsin, elected and re-elected a Socialist as its mayor in the 1970s. In the 1980s, Madison led the rest of the country with its adoption of three innovations dealing with foreign affairs. The city declared itself a nuclear-free zone, which means that no nuclear weapons can be developed, stored, or transported through the community, and it became a sanctuary for Central American refugees. In addition, the Madison city council adopted a resolution calling for a comprehensive nuclear testing ban. These actions placed the city at the forefront of a group of politically liberal communities scattered across the country.

Leadership and Capacity

In the final analysis, leadership remains somewhat ephemeral. But regardless of the difficulty in pinning it down, it is a central, critical concern in local government. For example, Oshkosh, Wisconsin, is hailed as a success story because of the rejuvenation of its declining economy. Replicating this success in other cities is a difficult task, though, since "so much is dependent upon the charisma, vision, skill, and commitment of particular business leaders, city politicians, and managers."[59] In other words, success depends on leadership.

Leaders see problems as opportunities. The challenge comes in devising effective solutions. For example, in a 1989 poll, New York City residents reported profound pessimism about the city's future and identified drugs and crime as intractable problems crying out for solution.[60] When asked about their long-range view of the city, only 22 percent believed that New York would be a better place to live; more than twice that figure thought that it would be a worse place. Which of the six mayoral candidates in America's largest city that year offered the greatest hope for leadership? When the dust settled from the primary and general election, David Dinkins was the voters' choice to lead them.

Summary

Leaders display a penchant for action, and leading communities behave similarly. In each community, there are a few leaders and many followers; the same is true for each region and its constituent communities. Whether the focus is on individual leaders or leading communities, some of the important characteristics are initiative, energy, persistence, and vision.

Researchers have found variations of elitism and pluralism when they have studied power in communities. As political scientists, we have concentrated on leadership positions in local government—mayors, managers, councils, and commissions—in this chapter, but this does not deny the existence of unofficial power and the central role played by the private sector.

Key Terms

Decisional method A method for studying community power in which researchers identify key issues and the individuals who are active in the decision-making process.

Elite theory A theory of government that asserts that a small group possesses power and rules society.

Pluralist theory A theory of government that asserts that multiple, open, competing groups possess power and rule society.

Reputational approach A method for studying community power in which researchers ask informants to name and rank influential individuals.

Strong mayor An elected chief executive who possesses extensive powers in the city government structure.

Weak mayor An elected chief executive who shares power with other officials in the city government structure.

13

State and Local Finance

The Principles of Finance
  Interdependence/Diversity

Revenues
  Criteria for Evaluating Taxes/Major State and
  Local Taxes/Two Revenue Devices

The Political Economy of Taxation
  Tax Revolt/Fiscal Stress/Limited Discretion

Borrowing and Debt
  Estimating Revenues/Rainy Day Funds/Other
  Cash and Investment Management Practices/
  State and Local Debt

State and Local Financial Relationships
  An Uneasy Relationship/What Local
  Governments Want from the States

State and Local Finance in the 1990s

In 1978 a political upheaval in California altered the state and local fiscal landscape as surely as a bulldozer alters a field of flowers. Using the initiative process to amend the state constitution, California voters overwhelmingly approved Proposition 13. This amendment slashed property taxes by 60 percent and imposed strict limitations on the ability of local governments to raise property and other taxes in the future. Government officials and critics reacted stridently, claiming that police stations would be padlocked, that parks, recreation areas, and libraries would be closed, and that schoolchildren would suffer.

Enactment of Proposition 13 was the event that kicked off a taxpayer revolt across the United States. Before the energy of the revolt was spent, most states had passed laws restricting state and local revenues and expenditures. Prior to Proposition 13, state and local taxes had been rising steadily. Ten years after its passage, only five states had taxes higher (on a per capita basis and adjusted for cost-of-living increases) than in 1978. Some local governments have been forced to cut back certain services in order to balance their budgets, but essential services generally have been maintained, and local officials have come up with creative new ways to extract money from the public. The results of the taxpayer revolt have been positive in most jurisdictions, in that elected officials think longer and harder before raising taxes. But in states with very stringent taxing limitations, such as California and Massachusetts, the taxpayer revolt has caused pain and disruption.

Today, largely as a result of the taxpayer revolt, state and local revenue systems have changed dramatically. Tax systems are more diversified and more equitable. Sizable cutbacks in national government spending have resulted in the concentration of revenue-raising and spending activity at the state level, and greater cooperation between state and local governments.

The Principles of Finance

A major purpose of government is to provide services to citizens. This costs money: equipment must be purchased and employees must be paid. Governments raise needed funds through taxes and fees. In a democracy, the voters decide what range and quality of services they desire and register those opinions through elected representatives. Sometimes, as in the case of Proposition 13, voters take matters directly into their own hands.

Citizens in the 1700s and 1800s expected few services from their state and local governments, and that is essentially what they received. The taxation of property was the major source of state and local revenue until the beginning of this century. Property taxes were augmented by business licenses, poll taxes, and a variety of miscellaneous sources. As the scope and level of services rose in response to citizen demands, states and localities developed a wider array of revenue-raising devices, including taxes on income, merchandise sales, auto license plates, alcohol, tobacco, and gasoline.

Two basic principles describe state and local financial systems as they have evolved to the 1990s: *interdependence* and *diversity*. State and local fiscal systems are closely interlinked and heavily influenced by national financial activities. Intergovernmental sharing of revenues is a pronounced feature of our interdependent federal fiscal system. Yet our state financial structures and processes are also highly diverse. Although affected by national activities, their own economic health, and competitive pressures from one another, the states enjoy substantial autonomy in designing individual revenue systems in response to citizens' policy preferences.

Interdependence

The American governments raise huge amounts of money. In 1987 the national government took in over $915 billion, and the states and localities over $547 billion. That totals up to almost one and one-half trillion dollars.[1] Most of this money is **own-source revenue,** garnered from taxes, charges, and fees applied to people, services, and products within the jurisdiction of each level of government. Nonnational governments also benefit from **intergovernmental transfers.** The national government in 1985 transferred some $85 billion to the states and $22 billion to localities. For their part, states passed on over $116 billion to their cities, counties, and special-purpose governments.[2]

From 1902 (the first year such data were published) to the late 1970s, state and local governments gradually grew more and more dependent on federal revenue transfers. In 1980, 27.5 percent of total state revenues came from Washington, D.C., in the form of grants-in-aid and other sources; the corresponding percentage of intergovernmental contributions (i.e., national and state) to local governments was 44.1 percent.[3] Since 1980, the importance of intergovernmental sources has declined for both states and localities, primarily because of national aid reductions and the termination of the General Revenue Sharing program.

Figure 13.1 shows the rise and recent decline of national intergovernmental aid. Actually, the impact of federal cutbacks is significantly understated here. Some 52 percent of all federal aid to nonnational governments goes to *individual* recipients (for example, people receiving AFDC or Medicaid), not to state and local governments for general purposes. As a result, less than half of total grant dollars are available for the traditional functions of state and local governments, such as education, transportation, and public health.[4]

Local governments rely heavily on the states, and to a lesser degree on the national government, for financial authority and assistance. Only the states can authorize localities to levy taxes and fees, incur debt, and spend money. State constitutions and laws place many conditions on local govern-

Figure 13.1 The Rise and Decline of Federal Aid, 1958–1988
Federal aid as a percentage of total state and local government spending rose
from 1958 to 1978, and then declined rapidly. The broken line indicates a
projection of recent trends into the future.

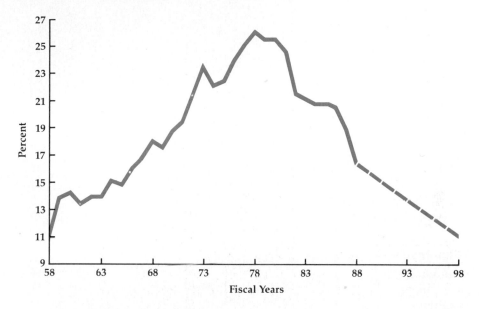

Source: U.S. Advisory Commission on Intergovernmental Relations, *Intergovernmental Perspective* 14 (Winter 1988): 13.

ment taxing and spending.[5] Recently, states have been increasing their
monetary support of local governments through state grants-in-aid and
revenue sharing and by assuming financial responsibility for activities previously paid for by localities, in particular school and social welfare costs.
The emergence of the states as "senior financial partners" in state-local
finance[6] is evident in the following statistics for 1986: states paid 54 cents to
local governments for every dollar raised from local sources, $1.17 to school
districts for each dollar raised locally, and 51 cents on each dollar raised by
counties.[7]

Although federal grants to local governments have dropped (in constant
dollars) since 1978, state-local finances continue to be linked very closely to
activities of the national government. When national monetary and fiscal
policies lead the nation into a recession, it is state and local governments
that suffer most. This fact was officially recognized until the early 1980s by
Congress, which would send substantial amounts of *countercyclical aid* to the
states and localities to help them recover from the ravages of recession.
During the severe recession of 1982–83, however, countercyclical aid was
very limited.

Table 13.1   State and Local Tax Revenue per $100 of Personal Income

	Level	Rank
New England		
Connecticut	$10.92*	25
Maine	12.63	7
Massachusetts	11.87	14
New Hampshire	8.48	50
Rhode Island	11.91	13
Vermont	12.51	9
Middle Atlantic		
Delaware	13.20	5
Maryland	11.37	22
New Jersey	11.19	24
New York	16.35	3
Pennsylvania	10.90	26
Great Lakes		
Illinois	10.49	32
Indiana	9.89	41
Michigan	12.36	10
Ohio	10.57	31
Wisconsin	12.53	8
Southeast		
Alabama	9.86	42
Arkansas	9.50	47
Florida	9.45	48
Georgia	10.29	33
Kentucky	10.63	30
Louisiana	10.74	29
Mississippi	10.28	36
North Carolina	10.88	27
South Carolina	11.52	19
Tennessee	9.80	44
Virginia	10.14	38
West Virginia	11.71	18

*Figures are estimates for fiscal year 1987.

Source: National Conference of State Legislatures, *State Legislatures*, March 1988, p. 5. Copyright © 1988 by National Conference of State Legislatures. Reprinted with permission from *State Legislatures*.

Table 13.1   State and Local Tax Revenue per $100 of Personal Income (*cont.*)

	Level	Rank
Plains		
Iowa	$11.36	23
Kansas	10.29	35
Minnesota	12.65	6
Missouri	8.98	49
Nebraska	10.26	37
North Dakota	9.80	43
South Dakota	10.11	39
Southwest		
Arizona	11.86	15
New Mexico	11.86	16
Oklahoma	9.70	45
Texas	9.66	46
Rocky Mountain		
Colorado	10.29	34
Idaho	10.09	40
Montana	11.78	17
Utah	12.22	11
Wyoming	17.53[†]	1
Far West		
Alaska	17.04[†]	2
California	11.47	20
Hawaii	13.51	4
Nevada	10.86	28
Oregon	11.94	12
Washington	11.46	21
U.S. Average	$11.35	

[†]The per capita tax burden for Alaska and Wyoming is exaggerated; most of these low-population states' revenues come from the taxation of oil production.

Diversity

The second basic principle of state and local finance systems is diversity. Each level of government depends on one type of revenue device more than others. For the national government it is the income tax; for the states, the sales tax; and for local governments, the property tax. Among the states diversity triumphs as well. Differences in tax capacity (wealth), tax effort, and tax choices are obvious to even the casual observer. Most states tax personal income and merchandise sales, but a handful do not. A growing number of states operate lotteries and pari-mutuel betting facilities. At least seventeen states have found a novel way of raising revenue, by requiring dealers in illegal drugs to purchase tax stamps. Someone caught selling drugs can be prosecuted for tax evasion as well as drug dealing. Minnesota's rates are $3.50 a gram for marijuana and $200 per gram for harder drugs. Dealers caught without stamps must pay the state double, and face up to five years in prison and an additional $10,000 fine. Minnesota has managed to collect some stamp tax dollars from apprehended dealers, along with automobiles and other property seized in lieu of taxes.[8]

There are high-tax states and low-tax states. Most fall somewhere in the middle. If the basic objective of taxing is to pluck the maximum number of

Table 13.2   Comparison of the States in Tax System Capacity and Effort

	Fiscal capacity	Tax effort
1. Alaska	177	168
2. Wyoming	151	117
3. Nevada	147	65
4. Connecticut	135	94
5. Massachusetts	124	103
6. District of Columbia	122	143
7. Delaware	121	81
8. New Jersey	121	103
9. New Hampshire	119	62
10. California	118	95
11. Colorado	117	83
12. Hawaii	113	105
13. Maryland	108	99
14. New York	107	152
15. Florida	105	77
16. Texas	104	79
17. Minnesota	102	108
18. Virginia	101	85
19. Vermont	99	91
20. Arizona	99	99
21. Oklahoma	98	85
22. Washington	98	103
23. Michigan	96	118
24. Illinois	96	106
25. Kansas	96	96

100 = U.S. average. Rankings are for 1986.

Source: U.S. Advisory Commission on Intergovernmental Relations, *Intergovernmental Perspective* 15 (Spring 1989), p. 17.

feathers from the goose with the minimum amount of squawking, the wealthy states hold a great advantage. They can reap high tax revenues with much less effort than poor states, which must tax at high rates just to pull in enough money to pay for the basics. Per capita state and local tax revenues vary from $4,489 in resource-rich, sparsely populated Alaska to $965 in poverty stricken Mississippi. The U.S. average in 1986 was $1,547. There is a fairly close relationship between state wealth (as measured by personal income) and tax revenues. Table 13.1 shows how the states compare in state and local tax revenues as a percentage of personal income. Note that joining Alaska as high-tax states are resource-rich Wyoming and New York. At the low end of the scale are New Hampshire, Missouri, Idaho, and several southern states. Most of the low scorers are resource-poor, rural, or both.

Table 13.2   Comparison of the States in Tax System Capacity and Effort (*cont.*)

	Fiscal capacity	Tax effort
26. Maine	95	99
27. Georgia	94	89
28. North Dakota	94	89
29. Oregon	93	98
30. Missouri	93	82
31. Rhode Island	92	111
32. New Mexico	91	88
33. Nebraska	91	96
34. Ohio	91	103
35. Louisiana	90	91
36. Pennsylvania	90	101
37. North Carolina	88	92
38. Montana	88	103
39. Indiana	87	94
40. Wisconsin	86	134
41. Iowa	84	113
42. Tennessee	84	84
43. Utah	80	107
44. South Carolina	79	94
45. South Dakota	78	95
46. Idaho	77	90
47. West Virginia	76	98
48. Kentucky	76	89
49. Alabama	74	86
50. Arkansas	73	91
51. Mississippi	65	97

The U.S. Advisory Commission on Intergovernmental Relations (ACIR), a federal agency composed of elected officials from national, state, and local government and a professional staff, has devised an index to measure states' **fiscal capacity,** or potential ability to raise revenues from taxes. It is calculated by applying identical rates to each state for twenty-six commonly used taxes. The national average for fiscal capacity is set at 100. States with scores above 100 have more than average capacity (in effect, greater wealth), while those below 100 have less than average. State fiscal capacity scores are found in Table 13.2, in the lefthand column. Note that there are regional dimensions to revenue capacity. In addition, high tax capacity is associated with high levels of urbanization, per capita income, industrialization, and natural resources.

Simply because a state has high revenue-raising capacity does not necessarily mean that it will maximize its tax-collecting possibilities. Indeed, many states with high revenue potential actually tax at relatively low rates. The degree to which a state exploits its fiscal potential, or tax capacity, is called *tax effort* by the ACIR. Tax effort depends on the scope and level of services desired by the people. Those in turn are related to historical factors, political culture, and other state-specific variables. In the righthand column of Table 13.2 are state scores on tax effort, as calculated by the ACIR. Comparison of capacity with effort shows some interesting deviations, such as in Nevada and New Hampshire. These two states have the fiscal capacity to generate about twice as much tax revenue as they presently take in. How fully does your state exploit its tax capacity?

Diversity in state and local finance is also evident in what the nonnational governments choose to do with their revenues. All of them are spending at a rapid pace. State and local spending rose nearly 2000 percent from 1950 to 1985, almost twice as fast as the gross national product and much faster than the level of inflation. The functional distribution of spending varies from state to state. Elementary and secondary education consumes the largest portion of total state and local spending (23.9 percent), followed by public welfare (12.3 percent), and higher education (9.3 percent). Health and hospitals is next (8.8 percent), then highways (8.1 percent) and police and fire protection (5.3 percent). Within each of these functional categories is a wide range of financial commitments. For instance, higher education expenditures run from 14.6 percent of total state and local spending in North Carolina to only 5.4 percent in New York. Georgia dedicates 18.7 percent to health and hospitals, while Alaska sets aside just 2.8 percent of its expenditures.[9] Such differences represent historical trends, local economic circumstances, citizens' willingness to incur debt to pay for services, and related factors.

The largest expenditure gains in recent years have been registered in corrections. Swelling prison populations, court-ordered changes in corrections practices, and tougher sentencing policies have propelled corrections spending upward at a rate twice that of other functional categories (see Chapter 17). Medical costs are also accelerating rapidly. The Medicaid program alone was expected to claim 11 percent of the average state budget in 1990, and 15 percent by 1995.[10]

Revenues

Although the fifty state and local finance systems have their own strengths, weaknesses, and peculiarities, certain trends are found in all of them. The property tax is increasingly unpopular. It is no longer a significant source of state revenue; its contribution to total own-source local coffers is still strong, but declining. User charges and other miscellaneous fees are gradually substituting for the property tax. States continue to depend heavily on the sales tax, but alternatives are being used more widely. Tax diversification is in fact an important trend in all state and local tax systems.

Criteria for Evaluating Taxes

Numerous criteria can be used to evaluate taxes. Moreover, what one person likes about a tax may be what another dislikes. Political scientists and economists agree that among the most important criteria are equity, yield, elasticity, ease of administration, and political accountability.

Equity If citizens or firms are expected to pay a tax, they should view it as fair. In the context of taxation, equity usually refers to distributing the burden of the tax in accordance with ability to pay: high income means greater ability to pay, and therefore a larger tax burden.

Taxes may be regressive, progressive, or proportional. A **regressive tax** places a greater burden on low-income citizens than on high-income citizens. This violates the ability-to-pay principle. It means that upper-income groups contribute a smaller portion of their incomes than lower-income groups do. Most state and local levies, including property and sales taxes, are regressive. For example, both low-income and high-income people pay a 5 percent sales tax. The latter will likely make more purchases and contribute more total dollars in sales tax, but at a lower percentage of total income than the low-income individuals.

A **progressive tax** increases as a percentage of a person's income as that income rises. The more you make, the greater proportion of your income is extracted by the progressive tax. Thus, those better able to pay carry a heavier tax burden than the poor. The federal income tax is the best example of a progressive tax. The more you earn, the higher your *income tax bracket*.

A **proportional tax** burdens everyone equally, at least in theory. For instance, a tax on income of, say, 10 percent, that is applied across the board is a proportional tax. Whether you earn $100,000 or $10,000, you pay a flat 10 percent of the total in taxes. Of course, it can be argued that a low-income person is more burdened by a proportional tax than a high-income person (as in the case of the sales tax).

In place of ability to pay, some people advocate the **benefit principle.** Under this principle, those who reap more benefits from government services should shoulder more of the tax burden than people who do not avail themselves of service opportunities to the same degree. For example, parents whose children attend public schools should pay higher taxes for education than should senior citizens, childless couples, or single people without children. The benefit principle is the theoretical underpinning for user fees, which charge a taxpayer directly for services received. Examples include water and sewer fees and trash collection fees.

Yield   Taxes can also be evaluated on the basis of efficiency, or how much money they contribute to government coffers compared to the effort expended to collect them. The administrative and other costs of applying a tax must be taken into consideration when determining yield. Taxes that return substantial sums of money at minimal costs are preferred to taxes that require large outlays for moderate revenues. Income and sales taxes have high yields because of the low costs of administering them. Property taxes have lower yields because they are more expensive to assess and collect.

Elasticity   This criterion is related to yield. Tax yields should be automatically responsive to changes in economic conditions, and revenue devices should expand or contract their yields as government expenditure needs change. Specifically, as per capita income grows within states and localities, revenues should keep pace without increases in the tax rate. Tax reductions should accompany economic recession and declines in per capita income, so that citizens' tax burdens are not increased during hard times. The federal income tax is considered to be elastic, because revenues increase as individuals earn more money and move into higher tax brackets and decline as income falls. Most state and local taxes, including sales, property, and user fees, generally do not move in tandem with economic conditions and are therefore considered to be inelastic.

Ease of Administration   Taxes should be simple to understand and compute. They should also be easy to apply in a nonarbitrary fashion. Under the so-called tax simplification of the 1986 Tax Reform Act, the federal income tax was rendered much more complex and confusing than it had been. However, it remains fairly easy to collect, because most people voluntarily compute and remit their tax to the national government. Local property taxes are difficult to administer, because of the time and expense involved in regularly appraising property values and the inherent subjectivity of placing a dollar value on buildings and land. The sales tax is easy to administer at the time and place of sale, and nearly impossible to evade.

Political Accountability Tax increases should not be hidden. Instead, state and local legislative bodies should have to approve them deliberately— and publicly. Citizens should know how much they owe and when it must be paid. For example, many state income taxes are silently hiked as wages rise in response to cost-of-living increases. After accounting for inflation, taxpayers make the same income as they did before, but they are driven into a higher income bracket for tax purposes. This phenomenon, known as bracket creep, can be eliminated by indexing income tax rates to changes in the cost of living.

Major State and Local Taxes

The principal types of taxes are property, sales, and income taxes, and user charges.

Property Tax In 1942, taxes on personal and corporate property accounted for 53 percent of all state and local tax revenues. By 1986, they represented less than 30 percent. States hardly utilize the property tax at all today—it accounts for less than 2 percent of their total revenues—but local governments continue to depend on it for three-quarters of all their own source revenues. Interestingly, average property tax rates have not decreased. Instead, other revenue sources have augmented the property tax, so that its proportionate contribution has diminished. As always, there is considerable state-by-state variation. New Hampshire, which has no sales or income taxes, depends on property taxes for 60.7 percent of its total tax revenues. The state least committed to this particular tax is New Mexico, which derives 11.5 percent of state and local tax revenues from property taxes.[11]

The best thing about the property tax is that it is certain; owners of property must pay it or the government will seize and sell their land, buildings, or other taxable possessions. But it has lost favor in recent years because it tends to be regressive, lacks political accountability, and is hard to administer. At first thought, it seems that property taxes cannot be truly regressive, because only those people who own property pay taxes on it directly; however, renters pay property taxes indirectly through their monthly checks to the landlord. When property tax assessments climb, so do rental charges. Property taxes can also violate the ability-to-pay principle, when housing values spiral upward, as they have done recently in parts of California, New Jersey, and Connecticut. Homeowners on fixed incomes, such as retired people, discover with alarm that their annual property tax bills are rising sharply as housing prices escalate.

Just this sort of situation helped precipitate Proposition 13 in California. In the Los Angeles and San Francisco Bay areas during the 1970s, property taxes doubled and then tripled in only a few years. Some senior citizens were forced to sell their homes in order to pay their property tax. Proposition 13 reduced property tax bills by approximately $7 billion in the first year, and California dropped from the eighth highest property tax state to the twenty-eighth. This illustrates the problem of political accountability: when property values rise to lofty heights, taxpayers' bills keep pace, even though elected officials do not explicitly vote to hike property taxes.

Property taxes are difficult to administer and somewhat arbitrary. The process of levying an annual fee on "real property" (land and buildings) begins with a government assessor making a formal appraisal of the market value of the land and the buildings on it. Then property values are "equalized" so that similarly valued real estate is taxed at the same level. Time is set aside to make corrections and to review appeals on appraisals that the owner believes to be too high. Next, an assessment ratio is applied to the property. For instance, houses might be assessed for tax purposes at 80 percent of market value. A rate is placed on the assessed value to calculate the annual tax amount. This might strike you as fairly straightforward, but ultimately the appraised market value depends on the findings of the assessor, who may or may not be properly trained for the job or fully aware of conditions in the local housing market. Property can be underappraised or overappraised. For the sake of equity, property should be appraised regularly (for example, every five years).

Property tax systems are further criticized for exempting certain types of real estate and buildings. Government buildings such as hospitals and state offices are not taxed, even though they receive police and fire protection and other local government services. Churches and church-owned property are also exempted in the vast majority of jurisdictions.

In an effort to make property taxation more equitable and more in keeping with ability to pay, thirty-two states have enacted some form of **circuit breaker.** For instance, the property of low-income individuals is excluded from taxation in some states; others assign lower assessment ratios to the homes of senior citizens or set a top limit on the tax according to the owner's income (for example, 4 percent of net income). At least ten states have promoted political accountability by enacting provisions for rolling back property tax rates as appraised values rise rapidly.[12] Many also offer homestead exemptions, in which owner-occupied homes are taxed at lower rates than rental homes or business property.

Despite such attempts to make property taxes fairer, differences in property values among cities, counties, and school districts still have important implications for the quality and distribution of services. Jurisdictions with many wealthy families or capital-intensive industries can provide high levels of services with low tax rates, while areas with weak property tax bases must tax at high rates just to yield enough revenues to maintain minimal services. To alter the unequal distribution of property values is essentially beyond the control of local governments. As a result, "wealthly suburbs remain wealthy, poor communities remain poor, and services remain unequal."[13]

Sales Tax   Mississippi was the first state to adopt this form of taxation, in 1932. Others followed suit very rapidly, and states collect more of their revenues today from the sales tax than from any other source. It accounted for 32 percent of own-source revenue in 1985, just ahead of the state income tax (29 percent).[14] Only five states do not levy a general sales tax: Alaska, Delaware, Montana, New Hampshire, and Oregon. State sales tax rates vary from 8 percent in Connecticut to 3 percent in Georgia, North Carolina, and Colorado. The national median is 5 percent. Some states are exceptionally dependent on this type of tax: Florida derives almost 50 percent of its own-source revenues from the sales tax; Texas and Washington raise over 40 percent of their revenues from it.[15]

Until enactment of the Tax Reform Act of 1986, the trend was for states to decrease reliance on income taxes in favor of sales taxes. There have been two major reasons for this. First, citizen surveys by the ACIR have shown consistently that when a tax must be raised, voters prefer the sales tax. Although the reasons are not entirely clear, this tax is perceived to be fairer than other forms of taxation (see Table 13.3). Second, there has been a growing (although empirically unsubstantiated) belief that high state income taxes depress economic development.[16] Some states have lowered taxes on income and increased taxes on sales. Between 1985 and 1987, ten states raised their sales tax rate, most by at least a penny.[17]

Twenty-nine states authorize at least some of their municipalities and counties to levy local sales taxes.[18] When state and local sales taxes are combined, the total tax bite can be substantial. In New Orleans, the purchase of a $1 item requires 9 cents in sales tax, the highest in the country in 1989. The rate on the dollar is 8.25 cents in New York City and Yonkers. Sales taxes are almost always optional for the local jurisdiction, requiring majority approval by the city or county legislative body. Most states impose ceilings on how many pennies the localities can attach to the state sales tax, and specify which sizes and types of local governments are permitted to exercise this option.

When applied to all merchandise, the sales tax is clearly regressive. Poor people must spend a larger portion of their incomes than rich people on basics, such as food and clothing. Therefore, the sales tax places a much heavier burden on low-income people. Most states have acted to alleviate

Table 13.3   "Which Do You Think Is the Worst Tax—the Least Fair?"

	1985	1986	1987	1988	1989
Federal income tax	38%	37%	30%	33%	27%
State income tax	10	8	12	10	10
State sales tax	16	17	21	18	18
Local property tax	24	28	24	28	32
Don't know	12	10	13	11	13

Source: Unpublished report by U.S. Advisory Commission on Intergovernmental Relations.

the regressivity of sales taxes by excluding certain "necessities." Twenty-eight states do not tax food, forty-five do not tax prescription drugs, thirty-two exempt consumer electric and gas utilities, and eight exclude clothing.[19]

States can improve the yield of the sales tax by broadening the base to include services. This passes on more of the burden to upper-income individuals, who are heavier users of services. Twenty-six states tax services such as household, automobile, and appliance repairs, barber and beauty shops, printing, rentals, dry cleaning, and interior decorating.[20] Hawaii, New Mexico, and South Dakota tax virtually all professional and personal services. However, Florida's 1987 move to broaden the base of its sales tax to services was repealed, following heavy lobbying efforts by the business community. Florida businesses found the taxation of advertising and other services sold in Florida by firms from other states to be especially offensive (see Politics and Policy 13.1).

The Florida debacle derailed incipient efforts to tax services in other states, but its effects are likely to be temporary. Services are the largest and fastest-growing segment of the U.S. economy. Eighty-five percent of new jobs are in services. As political journalist Neil Peirce asked, "How can one rationalize taxing autos, videocassettes, and toothpaste, but not piped-in music, cable TV, parking lot services, or $100 beauty salon treatments?"[21] Pet grooming services, legal services, financial services, and many others are likely to lose their tax-favored status in years to come.

Elasticity is not a strong point of the sales tax, although broadening the base helps. A few states have attempted to make the sales tax more responsive to short-term economic conditions by increasing it on a temporary basis. For example, Idaho raised its general sales tax by a penny in order to make up for lower-than-anticipated revenues in 1986, then reduced it when needed monies had been collected. A problem with this tactic is that consumers tend to postpone major purchases until the tax rate falls.[22]

The sales tax is relatively simple for governments to administer. Sellers of merchandise and services are required to collect it and remit it to the state on a regular basis. Political accountability is also an advantage, since legislative bodies must enact laws or ordinances to increase the sales tax rate. Many states directly tie, or earmark, portions of the sales tax to specific functions, such as public education or infrastructure.

Income Tax   Most states tax personal and corporate income. Wisconsin was the first, in 1911, long before the national government enacted its own personal income tax. Forty states have broad-based taxes on personal income, while three limit theirs to capital gains, interest, and dividends. Only Alaska, Florida, Nevada, South Dakota, Texas, Washington, and Wyoming leave all personal income untaxed. The last five of these also refuse to tax corporate income. Personal income taxes garnered 31 percent of all state own-source revenues in 1987, and the corporate tax brought in 8 percent.[23] West Virginia had the highest personal income tax rate in 1987 (13 percent),

POLITICS AND POLICY 13.1
Florida Lays a Tax Egg

Florida grew at a prodigious rate during the 1980s. It added a population equivalent to that of a new Miami nearly every year. To pay for this growth, which requires some two miles of new highways, two new teachers and police officers, and two new prison beds every day, Florida will need approximately $53 billion in new revenues during the 1990s. The options for raising monies are severely restricted by a constitutional prohibition on personal income taxes and constitutional limitations on property taxes.

With surprisingly little controversy and the strong support of Governor Bob Martinez, the state legislature on July 1, 1987, began applying its 5 percent sales tax to services as well as merchandise. By tapping new sources of revenue in the fast-growing service sector, the tax was projected to raise $800 million in the first year and $1.4 billion in the second. Although other states tax certain services, Florida was the pioneer in extending its sales tax to media advertising and services imported into the state. For example, an accounting firm with its home office in Atlanta would have to pay a 5 percent Florida tax for business in the Sunshine State.

The service tax lit a political firestorm that raged for six months and through several special sessions of the legislature. Major advertisers such as Kellogg's and Nabisco announced severe cutbacks in their Florida advertising budgets, which cost local broadcasters millions of dollars. About sixty scheduled meetings and conventions were canceled. The controversial tax was repealed on January 1, 1988, and replaced with a one-cent increase in the conventional merchandise sales tax.

This was not the first tax egg laid in Florida. In July 1983 the legislature passed a "unitary tax" on the worldwide income of corporations (instead of just their Florida income). That tax was repealed eighteen months later because of the wrath of big business. The Sunshine State's projected population growth rate in the 1990s is certain to result in new efforts to raise revenues. What will Florida try next?

Sources: Neil R. Peirce, "Service Tax May Rise Again," Public Administration Times 11 (August 12, 1988): 2; Marilyn Marks, "Florida's New Tax: The Budget 'Cure' That May Be Contagious," Governing (October 1987): 48–55; Steven D. Gold, "The Blizzard of 1987: A Year of Tax Reform Activity in the States," Publius 18 (Summer 1988): 17–35.

followed by California and Hawaii (11 percent).[24] Eleven states permit designated cities, counties, or school districts to levy taxes on personal income.[25]

State and local income taxes are equitable when they are progressive. This normally entails a sliding scale, so that high-income filers pay a greater percentage of their income in taxes than low-income filers do. Almost half of the states do not levy a personal income tax on people whose earnings fall below a certain floor—say, $5,000. Overall, personal income taxes in the states are moderately progressive and are gradually becoming more progressive.[26]

Personal and corporate income taxes are superior to other taxes on the criteria of yield and elasticity. By tapping virtually all sources of income, they draw in large sums of money and respond fairly well to short-term economic conditions. Through payroll withholding, income taxes are fairly simple to collect. However, many states have periodically manipulated income tax rates in response to annual revenue needs. In 1987 alone, thirty of the forty states with broad-based income taxes made some rate adjustments.[27]

As mentioned earlier, political accountability can be a problem with income taxes during periods of rising prices. Unless income tax rates are indexed to inflation, cost-of-living increases push salaries and corporate earnings into higher tax brackets. At least eight states have adopted indexing since 1978.

User Charges   Setting specific prices on goods and services provided by state and local governments is one method that clearly pursues the benefit principle: those who use the goods and services should pay. User fees have been in existence for many years. Examples include college tuition, toll roads, water and sewer charges, and garbage collection assessments. Today they are being applied broadly as state and especially local officials attempt to tie services to their true costs. User charges are increasingly being levied on "nonessential" local government services, such as parks and recreation, libraries, and public transit. In 1986 the average American paid $334 a year in user charges.[28]

User charges offer several advantages. If they are priced accurately, they are perfectly fair under the benefit principle. But those who do not have enough money to purchase these goods and services may have to do without, which, of course, violates the ability-to-pay principle. User fees yield whatever is needed to finance a particular service. An added benefit is that service-users who do not live in the taxing jurisdiction must also pay the price, say, for a day in the state park. Elasticity is achieved by varying the amount of the charge so that it always covers service costs.

User fees can be difficult to administer, since service users must be identified and charged. Political accountability is low, because the charges can be increased without legislative action. However, a special advantage of user fees is that they can be employed to ration certain goods or services. For instance, entrance charges can be increased to reduce attendance at an overcrowded public facility, or varied according to the day of the week in order to encourage more efficient utilization. If the municipal zoo has few visitors on Mondays, it can cut the entrance fee on that day of the week by one-half in order to encourage attendance. Table 13.4 rates the four major taxes based on the five criteria discussed above.

Miscellaneous Taxes   A wide variety of miscellaneous taxes are assessed by state and local governments. "Sin taxes" are especially lucrative. All states tax cigarettes; the median tax per pack is 18 cents. Minnesota discourages smokers with a 38-cent tax; North Carolina and Virginia, tobacco states, charge only 2 cents and $2\frac{1}{2}$ cents per pack, respectively. Alcoholic beverages are also taxed in all fifty states, although rates vary according to classification: beer, wine, or spirits. Beer drinkers steer clear of Hawaii, where the tax per gallon of nondraft beer is 81 cents; draft beer is tapped at 50 cents per gallon. Frequent imbibers are invited to visit New Jersey (3 cents per gallon) and California (4 cents per gallon). (The seventeen states that hold monopolies on wholesale distribution of alcoholic beverages or that have their own state-run liquor stores are not accounted for in these figures.) Although not a "sin," gasoline falls under the taxman's shadow as well. The highest tax on driving is in Wisconsin and Montana (20 cents per gallon); the lowest is in Florida (4 cents).[79] All states profit further from driving through taxes on vehicles and vehicle licenses.

Most states tax death in one form or another. Estate taxes must be paid on the money and property of a deceased person before the remainder is disbursed to the survivors. Nineteen states tax those who inherit the assets of the deceased. Rates are generally staggered according to the value of the

Table 13.4   Rating State and Local Taxes According to Five Criteria

Tax	Equity*	Yield	Elasticity	Administration	Political Accountability
Property	C	B	C	D	D
Sales	D	B	C	B	A
Personal and corporate income	B	A	B	B	C
User charges	C	B	A	C	C

A = excellent
B = good
C = fair
D = poor
*Ability-to-pay principle

estate. Other miscellaneous sources of revenues include hunting and fishing licenses, business licenses, auto license fees, and restaurant, meal, and lodging taxes.

Two Revenue Devices

In the continuous search for new ways to extract tax dollars, two old devices received renewed interest and attention during the 1970s and 1980s.

Severance Taxes   States blessed with petroleum, coal, natural gas, and minerals for many years have taxed these natural resources as they are taken from the land and sold. During the 1970s, several states hiked their severance taxes to very high levels. A fortunate few states are able to "export" a substantial portion of their tax bite to people living in other states. However, in-state users must pay the same tax as out-of-staters.[30] A large majority of states (thirty-four) place a severance tax on some form of natural resource, but just ten states collected 90 percent of all severance tax revenues in 1985. Taxes on oil and natural gas account for almost 85 percent of total state revenues in Alaska. Wyoming brings in almost 60 percent of its revenues from severance taxes on coal, oil, and gas. Other states leaning heavily on this form of taxation are Texas, Louisiana, Oklahoma, Montana, New Mexico, and North Dakota.

Severance taxes are popular in states rich in natural resources, because they help keep income, property, and sales taxes relatively low. Severance tax revenues also help to pay for environmental damage resulting from resource extraction operations, such as strip mining. The major disadvantage is that a state that is too dependent on severance taxes can be hurt badly if the price of its natural resources declines. During the late 1970s, oil and coal prices skyrocketed, enriching the bank accounts of Texas, Oklahoma, Louisiana, and Alaska. For several consecutive years, every man, woman, and child in Alaska received a rebate from the state's permanent fund. Checks totaled $403 per person in 1985 and $556.26 in 1986. All a person had to do to collect his or her share was to prove residence for six months or more—no small obligation, considering the severity of Alaska's climate. The share-the-wealth program was threatened with termination in the late 1980s, however, because of a dramatic decline in oil prices, from around $26 per barrel to an average of about $14 in 1988. Every $1 drop per barrel costs millions in foregone revenues for oil-dependent states like Alaska and Texas.

Lotteries   As of late 1989, thirty-three states operated lotteries; others are expected to follow suit in the next few years. The lottery is an old American tradition, popular from colonial days until the late 1800s. The first ones on record were established in the 1600s. During the nineteenth century lotteries flourished throughout the country as a means to raise money for such good causes as new schools, highways, canals, and bridges. But scandals and mismanagement led every state and the national government to ban them. From 1895 to 1963, no legal lotteries were operated. Then New Hampshire established a new one, followed in 1967 by New York. During the 1970s, a growing number of states created them. Total sales in 1986 came to over $11 billion, with $4.7 billion left over for the state treasuries after prizewinners and administrative costs were paid.[31]

Several factors account for the renewed popularity of lotteries. First, they bring in large sums of money. Pennsylvania generated $1.2 billion in 1986 lottery sales (but tiny Vermont could raise only $4.5 million). Second, they are very popular and entertaining—in only a single state, North Dakota, have voters disapproved a lottery during the past two decades. And they are voluntary—you do not have to participate. Third, lotteries help relieve pressure on major taxes. In some states, net lottery earnings take the place of a one-cent increase in the sales tax. Many states earmark lottery proceeds for special purposes (public education in California, senior citizens' programs in Pennsylvania). Fourth, state ownership of a game of chance offers a legal and fair alternative to illegal gambling operations such as neighborhood numbers games or betting (parlay) cards.[32]

But there are disadvantages as well. First of all, lotteries are costly to administer and have low yields. Prize awards must be great enough to encourage future ticket sales. Ticket vendors must be paid commissions. Tight (and expensive) security precautions are required to guarantee the game's integrity. As a result, lotteries generate a small percentage of total

The lines were long in April 1989 as Pennsylvanians (and many out-of-staters, too) purchased tickets for the record $115.5 million state lottery.

state revenue, usually less than 2 percent of own-source income. The average yield for players is low as well: about 50 percent of the total revenues are returned to players in prize money. This is far below the returns of other games of chance, such as slot machines, roulette, or craps.[33]

Lotteries can also be attacked on the grounds of equity and elasticity. Although the purchase of a ticket is voluntary and thus seemingly fair, studies indicate that low-income individuals are more likely to play.[34] The lottery is, then, a regressive way to raise revenues. Furthermore, lotteries tend to encourage compulsive gambling. In recognition of this problem, some states earmark a portion of lottery proceeds for treatment programs. Lotteries are said to be inelastic because earnings are cyclical and generally unstable. Sales depend on such factors as the legalized gambling activities in neighboring states, the size of jackpots, and the effectiveness of marketing efforts.[35]

If the present trend continues, virtually every state will operate a lottery by 1995. Most likely there will also be more experimentation with other forms of legalized gambling, such as pari-mutuel betting on horse and dog races and casino gambling. Revenues will definitely increase, but the net human costs are yet to be determined.

The Political Economy of Taxation

One of the most difficult decisions for an elected official is to go on record in favor of raising taxes. The political heat can scorch even the coolest incumbent. But when revenues do not equal service costs and citizens do not want to cut services, raising taxes is really the only answer. Unfortunately, most people do not want higher taxes. This is the familiar "tax-service paradox": people demand new and improved government services but do not want to pay for them through higher taxes. Is it any wonder that user charges have become a popular option? The political economy—the political choices that frame economic policy—has become much more imposing for state and local officials since the late 1970s. There are three major reasons: the tax revolt, fiscal stress, and limited discretion in raising new revenues.

Tax Revolt

Taxpayer resentment of property taxes, and the general perception that government was too big, too costly, and too wasteful, first took on a tangible form in 1978 with passage of Proposition 13 in California. Between 1977 and 1980, eighteen states enacted statutory or constitutional limitations on taxing and spending. Thirty-six states slashed personal or corporate income taxes, nine indexed their income taxes to the cost of living, twenty-two cut the sales tax. In some instances citizens took tax matters into their own hands through the initiative process. In other cases state legislators jumped in front of the parade and cut taxes and spending themselves. The taxpayer revolt continued at a much slower pace during the early 1980s, and for all practical purposes it is dormant today. Its legacy, however, remains enormously important. Public officials must work hard to justify tax increases or risk a citizen uprising and perhaps political death. They tend to view the taxpayer revolt as a smoldering but not quite dead prairie fire.

Most state and local jurisdictions managed the fallout of the tax revolt reasonably well. Many of them held large budget surpluses that they utilized to ameliorate the immediate effects of *taxation and expenditure limitations* (TELS). For example, California had a $3 billion surplus with which it temporarily replaced property tax revenues foregone by local governments. Only a handful of states followed California's stringent TELS, which cut property taxes by 60 percent. Massachusetts was one of them; approved on the general election ballot in 1980, Proposition $2\frac{1}{2}$ limited local property tax revenues to $2\frac{1}{2}$ percent of the total value of taxable property. Tax bills for Massachusetts homeowners soon dropped by $1.3 billion.[36] Forty states had some sort of property tax restriction in effect as of 1985, and many placed limitations on other forms of taxation as well.[37] Few states or localities significantly reduced service levels, opting instead to shift tax burdens or to find new sources of revenues, such as user charges.[38]

Overall, however, state spending as a percentage of the gross national product declined from 15.1 percent in 1975 to 13.5 percent in 1980. Political and economic consequences of the tax revolt have been much studied in its birthplace, California. Local governments in the Golden State have experienced serious impacts. Counties, special districts, and school districts have fewer revenue-raising opportunities than states, apart from the now highly constricted property tax. As a result, they are dependent on the state for funding. Since California's huge budget surplus was depleted, cities have creatively tapped a variety of available revenue sources to replace lost property tax income. User fees have increased substantially, as have franchise fees, lodging taxes, and other miscellaneous revenues. Cities have maintained expenditure levels for essential services like police and fire protection but made cuts in other areas, such as libraries, parks and recreation, and public works.[39]

Fiscal Stress

Following on the heels of the tax revolt was the most serious economic downturn since the Great Depression. As the Reagan administration strangled the national economy in order to control inflation, state and local revenues plummeted. Adding to the mounting woes of the nonnational governments were substantial reductions in federal aid. Grants-in-aid were eliminated or significantly pared back; revenue sharing contracted and

POLITICS AND POLICY 13.2
Can a State or Local Government Declare Bankruptcy?

The vision of a municipality or county auctioning off its streets, sewer system, fire trucks, and parking meters seems as ludicrous as that of a state advertising a going-out-of-business sale on colleges, office buildings, and prisons. But local governments have declared bankruptcy in the past. There was a wave of bankruptcies during the Great Depression, but with the exception of Ecorse, Michigan, no state, city, or county government has filed for bankruptcy in the past fifty years.

Bankruptcy entails a state or local government's legal declaration that it is unable to pay its lenders and creditors. A formal filing is made under Chapter IX of the federal bankruptcy code. The jurisdiction applying for bankruptcy status has to win the approval of two-thirds of its creditors for a plan to renegotiate and schedule the payment of its debt—a highly unlikely scenario. Unlike a private individual or firm filing for bankruptcy, governments do not liquidate their property and assets, with proceeds going to the creditors. Government property is held in trust for the citizens; it cannot be taken by creditors. Services must be continued to protect the health and safety of the citizens. As long as the government continues to tax, it is not truly insolvent, like a firm that no longer sells a product.

State or local bankruptcy

finally ended entirely. Unlike the case in earlier recessions, little special countercyclical aid was forthcoming to help the states and localities.

During this period, many state and local jurisdictions experienced severe **fiscal stress:** they were unable to pay for programs and provide services that citizens wanted and needed without taxing the citizens at unacceptably high levels. Many factors can contribute to fiscal stress. Typically, adverse social and economic conditions establish an environment conducive to these problems. Older industrial cities are particularly vulnerable. Many jobs and manufacturing industries have been lost because of the gradual but compelling shift to a service-based economy.[40] In cities such as Buffalo and Cleveland, the exodus of jobs and firms has eroded the value of taxable resources (mostly property), yet citizens left behind have increased their service demands. Concentration of the poor and minorities in deteriorating housing, the shortage of jobs, high levels of crime, and related factors have produced unfortunate situations. Declining infrastructure also plagues older cities: water and sewer lines, treatment plants, streets, sidewalks, and

would be a traumatic event for the government directly involved and for other affected parties as well. If the jurisdiction were large, its bankruptcy would shake the very foundations of the state and local bond market and jack up interest rates to precipitous heights. During the darkest days of New York City's financial crisis in the mid-1970s, it was estimated that bankruptcy would severely threaten the financial health of New York State (which held many of the debt instruments). In addition, at least sixty-nine banks would have failed.

Under the terms of Chapter IX, bankruptcy is not a viable option for states and localities. For example, a defaulted revenue bond backed by user fees could be transformed by legal actions into a full-faith-and-credit obligation. If a toll bridge collapsed or a municipal utility

failed, the jurisdiction would have to use general revenues in a financial bailout, which might threaten the fiscal stability of the city or county. The National League of Cities and various local officials are urging Congress to amend the bankruptcy code to permit a more reasonable use of bankruptcy as a means to reorganize debts.

Sources: Alberta M. Sbragia, "Politics, Local Government, and the Municipal Bond Market," in Alberta M. Sbragia, ed., *The Municipal Money Chase* (Boulder: Westview, 1983), pp. 67–111; Patricia Giles Leeds, "City Politics and the Market: The Case of New York City's Financing Crisis," in Sbragia, *The Municipal Money Chase*, pp. 124–27; Frank Shafroth, "NLC Urges Bankruptcy Legislation to Help Cities," *Nation's Cities Weekly*, September 12, 1988, p. 4; John A. Barnes, "The City That Privatized Everything," *The Wall Street Journal*, May 17, 1989, p. A-19.

other components of the urban physical landscape are in dire need of restoration or replacement.

Political sources of fiscal stress typically compound the economic problems of older cities. Mismanagement of resources and inefficient procedures and activities are common complaints. Pressures from city workers and their unions have also driven up service provision costs.[41] Thus, service demands and the costs of providing services grow while taxes and intergovernmental revenues decline. This is a well-tested recipe for fiscal stress,[42] evoking fears of bankruptcy (see Politics and Policy 13.2).

New York City in the 1970s offers an often-cited case study of fiscal stress. People, jobs, and industry fled the city for the suburbs and the Sunbelt in the early 1970s, reducing fiscal capacity. Public employees' pay and pensions grew to some of the highest levels in the United States, and welfare payments to the poor and a growing number of unemployed were generous. The tuition-free City University of New York (CUNY) had an enrollment of 265,000 students.

As revenues increasingly lagged behind expenditures, the city government played games with the budget and borrowed huge sums through municipal notes and bonds. Eventually it was poised on the brink of bankruptcy. Defaults on the city's bonds, notes, and other debt instruments seemed imminent. City officials cried out to the national government and New York State for help. Some people had little sympathy for a city that apparently had lived beyond its means for too long; for example, economist Milton Friedman urged New York City to "go bankrupt. The only other alternative is [to] live within its means and become an honest city again."[43]

Aided by national guarantees of new long-term loans, New York State and other large holders of New York City debt finally agreed to a bail-out.[44] Had this immense urban financial edifice collapsed, the fiscal shocks would have threatened New York State's economic stability and even had serious fiscal repercussions for states and localities throughout the United States.

Most jurisdictions have not had the misfortunes of officials in New York City. The taxpayer revolt and fiscal stress notwithstanding, budgets have been balanced, payrolls met, and services maintained. For their part, state officials have increasingly swallowed hard, held their noses, and raised taxes. In 1983, half the states imposed new taxes. Since that year, virtually every state has hiked at least one major tax. The only feasible alternative appears to be substantial spending reductions in critical areas such as public education, highways, law enforcement, and social welfare. Unlike the national government, states and localities do not have the luxury of incurring long-term debts in order to finance daily operating expenditures. Their fiscal environment requires much more discipline.

Limited Discretion

TELS have placed ceilings on rates and amounts of taxation and spending, which will probably limit the tax discretion of nonnational governments more in the future than they do at present, assuming that citizens continue to expect more from government. Other constraining factors also keep state and local governments from the temptation of taxing and spending orgies. An important one is interstate competition for jobs and economic development.[45] High-tax states run a serious risk of having jobs, firms, and investments "stolen" by low-tax states. It was just such a concern that convinced New York, Massachusetts, and other states to lower tax rates in the late 1980s.

When elected officials meet to consider a tax increase, two concerns tend to override all others: when to raise taxes and which taxes to raise. A tax increase is most likely to come during hard economic times, when government is struggling to maintain basic services. Recall that the taxpayer revolt was partly a response to cash-rich state governments that refused to alleviate severe property tax burdens on local taxpayers. A basic rule in political timing, however, is not to hike taxes during an election year. Taxation is a volatile and dangerous issue for elected officials. Although voting to increase taxes does not usually result in electoral defeat, enough horror stories exist of "tax-loss governors" and "tax-loss legislators" to make officials think long and hard about their electoral futures.

Typically, taxes are increased in the first year or two after a general election. A tactic increasingly being used that reduces political risk is to earmark new taxes for popular programs. Earmarking is well established: gasoline taxes have been set aside for road and highway programs since automobiles first left ruts in muddy cow pastures. What differs today are the levels of specificity and creativity in earmarking. For instance, gas tax hikes in several states are devoted to special projects such as bridge repair or construction of a new connecting road. Cigarette buyers in Washington cough up millions of dollars each year to help clean up Puget Sound. Earnings from the California state lottery are designated for public schools. Several states have earmarked penny increases in the sales tax for public education. Tax revenues from New Jersey casinos go to aid senior citizens and the disabled.[46]

The other critical concern is which tax to raise. This decision is largely determined by the size of the needed revenue increase. If the revenue needs are slight or moderate, the "sin taxes" are usually the first to be increased; user and license fees are alternative sources for moderate hikes. If the fiscal problem is more serious, sales and income taxes become the focus of attention.

Borrowing and Debt

Sometimes state or local government expenditures substantially outstrip revenues, because either revenue has been underestimated or too much money has been spent. A more pleasing development occurs when revenues exceed expenditures. Because the nonnational governments must balance their operating budgets each fiscal year, the reliability of revenue estimates is very important.

Estimating Revenues

Until fairly recently, state and local governments estimated their annual revenues simply by extrapolating from past trends. This approach works well during periods of steady economic growth, but it fails miserably during years of boom or bust. The states and most larger cities and counties are much more sophisticated today. Using computer technology, they employ econometric modeling to derive mathematical estimates of future revenues.

The method places key variables in equations to predict the fiscal year yield of each major tax. A wide variety of variables are used, including employment levels, food prices, housing costs, oil and gas prices, consumer savings levels, interest rates, and state and local debt obligations. Because state and local economies are increasingly linked to national and international factors, estimates often include measures for the value of the dollar, international trade and investment, and national fiscal policy.

Two critical factors determine the accuracy of revenue estimates: the quality of the data and the validity of the economic assumptions. Econometric modeling of state and local economies can be "a voyage into the unknown."[47] Data problems include difficulty in measuring key variables, periodic revisions of historical economic data (which require new calculations), and modifications in tax laws, but the major source of error is the economic assumptions built into the models. Examples are legion: the national economy may not perform as expected; oil prices may plummet or soar; natural disasters can disrupt state or local economic growth. Sometimes taxpayers foul up revenue estimates by making errors on tax returns, failing to comply fully with laws, or remitting payments later than usual.[48] Recessions are particularly damaging to fiscal stability, since state and local taxes are highly sensitive to economic downturns. Sometimes the miscalculations are enormous. In fiscal year 1988 and again in 1989, California misjudged its revenues by approximately $1 billion.[49]

Politics can also intrude in the revenue projection process. For instance, politicians can purposely overestimate revenues in order to fund a popular new program. When projected revenues do not appear, implementation of the program may be delayed, but it now has official standing. Overestimates can also defer cuts in politically sensitive programs or levels of public employment. When the revenue shortfall reaches serious proportions, cutbacks are much more palatable than they are when the shortfall is a mere projection. Actually, most jurisdictions err conservatively by underestimating revenues, because midyear cutbacks are painful and embarrassing for government officials.[50]

Rainy Day Funds

Because a balanced budget is mandatory but estimation errors are inevitable, many states and localities establish contingency funds. Popularly known as "rainy day funds," these savings accounts help insulate budgets from fiscal distortions caused by inaccurate data or faulty economic assumptions. Thirty-three states maintain some form of rainy day fund, many of which were put in place as a result of the severe recession of 1981–82.[51] In years of economic health, the funds accumulate principal and interest. When the economy falls ill, governments can tap them to balance the budget.

Deposits to rainy day accounts come through monies appropriated by the legislature or through a formula that links contributions to a general fund surplus or to the growth rate of the economy. In 1989 many states were worried that they had not properly built up their rainy day funds for the next recession. States were experiencing strong demands for more spending on education, corrections, and health care, even as federal grants for these and other functions declined. Some, including farm states like Iowa and energy-dependent states like Texas, Oklahoma, and Louisiana, were mired in recession in the mid- and late 1980s and could not set aside contingency funds. As one commentator put it, "When you're in the midst of a hurricane, it's too late to build up a rainy day fund."[52] More prosperous states feared that carrying a budget surplus would send the wrong message to taxpayers, who might once again revolt.

While rainy day funds have been widely adopted at the state level, they are rarely used by cities and counties. The task of balancing the budget is especially daunting in local governments, because of their lack of economic diversity, dependency on state taxes and financial aid, and sensitivity to economic dislocations. The departure of a single large employer can disrupt a local economy for years. Yet only a few of the nation's largest cities use rainy day accounts. A survey of the fifty-five largest cities conducted in the mid-1980s identified only six with a rainy day fund: Houston, Milwaukee, Omaha, St. Paul, San Antonio, and Virginia Beach, Virginia.[53] Nonetheless, the potential advantages of such a fund are numerous. As these advantages are accorded greater recognition in the future, more cities are likely to establish contingency accounts.

Other Cash and Investment Management Practices

State and local governments are becoming more knowledgeable about how to manage cash and investments. Cash reserves that once sat idly in non–interest-bearing accounts are now invested in short-term notes, certificates of deposit, and other financial instruments in order to maximize interest earnings. The process of spending and collecting monies is also manipulated to advantage. For example, large checks are deposited on the day they are received and payable checks are drawn on the latest date possible.[54] In general, state and local financial management today resembles that of a large corporation instead of the "mom-and-pop" approach of years ago.

State and local cooperation in investment management is found in such programs as bond banks. First established in Vermont in 1970 and now operating in eleven states, bond banks offer small localities the opportunity to sell bonds at competitive interest rates. Typically, the state gathers together a number of bonds from several small local jurisdictions and issues the total debt in a single state bond. This not only results in lower borrowing costs (interest rates), but saves in expenses involved in marketing the bonds to investors. For a very small or newly incorporated municipality, the bond bank may be the only way to borrow a substantial amount of money.[55] In the future, bond banks could also help meet capital requirements for the nation's growing problems with infrastructure (roads, bridges, and so forth).[56] Several states are expected to implement infrastructure bond funds during the next few years.[57]

State and Local Debt

Every state except Vermont is constitutionally or statutorily mandated to balance its budget each fiscal year. In turn, the states require their local governments to balance *their* budgets. However, these requirements apply only to **operating budgets,** which are used for daily financial receipts and disbursements. Capital budgets, used for big purchases that must be paid for over time, such as a new bridge or school building, typically run substantial deficits. Operating budgets may also go into deficit during the fiscal year, as long as expenditures equal revenues at the end of the year.

In order to deal with temporary revenue shortfalls and to finance expensive items that cannot be absorbed in the operating budget, governments borrow money, just as individuals use credit cards to make relatively small purchases that they will pay for when they receive next month's salary, or as they finance the purchase of an automobile or a house over a longer period of time. Borrowing is a major state and local government activity, amounting to approximately $20 billion per year.

Temporary cash-flow deficits in the operating budget are alleviated through tax anticipation or revenue anticipation notes. Investors such as banks lend money to a government on a short-term basis (typically thirty to ninety days). The loan is backed up by anticipated revenues from income, sales, and property taxes or other specified sources and is paid off as soon as the funds become available.

Long-term Borrowing Long-term debt obligations (typically five to twenty-five years) are financed through bonds. There are three major types: general obligation bonds, revenue bonds, and industrial development bonds. The principal and interest payments on **general obligation bonds** are secured by the "full faith, credit, and taxing power" of the state or local jurisdiction issuing them. General obligation bonds are used to finance public projects such as highways, schools, and hospitals. Lenders are guaranteed repayment so long as the bond-issuing government is solvent.

Revenue bonds are backed up by expected income from a specific project or service; examples include a toll bridge, toll road, or municipal sewer system. Revenue bonds are payable only from the revenues derived from the specified source, not from general tax revenues. They are generally a riskier investment than general obligation bonds and therefore command a higher rate of interest.

Industrial development bonds (IDBs) are a type of revenue bond, since the full faith, credit, and taxing power of the issuer are not pledged as security. The payment of principal and interest on IDBs depends solely on the ability of the user of the facilities financed by the bond (the industry) to meet its financial obligation. If the user fails to make payments, creditors can seize and sell any real or personal property associated with the facility. Private interests, such as shopping malls or firms, are the primary beneficiaries of IDBs. Conventionally, these bonds have been issued by local governments to attract economic activity and investments. IDBs are frequently used to furnish loans at highly favorable interest rates to small or medium-sized firms. This form of debt received a great deal of criticism in the early 1980s, because many local governments were using IDBs to finance low-wage commercial and retail operations like McDonalds and Kmart, which were fully capable of obtaining private financing. The abuse of IDBs led Congress in 1982 to prohibit their use for food establishments, entertainment facilities (such as cinemas), and related private purposes.

Limits on Borrowing   As of 1986, the states owed $248 billion to various creditors; local governments had incurred debts of $411 billion. The total state and local debt came to $2,390 per man, woman, and child in the United States. These gigantic sums pale in comparison to the national debt, which had reached a tidy sum of $2.4 *trillion* by 1987—almost $8,000 per person. State and local debt has remained at a fairly stable 12 to 13 percent of the gross national product since the early 1950s, although debt levels rose to 15.6 percent in 1986. The national debt leaped from 33 percent of the GNP in 1974 to more than 52 percent in 1987.[58]

Almost all states place constitutional or statutory restrictions on their own and local government borrowing. Some have set maximum levels of indebtedness; others require popular referenda to create debt or to exceed specified debt limits.[59] States tightly restrict local government debt, especially general obligation bonds. (State-imposed constraints normally do not apply to revenue bonds.) The impetus for these restrictions came from a series of bond defaults in the 1860s and 1870s and again during the Great Depression.

The bond market places its own informal limitations on debt by assessing the quality of bonds, notes, and other debt instruments. Investors in government bonds rely on Moody's, Standard and Poor, and other investment services for ratings of a jurisdiction's capacity to repay its obligations. Criteria taken into consideration in bond ratings include existing debt levels, market value of real estate, population growth, per capita income, employment levels, and other measures of overall financial health and solvency.[60] Highly rated bond issues receive ratings of Aaa, Aa, and A. Variations of B indicate medium to high risk. A rating of C is reserved for bonds in danger of default. The average interest rate on low-rated bonds usually exceeds that of top-rated ones by one and a half to two percentage points; this translates into a considerable difference in interest payments. Bond ratings can fall rapidly, as happened in Massachusetts: in 1989, the Bay State's credit rating dropped from Aa to A because of a deficit of $350 million, Medicaid debts of over $600 million, and the inability of the governor and the legislature to reach an agreement on how to deal with these problems. It was estimated that the lower credit rating would cost the state $4 million in interest payments.[61]

State and Local Financial Relationships

The most critical aspect of state and local relations has to do with dollars and cents. Increasingly, local governments are fixing their sights on the states rather than on Washington, D.C., as the most available financial target.

An Uneasy Relationship

An uneasy relationship exists between states and local governments when it comes to money. The status of localities is not unlike that of an eighteen-year-old with a part-time job. Since he still lives and eats at home, he remains dependent on his parents. He fervently wants to assert his independence, yet when he does, his parents often rein him in. As long as he dwells in his parents' house, he must bend to their authority.

Cities, counties, and other local governments will always live within the constitutional house of their parents, the states. They enjoy their own sources of revenue—property taxes, user fees, and business license fees—but depend on the states for the bulk of their income. They suffer the frustration of having to cope with rising expenditure demands from their residents while their authority to raise new monies is highly circumscribed by state law. No wonder they turned to their "grandparent"—the national government—in the 1960s and 1970s.

The historical insensitivity of states to the economic problems of their cities and counties began slowly changing in the 1970s, largely because reapportionment brought urban interests greater standing in state legislatures. In the 1980s, the states had to assume an even more attentive posture. National aid to localities declined substantially during the eight years of the Reagan administration, and although some "pass-through" grants-in-aid continue to go to cities for community development and infrastructure, approximately 80 percent of America's counties no longer receive direct aid from Washington, D.C.[62]

Today the single largest source of local revenues is the state. State aid represents more than one-third of all state expenditures ($127 billion in 1986). But like federal grants-in-aid, state grants come with lots of strings attached. Most state dollars ($3 out of every $4) are earmarked for public education and social welfare; state aid in 1986 accounted for more than 50 percent of total local education expenditures and 80 percent of public welfare spending.[63] Other state assistance is earmarked for roads, hospitals, and public health. The result is that local governments have very little spending discretion.

Naturally, there is a great amount of diversity in levels of encumbered and unencumbered state assistance to local jurisdictions, much of which is related to the distribution of functions between a state and its localities. Highly centralized states like Hawaii, South Carolina, and West Virginia fund and administer many programs at the state level that are funded and administered locally in decentralized states such as Maryland, New York, and Wisconsin. In states where taxation and expenditure limitations have hampered the ability of local jurisdictions to raise and spend revenues, the trend has been toward centralization. Once again California offers the prototype. Since Proposition 13, public education and several other functions formerly dominated by local governments have been brought under state control. Greater fiscal centralization has also resulted from state efforts to reduce service disparities between wealthly and poor jurisdictions and to lessen the dependence of local governments on the property tax.

Table 13.5 shows the diversity in state aid to cities, which varies from $1,276.19 per city resident in Alaska to $8.02 in West Virginia; the average is $166.48. This surprisingly large variation has recently been the subject of empirical research. It appears that the most important predictors of state aid to localities are centralization of functions (for example, more than 50 percent of Alaska's total aid is for education), state wealth (rich states provide more money than poor states), fiscal need (fiscally stressed localities need greater state aid), and legislative professionalism (professional legislatures are willing to spend more on education, social welfare, and other local programs).[64]

What Local Governments Want from the States

What local governments want from their states and what they actually get may be a cosmos apart. Today states and their local jurisdictions conduct a lot of dialogue over financial matters. Increasingly, the states are willing to recognize and respond to local financial problems.

Simply put, local governments want *more money*. The tax revolt, terminations and reductions in federal grants-in aid, and the death rattle of revenue sharing have left local jurisdictions in a financial bind. State governments must provide help, and in general they have done so. The $127 billion in state aid for 1986 was up from $82.8 billion in 1980; this increase outstrips inflation over that period by 25 percent.[65]

Most increases in state aid are devoted to education and social services. Recently, however, states have been more willing to share revenues that cities or counties may spend as they desire. Many states distribute a portion of their tax revenues based on local fiscal need. This tends to equalize or level economic disparities between local jurisdictions.

The specific means for sharing revenues takes many forms. Some states make special payments to local governments that host state buildings or other facilities, which are exempt from property tax but cause a drain on local services. This is a particularly relevant concern for capital cities, in which large plots of prime downtown property are occupied by state office buildings.

In addition, local governments want the *legal capacity to raise additional revenues themselves*, especially through local option sales and income taxes

Table 13.5   State Aid per City Resident (1986 figures)

	Total aid per municipal resident		Total aid per municipal resident
Alabama	$ 23.94	Montana	$ 44.02
Alaska	1,276.19	Nebraska	60.29
Arizona	171.57	Nevada	178.32
Arkansas	49.67	New Hampshire	67.81
California	102.72	New Jersey	209.16
Colorado	75.08	New Mexico	214.34
Connecticut	299.66	New York	773.88
Delaware	36.97	North Carolina	81.09
Florida	72.24	North Dakota	74.33
Georgia	21.55	Ohio	55.24
Hawaii	27.84	Oklahoma	17.05
Idaho	50.95	Oregon	48.88
Illinois	69.66	Pennsylvania	69.03
Indiana	100.54	Rhode Island	284.04
Iowa	85.11	South Carolina	30.39
Kansas	35.51	South Dakota	25.58
Kentucky	27.21	Tennessee	193.65
Louisiana	46.66	Texas	11.58
Maine	164.24	Utah	17.35
Maryland	451.54	Vermont	36.88
Massachusetts	424.97	Virginia	381.96
Michigan	173.67	Washington	100.38
Minnesota	151.51	West Virginia	8.02
Mississippi	126.91	Wisconsin	238.55
Missouri	34.15	Wyoming	333.47
U.S. Average	166.48		

Source: Douglas D. Peterson, *State Aid to Cities and Towns: Sharpening the Focus* (Washington, D.C.: National League of Cities, July 1988). Reprinted by permission of the National League of Cities.

(although a slice of gasoline, tobacco, and other tax benefits is greatly appreciated). The key is local option, in which jurisdictions decide for themselves which, if any, taxes they will exact. More than two-thirds of the states have authorized an optional sales or income tax for some local governments, and some permit localities to adopt optional earmarked taxes. For example, Florida empowers its counties to place an accommodations tax on local hotel and motel rooms. Revenues are dedicated to tourism development projects. Local option taxes are attractive because they provide local jurisdictions with the flexibility to take action as they see fit in response to local needs.[66] Protecting citizens against "taxaholic" local legislative bodies are the smoldering ashes of the taxpayer revolt and state requirements that local tax hikes must receive approval by the voters in a referendum.

Local governments also want *reimbursements for state mandates* that require them to spend money. Through constitutional provisions, statutes, and administrative regulations, all states require localities to undertake certain activities and operate programs in accordance with state standards and rules. These mandates are similar to the strings attached to federal grants-in-aid, and they are as distasteful to local governments as federal mandates are to states. Many state mandates are associated with local personnel policies, such as minimum wages, maximum hours, and safe working conditions. Others entail special education programs, environmental protection standards, and access for the handicapped.[67] They are designed to achieve uniformity in levels and quality of local government services throughout the state. Sometimes, however, state mandates appear to be nitpicking. Examples include requirements that public libraries carry a certain number of books per resident or that schoolbuses be refueled daily, whether their tanks are empty or not.

Local governments believe that states should reimburse them for expenses incurred in carrying out such mandates. Many states have responded to this request. Nearly forty states attach to any proposed legislation that involves local governments "fiscal notes" that estimate the local costs of implementing the legislation. An increasing number of states are required by law to go one step further and fully reimburse local governments for mandated expenditures.

State and Local Finance in the 1990s

The taxpayer revolt may be dormant, but it is not dead. Its legacy lives on in taxation and expenditure limitations that constrain the financial discretion of state and local officials. Similarly, economic recessions must be expected as a normal part of the economic cycle in the United States. What is frightening is the potential depth of the next one, given the huge national budget and trade deficits, which could create shortfalls in state and local budgets not seen since the Great Depression. Prospects for more national aid are very poor. When the national government finally takes serious steps to reduce the budget deficit, states and localities are likely to feel the pinch of further declines in grants-in-aid.

State and local governments are doing a great deal to ward off these and other threats to their fiscal well-being. Revenue systems are rapidly becoming more diverse. Tax structures are broader and more productive, as most states become more dependent on sales and income taxes and user fees, along with severance taxes, lotteries, and a variety of other revenue-raising mechanisms. States are more willing to share tax revenues and tax systems with cities, counties, and other local governments. Greater local flexibility in taxing is a trend that localities welcome. Citizens may also benefit from local taxes that are linked more directly to received services, and perhaps attuned more closely to local needs.

State and local financial relations represent yet another aspect of the diversity, innovation, and change that characterize the nonnational governments as they enter the 1990s. State and local interdependence has never been greater in matters of taxing and spending. Burden-sharing and cooperative relations are increasingly prevalent. With the financial uncertainties facing the national government, these trends are very positive.

Summary

State and local finance is characterized by interdependence and diversity. Major state and local taxes have been joined by severance taxes and user fees. All taxes can be evaluated using the criteria of equity, yield, elasticity, ease of administration, and accountability. State and local governments have been buffeted by a series of financial blows, including the taxpayer revolt, severe economic recessions, and painful reductions in national aid. All are likely to continue to affect the nonnational governments during the 1990s.

State and local governments are doing a better job than they used to in managing their money. Revenue and expenditure estimates are becoming more accurate in the face of growing economic complexity. Rainy day funds are used to set aside monies for hard times and the next economic downturn. Bonded indebtedness is being kept at reasonable levels. And, of course, operating budgets are balanced each fiscal year.

Key Terms

Benefit principle The principle that taxes should be levied on those who benefit directly from a government service.

Circuit breaker A limit on taxes applied to certain categories of people, such as the poor or elderly.

Fiscal capacity The taxable resources of a government jurisdiction.

Fiscal stress Financial pressure on a government from such factors as revenue shortfalls and taxing and spending limitations.

General obligation bond A debt instrument supported by the full financial resources of the issuing jurisdiction.

Industrial development bond A bond issued to fund the construction of a facility to be used by a private firm.

Intergovernmental transfers The movement of money or other resources from one level of government to another.

Operating budget The document that lists annual revenues and expenditures for short-term operations.

Own-source revenue Monies derived by a government from its own taxable resources.

Political economy Political choices that have economic outcomes.

Progressive tax A tax in which the rate rises as the base or taxable income rises.

Proportional tax A tax in which people pay an identical rate regardless of income or economic transaction.

Regressive tax A tax in which the rate falls as the base or taxable income rises.

Revenue bond A bond that is paid off from income derived from the facility built with the bond proceeds.

14

State-Local Relations

The Distribution of Authority
The Amount and Type of Authority/How
Distribution of Authority Works/A Tug of
War/State Mandates

State-Local Organizations
Task Forces/Advisory Commissions on
Intergovernmental Relations/Departments of
Community Affairs

**Metropolitics: A New Challenge for
State Government**
Accidental Cities/Shadow Governments/Regional
Government/Regional Coordination

States and Urban Policy
Housing Policy/Infrastructure Policy

States and Their Rural Communities

The Interaction of State and Local Governments

Building a new $210 million domed stadium in downtown Atlanta involved not only the city of Atlanta and Fulton County but the state of Georgia. Years of wrangling delayed the project, which, ironically, everyone considered an economic priority.[1] The problem was that each of the governments represented different constituencies and each had different financial and political concerns about the project. Georgia and the two local governments brought lists of demands to the negotiating table, and each ended up winning some and losing others when agreement was finally reached in 1989.

States and their communities have a strained relationship. On the one hand, it is state government that gives local governments life. Local governments exist only with state approval. On the other hand, state governments historically have not treated their local governments very well. It appears, however, that states are beginning to realize that mistreating their governmental offspring is counterproductive, and many have launched a sometimes uncoordinated process of assistance and empowerment of local government.

Capturing this evolution is the statement of the National Conference of State Legislatures (NCSL) Task Force on State-Local Relations: "Legislators should place a higher priority on state-local issues than has been done in the past. The time has come to change their attitude toward local governments—to stop considering them as just another special interest group and to start treating them as partners in our federal system."[2] Stronger, more competent local governments are an asset to state government.

Chapter 13 addressed the financial relationship between state and local governments. This chapter examines broader issues and related trends. Let us first consider the most fundamental issue: the distribution of authority between the state and its constituent units.

The Distribution of Authority

In the words of the U.S. Advisory Commission on Intergovernmental Relations, "State legislatures are the trustees of the basic rules of local governance in America. The laws and constitutions of each state are the basic legal instruments of local governance."[3] These statements denote the essence of the distribution of authority between a state and its localities. Simply put, it is up to the state to determine the amount and type of authority a local government may possess. As indicated by Dillon's Rule (see Chapter 2), local governments are creatures of the state; therefore they depend on the state to imbue them with enough powers to operate effectively.

The Amount and Type of Authority

There is wide variation in how much and what kind of authority states give their local governments. Some states grant their localities wide-ranging powers to restructure themselves, to impose new taxes, and to take on additional functions. Others are much more conservative with their power, and force local governments to turn to the legislature for approval to act. Empowerment also depends on the type of local government. General-purpose governments such as counties, cities, and towns typically have wider latitude than special-purpose governments like school districts. Even among general-purpose governments there are different degrees of authority; counties tend to be more circumscribed in their ability to modify their form of government and expand their service offerings than cities are.[4]

No local government today, however, suffers the powerlessness that South Carolina historically imposed on its counties. Until the late 1960s, the South Carolina legislature passed each county's budget (called a supply bill) and set local tax rates.[5] The legislative delegation was in fact the real government of the county. It was only two decades ago that the legislative changes brought by reapportionment and the pressures of urbanization forced the state to empower county governments.

The ACIR examined the distribution of authority between states and their cities and counties as the 1980s began.[6] It measured the amount of discretion a local jurisdiction possessed regarding its structure, personnel, finances, and functions and ranked the states according to the degree of local government discretionary authority present. Table 14.1 lists the states in descending order. The composite ranking covers not only cities and counties but smaller general-purpose governments like towns and villages as well.

Overall, local governments in Oregon, Maine, North Carolina, Connecticut, and Alaska enjoy substantially more discretion to manage their own affairs than do their counterparts in Idaho, West Virginia, New Mexico, South Dakota, and Nevada. The states at the bottom of the list keep their local governments on a short leash. Consequently, these jurisdictions are more dependent on state government for sustenance.

The rankings in Table 14.1 demonstrate that some states sharply distinguish between county and city governments. Texas stands at the top of the city list but ranks only forty-third on the county list. Arkansas, on the other hand, ranks sixth in the amount of discretionary authority held by county governments but only thirty-fourth with regard to its cities. Other states land at about the same point on each scale. California, for example, ranks seventeenth on both the city and the county list.

As Chapter 3 emphasizes, the 1980s saw a shift in power from the national government to state capitols. A smaller version of this phenomenon has occurred between states and their local governments. The more recently a state has adopted its constitution, the more likely the document is to contain provisions that strengthen local governments.[7] Some state constitutions set forth a provision for home rule (see Chapters 2 and 11), the true meaning of which becomes evident when state and local governments try to sort out which issues are local and which are of state concern. For the most part, real home rule has been somewhat elusive. Only about one-half of the states extend truly proprietary policymaking powers to their city governments; even fewer accord similar powers to counties.[8]

How Distribution of Authority Works

The concept of distribution of authority becomes clearer when we apply it to an actual situation, like highway planning, funding, and construction. State and local governments share the responsibility for this function and over time have fashioned a workable relationship.[9] For example, state officials consult local officials regarding the planning and construction of state roads and highways in their jurisdictions. Consultation does not mean that local approval is required; only occasionally is local approval sought. But consultation does guarantee room for local maneuvering, according to a 1987 nationwide survey of executive directors of state associations of counties, cities, towns, and regional councils (see Table 14.2).

Local officials are frequently able to convince state highway officials to modify highway plans to accommodate local preferences. Among city officials and regional councils, the reported ability to influence state highway officials is strong. The group with the least influence, township officials, represents the smallest jurisdictions, both in area and population. All in all, although local officials tend to be satisfied with the amount of highway consultation in their area, they would prefer more influence. This comparatively harmonious relationship does not necessarily extend to other interactions between state and local officials. Land management, for example, can generate considerably more friction, as explained in Politics and Policy 14.1.

A Tug of War

Local governments want their states to provide them with adequate funding and ample discretion. Local officials are supremely confident of their abilities to govern, given sufficient state support. But county officials express concern that neither their policymaking power nor their financial authority has kept pace with the increased administrative responsibilities placed on them by state government.[10] The recognition and correction of such conditions is the states' responsibility.

Evidence from New York in 1987 indicates that state and local officials evaluate the condition of their relations differently.[11] Using a scale on which 100 represented ideal state-local relations, state officials were generally

Table 14.1 States Ranked by Degree of Local Discretionary Authority, 1980

Composite (all types of local units)	Cities only*	Counties only†
1. Oregon	Texas	Oregon
2. Maine	Maine	Alaska
3. North Carolina	Michigan	North Carolina
4. Connecticut	Connecticut	Pennsylvania
5. Alaska	North Carolina	Delaware
6. Maryland	Oregon	Arkansas
7. Pennsylvania	Maryland	South Carolina
8. Virginia	Missouri	Louisiana
9. Delaware	Virginia	Maryland
10. Louisiana	Illinois	Utah
11. Texas	Ohio	Kansas
12. Illinois	Oklahoma	Minnesota
13. Oklahoma	Alaska	Virginia
14. Kansas	Arizona	Florida
15. South Carolina	Kansas	Wisconsin
16. Michigan	Louisiana	Kentucky
17. Minnesota	California	California
18. California	Georgia	Montana
19. Missouri	Minnesota	Illinois
20. Utah	Pennsylvania	Maine
21. Arkansas	South Carolina	North Dakota
22. New Hampshire	Wisconsin	Hawaii
23. Wisconsin	Alabama	New Mexico
24. North Dakota	Nebraska	Indiana
25. Arizona	North Dakota	New York

*Hawaii is not included in the list because, at the time of the study, Honolulu was the only city and it is a consolidated city-county government.
†Connecticut and Rhode Island are not listed because they do not have organized county governments.
Source: U.S. Advisory Commission on Intergovernmental Relations, *State and Local Roles in the Federal System* (Washington, D.C.: ACIR, 1982), p. 262.

more positive, scoring 56.2 to the local officials' range of 43.2 to 50.0 (depending on the type of local government). These scores reflect an improvement (a gain of 11.2 points) from state officials' assessment of the relationship five years ago. Local officials, however, did not think any progress had been made. The state received relatively high marks for its provision of technical assistance, but it fared less well on financial assistance provided to local governments and the discretion in the use of the funds.

To a certain extent, the evaluation of state-local relations depends on who

Table 14.1   States Ranked by Degree of Local Discretionary
Authority, 1980 (*cont.*)

Composite (all types of local units)	Cities only	Counties only
26. Florida	Delaware	Wyoming
27. Ohio	New Hampshire	Oklahoma
28. Alabama	Utah	Michigan
29. Kentucky	Wyoming	Washington
30. Georgia	Florida	Iowa
31. Montana	Mississippi	New Jersey
32. Washington	Tennessee	Georgia
33. Wyoming	Washington	Nevada
34. Tennessee	Arkansas	Tennessee
35. New York	New Jersey	Mississippi
36. New Jersey	Kentucky	New Hampshire
37. Indiana	Colorado	Alabama
38. Rhode Island	Montana	Arizona
39. Vermont	Iowa	South Dakota
40. Hawaii	Indiana	West Virginia
41. Nebraska	Massachusetts	Nebraska
42. Colorado	Rhode Island	Ohio
43. Massachusetts	South Dakota	Texas
44. Iowa	New York	Idaho
45. Mississippi	Nevada	Colorado
46. Nevada	West Virginia	Vermont
47. South Dakota	Idaho	Missouri
48. New Mexico	Vermont	Massachusetts
49. West Virginia	New Mexico	—
50. Idaho	—	—

is doing the assessment. State officials are apprehensive of awarding local governments carte blanche authority. Local officials, while they want more authority, really want more money. The tug of war will continue.

State Mandates

Although local governments generally want more autonomy, state governments share their policymaking sphere with reluctance. They have demonstrated a tendency to be fairly comfortable with a command approach. In other words, rather than let subgovernments devise their own solutions to problems, states frequently prefer to tell them how to solve them. They do this through a mechanism called a *mandate*, a subject that was discussed in

Chapter 13 in the context of state-local finances. The New York survey of state and local officials identified unfunded mandates as the most persistent source of friction between the levels of government.[12]

From the perspective of state government, mandates are necessary to ensure that vital activities are performed and desirable goals are achieved. State mandates promote uniformity of policy from one jurisdiction to another (for instance, the length of the public school year or the operating hours of precinct polling places). In addition, they promote coordination, especially among adjacent jurisdictions that provide services jointly (such as a regional hospital or a metropolitan transportation system).

Local governments see the issue quite differently. They have three basic complaints:[13]

1. State mandates (especially those that mandate a new service or impose a service quality standard) can be quite expensive for local governments.
2. State mandates displace local priorities in favor of state priorities.
3. State mandates limit the management flexibility of local governments.

Taken together, these problems make for unhappy local officials. A five-state study of mandates in the late 1970s found that the number of mandates varied from a high of 1,479 in California to a low of 259 in North Carolina.[14] Most of these dealt with performance standards and reporting requirements having to do with general government, health, and community development. The costs of nearly 75 percent of the "direct order" mandates

Table 14.2   Local Government Influence in State Highway Matters

Issue: If local officials wish to modify a state road or highway plan or project that affects their area, how likely are they to be able to convince state highway officials to make the changes they desire?

Likelihood of convincing state	Type of local official			
	Township	Municipal	County	Regional council
Very likely	0.0	15.2	8.3	20.0
Somewhat likely	44.4	72.7	52.8	63.3
Hardly likely	55.6	12.1	27.8	13.3
Not at all likely	0.0	0.0	0.0	0.0
Don't know	0.0	0.0	11.1	3.3

Source: U.S. Advisory Commission on Intergovernmental Relations, *Local Perspectives on State-Local Highway Consultation and Cooperation* (Washington, D.C.: ACIR, July 1987), p. 13.

POLITICS AND POLICY 14.1
A Battle Royal: State and Local Land Management Politics

L and is a valuable resource. Governments make decisions about how land is to be used through comprehensive plans and zoning. These decisions can spark intense conflict, not only between landowners and government but between state and local governments. If there is one power that local governments jealously guard, it is their authority to determine how land within their borders is to be used. This power was threatened, however, in the 1970s, as state governments increased their involvement in land management. Oregon, California, Vermont, and Hawaii took aggressive actions to manage land, and virtually without exception, state government forays into land management were resented and resisted by local governments.

Florida jumped onto the land management bandwagon in 1975. Concerned about the impact of growth on the state's fragile ecosystem, Florida enacted legislation that required every city and county to adopt a comprehensive land-use plan. The legislature did not allocate funds to assist local govern-

ments in the planning process (it cost an estimated $50 million), and despite the mandate, many cities and counties did not comply.[1]

A decade later, in the face of local noncompliance, the Florida legislature enacted a bill that requires local governments to design comprehensive plans that are consistent with state-determined criteria. Such a proviso effectively limits the amount of local government discretion in land use. The Florida law identifies three statewide policy goals: to rechannel development away from the coast, to prohibit development unless adequate infrastructure exists, and to discourage urban sprawl into existing open space and wetlands. Local government dismay over its eroding authority has been lessened somewhat by the availability of state funding for the planning process. This approach to land management is likely to generate more local compliance.

[1] John M. DeGrove, "Creative Tensions in State/Local Relations," in Douglas R. Porter, ed., *Growth Management: Keeping on Target* (Washington, D.C.: Urban Land Institute, 1986), pp. 169–72.

were paid for by local governments. Research in South Carolina indicated that smaller, poorer jurisdictions bore the heaviest financial burden in complying with such mandates.[15]

This issue is not going to fade away. It is no wonder that the NCSL's Task Force on State-Local Relations has urged states to consider relaxation or elimination of mandates and assumption of the cost of complying with them.[16] Mandates dealing with local personnel policies, environmental standards, service levels, and tax-base exemptions are due reconsideration. Massachusetts is well on the way to doing this; its Division of Local Mandates in the Department of the State Auditor reviews mandates every five years and recommends their continuation, modification, or termination. Other states are likely to adopt similar provisions.

State-Local Organizations

Although the structure of the federal system has created a set of legal, administrative, and financial ties between state and local governments, it has not necessarily embraced state understanding of or sympathy toward local governments. To rectify this condition, state governments have established numerous organizations such as local government study commissions and advisory panels of local officials. Three popular approaches are examined here.

Task Forces

Task forces tend to be focused organizations set up by the governor or the state legislature in response to a perceived local-level problem. If a state wants to investigate the ramifications of changing its annexation statutes, the legislature might create a Task Force on Annexation and Boundary Changes or something similar. The task force would probably be composed of state and local officials, community leaders, and experts on the subject of annexation.

The task force would proceed in this manner: first, it would collect information on how other states handle the annexation question. Then it would conduct a series of public hearings to get input from individuals and groups interested in the issue, and finally it would compile a report that included recommendations suitable for legislative action. Its work completed, the task force would then disband, although individual members might turn up as advocates when the task force recommendations received legislative attention.

Task forces are quick organizational responses to local problems that have become too prominent for state government to ignore. A task force is a low-cost, concentrated reaction that gives the appearance of action, and in some instances actually influences legislative deliberations.

Advisory Commissions on Intergovernmental Relations

To make an ongoing, comprehensive effort at state-local cooperation, many states have created state-level advisory commissions on intergovernmental relations, modeled after the commission created by the U.S. Congress in 1959. State-level ACIRs are designed to promote more harmonious, workable relations between the state and its governmental subdivisions.

They are intended to offer a forum for discussion of long-range state-local issues—a venue where local officials can be listened to and engaged in focused dialogue; conduct research on local developments and new state policies; promote experimentation in intergovernmental processes, both state-local and interlocal; and develop suggested solutions to state-local problems.[17]

By 1988, twenty-two states had instituted their own ACIRs. Two of these were Connecticut and Missouri. Connecticut established a twenty-five-member bipartisan commission composed of legislative leaders (such as the Speaker of the House), local government officials (appointed by the governor and local associations), and members of the public.[18] On its agenda were the development of "municipal powers" impact analyses and the creation of an intergovernmental fiscal data base.

Missouri took a slightly different approach. Its organization is called the Commission on Local Government Cooperation and was established by Governor John Ashcroft.[19] The goal of the thirty-member commission was to forge a partnership between the state of Missouri and its local governments. One of the first issues it tackled was the liability insurance crisis confronting local governments. The commission developed a risk management fund plan (basically a state-administered self-insurance pool) as a possible solution to the problem. It rallied local governments behind the plan and successfully lobbied the legislature to enact it. The commission's next target was a study of alternative revenue sources for local governments.

In both Connecticut and Missouri, the creation of a state-level ACIR quickly returned real benefits to local government. Whether in their narrowest form, as arenas for discussion of local issues, or in their broadest, as policy developers and initiators, ACIRs are useful to state and local governments. Their greatest impact will occur, however, if they are given the authority and resources to do something more than simply discussing issues. The 1990s will probably see other states exploring this organizational possibility.

Departments of Community Affairs

Another way in which states can generate closer formal ties with their local governments is through specialized administrative agencies. All fifty states have created departments of community affairs (DCA) that are involved in local activities. They have different labels (Kentucky calls its DCA the Department for Local Government; Ohio's is the Department of Economic and Community Development), but their function is similar: to offer a range of programs and services to local governments.[20] DCAs are involved in housing, urban revitalization, antipoverty programs, and economic development, and offer local governments such services as planning, management, and financial assistance.

DCAs vary on several dimensions: their niche in state government, the sizes of their budget and staff, and whether they include an advisory board of local officials. Each of these dimensions contributes to the clout that any DCA has. For example, a DCA that has cabinet-level status (as thirty-five of them do) is likely to be more influential than one located within another state agency (nine states) or within the governor's office (six states). DCAs with bigger budgets and staffs should have more influence. As of 1980, the budgets of these organizations ranged from under $200,000 to $70 million, and their staff sizes ranged from fewer than fifty to more than five hundred. The existence of an advisory board is problematic, however. Half of the DCAs have advisory boards, but few of these are active or effective in an array of local policy areas.[21]

Compared to their state-level ACIR counterparts, DCAs function much more as service deliverers and much less as policy initiators. Therefore, these two types of organizations tend to complement rather than compete with one another. Both, however, function as advocates for local government at the state level.

Metropolitics: A New Challenge for State Government

State governments find their dealings with local governments confounded by the side effects of urbanization. Regardless of which state we examine, its urban areas show the effects of three waves of suburbanization. An early wave occurred during the 1920s, when automobiles facilitated the development of outlying residential areas. Although the dispersion slowed during the Depression and World War II, its resurgence in the 1950s triggered a second wave, which saw retail stores follow the population exodus. The "malling of America" has led to the third wave of suburbanization: the development of office space beyond the central city.[22] This is happening with a vengeance in New York City and Atlanta, in Cheyenne and Nogales. It is this third wave that has caught the attention of state government.

The transformation of American metropolitan areas in the 1980s meant that central cities have lost their prominence as the social, economic, and political focal points of their areas. People have moved to surrounding suburbs and beyond; businesses and firms have sprung up in the hinterlands; communities have formed their own service and taxing districts. The outward flow of people and activities has fundamentally altered metropolitan areas, which are now composed of "a series of relatively self-contained and self-sufficient decentralized regional units."[23] Not simply residential, these new "boom towns" include business, retail, and entertainment activities. The de-emphasis of the central city suggests the need for changes in outmoded state government policy toward metropolitan jurisdictions.

A serious concern is that rapid, unplanned growth is producing "accidental cities" and fostering "shadow governments." A logical question is, what is state government doing while all of this is occurring? In the late 1980s, the answer was not much.

Accidental Cities

The term that the Conservation Foundation has coined for the conversion of suburban communities and small towns into homogenized, traffic-clogged places is **accidental cities.**[24] The forces of rapid, unplanned growth are said to threaten the distinctive character of small towns and the community life of extant suburbs. Residents watch the conversion occurring around them, as a stand of pine trees is leveled for a car wash, a locally owned drug store becomes the site of a new office tower, and homes located along two-lane roads are converted to professional offices, then razed when the road is widened to six lanes and the property rezoned as commercial.

The development of accidental cities has triggered apprehension over livability and quality of life. The areas surrounding Honolulu and Phoenix offer interesting cases of growth-related stress.

The Honolulu Area   Honolulu has taken an innovative approach in addressing the excesses of rapid urbanization on the eastern side of the island of Oahu. The state of Hawaii and Honolulu County have joined forces to create a new municipality twenty miles from Waikiki Beach.[25] Plans for the new city include waterfront resort hotels largely financed by Japanese investors, a defined downtown center, an industrial park, large residential neighborhoods, shopping centers, and office buildings. Government officials hope to recreate the look of old Honolulu in the new city of Kapolei and avoid the high-rise concrete jungle that characterizes downtown Honolulu today. Of course, it is much easier to improve on the past when you have the luxury of starting from the ground up (quite literally in this case) than when you are confronted with years of accumulated land uses.

The Phoenix Area   Phoenix, the fastest-growing large city in America, has four growth "hot spots," with the promise of nine by the year 2000.[26] Phoenix was the first city in the country to acknowledge these emerging urban centers officially in its planning process, which suggests that the growth areas will be targeted for public infrastructure investments—parks, libraries, government offices, hospitals—in anticipation of development rather than in reaction to it. Among city officials, the hope is that the state of Arizona will provide enough resources to help Phoenix prepare for the growth. As an initial step in the late 1980s, the legislature commissioned a study of growth management strategies for the area.[27]

Shadow Governments

Accidental cities are appearing and new forms of governance are emerging. **Shadow governments** may or may not be official government units, but in many important ways they behave like governments: they levy taxes, regulate behavior, and provide services. Three types of shadow governments exist: private enterprise shadow governments, such as a homeowners' association; public-private partnership shadow governments, a common example of which is development corporations (see Chapter 16); and subsidiaries of conventional governments with unusual powers, such as an areawide planning commission (see the discussion of regional coordination later in this chapter).[28] These bodies exist within the confines of state law, but thus far states have displayed a curious hands-off posture toward them.

Estimates place the number of private enterprise shadow governments at about 120,000, approximately 60 percent of which are located in suburban areas.[29] Condominium communities are a good illustration. The property owners' association makes rules for residents (from the speed limit on community streets to the color of the condo), provides services (security, maintenance, landscaping), and assesses fees (based on the size of the unit). Residents typically vote for the board of directors of the association (in some instances, developers of the project retain seats on the board), and votes tend to be weighted according to the value of the housing unit. Residents with a greater financial investment have a greater say in the governing of the community. This is a far cry from the one-person, one-vote principle.

Shadow governments, regardless of type, raise questions about matters of power and equity. (There are few questions about their efficiency, because by most accounts they tend to operate fairly efficiently.) The power issue centers on information, influence, and accountability. Shadow governments control information, restrict influence to those who belong or can pay, and have no public accountability. The equity issue addresses the class discrimination inherent in these governments. A poor family out for a Sunday drive may be able to traverse city streets, but if they turn their ramshackle automobile off onto a private street patroled by private police, they are likely to be followed and perhaps even stopped, questioned, and escorted out of the neighborhood.

Whatever our uneasiness over power and equity, the number of shadow governments is increasing, not decreasing. In metropolitan areas, where in the words of one observer "local government boundaries are totally out of whack with the realities of economic geography or development patterns,"[30] shadow governments are especially popular. Their vaunted efficiency makes them a force to be reckoned with.

The social and economic changes in America's metropolitan areas have had a tremendous impact on urban governance. Accidental cities and shadow governments make up extended webs of interdependent jurisdictions. How can these places best be governed? Thus far, state governments do not have much idea. Idealistic metropolitan reformers have called for regional government; more pragmatic observers have advocated regional coordination.

Regional Government

One alternative to specialized minigovernments is the creation of **regional government,** a structural recognition of the interdependence of proximate communities. Under a regional government, local jurisdictions give up some of their power and authority to a larger government in exchange for areawide solutions to local problems. State legislatures are important players in this process, because aside from the state constitution, they create the rules of the game. Their actions facilitate or hinder local government reorganization into regional units.

In the United States, the closest thing to regional government is **city-county consolidation,** where area jurisdictions are absorbed into a single countywide government. Structure and function are unified. In a pure form of consolidation, there is one police department, one fire department, one water and sewer system. The functions of local government—public safety, public works, health and human services, community and economic development, and recreation and arts programs—are provided by a single jurisdiction. There are twenty-four city-county consolidated governments; Indianapolis/Marion County, Indiana; Jacksonville/Duval County, Florida; and Nashville/Davidson County, Tennessee, are the most prominent examples. Table 14.3 lists the nineteen largest consolidated governments.

Regional government seems so rational, yet it has proven to be quite elusive, as many attempts at city-county consolidation were defeated at the polls in the 1960s and 1970s. The logic is straightforward: if small local governments in a metropolitan area merge to form a larger local government, two positive outcomes will occur. First, stubborn public policy problems can be tackled from an areawide perspective. For example, the pollution generated by city A that affects city B can be handled as a regional problem rather than as a conflict between the two cities. Second, combining forces produces *economies of scale* in service delivery. Instead of each jurisdiction constructing and operating jails, for example, one large regional facility can be maintained. Jail service can be provided at a lower cost to each participating jurisdiction.

Table 14.3   Consolidated City-County Governments

Jurisdiction	Year organized
Anaconda–Deer Lodge County, Montana	1976
Anchorage–Anchorage Borough, Alaska	1975
Baton Rouge–East Baton Rouge Parish, Louisiana	1947
Boston–Suffolk County, Massachusetts	1821
Butte–Silver Bow County, Montana	1976
Carson City–Ormsby County, Nevada	1969
Columbus–Muscogee County, Georgia	1970
Denver–Denver County, Colorado	1904
Honolulu–Honolulu County, Hawaii	1907
Houma–Terrebonne Parish, Louisiana	1984
Indianapolis–Marion County, Indiana	1969
Jacksonville–Duval County, Florida	1967
Juneau–Greater Juneau Borough, Alaska	1969
Lexington–Fayette County, Kentucky	1972
Nashville–Davidson County, Tennessee	1962
New Orleans–New Orleans Parish, Louisiana	1805
New York–New York County, New York	1847
Philadelphia–Philadelphia County, Pennsylvania	1854
San Francisco–San Francisco County, California	1856

Source: Victor S. DeSantis, "Profiles of Individual Cities and Counties," in International City Management Association, *The Municipal Year Book 1988* (Washington, D.C.: ICMA, 1988), pp. 199–200. Reprinted by permission.

Regional government does not always perform as expected. Recent research compared the taxing and spending policies of a consolidated jurisdiction with a comparable but unconsolidated area in the same state.[31] Both taxes and expenditures increased in consolidated Jacksonville/Duval County compared to those of unconsolidated Tampa/Hillsborough County, Florida. Another criticism of regional government is that it can be inaccessible and destructive of the hard-won political gains of minorities. Compared to a city or town government, regional government is farther away, both literally and figuratively. The effect on minority political strength, while not as obvious, is no less troublesome. Because the proportionate number of minorities may be lessened when jurisdictions are combined, their voting strength can be diluted. It is likely that minorities will find it more difficult to elect one of their own to the regional governing board.

Given the reluctance of voters to endorse consolidated city-county government, some reformers have turned their attention to an old-fashioned way of merging governments—by state legislative action. In the nineteenth century, legislatures simply combined local governments when they thought it necessary. The sole successful modern example of consolidation by a state legislature is Indianapolis/Marion County, Indiana. (Nevada's state legislature consolidated Las Vegas and Clark County in 1975, but the action was subsequently overturned by the state supreme court as unconstitutional.)[32] Since the action of the Indiana legislature, both Alabama and Georgia seriously considered consolidation of Birmingham and Jefferson County and Atlanta and Fulton County, respectively. In each case, the legislative action fell short of the necessary votes.

Regional Coordination

Regional coordination is an alternative to regional government. **Substate districts,** usually called councils of government or regional planning commissions, are examples. Substate districting does not involve a formal merger or combination of governments; instead, districts are loose collections of local governments designed to increase communication and coordination in an area. State governments were not active in the creation of substate districts; national government programs spurred their development. The Housing Act of 1954, for example, provided funds for metropolitan planning, but the real impetus came through the Model Cities Act of 1966, which required metropolitan planning agencies to review grant applications. The review process, known as A-95, stimulated the creation of regional planning organizations in both metropolitan and nonmetropolitan areas. By 1980, 650 such entities were supported by federal grants and payments from member governments.

Although areawide planning remains the most common activity of councils of government, they do other things as well. Member governments can turn to them for technical assistance (such as help in writing federal grant applications), professional services (planning, budgeting, engineering, legal advice), and information (economic data for the region).[33]

The impact of these councils has been less significant than their creators hoped, but they have had two positive effects. First, councils have elevated the concept of areawide policy planning from a pipe dream to a reality. They have been heavily involved in criminal justice, water quality, housing, and transportation planning. Second, councils have substantially improved the operational capacity of rural local governments, by providing expertise to small local jurisdictions that cannot afford to hire specialized staff.

During the 1980s, councils suffered several blows that threatened their survival. In 1983 the Reagan administration rescinded the A-95 order, thus ending their mandatory grant review function. In addition, less money was available from the national government for areawide planning. The councils' standing was further threatened by defections by member governments. In some instances, local officials resented their power; in other cases, the governments could no longer afford to pay the necessary dues.

Figure 14.1 Healthy and Distressed Cities
The UDAG program allocated points based on a city's socioeconomic conditions. The distressed cities shown here scored the maximum number of points in 1986; the healthy cities had scores of zero or below.

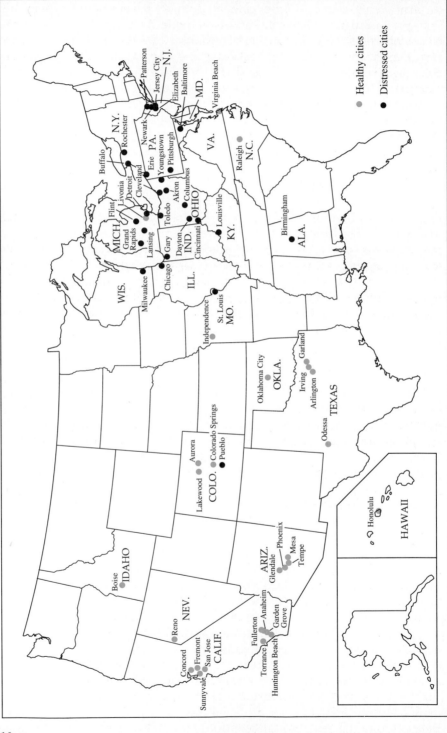

Source: U.S. Department of Housing and Urban Development, "Explanation of Items Appearing on the Large City and Urban County UDAG List of 4/25/86."

State governments will play an important role in determining the fate of regional councils in the future. The Reagan administration's substitute for A-95 was Executive Order 12372, which emphasizes a state-determined review process for federal financial assistance. Although states vary in their commitment to regional coordination, the majority have continued to utilize a regional council structure in their grant process.[34] North Carolina, for example, has chosen to use regional councils to link the state and its communities. In addition, the state hires regional organizations to conduct studies and produce research reports. Not all states have exhibited this level of support, however, and to survive regional councils have redirected their organizational mission toward providing services to member governments.[35]

States and Urban Policy

If you had attended an urban policy conference in the late 1980s, you would have heard the phrase "state government" used repeatedly. When people mentioned the national government, they did so more wistfully than hopefully. Even government interest groups that have built solid reputations on their ability to represent urban interests before the national government, such as the National League of Cities and the U.S. Conference of Mayors, are increasingly concentrating on state capitols.

One action that symbolized the cities' steep fall from national grace was congressional action in 1988 that eliminated the locally popular Urban Development Action Grant (UDAG) program. Members of Congress who wanted to kill the program argued that UDAG had accomplished much of the original intent (funneling money to the nation's distressed cities) and that significant diversion was occurring (amendments allowed economically healthy cities to receive one-third of the funds).[36] Regardless of the assets of the program and communities' need for it, congressional decision makers concluded that UDAG was not a priority and shifted its funds into space exploration. Such national actions make state government the alternative savior of urban areas.

Figure 14.1 provides a look at American cities through UDAG program criteria such as population loss, percentage of population below the poverty line, percentage of housing built before 1940, rate of per capita income growth, unemployment rate, and job lags. The map shows those cities with populations greater than 100,000 that in the mid-1980s were considered particularly worthy of UDAG funds. It also shows the cities that were free of distress, as measured by the UDAG criteria.

Two significant contemporary issues, housing and infrastructure, are of particular interest in an urban environment, simply because of the large number of people who are affected. Let us consider each of these in terms of state-local interaction.

Housing Policy

For middle- and upper-income city residents, the housing market can be counted on to produce "affordable" units, but what is affordable to these residents is out of reach for low-income households. The mechanics of market economics effectively shut them out of the system. Low-cost housing does not generate the return that higher-cost housing does. As a result, governments have intervened to create incentives for developers to produce low-income housing units, and, where incentives do not work, to become providers of housing themselves. One of the aims of the federal Housing Act of 1949 was "a decent home in a suitable living environment" for all Americans.

Over time, the national government has backed away from this aim and has altered its approach to housing. In 1968 it was willing to become the nation's houser of last resort, but by 1982 the push was to deregulate and let market forces prevail.[37] Modifications of the national tax laws have had a

Governors and mayors occasionally work together to resolve perplexing urban problems. In 1988 New York governor Mario Cuomo and New York City mayor Edward Koch supported a bond act to finance repair of the Williamsburg bridge.

negative effect on rental housing stock. Deliberate actions and inaction have resulted in a decline in home ownership, an increase in the proportion of household income that is spent on housing, a decrease in the number of affordable rental units, an increase in the number of physically inadequate and abandoned structures, and an increase in the number of homeless people.

In response, state governments have set up housing finance agencies, nonprofit corporations have entered the low-income housing market, and local governments have adopted regulations to preserve their affordable housing stock. In some places, housing vouchers—a form of consumer subsidy that would open up currently nonaffordable housing to low-income residents—are being discussed. Another approach is for local governments to require developers to include a fixed proportion of affordable units in their market-rate project as a condition for approval of a building permit. This approach works, however, only where developers are clamoring for access.

Connecticut has been particularly innovative in addressing its affordable housing problem. As part of its new statewide plan, the state conducted a "housing needs assessment."[38] The bottom line is that "poor people don't make enough money to buy decent shelter at a price that the market can economically provide."[39] In a pilot program, Connecticut will enter into mediated negotiations with local jurisdictions in a specified area to develop a fair-housing compact for the area. To encourage local jurisdictions to pursue the goals of the compact, Connecticut has established a housing infrastructure fund to provide state financial assistance. The state's effort to address the scarcity of affordable housing is likely to be emulated by other states.

Infrastructure Policy

Infrastructure—public works projects and services—is the physical network of a community, that is, its roads and bridges, airports, water and sewer systems, and public buildings. It is important because it is crucial for development; the simplest equation is, no infrastructure = no development. Infrastructure has become an issue in many communities because of its crumbling condition and the high cost of new infrastructure.[40]

States take different approaches in financing local public works, and tradition is a powerful explanation of this behavior.[41] Generally, they are providing more financial support for local public works today than they did in the early 1980s, through grants, dedicated revenues (the money collected from a particular tax), loans, and bonds. States that have been particularly inventive in public works assistance include Pennsylvania, Massachusetts, Virginia, Wisconsin, and Wyoming.[42] Pennsylvania, for instance, allows cities to become financial partners in constructing roads to shopping malls and industrial sites. Massachusetts, through its Aquifer Land Acquisition

Program, purchases property or development rights to protect public drinking water supplies.

Local governments face huge infrastructure demands. Consider the case of Akron, Ohio, which had a 1980 population of 237,000 and a land area of slightly over 57 square miles. Akron's Capital Investment Program is a six-year schedule for infrastructure maintenance and improvement. The funding for the projects comes from a variety of sources: the city's income tax, water and sewer user fees, the county's motor vehicle license tax, general obligation bonds, state transportation funds, and federal funds such as the Urban Mass Transportation Administration block grants.[43] With these funds, Akron will resurface roads, restore curbs and sidewalks, build new water mains, plant trees, and design bikeways. The strategy is, quite simply, one of continual reinvestment. These infrastructure expenditures are necessary so that, in the words of Akron's mayor, the city can move "gracefully into the future." Other cities are doing the same.

States and Their Rural Communities

When the local Dairy Queen closes its doors, a small town in rural America knows that it is in trouble. The Dairy Queen, like the coffee shop on Main Street, serves as a gathering place for community residents. Its demise symbolizes the tough times that a lot of rural communities face. In fact, some analysts argue that the major distinctions in regional economics are no longer between Sunbelt and Frostbelt or East Coast and West Coast but between metropolitan America and the countryside.[44]

Not all rural areas are suffering. Four community growth types can be identified from economic and demographic trends.[45] A dynamic growth community is one in which both population and economic growth are occurring. Its opposite is the declining community, which is losing both its population and its economic base. Typically, declining communities have had economies based on farming, mining, or manufacturing. "Strain" communities experience population growth without proportionate gains in personal income, and finally, preservation communities have stable or declining populations but enjoy growth in personal income. Even prosperous communities have difficulties, as leaders ponder whether growth will disturb their rural flavor and identity.

The distressing news for declining communities is that compared to the other types, their local leaders are the least supportive of administrative modernization and change.[46] Local governments in these communities are less capable of responding creatively to the problems they face. Consequently, the gap between places where dynamic growth is occurring and the declining communities is likely to increase. The fear is that this will become a self-perpetuating phenomenon, until some communities simply disappear. Research on rural communities in the Midwest lends some credibility to this contention: the communities that have withstood economic downturns are those that have had the administrative capacity to identify and pursue opportunities.[47] Macon County, Missouri, is an example. With "hard work, luck, and heads-up opportunism," Macon County transformed itself from a declining community into a dynamic growth community.

What can state governments do to encourage the right kind of growth in rural areas? Short of pumping enormous amounts of money into the local economy, they can encourage the expansion of local intergovernmental cooperation, so that small rural governments join together to increase their administrative capacity to deliver services and achieve economies of scale. Two state actions facilitate such cooperation. One is reform of state tax codes, so that jurisdictions can share locally generated tax revenues. Rather than competing with each other for a new manufacturing plant or a shopping mall, local governments can cooperate to bring the new facility to the area; regardless of where it is located, all jurisdictions can receive a portion of the tax revenue. A second useful state action is the promotion of statewide land-use planning. As one observer has noted, "Currently too many rural local governments engage in wasteful inter-community competition, mutually antagonistic zoning, and contradictory development plans."[48] The developmental efforts of two states are presented in Politics and Policy 14.2.

Not every problem in rural America can be traced to the decline of agriculture, but a substantial number can. As a result, state governments have launched programs to stimulate agricultural diversification. For example, legislation passed in Iowa in 1986 was designed to encourage farmers to turn to horticulture and alternative crops. Montana established an Agricultural Development Council in 1987 to invest in promising agricultural diversification projects.[49]

The New York Legislative Commission on Rural Resources, established in 1982, was one of the first state initiatives designed to anticipate and prevent rural decline.[50] The Commission on Rural Resources analyzes potential problems, identifies solutions, and makes recommendations to the legislature. Other states have followed New York's lead. In 1986, for example, twenty states enacted farm credit programs, agribusiness initiatives, and rural community job development efforts.

One approach suggested by the Council of State Governments is the establishment of commissions and task forces to undertake thorough analyses of rural communities. This is an important step, as comprehension of rural problems is not widespread among urban legislators. Even New York was unsuccessful in establishing a rural development authority, because most legislators believed that the existing Urban Development Commission could do the job.[51] Services designed for urban dwellers, however, may function poorly in a rural environment.

POLITICS AND POLICY 14.2
States and Their Uneven Local Economies

A state's economy is made up of a lot of local economies, which vary from one part of the state to another. Maryland and Virginia offer two interesting examples. In both states, the areas bordering Washington, D.C., have thriving local economies, but other areas are struggling. In Maryland, it is the western portion of the state; in Virginia, the southwestern region. In each case, the depressed areas are geographically remote from those places that are economically booming. Maryland and Virginia share another significant feature: both have governors who are committed to bolstering the economies of their troubled regions.

When a major tire manufacturer announced plans to close its western Maryland plant in late 1986, this appeared to be another devastating blow to an already depressed region. Enter William Donald Schaefer, the former Baltimore mayor who won a landslide victory in the governor's race. Although he had not yet assumed the governor's office, Schaefer negotiated a deal with the tire company, which agreed to retain its corporate headquarters in western Maryland in exchange for $9 million in financial incentives from the state. This action was just the beginning of Schaefer's efforts to retain businesses in Maryland.

Virginia adopted a variation on the technology transfer idea. In 1986 Governor Gerald Baliles assembled a group of northern Virginia movers and shakers to tour the troubled southwestern area of the state and offer tips on attracting business. Local leaders gratefully welcomed the entourage, and the delegation suggested an array of tactics ranging from infrastructure development to promotional activities. Whether these recommendations will bear fruit remains to be seen; it is clear, however, that the state will not sit idly by as local economies wither.

The words of Maryland's Governor Schaefer sum up the situation: "Whenever you have a problem in any part of the state, the whole state must help."

Sources: Chris Spolar, "Cumberland Welcomes State Economic Efforts," *Washington Post*, February 9, 1987, pp. E1, E4; Donald P. Baker, "N. Va. Sends Advisers Downstate," *Washington Post*, December 6, 1986, pp. B1, B4; and Rudolph A. Pyatt, Jr., "Schaefer's Mind Is on the Jobs," *Washington Post*, December 9, 1986, p. D4.

The Interaction of State and Local Governments

State governments benefit from positive relationships with their local governments. Local governments benefit from positive relationships with their state government. Nonetheless, the two levels of government frequently clash.

Constitutionally, state governments are supreme in their dealings with local governments; even New York City, seven million strong and larger than many states, has to do what the government in Albany says. Yet there is evidence that the state-local relationship is shifting. Leaders in state government are increasingly aware that creating clinging vines—local governments with limited legal and fiscal authority—does not suit their purposes. During the 1990s, states will be strengthening those vines so that they can grow and prosper. Strong local governments make for resurgent state governments.

An interesting test of this prediction is likely to occur in western Washington. The Puget Sound region, a four-county, seventy-one-city area that is experiencing tremendous growth, faces infrastructure problems that crisscross the boundaries of individual jurisdictions.[52] Streets, bridges, and water and sewer systems need repair, replacement, and expansion. State government is ideally suited to devise a regionwide solution to these growth problems, but local jurisdictions are reluctant to give up their existing authority. Perhaps the best solution is something that has been called home-grown regionalism, in which regional goals are set at the local level and then implemented with state incentives.[53]

Of course, there are still examples of states withholding power from local governments. In its 1989 session, the Virginia legislature passed a bill that gives the state sole authority to regulate smoking.[54] Local governments are prohibited from enacting their own clean indoor air bills. The state's explanation for its action was uniformity: a state law would prevent a patchwork of different and perhaps conflicting local ordinances. An example like this not only speaks volumes about the power of the tobacco industry in Virginia politics, but it underscores the limitations of local government authority.

Summary

State-local relations are always in flux. The trend over the past two decades has been toward increased state assistance and empowerment of local jurisdictions. One issue that remains a sore point, however, is the use of mandates.

States have established a number of organizations in an effort to understand and assist local governments better. The consequences of growth (and, in some jurisdictions, stagnation) are likely to be an area of increasing state-local conflict. Local governments do not want to be neglected by the state, but neither do they want the state to become too involved in their affairs. There is a fine line between state assistance and state interference. Where the line is drawn depends on which level of government is holding the chalk.

Key Terms

Accidental cities The unplanned transformation of suburban communities and small towns into homogenized, congested places.

City-county consolidation The merger of city and county governments into a single jurisdiction.

Regional government An areawide structure for local governance, designed to replace multiple jurisdictions.

Shadow governments Entities, especially unofficial ones, that function like governments.

Substate districts Formal organizations of general-purpose governments in an area, intended to improve regional coordination.

15

Education Policy

The Crisis in Education
Standards/Students/Teachers

Intergovernmental Roles in Education
State and Local Roles/The National Role

Actors in Education Policy
The Education Establishment/The New
Policy Leaders

Educational Innovation in the States
Standards/Students/Teachers

The Continuing Challenge of Public Education

Early in 1989, the Educational Testing Service released the latest in a long string of studies documenting the dismal performance of American students in comparison with those in other countries. Scores in mathematics and science by American thirteen-year-olds were far below scores from South Korea, Ireland, Spain, the United Kingdom, and four Canadian provinces; American students ranked last in math and close to the bottom in science. Educators made dire predictions about declines in our technological sophistication and eventually in our standard of living.[1]

In the opinion of many Americans, education is the most important function performed by state and local government. The facts support this point of view. Education consumes more of state and local budgets than any other service. In 1988, approximately $309 trillion was spent on schooling in the United States.[2] That comes to around $1,280 per man, woman, and child. The importance of education is also associated with the sheer number of people involved in it. Fifty-five percent of the U.S. population is either enrolled in an educational institution or employed in the system that delivers educational services. Citizens have high expectations for their schools, assuming that they will teach everything from patriotism and good citizenship to driver and sex education. Furthermore, schools have served at the front lines in the battle against racial segregation.

Citizens also attribute problems in society to what goes on in schools, from "breakdowns in morality," as manifested by drug and alcohol abuse and lack of discipline, to the declining international competitiveness of American business. To a great extent, the future of this country and its economic expansion have always been explicitly linked to the quality of free public education.

In 1983 a prestigious national commission officially declared a crisis in the schools. In its much-cited report, *A Nation at Risk,* the National Commission on Excellence in Education lamented the erosion of the educational foundations of society "by a rising tide of mediocrity that threatens our very future." According to the authors, "If an unfriendly foreign power had attempted to impose on America the mediocre educational performance that exists today, we might well have viewed it as an act of war. . . . We have, in effect, been committing an act of unthinking, unilateral educational disarmament."[3]

The Crisis in Education

Education policy has always been controversial. For more than a hundred years policymakers, parents, teachers, and others have debated how educational institutions should be organized and financed, what should be taught, and who should receive the greatest benefit from public schooling. The most recent crisis is in many respects simply an extension of what has happened before. "Crises" in American education have been solemnly declared every thirty years or so. (Periodic public alarm followed by neglect characterizes other policies as well.)[4] Before the most recent one, a crisis was provoked in 1957 by the Soviet launching of Sputnik, the first orbiting space satellite. This momentous event led to a far-reaching effort to improve American education in science and mathematics, and eventually to American success in landing the first man on the moon.

The education crisis that began in the 1980s, however, appears to be more profound in two respects. First, the rapidity of world economic and social change means that education policy must be constantly reformulated and altered if schooling is to be relevant and the United States is to remain a dominant player in the international sphere. Second, improved analysis and data collection have provided a clearer picture of our specific shortcomings in education, and generated greater public awareness of them.

Public opinion reflects the education crisis. Each year since 1977 the Gallup Poll has asked Americans their opinions of community schools.[5] One question requires respondents to grade their local school on a scale of A to F. In the first year of the poll, 37 percent awarded the schools an A or a B, but by 1983 the proportion of A's and B's had dropped to 31 percent; 24 percent assigned a D or F. In a related question, the Gallup Poll measured citizens' confidence in schools, compared with their confidence in other important institutions such as churches, the military, banks, newspapers, and big business. Although the schools have not done badly on a comparative basis, the level of "substantial" public confidence in them declined from 58 percent in 1973 to 30 percent in 1983.[6]

One convincing piece of evidence of deterioration in the quality of schooling made headlines in newspapers throughout the country each year during the 1970s: student performance on standardized college entrance exams. Scholastic Aptitude Test (SAT) and American College Test (ACT) scores on verbal and math sections dropped almost annually from 1963 to 1982, below the levels existing at the time of the last declared crisis in education (see Figure 15.1).[7] Declining student performance is particularly disturbing when American students are compared to their peers in other countries, as we have noted.

What's wrong with the American education system? The policy problems widely recognized in the 1980s can be reduced to three major variables: standards, students, and teachers.[8]

Standards

During the 1960s and 1970s American schools suffered from a malady that might be called curriculum drift. Courses designed to teach basic verbal and mathematical skills were de-emphasized while numerous nonessential topics became popular. In the words of *A Nation at Risk,* school curricula were "diffused to the point that they no longer have a central purpose. In effect, we have a cafeteria-style curriculum in which the appetizers and desserts can easily be mistaken for the main courses."[9] For example,

Figure 15.1   Average SAT Verbal and Mathematics Scores,
1963–1988
Average SAT verbal and math scores began a prolonged period of
decline in the early 1960s, but turned upward in 1982. Although the
current trend is not entirely clear, scores seem to be leveling off.

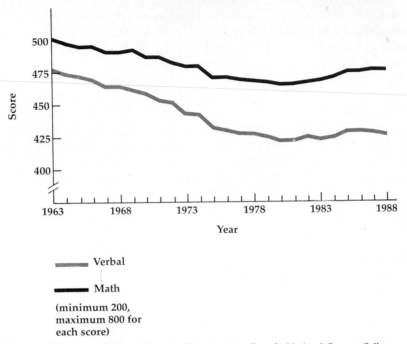

Verbal

Math

(minimum 200,
maximum 800 for
each score)

Source: Data from College Entrance Examination Board, *National Report: College-
Bound Seniors,* as cited in U.S. Department of Education, Center for Statistics,
Digest of Education Statistics, 1988 (Washington, D.C.: U.S. Government Printing
Office, 1988), p. 108.

courses on the secondary school menu included Self-awareness, Who Am I,
Skiing, Sailing, Love and Marriage, and Bachelor Living. Education seemed
to be aimed at helping students feel comfortable with themselves and have a
good time rather than at teaching them basic skills and the ability to think
analytically. Business, military, and university leaders complained about
having to invest millions of dollars in remedial education before ill-prepared
high school graduates were ready to work, serve in the armed forces, or
study.

The authors of *A Nation at Risk* strongly advocated tightening up the
curriculum requirements for all secondary school students to include four
years of English, three each of science, mathematics, and social studies, and
at least one half-year of computer science. College-bound students would
be expected to take two years of a foreign language. In 1982 not even 3

percent of U.S. high school graduates had fulfilled these suggested requirements.

Even more disturbing, the commission pointed out that some 23 million
Americans were functionally illiterate—unable to perform simple tasks of
reading, writing, and comprehension. Around 13 percent of American
seventeen-year-olds were classified in this hapless group. About two-thirds
of all students lacked the ability to solve a math problem involving several
steps, 80 percent could not write a persuasive essay, and 40 percent were
unable to "draw inferences from written material."[10] One shocking conclusion of *A Nation at Risk* was that "for the first time in the history of our
country, the educational skills of one generation will not surpass, will not
equal, will not even approach, those of their parents."[11] As a result, many
students have been graduating from high school prepared for neither college nor the job market. Since it is virtually impossible to argue that the
native intelligence of American youth has declined, considerable blame has
been placed on vacillating educational standards for curricula and courses.

Students

Students themselves have not escaped criticism. They choose to soften up
their curriculum with easy "life-style" courses rather than basic English,
math, science, and social studies. Today's students are said to be poorly
motivated and lazy in comparison to their predecessors. They are faulted for
seeking instant gratification through television, drugs, alcohol, and sex
instead of seriously applying themselves to coursework. In a typical year in
the 1980s, nearly one million students gave up school altogether by dropping out.

Clearly, however, the legal and moral responsibility for providing direction to a young person's life rests with his or her parents. This includes
encouraging the child to complete homework assignments and regulating
television time. The potential contribution of parental involvement in the
educational process was revealed by a six-year study of students in Japan,
Taiwan, and the United States, in which researchers found that American
children registered the lowest scores on math and reading tests principally
because they started the first grade with fewer academic skills than their
Asian counterparts. Japanese and Taiwanese parents gave their youngsters
a head start by regularly working with them at home before they entered
school. Coaching after school helped the Japanese and Taiwanese children
maintain their early advantage.[12] But American parents tend to abdicate to
the schools the responsibility for educating their children. Often they have
little choice; there has been a dramatic jump in the number of single-parent
and two-worker households in recent years, so parents have less time to
spend helping their children.

Teachers

Teachers are the linchpins between students and the process of education. Effective teaching can bestow lifelong learning skills on fortunate students, and poor teaching can result in indifference in good students and dropping out by marginal students. The problem with teaching is twofold. First, for many years the teaching profession declined in terms of the quality of individuals who chose to enter it. Second, teachers believed that their status and conditions of work had dropped substantially. Clearly, one part of the problem is closely related to the other.

The gradual decline in the quality of teachers is partly due to changes in the nature of the work force. Until about twenty-five years ago, most women had few job opportunities besides teaching, nursing, and clerical work. But in the mid-1960s, women began moving into traditionally male-dominated jobs in growing numbers.

In recent years, academically gifted women who once would have chosen the teaching profession were more likely to seek out higher-paying, more prestigious positions in government and the private sector. This meant that less able college graduates elected to become teachers, and in some states a severe shortage of qualified teachers resulted. SAT scores bear this out. Prospective teachers in 1982 earned average scores of 394 on the verbal section and 419 on the math; the national averages were 426 and 467. The fall in teacher quality was cruelly but honestly stated by Albert Shanker, president of the second largest teachers union (the American Federation of Teachers): "For the most part you are getting illiterate, incompetent people who cannot go into any other field."[13] In some situations, school districts have little choice but to hire substandard teachers. For example, Dallas gave a basic competency test over a six-year period to 13,700 applicants for teaching jobs. Only 3,700 passed, but Dallas had to fill 5,000 vacancies. The result was that hundreds of unqualified individuals entered the class-rooms.[14]

Part of the blame must also be placed on university and college education curricula that emphasize "educational methodology" courses, which aim to teach prospective instructors how to teach rather than giving them substantive knowledge of their subject matter. Another reason it has been difficult to find good teachers is that teaching has until recently been a low-wage occupation. The average starting salary was only slightly more than $12,000 in 1982; this compared very unfavorably with other fields for college graduates. Before the salary gains of the mid- to late 1980s, teacher compensation did not keep pace with the cost of living. Between 1973 and 1983 the average teacher lost over 11 percent of his or her purchasing power.[15]

The frustration of teaching is perhaps best illustrated by the responses of teachers when asked to identify the biggest problems public schools face in their community (see Table 15.1). Parents' lack of interest and support comes in first by a wide margin. Another concern is discipline. Disruptive

Table 15.1   Major Problems Facing the Public Schools, as Named by Teachers
and the Public, 1984

Problem	Percentage	
	Teachers	Public
Parents' lack of interest/support	31	5
Lack of proper financial support	21	14
Pupils' lack of interest/truancy	20	4
Lack of discipline	19	27
Problems with administration	10	3
Poor curriculum/poor standards	7	15
Use of drugs	5	18
Low teacher salaries	5	4
Difficulty getting good teachers	4	14
Large schools/overcrowding	4	4
Teachers' lack of interest	4	5
Integration/busing	2	6

Note: Fewer than 5 percent listed any other problem as major.
Source: "The Gallup Poll of Teachers' Attitudes Toward the Public Schools," *Phi Delta Kappan,*
October 1984. Reprinted with permission of *Phi Delta Kappan.*

behavior by students, which is most likely in large schools in urban areas,
spoils the learning environment. Further, more than 100,000 assaults on
teachers have been reported for a single year. Table 15.1 indicates that lack
of student discipline is also the paramount worry of the general public. The
stress created by disruptive classroom situations perhaps helps explain why
more than half of public school teachers in 1984 would not advise young
people to pursue a teaching career.[16]

Because of these and other dissatisfactions, the proportion of incoming
college freshmen declaring an interest in becoming teachers began a steady
decline in 1966. Severe shortages of teachers, especially of mathematics,
science, and foreign languages, developed in the late 1970s and early 1980s.
Meanwhile, the number of schoolchildren began increasing in 1986, following ten years of decline, and this trend is expected to continue until the
"baby-boom echo" leaves the classroom in ten to twenty years. Teacher
resignations and retirements have exacerbated the shortage. Between 1989
and 1994 the United States will require over one million new teachers, but
only 625,000 will be available if current trends continue.[17]

Before reviewing the far-reaching responses of the states and localities to
such critical problems in American public education, let us look at how
intergovernmental relationships have evolved.

Intergovernmental Roles in Education

The responsibility for establishing, supporting, and overseeing public schools is reserved to the states under the Tenth Amendment and specifically provided for in the state constitutions. Day-to-day operating authority is delegated to local governments by all states except Hawaii, which has established its system of public education as an arm of the state. Ninety percent of American primary and secondary school systems are operated by independent school districts, but counties or townships run the schools in some states. Although "local control" is the tradition, the states have always been the dominant policymakers, deciding such important issues as the duration of the school year, curriculum requirements, textbook selection, teacher certification and compensation, minimum graduation requirements, and pupil-teacher ratios. The selection and dismissal of teachers, certain budget decisions, and operating details are carried out locally.

Essentially, this will remain the pattern in the 1990s, although the scope of state involvement is growing substantially and is stronger than ever before, largely because of forceful actions taken to address the education crisis of the 1980s. Centralization of state authority in education policy has always been greatest in the South, where poverty and race relations have called for high levels of state intervention. The tradition of local autonomy is strongest in New England. However, it is difficult to identify a single important school policy issue today that is not subject to state, rather than local, determination.

State and Local Roles

Since around 1965 there has been a steady trend of more state involvement in the public schools, as citizens and policymakers have lost confidence in the schools' ability to provide a quality education. In several states, local school systems have for all practical purposes lost their independence as the state has assumed local responsibilities. Such centralization is happening primarily because local school districts are unable to cope successfully with political and financial pressures.

Political Pressures   Political pressures rose to new heights in the 1960s as teachers, minority groups, and parents made new and controversial demands on their schools. Teachers formed unions and sought to bargain collectively over salaries and working conditions. Minority groups wanted to desegregate all-white schools. Bilingual education became an issue in states with large Hispanic populations. Religious groups fought to keep prayer in the classroom. Many local school boards wilted under the crescendo of demands, and teachers, minority groups, parents, and other parties interested in education policy have taken their demands more and more often to the next highest political level—the governor, the state legislature, the courts, and the state board of education. In this way, school politics, once the province of school boards and professional educators, has evolved into interest group politics at the state level.

Financial Pressures   The second factor behind state centralization has to do with increased financial pressures on the schools. Historically, schools have been funded largely through revenues derived from a tax on property. A school district can assess taxes only on property within its local boundaries, so wealthy districts with a lot of highly valued residential and/or commercial property can afford to finance public schools at high levels, whereas poor districts (which often tax their property at much higher rates than wealthy districts) can raise fewer dollars because of their lower property values. The consequence of financial inequities is that some children receive a better education than others, even though their parents may contribute fewer tax dollars.

There is an important legal footnote to the states' assumption of financial responsibility for public schools. In the case of *Serrano* v. *Priest* (1971), the California Supreme Court declared that inequalities in school district spending resulting from variations in taxable wealth were unconstitutional. The court observed that local control is a "cruel illusion" where poor districts cannot achieve excellence in education because of a low tax base, no matter how highly property is taxed.[18] Therefore, education must be considered a fundamental interest of the state, which means that the state must ensure that expenditures on education are not determined primarily by the tax wealth of the school district.

Following *Serrano*, lawsuits were filed in other states by plaintiffs who sought to have their own property tax–based systems declared unconstitutional. One of these cases, *San Antonio Independent School District* v. *Rodriguez* (1973), made its way to the U.S. Supreme Court. A federal district court had found the Texas school finance system to be unconstitutional under the equal protection clause of the Fourteenth Amendment. However, the Burger Court reversed the lower court, holding that education is not a fundamental right under the Constitution (it is not even mentioned). Although the finance system in Texas resulted in unequal school expenditures, the Court did not find "that such disparities are the products of a system that is so irrational as to be invidiously discriminatory."[19] The issue was thus placed exclusively in the constitutional domain of the states, which would have to rely on their own constitutions to prevent arbitrary circumstances from predetermining the quality of a child's education.

Generally speaking, the states have responded well to the challenge. Since *Rodriguez*, more than thirty state supreme courts have heard cases on educational financing. Around half of them have determined that existing aid schemes were unconstitutional; Kentucky was the most recent, in 1989. All states have made efforts to equalize funding among school districts, usually by applying distribution formulas (the equalization formulas brought up in Chapter 11) for state aid that take property values and property tax effort in individual districts into account. Most increased state financing has been targeted to districts with low property values through "foundation programs," which seek to provide all school districts with a minimum level of funding per pupil while furnishing extra financing to poor districts.[20] From 1969 to 1979, state aid to the schools grew by 44.5 percent in real (noninflated) dollars, substantially surpassing new local and national allocations,[21] and the percentage of total state aid to education exceeded local government contributions for the first time in 1979. Figure 15.2 displays the increasing state revenue contributions for public schools since 1920. Note that local governments' share has plummeted since data were first collected in 1919.

The Impact of Property Tax Cuts   Additional impetus to state assumption of school costs was provided by Proposition 13 in California and by similar legacies of the taxpayer revolt of the late 1970s and early 1980s. Statutory and state constitutional limitations on taxing were typically aimed at the increasingly unpopular property tax. If public schools were to avoid closing

Figure 15.2   Trends in Revenue Sources for Public Elementary and Secondary Education, 1920–1986
Elementary and secondary education have received the greatest portion of revenues from state government since 1979. The national contribution declined markedly during the Reagan years.

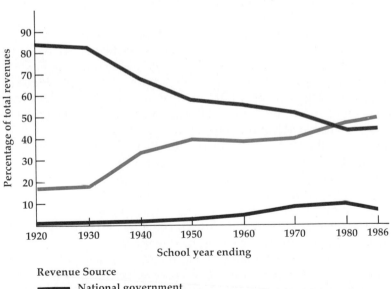

Source: U.S. Department of Education, Center for Statistics, *Digest of Education Statistics, 1988* (Washington, D.C.: U.S. Government Printing Office, 1988), p. 43.

their doors or other draconian measures to adjust to revenue shortfalls, the states had to increase their education contributions. In California, for example, Proposition 13 followed *Serrano* v. *Priest* by seven years. The consequence was a severe erosion of local property tax dollars for public education. The local share of school funding dropped from 70 percent in 1970 to 20 percent in 1982,[22] and the state picked up the difference.

The California case also illustrates an important principle of education policy in the 1980s: state centralization and control follow financial responsibility. A long tradition of local control of schools was displaced as California became the prime education policy decision maker. Local school districts in California and some other states have become mere administrative appendages of the state government.[23]

Remaining Inequities   Although centralization of state control of education and efforts to equalize funding for poor districts have proceeded in all states, inequities continue to exist. A recent study indicates that nine out of ten state aid dollars are distributed on the basis of the number of pupils in a district rather than according to need.[24] Anyone who compares a wealthy suburban school with one in a poor rural district or in an urban ghetto cannot fail to be impressed by the differences in facilities and resources.

Although a great deal of progress has been made and the worst disparities have been eliminated, comparisons of state education spending reveal some abiding inequities. The reason is simple: wealthy states can afford to allocate more money to schools than poor states can. Table 15.2 shows average state expenditures and national rankings for 1988.

Common sense tells us that money is related to the quality of schooling. Modern, well-designed buildings, up-to-date equipment, the latest learning materials, and an adequate heating and cooling system should enhance the quality of education. Schools that can afford to hire the best teachers and maintain low pupil-teacher ratios should be better than those with large classrooms and inexperienced or poorly prepared teaching staff. But research has revealed an astonishing paradox: there is no significant relationship between school resources and student performance.

The first research to reach this conclusion was the so-called Coleman Report in 1966.[25] Sociologist James S. Coleman examined thousands of school situations and discovered that curricula, facilities, class size, expenditures, and other resource factors were not associated with achievement. He *did* find that the family and socioeconomic backgrounds of students influenced performance. For example, black students performed better in predominantly white schools than in predominantly black schools—a finding that later served as the grounds for busing to put an end to school segregation. Coleman's staggering conclusions have been followed by more than 150 related studies. An extensive review of 120 of these determined that only 18 found a statistically significant positive relationship between school expenditures and student performance. The conclusion is that no strong or systematic relationship exists between them.[26]

Table 15.2   Elementary and Secondary School
Expenditures by State, 1988

State	Average expenditures per pupil*	
	Amount	Rank
Alabama	$2,752	49
Alaska	7,038	1
Arizona	3,265	40
Arkansas	2,410	51
California	3,994	26
Colorado	4,359	17
Connecticut	6,141	5
Delaware	4,994	10
District of Columbia	5,643	6
Florida	4,389	16
Georgia	2,939	46
Hawaii	3,894	30
Idaho	2,814	47
Illinois	4,217	20
Indiana	3,616	35
Iowa	3,846	32
Kansas	4,262	19
Kentucky	3,355	38
Louisiana	3,211	41
Maine	4,726	18
Maryland	4,871	13
Massachusetts	5,396	8
Michigan	4,122	22
Minnesota	4,513	15
Mississippi	2,760	48
Missouri	3,566	36

*Based on average daily attendance

Source: U.S. Department of Education, Center for Statistics, *Digest of Education Statistics, 1988* (Washington, D.C.: U.S. Government Printing Office, 1988), p. 140.

If specific factors that affect educational performance can be identified, it will probably be the states that pinpoint them. The 1970s and 1980s were decades in which states led in policymaking, innovation, and research in public education. This impressive growth is unlikely to go much further in the 1990s, however. Once a state achieves an acceptable level of performance throughout its school districts, responsibility and policy activity may

Table 15.2   Elementary and Secondary School
Expenditures by State, 1988 (*cont.*)

State	Average expenditures per pupil*	
	Amount	Rank
Montana	$4,061	24
Nebraska	3,641	34
Nevada	3,829	33
New Hampshire	3,990	27
New Jersey	6,910	2
New Mexico	3,880	31
New York	6,864	4
North Carolina	3,911	28
North Dakota	3,353	39
Ohio	4,019	25
Oklahoma	3,051	45
Oregon	4,574	14
Pennsylvania	5,063	9
Rhode Island	5,456	7
South Carolina	3,075	44
South Dakota	3,159	43
Tennessee	3,189	42
Texas	3,462	37
Utah	2,658	50
Vermont	4,949	12
Virginia	4,145	21
Washington	4,083	23
West Virginia	3,895	29
Wisconsin	4,991	11
Wyoming	6,885	3
U.S. Average	$4,209	—

begin to flow back to the local level. The national government may also upgrade its interest and programmatic support for schools in the years ahead.

The National Role

The United States government has traditionally played a minimal role in primary and secondary education, especially when compared with most other countries, where public education is treated as a national responsibility. For instance, the first grant of money for education came only in 1917, when the Smith-Hughes Act financed vocational education in secondary schools. Much later, the National Defense Education Act provided funds to improve math, science, and foreign-language education following the humiliation of the Soviet Sputnik launching.

The national role was substantially enlarged during the 1960s and 1970s, primarily through the Elementary and Secondary Education Act of 1965 (ESEA), which emerged after years of negotiations among groups interested in public education. The ESEA established a direct national subsidy for education, providing funds to virtually every school district in the United States. Amounts were allocated for library acquisitions, audiovisual materials, teachers' aides, and compensatory programs for children of poor families and for the mentally and physically handicapped. ESEA monies were originally distributed in accordance with a formula that favored wealthy states, even though the program was considered to be an important component in the Johnson administration's War on Poverty.[27] Later the formula was amended to the advantage of poor states. Parochial (religious) schools also benefited from ESEA funding, although no funds were provided for religious materials or courses or for teacher salaries.

During this period the national government assumed policy leadership in education. Matching grants encouraged states and localities to experiment with programs, and research findings, statistics, and new policy information were disseminated by the National Institute of Education and the National Center for Education Statistics. Other national entities furnished consulting and technical aid to local schools and state education departments. The national commitment to public schools received a symbolic boost in 1979, when the Carter administration created the U.S. Department of Education. (Education previously held "office" status as part of the Department of Health, Education, and Welfare.)

These new commitments brought the national share of total school expenditures from 4.4 percent in 1960 to 9 percent in 1980. Ronald Reagan unsuccessfully sought to abolish the U.S. Department of Education, but did succeed in drastically cutting national aid to education. By 1985 the U.S. government's proportion of education expenditures had declined to 6.4 percent, the lowest level in over twenty years (see Figure 15.2). The president of the largest teachers' union, Mary Futrell of the National Education Association, echoed *A Nation at Risk* by accusing the Reagan administration of "educational disarmament."[28]

This de-emphasis of education policy by the national government, combined with the growing inability of local school districts to confront successfully the school problems plaguing them, has forced the states to fill a policy vacuum. With determination, the states have accepted the difficult challenge of school reform. So far they have proved equal to the task.

Actors in Education Policy

The proliferation of independent school districts in the latter part of the nineteenth century was accompanied by intensive politicization. School districts in big cities and rural areas alike were as likely to hire teachers and principals on the basis of patronage as for professional competence. Reformers (mostly professional educators) struggled to remove partisan politics from the public schools by electing school boards on a nonpartisan, at-large basis, and by giving the primary responsibility for running school systems to professionals.[29] These efforts were successful, but a new type of politics arose as teachers, school administrators, and state-level education actors began to dominate policy decisions.

First let us consider the "education establishment": the teachers, local school boards, chief state school officers, the state board of education, and the state department of education. Next we will turn to the new power-wielders in school policy: the governors, legislators, and judges.

The Education Establishment

In the past, the members of the education establishment tried to dominate school policymaking by resolving issues themselves, then presenting a united front before legislative bodies and the governor. They constituted a very powerful political coalition that managed to win substantial financial commitments to the schools. Because of the political pressures we have already mentioned, however, the education establishment is fractured today in most states.

Teachers   Teachers had little power or influence outside the classroom until they began to organize into professional associations and unions. Before the 1960s, teacher organizations, particularly the National Education Association (NEA), focused their attention on school improvement rather than on the economic well-being of teachers themselves. Teachers and administrators maintained a common front before the state legislature. Gradually, however, a newer teacher organization began to challenge the dominance and docility of the NEA, especially in large cities. This rival organization, the American Federation of Teachers (AFT), openly referred to itself as a labor union and struggled to win collective bargaining rights for teachers. When the AFT was elected in 1961 as the bargaining agent for teachers in New York City, the handwriting was on the blackboard. Both the NEA and the AFT lobbied for state legislation permitting collective bargaining in the late 1960s and 1970s and concentrated their efforts on winning better pay and working conditions for teachers. Today over two-thirds of the nation's schoolteachers belong to one of these groups. Many NEA locals, however, primarily in southern and western states, still do not engage in collective bargaining, either because they choose not to or because the state restricts them legally.

Teacher militancy accompanied unionization. Strikes and other job actions disrupted many local school districts as teachers battled for more money, fewer nonteaching duties, and related demands. The explosion of teacher unions forever fragmented the education lobby in most states, as teachers sought to look out for their own interests rather than the interests of school administrators. Generally speaking, teachers have done an effective job of representing themselves through the NEA and AFT, enjoying strength through numbers. They operate through political action committees, professional lobbyists, campaign contributions, and individual efforts, such as telephoning local legislators or working for the election of a political candidate who is known to be a friend of education. All things considered, teachers are the most influential of education interest groups at the state level.[30]

Local School Boards   Another member of the education establishment, the local school board (LSB), is a legislative body that is responsible for administering public education at the local level. There are approximately 16,000 of these local bodies in the United States, with around 97,000 members. Local school boards are made up of laypeople, not representatives of the professional education community. Board members are elected by voters in independent school districts in most states, although some or all of them are appointed by local legislative delegations in several southern states. The average board size is five to seven members.

The original American ideal of local control of public schools lodged its faith in local school boards, which were popularly elected and therefore responsive to citizens' opinions and points of view. In fact, their true authority has never equaled the myth of local control. Recently, the influence of LSBs has reached very low levels indeed. They still determine school taxes and levy them on real estate in the district, and they also continue to hire district superintendents of education and school administrators, approve teacher appointments, determine building and facility needs, set salary levels for certain personnel, and debate program needs. However, such issues are increasingly influenced by state standards and regulations. Moreover, LSBs often rely on their appointed superintendents to make such decisions. In one case, the management of a public school system has been turned over to a private university. In 1989 Boston University contracted to run the Chelsea, Massachusetts, schools after the Chelsea school board failed to deal successfully with the system's problems.

The decline of school board power is due to two factors. First, the triumph of education professionals (until quite recently, at least) effectively prevented the boards from making many policy decisions. Most boards defer to the expertise of superintendents, except in situations that generate strong public interest or controversy. Collective bargaining by administrators and teacher organizations often determines such matters as teacher compensation, working conditions, and even curriculum questions.

Second, local school boards suffer from low levels of citizen interest. A nationwide study by the Institute for Educational Leadership discovered "deep public apathy and indifference" to LSBs, "abysmally low" turnouts for board elections, and widespread ignorance of what LSBs are supposed to be doing.[31] About the only event that focuses citizen attention on LSBs is the occasional bond or tax referendum that threatens to raise property taxes in the school district. Such referenda were frequently voted down during the 1960s and 1970s but had better luck in the 1980s.

Other Policy Actors   Also known as the state education agency, the state board of education (SBE) exists in all states except Wisconsin. It exercises general supervision over all primary and secondary schools. The SBE members, ranging from three in Mississippi to twenty-four in Texas, are appointed by the governor (thirty-two states), popularly elected (twelve), elected by the legislature (two), elected by local school boards (one), or composed of *ex officio* members (two), who hold the position by virtue of some other office.[32]

SBEs are administrative boards, but most of them also make policy and budget recommendations to the governor and legislature. With few exceptions, however, they are not significant policy actors. They tend to lack political clout, policy expertise, and public visibility.[33] Like local school boards, state boards of education defer to the authority and expertise of another policy actor, in this case the chief state school officer (CSSO).

This person, known as the state superintendent of schools or the commissioner of education in some states, establishes and enforces standards for local school curricula, teacher certification, and certain other matters and provides technical and other assistance to the schools. She or he is appointed by the state board of education in twenty-six states, popularly elected on a statewide ballot in nineteen, and appointed by the governor in five states. Although the formal relationship between the CSSO and the state board of education varies, nearly all CSSOs serve as executive officers and professional advisers to their state boards of education.[34] Recently, however, as governors and state legislatures have increasingly provided policy leadership for the schools, their influence has declined.[35]

The state department of education (SDE) is responsible for furnishing administrative and technical support to the CSSO and the SBE. It also administers national and state aid programs for public schools. The state department of education is almost exclusively the habitat of education professionals.

Until the national government entered the school policy arena with ESEA and other programs in the 1960s, the SDEs were understaffed and underutilized. National and state financial support in the 1980s resulted in SDEs that are larger, much more competent and sophisticated, and more powerful. They have taken on the difficult job of monitoring the state education reforms of the 1980s, and they have significantly increased their capacities for program evaluation, data collection, and research.

The New Policy Leaders

Financial and political pressures on the education establishment, coinciding with a loss of public confidence in the schools, resulted in fragmentation of the coalition of actors described above. Simultaneously, state-level education actors were increasing their interest in school issues and their capacity to respond to them, and governors and legislatures were adding staff and augmenting their ability to collect data and conduct research. The strengthened state departments of education have now become handmaidens of the governors and legislatures. Education policymaking today orbits around state government rather than local education professionals.

Governors   In the past, governors were weak participants in school policymaking. They rarely exercised leadership on education issues, but left such matters in the hands of the education establishment. As school politics became energized in the 1960s, however, so did the governors, primarily because the American people tend to turn to their chief executives in times of crisis.

Recent gubernatorial attention to education began with school finance reform. Changing the means of funding the schools demanded major alterations in tax policy—a highly charged issue in any state, given an extra jolt by the fact that education makes up the largest portion of state and local spending.

Today, state chief executives are deeply involved in all major aspects of education policymaking. Education issues often receive a lot of attention during campaigns, in state-of-the-state addresses, and throughout a governor's term of office. During the first half of the 1980s, education completely dominated governors' policy agendas in quite a few states, particularly in the South: the bulk of governors' legislative efforts in Tennessee, Texas, Mississippi, Georgia, Arkansas, and South Carolina were directed toward education reform programs, and other pressing issues were placed on the back burner. This consuming passion has cooled somewhat in recent years, but education policy remains the most important "perennial issue" in most states.

In formulating, lobbying for, and implementing education policy, the governors rely heavily on their staff. Many governors have special divisions of education. Staff members facilitate the flow of information to and from the governor's office and the desks of other key education policymakers. They analyze information from all levels of government, in and out of state, and from national organizations. They also draft proposed legislation, lobby legislators and education groups, and attempt to influence public opinion on education issues.

Governors also rely on the education establishment for information and support. Chief state school officers provide helpful advice in some states, as does the state department of education.[36] Private-sector participation is obtained through education task forces that meet to study problems and issue recommendations to the governor. The most successful governors have managed to weave delicate coalitions among all significant education policy actors in order to enact substantial reform programs.

State Legislatures   Legislatures have always had the final responsibility for enacting broad educational policy and for state funding of public schools. They were the leading state policy actors until governors upstaged them, and it is still on legislative turf where the critical policy battles are fought. In a few states, such as Florida and California, legislatures continue to dominate education policy.

Lobbyists for the education establishment are quite active in the statehouse, but their influence has diminished as issue conflicts have precluded a united front. Numerous other interests, including minority groups, the handicapped, and the economically disadvantaged, also receive a hearing from legislators. As national funding tailed off during the 1980s, such groups increasingly turned their sights on state legislatures. One writer has suggested that these groups resemble an education shopping mall, with "sophisticated specialty shops each catering to a small segment of the populace," including female students, the gifted, blacks, Hispanics, native Americans, and more.[37] Sometimes the mall becomes rather boisterous and crowded, as competing shoppers fight for limited public education merchandise.

Although governors are the education policy leaders in most states, legislatures have been rapidly developing their capabilities. They have added education staff specialists, enhanced their research abilities, and extended oversight efforts. Two important legislative contributions are ensuring that reform laws are fully implemented and ensuring that education policy actors are held accountable to the people.

Courts   Federal courts, especially the U.S. Supreme Court, are important factors in public education. They have issued rulings on a variety of issues affecting students, such as censorship of school newspapers, personal grooming standards, female participation in sports programs, student discipline, and school prayer. Federal courts imposed desegregation policies on public schools through a series of decisions beginning with *Brown* v. *Board of Education of Topeka* (1954), which declared that racial segregation violated the Fourteenth Amendment's equal protection clause.[38] Court-ordered busing to achieve school desegregation was mandated in *Swann* v. *Charlotte–Mecklenberg County Schools* (in North Carolina) in 1971 and in other decisions involving districts that had practiced government-approved racial segregation.[39] These decisions, and the subsequent busing, were highly controversial, and in many places contributed to "white flight" to the suburbs. In some cities, like Boston, court-ordered busing led to violent protests.

POLITICS AND POLICY 15.1
South Carolina: A Model in Education Reform

In the past, one could take any statistical measure of quality in primary and secondary education, rank the states according to this measure, and find South Carolina at or near the bottom of the list. Per capita expenditures, pupil-teacher ratios, dropout rates, percentage of state adult population completing high school, teacher salaries, standardized test scores—the state did miserably on all of these until the mid-1970s, when education finance reforms began to have a slight impact. In 1984, South Carolina scored top marks in the nation on education improvement.

The state's Education Improvement Act was heralded in a Rand Corporation study as the most comprehensive of all state education reforms and a model for the nation, and was singled out for special praise in 1986 by the authors of *A Nation at Risk.* Largely through the leadership of a popular, talented, and determined governor, a coalition of business leaders, education groups, and junior legislators formulated a carefully crafted bill that was eventually adopted almost wholesale by the state legislature, in spite of strong early opposition. A one-cent increase in South Carolina's sales tax was earmarked to pay for the program costs.

Teachers received an immediate 16 percent across-the-board raise, and future salaries were adjusted to the average for southeastern states. Three merit pay plans are being pilot-tested; the most promising will be implemented. School districts that show the most improvement in

State courts, too, have stimulated and even ordered changes in education policy. As we have noted, a number of state supreme courts have mandated school finance reform to attain more equity in funding public education. State courts are also being asked to resolve numerous legal disagreements spawned by education reforms. It is likely that the role of these courts as education policymakers will continue to grow during the 1990s, since it is often only through the legal system that individuals and groups representing minority positions can capture the attention of top policymakers.

Educational Innovation in the States

In the short time since *A Nation at Risk* called national attention to the acute need for educational reforms, the states have responded on a large scale.

test scores, attendance rates, and other measures receive special grants. Districts that do not meet the new minimum standards are declared "impaired" by the state board of education and are subject to an administrative takeover until performance is up to par. Each school is assessed in an annual "report card" from the state.

South Carolina has begun an impressive climb in the state rankings on quality of education. Absenteeism has declined by around 30 percent; in fact, South Carolina had the highest school attendance rate in the country in 1985. In that year too, for the first time, state tenth-graders scored above the average in a national comprehensive test of basic skills. The number of first-graders passing a readiness test has jumped 14 percent, with the greatest gains registered by black students. South Carolina led the nation in gains in SAT scores from 1982 to 1988,

and high school graduation rates rose significantly. Enrollment in special programs for gifted and talented students has more than doubled.

Although South Carolina had further to go than most other states, its school improvements have been remarkable. Much remains to be done, and continued full funding of the Education Improvement Act is called into question by the legislature each year. But as of 1989, the Palmetto State had risen to the head of the class in education reform.

Source: Richard C. Kearney and Terry K. Peterson, "Public Education in South Carolina: The Struggle from Mediocrity to Excellence," in Charlie B. Tyer and S. Jane Massey, eds., *Government in the Palmetto State: Perspectives and Issues* (Columbia: Bureau of Governmental Research and Service, University of South Carolina, 1988), pp. 85–99. Copyright (1988) by the Institute of Public Affairs, University of South Carolina.

Some three hundred task forces have thoroughly studied school problems and issued recommendations for resolving them. Most of these recommendations have been enacted into law. Politics and Policy 15.1 relates the progress South Carolina has made.

First of all, the state share of school funding has risen dramatically. Many states have raised taxes specifically for aid to education. State support for schools jumped by more than 49 percent ($22 billion) from 1978 to 1983, and by another 31 percent from 1983 to 1986.[40] A broad and powerful coalition of state and local elected officials, professional educators, parents, and business interests has been important in the reform drive. Improvement in education is a bipartisan issue; Democrats and Republicans agree that the economic future of the United States depends on the quality of schooling. As the former Republican governor of Tennessee, Lamar

Alexander, put it, "Republicans always conceded the education issue to the Democrats, but that's changed . . . today you can't talk the Republican language of economic development without talking about education."[41]

A remarkable turnabout in the attitude of the American taxpayer has also been observed. After beating down school funding referenda all over the country during the 1970s, and enacting taxation and expenditure limitations that further deprived public education of needed resources, taxpayers became much more willing to support spending for the schools in the 1980s. In some states, such as South Carolina, they enthusiastically endorsed substantial tax increases for education. At the same time, they remained very concerned about how this money was being spent. One opinion researcher called the 1980s the "era of educational accountability."[42]

The states have moved forward with innovations in the three critical areas of standards, students, and teachers. Every state has recorded remarkable program achievements in at least one of these categories, and a majority have implemented reforms in all three areas.

Standards

Standards have been raised in virtually every state. Curriculum and graduation requirements have been strengthened, instructional time and the length of the school day have been increased, steps have been taken to minimize overcrowding, minimum competency tests in the basic skills have been introduced, and special programs have been developed to encourage gifted students.

For example, crowded school districts in some locales have begun experimenting with the rather radical concept of year-round schools. Los Angeles, Houston, Las Vegas, and other Sunbelt cities have adopted this idea, less to improve the quality of schooling than to ease overcrowding and save money. Typically, students are organized into four groups, which attend classes for forty-five, sixty, or ninety days at a time, then go on break for two or three weeks. Class schedules within grades overlap during a calendar year. Up to one-third more students can attend a school under such a plan. Teachers seem to like the concept, because classes are smaller and they do not have to reteach as much after the shorter vacation periods. An important point is that students appear to respond well to year-round schooling too, by learning more material at a faster rate. However, the plan does cause certain difficulties: air-conditioning may be needed, teachers have to give up summer jobs, and maintenance on buildings and equipment becomes difficult to schedule. Staggered vacations also can interfere with sports, extracurricular activities, and family vacations.[43]

Minimum competency testing for basic skills has been another widely adopted reform. More than forty states test students at several grade levels in order to monitor progress in the basics, and at least twenty-five now

Team teaching is being tried in a number of schools, including Boston's Timilty School, to create a better environment for learning.

require students to pass a competency test before graduating from high school. The tests can also be used to identify outstanding student achievement, as in California and New York, or to diagnose students who need remedial instruction, as in South Carolina and Texas.[44] Gifted students are singled out for special opportunities in several states. The North Carolina School of Science and Mathematics, established in 1980, places around 475 talented high school juniors and seniors in a college campus setting. The state pays all operating costs for the school—$6.2 million in 1986 ($10,000 per student). Students are expected to balance high levels of academic work with weekly chores and community service.[45] Similar state schools for promising high school students have been established in Louisiana, Illinois, South Carolina, Texas, and elsewhere.[46]

Students

Students, of course, are the intended beneficiaries of the improvements and strengthening of standards. In general, expectations for student academic performance and classroom behavior have been raised, and preliminary results indicate that the reforms are having their intended effect. SAT scores

POLITICS AND POLICY 15.2
Voucher Plans: Privatization for the Schools?

For more than a decade, conservatives have promoted the adoption of an education voucher system. Although specific plans vary, most would give parents a voucher, or check, to spend each year on primary and secondary schooling for their children. They could use the voucher in public schools, where no additional payments would be required, or for partial payment of private school tuition.

In theory, parents could freely match the needs of their children with the most suitable mix of programs available. An artistically inclined child could go to a school with a strong arts program, a marginal student could be placed in an institution emphasizing basic skills, a mechanically inclined student could learn a trade, and so on. Also, in theory, a voucher system would encourage healthy competition between schools as each sought to win its fair share (or more) of the community's vouchers.

One implicit purpose of a voucher plan is to promote private schools. This provokes a hostile reaction from liberals and the entire education establishment. Albert Shanker, president of the American Federation of Teachers, harshly attacked a voucher proposal from the Reagan administration by suggesting that Reagan was "bent on virtually eliminating public schools and turning those

in 1985 showed the biggest nationwide gain since 1963, with verbal scores rising five points and math scores up by four points. This came in spite of the fact that the number of test-takers increased, which should depress average scores somewhat, as more marginal students participate. However, since 1985 SAT math scores have leveled out and verbal scores have declined slightly. (See Figure 15.1 again.) Scores for 1988–89 followed this trend, with the average math scores unchanged from the year before at 476 and average verbal scores down one point to 427. Further improvements in test scores do not seem likely without new attention to the problems in education.[47]

Student classroom behavior has been a target of reformers in many states. Strict discipline codes are being enforced, as are stronger attendance policies. In especially difficult school settings, police officers, closed-circuit television monitors, and other devices help maintain order. Most of the states that have adopted more stringent discipline policies in the past few years have made it easier to remove troublemakers from the classroom and to expel them.

classrooms into a wasteland for the poor, minorities, and the difficult to educate." In this view, vouchers would create a dual system of education in which the children of the disadvantaged would be corraled in public schools while the better-off enjoyed subsidized private schooling (since vouchers would defray only a portion of private tuition, poor children would still be unlikely to attend). The children most in need of exceptional schooling would suffer most.

The alleged benefits of a voucher plan have been criticized as illusory. Parents would exercise greater freedom of choice in selecting a school for their child, but how many parents actually understand the child's educational needs? Further, the consequences of increased competition are un-known. It could damage the quality and availability of public education instead of being helpful.

Although a nationally funded voucher system is not likely to pass Congress while the country has an enormous budget deficit, at least three states (Colorado, Minnesota, and South Dakota) are experimenting with their own versions. Rather than offering a true voucher, these states provide a state income tax credit or a deduction for private school tuition along with a choice of schools.

Sources: Michael Krashinsky, "Why Education Vouchers May Be Bad Economics," *Teachers College Record* 88 (Winter 1986): 139–51; Edwin G. West, "An Economic Rationale for Public Schools: The Search Continues," *Teachers College Record* 88 (Winter 1986): 152–62; and Mary Anne Raywid, "Public Choice, Yes; Vouchers, No!" *Phi Delta Kappan* 68 (June 1987): 762–69.

Incentives for regular, punctual attendance are being offered in many locales. For example, Boston, Baltimore, and Los Angeles reduce truancy and dropout rates by guaranteeing a job or admission to college to all graduating seniors with a minimum grade point average and regular attendance (Los Angeles specifies a 2.5 average and 95 percent attendance). Similar programs are being experimented with elsewhere in an effort to keep in school some of the 700,000 students who drop out each year, at an estimated annual cost of $77 billion in lost tax revenues and increased expenditures associated with welfare, unemployment, and crime. The participation of business makes this kind of program possible. Firms can set aside jobs for new graduates, offer placement services, and even teach students how to dress and act in the world of work.[48] West Virginia and several other states have chosen a punitive approach, by denying or suspending driver's licenses of high school dropouts.[49] Another idea to improve student performance and participation is to issue vouchers that would allow parents and students to choose a school. This very controversial proposal is examined in Politics and Policy 15.2.

Teachers

Teachers have been the beneficiaries (or victims, depending on one's point of view) of the most extensive and far-reaching educational reforms of the 1980s. They have universally welcomed higher pay, improved fringe benefits, and more opportunities for professional improvement. They have been less pleased with teacher merit pay schemes and competency testing.

After falling behind in real dollar terms during the 1970s, teacher salaries have begun to catch up with the cost of living. They increased 33 percent in current dollars and 9 percent in inflation-controlled dollars between 1980 and 1985. The comparable figures for all workers with college degrees were 18 percent and 5 percent, respectively.[50] Variations among the states continue to be rather pronounced, in response to differences in the cost of living, labor market conditions, and other factors (see Table 15.3). In 1987 Alaska teachers earned an average salary of $43,970; those in South Dakota averaged $18,781.

Teacher Shortages   Unfortunately, critical shortages of qualified teachers for math and science courses continue to exist in virtually all states, and projections of the total need for classroom teachers in the 1990s indicate even worse problems in teacher supply. Vacancies were expected to exceed greatly the supply of new teachers in states like Florida, which needs 11,500 more teachers by the year 2000 but expects to graduate only 1,000 from its higher education institutions.

The states are experimenting with several strategies to relieve teacher shortfalls. Most are taking steps to entice former teachers and education majors who are working in other fields back into the classroom. Others are setting up streamlined systems to certify noneducation majors. Several states (Connecticut, Maine, Oregon) no longer require teachers to be education majors, and accept regular academic majors instead. One particularly promising pool of new teachers consists of people who have retired early from military service, business, or government. Some school districts cast their recruiting nets amazingly far: Atlanta recruits math and science teachers from Belgium, and New York City fills teacher vacancies by hiring in Spain and Puerto Rico.

Not only the quantity but the quality of teachers needs improvement. Recall that average SAT scores of prospective teachers have lagged behind those of other college students. Empirical evidence indicates that states offering high teacher salaries attract a larger number of bright college students into education careers than states with low salaries do.[51] Other material incentives can be helpful as well. More than thirty-eight states offer special scholarships and loans to attract college students into the teaching profession. Kentucky, for example, instituted a program in 1982 that provided loans for room, board, tuition, and fees for students committing to teaching math or science in Kentucky schools. For each year they teach, the state pays back one year's loan and interest.

Table 15.3   Estimated Average Annual Salary of Teachers in Public Elementary and Secondary Schools, by State: 1986–1987

State	Salary	State	Salary
Alabama	$23,500	Montana	$23,206
Alaska	43,970	Nebraska	22,063
Arizona	25,972	Nevada	26,960
Arkansas	19,904	New Hampshire	22,011
California	31,219	New Jersey	28,718
Colorado	27,387	New Mexico	23,977
Connecticut	28,902	New York	32,000
Delaware	27,467	North Carolina	23,775
District of Columbia	33,797	North Dakota	21,284
Florida	23,785	Ohio	26,288
Georgia	24,200	Oklahoma	22,060
Hawaii	26,815	Oregon	26,690
Idaho	21,469	Pennsylvania	27,422
Illinois	28,238	Rhode Island	31,079
Indiana	26,083	South Carolina	23,190
Iowa	22,603	South Dakota	18,781
Kansas	23,427	Tennessee	22,627
Kentucky	22,612	Texas	24,588
Louisiana	20,054	Utah	23,035
Maine	21,257	Vermont	21,835
Maryland	28,893	Virginia	25,473
Massachusetts	28,410	Washington	27,527
Michigan	31,500	West Virginia	21,446
Minnesota	28,340	Wisconsin	27,976
Mississippi	19,447	Wyoming	28,103
Missouri	23,468		
U.S. Average	$26,551		

Source: U.S. Department of Education, Center for Statistics, Digest of Education Statistics, 1988 (Washington, D.C.: U.S. Government Printing Office, 1988), p. 73.

Merit Plans   A controversial approach to keeping good teachers on the job is to reward them with higher pay and professional status through various merit plans. **Merit pay plans** assess teacher performance in the classroom and grant larger salary increases to the best performers. **Career ladders** provide several promotional steps for teachers. Those who are promoted up the ladder receive higher professional status and substantial pay increases. Tennessee, Texas, and several other states are experimenting with this approach.

Merit pay plans and career ladders are criticized by teachers when they feel that the evaluation procedure that determines promotions and pay hikes is not fair. If principals do the ratings, they might unduly reward their personal favorites and sycophants. Where teachers are included on evaluation committees, acceptance of career ladder and merit pay plans is much more likely. In Arizona's career ladder plan, introduced in fifteen school districts in 1988, teachers are evaluated by principals and fellow teachers. Student test performance is also taken into account. Evaluating teacher performance is not an exact science, but multiple measures and teacher participation help make the process more equitable.

The goal of improving the quality of teaching is to attract and keep better people while weeding out the incompetent, unqualified, and uninterested. Teacher competency testing of those seeking to enter the profession is authorized in thirty-five states. Arkansas became the first state to require basic skills tests of working teachers in 1983. Texas and Georgia soon followed suit. Not surprisingly, subjecting certified teachers to competency testing is not accepted cheerfully by the teaching profession.

The Continuing Challenge of Public Education

The wave of school reform sweeping across the states during the 1980s represents the single greatest state policy achievement of the past several decades. The states have linked their plans for economic development to excellence in education, providing the sort of national direction and leadership once thought to be possible only through efforts of the national government. Nowhere is the vitality, innovation, and capability of the states in better evidence than in education policy.

But we should not be overly generous in our praise as yet. A wide gap separates policy enactment from policy implementation. Several more years must pass before we can accurately gauge the consequences of new state programs. It will take a tremendous act of political will and much hard work to bring to fruition the educational improvement goals represented in state legislation. We cannot pass well-meaning laws, then smugly walk away from them, expecting automatic implementation.

Putting state education reforms into practice requires the enthusiastic cooperation of teachers, school administrators, superintendents, students, and parents. The unfinished portrait for educational excellence has been framed by governors, legislatures, and the state education community. The local schools must now fill in the details. The states must encourage innovation and creative thinking at the local level, while maintaining standards and accountability.

Summary

In spite of a crisis in public education, for the past twenty years the national government has played a diminished role in public education finance and policymaking, while the state role has grown. Education is the single most important, and costly, function performed by state and local government.

The activities of the education lobby and intergovernmental actors in this important policy field largely determine policy outcomes. A wave of reform in the 1980s swept all state education systems into a richness of innovation and change unequalled in any other policy area. The basic characteristics of the reforms pertain to standards, students, and teachers.

Key Terms

Career ladder A merit plan in which high-performing teachers are promoted up several career steps, each involving an increase in status and pay.

Merit pay plan A merit plan that seeks to reward high-performing teachers with special pay increases.

16

Economic Development

Regional Differences in Economic Prosperity
New England/The South/The Midwest/The West

Approaches to Economic Development

Issues in Economic Development
Do State and Local Government Initiatives Make
Much Difference?/Does Government Spend Too
Much?/Does Government Spend Fairly?

Tools of Economic Development Policy
Taxation and Regulation/Government
Intervention

Competition and Cooperation

State Policy Development and Implementation
The Politics of Economic Development/Blue-
Ribbon Panels, Task Forces, and Advisory
Boards/Economic Development Agencies/Public-
Private Partnerships

Current Initiatives
Strategic Planning/High-Technology
Development/Small-Business Incubators/
Enterprise Zones/International Trade Promotion

Cities and Development
Local Initiatives/Deal Making/Growth Problems

The Implications of Economic Development Policy

State was pitted against state during the late 1980s in competition for the superconducting super collider (SSC) project, the largest single construction project ever conceived, with a price tag in the $4.5 to $6 billion range.[1] Twenty-five states fought for the chance to host this huge atom smasher, considered by many to be the high-tech prize of the century. The winner, Texas, expects the SSC to launch its economy into the stratosphere, and with good reason. Thousands of jobs in both construction and operation of the facility will be created, and the SSC will also pump millions of dollars into Texas.

The competition for the SSC project is an example of **economic development,** a hot topic in state and local government. These governments adopt policies, enact laws, create programs, and spend money in its name. Although there is no single definition of economic development, it traditionally has meant increases in per capita income and community investment. Cities and states with higher per capita incomes and higher levels of capital investment are considered more economically developed than their counterparts, and this translates into ample employment opportunities and an adequate tax base. Others define economic development more broadly, to include both the social well-being and the material well-being of a community.[2] Whatever the definition, economic performance is a major contributor to the resurgence of nonnational governments.

Regional Differences in Economic Prosperity

The United States continues to be a nation of diverse regional economies.[3] Regional prosperity has depended in the past on the fortunes of specific industries; for example, when domestic automobile production was riding high, so was the Midwest, and when it slowed, the whole region felt the effects. The 1980s, a decade marked by a growing trade imbalance, an unprecedented national budget deficit, and a drop in interest rates, saw various results in the different regions of the country.[4]

Within a region, states and communities vary in two important and related ways. First, they have different economic structures. Although the primary components in most local economies are services, manufacturing, and retail employment, communities have different proportions of these components. A city in which 25 percent of the work force is engaged in manufacturing is different from one in which manufacturing accounts for 10 percent of employment. This produces the second variation: states and communities face different economic conditions. Some jurisdictions have been widely affected by the nationwide decline in manufacturing, whereas others have felt a negligible effect. Some places are enjoying an economic boom because of the current emphasis on high-technology research and development, whereas in others, high tech has caused barely a ripple.

New England

The New England area enjoyed a remarkable economic surge in the 1980s.[5] One explanation for this is market factors—New England had the right mixture of industries and labor supply for the times. Another explanation credits state governments with creating a strong investment climate. Regardless of what is responsible, the critical question is whether New England's economic boom can be sustained.[6]

Massachusetts led the New England renaissance. The Boston area in particular has become a haven for entrepreneurs, especially those engaged in high technology. The state has encouraged this by creating development finance programs that provide capital to entrepreneurs. In addition, Massachusetts has actively sought to redirect economic growth to areas that have lagged behind the rest of the state.[7] This and other initiatives encouraged by Governor Michael Dukakis have been dubbed "creating the future."[8]

The South

In the South, economic indicators were problematic during the 1980s.[9] The Atlantic seaboard areas and large communities enjoyed an extended period of prosperity, but the oil-rich states of Louisiana, Oklahoma, and Texas and rural areas with agricultural economies found prosperity elusive. To boost their economies, southern states have engaged in industrial recruitment and pursued high-technology firms ("smokestack chasing" and "chip chasing," respectively).

Tennessee is one southern state that has been successful in promoting economic development. The state has relied on two tactics: attracting manufacturing branch plants, headquarters, and distribution facilities and improving basic public services.[10] It has been especially adept at recruiting Japanese firms. The personal salesmanship abilities of Governor Lamar Alexander, who served from 1979 to 1987, are thought to be the reason for many of Tennessee's economic coups.[11]

The Midwest

In the Midwest, the 1980s saw a continuation of a dramatic economic transformation.[12] The staples of the region's economy, manufacturing and agriculture, have been under siege. Most analysts identify the emergence of a global economy, lack of innovation, and a change in the national government's spending priorities as factors that contributed to the region's economic decline. How long this transformation will take is unclear. Depending on which statistics are used, researchers claim either that the region is trapped in a downward spiral or that it is on the brink of an economic recovery. One promising signal is that in the late 1980s, regional increases in manufacturing employment outpaced those in the nation as a whole.[13]

Michigan, one of the hardest-hit midwestern states, responded to its economic downturn aggressively. It abandoned the approach of "let's try to maintain what we've got" for a more hopeful strategy of "let's try to create new industries and enterprises."[14] The focus on innovation and investment produced immediate, although limited, results. Other states in the region are now trying similar tactics.

The West

In many areas of the West, the economy in the 1980s was robust.[15] Steady job growth was bolstered by a substantial increase in defense-related spending. But other areas, especially the northern group of mountain states, did not fare as well. These states depend on sectors of the economy that were less healthy: energy, mining, and agriculture.

Even in the state that is considered to be a microcosm of the nation—California—there are indications of economic vulnerability. One study described California's economy as "a fine luxury car cruising down the freeway with red warning lights on the dashboard."[16] The enduring competitiveness of the state's industries and the maturation of its economy are potential problems.[17] California's growth rate has slowed and the state government, like so many others, has begun a campaign to promote innovation and entrepreneurship.

Approaches to Economic Development

Governments devise elaborate strategies to promote economic development within their boundaries. These take three forms: (1) maintaining and retaining existing industries and firms; (2) attracting industries and firms from other states; and (3) creating new industries and enterprises. Given global economic transformations, simply pursuing the first strategy in isolation is not enough. Retaining existing economic activity does not generate enough growth, so states also engage in the second and third strategies: attraction and creation.

A historical example makes the point quite clearly. During the Depression, individual communities frequently offered grants and concessions to support private commercial and industrial ventures. Mississippi, an exceedingly poor state, was among the first to create a statewide program of industrial recruitment. Under its Balance Agriculture with Industry (BAWI) plan, local governments could issue bonds to finance the construction or purchase of facilities for relocating industry.[18] Its subsidies to industry gave Mississippi an edge in industrial recruitment.

More recently, many states have emphasized creation strategies. Innovation and entrepreneurship are the critical activities in creation, and individuals and firms with new ideas, products, and techniques are offered developmental support. Frequently, these innovators need *venture capital* to start up.

Whatever mix of strategies a state uses, the goal remains the same: a viable economy. According to the Council of State Planning Agencies, all states, regardless of their economic structure and conditions, need a similar foundation to pursue development.[19] This foundation includes a stable fiscal environment and a good educational system. In addition, states benefit from a regulatory structure that encourages private-sector competitiveness rather than one that is protectionist (one that favors certain existing businesses over others). Finally, it is important for states to have adequate infrastructure to support development. Such a foundation will make a state more attractive for development.

On this foundation, states build a variety of programs and actions designed to promote economic development. One of the most conventional activities is a **subsidy** (as Mississippi used through BAWI), by which the state reduces costs to business. For example, the government may build a highway or extend water and sewer lines to service a new plant, or it might offer tax abatements or below-market-interest-rate loans to a relocating firm. Some jurisdictions indirectly subsidize a facility by providing job training for its employees. These actions are undertaken to make the state more attractive for development.

Some jurisdictions have approached economic development by offering **amenities** that contribute to the quality of life. Amenities include parks, theaters, art museums and galleries, sports and recreational facilities, clean air, and pleasant streets. Pittsburgh's environmental cleanup, Seattle's arts program, Baltimore's mixed-use waterfront, and Indianapolis's amateur sports focus are examples of amenity-based economic development plans.[20]

Issues in Economic Development

An economy that is robust provides jobs for residents and revenues for governments. Therefore, economic health is a central public policy concern. Government actions intended to spark economic development are typically considered in the public interest.[21] Still, several questions are associated with government involvement in the economy. These include the impact, the extent, and the fairness of government action.

Do State and Local Government Initiatives Make Much Difference?

There are divergent views on the impact of government actions on the economy. Some studies suggest that many of the important factors that affect an economy are beyond the control of state and local governments.[22]

Others contend that government action can greatly influence the fate of a local economy.[23] Both views contain a kernel of truth. One widely cited study of the location decisions of large firms found that a favorable labor climate and proximity to suppliers and consumers were important criteria to most firms.[24] Governments can affect the first factor but not the second. Also, states vary in the degree to which their economies are influenced by external forces.[25]

The debatable effect of government actions on the economy contributed to Rhode Island voters' rejection of the Greenhouse Compact in 1984.[26] Under the compact, the state would have created research "greenhouses" to generate high-technology products, and would have provided subsidies to promising industries.[27] Forty million dollars of the total project costs (estimated to be $250 million) were to be generated by new taxes. The overwhelming defeat of the project at the polls was linked to persistent doubts about the actual economic benefits that the state would derive from the compact.

Does Government Spend Too Much?

Some observers claim that government gives away too much in its pursuit of economic health.[28] This concern develops out of the fundamental relationship between a federal system of government and a capitalistic economic system. Governmental jurisdictions cover specific territories, but capital is mobile, so business firms can move from one location to another. Because these firms are so important to a local economy, governments offer incentives to influence their location decisions. The impact of these incentives on firms' decisions is not clear, but most jurisdictions believe that they cannot afford not to offer them.[29] However, there is increasing concern that competition among jurisdictions to attract business may be counterproductive and costly to government. As a consequence, citizens are beginning to look more closely at the **incentive packages**—tax breaks, low-interest loans, and infrastructure development—that their governments offer business.

These incentive packages can be extensive. For example, to lure Volkswagen (VW) during the 1970s, the state of Pennsylvania agreed to buy and refurbish an old Chrysler plant (at a cost of $40 million) and lease it to VW at a negligible interest rate.[30] Under a deal negotiated by the state, 95 percent of VW's local taxes were forgiven for the first two years, and 50 percent were forgiven for the following three years. In addition, Pennsylvania provided infrastructure support for VW in the form of a railway spur and highway construction. To the state, the VW plant meant jobs and a boost to the area's sagging economy. Supporters hoped that the plant would have a ripple effect and spark additional investment. In 1988, however, VW announced plans to close the Pennsylvania plant, which had been operating at less than half its capacity for five years.

Examples of government concessions to the automobile industry abound—the Honda plant in Ohio, the Mazda facility in Michigan, the

General Motors Saturn operation in Tennessee.[31] The fundamental question is how extensive these incentives should be. An examination of one recent case helps shed light on the answer.

In 1987, Kentucky taxpayers provided an incentives package worth an estimated $325 million for a new Toyota assembly plant in the community of Georgetown.[32] Half of the state's costs ($167 million) were in the form of interest payments to purchasers of economic development bonds (the primary source of capital for the project). Land and site preparation expenses were estimated at close to $33 million. Local highway construction absorbed $47 million in state funds. Another $65 million was spent for employee training. Opposition to the incentives package came from local small businesses, unionized labor, and environmental protection advocates,[33] but their opposition was blunted by a study predicting that the state will reap $632 million in taxes from Toyota and the industrial and commercial development that will follow.[34] The package was presented to taxpayers as a wise business decision.

Does Government Spend Fairly?

Traditionally, government involvement in economic development has taken the form of efforts to reduce costs to business. According to economic development professionals, the central business district, local developers, the local labor force, and existing business firms derive the greatest benefit from city-sponsored economic development activity.[35] However, as citizens began to ask who benefits, some state governments refocused their efforts toward direct investments in human resources. An outstanding illustration of this reorientation can be found in Massachusetts—a model of successful economic revitalization. At the top of the Massachusetts agenda for economic development are the goals of strengthening higher education and increasing skills training.[36]

Local governments have been especially active in expanding the concept of economic development beyond a narrow concern with business investment. Led by the pioneering efforts of San Francisco and Boston, some local governments are tying economic development initiatives to the achievement of social objectives, an approach called **linkaging.** A growing number of U.S. cities are linking large-scale commercial development (office and retail buildings and hotels) to such concerns as housing and employment. This movement grew out of frustration over the disappearance of older low-income neighborhoods from revitalized, commercially oriented downtown areas.[37] With linkaging, developers are required to provide low- or moderate-income housing or employment to targeted groups or to contribute funding to programs that support these objectives. In return for the opportunity to enter a lucrative local market, a developer pays a price. This process has been called "the cities' attempt to share the profits of their prospering sectors with their poor."[38]

Linkaging works best in cities with booming economies. But even in cities with more stable economies, local government can negotiate with developers for social concessions. In Richmond, Virginia, for example, city officials convinced developers to provide substantial minority participation in a major retail project in the downtown area. In return for city approval of a massive redevelopment project in Jersey City, New Jersey, developers agreed to reserve a certain percentage of dwelling units for low- and moderate-income individuals.

Concern over the relative fairness of government actions is spreading, as reflected in the discussion of Baltimore's redevelopment activity in Profile 16.1. Court cases challenging a city's right to use linkaging have not met with success. By mid-1987, neighborhood groups in cities as different as Hartford and Chicago were pushing their governments to enact such policies.

Tools of Economic Development Policy

All levels of government make economic development policy. They do this indirectly, through taxing, spending, and regulatory policy, and directly, through government intervention in the economy. Despite the nagging questions about return on investment, excessive costs, and fairness, state and local governments are steaming full speed ahead with economic development initiatives.

Taxation and Regulation

A government makes economic development policy through the basic exercise of its taxation and regulatory powers and through its spending decisions. For example, when the national government increases defense spending, communities with defense-related economies surge. When a state extends its sales tax to cover services or adopts a corporate income tax, ripples are felt throughout its economy. When a city alters its land-use plan, economic consequences abound. Although the avowed intent of such actions may be something else—to beef up the country's military capability, to raise revenues to fund state programs, or to allow residents to convert their homes into apartments—they affect economic development.

Government Intervention

In addition, there are governmental actions that are explicitly intended to influence economic development. For example, until 1988 the national government funded the Urban Development Action Grant (UDAG) program, which provided **gap financing**—the amount needed to make the project go—for commercial, residential, or industrial development projects in dis-

PROFILE 16.1
Baltimore: A Tale of Two Cities

The dazzling Inner Harbor area of Baltimore, Maryland, stands as a testament to the impact of money, power, and vision. A once-crumbling waterfront has been transformed into a vibrant commercial, retail, and residential mecca. Tourists visiting the nation's capital make the thirty-five-mile trip north to see Baltimore's Inner Harbor.

A few miles away is a black neighborhood where 25 percent of the residents are unemployed and 50 percent live below the poverty line. Conditions are worse now than they were in 1970. If tourists unwittingly encounter the area, they beat a hasty retreat. The renaissance of the Inner Harbor and the surrounding downtown area of Baltimore has had little effect on these Baltimoreans.[1] As one critical analysis of the city concluded, "There is rot beneath the glitter."[2]

The revitalization of the Inner Harbor area was on the drawing boards from the mid-1960s, but it took the election of William Donald Schaefer as mayor in 1971 to get the project under way. Schaefer, elected governor in 1986, was an aggressive booster of Baltimore during his fifteen years as mayor. His goal was to develop a probusiness economic development strategy that would trigger corporate investment in the city. By skillfully using public dollars to stimulate private investment, the strategy worked. A moribund central business district has been revitalized, but the city continues to face serious problems.

One central question is whether the intensive focus on redeveloping the downtown area cushioned the deteriorating neighborhoods from a steeper fall or accelerated their decline. Statistics can be marshaled to support either argument.[3] The debate touches on the important question of equity. In whose interests does government promote economic development? Does a strategy that emphasizes downtown development necessarily exclude neighborhoods?

In Baltimore, a more neighborhood-focused approach may be in the offing. As Mayor Kurt Schmoke said in 1987, "We must build upon the successes of our downtown redevelopment program and ensure that the benefits of growth reach the neighborhoods."[4]

[1] Marc V. Levine, "Downtown Redevelopment as an Urban Growth Strategy: A Critical Appraisal of the Baltimore Renaissance," *Journal of Urban Affairs* 9, no. 2 (1987): 103–23.

[2] Peter L. Szanton, *Baltimore 2000* (Baltimore: Morris Goldseker Foundation, 1986).

[3] Levine, "Downtown Redevelopment," and Bernard L. Berkowitz, "Rejoinder to Downtown Redevelopment as an Urban Growth Strategy," *Journal of Urban Affairs* 9, no. 2 (1987): 125–32.

[4] Levine, "Response to Berkowitz: Economic Development in Baltimore," *Journal of Urban Affairs* 9, no. 2 (1987): 133–38.

tressed areas. State governments have adopted a wide array of programs designed to improve their economies, such as small-business incubator programs, which support the development of undercapitalized new enterprises. Local governments are by no means left out of the action; cities and counties offer tax breaks, provide infrastructure for developers, and market their jurisdictions as friendly to business. All of this activity makes sorting out intergovernmental roles and legal relationships rather complex.

Since the Great Depression, the national government has actively funded an array of economic assistance programs. The most popular of these programs in recent years have been UDAGs, Community Development Block Grants (CDBG), and Economic Development Administration (EDA) grants. The stimulation of local economies is a central goal of UDAGs and EDA grants, and a subsidiary goal of CDBG. They have been quite important in arresting the spiraling decline that some communities have experienced, and even in localities with relatively healthy economies, they have been instrumental in halting the deterioration of poor areas.

The Reagan administration chose to emphasize productivity improvements and global competition in its economic policies. To a certain extent, this emphasis led to the termination of UDAG, and to cuts in CDBG and EDA. A 1987 survey of city economic development officials indicated that cuts in these programs would deal a devastating blow to local economies.[39] Other national actions that, in the assessment of knowledgeable local officials, would harm economic development include restrictions on industrial development bonds, cuts in highway and transit funds, and the elimination of general revenue sharing.

Competition and Cooperation

As the national government has reordered its economic priorities, state and local governments have become more innovative and active vis-à-vis their economies. The characteristic that distinguishes state and local economic development activity is competitiveness.[40] Nonnational governments are awash in competition for economic development, primarily for a structural reason: a fragmented federal system fosters interjurisdictional competition.[41] More than 82 percent of influential local officials in southeastern cities termed the economic development environment "very competitive" in a survey conducted in 1986.[42]

State and local governments have reacted to this situation by taking actions intended to make themselves more attractive to new and relocating enterprises. If a business firm is unhappy with conditions in a community, it may seek a new location, and it is likely to find other communities waiting with open arms. When the Mack Truck Company announced its intention to relocate its manufacturing facility from Allentown, Pennsylvania, it had an array of communities from which to choose. To make themselves more enticing, the beckoning jurisdictions (and their state governments) offered a panoply of incentives, including property tax abatements, below-cost land, infrastructure, and training programs for potential employees. Mack Truck decided to relocate in South Carolina.

Economic competition is most apparent when the stakes are high, that is, when the location decision will mean a substantial number of jobs, as in the case of General Motors' Saturn plant. State after state lined up to offer General Motors generous packages of financial incentives, promising an assortment of tax breaks, access roads, water and sewer systems, and employee training. The eventual winner was Tennessee.

There is a great deal of debate about the impact of interjurisdictional competition. As we noted earlier, incentives and concessions amount to a giveaway to business. Critics claim that competition for economic development is nothing more than the relocation of a given amount of economic activity from one community to another, with no overall increase in national productivity.[43] The solution, they argue, is increased cooperation. However, this is elusive. For example, governors of the Great Lakes states have been unsuccessful in establishing a "no pirating" pact within the region.[44]

Counties have found cooperation challenging, too. A National Association of Counties study of urban counties reported that only 5 percent frequently coordinated their economic development activities with other counties.[45] Only slightly more (19 percent) indicated frequent coordination with cities located within their boundaries. Economic development has tended to be a singular proposition, with each jurisdiction pursuing its own destiny.

This can be destructive to the jurisdictions involved. For example, the State Development Board in South Carolina, an agency devoted to promoting the state as a place for investment, has encouraged rural counties to band together and pursue a united economic development effort. But the board's encouragements do not square with political realities. Lingering rivalries between adjacent counties effectively blunt efforts at cooperation. Further, while the board advocates intrastate cooperation, it explicitly engages in interstate competition: the reason that South Carolina counties should work together, it argues, is to become stronger competitors against North Carolina counties.[46] Competition continues but in a different arena.

Economic conditions may ultimately serve as the catalyst for greater cooperation among jurisdictions. This is exactly what has occurred in the Monongahela River Valley area. This 7,400-square-mile section of southwestern Pennsylvania, northern West Virginia, and western Maryland has found that the markets for its products and traditional sources of investment are drying up. Individual jurisdictions have realized that the economic problems are too big for them to solve alone; the troubled economies of the cities and counties are symptoms of a region-wide malaise. After a series of false starts, local leaders have journeyed across county and state boundaries to develop a coordinated agenda for economic revival. Organizers of the first Monongahela River Valley economic summit conference put it bluntly: "Our theme is unity. We have no other choice."[47]

State Policy Development and Implementation

Economic development policy is formulated, adopted, and implemented at both the state and local level and involves government officials and public and private institutions with the private sector. All state governments have created economic development offices, although these offices operate with different labels and have different functions. Similarly, all but the smallest cities and counties have established economic development departments or councils. In a study of the nation's mayors, 86 percent indicated that economic development was among the top three priorities in their cities.[48]

The Politics of Economic Development

Economic development is assuming a central role in campaigns for state and local elective office. Like reducing crime and improving education, it is a consensus issue: everybody is in favor of it. Each candidate, then, tries to convince the voters that his or her approach to economic development will be the most effective. At both the state and local levels, the campaign rhetoric typically emphasizes jobs and employment.

Most states have created a variety of partnerships to aid in implementing economic development strategies.[49] Ideally, a state government should be internally united for its economic development effort, but several natural cleavages—partisan politics, legislative-executive disputes, and agency turf battles—make cohesion hard to come by. And because economic development is a central issue, a lot of political posturing goes on around it. In the end, a state government with a unified, cohesive approach to economic development is likely to be more successful than a state without one.

Blue-Ribbon Panels, Task Forces, and Advisory Boards

Once in office, the erstwhile candidate faces the challenge of transforming rhetoric into reality. As a state's top elected official and chief executive, the governor commonly takes the lead, creating staff task forces, blue-ribbon panels, and subject-specific public or private task forces.[50] In the 1980s, these approaches were quite popular. Arkansas governor Bill Clinton set up a staff task force, for instance, by asking the directors of five state agencies to create an economic development program for the state. The task force considered the availability of capital for investment, the skill level of the work force, the retention and expansion of existing business, and local-level promotion of economic development. Its recommendations, as modified by the governor, served as the basis for legislative proposals, some of which eventually became law.

The blue-ribbon panel approach was used by Iowa governor Terry Branstad, who appointed a group of citizens and officials to the Committee on Iowa's Future Growth and charged it with several tasks. The committee reviewed economic conditions in the state and recommended corrective public and private actions. One of its recommendations led to the creation of the Iowa Partnership for Economic Progress, a policy planning and coordinating organization that advises state government.

A different approach to economic development was adopted by Nebraska governor Robert Kerrey, who utilized a series of subject-specific public and private task forces to address small-business equity financing, public pension fund investments, communications and information systems technology, and agricultural finance and rural development. The governor appointed knowledgeable citizens and assigned staff from his own office and the Department of Economic Development. Each task force studied the relevant issues, produced reports containing recommendations, and subsequently disbanded, its work completed.

In these instances, the work of the governor's task force or blue-ribbon panel had to pass legislative muster. Although a governor can implement some recommendations through an executive order or by agency directive, major policy recommendations require legislative approval, especially if they involve spending money.

Most states use advisory boards to refine and adjust their economic strategies as changing conditions dictate. These committees vary in responsibility and authority. Their primary function is to provide input from a variety of perspectives. The composition of Washington's Economic Development Board is typical of a comprehensive board; it is composed of the governor, four legislators, directors of four development-related state agencies, five citizens, one economic development professional, and one representative each from different-sized manufacturing firms, organized labor, financial institutions, agriculture, education, tourism, forest products, female-owned businesses, and minority-owned businesses. Other advisory committees are less comprehensive and deal with specific subjects, such as small business, science and technology, international trade, or tourism.

Economic Development Agencies

Once an economic development strategy is in place, the next challenge is implementation. This is an important step, because grand strategies can fail if implementation is faulty. Implementation is the job of state agencies.

Three-quarters of the states assign the economic development function to a *line agency*, typically called an economic development department. Comprehensive economic development agencies are responsible for industrial development, international trade, small-business assistance, and, in some cases, tourism promotion. A few states make economic development a part of the governor's office, assign it to a division within a larger department, or turn it over to a private-sector board.

The Illinois Department of Commerce and Community Affairs exemplifies a comprehensive economic development agency. Created in 1979 by the combination of three state agencies, the department had 550 employees and a $550 million budget by the mid-1980s. Not only does it provide standard and entrepreneurial business assistance, it also handles job training, economic development promotion, and tourism. The advantage of such an agency is that it maximizes coordination and minimizes duplication. (The or-

Figure 16.1   The Organization of Tennessee's Department of Economic and Community Development
State economic development agencies are active in many areas. Trying to attract movie makers and car manufacturers is all in a day's work for Tennessee's agency.

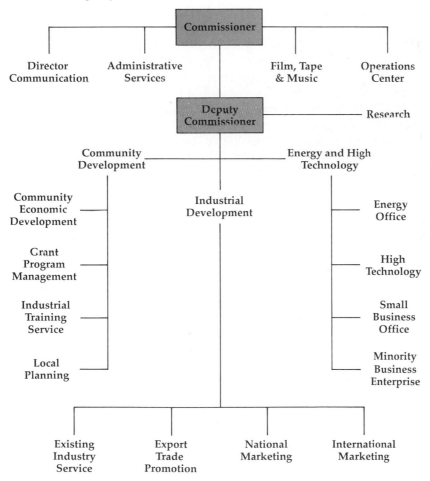

Source: Timothy J. Bartik, "Recruitment and Fundamentals: A Description of Tennessee's Economic Development Policies," in *The New Economic Role of American States: Strategies in a Competitive World Economy.* Edited by R. Scott Fosler. © 1988 Committee for Economic Development. Reprinted by permission of Oxford University Press, Inc.

ganization chart for another comprehensive agency, Tennessee's Department of Economic and Community Development, is displayed in Figure 16.1.)

Public-Private Partnerships

A critical partnership for any state government is with its private sector. This partnership is often difficult to forge, given the traditional differences in the public and private sectors. State government has to contend with demands from a variety of interests, of which business is one, albeit a powerful one. Business leaders believe that because their success is central to a state's economy, they ought to be treated as a public interest rather than a special interest group.[51] States differ in the degree to which they accommodate this contention.

Because states compete with one another for economic development, the public-private partnership can be tenuous. Business is in a position to extract favorable treatment from government. A state may feel that it is less a partner than a captive. In response to the question "Who runs Massachusetts?" one state legislator responded: "The businesses that threaten to move out of the state. They have a chokehold on us."[52] This statement may be extreme in tone, but it conveys the frustration that some state officials feel about their government's relationship with business.

One partnership that has developed in some states is that between industries and universities. The Committee for Economic Development, a national group of prominent business executives and educators, identifies five ways in which states can facilitate these partnerships: state-established centers, state grants to university research centers, research incubators, small-business development centers, and research parks.[53]

One means of channeling state funds into university research is through "centers of excellence," a designation that makes the related research activity eligible for special grants from the state. For example, at Arizona State University's Center for Excellence in Engineering, the legislature provides matching funds for research in solid-state electronics and thermosciences, among other topics. (The genesis of Arizona's actions is interesting: the center was created after the state lost out to Texas in the battle for a microelectronics computer consortium.)

The level of economic development activity in state government is extensive. The governor, the legislature, state agencies, task forces, universities are all involved; the list of actors is long and getting longer. Furthermore, this list does not include activity by local governments.

Current Initiatives

The nonnational economic development policy landscape is a cluttered one. State and local governments are busy proliferating new economic development strategies, policies, programs, and organizations. Fearful that some of this activity may be duplicative, counterproductive, and ineffective, state governments in particular are attempting to impose some order on this confusion. One of the primary means of doing so is called strategic planning.

Strategic Planning

Strategic planning can be useful for several reasons, according to the National Association of State Development Agencies.[54] First, it produces an understanding of the state's economic bedrock. Second, it provides a venue in which public- and private-sector leaders can exchange perspectives and develop a consensus about the state's economic future. In addition, strategic planning moves the economic development issue from goal setting to implementation. Finally, it provides a mechanism for adjusting and correcting the state's actions in reaction to emerging economic trends.

Six states adopted long-term strategic plans during the mid-1980s: Indiana, Michigan, Ohio, Pennsylvania, Washington, and Wisconsin. Wisconsin's approach is similar to actions taken in the other states. Its twenty-three-member Strategic Development Commission was established by the governor in 1984, in a time of economic turmoil in the state, caused in large part by the loss of industrial jobs. The commission's assignment was to analyze the Wisconsin economy and identify avenues for government action.

The commission's analysis revealed an interesting combination of strengths and weaknesses compared to other states. On the "strengths" side were a diverse economy, a skilled labor force imbued with a strong work ethic, a sound infrastructure, and a world-class university system, among others. On the "weaknesses" side, Wisconsin was considered to have relatively high personal taxes, an expensive government, a lack of entrepreneurial characteristics, and fairly high wage rates in certain industries.[55] Armed with this understanding of the economic context, the commission commenced an exhaustive study of the job-creation process. Eighteen months and $500,000 later, it produced its strategic plan. (One-half of the cost of the report was paid for by state government; the remainder was picked up by major corporations in Wisconsin.)[56]

The Wisconsin plan differed from some in that it set out three specific objectives for the year 1990: to create 150,000 new jobs in Wisconsin, to lower the unemployment rate to 5 percent, and to increase per capita disposable income by 18 percent. These objectives should be achieved by preserving the existing job base, fostering new jobs, and adopting an ethos that "Wisconsin is first in quality." Over one hundred specific recommendations were included in the plan. Some of them were aimed at improving government performance through the creation of a business-labor council, the establishment of an office of industrial economics in the Department of Natural Resources, and the strengthening of the Department of Development's economic adjustment team. Other recommendations were more financial in nature, such as the creation of different funds for seed capital, start-up capital, and growth capital for Wisconsin firms. Still others sought to expand markets by promoting international trade and establishing a product development corporation to invest in specific products. Ideally, these actions would increase demand for Wisconsin-produced goods.

The commission's strategic plan became the subject of a special legislative session on economic development and the focus of a series of public hearings throughout the state. The commission, its task completed, dissolved and was replaced by the Wisconsin Strategic Planning Council, a public-private partnership. The future will tell whether the strategic plan was correct in its objectives and recommendations.

Many states have a less developed strategic economic development plan and a more incremental, eclectic approach. The actual programs and tools that state and local governments use to accomplish their economic development objectives are many and varied. Four that are particularly popular are high-technology development, small-business incubators, enterprise zones, and international trade promotion.

High-Technology Development

High technology conjures up the image of white-coated researchers bent over microscopes in space-age laboratories. Whether microelectronics, robotics, or genetic engineering, a sense of "exotic technology" prevails. Many state governments have been seduced by the image and have jumped aboard the high-tech bandwagon: by 1987, more than forty had established high-technology programs, a 300 percent increase since 1980. The most popular programs are technology research centers (twenty-seven states) and technology transfer (twenty states).

One of the pioneering high-tech efforts was North Carolina's Research Triangle Park, an area bounded by Duke University in Durham, the University of North Carolina in Chapel Hill, and North Carolina State University in Raleigh. State leaders decided to take advantage of the location of the three universities and promote the park as a site for industrial research laboratories. They reasoned that it could attract the kind of research firms that would benefit from proximity to the knowledge and research capabilities of the universities. It took time, but Research Triangle Park is now an example to other states bent on high-technology development.

State assistance to high-technology development is more than simply facilitative. For example, the Massachusetts Technology Development Corporation provides capital to high-tech firms by using public funds to create a revolving loan pool. To be considered for funding, a firm must be working on innovative products and must exhibit employment growth potential.

Of course, not all states are suited for the high-tech challenge. As one observer remarked, "There is just never going to be a silicon bayou or a silicon prairie."[57] But regardless of the uncertainty of the venture, states appear to be fairly smitten with the idea.

Small-Business Incubators

In some states, high-tech development is part of a more comprehensive effort to stimulate small-business growth. State governments, especially those that have been burned in the competition to attract relocating businesses, have turned inward and are concentrating their efforts on creating, expanding, and retaining businesses within the state by improving their educational systems and installing infrastructure. In addition, states are encouraging small-business growth through *incubators,* facilities that nurture or "hatch" small businesses. By housing a number of small enterprises under one roof, an incubator provides affordable space, shared support services, management assistance, and financial support to its tenants. If it is successful, the businesses will flourish and jobs will be created.

Small-business incubators are being developed at a rapid pace. As of 1986, there were more than 120 publicly sponsored or nonprofit incubators around the country.[58] Each is different in design and management, and there does not appear to be a formula for successful operation. In 1985, the Illinois legislature adopted the Build Illinois Act, which provided $1 million for incubators, and in the same year Michigan agreed to subsidize the operating expenses of incubators that set up shop in abandoned buildings. (An approach like Michigan's has a payoff beyond job creation: it puts property back on the tax rolls.)

Some incubator programs have a "need" component built into them; in other words, they are targeted to areas and residents with the greatest need. In this way, they are similar to another popular economic development program, enterprise zones.

Enterprise Zones

Enterprise zones are designated areas of a community that qualify for special treatment in the form of tax incentives and regulatory relief. They are designed to transform an economically depressed section into an economically productive one. The idea was imported from Great Britain as the capstone of the Reagan administration's housing policy, but it languished in the U.S. Congress and eventually was taken up by state governments. Florida enacted its enterprise zone program in 1980 in reaction to rioting in the economically embattled Liberty City area of Miami. Since then, more than thirty-five states have followed suit.

Ohio has a fairly extensive enterprise zone program, enacted in 1981 as a response to an economy ravaged by deindustrialization. The program offers tax relief to businesses located in authorized zones, and was justified as a method for keeping Ohio competitive with other states. In the words of one official, "Attracting business to Ohio used to be like shooting fish in a barrel, but now you really have to compete."[59]

Although the ostensible purpose of enterprise zones is to encourage new investment and job creation in declining urban areas, two other rationales have evolved in Ohio. One is to retain business. The state's five largest enterprise zones were established at the request of an existing business. For example, when General Motors indicated that the modernization of its plant in Parma hinged on a tax abatement, Ohio created an enterprise zone for the plant.[60] The second rationale is related to a community's business climate: an enterprise zone symbolizes a community's commitment to business, so that it becomes more attractive to relocating firms. Whatever the rationale, by 1987 thirty-nine Ohio communities had created enterprise zones, and the state estimated that they had saved 8,363 jobs and created 4,024 new ones.

As with so many government-sponsored economic development actions, there is persistent uncertainty as to the long-term impact of enterprise zones. Is a state's investment in the form of foregone tax revenues worth it? Illinois offers one of the most comprehensive enterprise zone programs in the country: forty-nine areas of the state enjoy a package of tax exemptions and credits, fee waivers, and regulatory breaks. One criticism that has surfaced there is that without other state and local inducements, the zones have little impact on business investment decisions.[61] But the numbers are impressive: in 1986 Illinois's zones had their best year ever, recording $181.3 million in investments and 4,969 new jobs.[62] As states struggle with solutions to economic problems, enterprise zones are likely to remain high on the list.

International Trade Promotion

An economic development program that symbolizes just how far states have come in the past twenty years is international trade promotion. States are no longer content to concentrate on domestic markets—they are venturing abroad. All fifty states have international trade agencies of one kind or another, varying in scale from one employee in Idaho and Nevada to a staff of forty-one in Minnesota.

States pursue international trade for two reasons. First, foreign markets can be important consumers of state goods. Second, foreign investors may have capital to commit to projects in a state. International trade promotion is, then, a two-way street: exporting state products and importing investment capital.

One highly visible way in which state governments pursue international markets and investments is through trade missions, in which the governor, top business leaders, and economic development agency officials make formal visits, most often to Europe and the Far East. The state delegation

A handshake between a governor and an industrialist from Asia is not unusual these days. Here South Carolina governor Carroll Campbell welcomes the chairman of Formosa Plastics Group of Taiwan, which in 1989 announced plans for a $200 million factory in his state.

exchanges information with representatives of the country's public and private sectors and establishes ties that members hope will lead to exports and investments.

State governments perform three important roles in export promotion: brokering information, offering technical support, and providing export financing.[63] As information brokers, states conduct seminars and conferences, sponsor trade shows, publish export handbooks, and offer individual counseling to American businesses. Oklahoma has set up an international division in its economic development department to encourage export activity, and one of its key functions is to identify export opportunities for Oklahoma's business firms. Once an opportunity has been identified, the division provides technical support to help the relevant firm become more knowledgeable about the exporting process.

Technical support is critical, because U.S. firms may not be aware of the details involved in exporting: working with international banks, complying with another country's laws and regulations, securing the necessary licensing agreements, designing appropriate packaging for products, and the like. Export finance is also important, because without it, a state's information brokerage and technical support functions are meaningless. The first state to tackle the export finance issue was Minnesota, in 1983; it provides a firm with operating capital for the period between the signing of a sales agreement and the delivery of a product. In addition to working capital, some states offer insurance and export credit. The availability of financing converts the fantasy of exporting into reality. By 1986, sixteen states had established export finance programs.

State government is also involved in promoting the state as a place for foreign investment, although public sensitivity about foreign influences on the domestic economy necessitates a cautious approach. According to the U.S. Bureau of the Census, more than 2.8 million jobs are a direct result of foreign investment (10 percent of these are in California). The value of foreign-owned property, plants, and equipment was close to $300 billion in 1985, and one-quarter of this investment was in two states: Texas and California. Table 16.1 gives a state-by-state breakdown of the value of foreign investment and the number of jobs that directly result from it. One trend that is likely to continue is the establishment of joint ventures, in which domestic firms join with foreign ones to produce goods and services in the United States.

Cities and Development

Although states are key players in economic development, it is important to remember that their programs have a local impact. If a state is successful in attracting foreign investment, the investment ends up in a particular jurisdiction. The same is true for the firms that a state assists with exports—they are located in a local jurisdiction of some sort.

Local governments operate their economic development programs within a context defined by state government, and the state's commitment to educational quality and infrastructure sets the tone for local efforts. State laws, policies, and programs influence the direction of local activities.

Cities look to state government to provide leadership in economic development. They want the state to provide infrastructure, low-interest loan programs, education, and job training, which will contribute to the cities' goals of more jobs and increased investment.

Of necessity, the economic development package of a typical city consists of a variety of tools and techniques.[64] For example, cities invest in infrastructure improvements, they make low-interest loans available to businesses and developers, and they advertise, supported to a great extent by federal and state funds and by local groups such as the Chamber of Commerce. But the pursuit of economic development is easier for some cities than for others. In 1987, *Inc.* magazine ranked all of the metropolitan areas in the United States on the basis of three factors: job generation, the rate of significant new business start-ups, and the percent of young companies enjoying high growth rates.[65] At the top of the list was Austin, followed by Orlando and Phoenix. At the bottom of the list was Duluth, Minnesota. Austin is in the enviable position of being a government headquarters with a large research university and a maturing high-tech center. Duluth, in contrast, is struggling to transform its economy from a reliance on manufacturing and shipping raw materials to a more diversified, service-oriented base.[66] Given global economic trends, Duluth has a harder job than Austin.

Local Initiatives

The booming mining communities of yesterday that are the ghost towns of today symbolize the importance of a healthy economy to community survival. Mayors and council members often see their political futures intertwined with community economic development. Politicians want to be associated not with plant and mill closings but with ground-breaking ceremonies for new convention centers and office buildings.

To facilitate economic development, local governments adopt strategies, establish organizations, and try to put together deals. Their strategies typically are aimed at increasing employment opportunities and capital investment in the community. The organizations they create vary depending on the community's political system and the condition of the local economy. For example, in 1986 Des Moines, Iowa, confronted a declining tax base, loss of federal funds, and a tight budget. The city council voted to replace the city's existing fragmented economic development structure with a new Office of Economic Development within city government. It was charged with promoting commercial and industrial growth and expansion to increase the tax base and create jobs for Des Moines residents. Within a year, the office reported assisting about fifty projects, resulting in more than nine hundred new and retained jobs and over $40 million in new investment.[67]

Atlanta, on the other hand, has several organizations involved in economic development. Two of them, the Mayor's Office of Economic Development and the Atlanta Department of Community Development, operate within city government. Two others, the Chamber of Commerce and Central Atlanta Progress, are private-sector organizations with close ties to government. A fifth organization bridges the gap between the public and the private sectors: the Atlanta Economic Development Corporation (AEDC), a private, nonprofit corporation founded by the city and Central Atlanta Progress to promote and implement economic development projects. When it celebrated its first decade of existence in 1986, AEDC had developed two industrial parks, packaged more than 250 small-business projects, and established a venture capital network, and was undertaking the development of a hotel/conference center at the twenty-nine-acre site of the old Atlanta airport terminal.[68] AEDC considers itself Atlanta's "economic spark plug."

Deal Making

An increasingly popular activity in local economic development is *deal making*, which signifies a closer, reciprocal relationship between government and the business/development community. The government and the private sector act as partners in development projects. Sports stadiums, the subject of Politics and Policy 16.1, are frequently public-private ventures.

A National League of Cities study explored the particulars of deal mak-

Table 16.1   Foreign Investment in the United States, by State, 1985

	Value of property, plant, and equipment (in millions of dollars)	Direct jobs resulting from foreign investment
New England		
Connecticut	$ 1,917	43,496
Maine	1,266	21,130
Massachusetts	3,079	71,545
New Hampshire	582	16,486
Rhode Island	443	11,301
Vermont	457	6,591
Middle Atlantic		
Delaware	2,777	34,785
District of Columbia	1,136	5,703
Maryland	3,227	49,487
New Jersey	9,384	154,763
New York	15,292	241,933
Pennsylvania	8,531	150,182
Great Lakes		
Illinois	9,155	143,863
Indiana	2,700	54,143
Michigan	6,229	81,834
Ohio	8,671	138,147
Wisconsin	3,222	63,406
Plains		
Iowa	1,404	18,488
Kansas	1,216	14,642
Minnesota	4,294	35,712
Missouri	3,042	46,164
Nebraska	441	7,523
North Dakota	1,386	2,768
South Dakota	382	1,780

Source: U.S. Department of Commerce, Bureau of Economic Analysis, *Foreign Direct Investment in the United States: Operations of U.S. Affiliates of Foreign Companies,* rev. 1985 estimates, June 1988.

Table 16.1   Foreign Investment in the United States, by State, 1985 (*cont.*)

	Value of property, plant, and equipment (in millions of dollars)	Direct jobs resulting from foreign investment
Southeast		
Alabama	$ 3,057	31,507
Arkansas	1,061	18,399
Florida	9,751	94,812
Georgia	8,158	107,367
Kentucky	3,941	37,238
Louisiana	12,832	51,026
Mississippi	2,320	15,938
North Carolina	7,611	115,975
South Carolina	5,940	66,641
Tennessee	4,609	69,559
Virginia	5,160	69,385
West Virginia	5,670	32,404
Southwest		
Arizona	3,724	34,485
New Mexico	1,891	11,245
Oklahoma	4,922	26,900
Texas	38,020	211,663
Rocky Mountains		
Colorado	4,630	30,993
Idaho	356	2,755
Montana	1,865	2,910
Utah	2,647	9,912
Wyoming	2,455	3,121
Far West		
Alaska	14,474	7,122
California	35,323	298,796
Hawaii	1,777	18,680
Nevada	1,087	7,370
Oregon	1,730	18,586
Washington	3,680	35,534
Total	$295,181	2,862,153

POLITICS AND POLICY 16.1
Major-League Cities

Professional sports and big-league cities go hand in hand. Hosting a professional sports franchise is evidence that a city has arrived— that it is not simply a large city but a major-league city. Only fifty cities in the country host a professional baseball, basketball, football, or hockey team.

Major-league status is something that large cities desire. Acquiring or retaining professional sports teams is an important element in their economic development plans.[1] Just ask Baltimore and Indianapolis. In 1984 the National Football League's Baltimore Colts relocated to Indianapolis, and neither city has been the same since. Two of the newest cities to join the big-league ranks are Charlotte, North Carolina, and Orlando, Florida. In 1987 they were named as sites for expansion teams in the National Basketball Association. Two perennial also-rans in the major-league competition, Jacksonville, Florida, and Memphis, Tennessee, continue to bide their time.

Cities want professional sports franchises, but they do not come easy. In fact, cities have to bid for them, typically through some sort of public sub-sidy for the franchise. This usually comes in the form of below-market-rate leases and tax breaks for the stadium (depending on whether the facility is publicly or privately owned). City leaders defend these subsidies, arguing that the return, both economically and symbolically, is worth it. In some cities—Cincinnati and Seattle, for instance—the construction of a sports stadium in the downtown area has stimulated development activity.

A recent study on the impact of sports stadiums on nine local economies challenges these assumptions.[2] It found that the stadiums had negligible effects on jobs and development; instead, they diverted economic development from manufacturing to the service sector. City officials in Buffalo, New York, and St. Petersburg, Florida, where stadiums were under construction in the hopes that major-league baseball teams would follow, disagreed with the findings. Time will tell who is correct.

[1] Arthur T. Johnson, "Economic and Policy Implications of Hosting Sports Franchises: Lessons from Baltimore," *Urban Affairs Quarterly* 21 (March 1986): 411–33.
[2] Rodd Zolkos, "Cities Blast Stadium Study," *City and State* 4 (April 1987): 3, 53.

ing, including the roles played by individuals and groups interested in or affected by development deals.[69] The potentially important actors included the mayor, developers, nonprofit development corporations, neighborhood groups, the Chamber of Commerce, labor union leaders, banks, state officials, the local newspaper, national officials, and city agencies. Development projects need organizers and promoters, funders and arbitrators. They inevitably encounter opponents. Economic development professionals in 322 cities assigned individuals and groups to specific development roles, which are categorized in Figure 16.2.

The study found that the initiators and catalysts of development deals are the mayor, the developer, and the nonprofit development corporation. These are the pivotal actors who get the deal moving. Banks play a limited but important role as investors in a project, as do developers and nonprofit development corporations. The "fixers"—those who smooth the bumps in the process—include city agencies, the mayor, and nonprofit development corporations. Coordinators of deals tend to be city agencies, nonprofit development corporations, and the Chamber of Commerce. The Chamber of Commerce occupies an equivocal position, in that it is considered a "scene-stealer" or intruder, as are state officials. The troublemakers are the local newspaper, neighborhood groups, and labor union leaders, which can disrupt a carefully negotiated deal.

It is plausible to assume that the actors who play multiple roles are probably the most influential in development deals. Of special interest are nonprofit development corporations, which can be powerful. Organizational by-products of the growing interaction between public and private sectors, nonprofit development corporations have a flexible structure that makes them particularly attractive to both sectors. They offer improved access to and coordination of public and private resources, independence from city government, expansion of public powers, and privacy of negotiations.[70] But not everyone welcomes them; critics claim that they institutionalize existing power relationships and that "partnership" is a misnomer for a private-sector–driven, antidemocratic development machine.[71] While the debate continues, the number of local nonprofit economic development corporations grows.

Growth Problems

Even for the most fortunate of cities, economic development is not without problems. Examine the cases of Palo Alto, California, and Traverse City, Michigan, both of which are making concerted efforts to limit economic growth. Palo Alto, a highly desirable residential community and employment center in the San Francisco Bay Area, has adopted policies that effectively discourage the employment potential of the city.[72] In Traverse City, residents rejected a proposal to turn a bayfront parking lot into a shopping mall because of fears that it would stimulate additional growth.[73]

Figure 16.2   The Actors and Their Roles in Local Economic Development Deals

Development deals can be derailed if catalysts and investors are absent, or if the number of troublemakers rises.

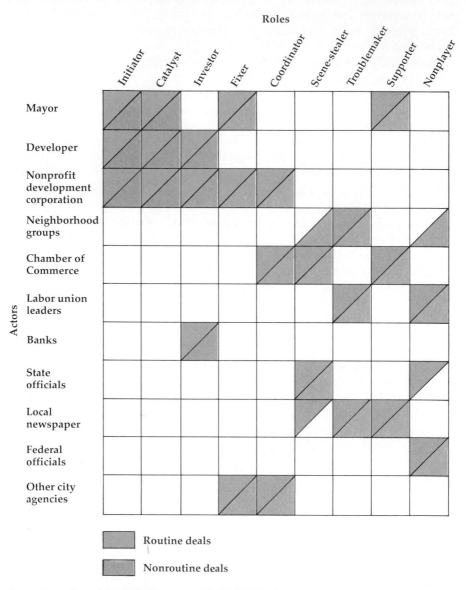

Source: Data from Ann O'M. Bowman, *The Visible Hand: Major Issues in City Economic Policy* (Washington, D.C.: National League of Cities, 1987).

For many cities, the problems associated with growth are ones they would gladly accept. They are busy trying to attract businesses from elsewhere, retain (and encourage the expansion of) the ones they already have, and stimulate new enterprises. Old factories and warehouses are being converted into festive marketplaces full of shops and restaurants. Office buildings, hotels, and convention centers are being constructed. Idle waterfronts are being transformed into parks. This activity underscores the efforts of city governments to harness private investment and stimulate the local economy. The dramatic rebirth of an old mill city like Lowell, Massachusetts, as a high-tech center fuels the hopes of cities across the country.

The Implications of Economic Development Policy

Greater government involvement (especially financial) in economic development is fraught with risk. Two headlines from major newspapers tell the story. The *Washington Post* carried this one in 1986: "P.G. [Prince George's County, Maryland] May Be Stuck With $675,000 Check if Restaurant Closes."[74] And the *Atlanta Constitution* ran this in 1987: "City [Atlanta] Suing Developer to Recoup $450,000 Lent in Property Deal."[75] Economic development is a high-stakes game, and one that jurisdictions cannot afford to sit out. A healthy economy is central to the functioning of government. State and local officials know this and act accordingly. The slogan for Rhode Island's 1989 economic development campaign sums up the attitude: "Every state says they'll move mountains to get your business. We're moving rivers."[76] The ad did not exaggerate: the state is redirecting two rivers as part of a $200 million redevelopment project in the capital city of Providence.

Yet when an observer steps back and ponders the strategies and deals, a degree of skepticism is inevitable. Could New York City have better spent the millions it committed to Chase Manhattan Bank to keep the financial institution from moving 4,600 office workers to New Jersey? The deal involved $235 million worth of tax abatements, discounted utilities, site improvements, and job training tax credits over the next twenty years.[77] Which state really won when a division of Eastman Kodak turned down Maryland's $4.5 million package of subsidized land, tax breaks, and employee training in favor of Pennsylvania's $14 million deal? Some might conclude that corporations are staging raids on public treasuries. But many state and local government officials would argue that concessions for business serve an important function by creating jobs and generating economic activity, thus improving the local tax base, which funds public services. Undoubtedly, the subject will continue to be debated.

Summary

State and local governments are immersed in economic development policy. They engage in a wide range of activities intended to improve their economies, yet there is tremendous uncertainty about the impact of government action, its relative cost, and its focus.

The importance of economic development to state and local governments means that despite the uncertainty, jurisdictions must press on. States have created a variety of organizations and agencies—including private-sector and citizen participants—in their quest to understand and help shape the economy. In the 1980s, state governments relied on strategic planning, high-tech development, small-business incubators, enterprise zones, and international trade promotion to stimulate their economies. Local governments are not without their own economic development tools and techniques, including infrastructure improvements, tax breaks, and job training as means of retaining and attracting business.

Key Terms

Amenities Comforts and conveniences that contribute to the quality of life.

Economic development A process by which a community, state, or nation increases its level of per capita income and capital investment.

Enterprise zones Areas of a community that offer special government incentives aimed at stimulating investment.

Gap financing The additional money that provides a development project with enough investment capital to proceed.

Incentive packages The enticements that state and local governments offer to retain or attract business and industry.

Linkaging A means by which local governments use large-scale commercial development projects to accomplish social objectives.

Subsidy Financial assistance given by government to a firm or enterprise.

Strategic planning An approach to economic development that emphasizes adaptation to changing conditions and anticipation of future events.

17

Criminal Justice

How Much Crime Is There?
Intergovernmental Roles in Criminal Justice

Actors in Criminal Justice Policy
Law Enforcement Officials/The Courts/The
Public's Involvement/The Victim

Two Policy Areas
Victimless Crime/Capital Punishment

Correctional Policy
Sentencing/Prison Conditions

Policy Alternatives for States and Localities
Back-Door Strategies/Front-Door Strategies/
Capacity Enhancement

The Continuing Crisis in Crime and Corrections

When Americans are asked what they believe to be the most important problems facing the nation, they often mention crime first. More than 40 million citizens were victims of crime in 1987—that is one out of every six men, women, and children. In large sections of America's cities, many people are afraid to leave their homes after dark. Inside homes there are more firearms than ever before, more dogs, and more electronic burglar devices. The fear in many cities is palpable.

Washington, D.C., "the capital of the free world," has become the murder capital of the United States, displacing Detroit. In 1988, 372 homicides took place in Washington—more than one per day. In 1989, more than 600 murders were expected. Many of these killings occur within blocks of the Capitol and the White House. Washington's escalating murder rate has been attributed to the influx of cheap drugs, especially crack, and handguns.[1]

How Much Crime Is There?

Crime data are available from two major sources, the FBI's *Uniform Crime Reports* and victimization surveys. The FBI's annual crime index covers four kinds of violent crime (assault, murder, rape, robbery) and four categories of property crime (arson, burglary, larceny, motor vehicle theft). It tracked a sharp increase in criminal behavior between 1960 and 1980, during which time the rate of violent crime tripled and that of property crime more than doubled. But beginning in 1981, the rates of both types of crime began to drop. Seven percent fewer offenses were reported to the FBI in 1985 than in 1981. However, the crime index for 1986 showed a 5 percent increase over the previous year, fueled by a jump in figures from the Sunbelt.

Is a new "crime wave" under way? One cannot judge by the *Uniform Crime Reports*. The FBI's statistics are suspect for three reasons. First, they only reflect crimes reported to local police departments. It is estimated that only one out of every three crimes is known officially by the police. If a greater proportion of criminal acts are discovered by the police through their data collection efforts or from citizen contacts, then the crime rate will show an increase, even though the true extent of criminal activity stays the same or actually declines. Second, some types of crime are more likely to be reported than others. Murders and auto thefts are almost always reported, whereas larceny and rape victims, out of embarrassment or fear, may remain silent. Third, the FBI's crime data include only eight types of criminal behavior. Most white-collar crimes are excluded, in spite of the fact that they may be growing faster than any other type of crime. Thus, the index provides only a partial picture of actual criminal activity.

Because of these disadvantages, a second, more accurate approach to measuring crime is now in use. *Victimization surveys* scientifically poll residents of certain jurisdictions, asking them whether they or members of their household have been victims of crime during a specified recent time period.

Long utilized by larger metropolitan areas and some states, victimization surveys have been conducted on a nationwide basis by the U.S. Bureau of the Census since 1973. According to the National Crime Survey, the true rate of crime is much higher than that reported by the *Uniform Crime Reports*.[2]

Studies predicting criminal activity in the 1990s tend to be contradictory. Some say that crime will drop because the proportion of fifteen- to twenty-nine-year-old males—the segment of the population that commits most crimes—will decline until the year 2000 and perhaps beyond. Others project that drug-related crimes and the growing black and Hispanic "underclass" will drive up the crime rate.

Prediction is problematic, because we do not really know what *causes* crime. We can, however, state authoritatively that it is associated with certain factors. As noted above, crime is most likely to be committed by young males. Approximately half of the arrests for FBI index crimes in any given year are of men under the age of twenty.[3] Crime rates are higher in densely populated cities and states than in rural areas. Urban areas present more targets of opportunity and a better chance of escape for criminals. Additionally, crime appears to be related to poverty, unemployment, drug abuse, and race.

But the issue is more complex than that. Businesspeople have recently been convicted of insider trading and other white-collar abuses on Wall Street that cost their victims millions of dollars. Some wealthy contractors rig bids on government construction projects and Pentagon defense contracts; some judges accept bribes; the occasional priest or minister sexually abuses a child. The underlying causes of these and other sad cases cannot be attributed to economic deprivation, race, age, or neighborhood. Their origins remain unknown.

Although reasonable people disagree about the causes of crime, virtually everyone with even a passing familiarity with the criminal justice system in the United States agrees that it is not effective in apprehending and deterring criminals. Fewer than 20 percent of all property crimes reported to police are "cleared" by an arrest. For violent crimes the record is better: about 75 percent of murders are cleared, 60 percent of assaults, 50 percent of rapes, and 25 percent of robberies.[4] Probably half of the arrests, however, do not result in a conviction or in any sort of punishment for the offender. Extrapolation from these somewhat rough estimates indicates that a criminal has only a slight chance of being arrested and punished for a crime.

Throwing money at the problem does not seem to do much good; research has been unable to find a link between higher police expenditures on personnel and materials and a subsequent reduction in crime.[5] Most criminal activities cannot be prevented by law enforcement officials, and unreported crimes are very difficult to investigate. The only factors that appear to be associated with higher arrest rates, and perhaps lower crime rates as well, are related to the attitude and tactical deployment of police officers. Aggressive and active police work in responding to calls from citizens and

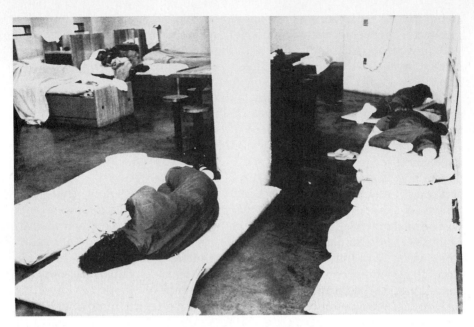

Overcrowding in county jails, like the King County Jail in Seattle, means that some prisoners have to sleep on the floor.

in investigating criminal events seems to help, as does using officers in one-person instead of two-officer patrol units.[6] One promising new strategy is community policing, in which officers are assigned specific territorial areas of responsibility and encouraged to use their imagination and experience in fighting crime.[7]

Intergovernmental Roles in Criminal Justice

The failure of the American system of criminal justice cannot be attributed to a lack of human and material resources. In 1985 there were 1,368,562 full-time employees in national, state, and local police and corrections agencies. Total state and local expenditures exceeded $35 billion.[8]

Responsibility for confronting crime rests primarily with the states and localities. Municipal police departments carry much of the load of law enforcement, employing approximately 60 percent of all sworn police officers; counties employ 30 percent, and the state law enforcement organizations (highway patrol and special agencies) just over 9 percent.[9] These state and local entities enforce state laws and local ordinances. Federal crimes such as treason, kidnapping, and counterfeiting are dealt with by the FBI and processed through the federal courts and correctional system. The two systems are separate, but some cooperation occurs. For instance, the FBI and state law enforcement agencies exchange such information as finger-prints and details of the movements of fugitives and drug smugglers.

Nine out of every ten dollars spent on police protection and corrections come from the coffers of state and local government—an illustration of the decentralized nature of criminal justice spending in the United States. The national government's resources are concentrated on its own enforcement and corrections agencies. However, Washington has provided certain forms of direct financial assistance to the states and localities.

One of the biggest programs was the Law Enforcement Assistance Administration (LEAA). Created through the Omnibus Crime Control and Safe Street Act of 1968, LEAA transferred hundreds of millions of dollars to state and local police agencies during the 1970s to meet equipment, man-power, and training needs. One of the first block grants, the LEAA program was downgraded into a formula grant with greatly reduced funding in 1979. Other national efforts to assist states and localities, such as the 1968 Juvenile Delinquency Prevention and Control Act and the 1970 Organized Crime Control Act, were also folded into other programs or drastically cut back. Among the few contributions during the Reagan years was the 1984 Comprehensive Crime Control Act, which provided limited funding for law enforcement projects, prison construction, and state victim compensation programs.

Greater national involvement in state and local law enforcement appears to be called for, given the rise in new types of computer-aided white-collar crime, the growing economic and political dimensions of organized crime and drug trafficking, and the fact that criminal activities do not respect state and local jurisdictional boundaries.

Actors in Criminal Justice Policy

There is a large cast of actors in state and local criminal justice systems. Policy leadership is exercised by the governor, who also has the job of replacing county sheriffs, city police chiefs, and other law enforcement officials who are accused or convicted of wrongdoing. Normally, the governor sets the tone for the pursuit of law and order through state-of-the-state addresses, proposed legislation, and public presentations. His role in the appointment of judges is also important, as pointed out in Chapter 10.

Besides being involved in judicial selection in several states, legislative bodies establish the structure of the legal system and decide which behaviors constitute a violation of law. Legislatures tend to be responsive to citizen pressures on law enforcement issues, as demonstrated by recent legislative activity in areas such as victimless crimes, gun control, the death penalty, and sentencing reform.

Law Enforcement Officials

The state attorney general formally heads the law enforcement function in most states; county and city attorneys and district attorneys generally follow the attorney general's lead. These positions call for a great deal of discretion in deciding whom to prosecute for what alleged crimes or civil violations. The prosecution of offenses is a politically charged endeavor, particularly when it involves people who are aiming for higher political office.

The state highway patrol, special state law enforcement divisions modeled on the FBI, sheriffs, police chiefs, and local line and staff officers are also important. They are responsible for enforcing the policies decided on by elected officials and for carrying out the basic day-to-day activities connected with enforcing the law.

The Courts

State and local courts decide the innocence or guilt of defendants brought before them, based on the evidence submitted. Courts also can influence the procedural aspects of criminal justice through rulings that specify correct policy procedures in criminal cases. In particular, a number of U.S. Supreme Court decisions have shaped the criminal justice process. The federal courts have the final word on cases in which the defendant claims that his or her federal civil rights have been violated by state or local law enforcement personnel.

Critics have alleged that the Supreme Court under Chief Justice Earl Warren made it more difficult to convict criminals through decisions that expanded the rights of the accused. The first of these famous cases was *Gideon* v. *Wainwright* (1963), in which the Warren Court said that all accused persons have a constitutional right to be defended by counsel. If they cannot afford to pay an attorney, the state or locality must provide one free of charge.[10] The second ruling, *Escobedo* v. *Illinois* (1964), required that the accused be informed of the right to remain silent at the time of his or her arrest.[11]

The often-cited case of *Miranda* v. *Arizona* (1966) further expanded the rights of the accused by requiring police officers to inform anyone suspected of a crime of the right to remain silent, the fact that anything said can and will be used against him in a court of law, and the right to be represented by counsel, paid for by the state if necessary.[12] Evidence obtained when the accused has not clearly indicated his understanding of these "Miranda warnings" and explicitly waived his rights is not legally admissible in the courtroom, as it is considered a violation of the Fifth Amendment right not to incriminate oneself.

The Supreme Court cited evidence showing that before the *Miranda* decision, it was not uncommon for police to extract confessions from suspects by wearing them down through physical or psychological abuse or misrepresenting or lying to them about their rights regarding self-incrimination and counsel. Many believed that *Miranda* would severely derail police efforts to obtain a confession and thereby result in some criminals getting off scot-free. Post-*Miranda* research seems to confirm that confessions are now less likely to serve as the basis for convictions.[13] However, many accused criminals decline to exercise their *Miranda* rights and spill the beans anyway, whether because of a strong sense of guilt or because they fail to comprehend the full implications of the warnings. In the vast majority of cases there is sufficient material evidence or testimony from witnesses to convict without a confession; law enforcement officers must, however, work a bit harder to obtain it. In fact, although the Supreme Court threw out Mr. Miranda's confession, he was later found guilty because of the overwhelming physical evidence against him. Under Chief Justice Warren Burger, the Supreme Court issued a series of decisions that narrowed the scope of *Miranda*. Further limitations are possible under the Rehnquist Court, but the basic principles are unlikely to be overturned.

The U.S. Supreme Court also influenced state and local criminal procedure in the case of *Mapp* v. *Ohio* (1961). Basing its decision on the due process clause of the Fourteenth Amendment, the Warren Court ruled that evidence obtained illegally by the police cannot be introduced in court.[14] This "exclusionary rule" extended the constitutional protection from illegal search and seizure. The police must have a search warrant specifying what person or place will be searched and what will be seized. However, the Supreme Court later eased this requirement, particularly in circumstances in which the police were acting in good faith. A recent case concerned a 1987 raid of an apartment by Baltimore police officers, which turned up heroin and drug paraphernalia. By mistake the officers searched the apartment next to the one for which they had a warrant, but they were permitted to use the seized materials as evidence to convict the unlucky defendant.

The Public's Involvement

Another participant in justice policy is the voting public. Citizens make demands on officials (the governor, legislators, judges, police, and so on) to conform to public opinion on crime and criminals. Generally, the pressure is for more law and order, and it results in criminal codes aimed at that end.[15] Citizens also participate directly in the criminal justice system by serving on juries, which are selected from driver's license lists, tax returns, or registered voter rolls. Most citizens consider it their public duty to serve on a jury from time to time, and such service does tend to be an interesting (if not always edifying) experience. Occasionally, a jury trial will drag out over a lengthy period; the longest was concluded in October 1987, in Belleville, Illinois, after a forty-four-month marathon concerning liability for a toxic chemical spill. Attorneys for the losing party announced that they would appeal.[16]

Citizens also participate in criminal justice by serving on grand juries. A **grand jury** (which is composed of up to twenty-three members, but averages twelve) serves as a check on the power of the state or local prosecutor by considering evidence in a case, then deciding whether to indict the accused. Twenty states require a grand jury indictment for serious crime; in other states it is optional, or a preliminary hearing before a judge is used instead. Grand juries are usually organized on a county or district basis. In practice, they are inclined to rubber-stamp whatever course of action is recommended by the prosecutor. Rarely does one question the professional legal opinion of the district attorney or attorney general.

An additional function of the grand jury is to act as an investigatory body for certain types of crimes, especially vice, political corruption, and organized crime. In this capacity it is empowered to issue subpoenas for suspects and evidence that it wishes to examine. A statewide grand jury is most appropriate for criminal investigations, because it can deal with activities that cross county or district boundaries. Among the states that provide for statewide grand juries are Arizona, Colorado, Florida, New Jersey, and Virginia.

The Victim

The last influence on criminal justice policy is the one most frequently ignored in the past—the victim. Many victims are left psychologically, physically, and/or financially injured for lengthy periods after the crime. Since 1965 some forty states have responded to this sad fact by developing victim compensation programs. These are typically administered by a board, which assesses the validity of victims' claims and determines a monetary award to help compensate for hospital and doctor bills, loss of property, and other financial needs resulting from the crime. Maximum benefits vary from $1,500 to $45,000, depending on the state. Rarely is a victim "made whole" by these limited payments, but at least some assistance is provided to help the person deal with the various traumas of the crime.

Two Policy Areas

The nature of any state's approach to crime is determined by the interactions of the various participants in the system. The states' handling of victimless crimes and capital punishment illuminates this important point.

Victimless Crime

Statutes enacted by legislative bodies define what constitutes criminal behavior, and public opinion usually influences what activities the legislatures treat as criminal. *Victimless crimes* are voluntary acts that violate the law but are perceived by some to present little or no threat to society. Examples are the production, consumption, and sale of illegal drugs; gambling; pornography; prostitution and other prohibited sexual behavior. It is estimated that 50 percent of all arrests in urban areas are for victimless crimes.[17]

Some people argue that such crimes should be wiped off the books, because those who engage in these activities suffer willingly. A strong case can be made for legalizing, regulating, and taxing gambling, drugs, and prostitution. People are going to do these things anyhow, so why criminalize a large portion of the population unnecessarily? Instead, why not get a little piece of the action for the public purse? Moreover, state regulation of gambling could help diminish the role of organized crime, and regulation of prostitution could help prevent the spread of sexually transmitted diseases by requiring regular medical checkups for the prostitutes. Almost every state permits some form of gambling, such as lotteries, bingo, and betting on horse or dog racing, but only Nevada has legalized and regulated prostitution.

Opponents claim that "victimless" is the wrong word to describe these actions. For example, gambling can become an addictive social disease that can destroy individuals and their families. Studies have shown that gamblers tend to come from lower socioeconomic groups—those who can least afford to lose their money. As for selling sex, prostitutes and their clients can become infected with AIDS and other diseases. Legalization of drugs such as heroin or crack cocaine might lead to a significant rise in addiction rates and require higher taxes for treatment and health care.

In states where legislative bodies define the scope of criminal behavior broadly, to include victimless crimes, an extra burden is placed on other actors in the criminal justice system. Prosecutors and law enforcement authorities find much of their time consumed by these relatively minor and nonthreatening activities when they could be concentrating on more serious crimes, like murder, rape, and robbery. The courts, too, must spend a great deal of time on processing these cases. The legalization of victimless crimes could immediately shorten the dockets of prosecutors, the police, and judges and keep the process more manageable. A less radical strategy is *decriminalization*—prescribing a minor penalty (usually a small fine) for certain crimes. For example, Oregon and a handful of other states and localities have decriminalized possession of small amounts of marijuana.

In practice, hard-pressed prosecutors often drop charges against perpetrators of victimless crimes, and judges dismiss the least offensive cases or administer a small fine or a suspended sentence. Law enforcement person-

Figure 17.1 States with Capital Punishment
Most states permit capital punishment, although some have not actually carried out the death penalty for many years.

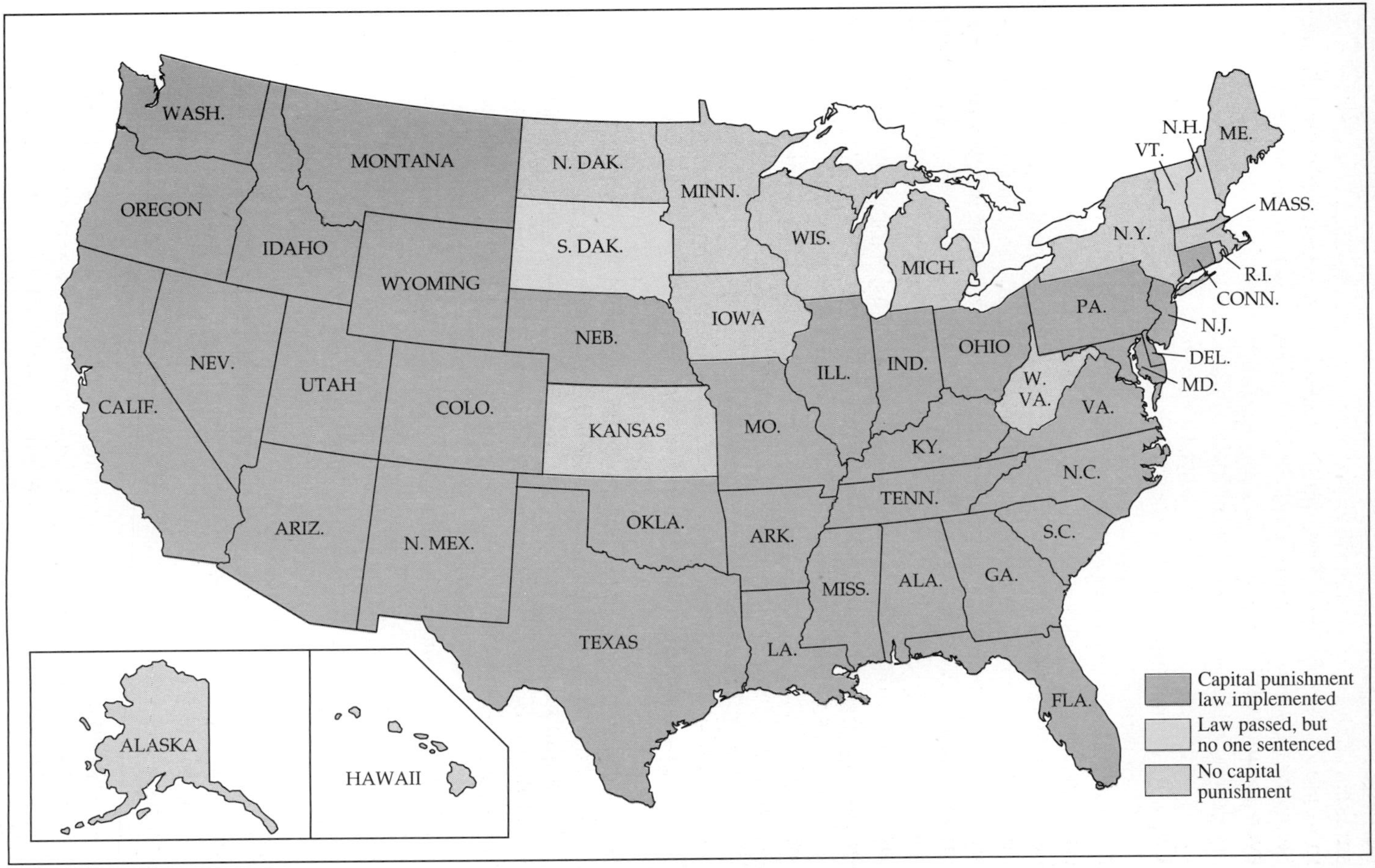

Capital punishment law implemented

Law passed, but no one sentenced

No capital punishment

Source: NAACP Legal Defense and Educational Fund Inc., as cited in Andrew H. Malcolm, "Society's Conflict on Death Penalty Stalls Procession of the Condemned," *New York Times*, June 19, 1989, p. B10. Copyright © 1989 by The New York Times Company. Reprinted by permission.

nel tend to look the other way when passing near a streetwalker or a pot smoker. De facto decriminalization is the norm for many victimless crimes in much of the United States. This is especially true for prohibited sexual behavior between consenting adults, including sodomy, adultery, and the ever-popular fornication.

Capital Punishment

Capital punishment offers a second example of how a state's approach to crime is affected by the interaction of various participants. Public opinion helps determine a legislature's propensity to enact a death penalty statute. Prosecutors must decide under what circumstances to seek the death penalty. Only juries can find a defendant guilty or innocent in a capital case. Judges must enforce the penalty of death, subject to lengthy appellate review. The federal courts have also played an important role in determining the conditions under which a state can legally put a person to death for a crime.

Before the 1960s, criminal executions were commonplace in the United States, and the appeals process was much shorter than it is today. A total of 717 people were legally executed during the 1950s. States took the lives of 199 human beings in 1935 alone. But public opinion began to turn against capital punishment (only two were executed in 1967), and so did the U.S. Supreme Court. In the 1972 case of *Furman* v. *Georgia,* a 5-to-4 majority held that in principle the death penalty did not represent cruel and unusual punishment, in violation of the Eighth Amendment, but that in practice it had been applied in a cruel and unusual manner by the states.[18]

The Supreme Court expressly declared unconstitutional the capital punishment statutes in Louisiana and North Carolina and implicitly invalidated similar laws in many other states. It held that death penalty laws could be valid only if used in accordance with correct procedures and standards, and could be invoked solely for lethal crimes. This position was confirmed in a later case, *Gregg* v. *Georgia* (1976), in which the Court struck down a law permitting imposition of the death penalty for rape of an adult female.[19]

Recently, however, the Rehnquist Court has taken a different, less restrictive direction on capital punishment. In a 1987 case involving Georgia, *McCleskey* v. *Kemp,* the Court dismissed an allegation that the new death penalty statute was being utilized in a discriminatory way.[20] And in 1989 the Court ruled that the use of the death penalty for the mentally retarded (*Penry* v. *Lynaugh*) and those who committed crimes while juveniles (*Stanford* v. *Kentucky*) is not unconstitutional.[21]

Several states voluntarily abolished capital punishment in the 1960s and 1970s. The majority, however, rewrote their statutes to conform with the Supreme Court's guidelines. Thirty-seven states have death penalty laws in place today (see Figure 17.1). In early 1989, 2,188 inmates were languishing on death row, and another 250 were expected to join them in 1990. Florida had 296 inmates awaiting execution, more than any other state. Texas (284),

California (238), Illinois (119), and Pennsylvania (115) enjoyed the dubious distinction of following.[22] While statutes were being rewritten and clarified between 1968 and 1976, no executions were carried out. Since January 1977, however, more than 111 people have made the long walk from death row to the death chamber. Texas is the leading executioner, killing thirty-one people between 1976 and early 1989 (see Figure 17.2).

In spite of the increased popularity of capital punishment, it is still a rather tedious endeavor. The appeals process presents numerous opportunities for delay, and it is not unusual for an inmate to spend four or five years on death row before he escapes the death penalty through the legal process. Willie Darden waited thirteen years after his murder conviction before being executed in Florida's electric chair in March 1988.[23]

One troublesome aspect of the death penalty is that blacks receive it well out of proportion to their numbers. Although black people make up less than 12 percent of the U.S. population, 39 percent of those executed have been black and 40 percent of those on death row in 1989 were black.[24] A white person who murders is just as likely to be sentenced to death as a

Figure 17.2   Executions by State, 1976–1989
Southern states lead the nation in the number of executions since 1976. The figures are through June 1989.

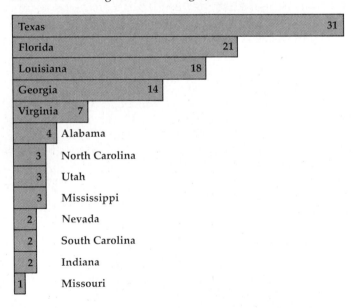

Total: 111

Source: NAACP Legal Defense and Educational Fund Inc., as cited in Andrew H. Malcolm, "Society's Conflict on Death Penalty Stalls Procession of the Condemned," *New York Times,* June 19, 1989, p. B10. Copyright © 1989 by The New York Times Company. Reprinted by permission.

black murderer, but blacks are involved in a disproportionate number of capital offenses.

A great deal of controversy continues to surround the issue of executing criminals. Researchers generally agree that if punishment is to discourage future criminal behavior, it must be swift and certain. Neither of these conditions is met by the death penalty in the United States. Few reasonable and informed people today argue that capital punishment acts as a deterrent, except in the specific case of the unfortunate individual who is executed. Studies comparing homicide rates between states with and without death penalties either find no significant differences or determine that states with capital punishment actually have higher rates of homicide.[25] For example, Virginia, which imposes the death penalty, has a higher homicide rate than Oregon, Maine, and West Virginia, which do not.

On the other side is the argument for the legitimacy of *lex talionis*, the ancient principle that the punishment should fit the crime. In contemporary terminology this is known as retribution. In this view, some crimes are so heinous that only the death of the perpetrator can balance the scales of justice and relieve the moral outrage of society. The argument for justice as retribution cannot be validated on empirical grounds; it is an ethical question that each individual must personally resolve. Recent public opinion polls tell us that the majority of Americans do believe in this justification for executing convicted murderers.

Correctional Policy

A person convicted of a crime in a court of law becomes the object of correctional policy, which, as its name implies, aims to "correct" behavior that society finds unacceptable. It proposes to accomplish this daunting task in several ways. First, an offender should be punished, both for retribution and to deter future criminal behavior by the offender and by other potential criminals. Second, convicted lawbreakers should be rehabilitated, so that they can become productive, law-abiding citizens after fulfilling the terms of their punishment. Third, criminals who represent a danger to society should be physically separated from the general public.

If correcting criminal behavior is the overarching goal of correctional policy in the states, we have a terrible policy failure on our hands. As we have already noted, most crimes do not result in an arrest. Even when an offender is detained by the police, she stands a good chance of avoiding conviction or incarceration. Thus, deterrence is a fallacy. Remember that the best way to prevent undesirable behavior is through swift and certain punishment. Those of us who quizzically stuck a tiny finger into an electrical outlet in childhood received the shock of swift punishment. If we were foolish enough to try it a second time, we discovered that the punishment was certain. Only idiots and masochists subject themselves to such abuse a third time. That is how our correctional policy would have to work if deterrence is to be achieved. But for a variety of reasons, swift and certain punishment is improbable as long as we live in a humane, democratic society.

Rehabilitation was a correctional fad of the 1960s and 1970s that was largely ignored in the 1980s. The U.S. Justice Department estimates that over 60 percent of all felonies are committed by previous felons, many of them recently released from prison.[26] It appears that prisons actually increase the likelihood that an individual will commit additional crimes when he is freed. Our state prisons have been called breeding pens for criminals. Instead of being rehabilitated, the first-time offender is likely to receive expert schooling in various criminal professions. Overcrowding, understaffing, physical and sexual brutality, and rampant drug abuse make it unlikely that an offender will become a law-abiding citizen. Many schemes have been tried—counseling, vocational training, basic education, and others—but nothing has been able consistently to overcome the criminalizing environment of state prison systems.

Without doubt, most incarcerated offenders do see deprivation of their freedom as punishment, and so retribution does occur. Just as surely, prison effectively removes undesirable characters from our midst. These objectives of correctional policy are achieved to some degree, although cynics point out that sentencing tends to be rather inconsistent and few criminals serve even half of their sentences before release.

Sentencing

Sentencing reform has recently received a great deal of attention in the states. The inconsistency of criminal sentencing is obvious if we examine incarceration rates. In 1988 they varied from 452 inmates per 100,000 population in Nevada to 62 in North Dakota (see Table 17.1). Southern states tend to be toughest on crime: they are more than twice as likely as other states to convict people arrested on felony charges, and their sentences are more severe than those in other regions. It is interesting to note that crime rates and incarceration rates are not closely related. A state with a relatively high rate of crime, like New York, locks up fewer people than a state with a lower crime rate, such as Delaware.

Historically, sentencing in state courts has been **indeterminate,** which means that judges have great discretion in deciding for how many years an offender should be sentenced to prison. The offender then becomes eligible for parole after a minimum period is served. For instance, a ten- to twenty-year sentence for armed robbery will require the inmate to serve at least ten years. After that time he becomes eligible for parole, subject to the judgment of a parole board (usually appointed by the governor), which reviews his case and behavior in prison.

The trend today is toward **determinate sentencing,** in which offenders are given mandatory terms that they must serve without possibility of parole. Twenty-one states now provide for the extreme sentence of "life without possibility of parole." Determinate sentencing is designed to reduce sentencing disparity among judges. It also eliminates the need for parole. Inmates who stay out of trouble can be awarded "good time," which will deduct a limited amount of time from their terms.

Naturally, determinate sentencing keeps prisoners incarcerated for longer periods than indeterminate sentencing does. In conjunction with a generally punitive public attitude toward criminals in the 1970s and 1980s, which helped stiffen the sentences awarded by judges as well as the judgments of parole boards, determinate sentencing has contributed to a dramatic rise in prison populations across the United States. The increasing crime rate of the 1960s and 1970s did its part as well. The result is prison overcrowding—the nation's greatest crisis in corrections policy.

Prison Conditions

As shown in Table 17.1, more than 600,000 people were confined to state and federal prisons in the United States in 1988, an incarceration rate of 244 inmates for every 100,000 citizens. It is estimated that another 200,000 reside in local jails. Because criminals are more likely to receive prison sentences today (as well as longer sentences), and because probation and parole have fallen into disfavor with the advent of determinate sentencing, the number of prisoners literally increases each day, which means overcrowding. At the end of 1987, for instance, 533,000 inmates were incarcerated in state institutions designed to hold fewer than 500,000.[27]

The Role of the Federal Courts   In the past, exceeding maximum intended inmate capacity was not a serious problem for the state correctional systems. The courts assumed a hands-off policy toward offenders once they were behind prison walls. The administration of state correctional systems was the sole responsibility of corrections officials. But the prime mover of correctional policy during the past twenty-five years has been the federal courts.

In a series of decisions, the federal courts have applied the Eighth Amendment prohibition on cruel and unusual punishment and the Fourteenth Amendment provision for due process and equal protection of the laws to prison inmates. In addition, the Supreme Court has permitted inmates of state and local facilities to bypass less sympathetic state courts and file suits alleging violations of their civil rights in federal courts. As a consequence of various federal court rulings, the nature of correctional policy has been vastly changed.

Much of the litigation has been concerned with overcrowding. As more and more people were sentenced to prison, corrections officials responded by doubling, tripling, and even quadrupling cell arrangements. It was not

Table 17.1   Prisoners in State or Federal Prisons, 1988

	Total number of prisoners	Incarceration rate*
Northeast		
Connecticut	8,005	146
Maine	1,297	100
Massachusetts	6,733	114
New Hampshire	1,019	93
New Jersey	16,936	219
New York	44,560	248
Pennsylvania	17,879	148
Rhode Island	1,906	118
Vermont	811	97
South		
Alabama	12,610	300
Arkansas	5,519	230
Delaware	3,166	354
District of Columbia	8,705	1,031
Florida	34,732	278
Georgia	18,787	281
Kentucky	7,119	191
Louisiana	16,149	368
Maryland	14,276	291
Mississippi	7,438	279
North Carolina	17,069	250
Oklahoma	10,448	323
South Carolina	13,745	370
Tennessee	7,491	152
Texas	40,437	240
Virginia	14,184	230
West Virginia	1,458	78

*The number of prisoners sentenced to more than one year per 100,000 resident population on December 31, 1988.

Source: Bureau of Justice Statistics, *Prisoners in 1988* (Washington, D.C.: U.S. Department of Justice, 1989), p. 2.

unusual for inmates to be crowded together at the rate of one per ten square feet of floor space.

Drastic improvements were long overdue in Arkansas and Alabama, for instance. At Arkansas's maximum security institution, Cumming Farms, inmates were worked in the fields like slaves, ten hours a day, six days a week, in all types of weather. At night they slept in 100-man barracks.

Table 17.1 Prisoners in State or Federal Prisons, 1988 (*cont.*)

	Total number of prisoners	Incarceration rate
Midwest		
Illinois	21,081	181
Indiana	11,406	202
Iowa	3,034	107
Kansas	5,936	237
Michigan	27,714	299
Minnesota	2,799	64
Missouri	12,354	239
Nebraska	2,205	131
North Dakota	466	62
Ohio	26,113	240
South Dakota	1,020	143
Wisconsin	6,287	126
West		
Alaska	2,588	355
Arizona	12,158	329
California	76,171	257
Colorado	5,997	181
Hawaii	2,367	136
Idaho	1,548	154
Montana	1,272	158
Nevada	4,881	452
New Mexico	2,825	180
Oregon	5,991	215
Utah	2,004	117
Washington	5,816	124
Wyoming	962	203
U.S. total	627,402	244
Federal	49,928	17
State	577,474	227

Homosexual rapes and other forms of physical violence occurred regularly. A 1970 federal court suit led to a finding that Arkansas's entire penal system was in violation of the Eighth Amendment. Similarly, in 1976 a federal judge ordered the Alabama state prison system to surrender to federal authority. Federal officials assumed the responsibility for day-to-day management decisions, including cell size, the placement of urinals, water temperature in the showers, and the number of inmates permitted in various institutions.[28]

By 1987, the entire prison systems of nine states were being overseen by the national government under federal court orders. Another twenty-eight states were subject to a more limited type of federal court order, and four others were involved in litigation in federal courts (see Table 17.2). State officials faced the disturbing choice of balancing the stringent law-and-order approach sought by the public and elected representatives with court

Table 17.2   States Under Court Order or Facing Litigation Because of Prison Conditions, 1987

Entire prison system under court order:	Alabama*	Rhode Island
	Florida	South Carolina
	Hawaii	Tennessee
	Mississippi	Texas
	Oklahoma*	
One or more facilities under court order:	Arizona	Michigan
	California	Missouri
	Colorado	Nevada
	Connecticut	New Hampshire
	Delaware	New Mexico
	Georgia	North Carolina
	Idaho	Ohio
	Illinois	South Dakota
	Indiana	Utah
	Iowa	Virginia
	Kansas	Washington
	Kentucky	West Virginia
	Louisiana	Wisconsin
	Maryland	Wyoming
One or more facilities in litigation:	Alaska	Massachusetts
	Arkansas	Pennsylvania
No litigation pending:	Maine	New York
	Minnesota	North Dakota
	Montana	Oregon
	Nebraska	Vermont
	New Jersey	

*In these states, the federal court no longer maintains a compliance mechanism but the court order is still in effect.

Source: North Carolina Insight 9, no. 3 (March 1987): 2–10. Reprinted with permission of *North Carolina Insight.*

orders that seemed to require them to turn convicted criminals onto the streets to relieve overcrowding. Some took what seemed to be the easiest path out of the dilemma by seeking to acquire or construct additional space for incarceration. Unfortunately, this option requires states to raise new revenues for prison construction or divert money from more popular programs such as education and health care.

The intrusion of the federal courts in state correctional policy is quite controversial, particularly when they have taken over full operating responsibility or ordered increased state and local expenditures for prisons. Important questions concerning the proper division of power between the national government and the states have been raised, as have questions about the competence of federal court officials to run state prison systems.[29] Still, there is no denying that some states have operated prisons under less than humane conditions.

State Response to Federal Orders However these important issues in federalism are ultimately resolved, the immediate problem for most states is producing more space for their growing prison populations (and finding the money to pay for it). The only short-term alternatives are to release inmates, to sentence all newly convicted offenders to something other than incarceration, or to find new space for lockup. Following a federal judge's ruling in late 1985 that Tennessee prisons could not accept any additional inmates without special permission, prison officials locked up inmates in school gyms, public libraries, and prison reception centers. They also transferred state inmates to overpopulated and understaffed local jails. At one point in the crisis the sheriff of Shelby County, Tennessee, removed twelve state prisoners from the overcrowded county jail and defiantly chained them to a fence at the state penitentiary.

Court orders to relieve prison overcrowding have brought some states to the point of fiscal disaster. In the 1980 case of *Ruiz* v. *Estelle,* a U.S. District Court judge ordered the Texas Department of Corrections to make sweeping changes in its prison system. Prison officials were instructed to halt triple and quadruple celling, reduce the use of force by prison employees, hire more guards, eliminate internal inmate control of prison activities, upgrade inmate health care, improve inmate disciplinary practices, and correct problems concerning fire and safety standards. In January 1987 U.S. District Court Judge William Wayne Justice ruled that these requirements had not been met and that the state of Texas was therefore in contempt of court, even though it had spent millions of dollars. Judge Justice stated that if the problems were not remedied by April 1987, he would fine the state approximately $800,000 per day.

Texas, hurt critically by a huge drop in the price of oil, already faced a $56 million budget shortfall for the 1988 fiscal year. Governor William P. Clements halted new prison admissions on at least ten occasions during 1987 until inmate releases opened up new space. An admissions procedure was set up so that prisoners could be transferred to state institutions on

POLITICS AND POLICY 17.1
The Effects of Federal Judicial Intervention on Life in a Texas Prison

Before *Ruiz* v. *Estelle* (1980), inmates in Texas prisons, like their counterparts in other states, regulated their own daily activities and helped to enforce discipline. In the Eastham unit, a select group of inmates was granted special privileges (such as open cells, weapons, separate bathing and recreational periods) in exchange for their assistance in controlling ordinary prisoners in the cell blocks and living areas. These "building tenders," or BTs, served as mediators and enforcers, maintaining order through fear and physical punishment. As long as operations ran smoothly enough, guards let the BTs rule the roost. Guards also regularly applied force to inmates, particularly to those who refused to conform to the established system. There were three categories of physical force. "Attitude adjustments" usually involved slapping, a kick in the buttocks, or a punch in the stomach to instill terror without serious physical injury. For more serious problems, guards used fists, boots, blackjacks, or flashlights to beat an inmate, again without severe damage. Real troublemakers— those who injured another inmate, destroyed prison property, attempted to start rebellion, tried to escape, or violated other "sacred" rules— received the third treatment: a severe beating, often involving serious cuts, concussions, or broken bones.

In short, before *Ruiz* v.

Tuesdays and Wednesdays only. When capacity was reached, admissions were stopped. Local jails took up the slack.

Corrections officials proposed that $1.37 billion be allocated for the construction of two new maximum security prisons and five minimum security camps for trustees. Even though these expenditures would add some 9,950 beds to the system, projections indicated that another 10,000 beds would be necessary by 1990 to meet the terms of the court order.[30] Meanwhile, federally ordered prison reforms were playing havoc with inmate discipline and safety, as described in Politics and Policy 17.1.

For other states, prisons were becoming "budget rat holes," diverting state expenditures from education, highways, and social services. In 1986, states were doling out approximately $9 billion for the construction and operation of correctional institutions. By 1989, room, board, and care for a state prison inmate averaged $25,000 per year. Each new prison bed space

Estelle, guards and specially selected inmates worked together to keep order, peace, and the status quo. Fear and paranoia kept Eastham a "well-run" institution. However, the federal court abolished the prisoner control system (as one of several changes). BTs were stripped of their power and privilege, and the use of physical force by guards was prohibited. Court-appointed investigators monitored prison operations. The number of correctional officers was doubled.

Soon a new relationship developed between the keepers and the kept. Not having to fear physical punishment, inmates became confrontational and belligerent. During the two years following *Ruiz*, inmate threats and attacks on guards increased 500 percent. Moreover, with no BTs to maintain internal control, a marked increase in violence among inmates was recorded. Instead of settling disputes with fistfights refereed by BTs, prisoners used knifes or clubs. As the number of killings and serious injuries mounted, gang-related violence, especially along racial lines, created a crisis that even twice the number of guards could not handle. Guards became embittered over their lack of authority, and fearful of the inmates.

Thus, the civil rights of the prisoners were enhanced substantially at Eastham, yet, ironically, their lives are now in constant danger. An authoritarian system of control based on fear and force was exchanged for a system that espouses fairness and civil rights but that has developed into a lawless prison society. Is either acceptable?

Source: James W. Marquart and Ben M. Crouch, "Judicial Reform and Prisoner Control: The Impact of *Ruiz* v. *Estelle* on a Texas Penitentiary," *Law & Society Review* 19, no. 4 (1985): 557–87.

for the growing ranks of confined criminals cost from $50,000 to $100,000.[31] There seems to be no end in sight for prison spending, because of "Murphy's Law of Incarceration": the number of inmates expands to fill all available space, or "if you build them, you'll fill them."[32]

Local jails have entered the litigation battlefield in increasing numbers. Almost every county and good-sized municipality has a jail, and many have been the target of prisoners' rights lawsuits.[33] The overcrowding and legal vulnerability of local jails, and their increasingly intimate links to state prison systems, have prompted states to mandate operational standards and to conduct inspections to enforce those standards.[34] Alabama, Connecticut, Delaware, Hawaii, Rhode Island, and Vermont now have state-run systems. Other states, like Kentucky, have dedicated large sums of money to rehabilitating local corrections facilities.

Policy Alternatives for States and Localities

In addition to the immediate responses made necessary by federal court actions, states and localities are attempting to devise a more comprehensive approach to coping with the problem of overcrowding. Whatever their past failings, today they are demonstrating an increasing propensity for experimentation and innovation. Three basic strategies are being employed to bring and keep inmate populations in line with institutional capacity: back-door strategies, front-door strategies, and capacity enhancement.

Back-Door Strategies

Back-door strategies include several methods for releasing offenders from prisons before they have served their full sentences. This is the most conventional of the three strategies, but some interesting innovations are being tested.

An unimaginative but nonetheless quite effective way to deal with prison overcrowding is to grant early release to enough inmates so that new admissions do not push the institutional population beyond capacity. Most states have early release programs in place, but the method of implementation varies. In some states the governor or parole board simply lops off the last few months or weeks of sentences that are nearly completed, until the necessary number of inmates has left the prison. Other states apply a formula that predicts the likelihood that released inmates will commit another serious offense. For example, nonviolent offenders are freed before violent offenders, larcenists before burglars, drunk drivers before heroin dealers, and so on. An inmate's personal characteristics and work history may also be taken into consideration.

Early release reduces inmate population quickly, but human behavior is not entirely predictable. Public outcries are certain to follow when an offender released before expiration of his sentence commits a highly publicized violent crime.

Traditionally, prisoners released early for good behavior have been placed on parole. Conventional parole is not a very popular or effective program today. In most states that continue to utilize this technique, the parole officers, whose duty it is to keep up with the progress of parolees, are terribly overworked. It is not unusual for a parole officer to be responsible for 100 to 150 offenders—a nearly impossible task.

Electronic House Arrest   An interesting new approach to parole that is being tested by several state and local governments takes advantage of fairly sophisticated technology to monitor parolees' whereabouts. Sometimes called *electronic house arrest*, this technique requires released inmates to wear a transmitter (usually on their ankle) that steadily emits signals to a receiver in their home. Failure to detect a signal causes the receiver to dial a central computer automatically. The computer is programmed to know when the inmate is permitted to be away from home (usually during work hours). If something unusual appears, the computer prints out the anomaly for review by law enforcement officers. Removal of the transmitter also triggers an alarm at the central computer.

Electronic monitoring has been tried successfully in New Jersey, New Mexico, Oklahoma, and several other states, as well as in numerous counties. It is cheaper than jail or prison, and enables a working prisoner to pay her own share of the program, and in some cases to repay the victim of the crime as well. The electronic house arrest program of Palm Beach County, Florida, which has been in effect since December 1984, requires each inmate to pay a rental fee for the electronic equipment, and saves $42.50 per day by keeping the inmate out of the county jail.[35]

Vocational Programs   Another back-door strategy reduces the sentences of prisoners who participate in educational and vocational programs. These programs are intended to teach convicts skills that can help them obtain jobs once they are out of prison, and they have the added benefit of keeping inmates involved in productive, rather than destructive, activities while behind prison walls.

The idea of "factories with fences" has considerable appeal.[36] In addition to using their time productively and learning marketable skills, inmates earn wages that can help defray the cost of their room and board, provide monetary restitution to victims, and fund savings accounts for the inmates to have when they are released. Several experiments have had encouraging results. One example is Best Western International's reservations center in the minimum security Arizona Center for Women: more than thirty inmates have accepted jobs with Best Western after their release.[37]

Prison industry experiments in other states are now being planned. The major source of opposition to this idea is private business, which feels threatened by the low cost of prison labor. Many states have laws restricting production in prison industries or prohibiting the sale of prison-made goods. These laws will have to be repealed if factories with fences are to proliferate.

Front-Door Strategies

The second basic strategy being used to balance the number of prisoners with the supply of beds is the front-door approach, which aims to keep minor offenders out of prison in the first place by directing them into alternative programs.

Creative Sentencing   One method is to grant judges more flexibility in determining sentences. **Creative sentencing** permits judges to match the punishment with the crime while keeping the nonviolent offender in society. One option that has gained increasing acceptance is community service—sentencing the offender to put in a specified number of hours cleaning up parks or streets, working in a public hospital, painting public buildings, or performing specialized tasks related to her professional expertise, like dentistry or accounting. At least eight states allow their judges to assign community service in lieu of incarceration. Another option is to link the sentence to available prison space. This about-face from determinate sentencing was first undertaken by Minnesota, and was being adopted or actively considered by many states in the late 1980s.[38] In addition, judges can assess fines in lieu of prison for relatively serious nonviolent crimes. A substantial fine, some argue, is just as strong a deterrent as a short stay in jail.

A municipal court judge in Los Angeles provided an especially edifying example for any renter who has ever lived in a substandard building ignored by the landlord. A Beverly Hills neurosurgeon who had earned the nickname "Ratlord" because of numerous city citations for health, fire, and building code violations in his four apartment buildings was sentenced to move into one of his own apartments for a term of thirty days. The apartment contained mounds of rodent droppings, an army of cockroaches, inadequate plumbing, faulty wiring, and other problems. Ratlord was fitted with an electronic anklet to ensure that he remained in his "cell" from 5:30 P.M. to 8:30 A.M. Permanent residents soon noted improvements in the building's conditions.[39]

Regional Restitution Centers   Another front-door strategy is *regional restitution centers*, a variation on the standard work-release center. Nonviolent offenders are housed in restitution centers near their homes and work in the community during the day. Their paychecks are turned over to center staff, who subtract expenses for food and housing and distribute the remainder to the offenders' victims as restitution, to the court for payment of fines, and to the offenders' spouses and children for support. Anything left over belongs to the inmates.

Intensive Probation Supervision   A third front-door strategy is *intensive probation supervision* (IPS), which was pioneered by Georgia in 1982. Southern states are in the forefront of corrections policy innovation, largely because they have the biggest problems with prison overcrowding. More than eight states are now experimenting with IPS.

IPS is somewhat like house arrest in that it is designed to keep first-time offenders guilty of a serious but usually nonviolent crime out of state institutions. Those who qualify for the program face intense, highly intrusive supervision and surveillance for a prescribed period. IPS requires at least five face-to-face contacts between offenders and the IPS staff each week in the office, on the job, or in the home; random alcohol and drug testing; weekly employment verification; an early nightly curfew (usually

8:00 P.M.); weekly monitoring for any contact with state or local law enforcement personnel; and at least eight hours per week of unpaid community service for employed probationers and up to forty hours for those who are not working.[40]

IPS officers usually work in a team consisting of a professional probation officer and a surveillance officer, who generally has law enforcement experience. Caseload is limited to twenty-five. In addition to surveillance, the team helps probationers locate a place to live and a job. People who progress without problems are gradually eased into regular probation status; serious problems result in imprisonment.

The track record for IPS in Georgia is impressive. IPS probationers have been much less likely to commit subsequent crimes than conventional probationers or other former inmates. The program is basically self-supporting, since probationers pay from $10 to $50 per month to the program, as well as provide restitution to their victims. Approximately 1,400 Georgians were in the program in mid-1987, which has given Georgia prisons much-needed breathing space.[41] Annually, some 13,000 criminals are sentenced to do time in Georgia; the total prison capacity is less than 16,000. Politics and Policy 17.2 describes another controversial front-door approach initiated in Georgia.

Capacity Enhancement

Capacity enhancement is the third major strategy for matching available prison beds with the number of inmates. Usually it entails construction of new prison facilities, which cost the states billions of dollars in the 1980s. A 500-bed prison in 1988 cost around $30 million to build. As we have noted, this money could be allocated instead to education, health care, or a tax reduction, and many taxpayers resent spending it on the care and feeding of criminals.

When capacity enhancement is the selected strategy, states have few alternatives to new construction. There have been some rather interesting types of construction, however. The New York City Department of Correction is building a floating jail five stories high and the length of two football fields, to be moored off the Bronx in 1990. It will hold 800 beds.[42] Floating jails have been discussed in Texas as well. A less expensive means of building prisons, known as modular construction, is also being examined in various states.

Private Prisons   One long-term capacity enhancement innovation worthy of serious consideration is private prisons or "prisons for profit," a new idea spawned from the near hopelessness of many overcrowded state correctional systems. The private sector has for many years provided limited services and programs to prisons, including health care, food services, alcohol and drug treatment, education and training, counseling, and con-

POLITICS AND POLICY 17.2
Shock Probation

Another front-door approach to easing prison overcrowding is *shock probation*. Louisiana, Georgia, Mississippi, Florida, Oklahoma, and South Carolina are among those states experimenting with the method. Young (seventeen-to twenty-five-year-old) first-time felony offenders are given the option of serving their prison term or undergoing three to four months in a shock probation center, or "boot camp," which resembles boot camp in the U.S. Marine Corps. In fact, former Marine drill instructors are often in charge. Inmates are up by 4:30 or 5:00 A.M. to begin a rigid schedule of manual labor, physical training, and discipline. They clean their barracks, march, do calisthenics, perform work details, and undergo inspections. Psychological, drug, and alchohol counseling are required. Those who successfully complete the program win early release. Those who fall short the first time can try again. A second failure results in assignment to the regular prison population.

Shock probation is aimed at more than just relief of prison overcrowding: it is also intended to take young people who typically come from broken homes and selfish, undisciplined personal backgrounds and teach them self-control and self-discipline. Shock probation costs about the same, on a daily basis, as prison, but it can save a state millions of dollars from the early release of those who complete the program. If it has the long-term impact its advocates claim, it will keep thousands of young offenders from becoming recidivists (ex-inmates who commit further crimes). Preliminary evidence from several states indicates that boot-camp graduates are less likely to return to prison than regular prisoners are.

The director of the national antidrug program, William J. Bennett, has endorsed Georgia's program (one of the first to be established) as a model. "Instead of putting the guy in the company of hardened offenders, we can put him in a boot camp," Bennett says. "He gets a clear message that this is it: if he messes up again, he's going to be warehoused."[1]

Critics, however, say shock probation is simply a public-relations fad with no lasting effect on young felons' lives. The programs have not yet been in place long enough to permit empirical evaluation.[2]

[1] Richard L. Berke, "For Criminals, Camp Is No Vacation," *New York Times*, May 30, 1989, p. A14.
[2] Ibid.

struction. But the actual management of a correctional facility by a private firm is a recent innovation.

In 1989, adults and juveniles were held in privately run correctional institutions in at least twelve states. These included a delinquent treatment unit in Pennsylvania, the Okeechobee School for Boys in Florida, a 250-bed adult medium security prison in Tennessee, and several county jails in Texas and Wyoming. Many additional projects were under construction or being planned.[43]

Prison privatization is a controversial idea. Those who support it claim that prisons built and operated by the private sector will save the taxpayers money. Because of less red tape, facilities can be constructed relatively quickly and cheaply. Because personnel policies are more flexible in the absence of civil service protections, operations will be more economical. Most important, they claim, private prisons will reduce overcrowding. Opponents of privatization, however, question whether firms can in fact build and operate correctional facilities significantly less expensively than state or local governments. They believe that the profit motive is misplaced in a prison setting. A company whose business is prisons benefits from filling up cell space as soon as it is built, and might even run advertisements encouraging fear of crime to foster a "lock 'em up and throw away the key" approach. Such a firm might also lobby legislators for stricter sentencing and additional prisons.

Preliminary evidence on the economics of prison privatization is mixed. Most of the experimentation has been with juveniles, illegal aliens, and minimum security offenders. Cost savings have been marginal (Pennsylvania's juvenile facility in Weaversville) or nonexistent (Kentucky's adult facility at Marion), according to most studies.[44] Overcrowded conditions may be relieved more promptly, but the burden on the taxpayers appears to be about the same.

Who Should Be Responsible for Prisons?   Although economic considerations are obviously important, constitutional and legal issues may ultimately be the undoing of prisons for profit. One of the basic questions is whether the delegation of the corrections function to a private firm is constitutionally permissible. Under the necessary and proper clause, Congress can "delegate authority . . . sufficient to effect its purpose." The U.S. Supreme Court and state courts will have to determine whether incarceration, punishment, deterrence, and rehabilitation can properly be delegated, and who is legally liable for running a private facility.[45]

Another set of legal considerations concerns practical accountability for the day-to-day operation of jails and prisons. Who is responsible for developing operational rules, procedures, and standards and ensuring that they are carried out? Who is responsible for maintaining security at the institution and using force against a prisoner? Who will implement disciplinary actions against inmates? What happens if prison employees go out on strike? (Strikes by state correctional employees are illegal, but those by

their private-sector counterparts are not.) What if the corporation hikes its fees substantially? Or declares bankruptcy?

Economic and legal issues aside, perhaps the most important question is who *should* operate our jails and prisons. Legal scholar Ira Robbins suggests that we should remember the words of the novelist Dostoevsky: "The degree of civilization in a society can be judged by entering its prisons." Robbins adds:

> . . . just as the prisoner should perhaps be obliged to know—day by day, minute by minute—that he is in the custody of the state, perhaps too the state should be obliged to know—also day by day , minute by minute— that it alone is its brother's keeper, even with all of its flaws. To expect any less of the criminal-justice system may simply be misguided.[46]

The state, after all, administers justice in the courtroom. Should it not also be responsible for carrying out justice in the correctional facilities?

The Continuing Crisis in Crime and Corrections

The idea of placing people in prisons in order to punish them with deprivation of their freedom was devised only two hundred years ago. Until recently, brutality was the operating norm. Deliberately painful executions, maiming, flogging, branding, and other harsh punishments were applied to both serious and minor offenders. Misbehavior in prison was likely to be met with beatings, or with more elaborate tortures such as "stretching" from ropes attached to a pulley in the ceiling or long confinement in a unventilated "sweat box." Troublemakers in some prisons were shackled naked to a wall, then "cooled down" with a high-pressure hose targeted for maximum discomfort. By contrast, prison conditions in the states today seem almost luxurious. Inmates typically enjoy recreational activities, training and educational opportunities, the use of televisions, stereos, and VCRs in their cells, and other amenities. Rule enforcement is much more civilized and respectful of inmates' human rights.

But many prisons are very overcrowded, and they still don't do a very good job of preparing inmates for a productive, law-abiding life outside institutional walls. There appears to be very little that police can do to fight crime, short of apprehending criminals and sending them through the overloaded criminal justice system.

Crime and corrections present major challenges to state and local governments. How they meet these challenges will go far in determining their future role in American federalism. Certainly, any long-term success will have to come from the recognition that all major criminal justice system components are interrelated to some extent. Thus, a broad approach to fighting court, crime, and corrections challenges is called for. A U.S. Justice Department report released in early 1988 illustrates the need for a comprehensive treatment.[47] The report found that 50 to 75 percent of men arrested for serious crimes in various U.S. cities tested positive for illegal drug use. The purported link between drug use, criminal activity, and prison overcrowding was finally empirically verified. Before the states can successfully cope with the challenges described in this chapter, we must understand such complex relationships fully.

Summary

Dealing with crime today is almost entirely the responsibility of the states and localities. The national government offers little financial support. But the federal courts have been the most influential policy instigators of the 1970s and 1980s in the field of corrections. Concern for prison overcrowding and harsh conditions resulted in a series of rulings that forced state corrections systems to increase spending and significantly modify longstanding policies.

As the 1990s proceed, the states are valiantly attempting to cope with crime, prison overcrowding, and related difficulties. They are experimenting and innovating at a dizzying pace, exploring new approaches to deterring criminal behavior and using back-door, front-door, and capacity enhancement strategies to redefine corrections policy and the handling of criminals. It is reasonable to anticipate continued innovation in this important policy field during the 1990s.

Key Terms

Creative sentencing Sentencing in which a judge is able to fit the punishment to the crime and to the characteristics of the convicted person.

Determinate sentencing Sentencing that requires an offender, by law, to serve a fixed period in jail or prison without possibility of parole.

Grand jury A group of citizens appointed to examine evidence in order to determine whether there is enough evidence to bring a person to trial.

Indeterminate sentencing Sentencing in which a judge sentences an offender to a variable number of years.

Victimless crime An illegal act that, in theory, does no one harm.

18

Environmental

Policy

The Political Economy of Environmental Protection

Intergovernmental Relationships in Environmental Policy
  The Recent National Role/Environmental Policy Today in the States and Localities/Resolving Environmental Conflict: The Role of the Courts

Solid Waste Management: Garbage and What to Do with It
  Incineration/Recycling

Hazardous Waste: The Politics of Confusion
  RCRA: An Effort to Manage Hazardous Waste/ Superfund: Cleaning Up Hazardous Waste/What Can States Do?

Nuclear Waste: The Lingering Horror
  Types of Nuclear Trash/Low-Level Waste and Interstate Compacts

Environmental Tradeoffs
  Economics versus the Environment/Energy versus the Environment

Environmental Challenges for State and Local Governments

On March 22, 1987, a 230-foot garbage barge named *Mobro 4000* put out to sea from a dock in Queens, New York. It was loaded with 3,186 tons of commercial trash from New York City, the town of Islip, and Nassau County. After an odyssey of 6,000 miles and four and a half months, the barge returned to anchor in New York harbor, its load still intact.

The owner had originally intended to unload it at a garbage-to-methane-gas plant in North Carolina, but the *Mobro* was turned away because it lacked the necessary permits. In succession, the trash was refused by Alabama, Mississippi, Louisiana, Texas, Florida, Mexico, Belize, and the Bahamas. Public officials feared it contained lead, cadmium, and other dangerous heavy metals.

After *Mobro 4000* spent some two and a half months at anchorage, state and local officials in New York agreed to burn the cargo in a Brooklyn incinerator and to bury the ash in a landfill in Islip, where the bulk of the trash had originated. Following court battles to block first the incineration and then the burial of the ashes, the infamous garbage was finally disposed of.

The incident of the *Mobro 4000* graphically illustrated an increasingly critical environmental policy problem in the United States: what to do with the huge quantities of garbage produced by individuals, households, and industries. Similar dilemmas confront national, state, and local governments with regard to toxic wastes and nuclear wastes. Across America the NIMBY (Not in My Back Yard) syndrome has run rampant.

The late 1980s may be remembered as the time the earth screamed in anguish. Garbage barges sailing around aimlessly were the least of our global problems. Consider the following environmental crises, which led *Time* magazine to name earth "planet of the year" in 1988.

The ozone layer that protects us from dangerous ultraviolet radiation is thinning. An "ozone hole" twice the size of the continental United States has been discovered over Antarctica. The incidence of skin cancer, eye damage, and related conditions is expected to grow significantly.

The "greenhouse effect" is a global warming trend caused by the buildup of atmospheric gases that permit heat from the sun to penetrate but prevent this heat from escaping. The possible impacts are of tremendous—and frightening—magnitude. They include marked changes in weather patterns, with severe implications for world agriculture, and rising ocean levels as the polar icecaps melt.[1]

Acid rain and air pollution, principally from the burning of fossil fuels, menace the world's forests, lakes, and streams. Huge sectors of forests have been damaged in Europe, Canada, and other countries. Thousands of lakes have been "killed" by high acidity.[2]

Tropical rain forests are being cut and burned at astonishingly high rates as population growth drives Third World farmers onto marginal land. This leads to soil erosion and the accumulation of carbon dioxide in the atmosphere. Related to the devastation of the rain forests is the extinction of thousands of plant and animal species annually.

514

Surface and underground water supplies are being depleted by intensive use and poisoned by chemicals, pesticides, fertilizers, and other toxic substances. "Industrial disease" jeopardizes the lives of millions of people around the world. Life expectancies have actually declined in some countries. In Poland, 25 percent of the soil is so contaminated with chemicals that it is unfit for growing food.[3]

The 1986 nuclear disaster at Chernobyl in the Soviet Union irradiated much of Europe. In the United States, nuclear energy and weapons plants have spewed and leaked radioactive materials into the air, onto the land, and into the water.

In 1988 the U.S. Environmental Protection Agency estimated that eight million homes have dangerous levels of radon gas.[4] Up to 20,000 deaths from lung cancer per year were attributed to this colorless, odorless gas.

On beaches along the East Coast during the summer of 1988, sun worshippers were shocked to discover syringes, vials, and other medical wastes washing up on the sand. Some of the materials were contaminated with the AIDS virus.

And in 1989, as students flocked to the coasts for the spring-break ritual of sun and fun, the tanker *Exxon Valdez* ran aground, pouring 10 million gallons of oil into the pristine waters of Prince William Sound, Alaska.

The horror stories could go on and on. By 1990 it was crystal clear that our environment has become dangerously polluted. As the Worldwatch Institute put it, "Without a dramatic reordering of priorities, our grandchildren will inherit a less healthy, biologically impoverished planet, one lacking in aesthetic pleasures as well as economic opportunities."[5]

"America the Beautiful" (revised)

At first thought, these global problems may seem far removed from city halls and state capitols. There seems to be very little that state and local governments can do about acid rain, the greenhouse effect, or deforestation. Global problems require global solutions, as indicated by the multinational agreement to phase out production of industrial gases known as CFCs. Within the United States, environmental protection would seem to be a function properly assigned to the national government. Polluted air and water certainly do not respect state boundaries. But in the face of serious obstacles, the states and localities have become increasingly important environmental protectors.

The Political Economy of Environmental Protection

Environmental policy choices are made especially difficult by their economic implications. Controlling pollution is a significant economic cost for many firms today. In the essentially nonregulatory era prior to the 1960s, this expense was either quite low or nonexistent. Increasing government regulatory intervention in industrial processes and output reflects the indisputable fact that market forces by themselves will not guarantee the protection of health and environment. Polluters have little or no economic incentive to stop polluting, but clean air and water are public goods that should be available to all of us.

Left unregulated, most firms tend to maximize profits by minimizing costs—including the costs of environmental protection. Determining exactly what constitutes pollution or environmental degradation and deciding how stringently to regulate polluting activities have tremendous economic implications for firms and governments. Too much regulation could depress economic growth at national, state, and local levels and even force some companies into bankruptcy.

The tradeoffs between economic growth and environmental protection spawn conflict, and are evident wherever these important objectives clash. In Oregon, powerful timber interests have to harvest trees in order to preserve the 68,000 jobs they contribute to that state's economy, yet environmentalists won federal court prohibitions on logging where the endangered spotted owl is threatened (loggers responded with T-shirt logos such as "Save a Logger—Eat an Owl.")[6] In Maryland, a 1989 law explicitly recognized and indeed mandated a tradeoff between economics and environment: it requires developers of nontidal wetlands to replace lost swamps and bogs so that "no net loss" of these ecologically valuable wetlands occurs.[7]

All of us are potential victims of environmental problems. Polluted air, water, and land offend us aesthetically, but, more important, they threaten the health and safety of ourselves, our children, and our grandchildren. People who drink contaminated water and breathe polluted air experience the costs very directly. From a different perspective, all citizens must help pay the price of a safe and clean environment. We do this through the portion of our taxes that goes to government pollution control efforts and through the prices we pay for goods, which include the cost of pollution control. The costs to consumers are especially heavy for the products of chemical companies, the auto industry, and coal-burning power plants. Not surprisingly, these industries have lobbied heavily against what they perceive to be excessive regulation.

Government's role is to balance economic growth with environmental protection by regulating polluters. The political economy of environmental protection argues strongly for national domination of policymaking. Because states and local governments compete for industry, a nonnational jurisdiction might be tempted to relax environmental protection standards in order to influence a firm's decision on where to construct or expand a new manufacturing facility. Only national policies and standards can prevent the sacrifice of environmental quality in jurisdictions that seek growth and development at virtually any cost. By imposing minimum environmental protection standards on all states and localities, the national government helps limit interstate competition for polluting firms, since all prospective polluters must adhere to national standards.

Intergovernmental Relationships in Environmental Policy

The first government forays into the now-tangled jungle of environmental protection policy began in the early 1800s with local ordinances aimed at garbage, human and animal waste, contaminated drinking water, and other unsanitary, health-endangering conditions in American cities. Local failures to contain and control such problems were punctuated by cholera and typhoid epidemics throughout the nineteenth century. In 1878 a yellow fever epidemic caused 5,000 deaths and the exodus of another 25,000 fearful residents from Memphis, Tennessee. The population of that city dropped by more than half over a period of just two months.[8]

Such episodes prompted the states to begin regulating conditions causing waterborne diseases, thereby redefining what had been a private problem into a problem for state government. By 1948, states had taken over responsibility for water pollution control. Their early regulatory efforts were rather weak, however.[9]

The issue of water pollution control shows the evolving centralization of national government authority in environmental decision making. The national government paid little attention to environmental problems until after World War II, when urbanization and industrial production began to draw attention to the national dimensions of environmental dangers. The initial federal statutory step into the policy field was the Water Pollution Control Act of 1948. Under the original version of this act, the national government assumed limited enforcement authority for water pollution. Since then, seven other major federal statutes or amendments have been enacted to address the problem. Under this overall statutory framework, the national government pre-empted existing state and local water quality standards and substituted national standards.

The reasons for this are not difficult to fathom. We have already noted the economic dimensions. Polluted water, like contaminated air, cannot be contained within state or local boundaries. It does little good for a down-stream state to regulate water quality strictly if an upstream state is cavalier about dumping. A classic example of border-crossing water pollution is the Pigeon River in the southeastern United States, as explained in Politics and Policy 18.1.

Increasingly strong federal statutes also addressed the problems of air pollution, pesticides, and hazardous waste. By the late 1970s the national government had extended its authority to endangered species, strip mining, coastal zones, and many other areas (see Table 18.1). Thus, environmental protection was redefined as a national problem requiring national solutions. However, the national government does not operate alone; it has many state and local traveling companions.

The Recent National Role

The lead agency in national environmental policy is the Environmental Protection Agency (EPA), which was created in 1970 as an independent regulatory body for pollution control. With a director appointed by the president, the EPA's task is to coordinate and enforce the broad array of environmental protection programs established by Congress. The scope of the EPA's responsibility can be overwhelming, involving regular interaction and conflict with other national agencies, powerful private interests, and state and local governments. Its job is complicated by the tendency of Congress to pass environmental legislation that sets unattainable program goals and implementation dates. Most deadlines for compliance with federal laws have been missed by the EPA, which lends ammunition to its critics on all sides.[10] Litigation brought by regulated industries and environmental groups has further ensnarled the agency.

An example of the scope of the EPA's responsibilities is water pollution control. Every private and public facility that discharges wastes directly into waters must obtain a permit from the EPA or, in some instances, from its state counterpart. The national government, through the EPA, establishes specific discharge standards. Day-to-day oversight and implementation, however, are performed by the states. In effect, the national government makes the rules and lets the states enforce them according to their own circumstances. The national government also disburses grants to state and local governments for the treatment and monitoring of water resources. Over $30 billion was transferred to the nonnational governments for the

POLITICS AND POLICY 18.1
The Wake of the Pigeon

Near its source in the Great Smoky Mountains of North Carolina, the Pigeon River's waters are pristine and replete with trout. But as the Pigeon flows past the Champion International paper plant in Canton, North Carolina, it becomes a brown, ugly mess that smells like rotten eggs. Fifty miles below Canton the malodorous Pigeon invades Tennessee's Cocke County, provoking an "indignation that sometimes seems as rank as the river itself."[1]

Cocke County's high unemployment rate (15 percent in mid-1988) contrasts sharply with the area around Canton (less than 6 percent).[2] Tennesseans attribute many of their economic development problems in Cocke County, and a marked lack of tourists, to the color and stench of the Pigeon River. Tennessee filed suit against Champion International and North Carolina, seeking to force a cleanup. The company warned that it would have to shut down and lay off its 1,900 workers, but a compromise was reached with the help of the EPA, and Champion agreed to spend $200 million over a period of three years to improve the river's water quality. The agreement soon was jeopardized by the alleged appearance of a cancer "hot spot" in Cocke County: residents of tiny (pop. 500) Hartford were reporting an unusually high number of cancer cases. Tests of the Pigeon's water detected dangerous levels of dioxin in the fish caught near Hartford.[3] In January 1989 the state of Tennessee refused to issue a water quality variance for the treated water from Champion's plant. Negotiations between the EPA and the two states continued into late 1989 over the future of the plant and the Pigeon.

[1] Frank Trippett, "A Big Stink on the Pigeon," *Time*, June 6, 1988, p. 37.
[2] Ibid.
[3] Orville E. Bach, Jr., "Battle over a Big, Two-Hearted River," *Southern*, June 1988, p. 16.

construction of waste-water treatment plants in the 1970s and 1980s.[11] Millions more went for technical assistance and research and development.[12]

During the 1980s, state and local environmental protection roles began expanding because of several factors. One was the increased capability of the states and localities to assume more control over their environmental destinies. Another was the growing propensity of the national government to turn over program responsibilities to the states. But the most important

Table 18.1   Major Congressional Environmental Legislation

Date	Legislation	Major Provisions
1948	Water Pollution Control Act	Provided loans for construction of treatment plants
1956	Amendments to Water Pollution Control Act	Provided grants for construction of treatment plants
1963	Clean Air Act	Provided grants to state and local programs
1965	Water Quality Act	Provided grants for research and development of sewers
1965	Motor Vehicle Air Pollution Control Act	Set national standards on auto emissions
1967	Air Quality Act	Set deadlines for state air pollution standards; state implementation
1969	National Environmental Policy Act	Required environmental impact statements
1970	Amendments to Clean Air Act	Set national standards on air quality; state implementation
1972	Amendments to Water Pollution Control Act	Set national water quality goals; established national pollution discharge permit
1972	Environmental Pesticide Control Act	Required registration of all pesticides
1972	Coastal Zone Management Act	Provided federal grants for state development of coastal management

immediate factor in greater state involvement was the environmental policy decisions of the Reagan administration, which resulted in severe financial aid reductions and a general de-emphasis of national activities.

Ronald Reagan was openly hostile to environmental causes.[13] During the 1980 presidential campaign he repeatedly attacked the Clean Air Act and "excessive" environmental regulations, and during his eight years in office he sought to disembowel or terminate most existing antipollution programs. Reagan's attitude toward the environment was exemplified by his first appointees to direct the EPA (Anne Gorsuch) and the Department of the Interior (James Watt), both of whom were seen as openly biased in favor of industry and against environmentalists. Watt appointed many former employees of industries regulated by the Interior Department; when environmental groups criticized his decisions, Watt called them members of "a

Table 18.1   Major Congressional Environmental Legislation (*cont.*)

Date	Legislation	Major Provisions
1973	Endangered Species Act	Required protection of all "threatened" and "endangered" species
1974	Safe Water Drinking Act	Set national standards for quality of public drinking water supplies
1976	Toxic Substances Control Act	Allowed EPA to ban chemicals that threaten health or the environment; prohibited PCBs
1976	Resource Conservation and Recovery Act	Set standards for hazardous waste treatment, storage, transportation, and disposal
1977	Surface Mining Control and Reclamation Act	Set controls on strip mining and required land restoration
1980	Comprehensive Environmental Response, Compensation, and Liability Act	Created Superfund
1980	Low-Level Radioactive Waste Policy Act	Required interstate compacts for LLW disposal
1984	Asbestos School Hazard Abatement Act	Provided funds to remove asbestos from schools
1986	Superfund Reauthorization Act	Increased Superfund to $9 billion

left-wing cult."[14] Gorsuch was soon accused of mismanagement, intentional delays, conflicts of interest, and using political criteria to determine which states would receive grants for the cleanup of hazardous waste sites. Congress soon had enough of her, and cited her for contempt, among other things. After little more than two years in office, Gorsuch was forced to resign. Watt, too, eventually resigned under fire, after making an especially insensitive remark about the handicapped and racial minorities.[15]

Although national funding of environmental programs was cut by 50 percent during the first few years of Reagan's administration, few programs were actually terminated. Instead, the severe cutback in funding and qualified, experienced personnel seriously hindered the EPA's effectiveness. Even more drastic cuts sought by Reagan in later years were not granted by Congress. By that time environmental policy had become highly institutionalized and enjoyed widespread support in both political parties and in the general public. Large and influential interest groups such as the Sierra Club and the National Wildlife Federation rallied their troops to fight further cutbacks and to sabotage Reagan's policy efforts. Most added many new members. The Sierra Club's enrollment nearly doubled, to 335,000, in just three years.[16] In the end, Reagan's budget cuts, staff reductions, and hostile political appointments seriously damaged environmental protection policy at the national level but could not deal it a death blow.

George Bush entered the White House in 1989 with a much more benign attitude toward the environment. An ardent sportsman, Bush appointed William K. Reilly, former president of the World Wildlife Fund and the Conservation Foundation, as director of the EPA. In his first year in office, President Bush proposed significantly strengthening the Clean Air Act and showed strong interest in environmental issues generally.

Environmental Policy Today in the States and Localities

As the resolve of the national government weakened during the 1980s, the determination of the state and local governments grew. Increasingly, the nonnational governments are taking on greater responsibility for financing and operating environmental protection programs. For example, Congress was stalled on acid rain legislation for years, but several states took unilateral actions to cut sulfur dioxide emissions within their borders (New Hampshire and New York were the first). Several states, including New Jersey and Ohio, have passed legislation requiring firms to clean up hazardous wastes from industrial property before they can sell it. This helps prevent companies from abandoning polluted sites that present health risks and leaving them for the states to clean up. California voters used the initiative process in 1986 to impose criminal penalties of up to $100,000 per day on firms that illegally dump harmful chemicals.

States continue to operate their pollution control programs under the auspices of national legislation and the EPA. They must develop and implement plans and standards under the host of laws listed in Table 18.1. If a state does not enforce national regulations properly, the EPA will take over and operate the program itself. However, most states have willingly taken on the cause of environmental protection. State officials chafe at the funding reductions that seem to accompany each new transfer of program authority, and they deeply resent the laborious paperwork and other strings attached to national grants-in-aid. But ultimately, state and local governments are closer to pollution problems and best situated to address them on a day-to-day basis. Table 18.2 ranks the states' performance in environmental protection, based on programs in air pollution reduction, soil conservation, hazardous waste management, solid waste and recycling, and renewable energy and conservation.

Drawing on their constitutional and traditional responsibilities for protecting the health and safety of their citizens, state and local governments have once again become environmental policy initiators.[17] In some cases they have joined together on a formal basis to promote policy cooperation. For example, six interstate compacts are in effect on water policy. The most recent involves an eight-state compact for cleaning up the Great Lakes.

Resolving Environmental Conflict: The Role of the Courts

Three types of legal conflicts arise in environmental law. First, the government may bring enforcement actions against industrial polluters who do not comply with national or state law. Second, the government may be sued by firms or by environmental organizations. Finally, one government may take legal action against another government. Often the EPA or its state counterpart—an agency such as Michigan's Department of Natural Resources or California's Department of Health Services—is party to a suit, largely because of the broad discretionary authority given to it by legislation. Industries, environmental groups, and state and local governments test the boundaries of this authority by appealing decisions of the EPA and its state partners.

Typically, the principal effect of litigation is simply to delay mandated actions. In the majority of cases involving a government, the courts side with the government, and the result is often a decision to send the case back to the enforcement agency for action.[18] Interestingly, state courts are just as likely as federal courts to rule against polluters,[19] contrary to the beliefs of those who still do not trust the states to police their environment aggressively.

The large number and broad scope of environmental laws and the increasing legal expertise of environmental policy actors ensure that the courts will remain deeply involved in environmental affairs. This involvement can be controversial: the competence of judges to make technical decisions on environmental issues may be called into question, and the courtroom is unlikely to produce any sort of coherent policy through case-by-case adjudication. It is more desirable to determine policy through the legislative process. Also, litigation is very time-consuming and expensive.[20] This accounts for the increased reliance on "environmental mediation" to resolve disputes and reconcile differences. In environmental mediation, a nonbiased, third-party mediator promotes a voluntary settlement between litigants. This technique is faster, cheaper, and usually more satisfying to everyone involved, but it is not appropriate in all disputes.[21]

Solid Waste Management: Garbage and What to Do with It

The tragicomic saga of the *Mobro 4000* is a metaphor for the problem of what to do with the vast quantities of household and industrial trash generated in the United States. On a per capita basis, Americans produce 3.5 pounds of garbage each day. The 160 million tons of solid waste generated in 1988 would fill up enough ten-ton garbage trucks to reach bumper to bumper halfway to the moon;[22] the figure is expected to reach 200 million tons by 1990. Our per capita waste is twice that of any other country. McDonald's restaurants alone account for 1.5 billion cubic feet of Styrofoam waste each year.[23]

Table 18.2   A Ranking of State Environmental Programs

Rank	State	Total points (out of 60)
1	Wisconsin	49
2	California	48
3	New Jersey	47
4	Connecticut	44
5	Michigan	43
	New York	43
7	North Carolina	42
8	Florida	41
	Illinois	41
	Massachusetts	41
11	Iowa	39
12	Minnesota	38
13	Maine	36
	Indiana	36
15	Oregon	35
16	Maryland	34
	Ohio	34
18	Virginia	33
19	New Hampshire	32
	Pennsylvania	32
21	Missouri	31
	Nebraska	31
	South Carolina	31
24	Rhode Island	30

Source: Fund for Renewable Energy and the Environment, *The State of the States 1987* (Washington, D.C.: FREE, 1987), p. 3. Copyright 1987. Used by permission of Renew America.

Approximately 90 percent of this trash is buried in sanitary landfills, but they are filling up fast. More than four thousand have been closed down since 1980, and the pace is quickening. According to a national survey by the EPA, at least twenty-seven states confront serious landfill space problems.[24] The eleven operating landfills in New Jersey are due to be closed by 1991. Connecticut's may last only until 1990. One out of four large cities expects to exhaust its landfill space by 1992. To make matters even worse, the 56,000 still-functioning garbage dumps, along with the 14,000 that have been shut down, pose serious hazards to surface and underground water supplies.[25]

Like nuclear and hazardous waste, solid waste involves the NIMBY syndrome. Everyone generates garbage, and lots of it, but no one wants to have it smelling over the back fence or threatening the well water. The

Table 18.2 A Ranking of State Environmental Programs (*cont.*)

Rank	State	Total points (out of 60)
25	Kansas	29
	Oklahoma	29
	Tennessee	29
	Washington	29
29	Kentucky	28
	Vermont	28
31	Arizona	27
32	Georgia	26
	Texas	26
34	Delaware	24
	Colorado	24
36	Montana	23
	Nevada	23
	New Mexico	23
	South Dakota	23
40	Louisiana	21
41	Hawaii	19
42	Alaska	18
	Arkansas	18
	Idaho	18
45	Alabama	16
	North Dakota	16
	Utah	16
	Wyoming	16
49	West Virginia	15
50	Mississippi	14

shortage of sites has naturally driven up the price of land disposal in the dumps that still operate, and disposal fees have tripled in many localities during the past few years. Many cities must ship their waste 50 to 150 miles and across state lines to find an open dump site. As a consequence, the average "tipping fee" charged by landfill operators (most of which are local governments) leaped from $5 per ton in 1980 to $25 per ton in 1987.[26] By 1990, the cost of dumping reached $100 per ton in parts of the Northeast.

Solid waste management is primarily a local government responsibility. Garbage collection and disposal was one of the first local government services in American cities. In the 1800s most of the trash was piled up on vacant land outside urban areas, although some of it was hauled out to sea, a practice that continues today off the New Jersey shore. A 1988 national law will halt ocean dumping by 1992, which offers some reassurance that medical waste will not continue to wash up on East Coast beaches.

Although the national government has mostly left the states and localities to their own devices in dealing with the solid waste dilemma, the EPA enters the scene when water quality is threatened or when burning of trash pollutes the air, and some national grants are available to assist with alternative approaches. Essentially, however, state and local governments hold the policy mantle for solid wastes. They face the questions of how to dispose of existing garbage and how to reduce the quantity of solid waste generated in the future.

Concerned with the garbage disposal problem, Oregon enacted a law in 1983 that permits state officials to override local opposition to new landfills. Wisconsin uses a more cooperative approach, in which state officials negotiate with local officials and citizens to guarantee the value of nearby property or to provide cash grants to local areas and residents willing to host a landfill. Both approaches have shown signs of success.[27] For most states, though, incineration and recycling are the leading alternatives for reducing the quantity of garbage.

Incineration

Burning has for many centuries served as an alternative to burying or stacking up trash. In rural areas across America, homeowners and industries burn leaves, paper, and other organic wastes. Because burning presents a fire hazard to nearby land and buildings and pollutes the air, it is prohibited in most urban areas. Yet it remains the most common alternative to landfilling. It reduces waste volume by approximately 90 percent, and, depending on the extent of pollution controls and the size of the operation, it can be inexpensive. The remaining ash is usually buried in a landfill, although some of it must be treated as hazardous waste because it contains heavy metals and other toxic materials. Most of the large incineration operations in the United States utilize the principle of *cogeneration*, through which the heat from burning garbage is used to produce steam or electricity.

There is no disputing the fact that incineration drastically reduces the volume of solid waste. However, serious reservations about large-scale burning have been raised. First, incinerators are expensive. A 1,500-ton-per-day plant costs more than $150 million—quite a chunk of money for a local government to raise. The second big drawback to incineration is the environmental cost. The Sierra Club, the Environmental Defense Fund, and other environmental groups oppose burning because of its danger to public health. The process releases quantities of toxic substances, such as heavy metals, into the air around the site. Firms that build and sell the facilities claim that proper filtering of smoke and proper disposal of the contaminated ash make incineration a safe technology, but doubts seem to be growing. Many proposed incinerator projects were canceled during the late 1980s. Another threat to incineration comes from future tightening up of Clean Air Act standards. Further difficulties arise in siting incinerators in local communities, where they are rarely welcome.

Recycling

With landfill space diminishing, disposal fees climbing, and health concerns increasing, incineration began falling out of favor in the late 1980s. Recycling has been presented as a better option. It does not pollute, is relatively inexpensive, and is ecologically sound, since waste materials are utilized productively. Recycling programs are now in various stages of implementation in most states. Like other solid waste management activities, recycling is primarily a local government responsibility. States typically provide technical and financial assistance to the municipalities, which operate the programs.

Recycling is a promising technology that makes good sense. Only around 10 percent of the nation's trash is being recycled, but the percentage could grow to 25 percent by 1993.[28] The ports of New York and Boston already export more scrap metal and used paper than any other commodity. At least six states had some sort of mandatory recycling program in place in 1989. New Jersey's Source Separation and Recycling Act of 1987 requires all 567 local communities to implement programs for sorting and recycling household garbage, in order to reduce the total amount of waste by 25 percent.[29] Residents must separate their trash into that which is recyclable and that which is not, before placing it on the curb for pickup. A growing number of cities and counties have begun their own recycling efforts, independent of state legislation. One of the most unusual is the "cash for trash" program of St. Cloud, Minnesota. Residents who bag newspapers, glass, aluminum cans, and other reusable materials and place them on the curb for monthly pickup become eligible for a special cash award.[30]

Yard waste is recycled in many states and localities. Leaves, grass cuttings, shrub prunings, and similar materials make up about 18 percent of municipal solid waste and take up a large volume of precious landfill space.[31] This debris is biodegradable and valuable as a soil builder and fertilizer when composted. Even if there is no apparent use or market for the compost, the original amount of trash shrinks drastically at little or no cost.

Recycling is not a panacea for the solid waste problem. It requires citizen cooperation if it is to be affordable, and some people simply will not cooperate. San Jose, California, which operates the largest recycling effort in the United States, reports only 60 percent participation.[32] The city cannot refuse to collect nonparticipants' garbage without creating a public health problem. Another weakness of recycling is that there are not yet enough markets for the paper, aluminum cans, plastics, and other materials. As the director of environmental management in Rhode Island warned, "This is no garden club collecting a few bottles and cans. We are going to have to restructure fairly large pieces of the national and international economy to digest what we're going to feed it."[33]

Even if recycling were carried out to the fullest extent possible, substantial quantities of solid waste, particularly Styrofoam and plastics, would remain. One idea is to ban nonrecyclable beverage and fast-food containers. Suffolk County, New York, home of the long-suffering garbage barge, is the innovator. In 1981 it prohibited the sale of nonreturnable bottles, and in 1988 it banned plastic packages that are not biodegradable.[34] The technology for recycling plastics, including the 270 million pounds of plastic soda bottles and milk containers produced annually, is emerging.

All three techniques—landfilling, incineration, and recycling—will be needed in the future to manage the vast quantity of solid waste generated in our mass-consumption, throw-away society. Recycling is very appealing, and is likely to flourish in the 1990s. Simply recycling the Sunday editions of the *New York Times* would spare an estimated four million trees annually.[35] But we cannot recycle everything. Some of the garbage must therefore be incinerated or landfilled. Every new waste technology has its own difficult issues, and the states and localities, with virtually no assistance from Washington, D.C., are striving to deal effectively with the huge task of managing America's garbage.

Hazardous Waste: The Politics of Confusion

The image of garbage mountains rising above the horizon is disconcerting, to say the least. When New York City completes its Fresh Kills Landfill on Staten Island in 2005, the mammoth garbage mound is expected to rival the great pyramids of Egypt in size.[36] But solid waste is just one of several contributors to environmental destruction. A more insidious public health threat comes from hazardous waste—the poisonous by-products of industry. If these by-products possess toxic, corrosive, flammable, or reactive properties, they are considered hazardous. The industries that generate 90 percent of the hazardous waste in the United States are chemical and allied products, primary metals, petroleum and coal products, fabricated metal products, and rubber and plastic products.[37] Hazardous waste is even more ubiquitous than most people realize. Pesticide residues, used motor oil, discarded cadmium batteries, used refrigerants, and paint sludge are hazardous leftovers that are frequently found in households and in so-called nonpolluting industries.[38] It is no exaggeration to say that hazardous waste is all around us. More than 2.4 billion pounds of toxic substances poured into the air in 1987. Table 18.3 lists the ten states responsible for more than half of them.

The primary dilemma with hazardous waste is what to do with it. The discovery that wastes had not been properly or safely disposed of triggered government involvement; as hazardous liquids began seeping into people's basements from long-buried barrels, as children playing in fields uncovered rotting drums of toxic waste, as motorists developed unusual skin rashes from pesticides sprayed along the roadway, government was called in. Some states feared that the imposition of tough new hazardous waste regulations would make them less attractive to industry. Others were concerned that tightening the laws for waste disposal would actually increase the incidence of illegal dumping. A national policy initiative seemed preferable to state attempts at solving the problems.

The national government responded to the mounting crisis with two pieces of legislation: the Resource Conservation and Recovery Act of 1976 (RCRA) and the Comprehensive Environmental Response, Compensation and Liability Act of 1980 (known as Superfund). RCRA provides for "cradle-to-grave" tracking of waste and establishes standards for its treatment,

Table 18.3   The Toxic Ten

State	Millions of pounds of toxic pollutants released into the air, 1987
Texas	229.9
Louisiana	134.5
Tennessee	132.5
Virginia	131.4
Ohio	122.5
Michigan	106.2
Indiana	103.5
Illinois	103.1
Georgia	94.3
North Carolina	92.3

Source: U.S. Environmental Protection Agency, "National Air Quality and Emissions Trends Report," March 1989.

storage, and disposal. The Superfund program cleans up existing abandoned waste sites. If RCRA is successful, it should lessen the need for programs like Superfund in the future.

RCRA: An Effort to Manage Hazardous Waste

RCRA is considered partially pre-emptive in that states have a degree of discretion and flexibility in implementing it. Under RCRA, the EPA establishes minimum standards that state programs must meet and may exceed. Once the EPA is satisfied that a state program meets its standards and possesses adequate enforcement mechanisms, it authorizes the state to operate its own hazardous waste management program. If subsequent state regulatory behavior is insufficient or if a state chooses not to start its own program (as Wyoming has), the EPA steps in and operates the program. By March 1989, forty-two states had received authorization to run their own hazardous waste control systems (see Table 18.4).

State officials are not completely happy with the hazardous waste man-

Table 18.4   The States and their RCRA Status

States with authorization to operate their own hazardous waste management programs, grouped by year in which authorization was received

1984	1985		1986	1987	1988
Delaware	N. Hampshire	Oklahoma	Pennsylvania	Alabama	Maine
Mississippi	Vermont	Arkansas	Illinois		
Montana	New Mexico	Kentucky	Oregon		
Georgia	Tennessee	Massachusetts	Rhode Island		
North Dakota	Nebraska	Louisiana	Washington		
Utah	Maryland	Minnesota	Wisconsin		
Colorado	Florida	New Jersey	Indiana		
South Dakota	Kansas	Nevada	New York		
Virginia	S. Carolina	Arizona	West Virginia		
Texas	Missouri		Michigan		
North Carolina					

States without authorization, as of March 1, 1989

Alaska	Idaho
California	Iowa
Connecticut	Ohio
Hawaii	Wyoming

Source: U.S. Environmental Protection Agency, "States Granted Final Authorization for Pre-HWSA Program," no date.

agement system. Many use phrases like "too time-consuming," "burden-some," and "resource-intensive" to describe their state's experience with RCRA implementation.[39] Generally, they have difficulty adapting RCRA to the specific conditions and problems in their state. Ironically, while state officials lament the lack of flexibility in RCRA, some members of Congress believe that too much discretion is left to the states. EPA officials often hear from Congress because of inadequacies in state programs.

In its 1984 reauthorization of RCRA, Congress included specific dead-lines and **hammer provisions,** which penalize a state for failure to act. Although progress has been made, the complexity of hazardous waste regulation slows the process. For example, as of early 1988, the EPA and the states had issued operating permits to fewer than 15 percent of the nation's 4,000 active hazardous waste management facilities.[40]

Superfund: Cleaning Up Hazardous Waste

Superfund was passed in late 1980 in recognition of the fact that no matter how comprehensive and cautious hazardous waste management is in the future, the pollution of the past remains with us. Under Superfund, the national government can intervene to clean up a threatening hazardous waste site.

One of the first actions taken under Superfund was the identification of particularly dangerous sites that were in need of immediate cleanup. These sites formed what is known as the National Priorities List (NPL). In its first phase, the NPL listed 110 sites, and New Jersey contained more than any other state. By 1989 the list had grown to 1,163, with New Jersey continuing to have the dubious lead with 107 sites. (The number of NPL sites in each state for 1987 is shown in Figure 18.1.)

Despite its early promise, most analysts have concluded that Superfund has fallen far short of its goals. For example, five years from the inception of the act, only five sites had been cleaned up completely; another thirty-nine were partially completed.[41]

One factor confounding the Superfund program, aside from EPA's uncertain interest in it in the early 1980s, is the number of government and private interests that are inevitably involved in cleanups. Research on early cleanups found them hopelessly tangled in a web involving national, state, and local technicians, administrators, and politicians. Not surprisingly, very little was accomplished. Cleanup work bogged down over issues of responsibility and definition ("how clean is clean?"). As tensions escalated among local officials, environmental activists, nearby residents, state bureaucrats, EPA administrators, and the cleanup contractors, the hazardous waste sites remained.[42]

As with RCRA, congressional concern over the slow pace of implementation spurred legislative action. In renewing Superfund, Congress increased

Figure 18.1 Number of National Priority List (Superfund) Sites by State, 1987
The discovery of new hazardous waste sites outpaces the cleanup of existing sites.

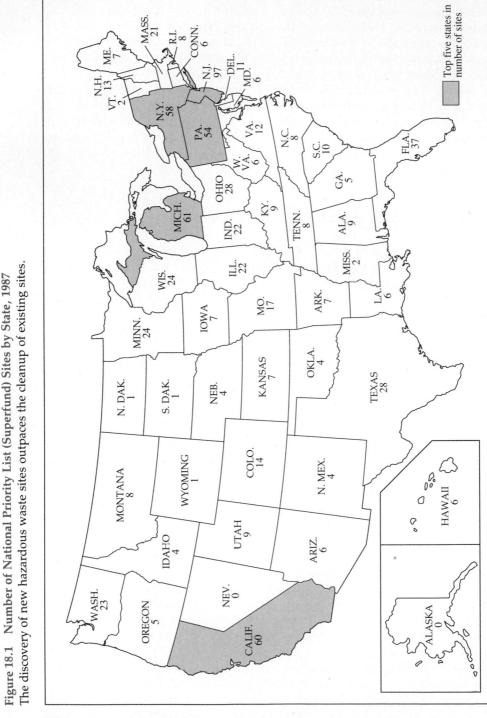

Top five states in
number of sites

MASS. 21
R.I. 8
ME. 7
CONN. 6
N.J. 97
DEL. 11
N.H. 13
MD. 6
VT. 2
N.Y. 58
VA. 12
N.C. 8
PA. 54
S.C. 10
FLA. 37
W. VA. 6
OHIO 28
GA. 5
MICH. 61
KY. 9
IND. 22
TENN. 8
ALA. 9
WIS. 24
ILL. 22
MISS. 2
MINN. 24
MO. 17
ARK. 7
LA. 6
IOWA 7
KANSAS 7
OKLA. 4
TEXAS 28
N. DAK. 1
S. DAK. 1
NEB. 4
WYOMING 1
COLO. 14
N. MEX. 4
HAWAII 6
MONTANA 8
UTAH 9
IDAHO 4
ARIZ. 6
ALASKA 0
WASH. 23
OREGON 5
NEV. 0
CALIF. 60

Source: U.S. Environmental Protection Agency, "National Priorities List: Final and Proposed Sites through Update 4," September 1987.

the funding level rather generously, from $1.6 billion (1980–85) to $9 billion (1986–91). The new law contained several key provisions affecting the involvement of state governments, which now play a greater role in selecting remedies but have a lessened obligation to pay for long-term cleanup. To address the problem of a lack of disposal facilities, Superfund now requires states to ensure that they have adequate disposal capacity in state or in other states, or risk losing their allocations.[43]

What Can States Do?

Some states have actively pursued their own hazardous waste control agendas. More than half have enacted mini-Superfund statutes that authorize them to conduct site assessments and initiate remedial cleanup actions or force a responsible party to do so.[44] Twenty-one states have enacted "community right to know" statutes, and seventeen have conducted household hazardous waste collection drives.

The issue that has caused the greatest trouble in the states is disposal. Hazardous waste disposal is *locally unwanted land use*, or a LULU. Which level of government should make decisions about LULUs, state or local? Some states have been aggressive in siting waste facilities, opting for an approach known as **state pre-emption.** Under this, state governments take the lead in evaluating the disposal potential of possible sites, conducting hearings, and approving construction and operation. New Jersey and Arizona are among the more than twenty states that have adopted this approach.[45] Other states, primarily in the South and West, have taken a different tack, allowing local governments to veto construction of a facility within their borders. An approach that falls between these extremes is a joint state/local decision-making process like the ones that Illinois, Maine, and Minnesota use. Another, which is being explored in Massachusetts and Wisconsin, is the use of negotiation and third-party arbiters in the site selection process. There is no single best way to make such decisions; of the 179 attempts to site new hazardous waste facilities between 1980 and 1986, 22 percent were approved, 25 percent were not, and 53 percent were on hold.[46]

Consider the way in which North Carolina settled the disposal of tons of PCB-contaminated dirt. The state considered more than a hundred possible sites; Warren County drew the short straw. The county government hastily adopted an ordinance prohibiting hazardous waste disposal in the area, but to no avail—the state's decision was final. Warren County residents organized protests and demonstrations in opposition to the dump, and protestors at the site locked arms in an attempt to form a human barricade, which only delayed the dumping. Eventually, North Carolina legislators threw a bone to the county by creating a special industrial development package for it, as partial compensation for the toxic waste dump.

Citizen interest in hazardous waste facility siting is potentially high. Across the country, rumors that a location is under consideration for a waste dump are enough to mobilize local residents. Unfocused local protests have evolved into sophisticated efforts at coalition building and legislative lobbying. In Ohio, for example, local groups like Independent Citizens Associated for Reclaiming the Environment (I-CARE) have teamed up with statewide networks of related groups such as Voting Ohioans Initiating a Clean Environment (VOICE) to influence policy implementation.[47]

California has launched an effort to involve local governments more intimately in hazardous waste decision making. In 1988, the General Assembly set up a $10 million grant program so that all fifty-eight counties could prepare local hazardous waste plans.[48] In developing their plans, the counties quickly encountered issues of fairness, as rural counties feared that they might become the dumping ground for waste produced in urban counties. The state agency, the Department of Health Services, fueled that speculation by reasoning that since California industries benefit the entire state, an individual county cannot refuse waste generated elsewhere. Counties that generate only a few thousand tons of hazardous waste consider this patently unfair; heavily populated and industrialized counties consider it the answer to their prayers.

One eminently plausible, if partial, solution to waste disposal dilemmas is to reduce the amount of waste generated. If less waste is produced, there will be less waste to dispose of. Yet this sensible solution is surprisingly difficult to impose. Reducing waste often means redesigning the production process, and that entails costs that industry has proven unwilling to absorb. New York developed the first waste reduction program in 1981; North Carolina (1983) and Minnesota (1984) followed suit. By 1986, ten states were operating waste reduction programs, inspired primarily by concern over vanishing land disposal capacity. One of the key features of the programs is the use of economic incentives to promote waste reduction.

Nuclear Waste: The Lingering Horror

Nuclear events have a particularly horrifying drama. The near meltdown of Pennsylvania's Three Mile Island nuclear reactor in 1979 continues to haunt the public and the industry; no new nuclear power plants have been ordered in the ensuing years, and many that were on the drawing boards have been canceled. Adequate safety has been the primary concern of the general public; increased costs, especially those dictated for safety reasons, have troubled investors. Additional fears have been triggered by revelations from defense-related nuclear facilities. The news that uranium has been regularly released into the environment at the Fernald nuclear weapons production facility in Ohio and that serious safety violations have occurred at the Savannah River site in South Carolina has raised troubling questions about contamination of air, soil, and water.

Types of Nuclear Trash

Nuclear power carries a heavy price: waste. As with solid and hazardous wastes, the key question is what to do with it. Nuclear waste is divided into three types—high-level, transuranic, and low-level—based on the persistence of toxicity. High-level wastes maintain their extreme toxicity for hundreds of thousands of years. Transuranic wastes are liquids that are dangerous for very long periods but are not as persistent as the high-level variety. Low-level wastes are much less toxic, in a relative sense, and break down to safe levels of radioactivity in anywhere from a few days or months to three hundred years.

The case of low-level radioactive waste (LLW) demonstrates the difficulties of the problem. LLW is produced by commercial nuclear power installations (54 percent), nuclear-related industries (11 percent), and medical and research institutions (35 percent). The waste, much of it stored in fifty-five-gallon steel drums, includes items such as contaminated laboratory clothes, tools, equipment, and leftover bomb materials as well as bulk wastes.

As burial sites exhausted their capacity or began to leak radioactive materials and were closed, the nation came to rely on three sites—Barnwell, South Carolina; Beatty, Nevada; and Hanford, Washington—for the disposal of LLW. Some citizens in these states began to question their role as a "dumping ground." They reasoned that since the waste was being produced in all fifty states, its disposal ought to be dispersed as well. The three governors met to develop a strategy for a national policy. They provoked action by increasing disposal fees, reducing the volume of waste they would accept, and periodically shutting down the LLW dumps. Washingtonians went so far as to pass an initiative that banned the disposal of out-of-state waste from states that were not developing their own burial sites.

The resulting clamor from the nuclear industry and from medical and research facilities precipitated congressional action, leading to the Low-Level Radioactive Waste Policy Act in 1980. Quite simply, the act made each state responsible for the disposal of the waste generated within its borders. States have the choice of managing LLW within their own jurisdictions (that is, developing their own burial sites) or entering into an interstate compact for out-of-state disposal. As expected, some states have opted to handle the problem alone, but most have joined with their neighbors to forge a regional solution to the disposal question.[49] Politics and Policy 18.2 tells the story of a planned New Mexico facility and of how New Mexico's problems have become other states' problems.

Low-Level Waste and Interstate Compacts

The use of interstate compacts to address the LLW problem was particularly inventive, since nuclear waste disposal has historically been considered a national responsibility. Under the act, states can venture into the arena of

POLITICS AND POLICY 18.2
Nuclear Waste? Let's Bury It in Southeastern New Mexico

Subterranean caverns in southeastern New Mexico are the site of the Waste Isolation Pilot Plant (WIPP), a $720 million (as of August 1989) facility designed to be the final resting place for low-level and transuranic waste generated at the nation's nuclear weapons facilities. The plan is said by its proponents to be technologically neat. The drummed waste will be placed in chambers that have been hollowed out of ancient salt beds 2,150 feet below ground. Over the site's twenty-five-year lifetime, up to one million barrels are expected to be buried there. Once it has reached its capacity, shafts leading to the caverns will be sealed, the aboveground area will be decontaminated, and the site will be abandoned. Within a hundred years, according to the U.S. Department of Energy (DOE), "the salt formation will creep inward, swallowing the waste forever." DOE is asking Congress for a five-year trial run to make certain that WIPP functions as hoped.

Concern over the facility's safety and the quality of its construction, however, led DOE to postpone its scheduled fall 1988 opening for at least one and a half years. Since then, DOE has had to respond to contentions from some scientists that the much-vaunted five-year test will not provide accurate data on the very serious problems of seepage. As moisture in the caverns interacts with the salt and corrodes the steel drums, the effects could be devastating to the Pecos River, a tributary of the Rio Grande.

Continued debate over WIPP's safety has caused some New Mexico officials, including the governor, to reconsider their strong support for the plan. The significance of WIPP, ten years in the making, was clarified in a recent three-state dispute. Because WIPP had not opened as scheduled, Idaho could not ship nuclear waste stored at the DOE facility within its borders to New Mexico. Faced with mounting waste, the governor of Idaho refused to accept incoming waste from the Rocky Flats, Colorado, bomb plant. Confronted with no place to send this waste, the governor of Colorado threatened to shut down Rocky Flats. Incidents like these underscore how anxious DOE is to have WIPP operational. WIPP's importance crosses state lines, a characteristic common to nuclear waste issues.

Source: Daniel Gibson, "Land of Disenchantment," *Sierra* 74 (March/April 1989): 38–44. Reprinted by permission of the author.

regulating interstate commerce, a territory typically off limits to them. Interstate LLW compacts are unique in another way. Usually interstate compacts distribute costs and benefits across a unified area. The "goods" (water systems or transportation networks) are to be enjoyed by all members; the "bads" (pollution or crime) are to be borne by all. Low-level waste compacting, however, actually concentrates public bads (the location of a nuclear waste disposal site) in one or two states while the benefits (the ability to use the site) are enjoyed by all member states.[50]

When they are successful, interstate compacts are a shining example of what the states, left to their own devices, can accomplish. The process can be somewhat tortuous, however, as initial enthusiasm encounters the hard realities of self-interested behavior. Interstate compacting begins with the negotiation of a draft document by delegates representing interested states. The draft must be ratified by the legislatures of potential member states, and then the compact must receive congressional consent. It is then ready for implementation. In a typical case, a compact commission composed of representatives of member states serves as the implementing agency.

Much attention has been focused on the Southeast compact, in which member states wrestled over which state would replace South Carolina as a host site in 1992.[51] No state volunteered for the role, and so decision makers developed a weighting system whereby they could evaluate the disposal potential of member states according to waste volume, population density, land suitability, transportation systems, and meteorological conditions. The process led to the designation of North Carolina as the successor to South Carolina. Many in the Tar Heel State contended that the designation process was biased, and some state legislators called for North Carolina to pull out of the Southeast compact and develop a disposal facility exclusively for its own use. The secession talk died down, however, and it appears that North Carolina will assume its regional nuclear responsibility.

Independent action could have been a costly course for North Carolina. Because it takes four or five years to identify, construct, and license a facility, North Carolina would have been forced to use out-of-state disposal facilities during that period. South Carolina probably would not have been very receptive to truckloads of toxins from its northern neighbor, and other states with disposal capacity might have used North Carolina's predicament to impose heavy surcharges on incoming waste. Congress might have forced North Carolina to accept waste from other states once its facility was operating.

Although a lot of time and negotiation was involved, by the late summer of 1987, nine interstate LLW compacts existed. Seven states remained unaligned, including three major LLW generators: Texas, Massachusetts, and New York. The compacts and member states are illustrated in Figure 18.2. The lack of guarantees about the future makes nuclear waste disposal fascinating and not a little bit frightening.

Figure 18.2   Low-Level Waste Compacts, through May 1989

By January 1, 1986, states were to have ratified compacts or enacted legislation to develop their own LLW facilities.

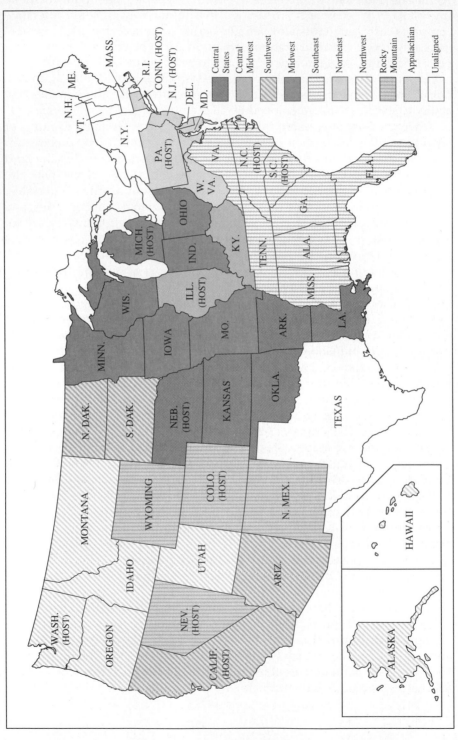

Source: Southeast Compact Commission for Low-Level Radioactive Waste Management, Raleigh, N.C.

Environmental Tradeoffs

Research tells us that Americans generally support the goals of environmental protection. Public opinion polls indicate that most people are in favor of increased government spending for environmental protection and oppose efforts to weaken environmental standards.[52] This resounding endorsement weakens, however, when environmental protection is pitted against goals such as economic growth and adequate energy. Environmental protection does not occur in a vacuum; achieving its goals comes at the expense of other valued objectives.

Economics versus the Environment

The proposed development of a cargo port on Sears Island along the central coast of Maine illustrates the economics/environment issue.[53] Supporters of the new port include business leaders and state and local officials. Lined up on the opposing side are the Sierra Club and the EPA. The dispute boils down to jobs versus coastline preservation. Proponents claim that the port will provide jobs, reduce shipping costs for local businesses, and stimulate additional development—a powerful lure to the economically depressed area. Opponents counter that the economic potential of the port does not justify the environmental damage that its construction and operation will cause. There are a multitude of side issues, such as whether an existing port might be modernized and how much the railroad company whose real estate subsidiary owns most of the island will profit. The chance of a compromise acceptable to both sides appears remote.

Slightly different themes emerged during the battle to clean up smog-shrouded southern California. A government-approved plan developed in 1989 aims to reduce the amount of harmful emissions released into the atmosphere by establishing tough new standards to be phased in over a twenty-year period. Already the key issue has become improving air quality without causing economic harm.[54] But achieving the goals of the plan is quite likely to disrupt the normal flow of business, especially in the transportation industry.

According to the plan, by 1998, 40 percent of all automobiles, 70 percent of trucks, and all buses are to use methanol or other "clean" fuels. By 2008, the plan envisions car dealers selling vehicles that run on electricity or other alternative fuels. Other industries are affected as well. The plan calls for reformulation of paints, solvents, and aerosol sprays, installation of filters at breweries and emission control devices at bakeries and dry cleaners, and a ban on gasoline-powered lawnmowers, bias-ply tires, and certain types of barbeque grills. Vast technological development and widespread public acceptance must occur for the plan to have a reasonable chance at success. Its announcement unleashed a flurry of discussion about the relative benefits and the substantial costs.[55]

Energy versus the Environment

The demand for energy raises a series of environmental questions. First and probably foremost is the question of just how much environmental degradation can be justified on behalf of energy production. Another is the degree to which those who enjoy the benefits of abundant energy should bear the costs of energy production. The seriousness of the issue was illustrated rather dramatically by the Alaskan oil spill in the spring of 1989.

Alaska owes much of its newfound prosperity to its plentiful supply of oil. In fiscal year 1988–89, oil sales and taxes collected from oil companies provided 85 percent of the state's budget.[56] At the same time that Alaska was basking in the glow of excess revenues, it allowed the oil industry to relax its preparations for environmental emergencies. But the state was shocked out of its complacency when the *Exxon Valdez* ran aground, spilling 240,000 barrels of oil and turning Prince William Sound into a marine graveyard. After much hand-wringing and finger-pointing, Alaska, the EPA, and Exxon sought to contain the damage.

Just how much this tragedy will affect future energy exploration remains unclear. What is clear is that issues like this will not disappear. The waters of the Atlantic off the coast of North Carolina offer another venue for a clash between environmental concerns and energy needs. Mobil Oil has applied to the U.S. Interior Department for a lease to drill for natural gas in a limestone reef off Cape Hatteras.[57] Opponents to the lease charge that

The garbage-laden *Mobro 4000* spent four and a half months searching for a place to dump its nasty cargo.

drilling could irreparably damage the ecosystem of the Outer Banks area. Proponents argue that in the fifty-two existing drilling sites off the East Coast, there has never been a well blowout or an oil spill. The risk is low, they argue, and certainly preferable to greater reliance on foreign sources of energy. But environmentalists counter that the "drain America first" strategy overlooks conservation and alternative energy sources.

Environmental Challenges for State and Local Governments

These examples—the development of Maine's new port, southern California's smog reduction plan, the Alaskan oil spill, and energy exploration off the North Carolina coast—raise fundamental questions about environmental quality in the future. The actions of state and local governments, as well as those of the national government, will chart the course.

Admittedly, the challenges posed by the environment will sorely test the capacities of state and local governments. Recognizing that there is a problem is the first step; designing workable solutions is the much tougher second step. Most state and local governments are aware of the problem, but their willingness and ability to do anything about it are another matter. The modernization and overall improvement in state and local governments during the past two decades is a promising sign. But the history of environmental policy in this country indicates that the national government will always play a major role in encouraging, and in some instances forcing, them to act. And even national action may be insufficient for problems that are global in scope.

One promising approach for state and local governments involves rethinking the entire issue. Rather than regarding environmental protection as pollution control, governments can think of it as pollution prevention. For example, waste that is not produced in the first place is waste that does not have to be treated, transported, and disposed. This fundamental reorientation to environmental protection will not happen overnight, but some of the examples cited in this chapter suggest that it can occur gradually, in one community after another.

Summary

Environmental protection policymaking is primarily a national government responsibility, but policy implementation is increasingly up to the states and localities. Funding cutbacks during the Reagan years weakened EPA, but opened the door to greater activity by the nonnational governments.

Modern America produces substantial quantities of solid, hazardous, and nuclear waste. State and local governments for the most part have followed the lead of the national government in attempting to address the environmental problems spawned by waste. Rather than relying solely on old technologies such as landfilling, governments are beginning to experiment with newer approaches, such as incineration and recycling.

Key Terms

Hammer provisions Automatic penalties if an agency or jurisdiction fails to meet deadlines specified in a statute.

State pre-emption State government assumption of the authority to take action, thereby precluding local government action.

References

Chapter 1 New Directions for State and Local Government pp. 1–19

1. "What's in a Name? Ask North Dakotans," *New York Times*, March 23, 1989, p. 11.

2. Bill Richards, "North Dakotans Find Themselves in a State of Flux," *Wall Street Journal*, March 17, 1989, pp. A1, A6.

3. Juan R. Palomo, "Texas' Growth in 1980s 2nd in U.S.," *Houston Post*, March 30, 1989, p. A-3.

4. U.S. Bureau of the Census, *Projections of the Population of States, by Age, Sex, and Race: 1988–2010* (Washington, D.C.: U.S. Government Printing Office, 1988).

5. "Estimating State Population," *State Policy Reports* 7 (January 1989): 2–5.

6. Daniel J. Elazar, *American Federalism: A View from the States*, 3rd ed. (New York: Harper & Row, 1984).

7. Eric B. Herzik, "The Legal-Formal Structuring of State Politics: A Cultural Explanation," *Western Political Quarterly* 38 (September 1985): 413–23.

8. Jody L. Fitzpatrick and Rodney E. Hero, "Political Culture and Political Characteristics of the American States: A Consideration of Some Old and New Questions," *Western Political Quarterly* 41 (March 1988): 145–53.

9. John Kincaid, "Introduction," in John Kincaid, ed., *Political Culture, Public Policy and the American States* (Philadelphia: Institute for the Study of Human Issues, 1982), pp. 1–23.

10. Bruce Wallin, "State and Local Governments Are American, Too," *The Political Science Teacher* 1 (Fall 1988): 1–3.

11. Gov. Mike Sullivan, as quoted in "Wyoming's Governor Signs Law to Restructure State Government," *Denver Post*, March 5, 1989, p. 8B.

12. "Tales of Ten Governments That Show What Innovation Is All About," *Governing* 2 (October 1988): 29–40.

13. Beth Walter Honadle, "Defining and Doing Capacity Building: Perspective and Experiences," in Beth Walter Honadle and Arnold M. Howitt, eds., *Perspectives on Management Capacity Building* (Albany, N.Y.: SUNY Press, 1986), pp. 9–23.

14. John Herbers, "The New Federalism: Unplanned, Innovative, and Here to Stay," *Governing* 1 (October 1987): 28–37.

15. Ibid., p. 28.

16. Ann O'M. Bowman and Richard C. Kearney, *The Resurgence of the States* (Englewood Cliffs, N.J.: Prentice-Hall, 1986).

17. Ibid., p. 12.

18. Terry Sanford, *Storm over the States* (New York: McGraw-Hill, 1967).

19. Ann O'M. Bowman and Richard C. Kearney, "Dimensions of State Government Capability," *Western Political Quarterly* 41 (June 1988): 341–62.

20. Larry Sabato, *Goodbye to Good-time Charlie: The American Governor Transformed*, 2nd. ed. (Washington, D.C.: Congressional Quarterly Press, 1983).

21. Deil S. Wright, *Understanding Intergovernmental Relations*, 3rd ed. (Pacific Grove, Calif.: Brooks-Cole, 1988).

22. James L. Garnett, *Reorganizing State Government: The Executive Branch* (Boulder: Westview, 1981).

23. Alan Rosenthal, *Legislative Life: People, Process, and Performance in the States* (New York: Harper & Row, 1981).

24. Robert A. Kagan et al., "The Evolution

of State Supreme Courts," *Michigan Law Review* 76 (1978): 961–1005.

25. Jacqueline Calmes, "444 North Capitol Street: Where State Lobbyists Are Learning Coalition Politics," *Governing* 1 (February 1988): 17–21.

26. Dabney T. Waring, Jr., "Deregulation Puts Trucking Safety in the Back Seat," *State Government News* 30 (April 1987): 12–13.

27. Dag Ryen, "States Take Lead in Health Care," *State Government News* 30 (August 1987): 4–5.

28. Raymond E. Glazier, Jr., "State Remedies for the AIDS Epidemic," *State Government News* 30 (February 1987): 27–30.

29. Lisa W. Foderaro, "Teachers as Social Workers: Experiment Finds Resistance," *New York Times*, April 14, 1989, pp. 1, 24.

30. James Edwin Kee and William Kiehl, *Assessing the Costs of Federal Mandates on State and Local Government* (Washington, D.C.: Academy for State and Local Government, 1988).

31. Kathy Kiely, "Washington Has a Big Beef over Texas 'Foreign Policy,'" *Houston Post*, February 6, 1989, pp. A1, A10.

32. Phillip J. Cooper, *Hard Judicial Choices* (New York: Oxford University Press, 1988).

33. Lyle J. Denniston, "O'Connor, Rehnquist and Uncertainty: The States and the Supreme Court," *State Legislatures* 9 (April 1983): 10–13.

34. Al Kamen, "States Win Dispute on Mine Rules," *Washington Post*, March 25, 1987, pp. A1, A11.

35. Stuart Taylor, Jr., "Congress Can Tax Municipal Bonds, High Court Rules," *New York Times*, April 21, 1988, p. 1.

36. Linda Greenhouse, "Court, in Consumer Victory, Allows State Antitrust Laws," *New York Times*, April 19, 1989, pp. 1, 29.

37. "Illinois Taxpayers' Checks Are Not in the Mail," *Governing* 1 (February 1988): 16.

38. Peter Applebome, "Louisiana Has a Lot Riding on Tax Drive by Governor," *New York Times*, March 22, 1989, p. 10.

39. Frances Frank Marcus, "Louisiana Crushes Tax Overhaul in a Defeat Damaging to Governor," *New York Times*, May 1, 1989, p. 8.

40. Steven D. Gold, "Are States Playing Budget Roulette?" *State Legislatures* 14 (March 1988): 28–30.

41. Ibid., p. 28.

42. Neal R. Peirce, "Cities Must Learn When to Say No," *Houston Chronicle*, February 13, 1989, p. 12A.

43. John Shannon, "The Return to Fend-for-Yourself Federalism: The Reagan Mark," *Intergovernmental Perspective* 13 (Summer/Fall 1987): 34–37.

44. Ibid., p. 35.

45. Ibid.

46. U.S. Advisory Commission on Intergovernmental Relations Staff Report, "Public Assistance in the Federal System," *Intergovernmental Perspective* 14 (Spring 1988): 5–10.

Chapter 2   The Evolution of Federalism   pp. 20–49

1. Richard Hofstadter, *The American Political Tradition* (New York: Vintage Books, 1948), p. 5.

2. Ibid., p. 9.

3. Ibid., pp. 9–10.

4. Ibid., pp. 8–9.

5. Richard H. Leach, *American Federalism* (New York: W. W. Norton, 1970), p. 1.

6. David B. Walker, *Toward a Functioning Federalism* (Cambridge, Mass.: Winthrop, 1981), p. 25.

7. Leach, *American Federalism*, p. 5.

8. James Madison, *The Federalist*, No. 45, 1788.

9. Walter Berns, "The Meaning of the Tenth Amendment," in Robert A. Goldwin, ed., *A Nation of States* (Chicago: Rand-McNally, 1961), p. 130.

10. Walker, *Functioning Federalism*, pp. 47–48.

11. Hofstadter, *American Political Tradition*, p. 72.

12. *McCulloch* v. *Maryland*, 4 Wheaton 316 (1819).

13. *Gibbons* v. *Ogden*, 9 Wheaton 1 (1824).

14. Franklin Pierce, *Congressional Globe*, 33rd Congress, 1st Session, May 3, 1854, p. 1062.

15. *Brown* v. *Board of Education*, 347 U.S. 487 (1954).

16. Berns, "The Meaning," p. 130.

17. *National League of Cities* v. *Usery*, 426 U.S. 833 (1976).

18. *Garcia* v. *San Antonio Metropolitan Transit Authority*, 105 S.Ct. 1007, 1011 (1985).

19. Ibid.

20. William H. Stewart, "Metaphors, Models and the Development of Federal

Theory," *Publius* 12 (Spring 1982): 5–24.

21. Morton Grodzins, *The American System: A New View of Government in the United States* (Chicago: Rand-McNally, 1966), pp. 42–53.

22. Deil S. Wright, *Understanding Intergovernmental Relations,* 2nd ed. (Monterey, Calif.: Brooks/Cole, 1982), pp. 40–42.

23. Walker, *Functioning Federalism,* pp. 46–65.

24. Ibid., p. 52.

25. Morton Grodzins, "Centralization and Decentralization in the American Federal System," in Robert A. Goldwin, ed., *A Nation of States* (Chicago: Rand-McNally, 1961), pp. 1–3.

26. Wright, *Understanding,* pp. 38–41.

27. Walker, *Functioning Federalism,* p. 101.

28. Terry Sanford, *Storm Over the States* (New York: McGraw-Hill, 1967), p. 80.

29. Wright, *Understanding,* p. 63.

30. James Madison, *The Federalist,* No. 10, 1788.

31. Michael Kinsley, "The Withering Away of the States," *The New Republic* (March 1981), pp. 3–7.

32. *Merriam* v. *Moody's Executors,* 25 Iowa 163, 170 (1868). Dillon's Rule was first written in the case of *City of Clinton* v. *Cedar Rapids and Missouri Railroad Co.* (1868).

33. Daniel J. Elazar, *American Federalism: A View from the States,* 3rd. ed. (New York: Harper and Row, 1984), p. 203.

34. *Community Communications Company, Inc.* v. *City of Boulder,* 102 S.Ct. 835 (1982).

35. Richard C. Kearney and John J. Stucker, "Interstate Compacts and the Management of Low-Level Radioactive Waste," *Public Administration Review* 45 (March/April, 1985): 210–20.

36. Wright, *Understanding,* pp. 333–34.

37. Samuel H. Beer, "The Future of the States in the Federal System," in Peter Woll, ed., *American Government: Readings and Cases* (Boston: Little, Brown, 1981), p. 92.

Chapter 3   Federalism and Public Policy   pp. 50–83

1. John Shannon, "The Return to Fend-for-Yourself Federalism: The Reagan Mark," *Intergovernmental Perspective* 13 (Summer/Fall 1987): 34–37.

2. Michael D. Reagan and John G.

Sanzone, *The New Federalism* (New York: Oxford University Press, 1981).

3. U.S. Advisory Commission on Intergovernmental Relations, *A Catalog of Federal Grant-in-Aid Programs to State and Local Governments: Grants Funded FY 1989* (Washington, D.C.: U.S. Government Printing Office, 1987).

4. Deil S. Wright, *Understanding Intergovernmental Relations,* 3rd ed. (Pacific Grove, Calif.: Brooks/Cole, 1988).

5. ACIR, *A Catalog of Federal Grant-in-Aid Programs,* pp. 15–35.

6. Paul E. Peterson, Barry G. Rabe, and Kenneth K. Wong, *When Federalism Works* (Washington, D.C.: Brookings Institution, 1986).

7. U.S. Office of Management and Budget, *Budget of the United States Government, Fiscal Year 1989, Special Analyses* (Washington, D.C.: U.S. Government Printing Office, 1988).

8. U.S. Office of Management and Budget, *Budget of the United States Government, Fiscal Year 1989, Special Analysis H* (Washington, D.C.: U.S. Government Printing Office, 1988), p. H-23.

9. ACIR, *Significant Features of Fiscal Federalism, 1989,* vol. 1. (Washington, D.C.: U.S. Government Printing Office, 1989), p. 21.

10. "Federal Spending Patterns," *State Policy Reports* 7 (April 1989): 2–12.

11. Richard P. Nathan and Fred C. Doolittle, eds., *Reagan and the States* (Princeton, N.J.: Princeton University Press, 1987).

12. Michael A. Pagano, *The Effects of the 1986 Tax Reform Act on City Finances* (Washington, D.C.: National League of Cities, 1987).

13. Quoted in *The New York Times,* January 27, 1982, p. 16.

14. Ronald Reagan, "National Conference of State Legislatures," *Weekly Compilation of Presidential Documents* 17 (August 3, 1981), p. 834.

15. Robert D. Reischauer, "Fiscal Federalism in the 1980s: Dismantling or Rationalizing the Great Society," in Marshall Kaplan and Peggy L. Cuciti, eds., *The Great Society and Its Legacy* (Durham, N.C.: Duke University Press, 1986), pp. 179–97.

16. Richard S. Williamson, "A New Federalism: Proposals and Achievements of

President Reagan's First Three Years," *Publius* 16 (Winter 1986): 11–28; and Richard L. Cole and Delbert A. Taebel, "The New Federalism: Promises, Programs, and Performance," *Publius* 16 (Winter 1986): 3–10.

17. Ann O'M. Bowman and Richard C. Kearney, *The Resurgence of the States* (Englewood Cliffs, N.J.: Prentice-Hall, 1986).

18. Timothy J. Conlan, "Federalism and Competing Values in the Reagan Administration," *Publius* 16 (Winter 1986): 29–47.

19. Demetrios Caraley and Yvette R. Schlussel, "Congress and Reagan's New Federalism," *Publius* 16 (Winter 1986): 49–79.

20. Working Group on Federalism of the Domestic Policy Council, *The Status of Federalism in America*, unpublished report, November 1986.

21. "The Test of Vital National Interest: Necessary and Sufficient Conditions for Activity by the National Government," *Intergovernmental Perspective* 12 (Summer 1986): 13.

22. Caraley and Schlussel, "Congress and Reagan's New Federalism," p. 79.

23. Peterson, Rabe, and Wong, *When Federalism Works*, pp. 219–29.

24. Ibid., p. 3.

25. U.S. Bureau of the Census, *Statistical Abstract of the United States, 1989* (Washington, D.C.: U.S. Government Printing Office, 1989).

26. Michael Novak et al., *The New Consensus on Family and Welfare* (Milwaukee: American Enterprise Institute for Public Policy Research, 1987), p. xiii.

27. Fred Block et al., *The Mean Season: The Attack on the Welfare State* (New York: Pantheon Books, 1987), p. 92.

28. Charles A. Murray, *Losing Ground: American Social Policy, 1950–1980* (New York: Basic Books, 1984).

29. John E. Schwarz, *American's Hidden Success*, rev. ed. (New York: W. W. Norton, 1988); and Block et al., *The Mean Season*.

30. U.S. Bureau of the Census, *Money, Income and Poverty Status in the United States, 1987* (Washington, D.C.: U.S. Government Printing Office, 1988).

31. Novak et al., *The New Consensus*.

32. Ibid., pp. 4–5; also see Harry J. Holzer, ed., *The Black Youth Employment Crisis* (Chicago: University of Chicago Press, 1986); and Ken Auletta, *The Underclass* (New York: Random House, 1982).

33. Novak et al., *The New Consensus*, p. 5.

34. *Statistical Abstract of the United States, 1988.*

35. U.S. House of Representatives, Committee on Ways and Means, *Background Material and Data on Programs within the Jurisdiction of the Committee on Ways and Means* (Washington, D.C.: U.S. Government Printing Office, 1978), p. 388.

36. Daniel Patrick Moynihan, "Our Poorest Citizens—Children," *Focus* 11 (Spring 1988): 5.

37. U.S. Bureau of the Census, *Statistical Abstract of the United States, 1989.*

38. Moynihan, "Our Poorest Citizens," p. 4.

39. Irwin Garfinkel, "The Evolution of Child Support Policy," *Focus* 11 (Spring 1988): 12–13.

40. Neal R. Peirce, "Children's Agenda Makes Headway," *P.A. Times* (December 1, 1986): 2; and *State Government News* 30 (November 1987): 27.

41. See Charles Garvin, Audrey Smith, and William Reid, eds., *The Work Incentive Experience* (Montclair, N.J.: Allenheld, Osman, 1978).

42. John Herbers, "Governors Ask Work Plan for Welfare Recipients," *The New York Times*, February 22, 1987, p. 30; and Julie Rovner, "Welfare Reform: The Issue that Bubbled up from the States to Capitol Hill," *Governing* 1 (December 1988): 17–21.

43. Joel F. Handler, "Consensus on Redirection—Which Direction?" *Focus* 11 (Spring 1988): 31–32.

44. U.S. General Accounting Office, *Work and Welfare: Current AFDC Work Programs and Implications for Federal Policy* (Washington, D.C.: U.S. Government Printing Office, 1987).

45. See Judith M. Gueron, *Reforming Welfare with Work* (New York: Ford Foundation, 1987).

46. Robert B. Albritton and Robert D. Brown, "Intergovernmental Impacts on Policy Variation Within States: Effects of Local Discretion on General Assistance Programs, *Policy Studies Review* 5 (February 1986): 529–35.

47. Bryan D. Jones and Arnold Vedlitz,

"Higher Education Policies and Economic Growth in the American States," paper presented at the annual meeting of the Midwest Political Science Association, April 1987.

48. U.S. Department of Education, Center for Statistics, *Fall Enrollment in Higher Education, 1984* (Washington, D.C.: U.S. Government Printing Office, 1985).

49. Three states combine coordination of higher education with primary and secondary education under a single state administration agency.

50. The Carnegie Foundation for the Advancement of Teaching, *The State and Higher Education* (San Francisco: Jossey-Bass, 1976), p. 19.

51. See Samuel K. Gove, "Governors and Higher Education, 1983," *Publius* 14 (Summer 1984): 111–19.

52. Frank Newman, "Building a Partnership," *State Government News* 30 (October 1987)· 10.

53. Ezra Bowen, "Wanted: Fresh, Homegrown Talent," *Time* (January 11, 1988): 47.

54. Newman, "Building a Partnership," pp. 10–11.

55. Richard H. Leach, *American Federalism* (New York: W. W. Norton and Co., 1970), p. ix.

56. Ibid., p. 45.

57. Timothy Conlan, *New Federalism: Intergovernmental Reform from Nixon to Reagan* (Washington, D.C.: Brookings Institution, 1988).

58. Michael A. Pagano and Ann O'M. Bowman, "The State of American Federalism—1988–89," *Publius* 20 (Summer 1989): 1–17.

Chapter 4   State Constitutions
pp. 84–111

1. *Lloyd Corp.* v. *Tanner,* 407 U.S. 551 (1972); *Hudgens* v. *NLRB,* 424 U.S. 507 (1976).

2. *Robins* v. *Prune Yard Shopping Center,* 23 Cal.3d 899, 592 P.2d 341 (1979).

3. G. Alan Tarr and Mary Cornelia Porter, "Introduction: State Constitutionalism and State Constitutional Law," *Publius* 17 (Winter 1987): 5.

4. Daniel J. Elazar, "The Principles and Traditions Underlying State Constitutions," *Publius* 12 (Winter 1982): 11.

5. Albert L. Sturm, "The Development of American State Constitutions," *Publius* 12 (Winter 1982): 61.

6. Ibid., pp. 62–63.

7. Paul G. Reardon, "The Massachusetts Constitution Makes a Milestone," *Publius* 12 (Winter 1982): 45–55.

8. James Bryce, "Nature of the American State," in Bruce Stinebrickner, ed., *State and Local Government,* 3rd ed. (Guilford, Conn.: Dushkin, 1987), pp. 20–23.

9. U.S. Advisory Commission on Intergovernmental Relations, *The Question of State Government Capability* (Washington, D.C.: ACIR, 1985), p. 36.

10. David Fellman, "What Should a State Constitution Contain?" in W. Brooke Graves, ed., *Major Problems in State Constitutional Revision* (Chicago: Public Administration Service, 1960), p. 146.

11. Sturm, "American State Constitutions," p. 64.

12. Lewis A. Froman, Jr., "Some Effects of Interest Group Strength in State Politics," *American Political Science Review* 60 (December 1966): 956.

13. David C. Nice, "Interest Groups and State Constitutions: Another Look," *State and Local Government Review* 20 (Winter 1988): 21–27.

14. Ibid., p. 22.

15. Ibid., pp. 23, 26.

16. ACIR, *A Report to the President for Transmittal to the Congress* (Washington, D.C.: U.S. Government Printing Office, 1955).

17. National Municipal League, *Model State Constitution,* 6th ed. (rev.) (New York: National Municipal League, 1968).

18. Council of State Governments, *Modernizing State Constitutions 1966–1972* (Lexington, Ky.: Council of State Governments, 1973), p. 4.

19. Thomas C. Marks, Jr., and John F. Cooper, *State Constitutional Law* (St. Paul: West, 1988).

20. Ibid., p.38.

21. Ibid., pp. 38–42.

22. Ibid., p. 46.

23. Ibid.

24. Sue Davis and Taunya Lovell Banks, "State Constitutions, Freedom of Expression, and Search and Seizure:

Prospects for State Court Reincarnation,'' *Publius* 17 (Winter 1987): 13–31.

25. Paulette Thomas, ''Mississippi's Quirky Constitution Regulates Duels and Prevents Governors from Governing Too Much,'' *Wall Street Journal,* August 19, 1986, p. 56.

26. Marks and Cooper, *State Constitutional Law,* p. 47.

27. Tarr and Porter, ''Introduction,'' p. 9.

28. Stanley H. Friedelbaum, ''The Complementary Role of Federal and State Courts,'' *Publius* 17 (Winter 1987): 48.

29. Susan P. Fino, ''Judicial Federalism and Equality Guarantees in State Supreme Courts,'' *Publius* 17 (Winter 1987): 66–67.

30. Albert L. Sturm, *Thirty Years of State Constitution-Making: 1938–1968* (New York: National Municipal League, 1970), pp. 27–28.

31. Elmer E. Cornwell, Jr., Jay S. Goodman, and Wayne R. Swanson, *State Constitutional Conventions: The Politics of the Revision Process in Seven States* (New York: Praeger, 1975), p. 72.

32. Ibid., p. 62.

33. Sturm, 1970, p. 69.

34. Jay S. Goodman et al., ''Public Responses to State Constitutional Revision,'' *American Journal of Political Science* 17 (August 1973): 571–96.

35. Philip G. Schrag, *Behind the Scenes: The Politics of a Constitutional Convention* (Washington, D.C.: Georgetown University Press, 1985).

36. Wayne R. Swanson, Sean Kelleher, and Arthur English, ''Socialization of Constitution-Makers: Experience, Role Conflict, and Attitude Change,'' *Journal of Politics* 34 (February 1972): 183–98.

37. Ibid.

38. Cornwell, Goodman, and Swanson, *State Constitutional Conventions,* p. 81.

39. Sturm, ''American State Constitutions,'' p. 85.

40. Ibid., p. 84.

41. Ibid., p. 104.

42. W. Brooke Graves, ''State Constitutional Law: A Twenty-five Year Summary,'' *William and Mary Law Review* 8 (Fall 1966): 12.

43. Donald S. Lutz, ''The Purposes of American State Constitutions,'' *Publius* 12 (Winter 1982): 27–44.

44. ACIR, *State Government Capability,* p. 60.

45. Richard H. Leach, ''A Quiet Revolution:

1933–1976,'' *The Book of the States, 1975–76* (Lexington, Ky.: Council of State Governments, 1976), p. 25.

46. Terry Sanford, *Storm Over the States* (New York: McGraw-Hill, 1967), p. 189.

Chapter 5 Participation and Interest Groups pp. 112–142

1. Lyn Riddle, ''Maine Town of 607 Weighs Its Fate,'' *New York Times,* March 18, 1989, p. 6.

2. William E. Lyons and David Lowery, ''Citizen Responses to Dissatisfaction in Urban Communities: A Test of a General Model,'' paper presented at the annual meeting of the Southern Political Science Association, Charlotte, N.C., 1987.

3. Sidney Verba and Norman H. Nie, *Participation in America* (New York: Harper & Row, 1972).

4. Ibid., and Richard Murray and Arnold Vedlitz, ''Race, Socioeconomic Status, and Voting Participation in Large Southern Cities,'' *Journal of Politics* 39 (November 1977): 1064–72.

5. Virginia Sapiro, *The Political Integration of Women* (Urbana: University of Illinois Press, 1983).

6. Earl Black and Merle Black, *Politics and Society in the South* (Cambridge, Mass.: Harvard University Press, 1987).

7. U.S. Bureau of the Census, *Statistical Abstract of the United States, 1988* (Washington, D.C.: U.S. Government Printing Office, 1987).

8. Richard Smolka, ''Election Legislation: 1986–87,'' in *The Book of the States, 1988–89* (Lexington, Ky.: Council of State Governments, 1988), pp. 179–82.

9. ''Voter Registration Information,'' in *The Book of the States, 1988–89,* p. 211.

10. Ibid.

11. E. J. Dionne, Jr., ''If Nonvoters Had Voted: Same Winner, But Bigger,'' *New York Times,* November 21, 1988, p. 10.

12. David B. Magleby, ''Taking the Initiative: Direct Legislation and Direct Democracy in the 1980s,'' *PS: Political Science and Politics* 21 (Summer 1988): 600–11.

13. Ibid., p. 600.

14. Ibid., p. 602.

15. David D. Schmidt, ''Initiative

Pendulum Begins Leftward Swing," *P.A. Times* 5 (September 15, 1982): 1, 10.

16. R. R. Reid, "The Governed Will Be the Rulers on 226 Statewide Questions," *Washington Post*, October 29, 1986, p. A6.

17. Bob Dart, "Voters Speak Out for English and Lotteries in State Referendums," *Atlanta Journal and Constitution*, November 10, 1988, p. 9A.

18. Robert Reinhold, "Three State Referendums Give New Impetus to Anti-Abortion Efforts," *New York Times*, November 10, 1988, p. 13.

19. Bill Halldin, "Rejection Looms for Damages Cap," *Tampa Tribune*, November 9, 1988, 1B.

20. Reinhold, "Three State Referendums."

21. W. John Moore, "Election Day Lawmaking," *National Journal* 20 (September 17, 1988): 2296–2301.

22. Dart, "Voters Speak Out."

23. "The Prop 13 'Prairie Fire,'" *Newsweek*, May 15, 1989, p. 50.

24. Moore, "Election Day Lawmaking," p. 2296.

25. Lucinda Simon, "Representative Democracy Challenged," *State Legislatures* 10 (August 1984): 111–15.

26. As quoted in William Pound and Lucinda Simon, "A Political Tide Continues to Ebb and Flow," *State Legislatures* 11 (January 1985): 11–17.

27. Joann S. Lublin, "Rising Use of Ballot Initiatives Threatens Legislatures' Powers," *Wall Street Journal*, October 30, 1984, p. 33.

28. F. Christopher Arterton, "Political Participation and 'Teledemocracy,'" *PS: Political Science and Politics* 21 (Summer 1988): 620–27.

29. Ibid., p. 521.

30. George B. Merry, "Citizen-Initiated Legislation May Be on the Ballot in 19 States," *Christian Science Monitor*, May 15, 1984, p. 7.

31. Paula D. McClain, "Arizona 'High Noon': The Recall and Impeachment of Evan Mecham," *PS: Political Science and Politics* 21 (Summer 1988): 628–38.

32. Judge Archie Simonson, as quoted in Laura R. Woliver, "Sputtering Interests: Ad Hoc, Grass Roots Interests in the United States," unpublished doctoral dissertation, University of Wisconsin, Madison, 1986, p. 47.

33. McClain, "Arizona 'High Noon,'" p. 629.

34. Joseph F. Zimmerman, *Participatory Democracy: Populism Revived* (New York: Praeger, 1986).

35. Jim Cleary, as quoted in "Fighting City Hall—and Winning," *The State* (Columbia, S.C.), May 26, 1987, p. 7A.

36. Thomas E. Cronin, "Public Opinion and Direct Democracy," *PS: Political Science and Politics* 21 (Summer 1988): 612–19.

37. L. Harmon Zeigler, "Interest Groups in the States," in Virginia Gray, Herbert Jacob, and Kenneth N. Vines, eds., *Politics in the American States*, 4th ed. (Boston: Little, Brown, 1983), pp. 97–131.

38. Clyde Brown, "Explanations of Interest Group Membership Over Time: The Farm Bureau in Five Midwestern States," *American Politics Quarterly* 17 (January 1989): 32–53.

39. Mitzi Mahoney, "Interest Group Use of the Legislative Rule Review Process in Three States," paper presented at the annual meeting of the Southern Political Science Association, Charlotte, N.C., 1987.

40. L. Harmon Zeigler and Hendrik van Dalen, "Interest Groups in the States," in Herbert Jacob and Kenneth N. Vines, eds., *Politics in the American States*, 2nd ed. (Boston: Little, Brown, 1971), pp. 122–60.

41. Zeigler, "Interest Groups in the States," pp. 111–19.

42. Sarah McCally Morehouse, *State Politics, Parties and Policy* (New York: Holt, Rinehart and Winston, 1981).

43. Zeigler, "Interest Groups in the States," p. 117.

44. Clive S. Thomas and Ronald J. Hrebenar, "Comparative Interest Group Politics in the American West," *State Government* 59 (September/October 1986): 124–36.

45. Allan J. Cigler and Dwight Kiel, "Special Interests in Kansas: Representation in Transition," paper presented at the annual meeting of the Midwest Political Science Association, Chicago, 1987.

46. Ibid., p. 28.

47. *The Book of the States, 1988–89.*

48. Ibid., pp. 142–44.

49. Theodore B. Pedeliski, "Interest Groups in North Dakota: Constituency Coupling in a Moralistic Political Culture," paper presented at the annual meeting of the

Midwest Political Science Association, Chicago, 1987.

50. William P. Browne and Delbert J. Ringquist, "Michigan Interests: The Politics of Diversification," paper presented at the annual meeting of the Midwest Political Science Association, Chicago, 1987, p. 15.

51. Thomas and Hrebenar, "Comparative Interest Politics in the American West," p. 130.

52. Keith E. Hamm, Charles W. Wiggins, and Charles G. Bell, "Interest Group Involvement, Conflict and Success in State Legislatures: A Comparative Assessment," paper presented at the annual meeting of the American Political Science Association, Chicago, 1983; and William P. Browne, "Variations in the Behavior and Style of State Lobbyists and Interest Groups," *Journal of Politics* 47 (May 1985): 450–68.

53. Charles W. Wiggins and Keith E. Hamm, "Iowa: Interest Group Politics in an Undistinguished Place," paper presented at the annual meeting of the Midwest Political Science Association, Chicago, 1987.

54. Ibid., p. 8.

55. Browne and Ringquist, "Michigan Interests: The Politics of Diversification," p. 24.

56. Howard A. Faye, Allan Cigler, and Paul Schumaker, "The Municipal Group Universe: Changes in Agency Penetration by Political Groups," paper presented at the annual meeting of the American Political Science Association, Washington, D.C., 1986.

57. Glenn Abney and Thomas P. Lauth, *The Politics of State and City Administration* (Albany: State University of New York Press, 1986).

58. Steven H. Haeberle, "Good Neighbors and Good Neighborhoods: Comparing Demographic and Environmental Influences on Neighborhood Activism," *State and Local Government Review* 18 (Fall 1986): 109–16.

59. U.S. Advisory Commission on Intergovernmental Relations, *Citizen Participation in the American Federal System* (Washington, D.C.: ACIR, 1979).

60. Ibid.

61. Zimmerman, *Participatory Democracy*, pp. 145–54.

62. Harry P. Hatry et al., *How Effective Are Your Community Services?* (Washington, D.C.: Urban Institute, 1977).

63. Michael D. Reagan and John G. Sanzone, *The New Federalism*, 2nd ed. (New York: Oxford University Press, 1981).

64. Steve Millard, "Voluntary Action and the States: The Other Alternative," *National Civic Review* 72 (May 1983): 262–69.

65. Harry P. Hatry and Carl F. Valente, "Alternative Service Delivery Approaches Involving Increased Use of the Private Sector," in International City Management Association, *The Municipal Year Book 1983* (Washington, D.C.: ICMA, 1983), pp. 199–216.

66. Mary A. Culp, "Volunteering as Helping," *National Civic Review* 77 (May/June 1988): 224–30.

67. Neal R. Peirce, "Denver Campaigns for Generous Giving," *P.A. Times*, April 15, 1987, p. 2.

68. Ronald K. Vogel and Bert E. Swanson, "Setting Agendas for Community Change: The Community Goal-Setting Strategy," *Journal of Urban Affairs* 10, no. 1 (1988): 41–61.

Chapter 6   Political Parties, Elections, and Campaigns   pp. 143–172

1. Peter Applebome, "Klan's Ghost Haunts G.O.P. on Louisiana Political Trail," *New York Times*, February 16, 1989, pp. 1, 8.

2. "Ex-KKK Leader Defeats Treen," *Houston Chronicle*, February 19, 1989, pp. 1A, 24A.

3. Larry J. Sabato, *The Party's Just Begun* (Glenview, Ill.: Scott Foresman, 1987).

4. Kenneth Janda, Jeffrey M. Berry, and Jerry Goldman, *The Challenge of Democracy: Government in America*, 2nd ed. (Boston: Houghton Mifflin, 1989), p. 304.

5. Coleman L. Blease, as quoted in George Brown Tindall, *The Disruption of the Solid South* (Athens: University of Georgia Press, 1972), p. 47.

6. Denise L. Baer, "Interest Intermediation and Political Party Reform: A Comparative Study of State Party Charters," paper presented at the annual meeting of the American Political Science Association, Washington, D.C., 1988.

7. Malcolm E. Jewell and David M. Olson, *Political Parties and Elections in American States*, 3rd ed. (Chicago: Dorsey Press, 1988).

8. James L. Gibson et al., "Whither the

Local Parties?: A Cross-Sectional and Longitudinal Analysis of the Strength of Party Organizations," *American Journal of Political Science* 29 (February 1985): 139–60.

9. Dwaine Marvick, "Stability and Change in the Views of Los Angeles Party Activists," in William Crotty, ed., *Political Parties in Local Areas* (Knoxville: University of Tennessee Press, 1986), p. 124.

10. William Crotty, "The Machine in Transition," in William Crotty, ed., *Political Parties in Local Areas* (Knoxville: University of Tennessee Press, 1986), p. 190.

11. Ibid., p. 54.

12. "County GOP Sundered by Evangelicals," *Governing* 1 (July 1988): 64–65.

13. Frank J. Sorauf and Paul Allen Beck, *Party Politics in America,* 6th ed. (Glenview, Ill.: Scott, Foresman, 1988).

14. Ibid., p. 47.

15. Euel Elliott, Gerard S. Gryski, and Bruce Reed, "Alternative Models of Non-Major Party Support in State Legislative Elections, 1976–1984," paper presented at the annual meeting of the American Political Science Association, Washington, D.C., 1988.

16. Ibid.

17. Ibid., p. 11.

18. Jewell and Olson, *Political Parties and Elections,* p. 29.

19. "Something Is Gaining on State's Democrats," *Atlanta Journal and Constitution,* November 10, 1988, p. 22.

20. Ibid.

21. Stephen C. Craig, "The Decay of Mass Partisanship," *Polity* 20 (Summer 1988): 705–13.

22. Cornelius P. Cotter et al., *Party Organizations in American Politics* (New York: Praeger, 1984).

23. Paul S. Hernnson, "The Importance of Party Campaigning," *Polity* 20 (Summer 1988): 714–19.

24. "Methods of Nominating Candidates for State Offices," *The Book of the States, 1988–89* (Lexington, Ky.: Council of State Governments, 1988), pp. 184–85.

25. William J. Keefe, *Parties, Politics, and Public Policy in America,* 5th ed. (Washington, D.C.: Congressional Quarterly, 1988).

26. Jewell and Olson, *Political Parties and Elections.*

27. Priscilla L. Southwell, "Open Versus Closed Primaries and Candidate Fortunes, 1972–1984," *American Politics Quarterly* 16 (July 1988): 280–95.

28. Charles S. Bullock III and Loch K. Johnson, "Runoff Elections in Georgia," *Journal of Politics* 47 (August 1985): 937–46.

29. Ibid., p. 940.

30. Steven H. Haeberle, "Rundown on the Runoff: Party Runway Run Amok," paper presented at the annual meeting of the Southern Political Science Association, Charlotte, N.C., 1987.

31. Barbara G. Salmore and Stephen A. Salmore, "The Transformation of State Electoral Politics," in Carl E. Van Horn, ed., *The State of the States* (Washington, D.C.: Congressional Quarterly, 1989), pp. 175–208.

32. Ibid.

33. Tari Renner, "Municipal Election Processes: The Impact on Minority Representation," in International City Management Association, *The Municipal Year Book 1988* (Washington, D.C.: ICMA, 1988), pp. 13–21.

34. Carol A. Cassel, "The Nonpartisan Ballot in the United States," in Bernard Grofman and Arend Lijphart, eds., *Electoral Laws and Their Consequences* (New York: Agathon, 1986), pp. 226–41.

35. Ibid.

36. Lana Stein and Arnold Fleischmann, "Newspaper and Business Endorsements in Municipal Elections: A Test of Conventional Wisdom," *Journal of Urban Affairs* 9, no. 4 (1987): 325–36.

37. Ibid., p. 331.

38. "For Mayor: Sandy Freedman," *The Tampa Tribune,* February 25, 1987, p. 8A.

39. Charles S. Bullock III and Susan A. MacManus, "Endorsements, Spending, and Minority Group Success in Municipal Elections," paper presented at the annual meeting of the American Political Science Association, Washington, D.C., 1986.

40. Ibid., p. 14.

41. W. John Moore, "Statehouse Status Quo," *National Journal* 20 (November 12, 1988): 2883–88.

42. Andrew Rosenthal, "G.O.P. Makes Few Legislature Gains," *New York Times,* November 11, 1988, p. 11.

43. "Indiana Legislators Break Tie, Avoid

Holiday Session," *Nashville Banner,* November 24, 1988, p. A2.

44. Isabel Wilkerson, "Indiana Lawmaking Is Fit to Be Tied," *New York Times,* March 20, 1989, p. 9.

45. *Campaigns and Elections* 9 (May/June 1988): 1.

46. Jerry Hagstrom and Robert Guskind, "Selling the Candidate," *National Journal* 18 (November 1, 1986): 2619–26.

47. Karl Struble, as quoted in ibid., p. 2626.

48. Ibid.

49. Ibid., p. 2619.

50. Thad Beyle, "The Cost of Becoming Governor," *State Government* 59 (September/October 1986): 95–101.

51. Ibid., p. 95.

52. "Governors," *The Book of the States, 1988–89,* p. 25.

53. Micheal W. Giles and Anita Pritchard, "Campaign Expenditures and Legislative Elections in Florida," *Legislative Studies Quarterly* 10 (February 1985): 71–88.

54. Stephen A. Salmore and Barbara G. Salmore, "Determinants of State Legislative Elections: The Case of New Jersey," paper presented at the annual meeting of the American Political Science Association, Chicago, 1987.

55. Ibid., pp. 3–4.

56. Sarah M. Morehouse, "Money Versus Party Effort: Nominating for Governor," paper presented at the annual meeting of the American Political Science Association, Chicago, 1987.

57. Common Cause, "Should State Elections Be Publicly Financed?" in Herbert M. Levine, ed., *The Politics of State and Local Government Debated* (Englewood Cliffs, N.J.: Prentice-Hall, 1985), pp. 84–85.

58. Robert J. Huckshorn, "Who Gave It? Who Got It?: The Enforcement of Campaign Finance Laws in the States," *Journal of Politics* 47 (August 1985): 773.

59. "Campaign Finance Laws: Limitations on Contributions by Organizations, by Individuals," *The Book of the States, 1988–89,* pp. 193–202.

60. Ibid., p. 98.

61. Charles W. Wiggins and Keith E. Hamm, "Iowa: Interest Group Politics in an Undistinguished Place," paper presented at the annual meeting of the Midwest Political Science Association, Chicago, 1987.

62. Salmore and Salmore, "The Transformation of State Electoral Politics."

63. "Funding of State Elections: Tax Provisions and Public Financing," *The Book of the States, 1988–1989,* pp. 209–10.

64. Ruth S. Jones, "State Public Financing and the State Parties," in Michael J. Malbin, ed., *Parties, Interest Groups, and Campaign Finance Laws* (Washington, D.C.: American Enterprise Institute, 1980), pp. 283–303.

65. Elizabeth G. King and David G. Wegge, "The Rules Are Never Neutral: Public Funds in Minnesota and Wisconsin Legislative Elections," paper presented at the annual meeting of the Midwest Political Science Association, Chicago, 1984.

66. James M. Penning and Corwin E. Smidt, "Views of American State Legislators on Public Funding of Legislative Elections," *Legislative Studies Quarterly* 8 (February 1983): 97–109.

67. Ruth S. Jones, "State Public Campaign Finance: Implications for Partisan Politics," *American Journal of Political Science* 25 (May 1981): 342–61.

68. Jones, "State Public Financing and the State Parties."

Chapter 7   Governors   pp. 173–211

1. Ann O'M. Bowman and Richard C. Kearney, *The Resurgence of the States* (Englewood Cliffs, N.J.: Prenctice-Hall, 1986), p. 52.

2. For a more detailed discussion of the processes and results of the state government reform movement, see Bowman and Kearney, *Resurgence,* pp. 47–54.

3. Eric B. Herzik, "Governors and Issues: A Typology of Concerns," paper presented at the annual meeting of the Southern Political Science Association, Memphis, Tenn., November 1981.

4. Ibid.

5. Coleman B. Ransome, Jr., *The American Governorship* (Westport, Conn.: Greenwood Press, 1982), p. 125.

6. Thad L. Beyle, "The Governor as Chief Legislator," *State Government* 51 (Winter 1978): 2–10.

7. Sharon Sherman, "Powersplit: When Legislatures and Governors Are of Opposing Parties," *State Legislatures* 10 (May/June 1984): 9–12.

8. Sarah McCally Morehouse, "The Governor and His Legislative Party,"

American Political Science Review 60
(December 1966): 933–41.

9. Wayne L. Francis, *Legislative Issues in the
Fifty States: A Comparative Analysis* (Chicago:
Rand-McNally, 1967), p. 35.

10. National Governors' Association,
Reflections on Being Governor (Washington,
D.C.: NGA, 1978), p. 45.

11. Beyle, "Governor as Chief Legislator,"
p. 8.

12. Ibid., p. 9.

13. Martha W. Weinberg, *Managing the
State* (Cambridge, Mass.: MIT Press, 1977),
p. 75.

14. Lynn Muchmore, "The Governor as
Manager," *State Government* 54 (March
1981): 72.

15. Ibid., pp. 73–74.

16. See Michael J. Del Giudice, "Mario
Cuomo as New York's Chief Executive
Officer," *State Government* 59 (July/August
1986): 70–76.

17. H. Edward Flentje, "Governor as
Manager: A Political Assessment," *State
Government* 54 (Summer 1981): 76–81.

18. Robert Dalton, "Governors' Views on
Management," in Thad L. Beyle and Lynn
R. Muchmore, eds., *Being Governor: The
View from the Office* (Durham, N.C.: Duke
University Press, 1983), pp. 100–101.

19. Beyle, 1978.

20. Thad L. Beyle and Lynn R. Muchmore,
"The Governor and the Public," in Beyle
and Muchmore, eds., *Being Governor,* p. 24.

21. Thad L. Beyle and Lynn R. Muchmore,
"Governors and Intergovernmental
Relations: Middleman in the Federal
System," in Beyle and Muchmore, eds.,
Being Governor, p. 193.

22. Thad L. Beyle and Lynn R. Muchmore,
"The Governor as Party Leader," in Beyle
and Muchmore, eds., *Being Governor,* pp.
44–51.

23. Larry Sabato, *Goodbye to Goodtime
Charlie: The American Governorship
Transformed* (Lexington, Mass.: Lexington
Books, 1978), p. 13.

24. Ibid.

25. Ibid., p. xi.

26. Ibid., pp. 27–31.

27. Thad L. Beyle, "Introduction," *State
Government: CQ's Guide to Current Issues and
Activities 1987–88* (Washington, D.C.: CQ
Press, 1987), pp. 89–90.

28. Ibid., pp. 95–101.

29. Thad L. Beyle, "The Cost of Becoming

Governor," *State Government* 59 (Sept./Oct.
1986): 97.

30. Ibid., p. 95.

31. Ibid., p. 96.

32. Quoted in George Weeks, "Statehouse
Hall of Fame, Ten Outstanding Governors
of the 20th Century," paper presented at
the annual meeting of the Southern Political
Science Association, Memphis, Tenn.,
November 1981.

33. Samuel R. Soloman, "Governors:
1960–1970," *National Civic Review* (March
1971): 126–46.

34. Thad L. Beyle and Robert Dalton,
"Appointment Power: Does It Belong to the
Governor?" *State Government* 54 (Winter
1981): 4.

35. Ibid., p. 5.

36. Ibid., p. 8.

37. Diane Kincaid Blair, "The Gubernatorial
Appointment Power: Too Much of a Good
Thing?" in Beyle and Muchmore, eds.,
Being Governor, p. 117.

38. Ransome, *American Governorship,* p. 121.

39. Beyle and Muchmore, "Governors and
Intergovernmental Relations," p. 197.

40. Neal R. Peirce, "State Local
Report/Structural Reform of Bureaucracy
Grows Rapidly," *National Journal Reports* 7
(April 5, 1975): 504.

41. Beyle and Dalton, "Appointment
Power."

42. Gerald Benjamin, "The Diffusion of the
Governor's Veto Power," *State Government*
55 (March 1982): 99–105.

43. Sabato, *Goodtime Charlie,* p. 77.

44. Charles W. Wiggins, "Executive Vetoes
and Legislative Overrides in the American
States," *Journal of Politics* 42 (November
1980): 1110–17.

45. See, for example, *The Book of the States,
1980–81* (Lexington, Ky.: Council of State
Governments, 1980), pp. 110–11.

46. Beyle, "Governor as Chief Legislator."

47. Glenn Abney and Thomas P. Lauth,
"The Governor as Chief Administrator,"
Public Administration Review 43 (Jan./Feb.
1983): 40–49.

48. Ibid., p. 46.

49. Thad L. Beyle, "The Governor's Formal
Powers: A View from the Governor and
Chair," *Public Administration Review* 28
(Nov./Dec. 1968): 540–45.

50. E. Lee Bernick and Charles W. Wiggins,
"The Governor's Executive Order: An
Unknown Power," *State and Local*

Government Review 16 (Winter 1984): 3–10.

51. U.S. Advisory Commission on Intergovernmental Relations, *The Question of State Government Capability*, A-98 (Washington, D.C.: ACIR, 1985), pp. 143–55. Also see James L. Garnett, *Reorganizing State Government: The Executive Branch* (Boulder, Col.: Westview Press, 1980).

52. James D. Carney, "Downsizing Government: Iowa's Challenge," *State Government* 60 (July/August 1987): 183–90.

53. Lydia Bodman and Daniel B. Garry, "Innovations in State Cabinet Systems," *State Government* 55 (March 1982): 93–97.

54. Ibid., pp. 217–18.

55. James Conant, "State Reorganization: A New Model?" *State Government* 58 (April 1985): 130–38. On the New Jersey reorganization, see also James Conant, "Reorganization and the Bottom Line," *Public Administration Review* 46 (Jan./Feb. 1986): 48–56.

56. Garnett, *Reorganizing State Government*, pp. 124–25.

57. Quoted in Flentje, "Governor as Manager," p. 70. For a description of failure in reorganization in Florida, see Less Garner, "Managing Change Through Organization Structure," *State Government* 60 (July/August 1987): 191–95.

58. Thad L. Beyle, "Governors' Offices: Variation on Common Themes," in Beyle and Muchmore, eds., *Being Governor*, pp. 158–73.

59. ACIR, *State Government Capability*, p. 137.

60. Ransome, *American Governorship*, p. 132.

61. Bowman and Kearney, *Resurgence*, p. 69.

62. Richard C. Kearney, "How a 'Weak' Governor Can Be Strong: Dick Riley and Education Reform in South Carolina," *State Government* 60 (July/August 1987): 150–56.

63. Dan Durning, "Change Masters for the States," *State Government* 60 (July/August 1987): 145–49.

64. Ransome, *American Governorship*, p. 156.

65. Lee Sigelman and Roland Smith, "Personal, Office, and State Characteristics as Predictors of Gubernatorial Performance," *Journal of Politics* 43 (February 1981): 169–80.

66. Scott M. Matheson, with James Edwin Kee, *Out of Balance* (Salt Lake City: Peregrine Smith Books, 1986), p. 186.

67. Dan Durning, "The Governor's Internal Campaign: Managing State Government by Influencing Attitudes and Values," *State Government* 59 (July/August 1986): 77–81.

68. Ibid.

69. Thad L. Beyle, "The Governors, 1984–85," in *The Book of the States, 1984–85* (Lexington, Ky.: Council of State Governments, 1986), p. 26.

70. W. John Moore, "New Cops on the Beat," *National Journal* 19 (May 23, 1987): 1338–42.

71. Alice Chasan Edelman, "Is There Room at the Top?" in Beyle and Muchmore, eds., *Being Governor*, p. 107.

72. Council of State Governments, *The Lieutenant Governors: The Office and the Powers* (Lexington, Ky.: CSG, 1983), p. 10.

73. Ibid.

Chapter 8   The Bureaucracy   pp. 212–245

1. U.S. Bureau of the Census, *Statistical Abstract of the United States, 1989* (Washington, D.C.: U.S. Government Printing Office, 1989), p. 293.

2. Ibid., p. 272.

3. Jay Shafritz, "The Cancer Eroding Public Personnel Professionalism," *Public Personnel Management* 3 (November/December 1974): 486–92.

4. U.S. Advisory Commission on Intergovernmental Relations, *The Question of State Government Capability*, A-98 (Washington, D.C.: ACIR, 1985), pp. 168–69.

5. See, for example, Kenneth J. Meier, "Representative Bureaucracy: An Empirical Analysis," *American Political Science Review* 69 (June 1975): 526–42; and Samuel Krislov and David H. Rosenbloom, *Representative Bureaucracy and the American Political System* (New York: Praeger, 1981), pp. 31–73 and 75–107.

6. U.S. Equal Employment Opportunity Commission, *Affirmative Action and Equal Employment: A Guidebook for Employers* (Washington, D.C.: U.S. Government Printing Office, 1974).

7. *Regents of the University of California* v. *Bakke*, 438 U.S. 265, 98 S.Ct. 2733 (1978).

8. *United Steelworkers of America, AFL-CIO* v. *Weber*, 443 U.S. 193 (1979).

9. *Memphis* v. *Stotts*, 467 U.S. 561 (1984).

10. *Martin* v. *Wilks*, 87–1614 (1989).

11. See, for example, James D. Slack, "Affirmative Action and City Managers: Attitudes Toward Recruitment of Women," *Public Administration Review* 47 (March/April 1987): 199–206; Albert Karnig et al., "Employment of Women by Cities in the Southwest," *Social Science Journal* 21 (Fall 1984): 41–48; Nelson C. Dometrius and Lee Sigelman, "Assessing Progress Toward Affirmative Action Goals in State and Local Government: A New Benchmark," *Public Administration Review* 44 (May/June 1984): 241–46.

12. Peter J. Haas and Deil S. Wright, "The Changing Profile of State Administrators," *Journal of State Government* 60 (November/December 1987): 270–78.

13. See Karen Torry, "Comparable Worth: A Developing Issue or One Losing Steam?" in Thad L. Beyle, ed., *State Government: CQ's Guide to Current Issues and Activities, 1986–87* (Washington, D.C.: Congressional Quarterly, 1986), pp. 116–21.

14. Keon S. Chi, "Comparable Worth in State Governments," *State Government News* 27 (November 1984): 4–6.

15. See M. Dawn McCaghy, *Sexual Harassment: A Guide to Resources* (Boston: G. K. Hall, 1985); Dail Ann Neugarten and Monica Miller-Spellman, "Sexual Harassment in Public Employment," in Steven W. Hays and Richard C. Kearney, eds., *Public Personnel Administration: Problems and Prospects* (Englewood Cliffs, N.J.: Prentice-Hall, 1983).

16. Cynthia S. Ross and Robert E. England, "State Governments' Sexual Harassment Policy Initiatives," *Public Administration Review* 47 (May/June 1987): 259–62.

17. U.S. Department of Commerce, *Labor-Management Relations in State and Local Government 1972–1980*, Series GSS No. 102 (Washington, D.C.: U.S. Government Printing Office, 1981), pp. 9–10.

18. *National League of Cities* v. *Usery*, 426 U.S. 833 (1976).

19. Jay F. Atwood, "Collective Bargaining's Challenge: Five Imperatives for Public Managers," *Public Personnel Management* 5 (January/February 1976): 24–32.

20. See Richard C. Kearney, "Monetary Impact of Collective Bargaining," in Jack Rabin et al., eds., *Handbook on Public Personnel Administration* (New York: Marcel Dekker, 1983).

21. See M. S. March, "Pensions for Public Employees Present Nationwide Problems," *Public Administration Review* 40 (July/August 1980): 382–88.

22. See Raymond D. Horton, David Levin, and James W. Kuhn, "Some Impacts of Collective Bargaining on Local Government: A Diversity Thesis," *Administration and Society* 7 (February 1976): 497–516.

23. Glenn Abney and Thomas P. Lauth, *The Politics of State and City Administration* (Albany: SUNY Press, 1986), pp. 76–78, 178–81.

24. John T. Scholz and Feng Heng Wei, "Regulatory Enforcement in a Federalist System," *American Political Science Review* 8 (December 1986): 1249–70; see also Abney and Lauth, *Politics of Administration*.

25. Abney and Lauth, *Politics of Administration*, pp. 132–53.

26. See Richard C. Kearney and Chandan Sinha, "Professionalism and Bureaucratic Responsiveness: Conflict or Compatibility?" *Public Administration Review* 48 (January/February 1988): 571–79.

27. See Frederick C. Mosher, *Democracy and the Public Service*, 2nd ed. (New York: Oxford University Press, 1982).

28. Robert Bell, "Professional Values and Organizational Decision Making," *Administration and Society* 17 (May 1985): 21–60.

29. Kearney and Sinha, "Professionalism and Bureaucratic Responsiveness," pp. 571–79.

30. Ibid.

31. Charles T. Goodsell, *The Case for Bureaucracy: A Public Administration Polemic* (Chatham, N.J.: Chatham House, 1983), pp. 44–48; also see Abney and Lauth, *Politics of Administration*, pp. 209–10.

32. Kearney and Sinha, "Professionalism and Bureaucratic Responsiveness."

33. Ibid.

34. Goodsell, *The Case for Bureaucracy*, p. 260.

35. Harold D. Lasswell, *Politics: Who Gets What, When, Where, How?* (Cleveland: World, 1958).

36. See Robert B. Albritton and Ellen M. Dran, "Balanced Budgets and State Surpluses: The Politics of Budgeting in Illinois," *Public Administration Review* 47 (March/April 1987): 143–52.

37. See Donald Axelrod, *A Budget Quartet* (New York: St. Martin's, 1989).

38. Aaron Wildavsky, "Toward a Radical Incrementalism," in Alfred De Grazia, ed., *Congress: The First Branch of Government* (Washington, D.C.: American Enterprise Institute, 1966).

39. Aaron Wildavsky, *The Politics of the Budgetary Process* (Boston: Little, Brown, 1964), pp. 1–13.

40. Abney and Lauth, *Politics of Administration*, pp. 110–11, 115, 142–43.

41. Charles E. Lindblom, "The Science of Muddling Through," *Public Administrative Review* 19 (Spring 1959): 79–88.

42. Allen Shick, "The Road to PPB: The Stages of Budget Reform," *Public Administration Review* 26 (December 1966).

43. James Ramsey and Merlin H. Backbart, *Innovations in State Budgeting: Process, Impact* (Lexington, Ky.: Center for Public Affairs, 1980), p. 7.

44. S. Kenneth Howard, *Changing State Budgeting* (Lexington, Ky.: Council of State Governments, 1973), p. 359.

45. ACIR, *The Question of State Government Capability*, p. 179.

46. Stanley B. Botner, "The Use of Budgeting/Management Tools by State Governments," *Public Administration Review* 45 (September/October 1985): 616–20.

47. Ibid., pp. 130–32.

Chapter 9   State Legislatures   pp. 246–278

1. Alan Ehrenhalt, "How a Party of Enthusiasts Keeps Its Hammerlock on a State Legislature," *Governing* 2 (June 1989): 28–33.

2. James N. Miller, "Hamstrung Legislatures," *National Civic Review* 54 (April 1965): 178–87.

3. Ibid.

4. *The Book of the States, 1988–89* (Lexington, Ky.: Council of State Governments, 1988).

5. Elizabeth Kolbert, "As Workload Grows, Number of Part-Time Legislators Falls," *New York Times*, June 4, 1989, p. 13.

6. National Municipal League, *Apportionment in the 1960s*, rev. ed. (New York: National Municipal League, 1970).

7. *Baker* v. *Carr*, 369 U.S. 186, 82 S.Ct. 691 (1362).

8. *Reynolds* v. *Sims*, 84 S.Ct. 1362 (1964).

9. *Davis* v. *Bandemer*, 106 S.Ct. 2797.

10. Charles S. Bullock III, "Redistricting and Changes in the Partisan and Racial Composition of Southern Legislatures," *State and Local Government Review* 19 (Spring 1987): 62–67.

11. Kimball Brace, Bernard Grofman, and Lisa Handley, "Does Redistricting Aimed to Help Blacks Necessarily Help Republicans?" *Journal of Politics* 49 (February 1987): 169–85.

12. Timothy G. O'Rourke, *The Impact of Reapportionment* (New Brunswick, N.J.: Transaction Books, 1980).

13. David C. Saffell, "Reapportionment and Public Policy: State Legislators' Perspectives," in Bernard Gronfman et al., eds., *Representation and Redistricting Issues* (Lexington, Mass.: D.C. Heath, 1982), pp. 203–19.

14. William T. Pound, "The State Legislatures," in Council of State Governments, *The Book of the States, 1988–89 Edition* (Lexington, Ky.: CSG, 1988), pp. 76–83.

15. Ibid., p. 80.

16. Peverill Squire, "Member Career Opportunities and the Internal Organization of Legislatures," *Journal of Politics* 50 (August 1988): 726–44.

17. Robert Harmel and Keith E. Hamm, "Development of a Party Role in a No-Party Legislature," *Western Political Quarterly* 39 (March 1986): 79–92.

18. Joel A. Thompson, "Bringing Home the Bacon: The Politics of Pork Barrel in the North Carolina Legislature," *Legislative Studies Quarterly* 11 (February 1986): 91–108.

19. Keith E. Hamm, "The Role of 'Subgovernments' in U.S. State Policy Making: An Exploratory Analysis," *Legislative Studies Quarterly* 11 (August 1986): 321–51.

20. Alan Rosenthal, *Legislative Life: People, Processes, and Performance in the States* (New York: Harper & Row, 1981).

21. *The Book of the States, 1988–89*, p. 117.

22. Harvey J. Tucker, "Legislative Logjams: A Comparative State Analysis," *Western Political Quarterly* 38 (September 1985): 432–46.

23. E. Lee Bernick and Charles W. Wiggins, "Legislative Norms in Eleven States," *Legislative Studies Quarterly* 8 (May 1983): 191–200.

24. Roy Brasfield Herron, "Diary of a Legislator," *Southern Magazine* 2 (May 1988): 31.

25. Squire, "Member Career Opportunities."

26. Peverill Squire, "Career Opportunities and Membership Stability in Legislatures," *Legislative Studies Quarterly* 13 (February 1988): 65–77.

27. Herron, "Diary of a Legislator."

28. Eric M. Uslaner and Ronald E. Weber, "U.S. State Legislators' Opinions and Perceptions of Constituency Attitudes," *Legislative Studies Quarterly* 4 (November 1979): 563–85.

29. Donald R. Songer et al., "The Influence of Issues on Choice of Voting Cues Utilized by State Legislators," *Western Political Quarterly* 39 (March 1986): 118–25.

30. Jon Hurwitz, "Determinants of Legislative Cue Selection," *Social Science Quarterly* 69 (March 1988): 212–23.

31. Citizens' Conference on State Legislatures, *The Sometimes Governments: A Critical Study of the 50 American Legislatures,* 2nd ed. (Kansas City, Mo.: CCSL, 1973), pp. 41–42.

32. The Council of State Governments, "Stated Briefly," *State Government News* 31 (June 1988): 30.

33. Pound, "The State Legislatures," p. 79.

34. Ibid., p. 82.

35. John Grumm, "The Effects of Legislative Structure on Legislative Performance," in Richard Hofferbert and Ira Sharkansky, eds., *State and Urban Politics: Readings in Comparative Public Policy* (Boston: Little, Brown, 1971), pp. 298–322.

36. Albert K. Karnig and Lee Sigelman, "State Legislative Reform and Public Policy: Another Look," *Western Political Quarterly* 28 (September 1975): 548–52.

37. Phillip W. Roeder, "State Legislative Reform: Determinants and Policy Consequences," *American Politics Quarterly* 7 (January 1979): 51–70.

38. Ann O'M. Bowman and Richard C. Kearney, "Dimensions of State Government Capability," *Western Political Quarterly* 41 (June 1988): 341–62.

39. Alan Rosenthal, "The New Legislature: Better or Worse and for Whom?" *State Legislatures* 12 (July 1986): 5.

40. Andrea Paterson, "Is the Citizen Legislator Becoming Extinct?" *State Legislatures* 12 (July 1986): 22–25.

41. Charles W. Wiggins, as quoted in Paterson, p. 24.

42. Representative Vic Krouse, as quoted in Paterson, p. 24.

43. Alan Rosenthal, "The State Legislature," paper presented at the Vanderbilt Institute for Public Policy Studies, November 1987.

44. Lucinda Simon, "Legislatures and Governors: The Wrestling Match," *State Government* 59 (Spring 1986): 1.

45. Ted Strickland, as quoted in Simon, p. 5.

46. Sharon Randall, "From Big Shot to Boss," *State Legislatures* 14 (June 1988): 34–38.

47. Governor Tommy Thompson, as quoted in Randall, p. 36.

48. Tom Loftus, as quoted in Randall, p. 36.

49. Madeleine Kunin, as quoted in Randall, p. 34.

50. Simon, "Legislatures and Governors."

51. Samuel K. Gove, "State Management and Legislative-Executive Relations," *State Government* 54, no. 3 (1981): 99–101.

52. Rosenthal, *Legislative Life.*

53. Richard E. Brown, "Legislative Performance Auditing: Its Goals and Pitfalls," *State Government* 52 (Winter 1979): 31–34.

54. William M. Pearson and Van A. Wigginton, "Effectiveness of Administrative Controls: Some Perceptions of State Legislators," *Public Administration Review* 46 (July/August 1986): 328–31.

55. Rosenthal, "The New Legislature," p. 5.

56. Bill Halldin, "Soil, Toothpicks, and Mothers All on Lawmakers' Agendas," *Tampa Tribune,* April 3, 1988, p. 7B.

Chapter 10   The Judiciary   pp. 279–309

1. "Ruling in Montana Puts Heat on Ski Operators," *Governing* 2 (January 1989): 17.

2. Henry Robert Glick and Kenneth N. Vines, *State Court Systems* (Englewood Cliffs, N.J.: Prentice-Hall, 1973), p. 19.

3. Ibid., p. 21.

4. See, for example, Robert A. Kagan et al., "The Evolution of State Supreme Courts," *Michigan Law Review* 76 (May 1978): 961–1005.

5. See Larry Berkson and Susan Carbon, *Court Unification: History, Politics and Implementation* (Washington, D.C.: U.S. Department of Justice, National Institute for Law Enforcement and Criminal Justice, 1978).

6. U.S. Advisory Commission on Intergovernmental Relations, "State Court Systems," in *The Question of State Government Capability* (Washington, D.C.: ACIR, 1985), p. 191.

7. American Bar Association, *Standards Relating to Court Organization* (New York: ABA, 1974), pp. 43–44.

8. Ibid., p. 43.

9. *The Book of the States 1985–86* (Lexington, Ky.: Council of State Governments, 1985), p. 159.

10. Herbert Jacob, "The Effect of Institutional Differences in the Recruitment Process: The Case of State Judges," *Journal of Public Law* 33, no. 113 (1964): 104–19.

11. Francis Graham Lee, "Party Representation of State Supreme Courts: 'Unequal Representation' Revisited," *State and Local Government Review* 11 (May 1979): 48–52. Also see Herbert Jacob, *Justice in America* (Boston: Little, Brown, 1965), p. 98.

12. "Is Texas Justice for Sale?" *Time*, January 11, 1988, p. 45.

13. Sheila Kaplan, "Justice for Sale," *State Government: CQ's Guide to Current Issues and Activities 1986–87* (Washington, D.C.: CQ Press, 1987), pp. 151–57.

14. Ibid., p. 152.

15. John H. Culver, "Politics and the California Plan for Choosing Appellate Judges: A Lesson at Large on Judicial Selection," *Judicature* 66 (September/October 1982): 152–53.

16. See, for example, Richard A. Watson and Ronald C. Downing, *The Politics of the Bench and Bar* (New York: John Wiley and Sons, 1969), pp. 43–48, 136–38.

17. Ibid.

18. Susan Carbon, "Judicial Retention Elections: Are They Serving Their Intended Purpose?" *Judicature* 64 (November 1980): 210–33.

19. Ibid., p. 221.

20. Bradley C. Canon, "The Impact of Formal Selection Processes on the Characteristics of Judges—Reconsidered," *Law and Society Review* 6 (1972): 575–93; Burton M. Atkins and Henry R. Glick, "Formal Judicial Recruitment and State Supreme Court Decisions," *American Politics Quarterly* 2 (October 1974): 427–49.

21. John Paul Ryan et al., *American Trial Judges* (New York: Free Press, 1980), pp. 125–30.

22. Philip L. Dubois, *From Ballot to Bench: Judicial Elections and the Quest for Accountability* (Austin: University of Texas Press, 1980), Chapter 4.

23. Philip L. Dubois, "State Trial Court Appointments: Does the Governor Make a Difference?" *Judicature* 69 (June/July 1985): 22; Bradley C. Canon, "Characteristics and Career Patterns of State Supreme Court Justices," *State Government* 45 (Winter 1972): 34–41.

24. Dubois, "State Trial Court Appointments."

25. Glick and Vines, *State Court Systems*, p. 44.

26. Ibid.

27. Dubois, "State Trial Court Appointments."

28. Ibid., pp. 24–25.

29. ACIR, *State Government Capability*, p. 190.

30. Ibid.

31. Harry Kalven, Jr., and Hans Zeisel, *The American Jury* (Boston: Little, Brown, 1966), pp. 502–3.

32. Glick and Vines, *State Court Systems*, p. 78.

33. Ibid., pp. 81–82.

34. Gregory A. Caldeira, "The Transmission of Legal Precedent: A Study of State Supreme Courts," *American Political Science Review* 79 (March 1985): 178–93.

35. Ibid., p. 190.

36. Stuart Nagel, "Political Party Affiliation and Judges' Decisions," *American Political Science Review* 55 (December 1961): 843–60.

37. See Beverly Cook, "Women Judges and Public Policy in Sex Integration," in Debra Stewart, ed., *Women in Local Politics* (London: Scarecrow Press, 1980); Gerald S. Gryski, Eleanor C. Main, and William J. Dixon, "Models of State High Court Decision Making in Sex Discrimination Cases," *Journal of Politics* 48 (February 1986): 143–55; Diane E. Wall and David W. Allen, "Elite Female Justices' Decision Making Within the South," paper presented at the annual meeting of the Southern Political Science Association, Charlotte, N.C., November 1987.

38. Bradley C. Canon, "Defining the Dimensions of Judicial Activism," *Judicature* 66 (December/January 1983): 236–47.

39. Ibid., pp. 238–39.

40. Quoted in Stanley M. Mosk, "The

Emerging Agenda in State Constitutional Law," *Intergovernmental Perspective* 13 (Spring 1987): 21.

41. Ibid., p. 22.

42. See John Patrick Hagan, "Patterns of Activism on State Supreme Courts," *Publius* 18 (Winter 1988): 97–115.

43. Canon, "Defining the Dimensions," pp. 246–47.

44. American Bar Association, *Standards*, pp. 97–104.

45. Charles G. Douglas III, "Innovative Appellate Court Processing: New Hampshire's Experience with Summary Affirmance," *Judicature* 69 (October/November 1985): 147–52.

46. Ibid., p. 148.

47. Jef Feeley, "Appellate Arbitration Set in South Carolina," *The National Law Journal* (January 14, 1985): 11, 38.

48. Marcia J. Lim, "State of the Judiciary," in *The Book of the States 1985–86.*

49. Ibid., p. 148.

50. "The Cameras Are Rolling in Kentucky Courts," *Governing* 2 (October 1988): 32–34.

51. Thomes B. Marvell, "Judicial Salaries: Doing More Work for Less Pay," *Judges Journal* 24 (Winter 1985): 34–37, 46 47.

52. Edward B. McConnell, "State Judicial Salaries: A National Perspective," *State Government* 61 (September/October 1988): 179–82.

Chapter 11   The Structure of Local Government   pp. 310–339

1. Richard Levine and Linda Greenhouse, "High Court Voids Governing Board in New York City," *New York Times*, March 23, 1989, pp. 1, 12.

2. "Local Government in Metropolitan Areas," *1982 Census of Governments* (Washington, D.C.: U.S. Department of Commerce, 1985).

3. John Kincaid, "Municipal Perspectives on Federalism," unpublished manuscript, 1987.

4. Dennis Hale, "The City as Polity and Economy," *Polity* 17 (Winter 1984): 205–24.

5. Kincaid, "Municipal Perspectives," p. 56.

6. Oliver P. Williams and Charles R. Adrian, *Four Cities: A Study in Comparative Policy Making* (Philadelphia: University of Pennsylvania Press, 1963).

7. Dennis R. Judd, *The Politics of American Cities: Private Power and Public Policy*, 2nd ed. (Boston: Little, Brown, 1988).

8. Ibid.

9. As quoted in Martin J. Schiesl, *The Politics of Efficiency* (Berkeley: University of California Press, 1977).

10. Samuel P. Hays, "The Politics of Reform in Municipal Government in the Progressive Era," in Harlan Hahn and Charles Levine, eds., *Urban Politics* (New York: Longman, 1980), pp. 53–72.

11. Paul D. Schumaker and Russell W. Getter, "Responsiveness Bias in 51 American Communities," *American Journal of Political Science* 21 (May 1977): 247–81.

12. Thomas R. Dye and Susan A. MacManus, "Predicting City Government Structure," *American Journal of Political Science*, 20 (May 1976): 257–71.

13. Herbert Sydney Duncombe, *Modern County Government* (Washington, D.C.: National Association of Counties, 1977).

14. Carolyn B. Lawrence and John M. DeGrove, "County Government Services," in National Association of Counties and International City Management Association, *The County Year Book 1976* (Washington, D.C.: NACO and ICMA, 1976), pp. 91–129.

15. U.S. Advisory Commission on Intergovernmental Relations, *State and Local Roles in the Federal System* (Washington, D.C.: ACIR, 1982).

16. Ibid.

17. Barbara P. Greene, "Counties and the Fiscal Challenges of the 1980s," *Intergovernmental Perspective* 13 (Winter 1987): 14–19.

18. John Herbers, "Seventeenth-Century Counties Struggle to Cope with Twentieth-Century Problems," *Governing* 2 (May 1989): 42–48.

19. John A. Gronouski and James L. Mercer, "A Consolidation Model: Austin/Travis County, Texas," *National Civic Review* 76 (September/October 1987): 450–54.

20. Douglas Yates, *The Ungovernable City* (Cambridge, Mass.: MIT Press, 1977).

21. Edward C. Banfield, *The Unheavenly City* (Boston: Little, Brown, 1968).

22. Joel C. Miller, "Municipal Annexation and Boundary Change," in *The Municipal Year Book 1988* (Washington, D.C.: ICMA, 1988), pp. 59–67.

23. Schiesl, *The Politics of Efficiency.*

24. Heywood T. Sanders, "The Government of American Cities: Continuity and Change in Structure," *The Municipal Year Book 1982* (Washington, D.C.: ICMA, 1982), pp. 178–86.

25. David R. Morgan, *Managing Urban America*, 2nd ed. (Belmont, Calif.: Wadsworth, 1984).

26. James H. Svara, "Dichotomy and Duality: Reconceptualizing the Relationship between Policy and Administration in Council-Manager Cities," *Public Administration Review* 45 (January/February 1985): 221–32.

27. Robert D. Thomas, "Metropolitan Structural Development: The Territorial Imperative," *Publius* 14 (Spring 1984): 83–115.

28. Richard H. Kraemer and Charldean Newell, *The Essentials of Texas Politics*, 2nd ed. (St. Paul: West, 1983).

29. Barry J. Kaplan, "Houston: The Golden Buckle of the Sunbelt," in Richard M. Bernard and Bradley R. Rice, eds., *Sunbelt Cities: Politics and Growth Since World War II* (Austin: University of Texas Press, 1983), pp. 196–212.

30. Michael Easterwood, "The Municipality and South Carolina Government," in Charlie B. Tyer and Cole Blease Graham, Jr., eds. *Local Government in South Carolina* (Columbia, S.C.: Bureau of Governmental Research and Service, 1984), pp. 9–49.

31. "Rankings of 75 Largest Cities for Selected Subjects," *County and City Data Book 1983* (Washington, D.C.: U.S. Government Printing Office, 1983).

32. Douglas D. Peterson, *City Fiscal Conditions 1989* (Washington, D.C.: National League of Cities, 1989).

33. Tari Renner, "Municipal Election Processes: The Impact on Minority Representation," in *The Municipal Year Book 1988*, pp. 13–21.

34. Susan Welch and Timothy Bledsoe, *Urban Reform and Its Consequences: A Study in Representation* (Chicago: University of Chicago Press, 1988).

35. Peggy Heilig and Robert J. Mundt, "The Effect of Adopting Districts on Representational Equity," *Social Science Quarterly* 64 (June 1983): 393–97.

36. Renner, "Municipal Election Processes."

37. Alva W. Stewart and Phung Nguyen, "Electing the City Council: Historic Change in Greensboro," *National Civic Review* 72 (July/August 1983): 377–81.

38. Peggy Heilig and Robert J. Mundt, *Your Voice at City Hall* (Albany: State University of New York Press, 1984).

39. Welch and Bledsoe, *Urban Reform and Its Consequences*.

40. ACIR, *State and Local Roles in the Federal System*.

41. Thomas L. Daniels, "Rationing Government Resources Calls for 'Small-Town Triage,' " *Governing* (March 1988): 74.

42. ACIR, *State and Local Roles in the Federal System*, p. 154.

43. John C. Bollens, *Special District Governments in the United States* (Berkeley: University of California Press, 1957).

44. Charlie B. Tyer, "The Special Purpose District in South Carolina," in Tyer and Graham, eds., *Local Government in South Carolina*, pp. 75–89.

45. Robert S. Lorch, *State and Local Politics* (Englewood Cliffs, N.J.: Prentice-Hall, 1983), p. 280.

46. Virginia M. Perronrod, *Special Districts, Special Purposes* (College Station: Texas A & M University Press, 1984).

47. Scott Bollens, "Examining the Link Between State Policy and the Creation of Local Special Districts," *State and Local Government Review* 18 (Fall 1986): 117–24.

48. Ibid.

49. Harvey Tucker and L. Harmon Zeigler, *The Politics of Educational Governance: An Overview* (Eugene: ERIC Clearinghouse on Education Management, University of Oregon, 1980).

50. Chester E. Finn, as quoted in Edward B. Fiske, "Parental Choice in Public Schools Gains," *New York Times*, July 11, 1988, p. 1.

51. Terry Minger and Parry Burnap, "A Metropolitan Crisis: The Mile High View," paper presented at the National Urban Policy Conference, Denver, 1986.

52. William R. Dodge, "The Emergence of Intercommunity Partnerships in the 1980s," *Public Management* 70 (July 1988): 2–7.

53. Ibid., p. 7.

54. Stephen Forman and Walt Crowley, "The Cultivation of Strategic Consensus: A New Mission for the Regional Citizen," paper presented at the Roundtable of Governments, Lincoln Institute of Land Policy, Denver, 1986.

55. Ibid., p. 6.

56. National Municipal League, "All-America Cities 1985–1986 Continue a Heritage of Achievement," *National Civic Review* 75 (May/June 1986): 130–37.

57. Harry P. Hatry, "Would We Know a Well-Governed City If We Saw One? *National Civic Review* 75 (May/June 1986): 142–46.

Chapter 12 Local Leadership
pp. 340–363

1. Jane Gross, "San Jose, That Upstart in Hinterland, Takes on San Francisco," *New York Times*, February 8, 1989, p. 8.

2. Jameson W. Doig and Erwin C. Hargrove, eds., *Leadership and Innovation* (Baltimore: Johns Hopkins University Press, 1987).

3. Bernard Sanders as quoted in Allan R. Gold, "Exit a Socialist, to Let History Judge," *New York Times*, March 6, 1989, p. 8.

4. Kathleen Sylvester, "In Search of Clout, America's Mayors Are Courting the Candidates," *Governing* (November 1987): 28–32.

5. Thomas J. Peters and Robert H. Waterman, Jr., *In Search of Excellence* (New York: Harper & Row, 1982).

6. Thomas J. Peters and Nancy Austin, *A Passion for Excellence: The Leadership Difference* (New York: Random House, 1985), p. 5.

7. Warren Bennis and Burt Nanus, *Leaders: The Strategies for Taking Charge* (New York: Harper & Row, 1985).

8. Wayne F. Anderson, Chester A. Newland, and Richard J. Stillman II, *The Effective Local Government Manager* (Washington, D.C.: International City Management Association, 1983).

9. George P. Barbour, Jr., and George A. Sipel, "Excellence in Leadership: Public Sector Model," *Public Management* (August 1986): 3–5.

10. Gaetano Mosca, *The Ruling Class* (New York: McGraw-Hill, 1939).

11. Robert Michels, *Political Parties* (New York: Free Press, 1962).

12. Robert S. Lynd and Helen M. Lynd, *Middletown* (New York: Harcourt Brace and World, 1929); Robert S. Lynd and Helen M. Lynd, *Middletown in Transition* (New York: Harcourt Brace and World, 1937).

13. Floyd Hunter, *Community Power Structure* (Chapel Hill: University of North Carolina Press, 1953); Floyd Hunter, *Community Power Succession* (Chapel Hill: University of North Carolina Press, 1980).

14. Hunter, *Community Power Succession*, p. 16.

15. Harvey Molotch, "Strategies and Constraints of Growth Elites," in Scott Cummings, ed., *Business Elites and Urban Development* (Albany: State University of New York Press, 1988), pp. 25–47.

16. Robert Dahl, *Who Governs?* (New Haven: Yale University Press, 1961).

17. Nelson Polsby, *Community Power and Political Theory* (New Haven: Yale University Press, 1963).

18. Charles M. Bonjean and David M. Olson, "Community Leadership: Directions of Research," *Administrative Science Quarterly* 9 (December 1964): 278–300.

19. Peter Bachrach and Morton S. Baratz, "Two Faces of Power," *American Political Science Review* 56 (December 1962): 947–53.

20. G. William Domhoff, *Who Really Rules?* (Santa Monica, Calif.: Goodyear, 1978).

21. Bonjean and Olson, "Community Leadership," p. 288.

22. Robert Agger, Daniel Goldrich, and Bert Swanson, *The Rulers and the Ruled*, rev. ed. (Belmont, Calif.: Wadsworth, 1972).

23. Anne B. Shlay and Robert P. Giloth, "The Social Organization of a Land-Based Elite: The Case of the Failed Chicago 1992 World's Fair," *Journal of Urban Affairs* 9, no. 4 (1987): 305–24.

24. Ibid., p. 320.

25. Ann O'M. Bowman, "Elite Organization and the Growth Machine," in G. William Domhoff and Thomas R. Dye, eds., *Power Elites and Organizations* (Newbury Part, Calif.: Sage, 1987), pp. 116–25.

26. Clarence N. Stone, "Systemic Power in Community Decision Making," *American Political Science Review* 74 (December 1980): 978–90.

27. Ibid., p. 989.

28. Clarence N. Stone, "The Study of the Politics of Urban Development," in Clarence N. Stone and Heywood T. Sanders, eds., *The Politics of Urban Development* (Lawrence: University of Kansas Press, 1987), pp. 3–22.

29. George J. Gordon, *Public Administration*

in America, 3rd ed. (New York: St. Martin's, 1986).

30. Glen Sparrow, "The Emerging Chief Executive: The San Diego Experience," *National Civic Review* 74 (November 1985): 542.

31. Ibid., p. 545.

32. Douglas Yates, *The Ungovernable City* (Cambridge, Mass.: MIT Press, 1977).

33. John P. Kotter and Paul R. Lawrence, *Mayors in Action* (New York: Wiley, 1974).

34. W. John Moore, "From Dreamers to Doers," *National Journal* (February 13, 1988): 372–77.

35. Ibid., p. 373.

36. Ibid., p. 375.

37. E. J. Dionne, Jr., "Blacks Study Politics of Polarization," *New York Times*, April 11, 1989, p. 7.

38. Clifford J. Wirth and Michael L. Vasu, "Ideology and Decision Making for American City Managers," *Urban Affairs Quarterly* 22 (March 1987): 454–74.

39. Anderson, Newland, and Stillman, *The Effective Local Government Manager*, pp. 45–73.

40. Ibid., p. 48.

41. Sparrow, "The Emerging Chief Executive," p. 545.

42. Anderson, Newland, and Stillman, *The Effective Local Government Manager*, pp. 18–21.

43. Larry Azevedo, as quoted in Alan Ehrenhalt, "How a Liberal Government Came to Power in a Conservative Suburb," *Governing* 1 (March 1988): 51–56.

44. Kenneth Prewitt, *The Recruitment of Political Leaders: A Study of Citizen-Politicians* (Indianapolis: Bobbs-Merrill, 1970).

45. Susan Welch and Timothy Bledsoe, *Urban Reform and Its Consequences* (Chicago: University of Chicago Press, 1988).

46. Robert D. Thomas, "The Search for Legitimacy and Competency in Mayor-Council Relations: The Case of Houston," paper presented at the annual meeting of the Southern Political Science Association, Charlotte, N.C., 1987.

47. Ibid.

48. James H. Svara, "Dichotomy and Duality: Reconceptualizing the Relationship between Policy and Administration in Council-Manager Cities," *Public Administration Review* 45 (January/February 1985): 221–32.

49. James H. Svara, "The Complementary Roles of Officials in Council-Manager Government," in International City Management Association, *The Municipal Year Book 1988* (Washington, D.C.: ICMA, 1988), pp. 23–33.

50. Ibid., pp. 25–26.

51. Thomas P. Ryan, Jr., as quoted in Jane Mobley, "Politician or Professional? The Debate over Who Should Run our Cities Continues," *Governing* 1 (February 1988): 42–48.

52. Ronald Reagan, as quoted in Peter A. Harkness, "Publisher's Desk," *Governing* 1 (March 1988): 6.

53. Doig and Hargrove, *Leadership and Innovation*, pp. 7–8.

54. Donald Rosenthal and Donald Crain, "Executive Leadership and Community Innovation: Fluoridation," *Urban Affairs Quarterly* 2 (March 1966): 39–57.

55. Thomas M. Scott, "The Diffusion of Urban Governmental Forms as a Case of Social Learning," *Journal of Politics* 30 (November 1968): 1091–1108.

56. Ann O'Meara Bowman, "Policy Innovation in Local Government," unpublished doctoral dissertation, University of Florida, 1979.

57. Richard W. Stevenson, "Challenging the Billboard Industry," *New York Times*, August 30, 1988, pp. 25, 38.

58. "Those Plastic Packages Aren't Welcome in Suffolk County, N.Y. Anymore," *Governing* 1 (July 1988): 14.

59. Lurton Blassingame, "Frostbelt Success Story: Oshkosh, Wisconsin," *Journal of Urban Affairs* 9, no. 1 (1987): 37–46.

60. Josh Barbanel, "New Yorkers Doubt Any Mayor Can Solve City's Worst Problems," *New York Times*, June 22, 1989, pp. 1, 22.

Chapter 13 State and Local Finance
pp. 364–399

1. U.S. Advisory Commission on Intergovernmental Relations, *Significant Features of Fiscal Federalism*, vol. 1 (Washington, D.C.: ACIR, 1988), p. 6.

2. Ibid.

3. Deil Wright, *Understanding Intergovernmental Relations*, 3rd. ed. (Pacific Grove, Calif.: Brooks/Cole, 1988), pp. 124–25.

4. ACIR, *Significant Features of Fiscal Federalism*, vol. 2, p. 14.

5. Susan A. MacManus, "State Government: The Overseer of Municipal Finance," in Alberta M. Sbragia, ed., *The Municipal Money Chase: The Politics of Local Government Finance* (Boulder: Westview, 1983), pp. 145–83.

6. ACIR, *The Question of State Government Capability*, A-98 (Washington, D.C.: ACIR, 1985), p. 308.

7. ACIR, *Significant Features of Fiscal Federalism*, vol. 2, p. 14.

8. "Tax Report," *Wall Street Journal*, December 10, 1986, p. 1; *Wall Street Journal*, August 30, 1989, p. 1.

9. See ACIR, *Significant Features of Fiscal Federalism*, vol. 2, p. 41.

10. Neal R. Peirce, "State Fortunes: Calm Now, Heavy Seas Ahead," *Public Administration Times* 12 (March 31, 1989): 2.

11. See Stephen D. Gold, "Developments in State Finances, 1983 to 1986," *Public Budgeting and Finance* 7 (Spring 1987): 16.

12. ACIR, *The Question of State Government Capability*, p. 209.

13. Mark Schneider, "Local Budgets and the Maximization of Local Property Wealth in the System of Suburban Government," *Journal of Politics* 49 (November 1987): 1114.

14. Michael J. Wolkoff, "Exploring the State Choice of Financing Options," *State and Local Government Review* 19 (Spring 1987): 74.

15. Ibid.

16. See Gold, "Developments in State Finances," p. 11.

17. ACIR, *Significant Features of Fiscal Federalism*, vol. 1, p. 56.

18. Ibid., p. 57.

19. Ibid., p. 54.

20. Ibid., pp. 54–55.

21. Neil R. Peirce, "Service Tax May Rise Again," *Public Administration Times* 11 (August 12, 1988): 2.

22. Thomas M. Fullerton, Jr., "Rational Reactions to Temporary Sales Tax Legislation: An Idaho Case Study," *Public Budgeting and Finance* 7 (Summer 1987).

23. Steven D. Gold, "The Blizzard of 1987: A Year of Tax Reform Activity in the States," *Publius* 18 (Summer 1988): 18.

24. Gold, "Developments in State Finances," pp. 12–13.

25. ACIR, *Significant Features of Fiscal Federalism*, pp. 46, 48–49.

26. Gold, "The Blizzard of 1987," p. 19.

27. Donald Axelrod, *Budgeting for Modern Government* (New York: St. Martin's, 1988), p. 218.

28. See Robert Cervero, "Paying for Off-Site Road Improvements Through Fees, Assessments, and Negotiations: Lessons from California," *Public Administration Review* 48 (January/February 1988): 534–41.

29. Data on tobacco, alcohol, and gasoline taken from ACIR, *Significant Features of Fiscal Federalism*, vol. 1, pp. 62–66.

30. Wolkoff, "Exploring the State Choice," p. 73.

31. Elder Witt, "States Place Their Bets on a Game of Diminishing Returns," *Governing* 1 (November 1987): 52–57.

32. John L. Mikesell and C. Kurt Zorn, "State Lotteries as Fiscal Savior or Fiscal Fraud: A Look at the Evidence," *Public Administration Review* 46 (July/August 1986): 312–13.

33. John L. Mikesell and Kurt Zorn, "State Lotteries for Public Revenue," *Public Budgeting and Finance* 8 (Spring 1988): 43.

34. See, for example, Charles R. Clotfelter, "On the Regressivity of State Operated 'Number' Games," *National Tax Journal* 32 (December 1979): 543–48.

35. Mikesell and Zorn, "State Lotteries for Public Revenue," pp. 40–41.

36. See Sherry Tvedt, "Enough Is Enough! Proposition 2 1/2 in Massachusetts," *National Civic Review* 70 (November 1981): 527–33.

37. ACIR, *Significant Features of Fiscal Federalism*, vol. 2, pp. 102–103.

38. Elaine B. Sharp and David Elkins, "The Impact of Fiscal Limitation: A Tale of Seven Cities," *Public Administration Review* 47 (September/October 1987): 385–92.

39. Gary J. Reid, "How Cities in California Have Responded to Fiscal Pressure Since Proposition 13," *Public Budgeting and Finance* 8 (Spring 1988): 20–37.

40. David R. Morgan and Robert E. England, "Explaining Fiscal Stress Among Large U.S. Cities: Toward an Integrative Model," *Policy Studies Review* 3 (August 1983): 73–78.

41. P. Nivola, "Apocalypse Now? Whither the Urban Fiscal Crisis," *Policy* 14 (Spring 1981): 371–94.

42. Morgan and England, "Explaining Fiscal Stress," pp. 73–78.

43. In Terry Nichols Clark and London Crowley Ferguson, *City Money* (New York: Columbia University Press, 1983), p. 2.
44. See Patricia Giles Leeds, "City Politics and the Market: The Case of New York City's Financing Crisis," in Sbragia, *The Municipal Money Chase*, pp. 113–44.
45. John Shannon, "The Return to Fend-for-Yourself Federalism: The Reagan Mark," *Intergovernmental Perspective* 13 (Summer/Fall 1987): 34–37.
46. Dan Goodgame, "It's Our Money: Voters Want a Say in Spending," *Time*, June 13, 1988, p. 36.
47. Axelrod, *Budgeting for Modern Government*, p. 220.
48. See Jon David Vasche and Brad Williams, "Optimal Governmental Budgeting Contingency Reserve Funds," *Public Budgeting and Finance* 7 (Spring 1987): 66–82.
49. Pamela Fessler, "State Revenue Forecasting Is No Science," *Governing* (November 1988): 64–65.
50. Irene S. Rubin, "Estimated and Actual Urban Revenues: Exploring the Gap," *Public Budgeting and Finance* 7 (Winter 1987): 83–93; Steven D. Gold, "Are States Playing Budget Roulette?" *State Legislatures* 14 (March 1988): 29.
51. Ibid., pp. 28–30.
52. Michael Wolkoff, "An Evaluation of Municipal Rainy Day Funds," *Public Budgeting and Finance* 7 (Summer 1987): 52–62.
53. Gold, "Are States Playing Budget Roulette?" p. 30.
54. Robert L. Bland, "The Effect of Cash Management Innovation on the Investment Income of Local Government," *State and Local Government Review* 18 (Winter 1986): 20–25.
55. Ibid.
56. C. Kurt Zorn and Shah Towfighi, "Not All Bond Banks Are Created Equal," *Public Budgeting and Finance* 6 (Autumn 1986): 57.
57. Nancy P. Humphrey and Diane Rausa Maurice, "Infrastructure Bond Bank Initiatives: Policy Implications and Credit Concerns," *Public Budgeting and Finance* 6 (Autumn 1986): 38–40.
58. Alberta M. Sbragia, "Politics, Local Government, and the Municipal Bond Market," in Sbragia, *The Municipal Money Chase*, pp. 90–93.

59. Data on national, state, and local debt taken from ACIR, *Significant Features of Fiscal Federalism*, vol. 2, pp. 28–29.
60. ACIR, *The Question of State Government Capability*, pp. 327–28.
61. Bruce Mohl, "State's Credit Rating Falls to 1975 Level," *Boston Globe*, June 22, 1989, pp. 1, 22.
62. John P. Thomas, "A Perspective on County Government Services and Financing," *State and Local Government Review* 19 (Fall 1987): 119–21.
63. Douglas D. Peterson, "State Aid to Cities—FY 1986," unpublished research report of the National League of Cities, May 1988, p. 5.
64. See David R. Morgan and Robert E. England, "State Aid to Cities: A Casual Inquiry," *Publius* 14 (Spring 1984): 67–82; and Keith J. Mueller, "Explaining Variation in State Assistance Programs to Local Communities: What to Expect and Why," *State and Local Government Review* 19 (Fall 1987): 101–107.
65. "More State Dollars for the Localities," *Governing* 1 (May 1988): 60–61.
66. Ann O'M. Bowman and Richard C. Kearney, *The Resurgence of the States* (Englewood Cliffs, N.J.: Prentice-Hall, 1986), p. 174.
67. Ibid., pp. 170–73.

Chapter 14   State-Local Relations
pp. 400–424

1. Peter Applebome, "Atlanta in Accord on Plans for a Domed Stadium," *New York Times*, June 7, 1989, p. 12.
2. Steven D. Gold, "NCSL State-Local Task Force: The First Year," *Intergovernmental Perspective* 13 (Winter 1987): 11.
3. U.S. Advisory Commission on Intergovernmental Relations, *The Organization of Local Public Economies* (Washington, D.C.: ACIR, December 1987).
4. Joseph F. Zimmerman, *State-Local Relations* (New York: Praeger, 1983).
5. Alan Ehrenhalt, "Power Shifts in a Southern City as Groups That Took Orders Learn How to Give Them," *Governing* 1 (September 1988): 48–53.
6. U.S. Advisory Commission on Intergovernmental Relations, *State and Local*

Roles in the Federal System (Washington, D.C.: ACIR, 1982).

7. David R. Berman and Lawrence L. Martin, "State-Local Relations: An Examination of Local Discretion," *Public Administration Review* 48 (March/April 1988): 637–41.

8. William L. Waugh, Jr., and Ronald John Hy, "Fiscal Stress and Local Autonomy: State-County Relations in a Changing Intergovernmental System," paper presented at the annual meeting of the American Political Science Association, Washington, D.C., August 1986.

9. U.S. Advisory Commission on Intergovernmental Relations, *Local Perspectives on State-Local Highway Consultation and Cooperation* (Washington, D.C.: ACIR, July 1987).

10. Waugh and Hy, "Fiscal Stress and Local Autonomy."

11. Paul D. Moore and Karen A. Scheer, "The 'State' of State-Local Relations: How Officials See It," *Intergovernmental Perspective* 14 (Winter 1988): 19–21.

12. Ibid., p. 20.

13. Jane Massey and Edwin Thomas, *State Mandated Local Government Expenditures and Revenue Limitations in South Carolina, Part Four* (Columbia: Bureau of Governmental Research and Service, University of South Carolina, March 1988).

14. Catherine H. Lovell et al., *Federal and State Mandating on Local Governments: An Exploration of Issues and Impacts* (Riverside: Graduate School of Administration, University of California, 1979).

15. Massey and Thomas, *State Mandated Local Government Expenditures.*

16. Gold, "NCSL State-Local Task Force," p. 12.

17. Ibid.

18. David W. Russell, "Spotlight on the Connecticut ACIR," *Intergovernmental Perspective* 14 (Winter 1988): 6–8.

19. Lois Pohl, "Spotlight on Missouri's Local Cooperation Commission," *Intergovernmental Perspective* 13 (Winter 1987): 5–7.

20. U.S. Advisory Commission on Intergovernmental Relations, *State-Local Relations Bodies: State ACIRs and Other Approaches* (Washington, D.C.: ACIR, 1981).

21. Ibid., pp. 38–40.

22. Anthony Downs, as cited in Joel Garreau, "From Suburbs, Cities Are Springing Up in Our Back Yards," *Washington Post,* March 8, 1987, p. A26.

23. Jack Meltzner, *Metropolis to Metroplex* (Baltimore: Johns Hopkins University Press, 1984).

24. Todd K. Buchta, "Will We Live in Accidental Cities or Successful Communities?" *Conservation Foundation Letter* 6 (1987).

25. Robert Lindsey, "The Crush on Waikiki Gives Birth to 2d City," *New York Times,* March 22, 1988, p. 8.

26. Joel Garreau, "Solving the Equation for Success," *Washington Post,* June 20, 1988, p. A8.

27. Arthur T. Johnson, *Intergovernmental Influences on Local Land Use Decision Making* (Washington, D.C.: National League of Cities, 1989).

28. Joel Garreau, "The Shadow Governments," *Washington Post,* June 14, 1987, p. A14.

29. Debra L. Dean, "Residential Community Associations: Partners in Local Governance or Headaches for Local Government?" *Intergovernmental Perspective* 15 (Winter 1989): 36–39.

30. Christopher Leinberger, as quoted in Howland, "Back to Basics," p. 7.

31. J. Edwin Benton and Darwin Gamble, "City/County Consolidation and Economies of Scale: Evidence from a Time-Series Analysis in Jacksonville, Florida," *Social Science Quarterly* 65 (March 1984): 190–98.

32. Howard W. Hallman, *Small and Large Together: Governing the Metropolis* (Beverly Hills, Calif.: Sage, 1977).

33. U.S. Advisory Commission on Intergovernmental Relations, *State and Local Roles in the Federal System* (Washington, D.C.: ACIR, 1982).

34. Cole Blease Graham, Jr., "State Consultation Processes after Federal A-95 Overhaul," *State and Local Government Review* 17 (Spring 1985): 207–12.

35. Ann O'M. Bowman and James L. Franke, "The Decline of Substate Regionalism," *Journal of Urban Affairs* 6 (Fall 1984): 51–63.

36. Marvin McGraw, "Congress Kills UDAG for Space Dreams," *Nation's Cities Weekly* 11 (June 27, 1988): 1, 13–14.

37. Langley Keyes, lecture on "Rebuilding a Sense of Community," at the Urban

Policy Roundtable, Boston, Mass., June 1988.

38. Byron Katsuyama, "State Actions Affecting Local Governments," in International City Management Association, *The Municipal Year Book* (Washington, D.C.: ICMA, 1988), pp. 85–99.

39. Robert Kuttner, "Bad Housekeeping: The Housing Crisis and What to Do about It," *The New Republic* (April 25, 1988): 22–25.

40. Pat Choate and Susan Walter, *America in Ruins: Beyond the Public Works Pork Barrel* (Washington, D.C.: Council of State Planning Agencies, 1981).

41. Terry Busson and Judith Hackett, *State Assistance for Local Public Works* (Lexington, Ky.: Council of State Governments, 1987).

42. Ibid., p. 32.

43. City of Akron, Ohio, *1987–1992 Capital Investment and Community Development Program*, 1987.

44. DeWitt John, as quoted in William K. Stevens, "Struggle for Recovery Altering Rural America," *New York Times*, February 5, 1988, p. 8.

45. Jim Seroka, "Community Growth and Administrative Capacity," *National Civic Review* 77 (January/February 1988): 42–46.

46. Ibid., p. 43.

47. Stevens, "Struggle for Recovery Altering Rural America."

48. Seroka, "Community Growth and Administrative Capacity," p. 45.

49. Gordon Meeks, Jr., and Sharon Lawrence, "The Challenges Ahead for Rural America," *State Legislatures* 14 (March 1988): 12–15.

50. Council of State Governments, *State Rural Development Policies: An Emerging Government Initiative* (Lexington, Ky.: CSG, 1987).

51. Meeks and Lawrence, "The Challenges Ahead for Rural America," p. 14.

52. John Herbers, "Seattle: Defeated by the Sprawl," *Governing* 2 (April 1989): 34–35.

53. William Fulton, "In Land-Use Planning, A Second Revolution Shifts Control to the States," *Governing* 2 (March 1989): 40–45.

54. Kathleen Sylvester, "The Tobacco Industry Will Walk a Mile to Stop an Anti-Smoking Law," *Governing* 2 (May 1989): 34–40.

Chapter 15   Education Policy   pp. 425–453

1. Gary Putka, "U.S. Students' Skills in Math and Science Are Below Average,"

Wall Street Journal, February 1, 1989, p. B4.

2. U.S. Bureau of the Census, *Statistical Abstract of the United States, 1987* (Washington, D.C.: U.S. Government Printing Office, 1987), p. 115.

3. National Commission on Excellence in Education, *A Nation at Risk: The Imperative for Educational Reform* (Washington, D.C.: U.S. Government Printing Office, 1983), p. 1.

4. See Anthony Downs, "Up and Down with Ecology — the 'Issue-Attention Cycle,' " *Public Interest* (Summer 1972): 38–50.

5. Joyce D. Stein and Mary Frase Williams, eds., *The Condition of Education* (Washington, D.C.: U.S. Government Printing Office, 1986), p. 90.

6. George Gallup, Inc., "Confidence in Institutions Trend," *The Gallup Report* (July 1985).

7. National Commission on Excellence in Education, *A Nation at Risk*, p. 405.

8. This discussion draws on Ann O'M. Bowman and Richard C. Kearney, *The Resurgence of the States* (Englewood Cliffs, N.J.: Prentice-Hall, 1986), pp. 206–12.

9. National Commission on Excellence in Education, *A Nation at Risk*, p. 7.

10. Ibid., pp. 4–5.

11. Ibid., p. 7.

12. Bowman and Kearney, *The Resurgence of the States*, p. 208.

13. David Savage, "Teaching: The Heart of the Problem," *State Legislatures* 9 (October 1983): 212–24.

14. Ann Cooper, "In the Real World of Educational Reform, Vigilance May Be the Key to Success," *National Journal* 17 (March 2, 1985): 460–66.

15. National Education Association, *Estimates of School Statistics* (Washington, D.C.: NEA, 1982).

16. Stein and Williams, *The Condition of Education*, p. 84.

17. William E. Blundell, "A Certified Need: Teachers," *Wall Street Journal*, May 19, 1989, p. 1. Also see U.S. Department of Education, National Center for Education Statistics, *Projections of Education Statistics to 1992–93* (January 1985).

18. *Serrano* v. *Priest*, 5 Cal.3d 584 (1971).

19. *San Antonio Independent School District* v. *Rodriguez*, 411 U.S. 1 (1973).

20. Frederick M. Wirt and Michael W.

Kirst, *Schools in Conflict* (Berkeley, Calif.: McCutchan, 1982), p. 237.

21. Ibid., p. 236.

22. Robert B. Hawkins, Jr., "Education Reform California Style," *Publius* 14 (Summer 1984): 100.

23. Ibid., pp. 99–109.

24. John P. Pelissero and David R. Morgan, "State Aid to Public Schools: An Analysis of State Responsiveness to School District Needs," *Social Science Quarterly* 68 (September 1987): 466–77.

25. James S. Coleman, *Equality of Educational Opportunity* (Washington, D.C.: U.S. Government Printing Office, 1966).

26. Eric A. Hanushek, "Throwing Money at Schools," *Journal of Policy Analysis and Management* (Fall 1981): 19–41; and "The Economics of Schooling: Production and Efficiency in Public Schools," *Journal of Economic Literature* 24 (September 1986): 1141–77.

27. See B. Guy Peters, "Educational Policy in the United States," in B. Guy Peters, ed., *American Public Policy* (New York: Franklin Watts, 1982), pp. 253–55.

28. Bowman and Kearney, *The Resurgence of the States*, p. 213.

29. Elisabeth Hanost and David Tyack, "A Usable Past: Using History in Education Policy," in Ann Lieberman and W. McLaughlin, eds., *Policy Making in Education* (Chicago: University of Chicago Press, 1982), pp. 1–10.

30. See J. Alan Aufderheide, "Educational Interest Groups and the State Legislature," in Roald F. Campbell and Tim L. Mazzoni, Jr., eds., *State Policy Making for the Public Schools* (Berkeley, Calif.: McCutchan, 1976), pp. 176–216.

31. See Neal R. Peirce, "Can School Boards Survive Reapproval?" *P.A. Times* 9 (November 15, 1986): 2.

32. Campbell and Mazzoni, *State Policy Making for the Public Schools*, pp. 287–90.

33. Ibid., pp. 28–80.

34. Ibid., p. 297.

35. Wirt and Kirst, *Schools in Conflict*, pp. 20–21.

36. Campbell and Mazzoni, *State Policy Making for the Public Schools*, pp. 134–75.

37. Jerome T. Murphy, "Programs and Problems: The Paradox of State Reform," in Lieberman and McLaughlin, *Policy Making in Education*, p. 207.

38. *Brown* v. *Board of Education of Topeka*, 347 U.S. 483 (1954).

39. *Swann* v. *Charlotte–Mecklenberg County Schools*, 402 U.S. 1 (1971).

40. U.S. Department of Education, Center for Statistics, *Digest of Education Statistics 1987–88* (Washington, D.C.: U.S. Government Printing Office, 1988), p. 124.

41. David Shribman, "Education Emerges as Hot Political Issue, and the GOP Seizes It," *Wall Street Journal*, September 11, 1987, pp. 1, 16.

42. See Patricia Lines, "First Reading," *State Legislatures* 9 (October 1983): 5–7.

43. Earl C. Gottshalk, Jr., "Cities Turn to Year-Round Schools as Answer to Crowded Conditions," *Wall Street Journal*, January 8, 1986, pp. 1, 3; Joseph Anthony, "Schools Cope with the New Baby Boom," *Governing* 2 (October 1988): 70–72.

44. Education Commission of the States, "State Activity — Minimum Competency Testing," *Clearinghouse Notes* (November 1985).

45. See Elaine S. Knapp, "North Carolina School for Excellence," *State Government News* 26 (September 1983): 3–5.

46. "Maryland Wants a New Whiz-Kid School," *Governing* 1 (November 1987): 11.

47. Gary Putka, "Scores on College Entrance Tests Fall, Adding to Concern about U.S. Schools," *Wall Street Journal*, September 12, 1989, p. A28.

48. Jay Mathews, "Guarantees for Inner-City Graduates," *Washington Post*, June 15, 1987, p. 89.

49. "West Virginia Law Returns Dropouts to Class," *Governing* 2 (March 1989): 18.

50. National Education Association, *Estimates of School Statistics 1985–1986* (Washington, D.C.: NEA, 1986).

51. Harvey J. Tucker and David B. Hill, "Teacher Quality and Expenditures for Public Education," *State Government* 58 (Fall 1985): 105–7.

Chapter 16 Economic Development
pp. 454–482

1. Julian Weiss, "The SSC: The Biggest Prize," *State Legislatures* 13 (November/December 1987): 29–32.

2. Ibid.

3. R. Scott Fosler, "The State Economic Role in Perspective," in R. Scott Fosler, ed., *The New Economic Role of American States*

(New York: Oxford University Press, 1988), pp. 8–18.

4. Timothy B. Clark and Richard Corrigan, "Ronald Reagan's Economy," *National Journal,* December 13, 1986, pp. 2982–99.

5. "A Concentration of Talent," *The Economist,* August 8, 1987, pp. 3–18.

6. Burt Solomon, "New England: Has the Boom Ended?" *National Journal,* December 13, 1986, pp. 3002–5.

7. Ronald F. Ferguson and Helen F. Ladd, "Creating the Future," in Fosler, ed., *The New Economic Role of American States,* pp. 62–87.

8. Ibid., p. 87.

9. Neal R. Peirce and Gregory Peterson, "South: A Tale of Two Souths," *National Journal,* December 13, 1986, pp. 3015–18.

10. Timothy J. Bartik, "Recruitment and Fundamentals: A Description of Tennessee's Economic Development Policies," in Fosler, ed., *The New Economic Role of American States,* pp. 165–84.

11. Timothy J. Bartik, "Assessing the Past and Looking toward the Future," in Fosler, ed., *The New Economic Role of American States,* pp. 185–200.

12. W. John Moore, "Midwest: Few Signs of Recovery," *National Journal,* December 13, 1986, pp. 3007–10.

13. William Robbins, "Rise in Exports Spurs Job Boom in Midwest," *New York Times,* May 2, 1988, pp. 1, 7.

14. John E. Jackson, "The Political Economy of Development in Mature Economies," in Fosler, ed., *The New Economic Role of American States,* pp. 100–111.

15. Jerry Hagstrom and Robert Guskind, "West: Losing a Little Glitter," *National Journal,* December 13, 1986, pp. 3020–23.

16. Cited in ibid., p. 3020.

17. Douglas Henton and Steven A. Waldhorn, "The Megastate Economy," in Fosler, ed., *The New Economic Role of American States,* pp. 203–25.

18. James C. Cobb, *The Selling of the South: The Southern Crusade for Industrial Development, 1936–1980* (Baton Rouge: Louisiana State University Press, 1982).

19. Robert J. Vaughan, Robert Pollard, and Barbara Dyer, *The Wealth of the States* (Washington, D.C.: Council of State Planning Agencies, 1986).

20. Robert McNulty et al., *Return of the Livable City: Learning from America's Best* (Washington, D.C.: Partners for Livable Places, 1986).

21. Institute for Public Policy Studies, *Economic Revitalization in the City: A Sourcebook* (Philadelphia: Temple University, 1985).

22. Richard S. Krannich and Craig R. Humphrey, "Local Mobilization and Community Growth: Toward an Assessment of the 'Growth Machine' Hypothesis," *Rural Sociology* 48 (Spring 1983): 60–81.

23. John M. Levy, *Urban and Metropolitan Economics* (New York: McGraw-Hill, 1985).

24. Roger Schmenner, "Location Decisions of Large Firms: Implications for Public Policy," *Commentary* 5 (January 1981): 307.

25. Paul Brace, "Isolating the Economies of States," *American Politics Quarterly* 17 (July 1989): 256–76.

26. Peter W. Bernstein, "States Are Going Down the Industrial Policy Lane," *Wall Street Journal,* June 13, 1984, p. 1.

27. Mark S. Hyde, William E. Hudson, and John J. Carroll, "Business and State Economic Development," *Western Political Quarterly* 41 (March 1988): 181–91.

28. Terry F. Buss and F. Stevens Redburn, "The Politics of Revitalization: Public Subsidies and Private Interests," in Gary Gappert, ed., *The Future of Winter Cities* (Beverly Hills: Sage, 1986), pp. 285–96.

29. Larry C. Ledebur and William W. Hamilton, *Tax Concessions in State and Local Economic Development* (Washington, D.C.: Aslan Press, 1986).

30. Neal R. Peirce, Jerry Hagstrom, and Carol Steinbach, *Economic Development: The Challenge of the 1980s* (Washington, D.C.: Council of State Planning Agencies, 1979).

31. Alex Kotlowitz and Dale D. Buss, "Localities' Giveaways to Lure Corporations Cause Growing Outcry," *Wall Street Journal,* September 24, 1986, pp. 1, 27.

32. Eugene Carlson, "What's a Toyota Plant Worth to Kentucky? Possibly Plenty," *Wall Street Journal,* June 9, 1987, p. 37.

33. Ernest J. Yanarella and Herbert G. Reid, "Labor, Environmentalist, and Small Business Opposition to the Georgetown/ Toyota Project: A Fragmented Challenge to State Economic Development and Multinational Capital," a paper presented at the annual meeting of the Southern Political

Science Association, Charlotte, N.C., November 1987.

34. Ibid.

35. Ann O'M. Bowman, *The Visible Hand: Major Issues in City Economic Policy* (Washington, D.C.: National League of Cities, 1987).

36. Committee for Economic Development, *Leadership for Dynamic State Economies* (Washington, D.C.: Committee for Economic Development, 1986).

37. Peter Waldman, "Cities Are Pressured to Make Developers Share Their Wealth," *Wall Street Journal*, March 10, 1987, p. 1.

38. Carol Steinbach, "Tapping Private Resources," *National Journal*, April 26, 1986, p. 993.

39. Bowman, *The Visible Hand*, pp. 23–26.

40. Enid F. Beaumont and Harold A. Hovey, "State, Local, and Federal Economic Development Policies: New Federal Patterns, Chaos, or What?" *Public Administration Review* 45 (March/April 1985): 327–32.

41. Susan E. Clarke, "Urban America, Inc. — Corporatist Convergence of Power in American Cities?" in Edward M. Bergman, ed., *Local Economies in Transition* (Durham, N.C.: Duke University Press, 1986), pp. 37–58.

42. Ann O'M. Bowman, "Competition for Economic Development among Southeastern Cities," *Urban Affairs Quarterly* 24 (June 1988): 511–27.

43. Robert Goodman, *The Last Entrepreneurs: America's Regional Wars for Jobs and Dollars* (Boston: South End Press, 1979).

44. Eugene Carlson, "Great Lakes Governors Split over Truce on Industry Raids," *Wall Street Journal*, July 12, 1983, p. 41.

45. National Association of Counties, "Economic Development Survey: Urban Counties," unpublished report, no date.

46. Michael Lewis, "Cooperation Key to Survival," *The State*, January 4, 1987, pp. B1, B7.

47. The Monongahela River Valley Steering Group, "An Interstate River Valley in Economic Transition," unpublished paper, October 1986, p. 3.

48. Bowman, *The Visible Hand*, p. 8.

49. Committee for Economic Development, *Leadership for Dynamic State Economies*, pp. 56–67.

50. Marianne K. Clarke, *Revitalizing State Economies* (Washington, D.C.: National Governors' Association, 1986). The discussion in this section is drawn from this study.

51. Charles E. Lindblom, *Politics and Markets* (New York: Basic Books, 1977).

52. Richard Reeves, *American Journey* (New York: Simon and Schuster, 1982).

53. Committee for Economic Development, *Leadership for Dynamic State Economies*, pp. 73–77. The examination of industry-university partnerships is drawn from this volume.

54. National Association of State Development Agencies, *The NASDAA Newsletter*, January 21, 1987, pp. 1–7.

55. Keon S. Chi, "Strategic Planning for Economic Development: The Wisconsin Experience," in *Innovations* (Lexington, Ky.: Council of State Governments, 1986).

56. National Association of State Development Agencies, *The NASDAA Newsletter*, p. 5.

57. W. John Moore, "High-Tech Hopes," *National Journal*, November 15, 1986, p. 2770.

58. Mt. Auburn Associates, "Designing a Small Business Incubator Policy," *The Entrepreneurial Economy* (November 5, 1986): 2–13.

59. DeLysa Burnier, "Urban Policy in the New Federalism Era: The Emergence of Enterprise Zones," paper presented at the annual meeting of the Urban Affairs Association, Akron, Ohio, April 1987, p. 10.

60. Ibid., p. 16.

61. Merrill Goozner, "Enterprise Zone May Be Overvalued," *Chicago Tribune*, May 11, 1987, pp. 1, 6.

62. Ibid., p. 6.

63. Clarke, *Revitalizing State Economies*, pp. 78–79.

64. Ann O'M. Bowman, *Tools and Targets: The Mechanics of City Economic Development* (Washington, D.C.: National League of Cities, 1987).

65. "Metro Report: Hot Spots, Inc.'s List of the 50 Fastest-Growing U.S. Cities," *Inc.*, April 1987, pp. 51–53.

66. Dale W. Olsen, "In Transition to a Service Economy: Incentives Support Duluth Paper Mill Construction," paper presented at the annual meeting of the

Urban Affairs Association, Akron, Ohio, April 1987.

67. Richard Clark, assistant city manager, Des Moines, Iowa. Correspondence with the author, July 30, 1987.

68. Atlanta Economic Development Corporation, *Progress Profile 1986* (Atlanta, Ga.: AEDC, 1986).

69. Bowman, *The Visible Hand*, pp. 41–45.

70. Ralph J. Basile, "The Changing Atmosphere for Dealmaking," *Nation's Cities Weekly* (October 6, 1986): 7–10.

71. Marc V. Levine, "Downtown Redevelopment as an Urban Growth Strategy: A Critical Appraisal of the Baltimore Renaissance," *Journal of Urban Affairs* 9, no. 2 (1987): 103–23.

72. George Zimmerman, Department of Planning and Community Environment, Palo Alto, California. Correspondence with the author, April 20, 1987.

73. Isabel Wilkerson, "Michigan Townspeople Resist the Lure of Growth," *New York Times*, April 5, 1987, p. 20.

74. Eugene L. Meyer and Sue Anne Pressley, "P.G. May Be Stuck with $675,000 Check if Restaurant Closes," *Washington Post*, October 9, 1986, pp. B1, B7.

75. Nathan McCall, "City Suing Developer to Recoup $450,000 Lent in Property Deal," *Atlanta Constitution*, October 1, 1987, pp. D1, D6.

76. "Taking Care of Business," *The Economist* (February 18, 1989): 28.

77. Neal Peirce, "Cities Must Learn When to Say No," *Houston Chronicle*, February 13, 1989, p. A12.

78. "Taking Care of Business," *The Economist*, p. 28.

Chapter 17   Criminal Justice   pp. 483–512

1. Carolyn Skorneck, "In D.C., Cheap Drugs and Guns Cheapen Lives," *The State*, February 23, 1989, pp. 1, 6.

2. Dag Ryen, "The Criminal Among Us," *State Government News* 30 (November 1987): 5.

3. See Federal Bureau of Investigation, *Crime in the United States* (Washington, D.C.: U.S. Department of Justice, various years). Also see Travis Hirschi and Michael Gottfredson, "Age and the Explanation of

Crime," *American Journal of Sociology* 89 (November 1983): 552–84.

4. Federal Bureau of Investigation, *Crime in the United States*.

5. See James Q. Wilson and Barbara Boland, *The Effect of Police on Crime* (Washington, D.C.: U.S. Department of Justice, 1979).

6. Ibid., pp. 12–17.

7. Andrew H. Malcolm, "Cities Try Out New Approach in Police Work," *New York Times*, March 29, 1988, p. A14.

8. Bureau of Justice Statistics, *Justice Expenditures and Employment, 1985* (Washington, D.C.: U.S. Department of Justice, 1987).

9. Federal Bureau of Investigation, *Crime in the United States*, 1988.

10. *Gideon* v. *Wainwright*, 372 U.S. 335 (1963).

11. *Escobedo* v. *Illinois*, 378 U.S. 478 (1964).

12. *Miranda* v. *Arizona*, 384 U.S. 486 (1966).

13. Richard Seeburger and Stanley Wetlick, "Miranda in Pittsburgh: A Statistical Study," in Theodore Becker and Malcolm Freely, eds., *The Impact of Supreme Court Decisions*, 2nd ed. (New York: Oxford University Press, 1973).

14. *Mapp* v. *Ohio*, 307 U.S. 643 (1961).

15. Samuel Walker, *Popular Justice: A History of American Criminal Justice* (New York: Oxford University Press, 1980).

16. "Free at Last, Free at Last," *Time* 44 (November 2, 1987): 55.

17. See Edwin M. Schur and Hugo Adam Bedan, *Victimless Crimes: Two Sides of a Controversy* (Englewood Cliffs, N.J.: Prentice-Hall, 1974).

18. *Furman* v. *Georgia*, 408 U.S. 238 (1971).

19. *Gregg* v. *Georgia*, 428 U.S. 153 (1976).

20. *McCleskey* v. *Kemp*, 481 U.S. 279 (1987).

21. *Stanford* v. *Kentucky*, 57 U.S. Law Week 4973; *Penry* v. *Lynaugh*, 57 U.S. Law Week 4958.

22. Stephen Wermiel, "Delays on Death Row Fuel Hot Debate," *Wall Street Journal*, March 6, 1989, p. B6.

23. Ibid.

24. NAACP Legal Defense and Educational Fund Inc., as cited in Andrew H. Malcolm, "Society's Conflict on Death Penalty Stalls Procession of the Condemned," *New York Times*, June 19, 1989, p. B10.

25. See Thorsten Sellin, *The Penalty of Death* (Beverly Hills, Calif.: Sage, 1980).

26. *Wall Street Journal,* April 4, 1989, p. A1.

27. Richard B. Abell, "Beyond Willie Horton: The Battle of the Prison Bulge," *Policy Review* (Winter 1989): 32–35.

28. Tinsley Yarbrough, "The Alabama Prison Litigation," *The Justice System Journal* 9, no. 3 (1984): 276.

29. Joel Rosch, "Will the Federal Courts Run the States' Prison Systems?" *North Carolina Insight* 9 (March 1987): 2–10.

30. "The Eyes of Justice Are on Texas," *Newsweek* (January 19, 1987): 55.

31. Abell, "Beyond Willie Horton."

32. See William Nagel, "On Behalf of a Moratorium on Prison Construction," *Crime and Delinquency* (April 1977): 154–72; and Michael Sherman and Gordon Hawkins, *Imprisonment in America: Choosing the Future* (Chicago: University of Chicago Press, 1981).

33. Jim Thomas, Devin Keller, and Kathy Harris, "Issues and Misconceptions in Prison Litigation: A Critical View," *Criminology* 24 (November 1986): 775–97.

34. Joel A. Thompson and G. Larry Mays, "State-Local Relations and the American Jail Crisis: A Study of State Jail Mandates," paper presented at the annual meeting of the Southern Political Science Association, Charlotte, N.C., November 1987.

35. "Electronic Detention Proves Successful," *P.A. Times* (June 16, 1987): 1, 3.

36. Warren E. Burger, "Prison Industries: Turning Warehouses into Factories with Fences," *Public Administration Review* 45 (November 1985): 754–57.

37. Ibid., p. 757 (fn. 7).

38. Fred Strasser, "Making the Punishment Fit the Crime . . . and the Prison Budget," *Governing* 2 (January 1989): 36–41.

39. Judy Farah, " 'Ratlord' Sent to Live in Own Dump," *The State,* July 14, 1987, p. 1.

40. John P. Conrad, "The Penal Dilemma and Its Emerging Solution," *Crime and Delinquency* (July 1985): 411–22.

41. Alan L. Otten, "Georgia Lets Some Offenders Do Time at Home Under Close Watch to Ease Crowding in Prisons," *Wall Street Journal,* July 23, 1987, p. 64.

42. "New York Building Floating Jail House," *The State,* March 26, 1989, p. A2.

43. Charles H. Logan and Sharla P. Rausch, "Punish and Profit: The Emergence of Private Enterprise Prisons," *Justice Quarterly* (September 1985): 303–18; and

Samuel Jan Brakel, "Give Private Firms a Greater Role," *Wall Street Journal,* March 21, 1989, p. A19.

44. See Logan and Rausch, "Punish and Profit," p. 231, and John D. Donahue, *Prisons for Profit: Public Justice, Private Interests* (Washington, D.C.: Economic Policy Institute, 1988).

45. For a helpful discussion of this issue, see Ira P. Robbins, "Privatization of Corrections: Defining the Issues," *Judicature* 69 (April/May 1986): 325–31.

46. Ibid., p. 33.

47. Peter Kerr, "Drug-Crime Link Underlined," *International Herald Tribune,* January 23–24, 1988, p. A3.

Chapter 18   Environmental Policy
pp. 513–542

1. See Lester R. Brown and Christopher Flavin, "The Earth's Vital Signs," in Lester R. Brown, ed., *State of the World* (New York: W. W. Norton, 1988), pp. 4–5.

2. Ibid., p. 6.

3. Ibid., p. 7.

4. Joseph A. Davis, "Radon Answers Are Surfacing in the States," *Governing* 2 (February 1988): 54–56; and Dag Ryen, "The Earth's Natural Waste," *State Government News* 30 (September 1987): 4.

5. Brown and Flavin, "The Earth's Vital Signs," p. 8.

6. "Still at Loggerheads: Oregon's Lumberjacks vs. Tree Huggers," *Time,* July 10, 1989, p. 24.

7. Neal R. Peirce, "Breakthrough for Wetlands: EPA's Reilly Lobbies a State Law," *P.A. Times* 12 (June 2, 1989): 2.

8. John J. Harrigan, *Political Change in the Metropolis,* 4th ed. (Glenview, Ill.: Scott, Foresman, 1989), pp. 22, 24.

9. J. Clarence Davies III, *The Politics of Pollution* (Indianapolis: Pegasus, 1970), p. 121.

10. Norman J. Vig and Michael E. Kraft, "Environmental Policy from the Seventies to the Eighties," in Norman J. Vig and Michael E. Kraft, eds., *Environmental Policy in the 1980s* (Washington, D.C.: Congressional Quarterly, 1984), p. 17.

11. Helen M. Ingram and Dean E. Mann, "Preserving the Clean Water Act: The Appearance of Environmental Victory," in

Vig and Kraft, *Environmental Policy in the 1980s*, pp. 251–71.

12. James L. Regens and Margaret A. Reams, "The State Strategies for Regulating Groundwater Quality," *Social Science Quarterly* 69 (March 1988): 53–69.

13. Henry C. Kenski and Helen M. Ingram, "The Reagan Administration and Environmental Regulation: The Constraint of the Political Market," in Sheldon Kamieniecki, Robert O'Brien, and Michael Clark, eds., *Controversies in Environmental Policy* (Albany: SUNY Press, 1986), p. 278.

14. Robert Cameron Mitchell, "Public Opinion and Environmental Politics in the 1970s and 1980s," in Vig and Kraft, *Environmental Policy in the 1980s*, p. 61.

15. J. Clarence Davies, "Environmental Institutions and the Reagan Administration," in Vig and Kraft, *Environmental Policy in the 1980s*, pp. 143–60.

16. Mitchell, "Public Opinion and Environmental Politics," p. 61.

17. Regens and Reams, "The State Strategies," p. 56.

18. Lettie Wenner, *The Environmental Decade in Court* (Bloomington: Indiana University Press, 1982).

19. Werner F. Grunbaum and Lettie M. Wenner, "Comparing Environmental Litigation in State and Federal Courts," *Publius* 10 (Summer 1980): 129–42.

20. See Barry G. Rabe, "The Politics of Environmental Dispute Resolution," *Policy Studies Journal* 16 (Spring 1988): 585–601.

21. Gail Bingham, *Resolving Environmental Disputes* (Washington, D.C.: Conservation Foundation, 1986).

22. Michael H. Levin, "The Trash Mess Won't Be Easily Disposed Of," *Wall Street Journal*, December 15, 1988, p. C12.

23. "Harpers Index," *Harper's* (February 1989): 13.

24. Paul Doyle, "The Garbage Crisis," *State Legislatures* (October 1987): 24.

25. Bill Paul, "Garbage Strains Planners' Ability to Handle It All," *Wall Street Journal*, June 8, 1987, p. 25; and Bill Paul, "Pennsylvania Town Finds a Way to Get Locals to Recycle Trash," *Wall Street Journal*, June 21, 1989, pp. A1, A10.

26. Doyle, "The Garbage Crisis," p. 24.

27. Ibid., p. 25.

28. Richards, "Energy from Garbage," p. 9.

29. Ibid.

30. "St. Cloud Gives Cash for Trash," *Governing* (April 1988): 16.

31. Susan Fine, "Composting Nature's 'Garbage,' " *World Watch* 2 (January/February 1989): 5.

32. Richards, "Energy from Garbage," p. 9.

33. Ibid.

34. "Those Plastic Packages Aren't Welcome in Suffolk County, N.Y., Anymore," *Governing* (July 1988): 14.

35. Neal R. Peirce, "Hats Off to the Parrah Barge," *The State*, May 5, 1987, p. 14.

36. Richard Severo, "Monument to Modern Man: 'Alp' of Trash Is Rising," *New York Times*, April 13, 1989, p. 13.

37. Congressional Budget Office, *Hazardous Waste Management: Recent Changes and Policy Alternatives* (Washington, D.C.: U.S. Government Printing Office, 1985).

38. Clifford S. Russell, "Economic Incentives in the Management of Hazardous Wastes," paper presented at the Colloquium on New Directions in Environmental Policy, Columbia University Law School, October 1987.

39. Ann O'M. Bowman and James P. Lester, "Implementing Intergovernmental Policy: The Resource Conservation and Recovery Act of 1976," paper presented at the annual meeting of the Southern Political Science Association, November 1987.

40. James E. McCarthy, "Hazardous Waste Management: RCRA Oversight in the 100th Congress" (Washington, D.C.: Congressional Research Service, March 4, 1988).

41. Ann O'M. Bowman, "Superfund Implementation: Five Years and How Many Cleanups," in Charles E. Davis and James P. Lester, eds., *Dimensions of Hazardous Waste Politics and Policy* (New York: Greenwood Press, 1988), pp. 129–44.

42. Ann O'M. Bowman, "Intergovernmental and Intersectoral Tensions in Environmental Policy Implementation: The Case of Hazardous Waste," *Policy Studies Review* 4 (November 1984): 230–44.

43. James P. Lester, "Superfund Implementation: Exploring the Conditions of Environmental Gridlock," *Environmental Impact Assessment Review* (1988): 63–70.

44. Scott Ridley, *The State of the States 1987* (Washington, D.C.: Fund for Renewable Energy and the Environment, 1987).

45. R. Steven Brown, "Siting Hazardous Waste Facilities," *State Government News* 30 (September 1987): 10–11, 17.

46. Richard N. L. Andrews, "Hazardous Waste Facility Siting: State Approaches," in Davis and Lester, eds., *Dimensions of Hazardous Waste Politics and Policy*, pp. 117–28.

47. Michael E. Kraft and Ruth Kraut, "The Impact of Citizen Participation on Hazardous Waste Policy Implementation: The Case of Clermont County, Ohio," *Policy Studies Journal* 14 (September 1985): 52–61.

48. Priscilla Hanford, "Local Planning for Hazardous Waste Management: California's 'Tanner Process,' " *Natural Resources & Environmental Administration* 12 (December 1988): 1, 3–4.

49. Ann O'M. Bowman and Richard C. Kearney, *The Resurgence of the States* (Englewood Cliffs, N.J.: Prentice-Hall, 1986).

50. Richard C. Kearney and John J. Stucker, "Interstate Compacts and the Management of Low-Level Radioactive Wastes," *Public Administration Review* 42 (January/February 1985): 14–24.

51. Ibid.

52. Riley E. Dunlap, "Public Opinion on the Environment in the Reagan Era," *Environment* 29 (July/August 1987): 6–11, 32–37.

53. Allan R. Gold, "Fight for Maine Coast Intensifies Over Port Plan," *New York Times*, July 20, 1988, p. 8.

54. Richard W. Stevenson, "Facing Up to a Clean-Air Plan," *New York Times*, April 3, 1989, p. 28.

55. Gina Kolata, "How Much Is Too Much to Pay to Meet Standards for Smog," *New York Times*, April 3, 1989, pp. 1, 11.

56. Keith Schneider, "Under Oil's Powerful Spell, Alaska Was Off Guard," *New York Times*, April 2, 1989, pp. 1, 11.

57. Peter Applebome, "Energy vs. Environment on Carolina Beaches," *New York Times*, January 30, 1989, pp. 1, 7.

Index

Abortion, 29, 30
  initiatives concerning, 123
  as 1990 campaign issue, 164
Absentee balloting, 118–119
Accidental cities, 411–412
Acid rain, 514
Acquired immune deficiency syndrome
  (AIDS), 14, 123–124, 515
Adams, John, 87
Administration, politics vs., 229–231
Administrative cases, 280
Administrative procedure acts, 138
Advertisements, political, 166
Advisory boards, 466
Advisory commissions on
    intergovernmental relations, 408. *See
    also* U.S. Advisory Commission on
    Intergovernmental Relations
Advisory committees, 138–139
Affirmative action, 218–221
  in Alabama, 220–221, 222
AFSCME v. *State of Washington,* 223–224
Agnew, Spiro T., 209
Agricultural Adjustment Act, 28
Agriculture, rural economy and, 421
Aid to Families with Dependent Children
  (AFDC), 65–67, 69–70, 72
Air pollution, 514
Air Quality Act, 31
Akron, Ohio, 420
Alabama
  affirmative action in, 220–221, 222
  1986 Democratic gubernatorial primary
    in, 158, 159
  prison conditions in, 499–500
Alaskan oil spill, 515, 540
Alcoholic beverage tax, 381
Alexander, Lamar, 180, 183, 193, 446, 456
Allain, Bill, 98
Amendments, legislative bill, 260

Amenities, economic development and,
  458
Amenities city, 312
American College Test (ACT), 427
American Federation of Teachers (AFT),
  439
Anaya, Tony, 185
Annexation, and city government, 327,
  328
Antitrust suits, 44
Appalachian Regional Commission, 45–46
Appellate courts, 299–300
Appellate jurisdiction, 281
Appointment power, gubernatorial, 192,
  194–197
Apportionment, legislative, 250, 252–253
Arkansas prison conditions, 498–499
Arrington, Richard, 351
Articles of Confederation, 23
Ashcroft, John, 409
Atlanta Economic Development
  Corporation, 475
At-large elections, 330, 332, 354–355
Attorney general, state
  election vs. appointment of, 194
  responsibilities of, 207–208
  role in law enforcement, 488
Atwood, Jay F., 228
Auditors, 274
  election vs. appointment of, 194
Audits, 238
Austin, Texas
  citizen group roles in, 162
  economic development in, 474
Automobile industry, 459–460
Automobile insurance initiatives, 124

Babbitt, Bruce, 198
Back-door strategies for criminals, 504
Baker v. *Carr,* 29, 249, 252

Balanced Budget and Emergency Deficit
    Control Act of 1985, 57
Balanced-budget requirements, 237,
    390–392. *See also* Budgeting
Baliles, Gerald, 422
Baltimore, Maryland, 71, 462
Barry, Marion, 107
Baxley, Bill, 159
Beer, Samuel H., 47
Behavioral dependency, 64
Bench trial, 299
Benefit principle of taxation, 373
Bennett, Robert F., 201
Bennett, William J., 508
Berkley, Richard, 349
Berns, Walter, 25
Bicameralism, 249–250
Bill of Rights, state, 94–95
Bill of Rights, U.S., 94, 95, 304
Bird, Rose, 293–295
Black Americans, 5. *See also* Affirmative
        action; Racial discrimination
    death penalty for, 494–495
    as mayors, 350–351
    political participation by, 42, 115, 116
    right to vote and, 115, 116
    voting strength of, 253, 254
Blanket primaries, 156–157
Blanton, Ray, 207
Block grants, 52, 58
Blue-ribbon panels, 466
Board of Estimate (New York City), 311
Bond banks, 391
Bonds
    general obligation, 243–244, 392
    industrial development, 392–393
    ratings for, 393
    revenue, 243–244, 392–393
Boosteristic city, 312
Borrowing, 392–393
Boss mayor, 350
Bracket creep, 375
Bradley, Tom, 188, 351
Branstad, Terry, 200, 466
Broker mayor, 350
Brokerage city, 312
Brown, Edmund G. "Jerry," 208–209,
    294–296
Brown, Edmund G. "Pat," 295–296
Brown v. *Board of Education*, 29, 443
Bryce, Lord James, 87
Buckley v. *Valeo*, 168
Budget cycle, 236–238
Budget deficit. *See also* Balanced-budget
        requirements
    legislation regarding, 57
    in state and local government, 16–17
Budgetary power, gubernatorial, 199

Budgeting, 234–236
    actors in, 238, 240
    pervasive incrementalism and, 240
Budgets, types of, 241–244
Bullfrog County, Nevada, 318
Bureaucracies, state and local
    budgeting in, 234–244
    employees of, 213–215
    personnel policy in, 215–229
    politics of, 229–234
Bureaucratic discretion, 230
Bureaucratic responsiveness, 232–234
Bureaucrats. *See* Public employees
Burger, Warren, 16, 302, 303, 489
Bush, George, 144
    campaign of 1988, 151
    on environmental issues, 522
Byrne, Jane, 346

Cabinet structure, 200–201
Caldeira, Gregory A., 301
Calhoun, John C., 25–26
California
    Bill of Rights, 95
    economic vulnerability in, 457
    hazardous waste disposal in, 534
    initiative process in, 122–125
    judicial selection in, 292–296
    organization of legislature in, 264–265
    political culture of, 7–8
    Proposition 13, 101, 123, 365, 375–376,
        384, 434
    smog reduction in southern, 539
    tax revolt in, 385
Campaign finance
    increases in, 167–168
    public funding as answer to, 170
    state efforts at reform in, 168–169
Campbell, Carroll, 473
Canada, federalism in, 42
Capacity enhancement in prisons, 507,
    509–510
Cape Cod, Massachusetts, 120
Capital budgets, 241, 243–244
Capital punishment, 492–495
Career ladders, 451–452
Caretaker city, 312
Carlin, John, 198
Carter, Jimmy, 63, 193, 213, 242
Carter administration, 438
Caseloads, judicial
    approaches to dealing with, 306–307
    as influence on judicial decision
        making, 301
Categorical grants, 52
Center for Policy Research (National
        Governors' Association), 182
Chase Manhattan Bank, 481

Chernobyl disaster, 515
Chicago, Illinois
  local party organization in, 147
  1992 World's Fair and, 346
Chief state school officer, 441
Child support payments, 70
Children
  poverty among, 62
  social welfare programs for, 65–67,
    69–70
Circuit breaker, 376
Cities, 322, 324. *See also* City government
  economic development in, 474–475,
    478–481
  growth problems in, 479, 481
  measuring health and distress in, 416,
    417
Citizen access. *See also* Public participation
  impact of, 139–140
  methods of, 137–139
Citizen advisory committees, 138–139
Citizen surveys, 139
Citizens' Conference on State Legislatures
  (CCSL), 249, 267–270
City commission form of government,
  324–327
City council members
  election of, 330, 332, 354–355
  profile of, 354
City councils
  conflict within, 354, 355
  interaction with city managers, 358, 359
City-county consolidation, 413
City government
  annexation and, 328
  authority of, 323
  financial issues in, 328–331
  representation issues in, 330, 332
  structure of, 324–327
City managers, 326
  interactions with city council, 355, 357
  as policy leaders, 352
  types of, 353
Civic republic, 311
Civil cases, 280
Civil Rights Act of 1964, 219, 224
  1972 amendment to, 220
  Supreme Court interpretation of, 221,
    223
Civil service. *See* Personnel policy; Public
  employees
Civil Service Reform Act of 1978, 216, 225
Civil War, U.S., 26
Clean Air Act, 520, 522
Clements, William P., 185, 501
Clientele groups, 230
Clinton, Bill, 184, 465
Closed primaries, 156–158

Coattail effect, 163
Cogeneration, 526
Coleman Report, 435
Collective bargaining, 225. *See also* Labor
  unions
  impact of, 227–229
  legislation regarding, 226
  teachers' union rights of, 439–440
Colleges. *See* Higher education institutions
Collins, Martha Layne, 185
Commerce clause, 27–30
Commission on Intergovernmental
  Relations (Kestnbaum Commission),
  91, 110
Committee for Economic Development,
  249, 468
Common Cause, 168
Communities, 2
  differing orientations of, 311
  metropolitan. *See* Cities
  rural, 420–422
  suburban, 410–411
  transformations in, 312–313
  types of, 312, 420
Community affairs departments, 409–410
Community Communications Co. v. *City of
  Boulder*, 44
Community Development Block Grant,
  59, 463
Community power. *See also* Leadership,
  local; Public participation
  dynamics of, 346–347
  theories of, 343–345
Comparable worth, 221–222
  debate over, 222–223
  Supreme Court on, 223–224
Compensation. *See* Salaries
Competency testing, 446–447
Comprehensive Environmental Response,
  Compensation and Liability Act of
  1980 (Superfund), 529–531
Confederacy, 21, 22
Connecticut
  advisory commission on
    intergovernmental relations in, 409
  affordable housing program in, 419
  LEAP coalition in, 151
  legislative elections in, 163–164
  organization of legislature in, 264, 265
Conservatism
  renewed popularity of, 147
  within Republican party, 147, 149
Constitution, U.S.
  commerce clause, 27–30
  Framers of, 21, 23–24
  full faith and credit clause, 44
  general welfare clause, 28–29
  interstate cooperation under, 44–46

Constitution (*cont.*)
  methods for altering, 98
  national supremacy clause, 26, 31
  necessary and proper clause of, 26–27
  privileges and immunities clause, 45
Constitutional Amendments, U.S., 35
  Fifth, 488
  Eighth, 493, 497, 499
  Tenth, 24–25, 31, 33, 432
  Fourteenth, 29, 218, 221, 443, 489, 497
  Fifteenth, 116
  Sixteenth, 30–31
Constitutional commission, 109
Constitutional Convention, U.S.,
  23–24, 98
Constitutional conventions, state,
  103–104, 105, 107
  delegates to, 104–105, 107
Constitutional reform, state
  contemporary, 91–94
  need for, 97–98
  state resurgence and, 109–110
Constitutional reform methods, 98–100
  constitutional commission, 109
  constitutional convention, 103–109
  initiative, 98, 101–103
  legislative proposal, 100–101
Constitutionalism, dual, 85
Constitutions, state, 92–93
  evolution of, 86–88
  model for, 91, 94–97
  weaknesses of, 88–91
Cooperative federalism, 37–38
  contemporary variations of, 38–40
Coordinate authority federalism, 36
Correctional system
  prison conditions and, 497–501
  purpose of, 495–496
  sentencing reform in, 496–498
Council-administrator plan, 320
Council-manager form of government,
  326, 327, 359–360
Council of State Governments, 46, 421
Countercyclical aid, 367
Counties, 316–317
County-council–elected executive plan,
  319–320
County government
  function of, 317, 319
  organization of, 319–320
  performance of, 321–322
  problems of, 320–321
Court systems. *See* Federal courts; State
  court systems; Supreme Court, U.S.;
  Supreme courts, state
Courts of the judiciary, 296–297
Cowper, Steve, 182
Creative federalism, 38

Creative sentencing, 505–506
Crime
  capital punishment for, 492–495
  extent of, 484–486
  victimless, 491–492
  victims of, 490
Criminal cases, 280
Criminal justice system
  actors involved in, 487–490
  correctional policy of, 495–503
  policy alternatives in, 504–510
Criminals
  back-door strategies for, 504–505
  front-door strategies for, 505–507
  prison capacity for, 507, 509–511
Crusader mayor, 350
Cuomo, Mario, 167, 180
Curb, Mike, 209
Custodial (caretaker) governors, 180

Dahl, Robert, 344, 345
Daley, Richard J., 341
Davis v. *Bandemer*, 253
Day care, 70
Deal making, in local economic
  government, 475, 479
Dealignment of political parties, 155
Death penalty, 492–495
Debt, state and local, 392–393
Decisional method of studying community
  power, 345
Declaration of Independence, 22
Declining community, 420–421
Decriminalization, 491–492
Delegates, legislators as, 265
Democratic party, 105
  ideology within, 147, 149
  image of, 145
  local organization of, 147, 148
  runoff elections and, 160
  state organization of, 146
Department of Education, U.S., 438
Departments of community affairs,
  409–410
Des Moines, Iowa, 475
Determinate sentencing, 496–497
Deukmejian, George, 176, 294
Dillon's Rule, 43
Direct action, 136
Direct cash transfers, 66–67
Direct initiative, 103
Discrimination. *See* Racial discrimination;
  Sex discrimination
District attorneys, 488
District of Columbia, 13, 105–107
District elections, 330, 332
Districts. *See* Legislative districts
Domestic Policy Council, 59

Domhoff, G. William, 345
Drinking age, 31, 32
Drug use, 491
du Pont, Pierre, 200
Dual constitutionalism, 85
Dual federalism, 36–37, 47
Dubois, Philip, 294
Due process, 29, 489
Dukakis, Michael, 193
  as governor, 456
  presidential campaign of, 151, 183
  on problems of legislative majority, 177
Duke, David, 144
Duluth, Minnesota, 474
Dynamic growth community, 420

Eastman Kodak, 481
Econometric modeling, 389–390
Economic development, 455
  agencies for, 466–468
  approaches to, 457–458
  competition and cooperation in,
      463–464
  conflict regarding, 17
  current initiatives for, 468–474
  governor as promoter of, 183
  implications of, 481
  issues in, 458–461
  politics of, 465
  public-private partnerships for, 468
  role of cities in, 474–475, 478–481
  tools of, 461–463
Economic Development Administration
    (EDA) grants, 59, 463
Economic development agencies, 466–468
Economic Opportunity Act of 1965, 63
Education
  actors involved in, 439–444
  crisis in, 426–427
  higher. See Higher education
      institutions; Higher education
      policy
  innovations in, 444–452
  national role in, 437–438
  public. See Public education
  standards in, 427–429, 446–447
  state and local roles in, 432–437
  state and local spending for, 372
  state constitutional provisions for, 97
  students' role in problems with,
      429–431, 447–448
Education voucher system, 448–449
Edwards, Edwin, 174, 207
Eighth Amendment, 493, 497, 499
Elasticity, tax, 374
Elazar, Daniel, 7
Elections. See also State elections
  at-large, 330, 332

Elections (cont.)
  general, 160–161
  of judges, 286–291, 293, 294
  legislative, 163–164, 167–168
  1988 state, 163–164
  1990 state, 164
  nonpartisan, 161–162, 287–291
  partisan, 287
  primary, 116, 156–159, 184
  runoff, 158–160
Electronic house arrest, 504–505
Elementary and Secondary Education Act
    of 1965, 438
Elite theory of community power, 343–344
Endorsements, newspaper, 162
Energy production, 540–541
English-language initiative, 123
Enterprise zones, 471–472
Entrepreneurial mayor, 350
Enumerated (delegated) powers, 25
Environment
  destruction of, 514–516
  economics vs., 539
  energy vs., 540–541
  political economy of protecting, 516–517
Environmental Defense Fund, 527
Environmental management
  activists concerned with, 122–123
  governmental challenges to, 541
  of hazardous waste, 528–534
  innovations concerning, 362
  of nuclear waste, 534–538
  of solid waste, 525–528
  state rankings in, 522, 524–525
Environmental mediation, 523
Environmental policy
  courts' role in, 523
  intergovernmental relationships in,
      517–518
  legislation, 517–518, 520–521
  national, 518–522
  state and local, 522–523
Environmental Protection Agency (EPA),
    515, 518, 526
  during Reagan administration, 521
Equal employment opportunity, 218
Equal Employment Opportunity Act of
    1972, 218
Equal Employment Opportunity
    Commission (EEOC), 218
Equal protection clause, 29, 443, 497
Equalization formula, 336–337
Equity, tax, 373–374
Escobedo v. Illinois, 488
Estate taxes, 381–382
Ethnic diversity, 5
Exclusionary rule, 489
Executive amendment, 198

Executive order, 59, 200
    12372, 417
    12612, 59–60
Expenditures, 51
    changes in federal, 53–57
Export promotion, 473
Extraterritorial jurisdiction, 328
Exxon Valdez, 515, 540

Factions, 21
FAIIR standards, 267–269, 271
Fair Labor Standards Act, 33
Family Support Act of 1988, 69–72
Fauntroy, Walter E., 106
Federal Bureau of Investigation (FBI)
    crime index, 484, 485
Federal courts, 497–501. *See also* Supreme
    Court, U.S.
Federal employees. *See* Public employees
Federalism, 2, 21, 22
    advantages and disadvantages of, 40–43
    and balance of power, 46–47
    Canadian, 42
    compact theory of, 25
    Congress, U.S., and, 29–33
    Constitution, U.S., and, 26–29
    cooperative, 37–40
    creative, 38
    dual, 36–37, 47
    foundation for, 23–24
    local government in, 43–44
    models of, 35
    nation-centered, 26
    New, 10–11, 39–40, 57–60
    picket fence, 38–39
    social welfare policy and, 61–72
    state-centered, 24–26
Federal pre-emption, 31
Feron, James, 323*n*
Fifteenth Amendment, 116
Fifth Amendment, 488
Finance systems, 365–366. *See also*
    Revenues; Taxation; Taxes
    diversity of, 368–373
    interdependence of, 366–367
Fiscal capacity, 372
Fiscal stress, 385–388
Fiscal year, 237
Floating prisons, 507
Florio, James, 185
Food stamps, 67
Ford Foundation, 9
Foreign investment in U.S., 472–474, 476,
    477
Formula grants, 52
Fourteenth Amendment, 29, 218, 221, 443,
    489, 497
Freedom Democratic party, 152

Freedom-of-information acts, 138–139
Froman, Lewis, 90
Front-door strategies for criminals,
    505–507
Full faith and credit clause, 44
Furman v. *Georgia*, 493

GAIN program (California), 72
Galveston, Texas, 324–325
Gantt, Harvey, 351
Gap financing, 461
Garbage. *See* Solid waste management
Garcia v. *San Antonio Metropolitan Transit
    Authority*, 33
Gasoline taxes, 381
General assistance, 67
General elections, 160–161. *See also*
    Elections
General Motors, 464, 472
General obligation bonds, 243–244, 392
General-purpose local governments, 315
General referendum, 119
General Revenue Sharing, 53, 58, 59
General welfare clause, 28–29
Georgia
    constitution of, 91
    intensive probation supervision in, 507
    runoff elections in, 159
    shock probation in, 508
Gerry, Elbridge, 253
Gerrymandering, 253–255
Gibbons v. *Ogden*, 28
Gibson, Kenneth, 350
Gideon v. *Wainwright*, 488
Goldberg v. *Kelly*, 29
Goodsell, Charles T., 234
Gorsuch, Anne, 520
Government. *See also* City government;
    County government; Local
    government; State government
    citizen access to, 137–140
    professionals in, 233–234
    regional, 413–415
    shadow, 412–413
    unitary, 21, 22
Governors, 174–175
    characteristics of, 205–206, 210
    formal powers of, 190–203. *See also*
        Gubernatorial powers
    impeachment of, 206–207
    informal powers of, 204–206
    legislature's relationship with, 272–274
    parties of current, 178
    profile of current, 184–189
    retirement of, 193
    roles of. *See* Gubernatorial roles
Graddick, Charlie, 159
Graham, Bob, 165, 206

Gramm-Rudman-Hollings bill. *See*
    Balanced Budget and Emergency
    Deficit Control Act of 1985
Grand juries, 490
Grant, Ulysses S., 215–216
Grants-in-aid, 31, 51–54, 366–367
    conditions for, 52–53
    during Great Society, 38
    during Reagan administration, 53
    impact of cuts in, 57
Grasso, Ella, 185
Graves, W. Brooke, 108
Great Depression, 28, 63
Great Society, 38
Greenhouse Compact, 459
Greenhouse effect, 514
Gregg v. *Georgia*, 493
Grodin, Joseph, 293–294
Gubernatorial campaign costs, 167,
    185–187, 189
Gubernatorial elections
    of incumbents, 189
    of 1988, 163
Gubernatorial powers, 189–190
    of appointment, 192, 194–197
    budgetary, 199
    in criminal justice system, 487
    on education issues, 77, 442–443
    of judicial appointment, 293–296
    relevance of, 202–203
    of reorganization, 199–201
    of staffing, 201–202
    of tenure, 190–192
    of veto, 197–198
Gubernatorial roles
    ceremonial leader, 181
    chief administrator, 179–181
    chief legislator, 176–178
    economic development promoter, 183
    intergovernmental coordinator, 181–183
    party leader, 183–184
    policymaker, 175–176
Gunther v. *County of Washington*, 223

Hall, David, 207
Hamilton, Alexander, 26–27
Hamm, Keith E., 135
Hammer provisions, 531
Harris County, Texas, 335
Hatcher, Richard, 350
Hazardous waste management, 528–530
    under Resource Conservation Recovery
        Act, 529–531
    states' role in, 533–534
    Superfund and, 529–533
Head Start, 63
Higher education institutions, 74–75,
    79–81, 430

Higher education policy. *See also*
    Education
    intergovernmental roles in, 75–76
    policy roles in, 76–78, 82
    in U.S., 74–75
High-level nuclear wastes, 535
High-technology development, 470–471
Hill, John, 289
Hobby, William P., 108
Home rule, 43–44, 319
Honolulu, Hawaii, 411
Housing and Community Development
    Act of 1974, 67–68
Housing policy, 418–419
Houston, Texas
    annexation in, 328
    city council elections in, 354
    city council reshaping in, 355, 357
    ideological distribution in, 147, 149, 150
Hughes, Howard, 42
Hunt, Guy, 159
Hunt, James, 200
Hunter, Floyd, 344
Hyperpluralism in interest groups, 132

Impeachment
    of governor, 206–207
    of state judges, 296
Implied powers, 27
Incentive packages, 459–460
Incineration, 526–527
Income tax, 378, 380
    administration of, 374
    voter perception of, 377
Incrementalism, 240, 241, 243
Incubators, small-business, 471
Indeterminate sentencing, 496
Indirect initiative, 103
Individualistic political culture, 7
Industrial development bonds, 392–393
Industrialization, 312–313
Infrastructure policy, 419–420
Initiatives, 119
    overuse of, 125–126
    process of, 98, 101–103, 121
    recent use of, 121, 123–125
In-kind programs, 67–68
Insurance commissioners, 194
Intensive probation supervision, 506–507
Intercommunity partnerships, 337–338
Interest groups, 127–128
    local-level, 134–136
    States-level, 130–132
    techniques used by, 132–135
    types of, 129–130
Intergovernmental Cooperation Program,
    337–338
Intergovernmental coordinator, 181–183

Intergovernmental financial relations
 grants-in-aid and, 51–53
 national expenditures and, 53–57
Interim committee, 257
Intermediate appellate courts, 282–284
International City Management
  Association, 352
International trade promotion, 472–474
Interparty competition, 152–155
Interposition, 25
Interstate compacts, 45, 535–538
Interstate rendition clause, 45

Jackson, Andrew, 26, 215
Jackson, Jesse, 5
Jackson, Maynard, 351
Jacksonian democracy, 192, 194
Jefferson, Thomas, 27, 91, 104
Job Corps, 63
Job Opportunities and Basic Skills (JOBS)
  program, 71
Johnson, Frank, 15
Johnson, Lyndon B., 38, 63
Joint committee, 257
Judges
 removal of, 296–298
 salaries of, 307
 selection of. See Judicial selection
Judicial activism, 303–304
Judicial decision making
 in appellate courts, 299–300
 legal system influence and, 300–302
 personal values and attitudes of judges
   and, 302
Judicial discipline and removal
  commissions, 296–297
Judicial federalism, 85
Judicial review, 99
Judicial selection
 comparison of methods of, 296, 297
 criteria for, 285–286
 by gubernatorial appointment, 293–296
 by legislative election, 286–291, 293, 294
 by merit plans, 291–294
 by nonpartisan popular election, 287–291
 by partisan popular election, 287
 state-by-state procedures for, 288–289
Judicial system. See State court systems
Judiciary Act of 1789, 26
Juries, 489, 490
Jurisdiction of state courts, 281–283. See
  also State court systems
Jury trials, 299
Justice, William Wayne, 501

Kansas interest groups, 132
Kean, Thomas, 201
Kennedy, John F., 82, 225, 341

Kentucky
 filming of trials in, 307
 financing public education in, 280
 Toyota plant in, 460
Kerner, Otto, 207
Kerrey, Robert, 466
Kestnbaum Commission, 91, 110
Kunin, Madeleine, 185, 188–189, 274

Labor unions. See also Collective
  bargaining
 in government, 225–227
 for teachers, 439–440
La Follette, Robert, 152
Lamm, Richard D., 192
Land-grant college system, 74–75
Land management, 403, 407
Lasswell, Harold, 235
Law enforcement, 486–488. See also
  Criminal justice system
Law Enforcement Assistance
  Administration, 487
Layer cake federalism, 36
Leach, Richard H., 21, 110
Leadership, local
 meaning of, 342–343
 political vs. professional, 358–361
 requirements for, 348
 theories of, 343–345
LEAP coalition (Connecticut), 151
Legislative address, 296
Legislative bills
 committee action regarding, 260–262
 floor action regarding, 262
 governor's action regarding, 263
 introduction of, 258–260
 legislative review and, 275
 Senate and House action regarding,
   262–263
Legislative casework, 231
Legislative committees, 256–258
 role in recommending legislative bills,
   260–261
 standing, 256, 257
 structure of, 270
Legislative districts
 gerrymandering of, 253–255
 malapportionment of, 250, 252–253
Legislative election of judges, 286
Legislative elections
 cost of, 167–168
 of 1988, 163–164
Legislative facilities, 270
Legislative investigation, 276–277
Legislative majority, 177
Legislative oversight committees, 276–277
Legislative party caucuses, 160–161
Legislative proposal, 100–101

Legislative review, 275–277
Legislative sessions, 248, 270
Legislative staff, 248–249, 269
Legislative supremacy, 87
Legislators
  leadership among, 256–257, 270
  salaries of, 255
Legislatures, local, 353–354
Legislatures, state
  changes in, 269–270
  cue-taking in, 265, 267
  effect of reform in, 271–272
  FAIIR rankings of, 267–269
  functions of, 247–248
  governor's relationship with, 176–177,
      272–274
  norms of, 264–266
  role in criminal justice system, 487
  role in education, 443
  role of overseeing bureaucracy, 274–277
  structure of, 249–250
  types of, 265, 266
Lehrman, Lewis, 167, 188
Levine, Marc V., 462
Lex talionis, 495
Liberalism
  within Democratic party, 147, 149
  in 1980s, 151
  tradition of, 147
Libertarian party, 152
Lieutenant governor, 208–209
Limited jurisdiction courts, 281–283
Line agency, 466
Line item budgets, 241
Line item veto, 197–198
Linkaging, 460–461
Lobbies, 133–134
  for education, 443
  intergovernmental, 13
Local government, 8–10, 14. See also
    State-local relations
  characteristics of, 338–339
  county. See County government
  employees in, 213–215. See also Public
      employees
  financial relationship between state and,
      394–397
  impact of reform movement on,
      314–315
  interjurisdictional conflict in, 17
  interjurisdictional cooperation in, 15,
      337–338
  origins of, 312–313
  political machines in, 313
  problems facing, 16–17
  restrictions on authority of, 90–91
  special districts in, 315, 333–335
  town and townships in, 332–333

Local government (cont.)
  types of, 315–316
Local-level interest groups, 134–136
Local political parties, 147, 148
Local school boards. See School boards
Long, Huey P., 174
Long-term borrowing, 392–393
Los Angeles, California, 147
Lotteries, 382–384
Louisiana
  constitution of, 91
  governors of, 174
Low-level radioactive waste, 535, 537–538
Low-level Radioactive Waste Policy Act of
    1980, 15, 535
Lynd, Robert S. and Helen M., 344

Mabus, Ray, 98, 184
McCall, Tom, 194
McCleskey v. Kemp, 493
McCulloch v. Maryland, 26
McNamara, Robert, 242
Madison, James, 21, 24, 27, 41–42
Magna Carta, 86, 87
Maier, Henry, 349
Major-league sports, 478
Major trial courts, 282
Malapportionment, 250, 252–253
Managerial governors, 180
Manchin, A. James, 209
Mandates, 15
  problems regarding, 397, 405–408
  purpose of, 407
Mandel, Marvin, 207
Mapp v. Ohio, 489
Marble cake federalism, 37
Marshall, John, 26–28
Martin v. Wilks, 220
Martinez, Bob, 185, 379
Massachusetts
  economic revitalization in, 456, 460
  health insurance plan in, 73
  initiative used in, 120
  state constitution in, 86–87
Massachusetts Technology Development
    Corporation, 470
Mass media, 162, 165–166
Matheson, Scott, 205–206
Mayor-council form of government, 324,
    325, 327
Mayors
  Black Americans as, 350–351
  leadership requirements for, 348
  power of, 324
  strong vs. weak, 347–349
  types of, 350
Mecham, Evan
  impeachment of, 206–207

Mecham (cont.)
  recall of, 126, 128–129
Media advertisement, 166
Media relations, 204–205, 273
Medicaid program, 67
Medicare program, 68
Memphis v. Stotts, 219–220
Merit pay plans for teachers, 451–452
Merit plan for judicial selection, 291–292
  politics of, 292–294
Merit system for public employees, 97,
  215–217
Michigan economy, 457
Middletown study, 344
Migration patterns, 4, 5, 7
Milliken, William, 193, 200
Minnesota tax stamps, 369–370
Minority voting strength, 253, 254. See also
  Black Americans
Miranda v. Arizona, 29, 488
Miranda rights, 488–489
Mississippi
  constitutional reform in, 98
  program of industrial recruitment in,
    457
Missoula County, Montana, Commission,
  356
Missouri, 409
Missouri Plan (merit plan), 291–292
Mobil Oil, 540
Mobro 4000, 514, 540
Model Cities Act of 1966, 415
Model State Constitution, 91, 94–97
Mofford, Rose, 185, 207
Monongahela River Valley, 464
Montana skier responsibility law, 280
Moralistic political culture, 7
Morial, Ernest, 350–351
Morrill Act of 1862, 74, 75
Morris, Gouverneur, 21
Multitracking approach to case
  management, 306
Municipal government. See City
  government
Murray, Charles, 62–63

Nagel, Stuart, 302
National Association for the Advancement
  of Colored People (NAACP), 220
National Association of Attorneys
  General, 208
National Association of Towns and
  Townships, 333
National Conference of State Legislatures,
  46, 125
National Council of State Legislatures
  Task Force on State-Local Relations,
  401, 408

National Defense Education Act, 438
National Education Association (NEA),
  439–440
National government
  Congress and power of, 29–33
  Constitution and judiciary and power
    of, 26–29
  role in education, 437–438
  state and local conflicts with, 15–16
National Governors' Association (NGA),
  39, 46
  Center for Policy Research, 182
  functions of, 176, 182
National Guard, 34–35
National Industrial Recovery Act, 28
National Institute of Education, 438
National Labor Relations Act, 28
National League of Cities, 39, 417
National League of Cities v. Usery, 33, 226
National Municipal League, 91, 96
National Priorities List, 531, 532
National supremacy clause, 26, 31
National Wildlife Federation, 522
Nation-centered federalism, 25, 26
Natural resources
  conflict regarding, 17
  severance taxes on, 382
Nebraska legislature, 249
Necessary and proper clause, 26–27
Negotiating skills, 205
Neighborhood organizations, 135–136
Neutral competence, 216
New Columbia, 106–107
New Deal, 28–29, 37
New Federalism, 39–40
  of Nixon administration, 58
  of Reagan administration, 10–11, 57–61
New Haven, Connecticut, 344–345
New Jersey, 250, 252–253
New Jersey Plan, 24
New Mexico, 536
News media
  endorsements by, 162
  image of governor in, 273
Newspapers, 162
New Vineyard, Maine, 113
New York Bureau of Municipal Research,
  315
New York City
  fiscal stress in, 387–388
  restructuring government of, 311
New York Legislative Commission on
  Rural Resources, 421
New York State legislature, 264
Nice, David, 90
Nigeria, 42
1988 state elections, 163–164
1990 state elections, 164

Nixon, Richard M., 39, 63
Nonparticipation, 115
Nonpartisan election, 161
    impact of, 162
    of judges, 287–291
    primaries, 157
North Carolina
    hazardous waste disposal in, 533
    high-technology development in, 470
North Carolina School of Science and
        Mathematics, 447
Nuclear power, 122–123
Nuclear waste, 534
    low-level waste and interstate compacts,
        535, 537–538
    in Nevada, 318
    types of, 535, 536
Nullification, 25

Objective responsibility, 232
Off-budget budget, 237
Ohio
    enterprise zone program in, 471–472
    hazardous waste policy in, 534
    race for supreme court justice in 1987,
        290–291
Omnibus Crime Control and Safe Street
        Act of 1968, 487
Open meeting laws, 137
Open primary, 156–158
Open records laws, 137–138
Operating budgets, 392
Organized Crime Control Act of 1970, 487
Original jurisdiction, 281
Orr, Kay, 185
Out-of-court settlements, 298–299
Oversight, legislative, 247, 248
Own-source revenue, 366

Package veto, 197
PACs. See Political action committees
Palo Alto, California, 479
Parole, 504–505
Partial veto, 273–274
Participation. See Public participation
Patronage, 205, 215
    governors' power of, 195–196
Pendleton Act of 1883, 215–216
People v. Anderson, 95
Performance budgets, 242
Perry v. Lynaugh, 493
Personnel policy, 215
    collective bargaining and, 225–229
    comparable worth issues and, 221–224
    merit system and, 215–217
    representative bureaucracy as part of,
        217–221
    sexual harassment and, 224–229

Pervasive incrementalism, 240
Petition, 122, 303
Phoenix, Arizona, 411–412
Picket fence federalism, 38–39
Picketing, 228
Pierce, Franklin, 28
Pigeon River, 518, 519
Planning, programming, and budgeting
        system (PPBS), 241, 242
Plea bargaining, 298–299
Pluralism in interest groups, 344, 345
Pluralist theory of community power,
        344–345
Plurality, 160
Pocket veto, 198, 263
Policymaking
    as function of legislatures, 247
    governors' role in, 175–176
    role of state courts in, 304–305
Political action committees (PACs), 134,
        135
    as financiers of state election
        campaigns, 169
Political campaigns
    financial issues of, 167–170
    new era of, 165–167
Political consultants, 166–167
Political cultures, 6–8
Political economy, 384–389
Political machines, 313
Political parties, 144–145
    governor as leader of, 183–184
    interparty competition among, 152–155
    local, 147, 148
    present state of, 155
    role in general elections of, 160–166
Political party organization, 145, 146
    local, 146, 148–149
    makeup of, 147, 149–150
    state, 146
Pollution
    impact of, 516–517
    types of, 514–516
Pollution control. See also Environmental
        management; Environmental policy
    national, 520, 522
    state and local, 522–524
Popular recall of judges, 296
Popular referendum, 119
Population, U.S., 4, 5, 7
Populist movement, 88
Pork barrel, 177, 205
Poverty, 61–62, 74
Poverty line, 62
Power dynamics, 346–347. See also
        Community power
Precedent, 301
Pre-emption, federal, 31

Preparatory commissions, 109
Preservation communities, 420
Primary elections, 156–159, 184
  right of blacks to vote in, 116
Prisons
  conditions in, 497–499, 510–511
  policy alternatives for dealing with
      problems in, 504–509
  private, 507, 509
  responsibility for, 509–510
  role of federal courts in, 497–501
  state response to federal orders
      regarding, 501–502
  statistics for inmates in, 497
Private-enterprise shadow governments,
  412
Private prisons, 507, 509
Privileges and immunities clause, 45
Professionalism
  legislative, 271
  in state and local government, 233–234
Professional responsibility, 233, 234
Progressive party, 152
Progressive reform movement, 88, 101,
  119, 314–315
Progressive tax, 373
Project grants, 52
Property crime, 484. See also Crime
Property taxes, 365, 374–376
  cuts in, 385
  impact on education funding of,
      434–435
  and Proposition 13, 123, 363
  unpopularity of, 373
Proportional tax, 373–374
Proposition 13 (California), 101, 123, 365,
  375–376, 384, 434
Proposition 103 (California), 124
Prostitution, 491
Prune Yard case, 85
Public administration. See Bureaucracies,
  state and local
Public campaign financing, 170
Public education. See also Education
  challenge of, 452–453
  financial inequities in, 303, 433–437
  impact of property tax cuts on, 434–435
  innovation in, 444–452
  national role in, 437–438
Public employees, 213–215
  governors' power to appoint, 192–196
  governors' power to fire, 197
  hiring practices for, 215–216
  personnel policy affecting. See
      Personnel policy
  statistics regarding, 213–215
  wages and salaries for, 229
Public interest, 231

Public participation
  citizen access and, 137–140
  in criminal justice, 489–490
  fragmentation as result of, 90
  impact of, 141
  by initiative, 101–103, 119–126
  by interest groups, 127–136
  nonvoting and, 11
  reasons for and methods of, 113–115
  by recall, 119, 126–127
  right to vote and, 115–116
  by voluntary action, 140
  voter turnout and, 116–118
Public policy. See Higher education policy;
  Social welfare policy
  citizen participation and direction of,
    113
  legislative decisions regarding, 265, 267
Public-private partnerships, 468
Puget Sound region (Washington State),
  423

Racial discrimination. See also Affirmative
  action; Black Americans
  in Alabama, 219–220
  campus, 78
  in language of state constitutions, 91
  in Yonkers, N.Y., 323
Rain forests, 514
Rainy day funds, 390–391
Rampton, Calvin L., 193
Randolph, Edmund, 24
Ratification, 100
Ray, Dixy Lee, 185
Reagan, Ronald, 39, 144, 193, 213, 361
  education aid cuts by, 438
  on environmental issues, 520–522
  as governor, 176, 295–296
  social welfare policy of, 63–64
Reagan administration
  defense expenditures under, 53
  economic policies of, 385–386, 463
  grant cuts during, 57
  New Federalism of, 10–11, 39–40, 57–61
Reapportionment, 164, 252–255
Recall, 119, 126–127
  to remove judges, 296
Recycling, 527–528
Referendum, general and popular, 119
Reform movement, 88, 101, 119, 314–315
Regents of the University of California v.
  Bakke, 218
Regional coordination, 415, 417
Regional differences, economic, 455
  in Midwest, 456–457
  in New England, 456
  in South, 456
  in West, 457

Regional government, 413–415
Regional restitution centers, 506
Regressive tax, 373
Rehnquist, William, 16, 303, 314
Reilly, William K., 522
Reorganization of state government
    gubernatorial power of, 199–200
    politics of, 201
    types of, 200–201
Representation
    in city government, 330, 332
    as function of legislature, 247–248
Representative bureaucracy, 217–218
    affirmative action to achieve, 218–221
    Supreme Court decisions regarding,
        219–220
Republican party
    background of, 150
    ideology within, 147, 149
    image of, 145
    local organization of, 146, 147
    runoff elections and, 160
    state organization of, 146
Reputational approach to study of
        community power, 345
Research Triangle Park, 470
Reserved powers, 24–25
Resource Conservation and Recovery Act
        of 1976 (RCRA), 529–531
Responsible party model, 144–145
Retention elections, judicial, 293, 294
Retribution, 495
Revenue bonds, 243–244, 392–393
Revenues, 51. *See also* Tax revenue;
        Taxation; Taxes
    borrowing to meet shortfalls in, 392–393
    cash investment management practices,
        391
    estimating, 389–390
    imbalances in city government, 329–331
    rainy day funds and, 390–391
    state-local government relations and,
        394–397
Revenue sharing, 52, 53
Reynolds v. *Sims*, 29, 249
Reynoso, Cruz, 293–294
Riley, Dick, 206
Robbins, Ira, 510
Rockefeller, Nelson, 180
Roe v. *Wade*, 29
Roemer, Charles "Buddy," 174, 184
Roll call vote, 262
Roosevelt, Franklin D., 28, 63
Rosenthal, Alan, 271
Ruiz v. *Estelle*, 501
Runoff elections, 158–160
Rural communities, 420–422

Sabato, Larry, 184
Safe Drinking Water Act, 31
Salaries
    of judges, 307
    of legislators, 255, 269–270
    of public employees, 229
    of teachers, 430, 450, 451
Sales tax, 374, 376–379
San Antonio city council elections, 354
San Antonio Independent School District v.
        Rodriquez, 303, 433
Sanders, Bernard, 341
San Diego, California, 348, 353
Sanford, Terry, 38, 110
Schaefer, William Donald, 343, 422, 462
Scholastic Aptitude Test (SAT), 422, 428
School boards, 335–336
    as member of education establishment,
        440–441
School districts, 315, 335–337
School segregation, 29, 435, 443–444
Scientific Games Inc., 125
Search and seizure, 489
Sears Island, Maine, 539
Seattle, Washington, 338
Secretary of state, 209–210
Segregation in public schools, 29, 435,
        443–444
Sentencing reform, 496–498
Severance taxes, 382
Sex discrimination
    comparable worth issue and, 222–224
    in language of state constitutions, 91
Sexual harassment, 224–225
Shadow governments, 412–413
Shafroth, Frank, 387
Shanker, Albert, 430, 449
Shapp, Milton, 180–181
Sherman Antitrust Act, 44
Shock probation, 508
Shopping centers, 85
Sierra Club, 522, 527
Simonson, Archie, 126
Single-purpose local governments, 315
Small-business incubators, 471
Small claims courts, 281–283
Smith, Alfred E., 190
Smith v. *Allwright*, 116
Smith-Hughes Act, 438
Snelling, Richard, 188
Social insurance, 68–69
Social Insurance Trust Fund, 68
Socialist party, 152
Social security, 68
Social Security Act of 1935, 68
    legal challenges to, 28–29
    1939 amendments to, 216

Social welfare policy, 61
  current, 64–65, 68–69, 81–82
  expenditures, 65
  federalism and, 72–74
  ideology and, 62–64
  origins of, 63–64
  state innovations in, 69–72
Social welfare programs
  direct cash transfers, 66–67
  in-kind, 67–68
  social insurance, 68–69
Socioeconomic status, 8, 113, 115
Solid waste management, 524–526
  by incineration, 526–527
  by landfill, 525, 526
  by recycling, 527–528
Source Separation and Recycling Act of
    1987 (New Jersey), 527
South Carolina
  annexation in, 328
  educational reform in, 444–445
  increased cooperation in, 464
Special districts, 315, 333–335
Split party control, 272
Staffing power, gubernatorial, 201–202
Standing committee, 257–258
Stanford v. Kentucky, 493
State boards of education, 441
State-centered federalism, 24–26
State court systems, 280
  activism in, 302–305
  delays in, 91
  development and structure of, 281–
    285
  excessive caseloads in, 306–307
  financial improvements for, 305
  judicial decision making in, 298–302
  modernization in, 307–308
  role in criminal justice, 488
  selection of judges in, 285–298. See also
    Judicial selection
State departments of education, 441
State elections. See also Elections
  finances of, 167–170
  1988, 163–164
  1990, 164
State government, 9, 14. See also
    State-local relations
  employees in, 213–215. See also Public
    employees
  financial relationship between local and,
    394–397
  interjurisdictional conflict in, 17
  interjurisdictional cooperation in, 14–15
  problems facing, 16–17
  professional jobs in, 195–196
  study of, 8–10

State-local organizations, 408
  advisory commissions on
      intergovernmental relations, 409
  departments of community affairs,
      409–410
  task forces, 408–409
State-local relations. See also Local
    government; State government
  challenges to, 410–417
  distribution of authority in, 401–408
  finances, 394–397
  rural communities and, 420–421
  urban policy and, 417–420
State party organizations, 146
State powers, 33–35
State pre-emption, 533
States. See also State court systems; State
    elections; State government
  cooperation among, 44–46
  population changes within, 4, 5, 7
Stokes, Carl, 350
Stone, Clarence, 346
Strategic Development Commission, 469
Strategic planning, 469–470
Strikes (labor), 228
Strong mayors, 347–349
Students
  discipline problems among, 430–431
  effect of educational reforms on, 447–448
  role in education crisis, 429
Study commission, 109
Subcabinet system, 200
Subjective responsibility, 232–233
Subsidy, 458
Substate districts, 415
Suburbanization, 410–411
Suffragists, 115–116
Sunset laws, 232, 276
Superconducting super collider project, 455
Superfund, 529–533
Supplemental Security Income, 67
Supremacy clause, 26, 31
Supreme Court, U.S., 24, 26
  on abortion, 29, 164
  activism of, 302–304
  on affirmative action, 218–221
  on campaign finances, 168
  on capital punishment, 492
  on comparable worth, 223–224
  conservatism of, 94, 304
  on education, 433, 443
  influence on criminal justice, 488–489
  on national-state conflict, 16
  on New York Board of Estimate, 311
  on state legislative apportionment, 252,
      253
  on state and local power, 33, 99

Supreme courts, state
  judicial federalism in, 85
  organization of, 282–284
  role in constitutional reform, 99
Surveys, citizen, 139
Swann v. *Charlotte–Mecklenberg County Schools*, 443

Task forces, 200, 408
  as approach to economic development, 465, 466
Taxation. *See also* Revenues; Tax revenues
  economic development policy through, 461
  fiscal stress and, 385–388
  limited discretion in, 388–389
  power of, 30–31
  revolt over, 365, 384–385
Taxation and expenditure limitations, 385, 388
Tax effort, 372
Taxes, 375–382
  criteria for evaluating and rating, 373–375, 381
  income, 374, 377, 378, 380
  lotteries to supplement, 382–384
  property. *See* Property taxes
  sales, 374, 376–379
  severance, 382
  user charges to raise, 380–381
  voter preferences regarding, 377
Taxing and spending power of Congress, 30–31
Tax Reform Act of 1986, 57, 70, 374, 377
Tax revenue. *See also* Revenues
  fiscal capacity and, 370–372
  listed by state, 368–370
Tax stamps, 369–370
Tax yield, 374
Teachers
  merit plans for, 451–452
  as part of education establishment, 439–440
  quality of, 430–431
  salaries of, 430, 450, 451
  shortages of, 450
Television. *See also* Media relations
  governors' use of, 204
  role in political campaigns, 165–166
Tennessee
  economic development in, 456, 464
  prison conditions in, 501
Tennessee Valley Authority, 28
Tenth Amendment, 24–25, 31, 33, 432
Texas
  annexation in, 328
  constitutional revision in, 107–109

Texas (*cont.*)
  judicial selection system in, 288–289
  prison reform in, 501–503
Third parties, 152
Thompson, James R., 183, 192
Three Mile Island disaster, 534
Ticket-splitting, 145
Tobacco taxes, 381
Town meeting, 125, 312
Towns, 332–333
Townships, 332–333
Trade missions, 472–473
Traditionalistic political culture, 7
Transuranic wastes, 535
Traverse City, Michigan, 479
Travis County, Texas, 321–322
Treasurer, state, 209
Trial by jury, 299
Trustees, legislators as, 267
Tsongas, Paul, 120
Two-party system, 150, 152

Unemployment compensation, 68
Unicameralism, 23, 249, 250
Unified court budgeting, 305
Unified court system, 284
Uniform Crime Reports, 484, 485
Unions. *See* Labor unions
Unitary government, 21, 22
U.S. Advisory Commission on Intergovernmental Relations (ACIR), 333, 334, 372, 401, 402, 409
U.S. Conference of Mayors, 417
United States v. *Paradise*, 220
United Steelworkers of America v. *Weber*, 218
Universities. *See* Higher education institutions
University research, 468
Urban Development Action Grants (UDAG) program, 59, 416, 417, 461, 463
Urbanization
  contemporary developments in, 411–412
  effect on state-local relations, 410–411
  industrialization and, 312–313
Urban policy
  housing and, 418–419
  infrastructure and, 419–420
User charges, 380–381
Utah gubernatorial races, 163

Veto power gubernatorial, 197–198, 273–274
Vetos, 197–198
Victimization surveys, 484–485
Victimless crime, 491–492
Violent crime, 484. *See also* Crime

Virginia
  House of Delegates in, 261
  regulation of smoking in, 423
  uneven local economies in, 422
Virginia Plan, 24
Vocational programs for criminals, 505
Volkswagen, 459
Volunteerism, 140
Voter turnout, 116–118
Voting as participation, 113
Voting rights, 115–116
Voting Rights Act of 1965, 31, 42, 116

Wages. *See* Salaries
Wallace, George, 152
War on Poverty, 63
Warren, Earl, 302, 488
Washington, Harold, 346, 351
Washington, D.C., 105–107
Washington state
  comparable worth policy in, 223–224
  nuclear waste disposal in, 535
Waste Isolation Pilot Plant, 536
Waste management. *See* Environmental
  management; Hazardous waste
  management; Nuclear waste; Solid
  waste management
Water pollution, 517–519
Water Pollution Control Act of 1948,
  517–518
Watt, James, 521

Weak mayors, 347–349
Webster v. *Reproductive Health Services,*
  29, 30
White, Mark, 185, 189
White primary, 116
Whitmire, Kathryn J., 342, 357
Wildavsky, Aaron, 238
Wilder, L. Douglas, 185
Wilson, Pete, 348
Wisconsin, strategic planning in, 469–470
Women
  discrimination against. *See* Sex
    discrimination
  harassment of. *See* Sexual harassment
  in legislature, 250, 251
  as local government leaders, 356
  poverty among, 62
  right to vote for, 115–116
  in teaching profession, 430
Work Incentive (WIN) Program, 70–71
Worker's compensation, 68
Workfare, 70–72

Yard waste, 527–528
Yellow dog Democrats, 145
Yield, tax, 374
Yonkers, New York, 323
Young, Coleman, 351

Zero-based budgets, 241–243